ALSO BY THOMAS POWERS

Diana: The Making of a Terrorist *(1971)*

The War at Home *(1973)*

The Man
Who Kept the Secrets

THE MAN WHO KEPT THE SECRETS

Richard Helms & the CIA

by THOMAS POWERS

 ALFRED A. KNOPF   NEW YORK   1979

THIS IS A BORZOI BOOK
PUBLISHED BY ALFRED A. KNOPF, INC.

Library of Congress Cataloging in Publication Data
Powers, Thomas, (Date).
The man who kept the secrets, Richard Helms & the CIA.
Bibliography: p.
Includes index.
1. United States.   Central Intelligence Agency.
2. Helms, Richard.   I. Title.
JK468.16P68   1979   327'.12'0924 [B]   79-2210
ISBN 0-394-50777-0

Manufactured in the United States of America

FIRST EDITION

Introduction

The Central Intelligence Agency and the career of Richard Helms are not neutral subjects. Just about everyone I talked to while working on this book wanted to know where I stood. Did I intend to attack or defend? Was I going to write an indictment or an apology? A short answer was desired. The question made me uneasy; it implied that my mind was firmly made up before I began, which I did not like to admit. It also implied that the only important thing to be asked of a book about Helms and the CIA was whose side it was on. It was a crowding sort of question, and I found various ways of evading short answers. But the book does have a point of view—a bias, if you will—and the reader has a right to know what it is before setting out.

Helms and the CIA have been charged with a good many specific failures or crimes in recent years, most of them familiar in outline from newspaper headlines. Naturally these make their appearance in the pages which follow, sometimes in considerable detail. But all the same, I have tried to avoid a prosecutorial approach, because it leads to a legalistic definition of the problem, and leaves out more than it includes.

Judging an intelligence service, or the career of a man who ran it, requires first of all a sense of what the job involves. The work of a service like the CIA can be broken down into three general categories: intelligence-gathering and analysis, the protection of its own integrity (or counterintelligence), and political intervention. Although all three are undertaken by a single institution, under the authority of one man, each of these functions has its own purposes and rationale. Criticism of the Agency, and of Helms, has touched in a scattershot fashion on all three aspects. CIA people are willing enough to concede the blunders and excesses of the past, but insist that the basic business of the Agency, if ugly in some of its particulars, is necessary too, one of the fatal facts of modern life, like taxes, prisons, and armies. An outsider naturally resents this argument—it smacks so much of an adult's explanation of the world to a child—but two thousand years of history, in which failures of intelligence were often as destructive as failures of arms, make it hard to dismiss. The trouble with the argument is that it lumps the CIA's work all together, and suggests that the rest of us must take it or leave it. This we do not have to do.

Intelligence services do not exist in a vacuum. A nation with neither an army nor enemies does not have much need for spies, but once it has both, an intelligence service is bound to follow. The development of missile systems since the German V rockets of World War II offers a particularly clear example of the almost symbiotic relationship between arms and intelligence. The simple subsonic guided missile with a conventional warhead has been succeeded by one generation after another of steadily more advanced systems, culminating (for the moment) in the Multiple Independently Targetable Re-entry Vehicle (known by its acronym as MIRV)—a single launch vehicle, defended by a host of sophisticated electronic devices, which can accurately threaten a number of targets with explosive power probably equal to that of all the bombs dropped in World War II. This doomsday marvel is not the result of any Strangelovian fascination with hardware, but of something not so widely recognized: the ability of the Soviet Union and the United States to keep precise track of each other's developments in missilery.

Assessing an enemy or potential enemy's military capacity is one of the two main functions of traditional intelligence; the other is the discovery of an enemy's intentions. Since spies[1]* are rarely in a position to answer such questions flatly, an intelligence service must infer the truth from whatever ancillary evidence it can gather. Some of this information is obtained secretly, most not. In theory, the CIA has no axe to grind and is accordingly objective in what it concludes from what it has learned. Where the U.S. Air Force, say, might be inclined to inflate the size of the Soviet bomber fleet, in order to boost expenditures for its own (as actually happened in the early 1950s), the CIA's role is to find out the simple facts, thus arming the President with an objective estimate to help him decide just how big a bomber fleet the United States really needs.

Up to a point, the process really does work this way. The weakness of the theory—we shall encounter a good many examples in the course of this book—is that some judgments can never be confirmed one way or the other (was Allende's election really a first step toward a Stalinist regime in Chile?), and that all of them have domestic political consequences. When these consequences grow beyond a certain point, they begin to exert a kind of gravitational pull on CIA estimates, skewing them around to fit the conventional wisdom. Broad questions (can the United States defeat Hanoi?) give

* There are a good many footnotes in this book. Some of them are simply source citations in the customary manner, but many are extensive and are intended to supplement the text. If the reader will browse through them at this point, he will quickly discover whether he wants to follow them up systematically. They are to be found at the back of the book because many of them would have overwhelmed the page, if printed literally at the foot.

way to narrow ones (what percentage of North Vietnam's oil reserves can be destroyed by X level of bombing?). This might be called innocent fudging, a deliberate neglect of the forest for the trees, but sometimes the fudging has not been so innocent, and the CIA would in effect surrender a point because the pressure to do so was simply too great to resist. But it is important to remember that the pressures have almost always come from above, not from below.

The point here is that a state of ongoing military confrontation between great powers—such as between the United States and the Soviet Union—does require intelligence of the traditional sort. One might scatter the CIA to the winds, as President Kennedy briefly threatened to do after the Bay of Pigs, but its job would only be picked up by some other agency with a different name. So far Helms and other defenders of the CIA are right: an intelligence service is one of the fatal facts of modern life.

They are right on another point as well. If one elects to have an intelligence service, then inevitably the necessity of counterintelligence must also be accepted. An intelligence service is a two-edged weapon. It is of no use unless policy-makers trust its honesty and heed its estimates, but the fact that they trust it leaves them dangerously vulnerable to its possible compromise. An intelligence service reduces the cacophony straining for a leader's ear: instead of forty estimates of the nature of a problem, a government elects to have one.[2] This serves leaders by minimizing confusion, but it also eases the job of enemies, giving them an ideal tool, and a narrow target, for penetration and deception. An intelligence service is like a missile system controlled by a single button. If an enemy can get at the button, he can cripple the system.

It is in the nature of counterintelligence that you never quite know how you're doing. This can make it appear silly or childish. Outsiders sometimes suggest that the melodramatic intrigue of the intelligence business be junked entirely; but even if all the spies were let go, and all the field stations closed down, counterintelligence would necessarily remain, for the reason that a vulnerable intelligence service is worse than none at all. Once that point has been conceded, all the rest of the clandestine enterprise comes tumbling after, because the best way to protect one's own service is to penetrate the enemy's. This is not something that happens only in spy novels.

But that still leaves the third CIA, which serves as an instrument of Presidents trying to work their will in the world—a tool of middle resort, lying somewhere between a note of diplomatic protest and sending in the Marines. The United States has perhaps five percent of the world's population, and uses perhaps a quarter of its resources. This makes for a vigorous foreign policy. Whenever a President wanted to make a point to a foreign power, which often happened in the last thirty years, the CIA offered a means for doing so secretly. Is intervention inevitable too? Does the United

States need an apparatus for the secret transfer of funds, the delivery of arms, the dissemination of propaganda, the training of allied intelligence agencies, and all the other means of pressing foreign opponents and propping up friends? The CIA's broad defense of what it does internationally—that it acts only at the direction of the President—is true, but inadequate, because it does not address the wisdom or utility of the undertaking itself.

The struggle for hegemony in Western Europe at the end of World War II was serious. Huge populations and a vast industrial capacity were at stake, not to mention the intellectual, spiritual, and artistic patrimony of the West. One might argue that the Soviet threat was feebler and less deliberate than it looked at the time, or that the struggle might have been pursued by other means, but at least the whole endeavor was about something large, which really mattered. This has not always been the case: Tibet, Angola, the Congo, Indonesia, Guatemala, Chile, and Vietnam were hardly prizes on a similar scale. Whether American interests were importantly involved or not is a matter of opinion, and always will be a matter of opinion; the American interest in Chile is not a knowable thing, like the temperature on the dark side of the moon. What is not a matter of opinion is the sheer extent of U.S. intervention in the postwar world.

It is not hard to draw up a long list of CIA crimes and failures. A biography of Richard Helms will inevitably include most of them; his career offers an ideal pathway through the secret history of thirty years. But there is more to be learned from Helms's role as a spymaster and Cold Warrior than from the crimes with which he has been charged, just as the CIA's offenses against common decency, while real and deplorable, lose some of their power to shock when they're compared to the normal activity of some other secret services. This has not been a generally held view in recent years, but it is so. The problem that ought to concern and trouble us is not primarily the existence of Agency wrongdoers who have escaped justice, but the nature of the role that the United States has chosen for itself in the world, a role importantly supported and implemented by the CIA. Four aspects of this problem strike me as paramount, and while they are implicit throughout the book, it will perhaps serve clarity to alert the reader to them here.

1) American intervention in foreign countries always matters more to the nation in question than it does to the United States. Yet the decision to proceed is often reached in a manner which is shockingly casual. Nixon's decision to try to prevent Salvador Allende from taking office in Chile, like Lyndon Johnson's to send Marines into the Dominican Republic, shows every sign of having been impulsive and flimsily justified by the vaguest of references to U.S. security. Kissinger's attempt to sustain a civil war in Angola had no better goal than to prove the American tiger could still bite. Even the U.S. decision to intervene in Vietnam, the work of years and

endless official paper, had little to do with Vietnam itself, but was based on nothing more solid than a desire to demonstrate American "will," and to "discourage" wars of national liberation. The result was a distressing failure for the United States, and a horrifying ordeal for Indochina.

It is tough enough for Americans to run their own country wisely; the idea that they can do better for someone else's is sheer presumption. The CIA lends itself to this presumption by smoothing the decision-making process, meticulously mapping the thread of American interest through the confusion of local reality, and thereby reducing the fate of peoples to option papers. The Agency does not decide what that interest is, but once it has been defined by the mood and preconceptions of the President and his advisers, the CIA ensures that it is at the heart of every briefing. The decision-making machinery supporting American foreign policy is too well organized. President Carter has described his job as like taking a multiple-choice exam. When X, Y, and Z are each represented by a piece of paper—and some Presidents were notorious for never reading beyond the one-page summaries—it should come as no surprise that policies are often adopted between breakfast and lunch, with no real comprehension of what that policy is going to mean to the people involved. The fear and resentment of the CIA around the world are justified, not because it is always on the wrong side—it is not—but because it represents an inevitable primacy of American interests which may be shallowly conceived and callously pursued.

2) Just as American power has more sway in other countries than it can claim by right, local CIA officers exert a disproportionate influence on local events, especially after a decision to intervene has been reached. It is one thing for Chilean army officers to decide that Allende poses a sufficient threat to justify a military coup: They are at least Chilean. They have spent their lives winning the power they wield, and have inevitably been tempered by the struggle. They may not have learned to be wise, but at least they comprehend what they are up against, are known and trusted by their followers, and must live with the consequences of what they attempt. But no amount of area expertise on the part of CIA people can alter the fact that they are outsiders, nor the fact that their very real power has been delegated to them by outsiders, rather than won through the normal give-and-take of political conflict.

Graham Greene's brilliant portrait of naïve political manipulators in *The Quiet American* might have been written as easily about Cuba, Chile, or Angola as it was about Vietnam. CIA officers often care very much about the countries in which they work; they may speak the language and master the literature. But when all is said and done, they are still the civil servants of a foreign power. Once the United States has embarked on a policy of intervention, it will find a local champion willy-nilly. If a first choice balks, he will be passed over for another, more pliable ally.[3] Thus a policy carelessly developed and casually adopted in Washington will be implemented on the local scene by rootless, alien, and presumably unknown CIA officers who are free to walk away from the wreckage.

3) The CIA has been too quick to surrender responsibility for what allies undertake with its aid, and other high officials in Washington have been too ready to let it do so. The Agency has helped train secret police in Vietnam, Iran, Argentina, the Dominican Republic, Chile, and many other countries, and then looked the other way when its former students have arbitrarily arrested, tortured, and murdered their opponents. The Phoenix program and the cramped "tiger cages" on Con Son Island in Vietnam, in which political prisoners often died or lost the use of their legs, are only the most egregious examples of the Agency's tendency to wash its hands of crimes it has materially supported, though not directly committed.

The United States should not, and in any event can not, run the countries it chooses to help, but this is a feeble defense against responsibility for everything which follows. The problem is not only an American one. China, for example, chose to support the regime of Pol Pot in Cambodia, just as Libya backed Idi Amin in Uganda, both of them indefensible clients if ever there were any. It is hard to say exactly where the line is crossed, but it's clear that the United States and the CIA have often crossed it. About the only ally Washington has ever declared beyond the pale, in fact, was Haiti, under the nightmarish rule of François ("Papa Doc") Duvalier. In other instances we have simply averted our eyes.

4) Perhaps the most troubling aspect of the CIA is the hardest to explain, because it represents at once both the field of its greatest success and its passive acceptance of fatal dangers about which there is very likely nothing to be done. To put the matter at its simplest, the CIA, like the government it serves, is fully committed to an international system that depends for its stability on a balance of power, and thus to the notion that war with the Soviet Union can best be avoided through a combination of intimidating military strength and the professional management of crises when they arise. The CIA's role in this seemingly perpetual confrontation is to provide intelligence in its purest, most classic form—timely information about an opponent's capabilities and intentions.

There have been lapses, but on the whole the CIA seems to have done its job well, especially where Soviet military capabilities have been concerned. There have been no major surprises, no sudden discoveries of developments in Soviet military technology that might leave the United States at a dramatic disadvantage. Even the boldest Soviet initiative in the postwar period—Khrushchev's decision to put nuclear missiles into Cuba—was discovered in sufficiently good time to give Kennedy an opportunity to respond. It goes without saying that Russian intelligence has been equally efficient in this regard, with the result that the one element essential for a working balance of power—that is, a genuine balance—has been maintained. Each side has generally known what the other was up to, even during periods of crisis when confusion or misunderstanding might have had disastrous consequences. One can search the records of Soviet-American relations since 1945 and find nothing like the blind guessing or outright blundering that preceded the First World War, much less the horrors of mismanagement and misinformation characteristic of the Crimean or Spanish-American War.[4]

From one point of view, this relative success might be taken as cause for self-congratulation. But it has also given the Agency a case of juggler's confidence: although no one in the intelligence community will say so directly, the truth is that they have all learned to live with the Bomb. The trouble with this twin dependence on military readiness and professional crisis management is that it must work forever. CIA people are not intimidated by the word "forever," because they don't use it; they speak of the "foreseeable future." But while success in the foreseeable future may be good enough for them, it need not be for the rest of us. CIA people, then, by training and instinct treat the danger of nuclear war in a manner that is at once professionally sober and almost childishly hopeful. The Agency is an integral part of what the social critic Randolph Bourne once called "the war system," and the fact that we don't know how to transcend it should not blind us to the very good chance it will eventually bring in the future what it has always brought in the past—war.

A Note on Procedure

A book about intelligence demands a word about sources and methods. Somewhat to my surprise, I found CIA people quite willing to talk about their careers. For one thing, a lot of them have retired since 1973; sensational headlines, public criticism, and time to brood have helped to put them into a communicative mood. For the most part, CIA people believe in what they have done, and are pained by what they take to be public misunderstanding. The habits of secrecy pull them in one direction, the desire to explain in another. The tug of the latter seems to be winning out. Of all the former Agency people I approached, more than forty over a two-year period, only three refused to speak to me at all.[5] The rest were all willing to talk, from field officers on up to Richard Helms himself, who surrendered four long mornings[6] to a book he probably wished no one would write. Others gave up even more of their time.

With a half-dozen exceptions, the former CIA officers I talked to were still loyal to the Agency and simply wanted to set the record straight. Most began by telling me what they wouldn't talk about: the names of agents and fellow CIA officers, the details of operations which had not already been exposed by the press, and so on. As we talked, however, the force of these prohibitions seemed to erode. A name that popped up in one conversation would serve as a useful wedge in another. An operation alluded to by one former official would be elaborated on by a second, corrected by a third, amended by a fourth, and finally rounded off by the first, now that I had most of it anyway. If one keeps on asking questions, the answers will gradually begin to fit together.

The raw material of this book comes in about equal measure from published sources and from interviews. In the case of the former I have followed the usual practice of acknowledging all direct quotations, as well as accounts on which I have depended heavily. Interviews with former CIA people and other government officials present a stickier problem. With only one or two exceptions concerning technical matters, no one told me anything I wasn't free to use as I liked, but almost all said that they didn't want to be quoted directly by name. Occasionally this was because they didn't want to be identified as the source of a particular bit of information: they weren't divulging national secrets exactly, but they were talking about things it had long been the custom to conceal. The more general motive for anonymity, however, was a desire to avoid contention with old friends, or enemies. The business of intelligence, like other bureaucratic endeavors, tends to breed acrimony, and while CIA people were willing enough to talk about professional disputes and personality clashes of the past, they certainly didn't want to fight those battles all over again. This struck me as reasonable enough. As a result, I have generally refrained from stating directly who told me what, except in those cases where the source of a quotation or factual claim was an inherent and necessary part of the story.

This inevitably raises the question of whether I have been led down the garden path. The CIA, and the profession of intelligence in general, have a reputation for subtle deviousness, and the reader may wonder whether I have been the victim of a clever and meticulous plan. I worried about this a good deal myself when I first began working on the book, and was on the lookout for that suspicious consistency that reveals a line. It didn't take long to discover: CIA people, with few exceptions, believe that the United States faces many enemies, great and small; that it needs an intelligence service and deserves a good one; that it cannot afford to act abroad within the constitutional limits imposed at home; that the Agency observes standards of conduct a good deal stricter and more humane than those of other intelligence services; that the Agency has been unfairly maligned for doing as it was told to do, and unfairly accused of domestic intrigue by an administration up to its scuppers in intrigue. CIA people are not so much angry about their public reputation in recent years as they are hurt, puzzled, upset, and alarmed. They think the Agency is a fine organization. That is their line, and it is not slipped out through winks, hints, and sly remarks. Its very uniformity makes it all the more remarkable that a handful of ex-CIA officials—Victor Marchetti, Frank Snepp, John Stockwell, and a few others—have managed to step outside the consensus and raise fundamental questions about its validity.

The details of specific operations are something else again. Here the habits of secrecy are still strong. One reason is that questions necessarily proceed from the public record, and that record is a dismal list of crime, blunder, embarrassment, and failure; CIA people are as instinctively reticent about such things as anyone else. But the habit of secrecy runs deeper than that. Intelligence services tend to keep everything secret for three basic reasons: one never knows what will serve an opponent as a sufficient clue, exposure invites kibitzing, and clandestine political arrangements, almost as a matter of course, threaten embarrassment. (This will be discussed elsewhere at greater length.) The CIA people I interviewed wanted me to understand what the Agency had been up to all these years—namely, serving the President in his constitutional conduct of foreign policy—but without surrendering more details than absolutely necessary. Naturally I tried to acquire as many as I could. It was a constant tug-of-war. But with a single exception, I never caught a CIA official in an outright lie.

Agency people often told me things I felt were untrue, but they all (with the single exception) involved matters of judgment. Was the Phoenix program an assassination program? Is the CIA guilty of a positive preference for right-wing dictators? Did the Bay of Pigs planners count on forcing Kennedy to intervene in the end? Was Allende a threat mainly to Chilean democracy, or to American business interests? Was the CIA trying to topple Sukarno in 1958, or just put a little pressure on him? Did the CIA fudge intelligence estimates under political pressure, or merely admit the evidence was ambiguous and the other fellow might be right? The history of the CIA raises many such questions, but the answers are necessarily a matter of opinion. When I say I only once caught a CIA official in a lie, I refer to something different—a flat assertion that was untrue. The exception was pretty small potatoes—a claim that a CIA margin of error was X, when the man I was talking to knew perfectly well it was $3X$—but it was a lie. His motive for telling it was a characteristic reluctance to admit the military had been so dramatically right, and the CIA so wrong, in its estimate of North Vietnamese military supplies shipped through the Cambodian port of Sihanoukville.

My informants sometimes evaded questions, or retreated behind faulty memory and the mists of time, or softened the character of harsh events, but it was always the nature of things that was in contention between us, rarely the facts. They had many opportunities to mislead me with false claims, often on matters that I would have found it impossible to verify. A good example would be the question of authority for the attempts to kill Castro. Eisenhower, both Kennedys, Allen Dulles, and other high officials are now dead. CIA people, much embarrassed by the episode (but not always for the right reasons), might have concocted evidence that the orders came from above, or they might have shifted all the blame to a handful of officers acting on their own. They made no attempt to do either. They simply admitted the murkiness of the record, and left me to puzzle it out as I could.

This was typical of the way they handled the hard questions. I was never confronted with a blizzard of conflicting factual claims, but rather with a chronic incompleteness. The problem, in short, was not a single large mystery—secret control of the CIA by the Mafia, or something of the sort—but many small mysteries.

When the manuscript was completed, I sent copies to Helms and several other former CIA officers. They caught a number of errors of fact— spelling of names, dates, official titles, and so on—and often elaborated on particular episodes. We also reargued many old disputes; sometimes I was brought around, sometimes not. I'm not sure if the people I talked to regret it now, but for the most part they feel I have been too harsh on Helms, too preoccupied with the CIA's "crimes," too naïve about the dangers of the real world, too ambivalent about the vigorous defense of American interests, too unwilling to recognize the CIA's achievements, the importance of secrecy, the fickleness of democracies on questions of foreign policy, or the fact that intelligence services are organized as they are because reasonable men haven't been able to find better ways to go about it. Nonetheless, despite frequent differences of opinion, the people I talked to were always generous with their time, never flagged in their confidence that they had nothing to fear from a fair historian, and did their best to help me understand why they had done as they had done. I am grateful for their time, candor, and trust. Their contribution to this book has been very great, but of course its errors and conclusions are all my own. Among those who assisted me in gathering information for this book, I would like to thank Sam Adams, John Ansell, Mary Bancroft, Richard Bissell, Tom Braden, John Bross, George Carver, Ray Cline, William Colby, John Ehrlichman, John Gardner, Morton Halperin, Sam Halpern, Dennis Helms, Richard Helms, Gerald Hickey, Roger Hilsman, Lawrence Houston, John Huizenga, Norvale Jones, Thomas Karamessines, Robert Kiley, Lyman Kirkpatrick, Edward Korry, George Lawton, Jerry Levinson, Frank Lindsay, Victor Marchetti, Carl Marcy, Andrew Marshall, John Maury, Steven McClintic, Tom McCoy, Robert S. McNamara, Armin Meyer, Richard Moose, Frederick Oechsner, Thomas Parrott, David Phillips, Sylvia Press, Henry Rothblatt, F. A. O. Schwarz Jr., Gerard C. Smith, Maxwell Taylor, DeForrest van Slyck, William Watt, John Wilbur, and Robert Wood. There are others, who preferred to remain nameless, to whom I am also grateful.

Generous help was provided by many other people as well, including Abby Brett, Gordon and Holly Chaplin, and Robert and Hannah Kaiser, who welcomed me as a guest on many trips to Washington. Fred Childs,

Tim Ferris, Tom Lewis, my sister Susan Urstadt, and my father, Joshua Powers, all read the manuscript or discussed it with me at length. Carrie Maynard ably transcribed my interviews with Richard Helms, and Ian Love provided a useful index of stories from the *Los Angeles Times*. Marianne Partridge precipitated the project when she invited me to write an article on Helms for *Rolling Stone*. Finally, my wife Candace and our children, Amanda, Susan, and Cassandra, supported me during the book's writing with grace and good humor. When it was done, Susan said she hoped the next one would be shorter, "about half a month," so we could go ice skating.

February 16, 1979   Thomas Powers

The Man
Who Kept the Secrets

Chapter 1

In the spring of 1977, the isolation of Richard Helms was almost complete. It was not that he lacked friends and allies in Washington, where he had spent nearly thirty years in the practice of intelligence. He was both liked and respected there, on his chosen ground; he was taken to be an honest man, a dedicated public servant who deserved honorable retirement after a long career working his way up through the ranks of the Central Intelligence Agency. Not many people knew what Helms had been doing in the CIA, but those who did formed a circle of unusual power and influence—former Presidents, cabinet secretaries and other high officials, Congressmen, and leading journalists. If Helms had his troubles in the spring of 1977, at least the men who knew him best had not turned against him. But this phalanx of support, personally gratifying as it must have been, only emphasized his isolation. Outside Washington, the word "intelligence" had acquired a new and sinister shade of meaning. Four years of official investigations had cast the CIA in a dark light, and the name of Richard Helms had turned up on a great many embarrassing documents about Watergate intrigue, assassination plots, the testing of drugs on unwitting victims, attempts to foment coups in democratic countries. The Washington circle which excused these things, explaining them away as the prosaic facts of international life, was a decidedly small one, and Helms was trapped at its very heart.

Helms did not understand how this had happened. He certainly knew the details of recent history better than most; he had watched the awful progress of events from Watergate to a major investigation of the CIA by a Senate select committee, and he had resisted the process of exposure at every step of the way. Helms had feared two consequences from the hemorrhage of Agency secrets which was still continuing: the demoralization of the CIA, unaccustomed to public scrutiny; and a field day for hostile intelligence services rummaging through the Senate committee's voluminous reports. In Helms's view both had occurred, just as predicted. He was not a believer in catharsis. He was neither embarrassed nor repentant. Men of the world knew that the business of intelligence was more than a simple matter of spy and counterspy. What Helms did not understand was the relentless harping—especially on the part of certain Senate liberals and the press—on the "crimes" of the CIA. Of course Helms read the papers; he knew there was a large public that did not like the Agency and what it was taken to represent—the secret expedients of power and the failures of American Presidents who had tried to bull their way in the world. The wreckage of Vietnam was proof enough that something had gone terribly wrong. But in Helms's view the hostility focused on the Agency, and indirectly on him, was the result of an all-but-willful refusal to accept the reality of an anarchic international system, in which vigilance, power, and strength of will were a nation's best—indeed only—defense. Destruction of the CIA through exposure and recrimination was like spiking the guns. These contrary views of the Agency were very far apart, and it was characteristic of Helms that he did not surrender an iota of his.

Out of a job for the first time in nearly forty years, Helms was confused and even angry in a way he had never been before. This was not something he wanted to admit, even to his friends when they met for lunch in town or talked on the phone. He had plenty of time on his hands and was restless after so many years of running things. He had no choice in the matter; his lawyer had told him to keep out of the public eye. But it went against the grain. Temperament and years of habit had accustomed him to days of busy executive routine: office by eight thirty, meetings throughout the day, the review of endless pieces of paper, departure regularly at six thirty with a clean desk. CIA people like to tell stories about the Agency's great days and the adventurous men who ran its operations before everything fell apart, but they do not tell anecdotes about Helms; there aren't any. He is remembered as an administrator, impatient with delay, excuses, self-seeking, the sour air of office politics. Asked for an example of Helms's characteristic utterance, three of his old friends came up with the same dry phrase: "Let's get on with it." He had hired out to do a job, he did today what had to be done today, he left his desk clean at night.

Of course every desk at the CIA was clean at night. The security people roamed the building after the close of work and handed out demerits for unlocked safes, full trash baskets, classified documents left in desk drawers. Even the desk of a man like Richard Bissell had been clean at night, before he left the CIA, in disgrace, after the collapse of his plan to invade Cuba at the Bay of Pigs. It would be hard to imagine two men more unlike than Richard Helms and Richard Bissell. Helms had been unhappy when Bissell got the job Helms wanted back in 1958, but it wasn't solely personal disappointment which distressed him. Bissell was loquacious, inventive, the most open-minded of men; there was literally nothing you might propose to him which he would not turn this way and that in his logical mind, judging it strictly on its practical merits. A plan to invade Cuba, a poisoned handkerchief for an Arab general—he was ready to entertain them all. But Bissell's logical clarity was illusory. He sometimes fatally misjudged men. He worked out schemes for management and then broke his own rules. His desk was chaos. One look at it (and Helms did not get many; Bissell did not invite Helms's advice) and you might despair for the country. But even Richard Bissell's desk, straightened up by his secretary, was clean at night.

No branch of the American government was in better order at night than the CIA, in its huge headquarters in the middle of a woods in Langley, Virginia. Allen Dulles got his old friend and legal client Edward Durrell Stone to design the building, he got the Congress to put up $65 million, and he gave himself an office with a private dining room on the seventh floor. But Dulles never moved in; he left with Bissell, and for the same reason. The closest Dulles came to ruling there was showing President Kennedy around the place. It was the biggest thing of its kind in the world, much larger and more modern than the headquarters of the Committee for State Security—the KGB—in Moscow. At night security people roamed the halls, checking desks and testing doors. A duty officer would be there with a small staff, ready to warn the Director if something came up. Communications people decoded cables as they came in from the CIA's hundreds of stations and bases around the world. Beginning at 3:00 a.m. a small group in the Office of Current Intelligence would be working on the President's daily briefing, a document whose name and style changed over the years to reflect the preference of the only reader who mattered. But for the most part the CIA was empty at night, the safes and color-coded office doors were all locked, and every desk was as clean as the day it arrived from the General Services Administration. The nation's secrets were each in their appointed place, and you might have thought, if you had made the rounds with the security officers checking for violations, that the country must be in good order, that everyone knew his job and accepted the ground rules and agreed on the importance and purpose of the business at hand. An illusion, as Richard Bissell abruptly discovered in April 1961.

Helms had not been much surprised by Bissell's failure at the time. But he cannot have imagined, as he picked up the pieces as Bissell's successor, that his own gifts as an administrator, his long experience in managing secret operations, his devotion to their secrecy, his caution and cool judgment would all fail, too. Indeed, before his government was through with him, Helms would have reason to envy Bissell's quiet departure. The problem, as Helms would have plenty of time but little temperamental inclination to reflect in the spring of his discontent in 1977, was not the way he or Bissell or anyone else in the CIA had been going about his job, but the job itself. The problem was what they did. The meticulous routine and order of the Agency, the tables of organization, the well-established and accepted dealings with the other branches of government, the procedures for internal and external control, the apparent consensus of official Washington on the importance of the CIA's work—all were illusory. The structure was jerry-built. The agreement was mostly confined to a small circle in Washington.

The arrangement had worked so well for so long it was hard to see how fragile it was. The foreign policy establishment in Washington trusted the CIA (and still trusts it, for that matter); but outside governing circles the political foundation of the CIA rested on nothing more substantial than a popular fascination with espionage and a conviction that we are the good guys. The American public, in short, had been taught a kind of child's history of the world, sanitized of the rougher facts of international life. A high-minded, almost Victorian political morality obtained. Presidents, congressional leaders, the Pentagon, and the State Department all found it convenient to let the public assume that only the Other Side did things like that. We did not bribe foreign politicians. We did not undermine other governments. We did not invade other countries with secret armies. We did not spread lies, conduct medical experiments, put prisoners in padded rooms for years on end, build stocks of poison, sabotage factories, contaminate foodstuffs, pass machine guns to men who planned to turn them on their national leaders. Above all, we did not plot to kill men for nothing more than displeasing Washington. To discover oneself the victim of so many illusions, all at once, is disorienting. The result has been a profound shift in public attitudes and deep confusion in Washington, where simultaneous efforts are under way to make sure the high-minded morality really obtains this time; to deny that it was ever seriously breached; and to get the CIA back on the job.

The questions of what the CIA does, and for whom, are not of much moment to Helms; there was never any doubt in his mind about either of those. He did not give much credit to the notion that now things were going to change, because he did not believe the CIA had ever done much that was wrong. One of the things which made him angry in the spring of 1977—and there were several—was this idea that the CIA was guilty of heinous crimes. What crimes? Three major investigations[1] had studied the Agency from top to bottom, and in thirty years of CIA history—busy every day—nothing much worse turned up than lapses, indiscretions, technical infractions of the Agency's charter, overzealousness in the pursuit of spies, too-willing accommodation of the wishes of a recent President, faulty judgment, and other avoidable errors. It wasn't much, stacked up against the records of a few other intelligence agencies, and not all of them Communist either. Helms was not ashamed of his record.

Then why the public air of horror? Not just on the part of the multitudes who only knew what they saw on television, but on the part of well-informed men in Washington? No one had seriously proposed doing things any differently. Stripped of persiflage, the recommendations of the three groups of investigators reduced to tinkering with the machinery, a lot of it,

Helms suspected, purely for effect. The idea, for example, that all covert operations should be approved on paper—really approved, not just glossed for the record. Helms did not exhibit profound respect for the authors of that proposal. He knew something of the way the world worked. It was not carelessness which explained the scanty record where certain operations were concerned.

If Helms and other CIA officials had been vague in their testimony about the authorization of certain operations—proposals to kill Patrice Lumumba and Fidel Castro, for example—it was not because they did not know who gave the orders, in what frame of mind, to whom, in which words, but because they had sworn not to reveal the secret, of course . . . and because there would not be one single piece of paper to support anyone who had the temerity to tell the truth.

Kennedy people like Robert McNamara, Maxwell Taylor, Richard Goodwin, Theodore Sorensen, and McGeorge Bundy had been strangely quiet while CIA officials had groped through the past like amnesia victims for the source of orders to kill Castro. The Senate Intelligence Committee headed by Frank Church had concluded that authority for the plot could not be pinned down definitively. Could anyone believe the Kennedy people would all have been chewing on pencils and murmuring disbelief if the CIA had truly been off on its own where Castro was concerned? They would have raised the roof. Could anyone believe that the CIA as an institution much cared who ruled Cuba? Could anyone doubt the response of the Kennedy people, and very likely the Senate Intelligence Committee itself, if some CIA official had risked the complete absence of a single piece of paper to back him up and had said: Well, who do you think ordered Castro's assassination, the office boy? *It was John F. Kennedy and his brother Bobby.* If Helms had said that (which in my opinion he could have), he not only would have been the target of some extremely caustic comment, but from that day forward he would have lunched alone.

There is an argument to be made that the Church Committee answered the question of responsibility in the only way it could: Not proved. But a recommendation that all covert operations in future ought to be authorized in writing was, in Helms's view, disingenuous. That's putting it kindly. Church knew how the world worked. Presidents don't sign orders to kill people. Only a bubblehead or a man plumping himself for higher office would even consider such a proposal. If Church's ambitions in that line had been fulfilled—and there wasn't a single CIA officer who doubted he was trying to launch himself toward the White House from the CIA's prostrate back—he would have acted in these matters exactly as his predecessors. Boys, you know what I want. Do it. *But nothing on paper.* A classic case of hypocrisy. *That isn't the way you do these things.*

The recommendations were all the same: tinkering with the machinery. An exercise in hypocrisy and grandstanding. Take the Rockefeller Commission's criticism of Helms for surrendering certain sensitive CIA files to Richard Nixon.[2] The Commission implied that Helms ought to have known Nixon intended to misuse those files for domestic political purposes, and it concluded that the Director of Central Intelligence should be a man with a political base outside the Agency so that he might be in a better position to refuse illegitimate requests.

In the spring of 1977, two years after the Rockefeller Commission's report, Helms was still bitter about the injustice of this personal attack. The Commission had implied it was Nixon who called in Helms and put him on the carpet, after John Ehrlichman had asked for the files. Well, it was Helms who insisted on that meeting, not Nixon, and the Commission knew it. Helms told them they ought to get the tape of the meeting; he knew there was one because a Washington journalist, Walter Pincus, had quoted from it in an article.[3] But this was Ford's commission; it wasn't about to start rooting around in Nixon's past. It was easier to blame Helms for giving in. Helms didn't appreciate that, just as he didn't appreciate old friends saying he never had money of his own—unlike a lot of early CIA people—and as a result was never quite independent.

Helms didn't think he had kowtowed to Nixon. What else could he have done? Nixon was the President, however much the Monday-morning quarterbacks might lament the fact with the safety of hindsight. The DCI worked for only one President at a time. You can't tell a President you won't give him a piece of his own government's paper. Could anyone doubt how a perennial presidential candidate like Nelson Rockefeller would have responded if he had ever gone all the way and some DCI—*his* DCI—had demurred at such a request? Rockefeller would have demanded those files *right now*. Another classic case of hypocrisy.

It was hard for Helms to see that anything much had changed by the spring of 1977. No one was suggesting the CIA ought to be disbanded. No one was seriously suggesting that covert operations ought to be stopped altogether, at least no one with much prospect of being heeded. The recommendations were all for tinkering with the machinery: move the DCI downtown, give him real authority over the intelligence community (as opposed to the responsibility without authority with which every DCI had been burdened since 1947), introduce some new pieces of paper, reroute the flow of some old pieces of paper, etc., etc. There had been a lot of talk, expressions of shock about CIA "excesses," highfalutin proposals for reform, various changes of name—the Directorate for Plans had become the Directorate for Operations, a quantum jump in candor, perhaps, but it didn't change by an iota what it did. In the same spirit, the 40 Committee which approved covert operations had become the Operations Advisory Group. Some old groups had been disbanded (the President's Foreign Intelligence Advisory Board; the CIA's Board of National Estimates), some new ones formed.

Perhaps the biggest change of all was the creation of a Senate Intelligence Oversight Committee with its own staff and its own files; earlier attempts in 1955 and 1966 had both been defeated by CIA lobbying and presidential hostility.

But for all the tinkering, the machinery itself was not much changed. The CIA still worked for the President, and in addition to its job of preventing unpleasant surprises by watching the world with an educated eye, it remained the covert arm of American policy. A President needed more choices than the dispatch of a white paper or the Marines. When Jimmy Carter took over the White House and immediately began looking for ways to protect the secrets, Senator Daniel Patrick Moynihan wryly remarked, "He's just discovered it's *his* CIA."

But this absence of change, this inability of the U.S. government to alter fundamentally what the CIA did, and how it did it, was also an illusion. Helms and his friends might all agree there was no other way to do these things, but the public was not to be coaxed back into the consensus so easily. A kind of geological fault had opened between the CIA as it was and the world the public thought it lived in. In the spring of 1977 Helms found himself on the far side of the fault, in some sense a ruined man, destroyed by the very thing—the cold recoil of a people nurtured on a child's history of the world—which had ended the career of his old rival Richard Bissell fifteen years earlier.

Ruined? Destroyed? Here Helms would protest with all the heat of a man who knows (even if he dare not say in every instance) that he has never done one thing in any of his jobs—with the Office of Strategic Services (OSS) in World War II, as an official in the CIA's clandestine arm, as director of it or the Agency, as ambassador to Iran—which he had not been directed to do by lawful authority. If you want to argue the merits of this decision or that he will argue, perhaps even surrender the odd point; no man achieves everything he tries. But how could he have been "ruined" or "destroyed" in the honest service of his country, under the direction of its elected and appointed representatives, for purposes which Monday-morning quarterbacks might sneer at but which were shared by every leading element in American government and life at the time?

But certain facts dispute him. The geological fault was there. He had time for phone calls and lunch with friends, for tennis and evenings out, for mowing the lawn and weeding the garden if he cared to do so (which he did not), because he was not free to find a job. He had toyed with the idea of writing his memoirs and straightening out a thing or two, but his better judgment and his lawyer told him that now was not the time. He'd get about halfway through and the Justice Department would subpoena his manuscript and notes.

Helms was the sort of man who greeted a visitor at nine o'clock on a sunny morning on his front doorstep, as lean as a long-distance runner and looking just about as restless, dressed in a suit and tie. He would not have been dressed any differently if he'd been on his way to present an annual report to a board of directors, but he was not going anywhere. The reason was not that he was looking forward to a chance to read the collected novels of Balzac at last, or that he wanted to stay home to work on his stamp collection, or that he welcomed the freedom to watch a whole season of baseball on television. The reason was that his whole life was hanging fire while he waited to learn if a special grand jury in the District of Columbia would vote to indict him for certain acts committed shortly after he ceased to be the Director of Central Intelligence.

Indicted *for what?* Helms would ask in his own defense. The question would not be frivolously put. It was precisely what he could not understand. Helms is a man with an oddly appealing grin. His lower jaw juts out a trace, giving his otherwise ordinarily handsome face a singularity. His grin, lower jaw out, eyes wide, hands up, has about it an ironic, incredulous air; he can be amused, bewildered, and angry at the same time. *For what?*

He knows perfectly well for what, but intends to convey his own contention that he had never done anything he was not asked, ordered, expected, or required to do by the nature of his job. In particular, the Director of Central Intelligence had a responsibility not to answer every idle question put to him. He was charged under the National Security Act of 1947 with protection of the CIA's sources and methods. No one has ever spelled out what powers are thereby granted to the DCI. The FBI under J. Edgar Hoover, who tried to abort the CIA at birth and once broke off liaison with the Agency out of sheer pique, was not much help where protecting the secrets was concerned. He would not institute a search for leaks without a written order from the Attorney General. Sometimes he had to be all but begged to install a perfectly legal wiretap or bugging device in some Washington embassy. Helms had to protect the CIA's secrets by himself. It was his job and he did it. Indicted *for what?*

The narrow answer was for perjury before the Senate Foreign Relations Committee on February 7, 1973, when Helms answered a question by Senator Stuart Symington—"Did you try in the Central Intelligence Agency to overthrow the government of Chile?"—with an unequivocal, "No, sir."

"Did you have any money passed to the opponents of Allende?"

"No, sir."

"So the stories you were involved in that war are wrong?"

"Yes, sir."[4]

After his testimony on that day, during confirmation hearings on his appointment as ambassador to Iran, Helms asked the CIA's general counsel, Lawrence Houston, to review his remarks—a standard procedure. Houston did so. He told Helms everything seemed okay to him, with one exception:

on this matter of Chile . . . Helms might have "a problem" there. Helms said he thought not. He knew what he meant. He let his testimony stand.

This was not feckless optimism on Helms's part. He knew very well that the CIA, in September 1970, had tried to mount a military coup in Chile in order to prevent the confirmation of Salvador Allende's victory in the Chilean presidential election. But the seven Senators present on February 7 were not specifically authorized to probe CIA secrets—not in that forum, at any rate—and thirty years of precedent in the CIA, not to mention two or three thousand years of precedent in the history of secret intelligence agencies, held that secrets were never idly disclosed. The attempt to overthrow the government of Chile in 1970 was such a secret. It was so secret that not even the U.S. ambassador to Chile at the time, Edward Korry, knew the effort was being made. This had been at the specific direction of President Nixon. If Helms felt his testimony about Chile was not "a problem," it was because he had done exactly what was expected of him by the authorities to whom he was responsible as DCI, which did not include the full membership of the Senate Foreign Relations Committee, just as it did not include the membership of the Committee's Subcommittee on Multinational Corporations, when it asked him all the same questions on March 6, 1973, and got the same answers.

But Chile was a problem. Helms might affect angry incredulity at the suggestion he was liable for indictment, but the Department of Justice had been considering the matter since December 1974; a grand jury had been hearing evidence, Helms had been formally notified of the proceedings against him, he had retained a lawyer (Edward Bennett Williams, the sort of lawyer retained by people who know they really do have a problem), and the new President, Jimmy Carter, had publicly stated that the matter of Helms's indictment was in the hands of the Attorney General, Griffin Bell. A number of Helms's friends, including Larry Houston, had reluctantly concluded that an indictment was quite probable. Houston knew the CIA was still being pressed for documentation, and that the grand jury was looking into possible conversations about Chile which might have taken place among Helms, John McCone—a former CIA director, and now a member of the board of International Telephone and Telegraph (ITT)—and ITT's president, Harold Geneen. The implication was that some sort of conspiracy indictment was under consideration.

Taken together with claims by some of Helms's friends that he would defend himself vigorously, and that Henry Kissinger and Nixon would inevitably find themselves in the middle of things, Helms's problem added up to a general mess of a sort unthinkable in previous years. But the dimensions and possible consequences of the mess had not yet halted the investigation, despite quiet appeals to the Justice Department by distinguished Washington figures who thought Helms was getting a raw deal. *In toto,* these facts explained why Helms, who ought to have encountered little difficulty in finding a job, was not free to write his memoirs or accept employment or do much of anything except play tennis, dine with friends, and wait for his lawyer to straighten things out.

Not far from the home of Richard Helms in Washington lived another former director of the CIA, William Colby, just across the district line in Bethesda, Maryland. The two men had somewhat similar histories. Both had joined OSS during the war, served in the CIA from its earliest years,[5] and worked their way up through the Directorate for Plans. Colby was a good deal shorter than Helms but just as lean, with an even greater mastery of the poker player's blank gaze. Actually, poker players are open books compared to former Directors of the CIA. A lot of retired CIA officials have faces which betray them. Perhaps it is the fact that until recently they have rarely dealt with journalists, and then only on their own terms. They have none of the average Congressman's ability to look you straight in the eye and say his only interest in the oil depletion allowance is what's best for the country. Practice makes perfect. Intelligence officers are supposed to have a passion for anonymity (Allen Dulles considered it a *sine qua non* for everybody but himself) and do not get the average Congressman's practice in protective dissimulation. Faced with a bald question about the source of orders for Castro's assassination, say, some former CIA officials will betray dramatic signs of psychological stress.

Helms and Colby, whose job involved the political dimension of dealing with official Washington, were not such men. When they wanted to keep a secret they either kept their mouths shut or found a way around it. Both were gifted with severe internal control, perhaps by temperament, certainly by training. They did not betray themselves, which led one to wonder what a meeting of the two would be like now.

Helms and Colby had never been close in a personal sense, but Helms did not make appointments on friendship alone. Back in 1962, in fact, he had fired a frequent tennis partner during a CIA manpower cutback very largely because the man had presumed on their tennis friendship in asking Helms to save his job. It was Colby's professional ability which led Helms to give him a series of jobs ending with the Agency's number three position, Executive Director/Comptroller, which put Colby in line to win the confidence of Helms's successor, James Schlesinger, and then to follow him in the job only a few months after Helms had gone to Iran.

Helms had a pretty clear head where the relations of high government officials were concerned, but still, there was such a thing as loyalty. He himself had referred more than once in his testimony before the Senate Intelligence Committee to the loyalty he felt toward John McCone, who had given him his job as DDP. At one point, for example, McCone's executive assistant Walter Elder had told the Committee that he had given Helms an explicit briefing on McCone's hostility toward the very idea of assassination, which, as a good Catholic, McCone took to be wrong. (He had even worried aloud, on the phone once to Robert McNamara, that he might be excommunicated if word got out that the government was talking about killing Castro.) Elder's testimony was extremely inconvenient to Helms. He said he did not remember the episode. He might have been a good deal more explicit and saved himself from the Committee's pointed skepticism, but he held back. "As I said, and I would like to repeat it, Mr. McCone had given me my job, he had promoted me, I felt close to him, I felt loyal to him, and I would not have violated an instruction he gave me if I could have possibly helped it."[6] That was a pretty soft way of saying Walt Elder never told him any such thing.

Helms had given Colby his job, and, in Helms's view, he had been oddly rewarded. In May 1973 the then-DCI James Schlesinger had issued an order, drafted and urged on him by Colby, ordering employees of the CIA to report all suspected violations of the law or the CIA's charter to the office of the Inspector General, at that time William Broe. One of the reports, investigated at length by three men appointed by Broe, concerned Helms's possible perjury on the subject of Chile. Back in September 1970, Broe had been chief of the Western Hemisphere Division of the DDP when the CIA looked under every rock in Chile trying to find someone who might block Allende's confirmation as President. One of the men the CIA talked to was General Arturo Marshall, a right-wing fanatic. When the Agency learned that Marshall was behind a series of bombings in Santiago, and was even toying with the idea of assassinating Allende, it dropped him as pure trouble. Broe knew all about Chile, and he certainly knew that Helms's bland denials on the subject were just plain false. But this was a legal question. Perjury is a hard charge to prove.

Larry Houston and other CIA officials protested to Colby that the IG investigators were not lawyers, did not understand the perjury laws, and suspected a crime where none existed. They urged Colby to suppress the report. Colby refused. He said he was under explicit instructions from the Attorney General to report all possible violations of the law. He had to comply. In December 1974, Colby personally turned over the IG's charges against Helms to the Justice Department. This was the proximate cause of all Helms's subsequent legal difficulties, and while Helms may have limited himself publicly to the reflection that Colby did not have to do that, in private he seems to have felt that Colby's action was one of reckless, even vindictive, disloyalty.

That was bad enough. Even worse was Colby's strategy—if you could call it strategy; it struck Helms and his friends as more like abject surrender —in dealing with the Senate Intelligence Committee. He simply handed over whatever he was asked for—postmortems, IG reports, cables to the

Washington, slyly hinting that Richard Helms had blackmailed his own President, threatening him with exposure unless he were given a job as ambassador. The reviewers pounced on Ehrlichman's book; was he trying to tell us something?

Helms had come to Washington thirty years earlier, he had lived on a government salary at a time when government salaries were so low you had to dragoon men into serving their country, he did his job as best he knew how, he won the respect of the handful of men who understood his work, he did what he was asked, even went out onto a limb or two. How was he rewarded? With a threat of jail and the innuendo of a goddamn liar like John Ehrlichman. It would be fair to say that in the spring of 1977, Richard Helms was neither repentant nor apologetic. But Helms might protest all he liked; there was another possible view of these matters, one which suggested that the exercise of American power in the postwar world had not always been so humane, reasonable, and inevitable as CIA people liked to argue. Helms's isolation was the result of the very last thing he had ever expected: the secrets had begun to leak out, the debate had grown general, and for the first time in his life, Helms was arguing with a public that knew something of what he had been doing.

Chapter 2

One bright, quiet morning in the early summer of 1947 a man in a plain business suit walked up to the door of a house on Bradley Lane, just behind the Chevy Chase Club in Maryland, and knocked precisely at 9:30 a.m. A moment later the door was opened by a ten-year-old boy named John Ansell. "Is your mother in?" asked the man standing there. "I'm from the FBI." He flashed his badge.

John said his mother was, and the man followed him into the house as he went to call her. The man sat down on a couch in the living room and watched the boy climb partway up the stairs. "Mom," he called out, "there's a man here to see you." His mother called back that she'd be down in a few minutes, would John please tell the man to drive around the block and come back. John returned with the message, but the man from the FBI did not get up to drive around the block. Instead he asked the boy's name. John told him.

"Do you know the family next door?" the man asked.

John said he did.

"Do you know Mr. Helms?"

"Yes."

"What do you think of him?"

The man's expressionless eyes watched John closely.

"He's a stern man and hard on his kids," said John.

"Have you been inside their house?" the man asked.

John said he had, and the man from the FBI asked a series of questions. What was it like in their house? What do they do? Did Mr. and Mrs. Helms get along? Does Mr. Helms drink? Is there anything unusual about Mr. Helms?

"Do you mean . . . something funny?"

"Yes."

John said there was. The man from the FBI sat up a degree straighter. Something like interest flickered across his cold face.

John blurted out, "He doesn't have any hair on his chest, and I think he . . . *waxes* it."

For a moment the FBI man's face registered nothing. Then his mouth dropped open.

The interview was over, but ten-year-old John Ansell had not revealed everything he'd learned about Richard Helms since he had moved in next door with his family in the spring of 1946. John had been delighted. There were two children: Dennis Helms, then three, and Helms's stepdaughter Judy, who was John's age. Not long after that, Helms invited his new neighbors in for a drink, to get acquainted. The reception was friendly enough, and John's father, Burr Ansell, fell into the inevitable conversation with Helms as their wives talked. The exchange went roughly like this:

HELMS: What do you do for a living, Burr?
ANSELL: I'm a lawyer in private practice, some routine legal work, some business with government agencies. What do you do, Dick?
HELMS: How about another drink?

Burr Ansell wasn't settling for that, and on perhaps the third try he elicited a laconic admission that Helms "worked for the government." When John overheard his parents talking about this later, his interest was piqued. One Sunday John's mother invited Helms's stepdaughter to go to church with them and on the way John turned to Judy in the back seat and said, "Judy, what does your father do?" Judy looked him right in the eye and said, "I can't tell you." John's interest naturally redoubled, and a couple of Sundays later he tried again. "John," she said this time, "I shouldn't tell you this, but . . . my father's a spy."

From that moment on, for nearly fifteen years, John Ansell watched Richard Helms, asked questions, and tried to put things together in an effort to find out just what it was, exactly, that Helms did. But Helms was an elusive man, laconic and reserved, most often seen coming and going, or on his way to the Chevy Chase Club in his tennis whites; or mowing his lawn, immaculate in white shirt and white duck trousers, until the middle 1950s when Helms's son Dennis was old enough to take over. At night Ansell sometimes heard Helms at the typewriter until ten or eleven, working in a room just off the second-story screened porch. A set of wind chimes hung on the porch, and when there was a breeze John Ansell would hear the tinkling of the chimes and the tap-tappeta-tap of Helms at his typewriter late into the night.

Mrs. Helms was a woman who made some impression on Bradley Lane. She was six years older than Helms, and she was a sculptress with a hobby of restoring old carousel horses, a woman as friendly and open, in John Ansell's memory, as Helms was elusive. His manner and dress announced very little about himself. His cars were old, conservative, unremarkable. It would be hard to imagine a deader black than the black of the 1950 Plymouth Helms drove to work for years, the sort of car it was easy to lose in traffic, hard to find in a parking lot. Later, around 1958 or 1959, Helms inherited a gray 1952 Cadillac from his father. That may sound like a step up in the world, but it was not. The Cadillac was as invisible as the Plymouth, a car like any other, a carefully muted statement of anonymity. Nothing about Helms suggested, much less announced, his profession. When he left for work promptly at eight in the morning he did not turn right on Connecticut Avenue and head directly for downtown Washington and his office in one of the four CIA buildings across from the reflecting pool. Instead, he crossed Connecticut and took the Brookville Road, the long way around, thereby disguising his destination.

Two or three times in the course of a summer Helms and his wife would give a good-sized garden party at night with lanterns hung in the backyard. These were formal, even genteel affairs of circulating couples and tinkling glasses, lasting perhaps until one in the morning. On other occasions four or five couples might come over in the evening and sit on the back porch. Then, and only then, John Ansell sometimes heard Helms laugh. It struck him because Helms had a big booming laugh—ho! ho! ho!—quite unlike his even, unemphatic voice at other times.

Helms was, in fact, a man who betrayed very little by way of emotion. Even in circumstances of danger or stress he remained under tight control. In May 1952, for example, a lot of Helms's neighbors literally saw him for the first time following a sudden, violent rain- and windstorm which swept Chevy Chase, uprooting forty or fifty big trees in the area immediately surrounding Bradley Lane. Light poles were down and the live electrical wires were dancing in the street, jumping wildly with cracks and sizzles from puddles of rainwater. When the wind died, people came out and approached the wires, not comprehending the danger. Burr Ansell was among them, and he was surprised to see Helms come out too, then amazed when Helms with only a word or two took charge of the situation, got people back out of the way. After the power had been turned off and the danger was past, Helms disappeared back into his house. The mystified Burr wrote John, away on a visit, "It was almost as if he had been trained to do that."

Helms's near-invisibility on Bradley Lane was no accident. He conducted his life, as he chose his cars, so that anyone who asked what is Richard Helms like? what does he think? what is he for or against? would be hard put to come up with a single word in reply. A man without qualities, to most of his neighbors at any rate. Later in 1952 John Ansell, by then sixteen, asked Mrs. Helms whom she favored in the presidential election. "Stevenson," she said.

"Who's Mr. Helms for?" asked John.

"We don't talk about that," said Mrs. Helms. "He can't be for anybody. Not in his position."

For fifteen years, from 1946 until Helms and his family moved away just after the turn of the year in 1961, John Ansell tried but failed to learn anything of substance about Richard Helms or his job. All he knew was what Judy had told him, that he was "a spy." Helms not only successfully concealed his work; he concealed himself. In all those years, John saw Helms express emotion only once. It had happened in May 1947. John was home working on a paper for school about South America when Judy rang the doorbell. She was terribly upset, in tears. No one explained in so many words, but John gathered that Judy, sick and home alone in bed, had been somehow frightened by a young man there to wash the windows. John never learned exactly what had happened, but he remembered Helms's face after he arrived. He was furious, his mouth was set, his eyes hard and angry, and when he spoke his teeth literally bared. John Ansell never saw Helms look like that again except once, on television in August 1973, when Helms was being cross-examined by the Senate Watergate Committee.

When Richard Helms moved to Washington in the spring of 1946 he was abandoning an old ambition for a career of anonymity and problematic advancement, going against the advice of friends who said he was making a mistake, the war was over, there was no longer a need for the arcane trade in which Helms had been trained. Helms's first ambition had been to own a newspaper. After he was graduated from Williams College in 1935, finishing second in his class and voted most likely to succeed, Helms approached Hugh Baillie, the president of United Press, for a job in Europe, where he had spent two high school years, one at Le Rosey in Switzerland, the other at the Realgymnasium in Freiburg, Germany. Most news organizations reserve foreign posts for reporters who have proved themselves, but the UP, a wire service with a need for bodies at minimum expense, would give foreign jobs to young men who were willing to pay their own travel expenses and to work for local wages. Helms wanted the experience, accepted Baillie's offer, and bought his own ticket to London, where he worked briefly before moving on to the UP bureau in Berlin.

The bureau chief in Berlin was Fred Oechsner, who later went on to join the State Department. Oechsner liked Helms, thought his German fair to good, and sometimes gave him the sort of assignments a veteran journalist might envy. In September 1936, Oechsner sent Helms down to Nuremberg to cover the Partaitag—the annual celebration of the National Socialist party. There Helms watched Hitler work himself and his crowd into a simultaneous frenzy, something he would not forget. After a rally, reporters in a press car followed Hitler across the city to the Nuremberg Castle, where they were startled to discover themselves being introduced to the Führer himself. He struck Helms as a small, unimposing figure, but as soon as Hitler spoke, Helms sensed a certain confidence and intelligence and, above all, clear-headedness. "A Europe led by cultural regimes one could understand," Hitler said to the reporters on the parapets of Nuremberg Castle. "But that Moscow, of all places, should seek to dominate Europe— that's something we Germans could never accept. Of course, we no longer fear Bolshevism inside of Germany. But, we have only one fear—I say it quite openly—that the countries around us into which this poison is slowly eating its way, will gradually succumb, one after another, to Bolshevism. To that we could not remain indifferent for we are, after all, a European nation. Of course, we could lean back and say, 'Let them slaughter their officers, slay their priests and intellectuals. It's none of our business.' Only someone with the mentality of a child would take that attitude."[1]

Helms wrote a story for UP about his meeting with Hitler, and then, eighteen months later, following Hitler's march into Austria on March 11, 1938, Helms wrote about the episode again, looking for what it was that drove Hitler forward. The man seemed split between the megalomania which fired his oratory and the calculating intelligence, cool and balanced, which he revealed in private. In Helms's final article on the subject, written for the Indianapolis *Times*, he guessed wrong: Hitler had learned caution from the beer hall *putsch*, Helms concluded, and would pick his way carefully.

But by that time Helms had deliberately given up the life of politics and great events. After two years in Europe he had learned a good deal about reporting and the ordeal-by-routine of wire service work, but more importantly that wherever the UP might lead (generally midnight pallor, liver trouble, and white hair at thirty-five), it was not toward his goal of owning a newspaper. For that, he was advised, he needed business experience, so in 1937 he left the UP and Europe for a job on the business side of the Indianapolis *Times*. By the time the United States entered the war in December 1941, Helms had risen to become the paper's national advertising manager. Helms immediately joined the Navy, applied for a commission, and after the usual bureaucratic delay (his file was lost under another letter of the alphabet for a number of months) he was sent to Harvard in July 1942 for a sixty-day training course. In September he was assigned to the office of the Commander, Eastern Sea Frontier, in New York City, where he spent a year in the Operations Department plotting German submarine activity in the North Atlantic.

Sometime during that year in New York Helms was contacted by his old Berlin bureau chief, Fred Oechsner, who had gone to work in the Morale Operations Department of the recently established Office of Strategic Services (OSS), then organizing itself in Washington as the first genuine foreign intelligence agency in U.S. history. With the help of the British Secret Intelligence Service (SIS, also known as MI 6), William Donovan, a Wall Street lawyer and World War I hero with access to President Roosevelt, was attempting to create overnight what it had taken the British centuries to evolve. A man of enormous crude energy and the open, adventurous mind which was to characterize American intelligence until the Bay of Pigs, Donovan was recruiting men for his new organization wherever he could find them—on Wall Street, in big corporations and Ivy League faculties, through the friends of friends. It had occurred to Fred Oechsner that Helms was just the sort of fellow the OSS needed—intelligent, spoke a couple of languages, knew his way around Europe. He called Helms to ask if he'd like to come down to Washington and sign on.

Helms thought not. Oechsner detected in Helms's refusal a note of caution natural to a young man of ambition, a question as to whether the OSS might fizzle. He already had a job of some importance, prospects of advancement. Oechsner's clearest impression of Helms was as a man who always knew what he intended to do, and how to go about it. He respected him for it. He was sorry to lose Helms, but not surprised.

But later Helms was simply assigned to the OSS by the Navy. A request had gone in for someone with a knowledge of German and a background in journalism; the names of Helms and two other men popped out of the files; the others were unavailable—and in August 1943, Helms reported to an OSS farm in Maryland for another round of training, this time as a secret intelligence operative.

His training was of the standard sort: how to fire a weapon, secret communications, the tradecraft of espionage, hand-to-hand combat. This last was under the instruction of a British colonel seconded to the OSS, a former chief of the Shanghai police who knew a great deal about the maiming or killing of an opponent in close-contact fighting. Helms never laid a hand on anyone during the war or thereafter, but there was another purpose behind such training. It put a man in the right frame of mind, it gave him a bearing of confidence, and it let him know the nature of the business in which he was engaged, which, office routine at one end, was treason, betrayal, and violence at the other.

When he had completed the OSS's short course in secret war Helms went to work for a time on the planning staff run by Kennett Hanks, where he shared an office with John Gardner,[2] before transferring to another office run by Edward Meyer. There Helms concentrated on the basic secret intelligence work which he was to defend throughout the rest of his career against the charms of covert political intervention, paramilitary activities, and other direct routes to secret ends. From the outside, espionage and covert action may seem all of a piece, but in fact they proceed in a quite different spirit. Paramilitary teams or covert political operatives necessarily draw attention to the people they support, if not always to themselves. That is the whole point. Far from trying to keep quiet, they are plunging directly into the struggle for power. This is not the sort of thing which can be done in perfect anonymity, and it is a dim target which does not quickly realize who is pulling the strings. But espionage, properly conducted, never announces itself. "Stolen" information remains in its accustomed place; the "spy" is a trusted civil servant; the spymaster betrays no sign of special knowledge; even the consumer of the purloined fact may not know whence it came. Helms's work for the OSS, at first organizing secret intelligence operations against Germany through Scandinavia, and later, in London and Europe in 1945, instilled in him a lifelong respect for the exacting art of espionage, the utility of a fact secretly learned, and the importance of secrecy.

It would be hard to exaggerate this matter of secrecy. At its heart is the simple fact that secret information is useful only as long as its acquisition remains secret. Once an opponent learns what you know, its utility either ceases altogether—as in the case of a compromised code, say—or diminishes very greatly. Even worse, if he secretly learns what you know, he is in a position to turn what you've learned against you. Mistakenly thinking the enemy is right *there* is more dangerous than plain ignorance. But worst of all is when an enemy gains control of your secret apparatus and begins to feed you information of his own choice. Outsiders do not quite believe in such things, but they happen.

Coupled with the danger of giving away what you've learned is the companion danger of compromising a source. This might be almost anything—a traditional spy, a way to intercept a diplomatic pouch, a vantage point from which to take photographs, a listening device, access to a trash basket. There is no end to the possibilities, but they all have in common that an enemy needs only to suspect the source to put it out of commission. Intelligence agencies do not proceed by the rules of evidence; any evidence where breaches of security are concerned amounts to a verdict of guilty. Hence the general rule, raised to the level of a theological principle, *that you can't be too careful.* Not knowing what clue might give away an operation, intelligence agencies proceed on the assumption that it's better to keep quiet about everything. Commitment to silence and the corresponding suspicion of questions sink deep into the personality of intelligence officers. Certainly they did in the case of Richard Helms, whose character early took on a certain opaque quality. Even those who knew him best are often hard put to say what he is like, and those who knew him from a distance retained little impression at all, like one woman in counterintelligence work in Washington during the war who often saw Helms in the corridors, but remembered only his tall frame and crisp Navy uniform and the cool air of a man for whom discretion has become not just second nature but the very bedrock of personality.

Helms did not stay long in London, in 1945, or later in Europe, but what he learned there stuck with him all the same. Friends said he carried away two abiding impressions: that secret intelligence matters, and that paramilitary derring-do doesn't. Early in the war Churchill had created a paramilitary organization called Special Operations Executive (SOE) whose job was to "set Europe ablaze" with sabotage, assassination, and partisan warfare. It can be argued that SOE blew up the odd ammunition train and power line, that it tied down German garrison troops throughout Europe, that it encouraged enmity and suspicion between occupation forces and the local population, and that it served to release Allied frustration during the long build-up for the invasion of Europe. But Helms was not impressed. In his opinion, friends said, it did not achieve results commensurate with the trouble it took. Secret intelligence gathered through the penetration of German military and political circles cost less, and was worth more.

From London, Helms moved on to Paris and Luxembourg. When Germany surrendered on May 8, 1945, Helms was at Eisenhower's headquarters at Rheims with General Walter Bedell Smith and Allen Dulles, the OSS's chief of mission in Berne, Switzerland. Dulles was already famous for his work in Berne, especially for his contact with German military officers plotting against Hitler. Helms had done nothing of that magnitude and Smith was purely a military man, but both men still had several things in common with Dulles. All would later be Directors of Central Intelligence, and all were convinced, even at that early date, that Russia would be no less of a threat to the peace of the world than Hitler, whose ashes had hardly cooled in Berlin.

The Cold War began long before it was named. In April 1945, Dulles asked an OSS officer named Frank Wisner to begin talks with Reinhard Gehlen, the former commander of Fremde Heere Ost (Foreign Armies East), an intelligence unit targeted on the Russians. Gehlen had hidden his files and escaped to the West in the firm conviction that the Americans would want his services. He was right. Soviet-American relations went sour from the beginning.

Not long after the shooting stopped, Donovan left Berlin to fly to Copenhagen with a young OSS officer, John Bross, who had been in charge of Jedburgh paramilitary teams which conducted operations against the Germans in Europe. As soon as they were in the air, Donovan turned to the pilot of the small plane and said, "My boy, you are flying west. We want to fly north."

The pilot explained that the area around Berlin was occupied by the Russians, who permitted overflights by the Allies only along a fixed East-West corridor between Berlin and the Allied-occupied zones to the west. Donovan was by nature something of an autocrat. He didn't know anything about this corridor and he didn't like it; he ordered the pilot to turn north *right now*. But the pilot refused; he was polite, but he had his orders. The Russians insisted everybody fly within the corridor, and that was what he was going to do.

The long debate over the origins of the Cold War would strike OSS veterans later as a silly exercise. In their experience the Cold War was a corollary of the shooting war from the beginning. OSS-supported resistance movements in France, Italy, Greece, Yugoslavia, and elsewhere were bitterly divided between right and left. In Yugoslavia, Tito's Communist partisans spent as much time fighting the Chetniks as they did the Germans, and when the war ended, Tito was in firm control. In Paris the Communist resistance had been only narrowly prevented from seizing power and establishing a de facto government before Charles de Gaulle entered the city. In Poland the Russians had waited patiently while the Germans destroyed an urban army loyal to the Polish exile government in England, and then moved in with their own Moscow exiles to take control of the country. Even the OSS had been polarized to a degree between right and left, one faction critical of the "leftists" Donovan recruited or was willing to work with in Europe. The history of OSS,[3] which is indistinguishable from the secret political history of the war, is marked by a preoccupation with Communism almost as intense as its commitment to victory against Germany. A woman who worked for Dulles in Berne thinks the focus of his attention—the kind of thing a man thinks about as he drifts to sleep at night, and wakes up to in the morning—was beginning to shift from Germany to Russia as early as Stalingrad. The OSS, including Helms, lived with the Soviet-American rivalry as a fact throughout the war. At the end of it Helms moved to Berlin with Dulles and Frank Wisner, where his efforts to penetrate the rapidly collapsing Nazi resistance groups gradually shifted to the problem of the Soviets.

Berlin was a nightmare of destruction at that time, a moonscape of rubble and haunted, half-starved civilians which no man who saw it seems ever to have forgotten. It was also the interface of East and West, the testing ground of Allied unity, but the formal division of the city into four zones of occupation disguised a deeper chaos in which the very streets designated as boundaries had sometimes wholly disappeared, leaving the armies of the victors to collide blindly. The U.S. military was charged with bringing order out of the chaos in the American zone, but it was impossible to know who was in charge, or to establish essential services, without knowing where the armies were. On this point, in the first days of the occupation, there was no certainty. The Russians simply refused to say. The American military government asked the OSS to tell them what the Russians wouldn't. Thus Helms quickly found himself trying to learn the same things about the Russians (the size and location of units; the organs of political control) in the same way (through agents) that he had pursued only weeks earlier against Germany. No one yet called Russia the enemy, but it was treated as if it were.

One day in the fall of 1945 Helms and a friend took a jeep into the Russian sector of Berlin, past suspicious, gun-happy guards, to the half-ruined Reichschancellerei where Hitler had ruled. There Helms poked about the empty building; it was as much a monument to failed megalomania as Ozymandias' trunkless legs of stone. The place was littered with smashed furniture, fallen plaster, spilled trash—the wreckage of defeat. One of the documents Helms lifted from the scattered books and papers was a watchlist of Britons to be arrested following a Nazi invasion of England. The Americans had just such a watchlist of Germans; many had already been arrested, some would be tried, a few hanged. The winner chooses. The Russians, too, had their watchlists, not only of Germans but of Poles, Czechs, Hungarians, Bulgarians, Rumanians, Latvians, Estonians. A handful would be openly tried; most would simply disappear.

Helms also came across some dinnerware and stationery with the chancellor's crest, and he took them as souvenirs. Later, using a sheet of stationery from Hitler's office, Helms wrote a letter to his three-year-old son, Dennis. The letter seems to have disappeared now, but Dennis, who read it when he was older, remembers it was short, even laconic, and concerned the evils of totalitarian power.

Even before the war was over, Donovan concluded that the age of America's innocent isolation was over. The country could not ignore the rest of the world again, and it would need an intelligence agency to keep an eye on the enemies of order. In November 1944, Donovan sent President Roosevelt a long memorandum describing the sort of agency he thought was needed: it was of a sort very like the OSS, to be run by a man very like Donovan. Roosevelt agreed, perhaps a sign that he intended to use more than charm in dealing with Stalin, and he drafted an executive order to establish a "general intelligence service."[4]

But Donovan's plan was not without opponents. The most important of them was the Director of the FBI, J. Edgar Hoover, who had fought creation of the OSS in the first place, had balked at internal security liaison with the British intelligence officers who helped organize OSS, and had successfully held on to an FBI intelligence network in Latin America. Early in 1945 Hoover personally handed copies of Donovan's memo and Roosevelt's proposed executive order to a Chicago *Tribune* reporter, Walter J. Trohan. The *Tribune* published Trohan's story on February 9, 1945, sparking a Washington controversy about an "American Gestapo" which effectively killed Donovan's initiative.

After Roosevelt's death in April, Donovan failed to establish a similar relationship of confidence with Truman, and on October 1, 1945, while Helms was still living in Berlin with Dulles, the new President summarily disbanded OSS and distributed some of its components to other departments, at least partly at the urging of Harold D. Smith, Director of the Bureau of the Budget, who had never liked Donovan's free and easy style. The Research and Analysis Branch was given to the State Department, while two other units, X-2 (or counterintelligence) and SI (or Secret Intelligence, for which Helms worked), went to the Department of War. There they were renamed the Strategic Services Unit (SSU) and put under the control of General John Magruder.

Truman's order initiated a period of confusing reorganization in which names, initials, lines of authority, and tables of organization were frequently shifted while the government found its peacetime footing and tried to decide just what sort of intelligence service it wanted, if any. The genesis of the CIA was erratic in a way typical of postwar Washington, a tangential result of attempts to unify the warring military services.

In June of 1945, James Forrestal, then Secretary of the Navy and a man whose name appears frequently in the early history of the Cold War,[5] asked a New York lawyer, Ferdinand Eberstadt, to make a study of merger proposals. His purpose was to preserve the independence of the Navy, and while Eberstadt recommended coordination in place of outright unification, the report he submitted in mid-September went much further to urge "a complete realignment of our governmental organizations to serve our national security. . . ." The United States, he said, needed "an alert, smoothly-working and efficient machine" for the purpose of "waging peace, as well as war."[6] Eberstadt's machine, as eventually implemented with only minor changes by the National Security Act of July 1947, was to include a National Security Council, an independent Army, Navy, and Air Force coordinated by a Joint Chiefs of Staff under the authority of a Department of Defense, and an intelligence agency.

The Central Intelligence Group (CIG), established by Truman on January 22, 1946, was feeble, indeed something of a joke. Two days after the order which founded it, Truman held a little party for its first director, Admiral Sidney Souers. The President presented the guests of honor with black hats, cloaks, and wooden daggers—an ironic gesture, since the CIG did not at that time have, and was not supposed to have, so much as a single spy. Its job was to coordinate information, period. Souers was just passing through[7] and was quickly succeeded by Lieutenant General Hoyt Vandenberg, a nephew of influential Republican Senator Arthur Vandenberg and an ambitious man in his own right who intended to balloon the CIG, win a fourth star, and become Air Force Chief of Staff, all of which he did.

When Vandenberg became the second Director of Central Intelligence the CIG had a staff of about a hundred. He hired three hundred more before the end of the year, saying, "If I didn't fill all the slots I knew I'd lose them."[8] He also won the right to collect intelligence in Latin America from the FBI, although not its agents or files, and Hoover was characteristically resentful later when some of his people transferred to the CIG (and later the CIA) on their own, and then began to recruit old friends. But Vandenberg's most important acquisition was the Strategic Services Unit, which he brought over from the War Department in August 1946 and renamed the

Office of Special Operations.[9] The SSU-OSO came with a thousand people, including six hundred attached to seven field stations overseas. Thus it was that Richard Helms found himself as an adopted child for the second time, having moved from the OSS to the SSU and then on to the CIG, with only a month out at the end of 1945 for a visit to the Indianapolis *Times*, where he learned that his old ambition was simply beyond him: he would never have the money to buy a newspaper. But despite the institutional metamorphosis which turned the OSS of World War II into the OSO of the Central Intelligence Group, Helms had not altered his ultimate boss—at the top of the chain of command was always the President—or the nature of his work, or indeed anything of substance except the name of the enemy. As chief of FDM (that is, Foreign Division M), Helms was responsible for OSO activities in Germany, Austria, and Switzerland. These consisted of classic intelligence and counterintelligence and were heavily dependent on liaison with foreign intelligence services. Helms is said to have resented especially the primacy in the field of the British, who made it clear they felt they ought to run all the spies, while the Americans provided all the money. But there was not much Helms could do about that at the time, and liaison provided as much as 70 percent of CIA reports until the 1960s.

By the late summer of 1946 the United States had largely re-created an intelligence service of the sort which Truman had summarily disbanded only a year earlier, with one exception: the Central Intelligence Group had neither the authority nor the capacity to conduct covert operations. The lack was not long in making itself felt. In the fall of that year the Soviet specialist George Kennan delivered a lecture discussing what by then was already a fact, the division of Europe between East and West with Russia firmly in control in the East, while the West was to a degree still in dispute following the British and American demobilization which George Marshall once likened to a rout. At the end of Kennan's lecture one of his listeners asked why this had to be so; couldn't something be done to challenge Russia in the East?

"Sorry," Kennan said, "but the fact of the matter is that we do not have power in Eastern Europe really to do anything but talk. You see what I mean. It seems to me this issue is rather a theoretical one. There is no real action we can take there except to state our case."[10]

Not everyone in the American government agreed. It was obvious the United States was in neither the position nor the mood to challenge the Russian armies of occupation, but the experience of the OSS in World War II suggested there might be quieter, cheaper ways to do these things. Nelson Rockefeller, a man of pugnacious enthusiasms, argued from his experience running a huge propaganda effort in Latin America during the war that much could be done with psychological warfare. Toward the end of

1946 Secretary of War Robert Patterson raised the question with Forrestal. Patterson proposed a study of ways in which psychological warfare might be used in Europe, and before the end of December 1946 a subcommittee of the State-War-Navy Coordinating Committee (SWNCC) drew up guidelines for what would later form the basis of covert action operations.[11]

Discussion of covert operations continued at high levels for the next year under conditions of extreme secrecy. In April 1947 a SWNCC subcommittee began planning for actual operations, and in June the group was given a degree of independence and a name, the Special Studies and Evaluations Subcommittee. A troubling question, the subject of much argument, was who should have the responsibility for actually running such operations? A proposal to put covert operations in the State Department was vetoed by Secretary of State George Marshall in November 1947, with the argument that their discovery would irreparably compromise American foreign policy. Marshall was not opposed to covert operations as such. He thought they were necessary and intended the Secretary of State to have a voice in their direction, but he wanted them to be run by somebody else.

The question of who was far from academic at the end of 1947. American policymakers were alarmed at the possibility of a Communist victory in the Italian elections to be held the following April, so much so that both Forrestal and Allen Dulles, who had returned to private practice as a Wall Street lawyer, separately raised private funds to help the Italian centrist parties. Truman and Marshall both wanted to mount a more ambitious effort than that, and failing to find anyone else with the organization or expertise to undertake it, they turned to the CIA.

By that time Helms and the Office of Special Operations had been at work for eighteen months. The National Security Act, passed in July 1947, had changed the CIG's name to the Central Intelligence Agency as part of the larger reorganization of the American defense community recommended by the Eberstadt Report. The struggle for Europe was well under way, and the National Security Council, at its first meeting on December 19, 1947, decided to use the CIA as an active tool in the Cold War. It seemed the most likely instrument after Marshall refused to run covert operations from the State Department, and a directive known as NSC 4/A, adopted at the first NSC meeting, ordered Admiral Roscoe Hillenkoetter, Vandenberg's successor as Director of Central Intelligence, to undertake a broad range of covert activities to prevent a Communist victory in the Italian election. Hillenkoetter asked the CIA's general counsel, Lawrence Houston, if he thought the National Security Act gave the CIA authority to carry on covert operations. Houston said he thought it did not. Having solicited Houston's opinion, Hillenkoetter ignored it. He gave the job to the OSO, which set up a Special Procedures Group (SPG) on December 22, 1947, to direct the effort.

One of those who took part was an OSS veteran who had worked in

Italy during the war, a tall, thin, unapproachable man named James Jesus Angleton. As an undergraduate at Yale he had published a literary magazine called *Furioso* which included poems by Ezra Pound,[12] but Angleton's true calling was intelligence, and in particular that subgenre of intelligence called counterintelligence, an exotic discipline which he was to practice the way other men play chess. In Italy, however, his job was somewhat more straightforward, and his success there secured his position within the CIA. He became one of the handful of men (another was Helms, whom he met for the first time in 1947) who dominated the Agency for twenty-five years.

The American intervention in Italy was large and well coordinated, very much the work of an "efficient machine" like the one conceived by Eberstadt. Wheat and other commodities were supplied to alleviate food shortages, a letter-writing campaign by Italian-Americans was mounted, congressional and business leaders gave frequent speeches, Truman threatened to withhold money from any Italian government which included Communists, and the Special Procedures Group of the OSO provided secret funds to the centrist Italian political parties. An air of crisis was generated as the election approached, and in March 1948, George Kennan, then head of the State Department's Policy Planning Staff, cabled U.S. representatives in Europe: "As far as Europe is concerned, Italy is obviously key point. If Communists were to win election there our whole position in Mediterranean, and possibly in Europe as well, would probably be undermined."[13] So seriously did Kennan take the matter that he even recommended outright American military intervention should the Communists win. The weapons, supplies, and technical advice given the Italian military were a broad hint[14] that Truman and the Italian government alike were not prepared to accept an election defeat as final, and more than one source has suggested that an anti-Communist coup would have followed a failure at the polls.

Threats of this sort are a heavy-handed form of psychological warfare. Angleton and the SPG worked with a lighter touch. Much of their effort involved traditional propaganda—posters, pamphlets, stories planted in newspapers, and the like—but the SPG did not stop there. All the arcana of disinformation was used as well, such as forged documents and letters purporting to have come from the Communist party. The brutality of the Russian army of occupation in Germany, notorious for its looting and raping, was vividly evoked in anonymous publications, and the fates of Poland and Czechoslovakia, the latter captured by the Communists only a few weeks earlier, were projected for Italy in a campaign which was based on fear. The non-Communist Italians, of course, were fearful enough without any help from the CIA, and the Poles and the Czechs would have been the first to warn them to take care. The point here is that the United States shared the fears of the Italian center, that it believed the stakes to be large, that it turned to the CIA as a tool of intervention, and that the CIA's energetic effort "worked." At any rate, it was not followed by failure, even if it was not actually responsible for success.

The result was a surge of American enthusiasm for covert operations as the weapon of choice in the back-alley struggles of the Cold War. A virtual war of spies was underway in Berlin and Vienna, where routes to the East and West were legally open under the rules of four-power occupation, but a much broader struggle was also unfolding throughout the rest of Europe. Communist parties and front groups fought for the control of labor unions, publishing houses, and a host of specialized organizations for women, students, professionals, and the like. A mood of foreboding and despair hung over much of Europe,[15] exhausted by the destruction and bloodletting of the war, beset by unemployment, crippled economies, and at times outright famine. Armies were of little use in a struggle under such conditions, and in any event there were no armies. Secret political forces were organized in their place.

In May 1948, Kennan recommended creation of a permanent organization to do for the world at large what the SPG, under the authority of NSC 4/A, had done for Italy alone. On June 18, 1948, only six days before a Russian blockade was imposed on Berlin, the National Security Council superseded NSC 4/A with a new directive, NSC 10/2, authorizing the creation of a covert action organization with the typically euphemistic name of the Office of Policy Coordination (OPC). The directive cited the "vicious covert activities of the USSR, its satellite countries and Communist groups to discredit the aims and activities of the United States and other Western powers" and limited the OPC's efforts to counter the Russians only with the stipulation that they be "so planned and conducted that any U.S. government responsibility for them is not evident to unauthorized persons and that if uncovered the U.S. Government can plausibly disclaim any responsibility for them." NSC 10/2 defined covert operations as activity related to "propaganda, economic warfare; preventive direct action, including sabotage, antisabotage, demolition and evacuation measures; subversion against hostile states, including assistance to underground resistance groups, and support of indigenous anti-Communist elements in threatened countries of the free world."

In addition to its broad charter, the OPC was given a most unusual structure. While its director was to be appointed by the Secretary of State, he was to report to the Secretaries of both State and Defense, despite the fact that he was to receive his funds from the CIA. This odd and clumsy arrangement had been vigorously opposed in May 1948 by the American with the longest experience in secret intelligence activities, Allen Dulles. Truman had appointed Dulles and two other men, William H. Jackson, later a Deputy Director of Central Intelligence, and Mathias F. Corea, a New York lawyer, to make a study of the CIA. Anticipating that Thomas E.

Dewey would defeat Truman in the presidential election that November, and that his brother, John Foster Dulles, would become Dewey's Secretary of State, Allen Dulles used the opportunity Truman gave him to describe exactly the sort of CIA he would like to run. That certainly did not include an independent OPC running secret operations all over the world. Citing British experience in World War II, when the Special Operations Executive and SIS frequently ran afoul of each other, Dulles and the others argued for assignment of covert operations to the OSO, which already existed within CIA. But Dulles was ignored. Marshall wanted a separate organization at least partially under his direction, and that is what he got.

But Dulles was luckier in Marshall's choice of a director for the OPC, announced at the beginning of September 1948. It was Frank Wisner, an OSS veteran of Eastern Europe who had shared a house in Wiesbaden with both Dulles and Helms at the end of the war. Wisner had returned briefly to the practice of law, then joined the State Department as Deputy Assistant Secretary of State for Occupied Areas, where he argued for a frank recognition of the East-West partition of Germany. Wisner was a Southerner with money, a man with a facile intelligence and a broad interest in world affairs. The British defector Kim Philby, who drank martinis in Washington in 1951 with just about everyone who was anyone in CIA, described Wisner unkindly—all his descriptions are unkind—as "running self-importantly to fat." A pompous and oracular speaking style seemed to irritate Philby particularly. He quotes Wisner on the subject of secret funding for CIA fronts as saying, "It is essential to secure the overt cooperation of people with conspicuous access to wealth in their own right"[16]—that is, people who are rich.

Yet all accounts agree that Wisner was a hard worker, a man who wanted to read everything, know everybody, argue every question, involve himself in every dispute over policy—clearly a logical choice as Director for the OPC, where the whole world would be open to his intervention. When William H. Jackson heard that Wisner had been offered the job as OPC's Director he told a friend he hoped Wisner would turn it down. Jackson had worked in Army intelligence during the war, he had helped Dulles write a study of the CIA for Truman, and he knew Frank Wisner. Wisner would be insane to take a job like that, Jackson said; it would kill him.

But Wisner wanted to do things. He was intrigued by the idea of what he might achieve with a little imagination and hard work. He even fancied he would have something of a role in the very formation of American foreign policy. Wisner took the job, and from the beginning he took it seriously. He guarded his charter closely. Whenever someone in the OPC wanted to read NSC 10/2 he had to sign a special access document. Then he would be handed one of the two or three copies of the directive which Wisner kept in a safe in his office.

One of the men who worked for Wisner in the early days could never understand why he surrounded NSC 10/2 with such an aura of mystery. He thought there ought to be a copy pinned on every office wall. There wasn't much in it, the man remembered. "All it said was, they do it, and therefore we have to do it too."

Chapter 3

Richard Helms blossomed during his six years as Director of Central Intelligence. For the first time in his life, after years of anonymity buried two or three levels down in CIA, Helms began to step out. He spent weekends with the Mellons in Pittsburgh, visited the arms negotiator Gerard Smith's summer place in Southampton, lunched with high government officials, important Senators and leading journalists. But unlike Allen Dulles, Helms did not pursue a public reputation; he made only one public speech during his tenure as DCI, rarely showed up in the *New York Times Index*, and was rarely noticed by *Time* and *Newsweek*,[1] which had a hard time trying to penetrate his bland anonymity. But Helms won something much more substantial: support in the congressional committees where he needed it, the power to run his agency as he saw fit, a wide acquaintance among the men who counted, a seat in the highest councils of government. His celebrity was a quiet one, but nonetheless real. Men remembered their meetings with him, were pleased to share his confidence, noted his presence at dinners and diplomatic functions, saved his letters, jotted down his remarks in their diaries. One of those Helms lunched with often was Cyrus Sulzberger, a columnist for the *Times* and a man whose appointments calendar might have served as a Who's Who of Washington. "You know," Helms told Sulzberger at lunch in March 1972, "I tell you just about everything."[2] Sulzberger was flattered. He quoted the remark in his diary and later published it, pleased to be trusted by the director of the CIA.

Those years—1966 through 1972—ought to have been uncertain soil for the blooming of a bureaucratic career, especially for the career of a man whose job demanded that he tell two Presidents they were losing a war. Lyndon Johnson sometimes sulked and scowled at the news Helms brought him about Vietnam, just as Nixon muttered and complained and pondered the ax when he thought he'd been defied, but Helms lasted longer than any other DCI except Allen Dulles, who all but invented the job. Helms managed to placate Walt Rostow and Henry Kissinger, who both complained the CIA was not getting on the team, and he won a quiet reputation for honesty in Washington during the very period when Congress and the press finally began to admit they were being manipulated, deceived, even blatantly lied to about the war. Survival in such a situation was the achievement of a sure-footed man.

At the height of his career, as a fixture in Washington, Helms seemed the inevitable man, but in fact his rise had been erratic and improbable, his path blocked on no less than three occasions by men his equal in ability, with wider connections and the skill to exploit them. Helms had other disadvantages as well. He had a reputation for administrative ability, but that was a dull virtue, without much appeal to the men who valued imagination above all in the CIA's early years. Allen Dulles, whose love of The Great Game was the deepest of his life, once groped for a description of Helms and finally said he was "useful," and he "knew how to keep his mouth shut." When Dulles undertook the delicate job of getting a Postmaster General's okay for an illegal mail-opening program, it was Helms he picked to go with him. Helms had his friends from the years with OSS, the SSU, and the OSO; one old acquaintance described Helms and his admirers as resembling nothing so much as a cardinal surrounded by his bishops. But the new men who joined Frank Wisner's Office of Policy Coordination after 1948 were a different breed. Their line on Helms had a hostile edge. They thought he had a certain slippery ability to avoid the crisis situations in which failure might wreck a career, and they resented his skepticism of covert action. Helms was a champion of traditional intelligence gathering, of the value of exact reports from well-placed agents. Fair enough. No one denied it. But the OPC people resented the OSO's air of superiority, of being the only true intelligence professionals. OPC people would grant the value of a spy; but how many spies did the OSO have? All you got from a fellow like Helms was enigmatic smiles.

These early hostilities should not be dismissed as the usual sour air of office politics. They ran deep, and help explain the bitter rivalries which have sometimes emerged in public debate. Since 1948 and the creation of the OPC the Central Intelligence Agency has been shared by three distinct types of personality: the spy runners, the analysts, and the political operators. For the most part, they have been cool toward one another, skeptical within the bounds of politeness; but occasionally civility is strained, differences grow acerbic, and conflicts of style and outlook erupt into something very like open warfare, with all the incestuous bitterness of an argument in the family. It is this which explains certain initially startling charges —that the attempt on Castro's life, for example, was the work of flat-footed recruits from the FBI; or that a well-known high Agency official betrayed all the signs of being an agent for the KGB. Unfair as such charges are, they only exaggerate the bristling resentments which the three personalities betrayed from the beginning.

Richard Helms was a classic embodiment of the first personality, a man with the discretion, restraint, and exactitude traditional among the bureaucrats of espionage, whose work is equally divided between the penetration and the preservation of secrets, and whose ideal style is brisk invisibility. Small-town bankers and estate lawyers are boisterous by comparison. Helms has an engaging character, and people tend instinctively to like him, but there is an inner reserve about the man remarked upon even by his oldest friends. He also seems to have shared a certain lucidity characteristic of spy-runners, who get nowhere if they do not begin with an exact definition of what it is they are after.[3]

But espionage is the most disappointing of professions. It meets more often with failure than success, especially now, when the techniques of security have grown so sophisticated, and especially for Americans, whose principal target is a nation with a long history of rigid social control and the largest, most efficient security service the world has ever known. CIA people speak with great respect of the KGB, and wistfully of the easy target presented by the wide-open society, porous borders, and trusting citizenry of the United States. The CIA's agents have not often penetrated Russian secrets, and the gap left by their failure has been filled by analysts, whose job at least in part is to deduce what the spies have failed to learn.

Analysts born rather than merely assigned to the job have a glutton's appetite for paper—newspapers and magazines, steel production statistics, lists of names at official ceremonies, maps, charts of radio traffic flow, the text of toasts at official banquets, railroad timetables, photographs of switching yards, shipping figures, the names of new towns, the reports of agents, telephone directories, anything at all which can be written down, stacked on a desk, and read.

Whereas spies are obsessed with the missing pieces, the analysts are devoted to patterns. The spy (and the counterintelligence specialist, whose mentality is that of the spy cubed) is haunted by the possibility he has been denied the one clue which explains all. The analyst is convinced the pattern will always jump the gap. He proceeds on two basic assumptions: that the best clue to future behavior is past behavior, and that no nation will run a risk without a substantial chance of success in achieving a commensurate gain. In short, analysts believe nations are consistent and rational. It is above all an awesome appetite for paper, and their confidence in extrapolation, that characterizes intelligence analysts, even when bureaucratic caution leads them to hedge their estimates with protective waffling.

The third personality in the CIA, and the last to join up when the OPC was founded in 1948, is that of the covert operator. Here, for reasons which the spies and the analysts would be only too ready to identify, many names might serve as examples: Frank Wisner, Desmond FitzGerald, Richard Bissell, Mike Burke, Tracy Barnes, Kim Roosevelt. All were gregarious, intrigued by possibilities, liked to do things, had three bright ideas a day, shared the optimism of stock market plungers, and were convinced that every problem had its handle, and that the CIA could find a way to reach it.

They also tended to be white Anglo-Saxon patricians from old families with old money, at least in the beginning, and they somehow inherited traditional British attitudes toward the colored races of the world—not the pukka sahib arrogance of the Indian Raj, but the mixed fascination and condescension of men like T. E. Lawrence, who were enthusiastic partisans of the alien cultures into which they dipped for a time and rarely doubted their ability to help, until it was too late. Some of the men in the field were very good at this sort of thing, but the Agency itself must be remembered with a mixture of regret and bitterness by the out-of-the-way peoples or groups it encouraged out onto shaky limbs, and then abandoned—not only the Cubans in Miami, but the Khambas in Tibet, the Sumatran colonels in Indonesia, the Meos in Laos, the Montagnards in Vietnam, the Nationalist Chinese in Burma, the Ukrainians in Russia, and the Kurds in Iraq, who exercised a special fascination for Allen Dulles.

It might be objected here that the CIA was equally acting on orders when it picked up their separate causes, and when it put them down, and that the adventurers were more successful elsewhere, notably in the Philippines and the Congo. But that is not the point. The point is the spirit of the enterprise, which was aggressive, enthusiastic, and too often morally careless.[4] The adventurers thought of the world as being infinitely plastic; they thought they could do anything with funds and a broad okay from the top, and they offered policymakers in the late 1940s and early 1950s an irresistible promise: that they might achieve secretly what the United States government felt it could not attempt openly. Thus Helms began his career on the periphery of what would become the Agency's heart, a trusted aide— not the chosen protégé—of Allen Dulles, and by instinct a skeptic among ebullient men confident they could work America's will with bright ideas, suitcases of money, or a few more turns of the screw.

During the height of the Cold War, between 1948 and 1952, the demands on the CIA were mostly set by the military. The Joint Chiefs of Staff drew up "requirements," some of them feasible (for agents in East Berlin, say), and some not. On one occasion in 1950 or 1951 a team of three Air Force liaison colonels paid a call on the Eastern European Division's operations staff in order to deliver a new "requirement" to Frank Lindsay, the division chief, and his chief of operations. The colonels had been thinking things over, they said. It struck them it would be a good idea to start preparing for the sabotage of Soviet airfields in the event of war.

All right. What did the Air Force have in mind?

The colonels said they'd like to have an agent assigned to each airfield by D-Day, which for planning purposes had been designated as July 1, 1952.

Sure, said Lindsay, perhaps thinking this would be easy compared to some of the things he'd been asked to do by that time. Sure, we can do that.

But Lindsay's chief of operations was not so sure. He asked, How many of these airfields are there?

About two thousand, said the colonels.

What are they like? asked Lindsay's chief of operations.

Some tarmac, some dirt.

Hmmmmm, said Lindsay's chief of operations. But he was thinking: My God. Two thousand airfields spread all over Russia and Eastern Europe. At least two thousand agents ready to go in less than two years. With God knows how much in the way of demolition equipment. After all, it would take a full-scale bombing raid to close down a dirt airfield, and even then it would probably be back in operation in a matter of hours. So Lindsay's chief of operations asked: How do you sabotage an airfield?

The colonels turned to one another. A few moments of low conversation followed. Then the colonels said, We'll let you have that, and departed. That, according to Lindsay's chief of operations, was the last the OPC's East European Division heard about *that* particular requirement.

But that is only an extreme example of the heavy demands the military placed on the CIA during its first five years. In the late spring of 1948 the Joint Chiefs of Staff dispatched a colonel to the CIA to brief the Agency on the military's intelligence needs. The very first priority, the colonel said, was a network of agents throughout Poland, East Germany, Czechoslovakia, and Hungary who might provide an early warning of Russian mobilization. That requirement was pretty well met by the OSO with the aid of the British, of Reinhard Gehlen's organization at Pullach, West Germany, and of its own spies recruited from the huge refugee population in DP camps throughout Europe. Spies run out of West Germany and Austria did a good job of monitoring the border areas, but beyond that they could not go. Gehlen's first priority, and greatest success, was penetration of East Germany. But later, partly under the prodding of the CIA, he began sending spies farther east. The CIA was Gehlen's sole support at that time, and it maintained a full-time office at Pullach under James Critchfield.[5] But despite Critchfield's urging and Gehlen's efforts Russia, in particular, remained a "denied area" which resisted penetration; no one really knew what the Kremlin intended to do, and everyone in the Western capitals feared the worst. Given the danger of war, and given the American military weakness in Europe, and given the astonishing success of some European undergrounds which fought Hitler, it was only natural that the U.S. government should turn to the CIA to re-create the sort of tool which had worked so well before.

So much was hoped from the CIA, in fact, that Frank Wisner, with his lawyerly appetite for contracts, jointly drafted a command relationship paper with the Pentagon which would give the CIA an independent status in any war zone on a level with the Army, the Navy, and the Air Force. This quadripartite arrangement struck some CIA people as the bureaucratic equivalent of an elephant-squirrel stew. You know, said an OPC veteran, one elephant and one squirrel. But if there was an element of unreality to early Cold War planning, a degree of overreaching and almost nutty optimism about what might be achieved secretly by the squirrel-sized CIA, there was also about it an air of perfect seriousness. In those early years the United States, and the CIA, determined to carry the fight to the enemy.

On September 5, 1949—only a few days after the United States learned that Russia had test-fired an atomic bomb—an American aircraft stripped of all identifying markings took off from a field in West Germany and flew southeast across Russian-controlled territory toward the heart of the Soviet Union itself, the Ukraine, where a partisan army, once encouraged by Hitler's Germany, still maintained itself in the Carpathian mountains. There a long and bitter struggle was entering a final phase, although neither the Ukrainian nationalists in Munich nor the CIA had yet admitted the cause was hopeless. During the war the Russians had gone so far as to air-drop poisoned foodstuffs to the partisans in crates with German markings, and the struggle in Munich and the DP camps was still, in the late 1940s, marked by intrigue, deception, kidnappings, and assassination.

The flight in September 1949 was not the first over Soviet-controlled territory. The British and Americans had initiated such flights soon after the end of the war, the British in regular RAF craft with British pilots in British uniform. The Americans, after much debate, had decided to "sheep-dip" their craft and crews, which simply meant disguising their American origin. The first flights over Eastern Europe for the most part only dropped propaganda as part of a general program of support for democratic forces in Soviet-occupied territory. Later the Air Force asked the CIA if the aircraft might not carry electronic gear as well, in order to pick up intelligence at the same time—radio traffic, radar signatures, photographs of military installations, and so on. Gradually, as the Soviets imposed Communist rule on Eastern Europe and the CIA switched its propaganda activities to the Munich-based Radio Free Europe and Radio Liberation,[6] the purpose of the secret flights was progressively changed to intelligence gathering. The 1949 flight to the Ukraine was a further departure not only for its deep penetration of Soviet airspace, but because it dropped two Ukrainians trained by the CIA in radio operation and intelligence collection to join the partisans in a furtive but nonetheless shooting war. Still more important, it was an initial effort in a three-year CIA program to establish a network of active resistance movements behind Russian lines which the U.S. military hoped to use in the war everyone[7] thought was coming.

The theory behind the military's program grew directly out of World War II experience with partisan movements, and it was based almost entirely on such anti-Communist remnants of those movements as still existed. A university professor, Robert McDowell, an OSS veteran and consultant to the Joint Chiefs of Staff, had convinced military planners that Russian control of Eastern Europe was inherently shaky. Russian heavy-handedness would only encourage resistance, McDowell said, just as it had in czarist times. He himself had worked with the Chetniks in Yugoslavia, and he blamed Tito's victory on the British decision to give him their all-out support. McDowell convinced the military that resistance movements in the East, even in Russia itself, might genuinely threaten Moscow's control if only the United States provided support.

This struck the Joint Chiefs as a promising approach, and the CIA, pressed to establish a partisan capability, began to work with émigré groups from Poland, the Baltic states, Yugoslavia, Albania, Soviet Georgia, and the Ukraine. The idea was to organize partisan armies which might harass Russian logistical activity in the event of war and to "retard" any Russian move west by blowing up bridges, railroads, and the like. Money and manpower were devoted to the program in plenty. Hundreds of agents were trained and air-dropped or sent in over the beach along the Baltic coast. Large caches of arms and munitions were established in Western Europe, to be air-dropped in the event of war. Supplies, including military supplies, and funds—sometimes in local currencies; more often in dollars and gold— were provided to resistance groups in Russian-occupied territory. In no way was this a reluctant or half-hearted effort.

A corollary effort organized stay-behind nets in the West—principally in Germany and Austria, but also in France, Italy, and Scandinavia, where the program was for a time under the control of William Colby, an early OPC recruit. The stay-behind nets were to go into operation in the event Western Europe was overrun by Russian armies. But the main emphasis of the program was on building resistance in the East, where in every instance the result was the same: failure. The reasons for the failure were not so much organizational error by the CIA (with a possible exception in the matter of security, as we shall see) as they were war exhaustion on the part of the peoples expected to rise. In addition, there was the unprecedented efficiency of the Soviet security forces with which to contend.

In the beginning, perhaps, the Soviets had been hampered by the confusion left by the war—wrecked cities, files lost or destroyed, huge populations uprooted. But in Russia itself, beginning in 1949, every member of the population was reregistered, and similar measures in Eastern Europe closed those societies to any but the most cautious penetration. By 1952 the resistance-building program was dead. The CIA's failure, in short, was largely the result of an attempt to do the impossible. If Robert McDowell had been right about the effects of oppression of the czarist sort, he had completely underestimated the resolution and efficiency of Soviet repression.

But the great awakening was slow in coming. Not long after John Bross joined the Eastern European Division of the OPC in April 1951, a man on the Polish desk asked him, "How many guerrillas do we deploy in Poland by D plus thirty?" (meaning thirty days after the war began). Without hesitating—plucking a figure from the air—Bross answered, "Thirty-seven thousand." But to his amazement his colleague seemed to find the figure a reasonable goal, especially in light of the fact that the CIA already had an ally inside Poland, a remnant of the Home Army named Wolność i Niepodlenosć (Freedom and Independence), or WIN for short.

After the Germans destroyed the Home Army during the great Warsaw uprising in October 1944, while the Russians waited patiently within sound of the guns, the surviving members, pitifully few in number, went underground. They maintained fitful communication with the Polish government in exile in London until 1947, when a determined Russian drive wiped out the remaining cells of resistance, including WIN. Or so Western security services believed.

But then, miraculously, a few years later a Pole escaped to the West and made contact in London with General Wladyslaw Anders. WIN, he told Anders, still existed; with funds and equipment from the West it might be revived. Anders informed the British SIS, and soon the CIA and the SIS were intimately involved in an effort to build up WIN as part of the resistance network to harass the Russians in the event of war.

The first question to which the CIA in Washington wanted an answer was who, exactly, was in WIN? General Anders and the London group, called WIN Outside, demurred. Surely the CIA recognized the extreme precariousness of WIN Inside. A single breach of security might destroy the whole organization. WIN Outside would not reveal the names and locations of its contacts with WIN Inside. CIA counterintelligence people in Washington protested that this violated the most fundamental rule of clandestine work—absolute knowledge of, and maximum control over, the people you're working with. But the OPC's Eastern European Division, perhaps guilty of a degree of overconfidence, imbued with an aggressive spirit that wanted to win the Cold War right away, and delighted to have a genuine Polish resistance group to work with, was inclined to give WIN the benefit of the doubt. Relations were established, the British were invited to take part, supplies and money were air-dropped to the resistance, and a serious effort was initiated to make Bross's light-hearted prediction of 37,000 Polish guerrillas by D plus 30 a reality.

This professional carelessness—the result partly of CIA's immaturity, partly of the military's pressing demands for results, and mostly of American ignorance of the reality of Russian control—was typical of the early years of the Cold War. Fearful of Russia, still in the first stages of building intelligence networks in the East, the West had a ferocious appetite for information from Soviet territory. One result was a reckless association with émigré groups which promised to do great things at home. Another was creation of an espionage industry, centered in Berlin and Vienna, run by men with the most shadowy antecedents, to feed the Western appetite for a price. A wide variety of intelligence entrepreneurs appeared from nowhere with information to sell. Some of it was narrow but accurate, coming from groups with genuine if tenuous connections to the East. Some of it was Soviet disinformation. The vast majority of it was concocted from news stories or whole cloth by a group of snake-oil salesmen called "fabricators." One such fabricator with an alleged network inside Czechoslovakia fed reports to the CIA about a huge (but entirely imaginary) resistance movement fighting the Russians and their local allies. Eventually the reports grew so fantastic— pitched battles, towns changing hands—as to collapse of their own weight.

The CIA was often burned by reports which turned out to be false in the early years of the Cold War, but gradually it learned to be skeptical of inflated claims. An officer in OPC's Eastern European Division, Walter Jessel, studied the operations of a number of early fabricators and wrote a paper describing their methods, after which the most egregious errors of naïveté were avoided. But as the CIA grew more sophisticated, so did the fabricators and the Soviet disinformation experts, and persistent military demands for information and resistance building continued to lead the CIA out onto some shaky limbs.

Part of the problem was the time it took for the CIA's counterintelligence branch to build up and index the voluminous files which are at the heart of all intelligence work. These were maintained in I Building, one of the World War II temporary structures—called "tempos"—alongside the Reflecting Pool in Washington, where a staff processed the river of CIA paper which came back from the Agency's proliferating stations and liaison with local intelligence services abroad. But so vast was the flood of reports that they burst the banks of three-by-five index cards, and a simple name trace on some potential agent might keep an OPC officer drumming his fingers in I Building for half a morning while the clerks took their sweet time coming up with the relevant files. By the early 1950s, according to Lyman Kirkpatrick, the system was out of control. Records simply disappeared into the sea of paper. Walter Jessel, who had written the OPC fabricator study, organized a computer system to bring order to the chaos, and after he left to take a job with IBM in the early 1960s the company received the first of many contracts which eventually would give the CIA a sophisticated file-retrieval system called "Walnut" which could pop out the 1934 graduating class of a Sverdlovsk high school at a moment's notice.

But nothing of that sort was available when the CIA first made contact with WIN. If an agent said he'd been in such-and-such a unit of the Polish army, or had lived in this or that suburb of Warsaw, it was not so easy to check his claim. In the case of WIN, much against the better judgment of the OSO and the Eastern European Division's counterintelligence experts under Jessel, the OPC elected to fly blind. The demands of WIN Inside grew steadily, and the CIA attempted to meet them, balking only at a request for an air drop of an American general, who, WIN claimed, would galvanize the growing Polish resistance. It was just as well. At the end of December 1952, the CIA was stunned by a Polish broadcast detailing the OPC's efforts, and it was quickly apparent that the entire operation from first to last had been a Soviet provocation. WIN Inside existed, all right, but it was entirely controlled by the Soviet and Polish security services with a twin purpose: to draw out such genuine Polish rebels as existed so they might be arrested, and thereby convince Poles in general that resistance was useless; and to teach the CIA a lesson in caution. The plan worked. So well, in fact, that the entire operation had been financed with American gold; the Soviets may even have come out of the deal with a cash profit. The lesson was bitter and well learned. It was like losing a chess match six-zero, and WIN's exposure just about ended the CIA-military program of resistance-building in the East.

In truth, it had never gotten very far, not because the will was lacking among the émigrés—their resentment of the Russian takeover was bitter and deep—but because the Americans, when it came down to it, were not willing to wage war in order to liberate Eastern Europe, and because they were unwilling to encourage the émigrés to undertake a twenty-year struggle of the sort the North Vietnamese conducted against the French and the Americans. The United States was not really trying to challenge Russian control of the East, only to create an internal threat which might be used in war. The motives for the program, in short, were not sufficiently robust to survive the early defeats. Guerrilla activity in the Baltic states, where the British SIS had used fast patrol boats to land agents along the Amber Coast, was sporadic at best.[8] The Russians penetrated the guerrilla organizations, controlled a phony Baltic underground much like WIN in Poland, rolled up agent networks, and annihilated the few armed bands that had attempted partisan warfare. In the Carpathian mountains of the Ukraine clandestine warfare continued intermittently until late 1952, when a major Russian military campaign finally destroyed the last of the Ukrainian partisans. During the winter months of the struggle, which lasted from 1945 until 1952, the partisans had been confined to caves deep in the mountains, unable to venture out for fear of leaving tracks in the snow. It was there that the last of the bands were cornered and exterminated. Until the very end, two CIA-trained Ukrainian radio operators continued to send out reports. When they fell silent the CIA's fragile drive to the east came to a permanent halt. Rosters of émigrés willing to fight in the event of war were maintained for a number of years, but finally even that program was abandoned.

The only CIA penetration of Communist countries with armed men thereafter was directed against China, where four-man agent teams were air-dropped at least until 1960. The program was fairly extensive—perhaps six teams a year, beginning with the Chinese entrance into the Korean

War—but it was no more successful than the similar programs in Russia and Eastern Europe. One typical team dropped in Tsinghai Province in 1960 to investigate reports of local resistance met the standard fate, according to a CIA interpreter who listened to its radio reports. The team had been trained in Taiwan, then flown to Thailand and thence to China, where it was air-dropped along with two tons of supplies. One of the men broke his leg on landing. The team radioed reports for a couple of weeks and then fell silent. The CIA case officers had no illusions about the meaning of such a silence. At best the team might have decided to pack it in and try to slip into the local population. More likely, they had been discovered and killed.

The most ambitious of such efforts had been directed against Albania beginning in 1949, when the British SIS made contact with a resistance group in the central mountains. Because of Albania's isolation between Greece and a renegade Yugoslavia, the British and later the American CIA felt it might be possible to build a sizable resistance movement which would actually overthrow the Communist government of Enver Hoxha. The British, as usual, were short of funds, so they invited the Americans to join the operation. A base was established on the British island of Malta, and an ambitious plan was drawn up by Frank Lindsay, chief of the OPC's East European Division, his deputy John Bross, an OSS veteran named Mike Burke[9] who had worked with partisans along the Adriatic during the war, and a group of Army colonels on the OPC's Paramilitary Staff. In outline the plan was to train Albanian émigrés, build an agent network inside the country in collaboration with the resistance group already there, and eventually to initiate open warfare.

There was plenty of doubt about the feasibility of the plan from the beginning. At an early meeting of the White House–State Department–Pentagon group established to oversee the operation, General John Magruder got into an argument with the State Department's Robert Joyce. Magruder said that Albania was unimportant; a military attempt to overthrow Hoxha would only anger Yugoslavia and Greece alike. But Joyce took the position that slicing off a Russian satellite would have a propaganda impact justifying the risk, and in any event, a recent agreement between Moscow and Tirana involved aid for Albania in return for a Russian right to build a naval base at Valona. Did the military want a Russian submarine base with direct access to the Mediterranean? In the end, largely because of the threat of Russian submarines, it was decided to go ahead.

Later, after Albanian agents were killed or arrested with eerie efficiency as soon as they landed on Albanian soil by boat or parachute, it was argued that the operation failed because it had been compromised by the Russian agent Kim Philby, at that time the British SIS's liaison with the CIA in Washington. No doubt Philby reported the Albanian operation to his Russian case officer, as he did so much else, but the real cause of the plan's failure was elsewhere. In the first place, according to several CIA people involved in its execution, the recruitment of Albanian émigrés was too hurried and insecure, with the result that word of the operation quickly spread throughout the émigré community and as quickly reached Russian agents. This enabled the Russians, aiding the Albanians, to penetrate the operation with an agent who corroborated Philby's more general reports and was in a position to state the time and place of planned agent drops. But a more important cause of failure was the ambitious scope of the operation.

In late 1952, already beginning to think of leaving the CIA for private industry, Frank Lindsay was asked by Allen Dulles (then Deputy Director of Central Intelligence following the resignation of William Jackson in August 1951) to draft a paper for the State Department and the National Security Council on the resistance-building program. Lindsay did not yet know about the Soviet control of WIN (probably revealed at the end of the year in order to warn the Eisenhower administration about to take office against efforts of that sort), but he had watched agent networks being rolled up all over Eastern Europe, and he had personally presided over the Albanian fiasco. By that time, Lindsay was out of phase with Dulles's enthusiastic, even exuberant, optimism. In wartime perhaps, he felt, you could build resistance groups, but in peacetime the Russians seemed to penetrate them with ease. They had decades of underground experience; the clandestine mentality was rooted in their very souls. They were much better at handling such threats than the Germans were.

But there was another reason Lindsay wanted to warn the new administration against pushing this any further. That had to do with the nature of resistance itself, something the military did not seem to understand or take into account at all. In 1944 Lindsay had spent nine months with Tito's partisans and he had seen firsthand what a resistance movement entails: horrifying loss of life, suffering which wracks every level of society, wholesale destruction, the murder of hostages, starvation. No population that had gone through such an ordeal could attempt it again without a generation of forgetfulness. It was wrong even to ask. In addition, Lindsay felt, the military did not appreciate the years of political organization that lay behind successful resistance movements like Tito's.

After finishing his draft of the paper, Lindsay spent one long Saturday arguing the matter with Allen Dulles, but Dulles would not be persuaded. He knew, of course, that his brother, John Foster Dulles, was to be Eisenhower's Secretary of State, and that Foster was committed to Eisenhower's campaign pledge for a "rollback" of Communism in Eastern Europe. Dulles was also listening to the colonels on the paramilitary staff who wanted to push the program. But a deeper reason for Dulles's resistance to Lindsay's pessimism was his own fascination with the whole clandestine enterprise.

But finally even Dulles gave up. In 1953, after he had replaced Walter Bedell Smith as DCI under Eisenhower,[10] Dulles began to close down the resistance-building program. On a trip back to Washington that year Harry Rositzke, who had been directing operations against the Soviet Union from Munich, told Dulles that agent drops in Russia were getting nowhere. Dulles accepted his judgment almost wistfully. "At least we're getting the kind of experience we need for the next war," he said.[11]

But the true end of the adventure came in June 1953, when the population of East Berlin suddenly spilled into the streets following Stalin's death, and the Russians sent in tanks to crush the revolt. The first night of the riots the CIA's chief of base in Berlin, Henry Heckscher, sent a cable to Washington asking for permission to arm the East Berlin rioters with rifles and sten guns. Heckscher had been born in Germany in 1910 but left for the U.S. before the war. He anglicized his name from Heinrich, joined the OSS, then stayed on with the SSU and OSO after the war was over. He was fully an American by that time—he always translated "Kaiser" into English for example, referring to *Emperor* Wilhelm, in whose government his father had once served. But Heckscher retained a sympathy for the Germans, along with a deep hostility for the Russians, and he hoped the Berlin riots might force a Russian withdrawal. By that time John Bross was the chief of the East European Division and he took Heckscher's cable to Frank Wisner. They tried to reach Allen Dulles, failed, and on their own authority sent a cable back to Heckscher saying he might offer the rioters sympathy and asylum, but no arms.

When Dulles learned about this the following day, he was unhappy. Not angry, because it was hard to argue in favor of giving rifles to people who faced twenty-three Russian divisions of infantry and armor, but unhappy all the same. This was precisely the sort of thing the CIA had been predicting and even trying to encourage. It was hard to admit that Russian control in the East was permanent, that it was free to crush whatever rebellions might break out. An aide on Eisenhower's White House staff, an OSS veteran and former publisher of *Fortune* magazine, C. D. Jackson, was not just unhappy; he was furious. He thought the Berlin riots were a God-given opportunity, the arms should have been sent, and if a lot of people had been killed as a result, well . . . so what? "The blood of martyrs," he told Bross, would be the very thing to discredit the Soviets around the world.

Dulles never entirely gave up hope that the CIA could find a way to operate inside the Soviet bloc. That fall he and his brother attended a White House meeting to discuss possible countermeasures against the Russians if anything like the Berlin riots should ever erupt again. Allen Dulles was asked to have the CIA make a study of the problem and draw up a list of possible retaliations it might take in the future—economic sanctions, blockading the Black Sea, fomenting political troubles in Soviet territory, and so on. Dulles asked Frank Lindsay if he knew of anyone who might make such a study, and Lindsay suggested the name of Richard Bissell, an economist who had worked on the Marshall Plan in Europe, a good friend of Frank Wisner, and a man with a wide range of social and professional acquaintance in Washington.

Bissell agreed to make the study, put together a small staff, and quickly concluded that there wasn't much hope for clandestine operations against the East. "I know I emerged from that exercise feeling that very little could be done," he said later. Psychological operations, for which Nelson Rockefeller expressed such enthusiasm while he was on President Eisenhower's staff, might have a limited role, but in Bissell's view it was a mistake to expect too much. Paying all due respect to the power of ideas, he didn't think you could come up with ones so strong they could resist Russian divisions.

But while he was working on the study with two or three aides from the OPC, Bissell came across an interesting document, a project study, complete with maps, of the operation the OPC's Paramilitary Staff had hoped to mount against Albania. Bissell was quite struck by this document. He was a man who loved plans the way small boys love the insides of watches, and this plan was more elaborate than most. It did not stop with agent drops or guerrilla warfare in the mountains, but was to escalate steadily until it culminated in a full-scale invasion of Albania with ships, aircraft, parachute drops, and thousands of men. Bissell thought the plan bordered on fantasy. Albania was in Russia's backyard; how did those OPC colonels think they could get away with a provocation of that magnitude? But at the same time Bissell was intrigued by the plan's boldness and scale. The invasion of Albania, Bissell said, with frank amazement in his voice as he described it twenty-five years later, called for a force several times larger than the one which he himself was to send to the Bay of Pigs.

In his study, however, Bissell told Dulles pretty much the same thing Lindsay had told him a year earlier, and the conclusions of the two men were confirmed yet again in 1956, after the Hungarian revolution, and in November 1958, when Khrushchev gave the West six months to agree to a "resolution" in Berlin. Dulles cabled the CIA station in Frankfurt to make plans for cranking up trouble in the East by way of retaliation, but the answer which came back was the old one: the CIA had no assets there, the Russian security services were in complete control, there was no way the CIA might contest them on their own territory. The battlegrounds of the Cold War, as a matter of practical realism and necessity, were to lie elsewhere.

The failure of the OPC's drive to the east came as no surprise to Helms. He and other OSO people had argued from the beginning that the OPC was not taking sufficient account of what they were up against. The attempt to send agents east through Berlin and Vienna, and to counter Soviet operations mounted against the West from the Karlshorst compound in East

Berlin, provided all the proof one needed of Russian efficiency in these matters. The uprooted populations in the DP camps of Western Europe were a rich mine for CIA agents, but they served the Russians equally well as a funnel for agents headed west. The two Ukrainian nationalist organizations in Munich—the OUN and OUN–B (the "B" standing for "Bandura," i.e., its leader, Stepan Bandura, assassinated by the Russians in 1957) —and the White Russian émigré organization NTS (Narodny Trudovoy Soyuz) in Frankfurt were the target of frequent penetration attempts, and occasional violence, as were other, smaller émigré organizations made up of the Russian national minorities—Uzbeks, Turkomans, Georgians, Tadzhiks, and so on. The difficulty of countering the Russians in the West was large enough. The Armenian émigré community—about 1.5 million people in all, roughly the size of Soviet Armenia itself—was a battleground for two organizations, the pro-Communist, KGB-controlled Hanzoieks (translated as "the band" or "the knot") and the anti-Communist Dashnaks ("allies") who worked with the CIA. If Western security services had their hands full with an Armenian operation run by the Soviets in the West, how could they hope to defeat them in the East? Thus it came as no surprise to Helms when WIN, the Baltic underground, and other allegedly dissident groups turned out to be the work of Soviet deception artists.

But Helms's skepticism of the OPC went deeper than that. Put simply, he thought its sometimes harebrained operations were wrecking the more important, long-term work of the OSO, threatening its agents with exposure. The mutual suspicion and dislike of the OSO and OPC were probably inevitable; espionage and covert intervention are two different sorts of enterprise, hard to reconcile in spirit or practice. But the OSO-OPC rivalry had a concrete side as well, stemming partly from their competition for funds and high-level interest in Washington, and more importantly from their competition in the field. By the end of Wisner's first year running the OPC he had three hundred employees and seven overseas field stations. Three years later it had grown to 2,812 full-time people, forty-seven overseas stations, and a budget which had grown in the same period from $4.7 million to $82 million a year.[12] To some extent Wisner's triumphant empire-building had been at the expense of the OSO. Outsiders had been brought in with high-level GS ratings, responsible jobs were parceled out to inexperienced newcomers, and the OSO was called on to surrender access to agents who might help the OPC to build up networks of its own. But at the heart of the conflict was a difference in temperament and experience, which was sometimes expressed in arguments over technique in agent handling and the like, and sometimes in darker allegations. Most of the OPC people were OSS veterans of World War II derring-do, grown bored with Wall Street or business or the daily round of teaching. But the OSS had also been notoriously porous. In point of fact, a lot of OSS "leftists" had been purged in a government-wide loyalty check ordered by President Truman in

1946, and now here comes the OPC opening the gates to every old friend and college crony who says he wants to fight Communism. The OSO, in short, not only distrusted the tradecraft of the OPC people, but on occasion went so far as to wonder just who they were working for, anyway.

In his protest against the National Security Council plan for a separate OPC in May 1948, Allen Dulles had predicted, "There would be duplication of effort, crossing of wires in the use of clandestine agents, and serious risk for the . . . agents used in the respective operations."[13] This proved to be the case. The competition, especially for agents, resulted in frequent cable blizzards to and from Washington. On more than one occasion the OPC simply "stole" an agent from OSO by offering him more money or a promise of power and influence. The OSO complained that its agents were being compromised by clumsy OPC efforts to recruit them; the OPC counter-charged that the OSO kept it in the dark, refused to say who was working for them, hid its operations, or warned potential recruits that the OPC didn't know what it was up to. The OSO retorted that the OPC didn't understand security, was naïve about Soviet guile, and was endangering established networks in its hurry to grow and show results.

The acrimonious rivalry was partly personal, partly professional, and wholly intractable, no matter how often the DCI—at first Hillenkoetter, then "Beedle" Smith after October 1950—urged cooperation on the directors of the two organizations. The only solution was to join the two services into one. Smith's first step in that direction was to annex the OPC shortly after taking over, but that only brought the problem still more directly to his attention without solving it. His next step was to bring Allen Dulles into CIA for the first time, naming him Deputy Director for Plans (DDP) in January 1951, with the idea that he might impose a "benign coordination"[14] on the two organizations. But not even that worked, and Smith began to think of an outright merger.

In the OSO two men in particular, Lyman Kirkpatrick and Richard Helms, feared that the OSO would disappear in any merger, and they urged an alternative on Smith—a kind of "absorption" of OPC which, in effect, would simply return the mandate for covert action to the older OSO, which had exercised it briefly in Italy in 1948. This plan foundered on the rock of Frank Wisner, who had an ally in Allen Dulles and whose support in both the State and Defense Departments was deep. He was quick to use it, too. Once, when the OSO seemed to have blocked a project, Wisner went to his friend Richard Bissell and asked Bissell to bring the problem to the attention of Averell Harriman. Bissell did so. "You can tell Frank that's going to be taken care of," Harriman said, and it was. Kirkpatrick and Helms did not wield clout of that sort. Smith rejected their plan, which was in any event a pretty bald bureaucratic bid for ascendancy, and began to prepare for an integration of the services from the field on up.

At that time Kirkpatrick was a leading contender for power within the

CIA. A handsome man, tall, articulate, and sure in manner, Kirkpatrick was an old OSS veteran—he had joined nearly a year earlier than Helms—and he had a close relationship with "Beedle" Smith after a period as his executive assistant. He was also an ambitious man. In the summer of 1951 Kirkpatrick was the second man in OSO, under Major General Willard G. Wyman, when Smith called a meeting of all OSO-OPC division chiefs and announced that the two organizations were going to be merged. This, of course, threatened to be an administrative problem delicate in the extreme, since a genuine merger meant that half the executives in the two groups would be demoted. But Smith insisted it would be done fairly, with the new chiefs of a merged organization chosen equally from the two parent groups. Later that year, in November, General Wyman left his job as Assistant Director for Special Operations (ADSO) to go to Korea, his departure subtly engineered, according to several sources, by Kirkpatrick himself. In any event, Kirkpatrick moved up to become ADSO in Wyman's place, thus finding himself (or putting himself, depending on whom you believe) in line for one of the two top jobs in the reorganized Directorate for Plans.[15] At the same time, Kirkpatrick took an additional step by appointing Helms to replace him in his old job as Deputy Assistant Director for Special Operations.

From a distance, perhaps, this may look like a promotion for Helms and an act of friendliness on the part of Kirkpatrick. That was not the way it was interpreted by their colleagues at the time. The two men were seen as rivals by others in OSO-OPC, and Helms's "promotion" was taken as a sign that his career was effectively blocked. "As Helms's boss," said one man in OPC at the time, "Kirk was in a position to chew him to pieces bureaucratically." Late that year Kirkpatrick interviewed a young OSO recruit and told him flatly, "I'm going to be director here some day." If it were not for what amounted to an act of God, he might have been.

By the spring of 1952 plans for the merger were nearly complete. Smith announced that Frank Wisner would be the new DDP, with Kirkpatrick as his Chief of Operations (COPS), or number two man. Helms was to be relegated to a lesser position in DDP, off the upward path and possibly eclipsed for good in the CIA. But things did not work out that way. Partly in order to settle a particularly violent OSO-OPC dispute in Thailand (where the OPC was trying to steal a government official working with OSO in Bangkok), and partly to deliver the merger plans in person to the field staffs of the OSO and OPC around the world, Kirkpatrick set off on a world tour with the then DDP, Colonel Kilbourne ("Pat") Johnson. It was probably in Bangkok, the doctors said later, that Kirkpatrick was exposed to poliomyelitis. In July 1952 he went into the hospital, a very sick man, and Helms was named Acting Chief of Operations in the new DDP to serve under Wisner in Kirkpatrick's absence.

But Kirkpatrick was gone a long time. For a while, as he slowly lost the use of one part of his body after another, his doctors feared he would never so much as sit up again. It was a time of great suffering, and later, when a friend asked why he didn't give up smoking, Kirkpatrick laughed and said that no medical prognosis would ever frighten him again after what he'd been through. At Princeton he'd been a football player, a big, strong, confident man, but when he finally returned to the CIA in March 1953, Kirkpatrick was in a wheelchair, he was thin and weak, and he had to raise his almost useless right arm with his left in order to shake hands.

He was still an ambitious man, perhaps even more so, and he went on to hold important jobs in the CIA for the next dozen years. But he had been eclipsed by Helms. It was bad enough, from Kirkpatrick's point of view, that Helms had been confirmed as the number two man in the DDP while Kirkpatrick had been in the hospital, but he particularly resented the fact that no one had told him so. He had to wait until his recovery to find out that Helms had taken his place on the upward path. He blamed Frank Wisner, and never forgave him.

Chapter 4

One day in the fall of 1977, Richard Helms had lunch with Ben Bradlee, the editor of the Washington *Post*. The moment was one of strain in Helms's life, something of which Bradlee was aware in only a general way. Helms's lawyer, Edward Bennett Williams, was trying to obtain an agreement with the Justice Department to settle the threat of a perjury indictment which had been hanging over Helms's head since December 1974. The federal prosecutors had been insisting they were ready to go to trial, but then, breaking with custom in such matters, they suggested to Williams that perhaps some, ah . . . arrangement . . . could be worked out.

Plea bargaining is rarely initiated by a prosecutor, and the Justice Department's quiet proposal in this instance convinced Williams that its heart was faint. If Helms stood fast, perhaps the Attorney General, Griffin Bell, would respond to the appeals of Helms's many friends and drop the matter altogether. Williams told the prosecutors that Helms considered himself an innocent man and would welcome his day in court, a chance at last to vindicate himself by laying it all out, and letting the facts . . . *all the facts* . . . speak for themselves. During that period Helms told friends the same thing: he was tired of caution and wounding innuendo; he'd rather go to trial than let this drag on any longer, and if the Justice Department chose to press him then by God he was going to *defend himself.*

It was a sensible strategy. Bell had been all but wringing his hands in public for months. It was an open secret that Helms's testimony on Chile back in 1973 had been only an episode in a broad policy of official denial where Chile was concerned. At that time the cat had only an ear out of the bag and the whole U.S. government was conspiring to get it back in. Of course, "conspiring" was not the word these men would have chosen to describe what they were doing. But it is the word the Justice Department would have used, if it had decided to pursue all the men fairly party to Helms's alleged perjury. By all accounts, Griffin Bell grew faint at the thought of their number and distinguished names. He simply did not want to prosecute all those men. This inclined him to listen attentively when Edward Bennett Williams said Dick Helms was no liar, but a loyal public servant who supported his President even after he had been unceremoniously dumped from his job, and when the highest officials of the government at the time got a chance to testify fully in open court about their role, then the whole truth would become apparent at last. Williams was scrupulously echoing what Helms was saying privately to friends: he was tired, he was more than a little angry, his patience was wearing thin, and he was ready for trial. Indeed, he told one old friend in counterintelligence, he even hoped for a trial now.

But whatever he may have been saying to friends along this line, it seems highly unlikely that Helms really wanted a trial. He knew a bit about Washington, he had been in a few, half-hidden dog-and-cat fights during the Church Committee's CIA investigation in 1975; he had no illusions that a public argument about Chile would be anything but a scenario for high-level bloodletting. The loyalty of some of his "friends" would end the day a trial began. They might do their damnedest to prevent a trial from taking place, but if they failed, their loyalty would switch from Helms to the established order. They would want Helms to lie down and take the rap, in the interest of maintaining what remained of the now-tattered public regard for the men and institutions which run the country. However much he protested his essential innocence, Helms knew his public reputation would never survive the merciless scrutiny of a trial, that a trial would further cripple the agency he had helped to build, and that it would open a whole new artery of animus in Washington. Williams may have been telling the Justice Department that Helms had a tiger's hunger for public vindication, but it was mostly bluff. Helms didn't need a trial; he needed a deal, so that he might preserve something of what he had built with his life, and free himself to get on with what remained of it.

But it wasn't that which Helms and Bradlee talked about at that September lunch, even though it might fairly be said that Bradlee's paper had helped put Helms where he was. Bradlee was a journalist first. One word in the public prints about the deal and the deal would be off. But if Helms was quiet about this final crisis of his public life, he was also in a reflective mood.

"Do you know what I worried about most as Director of the CIA?" he asked Bradlee.

Bradlee didn't. He was honestly baffled; it had never quite occurred to him to wonder. He ticked off the obvious possibilities, listing his own preoccupations. Nixon? The Press? Watergate? "I don't know," he confessed.

He had missed by a country mile.

"The CIA is the only intelligence service in the Western world which has never been penetrated by the KGB," Helms answered. "That's what I worried about."

. . .

Richard Helms liked spy novels. This seems to be a common diversion among men in intelligence, perhaps because so much of what they do in life forms the detailed middle of a narrative with no beginning or end. Operations are begun which go nowhere or turn up information which never quite falls into place. People emerge from doubtful circumstances, disappear without explanation. Suspicions are aroused but left hanging because there is no way to close the open questions. Dossiers will recount some middle episode from the career of a foreign agent known only by pseudonym.

A Soviet defector like Yuri Nosenko, who aroused a great many questions about his motives in 1964 when he told the CIA that the KGB had nothing to do with Lee Harvey Oswald, is still a subject of dispute within the CIA. Nosenko was held in virtual solitary confinement for years while counterintelligence interrogators from the Soviet Russia Division and the Office of Security pored over every detail of his account of himself. There was room aplenty for skepticism. Nosenko claimed he had handled Oswald's file when he defected to Russia in 1959. Intelligence officers tend to brood upon coincidence. An obvious possibility was that Nosenko had defected on KGB orders in order to divert suspicion from the Russian intelligence service, but this could never be proved positively, and of course nothing can be proved negatively. In 1964, while Helms was serving as the CIA's liaison with the Warren Commission's investigation of the assassination of John F. Kennedy, he privately told Chief Justice Earl Warren that the CIA could not vouch for Nosenko's *bona fides*. He might be lying. The CIA simply did not know, and it still did not know three years later when the CIA's Director of Security, Howard Osborn, went to Helms, by that time Director, and told him the interrogation had gone on long enough. Nosenko's defection had all the stuff of good spy fiction with one exception: the story had no resolution.

Helms liked the standard spy stories in which secret agents are given impossible assignments and carry them out with the sort of neat dispatch so lacking in life. He enjoyed the novels of Ian Fleming, for example, which are so egregiously improbable that even what is true in them (the sinister Russian action agency SMERSH, founded early in 1943, its name a contraction in the Russian mode of the words *smert shpionom*—"death to spies") has the air of fable. Fleming's novels bear about the same relation to the world of espionage as Western movies do to the Old West. Maybe not as much.

Helms found a similar charm in the novels of E. Howard Hunt, who wrote more than forty thrillers, mostly under pseudonyms, after Helms gave him permission to do so in the 1960s. Allen Dulles had encouraged the same sort of thing, sometimes even providing writers (Helen MacInnes, for example) with their plots on the theory that they helped build popular support for an agency which could not publicize its victories on its own. Helms may have had such a purpose in mind when he told Hunt to go ahead, but he also liked Hunt's books, with their innocent melodrama, and he kept copies of them in his office which he sometimes gave to visitors.[1]

But there was one spy novel Helms did not like—John le Carré's *The Spy Who Came In from the Cold*, a bitter and cynical story of violence, betrayal, and spiritual exhaustion.[2] It was not just the violence Helms minded, but the betrayal, the mood of defeat, the meanness, the numb loneliness of a man for whom loyalty has become a joke. In Helms's view the essence of intelligence work was trust. An organization which deceived and sacrificed its own agents with such cold disregard could not stay in business for long. This was a profession in which men stuck by their own. Le Carré was undermining the very bedrock of intelligence, the faith of men in the meaning of their work. Helms's son Dennis said his father didn't just dislike Le Carré's book; he *detested* it.

Helms's commitment to the principle of loyalty was not always apparent to those who knew him in a glancing way. He was a man of extraordinary personal coolness. In some ways he was quite like the other dozen or so men who held important positions in the CIA in its early years. As a group they tended to be tall, good-looking, ambitious, and able. Helms was somewhat more cosmopolitan than the others, having spent two years in school in Europe, where he learned passable French and good German. He went to Williams College, while so many of the others went to Harvard, Princeton, and Yale, and he was conspicuously lacking in the old money which allowed a man like Frank Wisner, for example, to leave his salary checks uncashed in a desk drawer for a year or more.[3] Helms's lack of a personal fortune was often cited as a factor in his career by colleagues, a tendency which Helms resented, first because it argued that only the rich could afford to serve their country, and second because it was condescending. It implied he was something of a time server, a man who needed his job and might truckle to keep it, unlike others who could resign on principle and live on dividends. To be taken in such a way could hardly fail to make a man cool. But whatever the reason, Helms did not share a certain light-hearted social gregariousness and enthusiasm, a confidence in position amounting to noblesse oblige which characterized many of his colleagues.

But despite this reserve (encountered even by men who had known Helms for years) he had a reputation for fairness, human concern, and loyalty. It is easy to collect stories demonstrating all three, but they could not be presumed upon. In late 1961, when the CIA had been ordered to cut back personnel as part of a general force reduction throughout government, Helms was approached in the CIA's gym by a man whose job was in danger. Helms did not like to talk business outside of his office[4] and he particularly resented the man's approach. He and Helms were friends, the man said; they played *tennis* together. Wasn't there a way to save the man's job for friendship's sake?

Undoubtedly Helms might have, but he did not. The man went. This was a harsh act. A lower-level CIA officer who did not qualify for retirement benefits[5] was in an unenviable position if he lost his job. What was he to tell a prospective employer? He was not supposed to tell him anything. But Helms did not relent; his sometime tennis friend had broken an unwritten rule. This was not the only time Helms was harsh.

And yet, it is much easier to collect stories about Helms's consideration as a boss. At times, indeed, he carried loyalty to a fault.[6] In addition to humane considerations there are, of course, good operational reasons for taking care not to offend intelligence officers. If resentments were allowed to build up, a man might decide to go over to the other side. Personal troubles, debts, love affairs, professional disappointment, and plain pique are the source of more defections than ideology. Allowing an intelligence officer to brood on grievances is asking for trouble. But Helms's reputation for consideration is not touched with calculation. Those who worked for him took it to come from the man himself. On the long drive back from his father's funeral in 1965 Helms told his son Dennis that the thing he had admired most about the man was his fairness. Helms tried to be fair himself, and his reputation in the CIA indicates he succeeded.

What Helms resented in *The Spy Who Came In from the Cold* was the climate of despair, the desperate human isolation, which was so far from the atmosphere which Helms himself tried to encourage in the CIA. Dulles and others did the same, and to a degree they were successful. CIA people maintain an extraordinary closeness. Until recent years they were encouraged for reasons of security pretty much to limit their friendships to Agency people, and they tended to do so. To join the Agency was to leave the world. Carl Marcy, for example, the staff director of the Senate Foreign Relations Committee under J. William Fulbright, had been friends with a State Department officer named James Reber before Reber left to join the CIA. Marcy and Reber had similar interests and for years they had talked about *everything*. But after Reber joined the CIA the relationship drifted off, they rarely saw each other, and when they did Reber simply went blank. In a similar way in the early 1960s, a young analyst of Soviet affairs in the CIA's Office of Current Intelligence found her old friendship with Bernard Gwertzman of the *New York Times* freezing over. She was supposed to report to the Office of Security every time she saw Gwertzman (or any other journalist for that matter), relating the circumstances and recounting in minute particulars what he asked and what she answered, no matter how innocuous. Naturally this sort of thing does not do much for a friendship—with the result that Agency people not only talk to each other, they marry each other, live close to each other, arrange for their children to play with each other, have affairs with each other, divorce and remarry each other.

Even after they leave the Agency, CIA people stick together. They call each other up, exchange letters and Christmas cards, invite each other for dinner, pass on Agency gossip, rally around with astonishing speed when they sense a threat to the CIA. When Lyman Kirkpatrick's name was floated as a possible successor to Henry Knoche as Deputy Director of Central Intelligence in July 1977, his old enemies shot it down in a matter of hours.[7]

When James Schlesinger arrived at the CIA at the end of January 1973 to take over from Helms, he is alleged to have said, "This is a gentleman's club, and I am no gentleman."[8] What he meant was that the CIA was run by a lot of old friends with a common background and outlook which tended to make them protective rather than critical of each other. The much-criticized "three Bs," for example—Bissell, Barnes, and Bross—had histories stretching back to childhood. All three had been at Groton together. Tracy Barnes and Richard Bissell went to Yale, Bross to Harvard. They diverged again during World War II—Barnes and Bross going into OSS, Bissell working as an economist in Washington—then reunited in the CIA.[9] When Barnes and Bissell were harshly criticized by Lyman Kirkpatrick's Inspector General's Report on the Bay of Pigs project, Bross helped rally their friends in CIA. Maybe the invasion failed, they said, but Kirkpatrick might have been more *understanding*. Schlesinger wasn't going to have anything like that in his CIA, and didn't. He remained only five months, just long enough to fire perhaps 1,400 people, including most of the old guard; and to request a report of CIA excesses in the past, which the old guard has been explaining ever since.

There is no reason an intelligence agency has to be run by gentlemen—and indeed, most of them are not—but there are reasons why the people who run them need to know and trust each other. At a bare minimum, you've got to trust the man you ask to deliver $3 million in a valise to Gamal Abdel Nasser, who may not be eager to sign a receipt.[10] The tendency to litter the files with self-protective memorandums for the record is strong enough under the best of circumstances. If intelligence officers darkly suspected that every order was a veiled attempt to get them out on the end of a plank, nothing would be achieved at all.

But most important is the fact that intelligence is the most political of professions. In the United States, as in every other country, it is subject to endless attempts at meddling by every sort of special interest across the spectrum of domestic politics: by Republicans who want to blame the Democrats for "losing" China, Air Force generals who suspect CIA analysts are deliberately underestimating Russian bomber production, liberals who think the CIA has a positive preference for right-wing military juntas, conservatives convinced Castro would never have come to power if the CIA weren't soft on Communism, State Department Arabists who think the

Agency is blinded by the intimacy of its ties to Israel, Jewish organizations which are sure the CIA deliberately ignores a fundamental Arab intention to destroy Israel. The history of CIA might be written as a history of attempts to politicize the Agency, some of them of appalling crudity, and more than a few successful.[11] Nixon's hostility toward the CIA stemmed from the so-called missile gap, which he blamed for his defeat by Kennedy in 1960; and his hostility toward Helms was based on Helms's refusal to get completely on the team where Vietnam, Soviet missilery, and Watergate were involved. But none of the attempts to get the CIA on the team was cruder or more potentially destructive than Senator Joseph McCarthy's in the early 1950s.

When Joe McCarthy gave his now-infamous speech in Wheeling, West Virginia, on February 9, 1950, charging the State Department was riddled with at least 205 Communists, the CIA had already been through two internal purges in addition to the standard investigation of every new employee before he or she was granted a security clearance. The first rooted out the most blatant examples of Russophilia inside OSS during the war. Despite Donovan's Wall Street background and his service as a U.S. representative to the White Army of Admiral Kolchak during the Allied intervention in Russia in 1919–1920, he had been relatively open-minded where "leftists" were concerned. Russia was an ally, and leftists were as interested in defeating Hitler as Donovan was. But in several instances OSS officers were engaged in what amounted to outright espionage for the Soviet Union, and they were fired as a result.[12]

After the war, while the CIA was passing through cocoonlike stages as the SSU and the CIG, new security checks were carried out by the FBI in light of changed circumstances, the principal change, of course, being the fact that Russia was now the enemy. The CIA never subscribed to quite the anti-Communist orthodoxy of the FBI, but the change in attitude was pronounced all the same. In his memoirs Harry Rositzke relates two run-ins with the then chief of the Office of Special Operations, Colonel Donald Galloway. Rositzke had written a brief analysis of Communist ideology and political tactics in the struggle for Europe, a kind of short course which he entitled "The Gospel According to Marx." He wanted to send copies of it to CIA stations in Europe in the fall of 1948, but Galloway at first denied him permission to do so. What if it fell into the hands of some Red-hunting congressional committee? CIA would be charged with spreading Marxist propaganda. But finally Rositzke won Galloway's reluctant consent by promising to classify the document, even though it was based entirely on published sources.

On another occasion Rositzke recommended hiring a European with a socialist background. Galloway refused: the man was a Red. Rositzke argued that nobody was more anti-Communist than a good European Social Democrat. Galloway was adamant; he did not admit the distinction. "I won't have a socialist in my organization," he said. "So far as I'm concerned, there's no difference between socialists and Communists."[13]

The CIA has always insisted on its liberal credentials. Charles McCarry, a CIA field officer who retired after ten years to write novels, said there were two things he'd never met in CIA: one was an assassin, and the other was a Republican.[14] David Phillips, who did what he could to prevent a legally elected Salvador Allende from assuming the Chilean presidency, insists he is a man of progressive sympathies, and that he voted for Adlai Stevenson twice.[15] In preparing for the Bay of Pigs invasion, Richard Bissell and Tracy Barnes demanded that the Cuban exiles draft a new Cuban constitution with provision for land reform, apparently unaware that both Batista and Castro had already enacted such laws. Bissell was quoted as saying, "They [i.e., conservatives in Eisenhower's administration] don't know it, but we're the real revolutionaries."[16] After funding of the National Student Association (NSA), the Congress of Cultural Freedom, and a whole host of unions and private foundations became public in 1967,[17] the CIA insisted it had aided mostly left-of-center groups at a time when McCarthyism made open support impossible.

There is something in this. CIA officers are extremely sensitive to the charge they are a kind of worldwide counterrevolutionary police, and of course can cite chapter and verse where the atrocities of Communist police regimes are concerned. A lot of CIA officers in the Santiago station—perhaps even most; it is not easy for an outsider to tell—felt more comfortable aiding Chilean peasant movements during the Kennedy years than they did later watching the Pinochet regime crush them after 1973. The CIA tried to create a left-of-center coalition to oppose Castro, they supported genuinely democratic unions in France and Italy during the great struggles with Communist unions at the time of the Marshall Plan, and the huge CIA station in Saigon during the Vietnam war was engaged in a running battle with Washington over attempts to create anti-Communist alternatives to Diem, Ky, and Thieu. In Tunisia and Morocco, and perhaps even in France, at the time of the French-Algerian war, local CIA officers felt closer to the FLN than they did to the government of de Gaulle, despite official Washington support for the French position.

But in another sense the CIA's self-image as a vaguely populist organ committed to the best interests of those with whom it works—a kind of latter-day American missionary movement, spreading the gospel of development—is a myth. No CIA official was more of a missionary than Richard Bissell, and no CIA operation was cruder in motive, or crueler in effect, than Bissell's plan for the invasion of Cuba. The idea that the CIA could help the poor and defend freedom was only a gloss on American national policy, which just as often supported repressive regimes defending the rich. Helms disagreed with Bissell in this as in so many other things. He thought the CIA should collect intelligence, and leave altruism to others. But the myth did not die easily. CIA officers in Southeast Asia were often aghast at the final consequences of their well-meaning efforts at nation-building. One who spent four years training Meo tribesmen in Laos in self-defense during the early 1960s watched in sick horror as the army of General Vang Pao (a man whom he greatly respected) was turned first into an instrument of the American war, and then destroyed. Other CIA officers saw the same thing happen to the Montagnards in South Vietnam. The CIA organized, trained, and paid the South Vietnamese Special Forces which were turned into a political police by Ngo Dinh Nhu, and then sent into the Buddhist pagodas in 1962 and 1963. Perhaps the CIA officers who helped organize the Saigon secret police were personally horrified by the tiger cages on Con Son Island, where "political criminals" were cramped into cages so small they lost the use of their legs. The CIA organized an army of agents throughout Vietnam, Laos, and Cambodia, and then not only left most of them behind when the end came in 1975, but abandoned the records which would incriminate them as well.[18] Whatever CIA officers privately felt about their part in these and similar situations throughout the world, what they did was to carry out U.S. policy, whether it was in Vietnam, or in Europe at the end of the war, or the Philippines, or Greece, or Indonesia, or the Dominican Republic, or Chile. When U.S. policy changed, what CIA did changed with it, and very often CIA officers found themselves defending the indefensible. If CIA people did not share the FBI's crew-cut suspicion of do-goodism, the difference was more often one of style than of substance. The belief of CIA officers that what they did was somehow for the benefit of others was not so much hypocrisy as it was a last defense against the harsh and cynical reality of international relations.

But where McCarthy was concerned, the record is clear. If John Foster Dulles truckled shamelessly before the men Dean Acheson called "the primitives,"[19] his brother Allen did not. McCarthy was a thoroughly cynical man with an instinct for newspaper headlines which might enhance his own power. Gifted with a talent for the techniques of publicity, he jerry-built his alleged conspiracies from FBI reports, the right-wing press, Washington rumor, the leaks of disappointed men, and pure innuendo. Allen Dulles's defense of the CIA, which tantalized McCarthy for years with its potential headline value, was two-pronged: he sacrificed those who by the custom of the time were considered "security risks," and he defended those more vaguely charged with pink histories.

One man in the first category, alluded to but not named in McCarthy's Wheeling speech, was Carmel Offie, a former Foreign Service officer who had served in Italy during the war. Offie was a man of charm, ability, and great enterprise. In one of his diaries, C. L. Sulzberger describes a visit shortly after the war to a Russian fur warehouse in Moscow where he was to be allowed—as a special favor of unheard-of rarity—to pick out some choice skins for his wife. Only a man with the best of connections—a man as thoroughly wired as Sulzberger, for example—could hope to enjoy such a breach of regularity. Whom should Sulzberger find there ahead of him, ordering the finest furs available in the Soviet Union, and ordering them by the *bale*, but Carmel Offie.[20]

Offie was not only a man who got about a good deal, as amusing government bachelors who can fill a seat at dinner tend to do; he was also gifted with a sort of split brain. He was ambidextrous, but to such an extreme degree that he could write a chatty personal letter with his right hand while drafting a government document with his left. After the war, Offie went to work as Frank Wisner's chief deputy in the OPC. As such he was always the last man to see a piece of paper before it went to Wisner, and one OPC officer at the time remembers taking Offie a document which he started to read just as the phone rang. Without hesitating, Offie conducted a complex conversation with his caller—not just "yes, uh-huh," but an active discussion, with precise responses, disagreements, and recommendations—while continuing to read the ten- or twelve-page document he had just been handed, filled with the usual paragraphs and subparagraphs and footnotes to subparagraph A-1, etc. Offie finished reading the document and hung up the phone at the same moment. Then, without hesitating for so long as it might take to breathe deeply, he said, "Okay, but it says here on page three . . . ," and he quoted a sentence exactly in which he wanted certain changes. A man with such gifts would obviously make a fine aide in a paper-rich organization like the CIA, and Wisner valued him highly.

But Joseph McCarthy had somehow learned from the Washington police that Offie had been arrested in Lafayette Park on a charge of loitering for immoral purposes. That is, Offie was a homosexual, by Washington custom the personal vice most subject to blackmail, and McCarthy knew it. Before long, Allen Dulles learned that Offie was the CIA security risk to whom McCarthy had alluded in his Wheeling speech. Wisner defended him hotly. Offie, confronted with his arrest record, was perfectly frank. Yes, he was a homosexual. Some men like pomegranates. "Why revoke my security clearance? I don't deny it. I'll stand up on the roof and admit it. Nobody can blackmail me."

This was an unprecedented defense at the time, and it almost worked. Wisner wanted Offie, and Dulles was prepared to let him have him, but then a Washington newsman got Offie's name the same way McCarthy had—from police records—and that was that. Offie had to go.[21]

Other CIA people went through private ordeals during the McCarthy era. Perhaps the best-known was Cord Meyer, Jr., a young Yale graduate who was badly wounded by a Japanese hand grenade on Guam during the war. Thereafter Meyer had a glass eye. He was a cigarette smoker with the unsettling habit of leaving a cigarette dangling from his lips. The smoke would slowly drift up and into his open left eye, curling around the glass orb, a sight which so disconcerted some companions that they found themselves furiously rubbing their own left eyes in a kind of sympathetic agony. In 1944 Meyer published a widely noticed short story in the *Atlantic*,[22] and after the war he became a peace activist with the United World Federalists and the American Veterans Committee. But his early experience with the AVC altered his view of the problem of peace. The infighting on that committee in 1947 was extremely fierce. The Communist party attempted to capture the group with a bitter parliamentary assault in which they packed meetings, shouted down speakers, and discredited opponents. After a thorough dose of crude Communist political tactics, which pictured every political dispute as black and white when Meyer took most of them to be gray, Meyer concluded there was an obstacle to world peace all right, only it wasn't the arms makers, international bankers, and general staffs of the West: it was the Communists. So in late 1950 Meyer went to work for the CIA, where he got a job in the International Organizations Division under Tom Braden in the OPC.

But in 1953 the FBI told the CIA they could not give Meyer a security clearance. Typically, they did not want to say why, but the CIA insisted and eventually the FBI listed its charges: (1) Meyer had appeared on a speaker's platform with the Harvard astronomy professor Harlow Shapley, a notorious "leftist"; (2) Informant X reported that while at college Meyer lived off campus and "lights burned all night in his room"; (3) Meyer had written letters in support of groups on the Attorney General's list of subversive organizations.[23]

Incredible as the charges were, the CIA, in the climate of the time, had to take them seriously. Dulles was out of Washington when the FBI's report was delivered, and in his absence the Deputy Director of Central Intelligence, General Charles Peare Cabell, ordered Meyer's summary suspension without discussion, a formal hearing, or pay. The man who brought the news to Cord Meyer was Richard Helms, and people who know them both say that Helms expressed himself in such a way that Meyer was thereafter the most loyal of friends. Helms told him he thought the FBI was wildly offbase, that Meyer ought to fight for his reinstatement, and that he, Helms, would help in any way he could.

Later, Meyer went to see John Bross, who told him much the same thing and advised him to get a lawyer. Meyer accordingly retained Abe Fortas, who told him it was not his presence on a platform with Harlow Shapley but his whole life which was at issue. In his defense Meyer wrote a detailed autobiography, beginning with his school days at St. Paul's and leading step by step to his recruitment by the CIA, arguing that his loyalty to the United States, his anti-Communism, and his commitment to peace were implicit at every stage of the way.

Meyer's own eloquence, and the intervention of powerful friends, overcame the flimsiness of the FBI's charges, and within six weeks he was back at work in the International Organizations Division—but not without paying a price. One man who knew him well, and who still likes and sees him, said that the shock of the FBI's charges significantly altered Meyer's personality. A note of harshness and rigidity entered his political thinking; he became more Catholic than the Pope, and from a commitment to peace and international amity he gradually shifted toward a purely anti-Communist fervor. In fact, said the man who knew him, Cord Meyer turned into something of a fanatic. When James Angleton held out against all the analysts and insisted the Sino-Soviet split was only a ruse to lull the West, Meyer was one of the few CIA people to share his suspicions.[24]

One of McCarthy's fiercest attacks on the CIA focused on William Bundy in July 1953. Bundy, then a young analyst in the Office of National Estimates, was a Yale graduate, intellectually able and well connected[25] and very far from being a man to succumb to a warm, naïve social enthusiasm of the sort likely to attract the attention of the FBI or Joe McCarthy. Even then, Bundy's was too frosty a temperament for that. His offense had a partisan edge to it. He was the son-in-law of Dean Acheson, the "Red Dean" blamed by Republicans for "losing" China, and suspect in a yet darker way for his support of Alger Hiss. A State Department Foreign Service officer with impeccable credentials, Hiss was charged as a Communist spy by Whittaker Chambers. He denied first the acquaintance and then the charges, but was convicted of perjury in January 1950. In a press conference a few days later Acheson had defended his friendship with Hiss and said, "I do not intend to turn my back on Alger Hiss."[26] His son-in-law William Bundy, going one step further, had contributed $400 to Hiss's legal defense. McCarthy announced that he intended to subpoena Bundy to testify before his Senate Subcommittee on Governmental Operations. Dulles was alarmed. With Bundy as a wedge, McCarthy might pry open the CIA, just as he had the State Department. This could not be allowed to happen. Dulles said no, McCarthy said yes, and the conflict rapidly built toward a confrontation.

McCarthy's method of attack reflected the undisciplined chaos of his own mind, but the anti-Communist panic of Washington at the time made the capital deeply vulnerable to his assaults. The city seethed with suspicion and resentment, and McCarthy's aides (described as "those wretched little people" by one CIA officer) found it easy to build their files. They proceeded, in fact, in rough approximation to an intelligence service, by probing the CIA for discontented, sullen men willing to blame their own professional failures on hostility from above, and eager to get even. A former CIA officer named Lyle Munson, for example, testified before a congressional committee in February 1952 that the CIA had considered hiring the "old China hands" fired by the State Department after the fall of China. That was next door to saying that the CIA was in the pay of the Kremlin. Others, darkly suspecting Tom Braden's motives in supporting "left-wing" unions, newspapers, and political parties in Europe through his International Organizations Division, quietly went to McCarthy with their suspicions. McCarthy's files grew. Disturbing reports reached Dulles of anonymous phone calls to CIA officers alluding to drinking problems or extramarital affairs in a manner which openly suggested blackmail: either they cooperated with McCarthy or they would be the talk of Washington in the morning.

To defend the Agency, Allen Dulles asked Lyman Kirkpatrick to oversee the CIA's own security investigations, a necessary first precaution if the CIA were to escape charges of faint vigilance. He also appointed Richard Helms to head a small committee which would counter McCarthyite attempts to penetrate the Agency with spies. Helms's job was to collect reports of clandestine approaches to CIA officers and to plug up such cracks in the dike as threatened to open. When a man is told that all Washington will soon be discussing his sexual life *unless*, it won't do to let him worry alone. The Helms committee held hands, kept an eye on McCarthy's progress, and allowed the CIA to keep one step ahead of him. In addition, Dulles held a meeting of six hundred top-level CIA officers and told them the Agency would protect any officer singled out by McCarthy, that no CIA officer would be allowed to testify before McCarthy's Senate committee, and, more pointedly, that he would fire any CIA officer who went to see McCarthy for any reason whatever without Dulles's express permission.

But that still left the problem of Bundy. The CIA thoroughly reinvestigated Bundy's past and found nothing. Colonel Sheffield Edwards, the Chief of Security, told the CIA's general counsel, Lawrence Houston, that he'd left no stone unturned and Bundy was about as clean as a man could be and live. "I've never had a case before where someone didn't at least say, 'Well, he drinks too much.' "

Thus armed, Dulles told Eisenhower he did not intend to give in and let Bundy testify. Eisenhower, according to one source, in effect said: Well, okay, if you can get away with it. Dulles and his aides agonized how to tell McCarthy no. The conclusion was hardly foregone. Dulles's own brother, a man of far greater weight in the government, treated McCarthy as a wolf out of control and fed him the meals of his choice. When an answer could be postponed no longer, Dulles went to McCarthy, and after the usual pleasantries behind which bureaucratic vendettas are waged, said, according to a man who accompanied him: " 'Joe, he's not going to come up.' And McCarthy said, 'Allen, that's all right.' It was as easy as that." Of course it wasn't quite as easy as that, but it was done. McCarthy did not neglect the CIA in his speeches thereafter, but the threat of a full-scale investigation was over.

But not everyone in the CIA fared as well during the McCarthy era as Cord Meyer and William Bundy, who were lucky enough to have both truth and powerful friends on their side. One who did not, Sylvia Press, described her long ordeal by interrogation at the hands of Robert Bannerman in a thinly fictionalized account called *The Care of Devils*,[27] a novel which truly fell stillborn from the press. Miss Press, a counterintelligence analyst who had joined the X-2 division of OSS in 1942 and then stayed on with CIA, never quite figured out why she was suspected by Bannerman, who later rose to become the CIA's Director of Security. It had something to do with an old lover and a trip to Mexico, but while Bannerman occasionally tried to trip her up with brutal questions like "When did you join the Communist party?" or "Was that when you went to work for the KGB?" he never laid out in so many words why he thought her a security risk. Eventually he recommended her dismissal, and Allen Dulles accepted the recommendation. Miss Press got an interview with Dulles but failed to persuade him to reconsider. She suspects that the price imposed on Dulles for defying McCarthy was super-security inside the CIA, and that meant finding and ejecting the occasional security risk. If they failed to find any, then they weren't looking. Miss Press suspects there was even a quota, and that she helped to fill it.[28]

In 1967, Miss Press wrote Richard Helms personally to explain what had happened to her, and to ask if there were some way she might collect a pension for her years with OSS-CIA between 1942 and 1958. Less than a week later she received an answer from Howard Osborn in the Office of Security, saying Helms had asked him to look into her situation. Osborn suggested he meet her for dinner in New York. Miss Press told Osborn how she had been summarily dismissed without ever receiving a hearing, or a list of the charges against her, or confronting a single witness. Now that she qualified by age, she felt she deserved the small pension she'd earned during fifteen years of work. Osborn was noncommittal but sympathetic. "Dick doesn't think there's anything wrong with you," he said.

"Then why am I having so much trouble?" asked Miss Press.

"The thing is, Sylvia," said Osborn, "if only you hadn't written *that book!*"

Over the next two years Miss Press met with Osborn perhaps a dozen times in all, always in New York. Osborn took copious notes. He was all sympathy and helpful affability. But she was neither granted the pension nor officially refused it. Her initiative simply faded off into nothing.

The investigation of Sylvia Press probably would not have taken place without McCarthy's threat as a goad, but it was not a McCarthyite investigation. That is, its object was not a suspect state of mind—left-wing "sympathies" or the like—but something more specific and threatening: a concrete chain of associations which might lead from Sylvia Press at one end to a hostile intelligence service at the other.

The question of security is not taken lightly by intelligence agencies.

For one thing an insecure service is not merely useless; it is positively dangerous, because it allows a hostile agency to manipulate the penetrated organization, as the British, for example, manipulated German intelligence during World War II. MI 5 turned German agents in Britain, used them to feed false information to Germany, and thereby thoroughly confused the Germans as to the probable site and nature of the invasion of Europe. The Germans would have done better with no agents in Britain at all. At the very least they would have been jumpily alert, not knowing where the blow was to land, rather than falsely confident.[29] It might almost be said that the better a service is, the more it is trusted by those for whom it works, the greater the potential danger it represents to its own masters. It is simultaneously the first line of defense, and the weakest link. It is an instrument perfectly designed for deception; an intelligence service is as close to a nation's vitals as a vault is to a bank's. There are enough horrible examples of manipulation in the history of espionage[30] to guarantee that intelligence services will always look first to their own defenses.

These defenses are of various sorts. The first line is to establish a protected area, not only by means of locked doors, barred windows, burglar alarms, guards, and 12-foot-tall cyclone fences but by limiting access to the protected area to persons whose trustworthiness has been established. The second is to lock up documents when they're not in use, and to make checks of such frequency, and to punish infractions with such severity, that intelligence officers will obey the regulations. The third, and perhaps most important, is to compartmentalize knowledge. This serves a double purpose: to limit what any one man can learn in order to minimize the damage which an agent inside might inflict, and to provide a ready tool for tracking him down once his existence is suspected. If the CIA should happen to learn, from a defector, for example, that the KGB has obtained documents X, Y, and Q from an agent inside CIA, the first step of counterintelligence would be to establish who was on the routing lists of the papers in question.

The point here is not the techniques but the importance of security within an intelligence service. This is so great, in fact, that a huge proportion of what intelligence agencies do is devoted to the penetration of hostile services, not simply because that provides a tool for deception and intelligence gathering by itself,[31] but because the surest way to discover one has been compromised is through the service which has done the compromising. They *know.* Thus the best security is to penetrate the counterintelligence branches of hostile services with agents willing to remain in place, a fact which helps explain the CIA's continuing obsession with Kim Philby.[32] Since this is extremely difficult (detection and execution, if not worse, being the usual fate of the agent-in-place), the next best source of such information is a defector. In that case the hostile service of course knows what the defector knows, but it does not know what he might suspect, or what the service to which he has defected might be able to piece together from the defector's scraps of the half-known.

The business of counterespionage is a Dantean hell with ninety-nine circles, and the men who dare its enigmas without exception have thick glasses, a midnight pallor, stomach ulcers, a love of fly fishing, and fretful wives. Richard Bissell says that his biggest failure as DDP was his failure to put himself at James Angleton's disposal for an uninterrupted week of instruction in counterintelligence. He never understood what Angleton was up to, and many other CIA people say that no one knew what was involved in some of Angleton's deeper operations. The ungenerous allege that not even *he* knew, losing his own tracks among the epicycles of deception. Others point to CIA's pristine record—pristine, that is, so far as is generally known, and certainly blemish-free compared to the horrifying security gaffes of the British, German, and French services. But the subject is complex in the extreme, and no one will ever know for sure.[33]

A lot of CIA people wanted to get Angleton out of the Agency years before William Colby finally fired him, but Angleton had a talent for establishing rapport with DCIs—Dulles, McCone, and Helms all stood by him in turn. Despairing of his actual removal, several DDPs tried to cut back his staff and limit his independence. Bissell assigned John Bross to draw up a reorganization plan, which Bross did. But when Bissell proposed it to Angleton, Angleton stood fast, argued that counterintelligence must be organized on a case-by-case basis demanding both independence and a large staff, and Bissell gave in. Later, Desmond FitzGerald drew up a similar plan to put Angleton in his place, but died—playing tennis on July 23, 1967[34]—before he could push it through.

It is obvious that no one outside the CIA is ever going to know if Angleton overdid it, because no one outside the CIA will ever have access to his files. The primacy of security explains a lot of the hocus-pocus of intelligence, the back-alley mucking about, the dangles, the doubling and redoubling[35] of agents, which leads most casual tourists of the profession to throw up their hands in despair with a heart-felt longing for the innocence of Henry Stimson, who alleged that gentlemen do not read each other's mail. But it is better to have no intelligence service at all than to have one which is insecure. Once a nation attempts to learn a thing or two about real or potential enemies, all the mystery and intrigue which make up the war of intelligence services necessarily comes tumbling in after.

But the question of security leads to another interesting aspect of the business of intelligence, a fundamental psychological fact which helps to explain why it is the way it is. Intelligence officers spend their lives on an existential tightrope between doubt and trust, simultaneously suspicious of everybody, while trusting their friends.[36]

In the fall of 1952, Walter Bedell Smith publicly admitted his conviction that the CIA had been penetrated by enemy agents.[37] "I believe there are Communists in my own organization," he said. "I do everything I can to detect them, but I am morally certain, since you are asking the question, that there are." This is a fundamental assumption of all intelligence services, since to neglect the possibility would be to leave themselves wide open. But of course one never knows who the enemy agents are, and yet one cannot suspect every old colleague or friend. That way madness lies. Trust is the bedrock of the work. When Frank Wisner or Dulles or Desmond FitzGerald or James Angleton or John Bross or Richard Helms knocked off for the day, or met a friend or colleague for lunch downtown, they could not raise a martini and drink a friend or colleague's health while at the same moment wondering: Why did he say that? *Why is this fellow asking about the Albanian operation?* And yet, and yet . . .

In the early 1950s the FBI and its British equivalent, MI 5, were slowly tracking down a KGB agent who had obtained certain secret documents from the British Embassy in Washington, an agent whose existence had been fortuitously discovered in the summer of 1945 when a Russian cipher clerk in New York inadvertently used a low-level commercial code to pass on his reports to Moscow. The error was quickly corrected, but enough messages had been intercepted to establish the fact of penetration, the agent's access to top-secret documents, and a single biographical fact: that the agent had traveled to New York twice a week to make his reports.

Tracking down the agent's identity was obviously a matter of high priority, and there was nothing odd or out of line about the interest in the case expressed by the British SIS liaison to CIA and FBI in Washington, a counterintelligence specialist with a stutter and a taste for martinis and a record of some first-rate intelligence coups during the war. A good-looking fellow, Cambridge graduate, face a bit worn, lines about the eyes, perhaps from all those martinis. Just about everybody above a certain level in CIA in those days has a story of a long martini-soaked lunch with Kim Philby ending at three in the afternoon. Philby must have had a wooden leg, because he drank with everybody from Dulles on down and did one hell of a job as liaison. He kept tabs on everybody and everything, carried out his own substantial duties, and still found time to photograph every document he could get his hands on, which he then passed on to his KGB case officer.

Philby's undoing happened like this: The spy in the British Embassy was Donald Maclean, who had moved on (to Cairo, where he suffered a mental breakdown) by the time Philby arrived in Washington in September 1949 and began his marathon of lunches. Many of them (they burned in the memory forever after) were with James Angleton, the CIA's counterintelligence specialist, a lean, chain-smoking man with a thin, wide, wide mouth—so wide its opposite ends could express two different emotions simultaneously. The most frequent combination was sardonic amusement, much muted, on the right, and despair on the left, almost as if he did not know whether to give up or persevere, and so attempted both.

Both the British and the Russians pressed on Philby the importance of keeping in close touch with the FBI–MI 5 progress on catching the man whom Philby probably knew to be Maclean. Early in 1951, as the hunters closed in, the Russians decided the time had come for Maclean's escape and Philby was the man chosen to organize it. His instrument was to be Guy Burgess, another Cambridge graduate whose social credentials were sufficiently firm to override a most chaotic personal history of drunkenness, homosexuality, and conduct of the sort the British call beastly—insulting one's hostess, throwing up on the bedroom rug, spilling the soup at dinner while arguing loudly, ostentatiously fondling the host's niece, staying until three in the morning and then falling asleep in the bathroom. Burgess had moved in with Philby in Washington, where he proceeded to set something of a record for making enemies in a matter of months. Hardly the sort of man to trust with a delicate exfiltration, but Burgess was all Philby had to work with, and in May 1951, just as MI 5 was closing in on Maclean in London, the escape took place. But with one horrible hitch. In a moment of panic at the last minute, *Burgess went with him.*

One gropes for a metaphor to describe the reaction at the CIA. If there's one thing an intelligence officer can do, it's to put two and two together. Burgess and Maclean added up to Philby. "Beedle" Smith, then the Director of Central Intelligence, wrote a letter to the head of SIS, Sir Stewart Menzies, and told him to get Philby out of Washington. Maclean was a spy of some importance. Bad show. Burgess was a spy of no importance, but he got Maclean out of London before MI 5 could lay hands on him. Bad show again. But Harold Adrian Russell Philby had been head of SIS counterintelligence. He had been SIS liaison with CIA in Washington, poking his nose into everybody's business with Allen Dulles's explicit recommendation. This was truly a disaster. For various reasons Philby was allowed to resign from SIS in London and was not publicly denounced as a spy until after he fled to the Soviet Union in January 1963, but there was little doubt about the truth in CIA, at least, and Philby is still a touchy subject even now.[38]

Helms had only a glancing contact with Philby. Like a lot of others, he knew him, lunched with him, and told him things, no doubt including a great many he has regretted ever since. But he has also lived within an intelligence service which knows it can be done, that the smiling man across the table—good old ———!—could be working for the opposition. The CIA is filled with old college friends who trust each other just as Kim's friends trusted him. Philby's domestic troubles were no worse than those of many CIA people, and if he consumed martinis the way a wounded man does plasma, well, this is also typical behavior in Washington, a hard-drinking town where the careers of many CIA people were cut short by alcoholism. CIA people trust each other, but their trust is of a deliberate, self-conscious character. Belief in a colleague in an intelligence agency is to some degree an act of the will: you don't *know* a man is to be trusted; you *believe* he is to be trusted, and decide to trust him. There is a difference. Most men never have to make any such judgment about their friends and colleagues. Those who do have a tighter bond, one more reason for defending each other from the misunderstanding of outsiders.

The CIA, of course, has never in fact been penetrated. The closest thing to it came in the person of Philip Agee, a CIA field officer in Latin America who resigned in 1968 and then wrote a book called *Inside the Company: CIA Diary.*[39] Agee offered himself to the world as a disillusioned former officer whose only interest was in bringing the truth to the public, a man whose motives were not unlike Daniel Ellsberg's in releasing the Pentagon Papers. CIA people consider Agee a defector, pure and simple. Why else would he expose so many operations and agents, endangering people's lives? And what was he doing on his trips to Cuba (where the local intelligence service, the Dirección Generale de Inteligencia, has allegedly been dominated by the KGB since 1969)? Agee has managed to convince much of the public he is not a traitor, but not the CIA. When his defection became apparent, the Agency proceeded exactly as it would have if he'd flown to Moscow, terminating agents and closing down operations about which Agee might have known.[40] Agency people are angry and disgusted with Victor Marchetti, Frank Snepp, and John Stockwell, but about Agee they are cold and bitter, and if Agee turns out the hall light before opening his front door at night, and thinks twice about switching on his car ignition, and doesn't accept candy from strangers, he is not being altogether melodramatic.

But Agee aside, the CIA has never been penetrated—unlike most other Western intelligence services. Or so the Agency says. But in fact there is a degree of quiet argument about this inside the Agency, and no one knows for sure. Those who knew about it still argue the details of a case in 1962, during the last months of Richard Bissell's tenure as Deputy Director of Plans, the case of a man who *might* have been a KGB agent—and then again, if the evidence is examined in a slightly different light, might not. According to Lawrence Houston and Lyman Kirkpatrick, perhaps a dozen CIA officers have been fired as security risks over the years, but this was the only case of suspected penetration. The others were more tenuous, having to do mainly with defects of character or breaches of procedure.

The case began in the classic manner: with a defector. Early in 1962 a high-ranking officer in the KGB, Major Anatoli Golitsin, secretly arrived in Washington for debriefing by counterintelligence experts on the staffs of James Angleton and of the DDP's Soviet Russia Division. Golitsin had been working for the CIA for some time before his defection in Helsinki, Finland, but clandestine meetings with a case officer are necessarily hurried and sketchy. It was not until his debriefing in Washington that Golitsin told the CIA about a KGB agent—called a "mole" in the vernacular of counterintelligence—placed at a high level inside the Directorate for Plans. Golitsin did not know the agent's name (which of course would have made the whole exercise bang-easy), but he did know the content of certain reports made by the agent, he had a physical description of the agent, and he knew the agent had met with the KGB on a certain date in London.

Angleton proceeded in the classic manner—that is, by triangulation. First he determined who might have known about the matters discussed in the agent's reports. Second, he looked for DDP officers who matched the defector's physical description of the agent. Third, he established who might have been in London on the date in question. Only one name appeared in all three categories.

So Angleton had a Suspect. But even after a great deal of investigation, that was all he had. No other incriminating evidence about The Suspect turned up—no unexpected bank deposits, unexplained trips, odd behavior in public places. If once a week he had attempted to elude a potential surveillance team (not knowing that he was now being followed, merely taking the standard precaution), that would have said a good deal. If the paper record showed that The Suspect had initiated an unusual number of name traces, or made an attempt to get his name on certain routing lists, or had otherwise betrayed a curiosity which went beyond narrow professional need, then Angleton could have put two and two together. But in this case he had only two plus X—a fact which refocused interest on Golitsin.

There was a possibility, of course, that Golitsin had not really "defected" at all, but had come over on Soviet orders in order to spread suspicion and confusion and perhaps end the career of an able DDP officer. But Golitsin's *bona fides* seemed solid. Not only did his story hold up, but he had delivered a great deal of other useful information, including the identities of KGB agents in various official bodies in Britain, Germany, France, and Italy. As a rule, counterintelligence people say, once you start looking in the right place all sorts of evidence turn up. In this instance: none. Of course Golitsin might simply be mistaken, or himself be the victim of some unknown KGB deception. But it was hard to drop the matter. There was the case of Walter Krivitsky, after all, a Russian defector in 1937 who reported one Soviet agent in the British Foreign Office, and another who worked in counterintelligence and had gone to Spain as a journalist during the Spanish Civil War. A perfect description of Kim Philby! Because British counterintelligence failed to put two and two together—good old Kim? nothing wrong with him—Philby delivered Allied secrets to the Russians for another fifteen years.

There was a good deal of argument about The Suspect within the DDP. According to Thomas Karamessines, Frank Wisner thought Golitsin was either lying or mistaken and wanted to keep The Suspect on. Two other CIA officers who knew about the case said they never doubted The Suspect's loyalty either, and one of them, Lawrence Houston, later helped The Suspect find a job. But they would hardly say anything else, since penetration is about the worst thing that can happen to an intelligence service. The probable truth is that they don't know for sure, one way or the other, and preferred to give the benefit of the doubt to the CIA, while at the same time protecting a friend.

Whatever arguments were raised by The Suspect or on his behalf at the time, however, they failed to convince Angleton. Despite Wisner's protests from his new position as chief of station in London, Angleton went to Dulles, laid out the evidence, and said the one thing which sealed The Suspect's fate: not that there was a 50–50 chance he was guilty, nor even that there was a 10 percent chance. All it took was *a* chance, and in Angleton's view the evidence pointed in that direction. It was possible.

Dulles agreed The Suspect had to go. Angleton next went to Bissell, who reached the same conclusion. The Suspect's departure was quiet. Lawrence Houston was surprised that he wasn't more indignant, but perhaps he grasped at once that indignation was useless. Golitsin had correctly claimed he'd been in London on such-and-such a date, and while the CIA could not prove The Suspect had met with the KGB, he could not prove he had not. He went so quietly that very few CIA people knew he'd ever been suspected, so quietly the rest of CIA would continue to claim, without a flicker of doubt, that the CIA had never been penetrated—its record was perfect.

But the inner circle—which included Richard Helms, who knew of the investigation and of its outcome—would defend the Agency's record of loyalty with that extra note of emphasis which comes from deciding what to believe, where it is impossible to know. Helms was not one of Angleton's detractors. If he only murmured interest when Angleton tried to unravel the secret motives in the larger issues of international affairs, he still valued the man's mastery of counterintelligence. It was Angleton who kept the KGB out of the CIA for more than twenty years—maybe—and saved Helms from ever having to explain an American Philby to Congress. The men remained friends after they both left the CIA, close friends by all accounts. Angleton frequently wrote Helms when he was ambassador to Iran, during the long investigations of the Watergate and Church committees, sometimes even sending him transcripts of television shows he thought Helms might be interested in. It was a friendship based on professional respect, and neither man ever expected to be understood by people who liked the novels of John le Carré.

Chapter 5

In retrospect, there were clues aplenty of the breakdown that ended Frank Wisner's career. The dinner, for example, where Wisner gave a humorous little speech as if he were a Soviet general. As the Deputy Director for Plans—perhaps the second most important officer in CIA, even if he did not technically rank second—Wisner probably knew as much about the personalities and professional quirks of Soviet generals as anybody around, specialists excepted. But there was something wrong about the speech, not just the fact that Wisner was a serious, in some ways even a self-important man, not generally given to wit or lightness. Frank Lindsay was one of the guests at Wisner's table that night, and it struck him that Wisner's monologue ran on too long, was too repetitive, too heavy, tendentious, insistent. But just at that moment when the guests might have begun to shift uneasily in their seats, Wisner stopped, and the conversation resumed, and Lindsay like the others allowed the incident to slip from his mind.

In retrospect, there were a number of clues of that sort, but they were all set aside. Wisner was a hard worker, an omnivorous reader, devoted to details, which he had to be if he were to know what his thousands of field officers, with their still-further thousands of contract officers and agents, were up to around the world. Tension was built into the job, and Wisner took his job seriously. People who worked with him say he fancied himself as a policymaker and squandered too much energy trying to ensure that everybody in Washington was on the team. Incoming paper might be a foot deep on his desk in L Building in the morning, but Wisner would neglect it all if he noticed a wrong-headed column by Scotty Reston in the morning's *Times*. Nothing took precedence over getting Reston straightened out. He would tell an aide to hunt up the facts of the matter and then call Reston to point out his error and get him back on the beam.

One man who knew him well remembers a spring evening at Wisner's house in 1957 when he was preparing a few remarks to deliver at a dinner later on. Nothing in the way of a speech was called for—it was a purely social gathering to which he had been invited—but there was Wisner, walking up and down the garden behind his house in Georgetown, Reston at his side, rehearsing his remarks until they satisfied him. He had a passionate desire that everybody *understand*, which was one reason why the CIA subsidized so many books in the United States at that time—accounts of Russian tyranny in Eastern Europe, the memoirs of apostate Communists, the Red Threat in Central America. The funds were sometimes passed to American publishers by an old friend of Allen Dulles, a partner in the Wall Street law firm of Sullivan and Cromwell, a delicate transaction but one necessary, Wisner thought, to ensure that Americans *understand*.

Not only did Wisner put in long days at the office; he conducted a tireless social life as well. He liked to get about, to know the people who counted, to hear all the news before it reached the papers. There was no surprise in finding Reston at Wisner's house. You might meet almost anyone there: George Kennan, Charles Bohlen back from Russia, journalists like Arthur Krock and the Alsop brothers, Randolph Churchill and Malcolm Muggeridge from England. No man in Washington lunched more often or changed more regularly for an evening out. It was easy to conclude, if Wisner rambled on too long and disjointedly in the guise of a Russian general, that he had simply been pushing himself too hard.

But there was more to it than that. Something was wrong. In the early fall of 1956 Wisner turned over the DDP to his chief of operations, Richard Helms, and left for one of his periodic tours of CIA stations in Europe. There was a lot on his mind, as usual, principally a developing conflict between Britain and Egypt over Suez, and the uncertainty of Khrushchev's intentions toward Hungary. But at the time of Wisner's departure Suez was at the head of the list.

Wisner's trip took him to England, France, Germany, Austria, Greece, and Italy, and the pace, as always, was grueling. But the thing which explained Wisner's state of mind on this trip was the combined French, British, and Israeli attack on Egypt at the end of October. Trouble had been building for some time, but when the British sent their bombers on October 31, 1956—at about the time Wisner was moving on from Britain to Germany —Wisner was incredulous, hurt, furious, alarmed: twenty things at once. Didn't Britain understand what this would do to Hungary, where Khrushchev had seemed on the verge of making important concessions? And not one word of warning. This hurt Wisner as much as the attack itself. He'd never trusted the French secret service; he didn't expect them to tell him a thing. But the British! The CIA and the SIS were almost fraternally close, and yet he had received not one word of warning during all his meetings with British diplomats and intelligence officials.

Wisner's chief aide on the trip, John Baker, told the CIA's chief of base in Berlin that it had been an impossible trip. Wisner ran from one appointment to another all day, then stayed up half the night talking, and started in the next day with only two or three hours of sleep. He never stopped talking. It was hard enough to get a word in edgewise with Wisner under the best of conditions, but on this trip it was impossible.

When Khrushchev abandoned attempts at conciliation (which may, in fact, have been only a feint) and sent his tanks into Budapest on November 4, Wisner flew on to Vienna, where local CIA officers noted the same excitement and tension and compulsive overwork. The moment was a horribly painful one. The CIA had encouraged nationalist resistance to the Russians in Eastern Europe and had even planned for clandestine military action in the late 1940s and early 1950s. In November 1956 there were still caches of sterilized arms waiting throughout Europe, and the émigré Hungarians who had volunteered to fight under CIA direction in the event of war began calling up their CIA case officers. The pressure on the Eastern European Division chief in Washington was tremendous. But there was nothing to be done. American intervention would have meant war, and the Hungarians who called for arms and aid had to be told no.

Wisner was there when the river of Hungarian refugees began to arrive in Vienna with stories of Russian brutality, tanks against men, bodies in the streets. When the rebel Hungarian radios fell silent, and the fighting ended, Wisner left Vienna for Greece and Rome before returning to the United States. In both cities local CIA officers noted his odd, insistent, and at moments outrightly erratic behavior. By this time he was also physically ill. It had not yet been diagnosed, but he had hepatitis, apparently acquired from a plate of raw clams in Athens.

Back in Washington, Wisner called a meeting of the chief officers of the DDP—Helms and all the Division chiefs—and asked John Baker to report on the trip. But before Baker could fairly begin, Wisner interrupted and thereafter continued to interrupt every three minutes, once in order to tell a long, detailed, thoroughly scatological story which involved some Russians, a confusion between the men's room and the women's room, and a great deal of toilet paper. A long, rambling, complicated, fairly funny story, but an odd choice for the present circumstances. Wisner seemed fascinated by the story. Later he called up Henry Cabot Lodge to tell him the story, and in the following days he told it again and again, at meetings and conferences.

And then he physically collapsed. With a fever of 106 degrees, Wisner went into the hospital, where a new idée fixe captured him. Indian Prime Minister Jawaharlal Nehru had recently visited the United States and was photographed climbing the White House steps to shake hands with Eisenhower. It was an amusing photo, Nehru up on his toes and looking a bit like a ballet dancer, hand out, big grin, bounding up the White House steps. Wisner, lying in his hospital bed, began to embroider the photo around the theme of *pas de deux, pas de dough,* etc., making fun of Nehru, who irritated the American foreign policy establishment by keeping one eye on his reputation as a neutralist man of peace and the other on foreign aid. Wisner decided it would make a terrific cartoon subject for Herblock, the editorial cartoonist of the Washington *Post*. He asked a hospital nurse to get him a phone so he could call the publisher of the *Post*, his friend Philip Graham.

Certainly not, said the nurse. It was late at night. Mr. Wisner was a sick man.

Wisner's eyes narrowed. He directed the full force of his personality at the hapless nurse. "You don't know who I am," he said, "but I have a very important job. And as part of my job I control thousand of *goons*. If you don't let me call Mr. Graham [and here the words were drawn out with terrible exactitude] *I'm going to set my goons on you.*"

The nurse gave in.

A groggy Graham finally answered his phone. "Phil," said Wisner, "I've got an idea for Herblock. . . ." And he proceeded to describe in detail the photo, and how Herblock should draw the cartoon, and what ought to go into the little insets which would surround the central drawing like medallions, each one a play on *pas de deux*. A long, detailed description, to which Graham listened in astonished silence. One man who heard Wisner describe the cartoon later said it was brilliant, in its way. . . .

While Wisner was in the hospital, Richard Helms again took charge of the DDP. Wisner returned to work early in 1957 and for a while seemed fine. His doctors of course told him to get plenty of rest and to quit drinking, but Wisner's temperament prevented him from taking his work lightly. For a year he was the old Wisner, active, interested, with a lawyer's crispness of mind, pushing himself on the social round. In March 1958 he set off on another round-the-world journey, covering the Far East this time.

Shortly after his return Wisner attended a Fourth of July party at the Virginia country home of Paul Nitze, a well-known Washington official, and it was immediately apparent to the dozen or so other guests that something was wrong with him. Richard Bissell was there, and he remembers Wisner as being quite voluble, not just talkative but insistent, tremendously excited, even euphoric as he described some silks he'd bought in Thailand. Bissell immediately concluded that Wisner was an extremely sick man.

This time his breakdown was unmistakably psychological. Wisner began writing long, contentious letters to friends. At meetings he swung from erratic insistence on matters of no importance to brooding silence. Even at Allen Dulles's regular Director's meetings, held on Monday, Wednesday, and Friday, he sometimes fell into long monologues on obscure points. People who worked for him directly were given impossible orders, criticized in a high wild voice, accused, abused. Wisner's secretary was often in tears that summer. Finally, at work one day in August, he broke down completely. An ambulance was called, and Wisner was subdued by hospital attendants and carried out of L Building by force, while DDP officials watched in shocked silence. Even then Wisner insisted there was nothing wrong with him—he did not need medical attention, a little rest would do the trick—but finally Desmond FitzGerald persuaded him that this was more than ordinary overwork, and Wisner consented to treatment in Shepherd Pratt hospital near Baltimore. The late 1950s were the great age of electroshock therapy, and Wisner's six months at Shepherd Pratt were an ordeal. He never talked about it to his old CIA colleagues except once, when he said to FitzGerald: "Des, if you knew what you'd done to me, you could never live with yourself."

For a second time Helms was appointed DDP during Wisner's absence. But this time it was clear Wisner was not coming back. Dulles had a theory that Wisner's trouble came from the nature of his job, where endless foreign policy crises allowed pressures to build to a killing level. Perhaps Wisner would do better as chief of station in London, where the pace was easier and Wisner had a lot of good friends and would be able to carry on the sort of social life he liked without the awful strain of work as DDP. So Wisner left the DDP for London in 1959, but later that year Richard Bissell stopped off to see him on a trip to Europe and thought he saw the first signs of a new breakdown. In 1961 Wisner left the CIA altogether; busying himself with various financial interests, he once again seemed to his friends to have recovered completely. He continued to take an interest in Agency affairs and none of his friends was much surprised in 1963 when he called them all to protest vigorously the projected appointment of Lyman Kirkpatrick as Inspector General/Comptroller of the CIA.[1] Didn't they see? This would make Kirkpatrick the number-three man in the agency, after the Deputy Director. It had to be stopped, Wisner said.

It wasn't—Kirkpatrick got the job, and held it until he resigned in 1965—but no one took Wisner's protests amiss. A lot of Agency people felt exactly the same way. Wisner's apparent recovery, however, was an illusion. In October 1965, with the onset of a new breakdown, Frank Wisner shot and killed himself.

When Wisner left the DDP, it was widely assumed that Dulles would appoint Helms to succeed him. It seemed a logical, indeed inevitable, choice. Helms had a reputation as an able administrator, a talent of no small importance under Frank Wisner's leadership. Wisner had his friends and his foes. The friends said he had a fine lawyerly mind, quick, crisp, and lucid. The foes said it was lawyerly all right: punctilious and shallow. But friends and foes agreed on one thing: Frank Wisner could not administer a dinner for two. When he wanted something done he'd ask four or five different people to do it and then call up every morning to find out how they were getting on. Without Helms as chief of operations to untangle the crossed wires, the DDP might have become mired down.

Helms's broad experience with clandestine operations was a result of his unique position under Wisner. As chief of operations, he was a kind of middle man between the field and Washington policymakers, approving and even choosing the wording of cables to the field describing "requirements"; and passing on concrete proposals for operations from the local CIA stations before handing them up to the policymaking apparatus for final approval.

This worked roughly in the following manner: For twenty years and more after World War II American policy in Italy, for example, had one abiding goal: prevent the Communists from coming to power. The requirement sent to the CIA station in Rome was for practical programs to strengthen the Christian Democratic party (and later the socialist parties which joined the Christian Democrats in a center-left coalition), and to weaken the neo-Fascist and Communist parties, with the emphasis on the latter. An official of the Christian Democratic party in contact with the CIA might say: If we had $25,000 we could put up a million wall posters blaming the Communists for X. If his CIA case officer agreed, he would draw up a poster proposal which the Rome station chief would send to Washington for approval. If Helms thought the proposal made sense, that the passage of money could be handled securely and so on, the proposal would go to Wisner with his okay and from Wisner to the Director, the White House, and the State Department. The State Department might ask what the U.S. ambassador to Italy thought, so the proposal would go back to Helms, and from Helms to Rome, where the station chief would get the ambassador on board and then resubmit the proposal to Helms.

In 1955 the National Security Council issued two directives establishing a special committee—formally known as the 5412 Committee—to provide final approval for all covert operations which the CIA considered large, important, or sensitive enough to require White House approval.[2] Eisenhower's first representative on the 5412 Committee, Gordon Gray, changed its everyday name to the Special Group for reasons of security. He was afraid his secretary would mark its meetings down on his calendar—"5412 Committee, State Department, 10 a.m."—and give the game away. "Special Group" had a nice, vague, anonymous ring to it. Before 1955 covert operations were approved in a haphazard way, pretty much at the discretion of the DCI. Afterward, the 5412 Committee, or Special Group, would say yes or no, before the proposal would pass back through Helms's hands on its way to the field.

If Helms did not exactly decide what the DDP ought to do, therefore, he nevertheless had a solid margin of control over how its operations were carried out, and he certainly had an unprecedented breadth of knowledge of what was in fact going on. He was one of the very few men in the CIA, in fact, who had a legitimate "need to know" pretty much everything. The reputation he won in this job was two-sided. He was credited with an ability to keep things moving, and for ensuring timely support once operations were under way. But Helms also had a reputation for indecisiveness and bureaucratic compromise.

This would take two forms, according to men who worked with him. For example, Helms did not like deciding the inevitable minor disputes which arose between competing interests within the CIA. One longstanding source of contention in the early years centered on the Soviet Division's need for "slots"—that is, the right to place its officers—in field offices controlled by other DDP divisions. For one thing, the CIA office in Moscow was naturally small and closely watched. For another, it is standard intelligence practice to mount operations against target countries—Russia, in this instance—from third countries like Germany, Austria, or France. Thus the Soviet Division might decide it would like five slots in the Paris station in order to pursue Soviet diplomats and trade officials. The head of the Western European Division might say good heavens no, five was far too many, he needed those slots for his own people; he might perhaps let the Soviet Division have, shall we say, two.

One former head of the Soviet Division remembered going to Helms's office with the head of the Western European Division after a long, fruitless wrestle with just such a problem in the early 1950s. They spent fifteen minutes in Helms's office in L Building, a quarter of an hour being Helms's allotted time for just about anything short of war. First the Soviet Division chief explained why he needed five slots in Paris. Then the Western European Division chief argued that two would strain his station to the breaking point. By that time only four minutes of the allotted fifteen still remained. Helms took 240 seconds to recognize the strength of the opposing arguments, emphasize how important it was to settle these things and get on with the job they'd hired out to do, and conclude that if there was any further problem of course he'd consider it, pressing schedule, thanks very much, carry on, men.

Out in the hall the Soviet Division chief turned to the Western European Division chief and said, "What did he decide?" For the life of them, they could not say. So they settled it themselves.

Helms was impossible in that regard; he just would not make a decision. After a time, the former Soviet Division chief said, he stopped taking problems of that sort to Helms; it was too frustrating. You'd go up the hall to Helms's office, and you'd come back down again, and you'd have to solve the problem yourselves anyway. Maybe, he reflected, that was Helms's technique. . . .

The other half of Helms's reputation was based on his coolness toward most covert operations, not only the ill-fated resistance-building programs in the Eastern bloc in the late 1940s and early 1950s, but the propagandizing that followed it as well. Wisner thought the United States could effectively combat Soviet influence around the world with a one-two punch—

support for political leaders and parties friendly to the United States, backed up by all the arts of propaganda. These ranged, in the system elaborated by a Johns Hopkins University professor named Paul Linebarger, from white to black.[3] White propaganda is simply an open, candid charge against an opponent. Black propaganda conceals its origin and works in devious ways. An example of black "disinformation" was the CIA's circulation of an allegedly Soviet anti-Islamic pamphlet in Egypt in October 1954.[4] But that was a minor, offhand effort compared to the CIA's use of Khrushchev's secret speech denouncing Stalin before the 20th Party Congress in February 1956.

Rumors of the speech quickly began to circulate throughout Communist party circles, and it was not long before the CIA picked them up. Dulles signed a "book message" (i.e., a cable to all CIA stations) putting the Agency's highest priority on obtaining a copy of the speech. This was accomplished within six weeks, apparently from a Communist party functionary in Poland who was in contact with the Israeli secret service, Mossad.[5] Wisner, Helms, and Angleton passed the speech on to Dulles, who asked for an estimate of its authenticity by an independent Agency analyst. Helms recommended Ray Cline, then a high official in the Directorate for Intelligence. Cline told the DDP officials, during a meeting in Wisner's office, that the speech seemed genuine to him, and urged its publication. After all, Khrushchev was confirming what had been charged for years— that Stalin's rule had been as arbitrary and bloody as Hitler's. But to Cline's amazement, Angleton and Wisner both wanted to sit on the speech and leak it piecemeal as part of a program to encourage Eastern European resistance to Russian rule.[6] After much argument Dulles decided Cline was right, but only after reaching a typical compromise with Angleton and Wisner.[7] Two versions of the speech were released, one by Dulles's brother at the State Department, who gave it to the *New York Times*,[8] and a second released secretly by the CIA, consisting of the *Times* text with the addition of 34 paragraphs to match gaps in the version obtained in Poland. The CIA additions were made up of compromising remarks about the Chinese and the Indians, for example, which Khrushchev was known by the CIA to have uttered at different times under different circumstances.

Wisner built his propaganda apparatus into a large but delicate instrument which he called his "mighty Wurlitzer." In its overt, white version it consisted mainly of two huge radio operations based in Germany, Radio Liberation (after 1956, Radio Liberty), which broadcast to Russia in fourteen languages, and Radio Free Europe, which broadcast to the satellite countries. They provided the base notes; the treble was played by propaganda assets throughout the world, from CIA-funded newspapers in English and other languages[9] to local publishers, editors, and reporters who could be counted upon to plant CIA stories from time to time. The range of these assets was very wide, and some of them even provided access to the Communist press in France and Italy.[10] Wisner's boast was that he could sit down at his mighty Wurlitzer and play just about any tune he liked, from eerie horror music (Moscow is planning a purge of the Western parties!!!) to light fantasias.

But not everyone shared Wisner's confidence in the Wurlitzer. Central direction gave it a broad impact, but much of it was so American-oriented that it only bewildered the out-of-the-way peoples who were its targets. One DDP officer in the 1950s, Sam Halpern, read an exquisitely worded Wisner editorial intended for Asian newspapers and asked, "How is that going to look in Urdu?" Wisner was not amused. Like Halpern, both Lyman Kirkpatrick and Helms felt the constant propaganda tremolo was something of a boondoggle, allowing local CIA stations to run up fantastic records of activity by planting three-paragraph stories of no consequence in newspapers no one read. In the same way, they were also skeptical of the CIA's largess in financing local political leaders, some of whom—in Chile, for example—all but considered the CIA their personal bankers. Once accustomed to such retainers and programmatic support, the local recipients proved hard to wean.

In Helms's view the larger-scale covert operations could be a positive menace. One typical plan of those years, approved at the height of the Korean War by President Truman, called for the opening of a secret second front in Burma with the aid of a 10,000-man Chinese Nationalist army under General Li Mi. The Pentagon hoped the operation would divert Chinese troops from Korea. General Walter Bedell Smith, then the DCI, vigorously opposed the plan, arguing that mainland China had troops aplenty, but Truman overruled him in a White House meeting and insisted that CIA carry out the operation. He also insisted that the operation be kept entirely secret from the American ambassador to Burma, David McKendree Key. In early 1952 Li Mi's army crossed the Burmese border into China and was immediately and decisively defeated.[11]

Helms's reservations about operations of this sort were purely pragmatic—covert operations threatened the security of local agent networks, were uncertain of success at best, and tended to get into the newspapers. There were many other skeptics about covert operations in the CIA, most of them veterans of the OSO who prided themselves on knowing what pure intelligence was and how to get it. But a lot of these skeptics, according to the operators, who had joined the OPC in the early days under Wisner, were only hedging their bets. Joseph Burckholder Smith, who loved the adventure of mounting operations in the field, was told by a sharper-witted office politician, "Look, the way to get ahead in this outfit is to be always opposed, or at least on the record as very doubtful, about any operation that's suggested. Never be enthusiastic. Almost all operations end up failures finally. If you get known as having been opposed to the idea from the beginning, people think you are very shrewd and must be a good administrator."[12] Undoubtedly there was an element of such bureaucratic caution in all the skeptics, but the real force of their objections lay in the potential dangers of the operations themselves. Lyman Kirkpatrick said that covert operations were as dangerous as nuclear weapons, and that most of them were better abandoned at the beginning, unless their secrecy could be guaranteed "from inception to eternity." Helms shared this attitude, feeling that if inherently noisy things had to be done, it was better to let someone else do them.

But the 1950s were the CIA's great age of clandestine operations. Dulles, Richard Bissell (who joined the CIA early in 1954), and Wisner were all activists by temperament. They had a new idea every ten minutes, and if Helms had flatly resisted covert operations as a matter of course he would not have lasted long. His job under Wisner was not to think up projects but to see they were carried out securely and efficiently. One second-level DDP official remembers Helms characteristically saying of a projected operation, "Let's do it right, let's do it quietly, let's do it correctly."

But Helms's instinctive caution in these matters was nonetheless apparent to everyone who dealt with him. He did not oppose operations, but he toned them down, cut them back, or suggested further testing of the water before going ahead. To say no made enemies; he preferred compromise. In June 1953, Desmond FitzGerald meticulously prepared a defense of an ambitious but operationally cumbersome plan to establish a chain of bookstores throughout Indonesia which might provide cover for CIA employees. The proposal, which was to cost $100,000 a year, was forwarded to the Project Review Committee which passed on large-scale operations. FitzGerald described what it was to do, why it was taking so long to get under way, and what might be gained by sending out a new CIA officer to study the situation further. FitzGerald wanted the full $100,000 for another year. "Well, I don't think we can give you a year's renewal," said Helms, who chaired the meeting, listened to FitzGerald's argument, and asked not a single question. "But we can approve $10,000 for the trip and we'll give you three months to write a recommendation."[13]

Thus Helms was to some degree an anomaly in Dulles's CIA. Dulles's personal history in secret intelligence went back to the First World War. His achievements for the OSS in Berne during the Second World War class him among the great spymasters of all time, in particular his establishment of contact with the German dissident circles trying to kill Hitler. His influence on the organization and style of the early CIA was often decisive, and his personality pervaded the Agency after his appointment as Director in January 1953. As an administrator he ranked even lower than Wisner, often keeping top Agency officials waiting in his outer office an hour or more while he chatted inconsequentially on the interoffice phone with Robert Amory, the Deputy Director of Intelligence.[14] Dulles's interest in the operational details of intelligence was so intense he was called "the great white case officer," but his quiet calls to operational officers down the line, with suggestions they do this or that *but not tell anyone,* frequently had the DDP working at cross-purposes.

The National Security Act of 1947 gave the DCI authority over the entire intelligence community, but Dulles never attempted to exercise that authority, partly in the interest of maintaining bureaucratic peace with the military, but more basically because he just didn't care. Operations were what interested him—how to recruit KGB officers, the vulnerabilities of uncooperative foreign governments, how to get information from friendly intelligence services without letting them know exactly what the CIA was after, or why, etc., etc.—not the lines of multimillion-dollar budgets. After Eisenhower created the President's Board of Consultants on Foreign Intelligence Activities (with ten members,[15] all suggested by Dulles) in January 1956, the Board frequently proposed ways to get Dulles to pay attention to his larger responsibilities—by putting him in the White House, or by getting him to hand over the CIA's internal administration to a special deputy. But Dulles wasn't having any. His brother at the State Department wanted an activist CIA, Dulles himself was as good at running such operations as anybody around, and Eisenhower, while regretting the lack of the sort of orderly intelligence apparatus a real administrator might have built, was content to settle for Allen Dulles as God made him.

"I'm not going to be able to change Allen," Eisenhower is quoted as having said. "I have two alternatives, either to get rid of him and appoint someone who will assert more authority, or keep him with his limitations. I'd rather have Allen as my chief intelligence officer with his limitations than anyone else I know."[16]

Dulles was a man everybody seemed to like. One former member of the CIA's Board of National Estimates (in the work of which the activist Dulles took the faintest possible interest) described him as a "perfectly delightful guy—so unlike his brother." Allen Dulles had about him a deceptively avuncular air, with his white brush mustache and his pipe and rimless spectacles and the bedroom slippers he wore to alleviate the sufferings of gout. The breadth of his acquaintance was truly astonishing; a chief of station in Germany in the mid-1950s said the number of Dulles's visitors during a stopover was simply incredible, not just government officials but international bankers, opposition political leaders, important journalists, and a host of others. He loved to talk, to swap stories, to ruminate on his long experience of the ways of international affairs. One of his favorite stories was about the time in Geneva during the First World War when an unknown Russian requested to see him and Dulles, anxious to leave the office, peeped out for a look at the bald-headed man with the dark spade beard—clearly another crazy exile with a smoldering harangue building up inside him—and decided to sneak off for a game of tennis instead. Well, the joke was on him! That man was none other than . . . Vladimir Ilyich *Lenin!* For years Dulles told this story to every incoming class of CIA recruits.

But Dulles was also a tough defender of the CIA's institutional interests. In 1961, for example, Roger Hilsman and Thomas Hughes, who had taken over the Bureau of Intelligence and Research (INR) at the State Department, tried to capture the Department's voice in the approval of covert operations. In the past a small group in the office of the Undersecretary of State for Political Affairs, run for years by Joseph W. Scott, had spoken for the State Department where covert operations were concerned. But Kennedy's choice for the Undersecretary was Chester Bowles, a man with a visceral dislike of covert operations, and he was inclined to surrender his prerogatives to Hilsman and Hughes. The State Department insisted it was up to them to decide to whom it would entrust its voice in these matters, but Dulles knew a power grab when he saw one, he fought the change tooth and nail, and he won.

Indifferent to broader organizational matters, Dulles was a master of bureaucratic infighting, adept at the arts of polite exchange when murder was in his blood, and never at a loss for someone to call when high-level aid was needed. His run-ins with McGeorge Bundy, Kennedy's Special Assistant to the President for National Security Affairs, were frequent. Bundy, a man whose arrogance was rawly apparent to almost everyone who dealt with him, had insisted that meetings of the Special Group be held in his office in the White House, instead of the Undersecretary's office in the State Department. He would sit there with his feet up on his desk, hands clasped confidently behind his head, and attempt to deal with Dulles as a professor might a promising student.

At one meeting in 1961 the Special Group discussed an incident in Singapore in which two CIA technicians had been arrested while trying to polygraph a potential recruit in Singapore's Special Branch of the national police. (The polygraph operator had literally tried to eat his graphs.)[17] The Prime Minister of Singapore, Lee Kuan Yew, was furious, and his anger only increased when an attempt was made to bribe him with $3 million in cash to drop charges against the CIA people.

Bundy, having given this matter perhaps three minutes of his divided attention, wanted to issue a ruling that henceforth all operations directed against a host government would have to be cleared in advance with the Special Group—which meant, of course, with him personally. To this Dulles refused to agree. For one thing, operations against host governments were legion; that's what the CIA did—recruit agents. This was the CIA's province, the very heart of its expertise. Bundy was in effect proposing that he be put in charge of Foreign Intelligence collection, and that he be entrusted with the identity of just about every agent in the CIA's employ. Dulles was not about to explain his objections to this young man; he just said no. "Now,

Allen," Bundy said, leaning back, hands clasped behind his head, "you must realize—this has a political aspect to it."

Dulles's tone was almost courtly, his voice soft, each word distinct. "Yes, Mac, I do understand there are some political aspects to this. Thank you very much for pointing this out to me." But Dulles knew how to say no, and Dulles won.

But that only brushes the surface of Dulles's underlying flint. He was a hard man; he did not shrink from ordering the assassination of foreign leaders, and as a general rule his charm, but not his power, stopped at the water's edge. In a State Department meeting about how to deal with Nasser around the turn of the year 1956–1957, Dulles told a State Department officer, Miles Copeland, "If that colonel of yours pushes us too far, we will break him in half."[18]

The threat was not an idle one. In the event, Nasser survived Dulles, but two other national leaders who elicited the anger of the Dulles brothers did not: Mohammad Mossadegh of Iran, and Jacobo Arbenz of Guatemala. The removal in August 1953 of Mossadegh, who had nationalized the British-owned Anglo-Iranian Oil Company, was a classic of quiet political subversion, accomplished by Kermit Roosevelt with a handful of aides and a suitcase full of money. Roosevelt's success, for which he was secretly awarded the National Security Medal, encouraged Eisenhower and the CIA to undertake a much more ambitious effort in 1954 to overthrow Arbenz, who was guilty of the cardinal sins of legalizing the Guatemalan Communist party and inviting it to join his government, and of expropriating nearly 400,000 acres of idle banana plantation owned by the United Fruit Company. By that time John Foster Dulles knew there would be no rollback of Communism in Eastern Europe, which served to redouble his determination to block other Communist regimes from coming to power, and to halt them especially in the Western Hemisphere.[19] Once Arbenz's exact political coloration had been identified—a shade of pink made up of reformism which inconvenienced American commercial interests, anti-Americanism, excessive tolerance of Communists—there was not much question what Foster Dulles's policy toward Guatemala would be. The question was not whether to remove him, but how.

In the Dulles brothers' youth the customary treatment for anti-American governments in Central America and the Caribbean had been military intervention, but for a variety of reasons (principally Latin American resentment), by the 1950s it was no longer considered possible to deal with Arbenz summarily by sending in the Marines. Instead, the job of his removal was turned over to the CIA, which came up with a sophisticated plan involving one part military action to nine parts propaganda and psychological warfare. In charge of the plan and its execution were Frank Wisner and Richard Bissell. Dulles assigned Bissell an anomalous role somewhere near the top of the operation—more than adviser, less than director. Because

Wisner disliked and distrusted the operations project director in Miami,[20] a further anomalous role was given to Tracy Barnes, who was theoretically in a kind of overall charge (under Wisner), while operating in practice as Washington-Miami liaison. Also involved were E. Howard Hunt, the operation's Political Action Officer; David Phillips, a propaganda expert in charge of the clandestine Voice of Liberation radio which broadcast from Honduras; and Henry Heckscher, who operated secretly inside Guatemala in quiet tandem with the local CIA station chiefs, Birch O'Neill and (from early June 1954) John Doherty.

Typically, the operation was closely held. J. C. King, the DDP's Western Hemisphere chief, was largely excluded (as he was to be later during the Bay of Pigs operation), and Richard Helms played only a tangential supporting role. He routinely accompanied Wisner to Dulles's regular Director's meetings held three times a week, but in the spring of 1954 Helms always left at the end of the regular meeting, before Wisner, Bissell, and sometimes Barnes would turn to the subject of Guatemala. From his office in L Building, Helms would send the DDP car back for Wisner an hour or so later.

The plan unfolded almost without a hitch, despite repeated protests by the Assistant Secretary of State for Latin American Affairs, Henry Holland, a Texas lawyer who was horrified to learn that the administration had earmarked $20 million for Arbenz's overthrow. His protests were overruled by the Undersecretary of State, General Walter Bedell Smith, but he continued to object to both the Americanization and the militarization of the projected coup, which was "led" by Colonel Carlos Castillo-Armas, a Guatemalan army officer who had been trained at the U.S. Army Command and Staff School at Fort Leavenworth, Kansas. Holland's objections were much like Helms's reservations about this and similar CIA undertakings: he did not so much oppose the goal of Arbenz's overthrow as he did the ostentatious scale of the CIA's role.

But that scale was very much part of the plan. Arbenz was not so much overthrown in the traditional sense as he was literally panicked into resignation. Beginning with well-publicized propaganda radio broadcasts on May 1, 1954, a Guatemalan holiday, a steadily escalating campaign of psychological pressures was brought to bear on Arbenz's government. It was no secret that Castillo-Armas was training a rebel army of several hundred men in Honduras, and official U.S. denunciation of Arbenz's regime by Foster Dulles and others led him to believe a full-scale U.S. effort was under way. Since the poorly equipped Guatemalan army and air force were obviously no match for a serious U.S.-backed invasion, Arbenz was very much alarmed, and his government was divided about how to deal with it. After the commander of the Guatemalan air force defected early in June, Arbenz grounded the rest of his pilots. He suspended civil liberties and considered use of a shipment of Czech weapons to arm a civilian militia, a step which alarmed the Guatemalan army.

On June 18, 1954, Castillo-Armas and his "army"—a small force in trucks—crossed the border from Honduras and encamped six miles inside Guatemala. His air force, a mixed handful of B-26s (some sources say C-46s) and P-47 fighter planes, dropped leaflets over Guatemala City, made strafing runs in outlying districts, and even dropped a bomb or two. Perhaps even so many as three, the point being that the attacks were militarily insignificant while contributing to widespread fear of all-out raids. Meanwhile, the Voice of Liberation was active around the clock, broadcasting meaningless "orders" to fictitious rebel forces, reporting "battles," and spreading rumors. Arbenz, bombarded with conflicting reports, did not know whom to believe and was psychologically isolated with a small group of advisers. Some of his leftist supporters urged all-out resistance while the military temporized and the heretofore neutral Guatemalan middle classes loudly called for anything but war. Even before a single serious military engagement, then, Arbenz was confused, excited, undecided, and alone.

In the middle of the campaign Castillo-Armas's air force lost two of his three P-47s, without which he was incapable of maintaining the show of force which had gained so much at the cost of so little. On June 22, Allen Dulles called on Eisenhower for more, and a meeting in the White House was held to consider the request. The only opposition came from Henry Holland, who argued that the request was illegal and excessive. Later Dulles said he knew he'd won the day when Holland arrived at the meeting with three fat legal tomes, hardly the way to appeal to a professional soldier like Eisenhower. The President himself later said Dulles convinced him when he candidly put the chances of success with more planes at only 50 percent. "If you'd said anything else I'd have turned you down," said Eisenhower, according to one CIA official. "But that's good enough. Go ahead."[21]

With the President's okay Richard Bissell then negotiated the "sale" of U.S. Air Force planes to the Nicaraguan Air Force, the CIA pilots flew additional sorties, and on June 27 Arbenz resigned. After a few days of further maneuvering, power was turned over to Castillo-Armas, who finally arrived victorious in Guatemala City on the embassy plane of U.S. Ambassador John Peurifoy.

From one point of view the whole operation was a resounding success. With next to no bloodshed and only indirect (if perfectly obvious) U.S. intervention, a "Red threat" to the Americas had been neatly removed. In the general euphoria Peurifoy's wife wrote a celebratory jingle, which appeared in *Time* magazine on July 26:

> *Sing a song of quetzals, pockets full of peace!*
> *The junta's in the palace, they've taken out a lease.*

The Commies are in hiding, just across the street;
To the embassy of Mexico they beat a quick retreat.
And pistol-packing Peurifoy looks mighty optimistic
For the land of Guatemala is no longer Communistic.

Even Holland, according to one source, was so impressed by the CIA's success he became a convert to clandestine operations. But not everyone in the CIA shared the elation of Dulles and the other CIA officials who had pulled it off.[22] Helms, several sources say, felt the price had been high—the CIA was more notorious than ever, its role being far too great to hide from any other intelligence agency, even if the American press had been deceived; and the scale and publicity surrounding the operation had inevitably compromised many CIA assets. If the Dulles brothers considered the operation a victory for the Free World, many Latin Americans did not agree. If anything, they liked the CIA even less than they liked the Marines. When Lyman Kirkpatrick made a tour of Latin America in 1956 he found resentment of the Agency for the coup wherever he went. Far from being secret, the CIA's role seemed so blatant to Latin Americans it amounted to an insult.[23]

But these reservations were lost in the euphoria of the back-to-back successes of Iran and Guatemala, where money and expertise had quickly solved nagging political problems with a minimum of publicity and international protest. In late 1954, when the CIA was under pressure from McCarthy and a proposal by Senator Mike Mansfield for serious congressional oversight of the CIA had been co-sponsored by twenty-seven Senators, Dulles launched a public-relations counterattack in which the CIA took quasi-official credit for overthrowing Mossadegh and Arbenz.[24] It was not until 1958, when a CIA attempt to sponsor an anti-Sukarno rebellion in Indonesia ended in abrupt, embarrassing failure, that the covert operators in CIA received a check. If that failure had been publicized the CIA might have been sufficiently cautioned to the dangers of the Cuban operation which began two years later, but Indonesia was far away, most of the press accepted the denials of Eisenhower and Foster Dulles as plausible, and the CIA's role was small enough in absolute terms to make the failure "embarrassing" rather than "costly." In short, they got away with it. Once again Helms had only a tangential supporting role, but he watched what happened, asked discreet questions afterward, and then, as usual, kept his own counsel.

Sukarno of Indonesia was a classic American "enemy" of the 1950s, a high-riding nationalist leader who exploited Russian-American hostility for foreign aid which he then "squandered" on prestigious public works such as government buildings, giant sports palaces, and six-lane highways to the airport. Foster Dulles's puritanical character and his practical thrift were equally offended by Sukarno's economic frivolity (as he considered it), but the full force of his anger was directed at Sukarno's "immoral" neutralism. In Dulles's eyes, playing footsie with the Communists (i.e., the Russians and the huge Indonesian Communist party, the PKI) amounted to supping with the devil with a short spoon, endangering not only the freedom of his own country, but the cause of the Free World. Not only was Sukarno dangerous, but his broad hints that money and political support for Indonesian claims to West Irian might wean him from his Red friends struck Dulles as the moral equivalent of blackmail. Publicly, the Secretary of State expressed high-minded disdain for such irresponsible national leaders. Sukarno was only one of many. Nasser was another. So were Nehru and Kwame Nkrumah and a host of others. Privately, Dulles was determined to show Sukarno that the United States was not to be trifled with. He was fully supported by a former ambassador to Indonesia, Hugh S. Cumming, who had forbidden his staff in Djakarta to read George Kahin's *Nationalism and Revolution in Indonesia*[25] because it was "too anti-Dutch," and who had taken over the State Department's Bureau of Intelligence and Research in 1957, from which position he peppered the rest of the government with alarming memos calling for action against Sukarno before it was too late.

Again, the job was given to the CIA. In the summer of 1956 a new station chief was sent to Djakarta, Val Goodell, an OSS veteran described by one of his colleagues as having "fewer scruples than any man I ever met elsewhere."[26] The head of the DDP's Far East Division at that time was Alfred Ulmer, an OSS veteran who had also worked in Greece at the height of the civil war[27] and who had ambitions of replacing Frank Wisner as DDP. In the fall of 1956 Wisner told Ulmer, "It's time we held Sukarno's feet to the fire."[28] Ulmer's first problem was a lack of CIA assets in Indonesia which might be used to teach Sukarno a lesson; but the following April, luck intervened. A representative of some dissident army officers on Sumatra approached the CIA in Djakarta with what gradually developed into a request for arms, money, and political support.

The moment was a delicate one. The new U.S. ambassador to Indonesia, John Allison, was driving Hugh Cumming at the State Department crazy with reports that Sukarno needed "understanding" and support on West Irian, not pugnacious muscle. The view from Washington was quite different. Navy reconnaissance had noted construction crews leveling an airfield-sized patch of land on the island of Natuna Besar, north of Sumatra; the U.S. Commander in Chief in the Pacific (CINCPAC) was alarmed that the new airfield would give Soviet fighter planes a refueling stop which would allow them to by-pass the SEATO countries and reach Indonesia, too distant from Soviet airfields on Hainan Island for a direct flight. Walter Robertson, the Assistant Secretary of State for Far Eastern Affairs, and Hugh Cumming both shared the Navy's alarm. The Dulles brothers did not want to overthrow Sukarno exactly, just force him to suppress the PKI, send the Russians packing, and get on the American team. Within the CIA it was decided to back the Sumatran army rebels quietly for use as a veiled threat that the United States might get mad someday, and would be in a position to do more than dispatch stiffly worded cables when it did.

By the end of 1957 the CIA had arranged for a rebel arms purchase and had infiltrated a CIA paramilitary expert and his radioman into Sumatra by submarine. In his memoirs Allison claims he was abruptly ordered to leave Indonesia early in January 1958, but a CIA official active in the operation says Allison requested reassignment after Undersecretary Christian Herter cabled him about the arms shipment. The CIA official said he knew this for a fact, because Allison used CIA radio channels, and the official read all his cables.[29]

But despite Foster Dulles's enthusiasm for putting pressure on Sukarno, and Allen Dulles's confidence the Sumatran rebels were just the thing, there was opposition within the DDP doubting the rebel policy was going to work. This principally came from Desmond FitzGerald, at that time chief of political and paramilitary warfare on the DDP's Covert Action Staff, who objected that the rebels were an unknown quantity, and that the State Department's caution (in the early stages the CIA was limited to one paramilitary expert and radioman with the rebels) was crippling the operation. One CIA officer who knew both Helms and FitzGerald said that Helms's reaction would have been doubly skeptical, that if FitzGerald (a decided covert action enthusiast) did not think much of the plan, then it was *hopeless*.

And so it was. The rebels sent Sukarno an ultimatum in February 1958, and when he failed to respond declared the island of Sumatra independent. Within days Sukarno's navy blockaded the rebels, his air force raided them, and his army began to move on Sumatra. The State Department reluctantly overcame its hostility to "white faces" and allowed the CIA to send two more paramilitary experts with their radiomen to join the rebels. One of them was Anthony Poshepny, called Tony Po, who had trained CIA client armies all over the Far East.[30] Tony Po was a hard, meticulous man, a veteran of many battles who habitually carried a boxer's mouthguard in his pocket because you never know what's going to happen when you walk into a bar—better safe than sorry. But no amount of paramilitary expertise could have saved the Sumatran rebels at that point. Even a rebel air force flown by CIA pilots and paid for with CIA funds—although the funds for security reasons were passed through a rebel bank account—failed to slow the rebels' defeat on Sumatra and retreat to the Celebes. At that point the CIA was reduced to the hope that its clients might hold on to an island or two for use as a "pressure point" in future dealings with Sukarno.

But on Sunday, May 18, Allen Lawrence Pope, one of the CIA pilots, was shot down in his B-26 after accidentally bombing a church and killing most of the congregation. When word of Pope's loss[31] reached Washington the same day, Allen Dulles decided to call off the operation and sent an emotional cable—this is the hardest thing I've ever had to do, brave men, etc.—to the senior paramilitary officer with the rebels in Menado, telling him to inform the rebels the United States must disengage. After telling the rebel leaders about the decision, the CIA officers simply abandoned whatever they could not destroy or carry, and left. One group of officers still in the heart of Sumatra, accompanied by a handful of Indonesians facing death if they remained, had to walk out to the coast through several hundred miles of jungle, and then put out to sea in rubber boats from which they were later picked up by the U.S. Navy.

The result, of course, was a humiliation for the United States, but it was a quiet humiliation. The Indonesians knew who had been behind the rebels, of course, but they elected to treat the matter calmly, knowing Foster Dulles would have to come around, as he did; and the American press somehow never got wind of the CIA's role. But within the CIA the covert operators were sobered by their failure. Al Ulmer was shortly thereafter replaced as chief of the Far East Division by Desmond FitzGerald, and that summer Frank Wisner left the DDP for good. Ulmer's chief executive officer throughout the operation had been Sam Halpern, and he was upset by its failure. Halpern had served as liaison with British MI 6, involved because of the CIA's use of British territory in Singapore during the operation, and he found it painful to watch their cool, professional equanimity the Sunday morning word arrived of Pope's loss. The CIA was in a full-scale flap, officers pulled in from home, people running about. The British attitude was implicit but clear: by the time an operation is blown it's too late to do anything about it: why all the excitement? couldn't things wait for Monday? One British intelligence official, watching the uproar, told Halpern, "This would never happen on our home territory."

Richard Helms took much the same attitude. After the dust had settled he casually raised the subject with Halpern, who happened to be in his office on another piece of business one day that summer. Helms asked, "What went wrong, Sam?"

Halpern told him. The rebels had been an unknown quantity, the State Department wanted an aggressive operation but refused to allow CIA to send more than one officer to deal with the rebels in the early stages. They were worried about white faces blowing the operation and embarrassing the United States. Al Ulmer argued again and again at the Ad Hoc Interagency Committee's meetings on the operation that you can't cover an operation like this with one guy. By the time the second and third men got in, it was too little and too late again, as usual. The rebels were given plenty of equipment, but they had little stomach for fighting.

Halpern did not go into great detail, but he laid it out clearly enough. Just about everything that can go wrong with a paramilitary operation, he told Helms, had gone wrong with this one. From confusion about aims and a bad estimate of clients, to a fatal caution about striking to kill, if you're going to strike at all. When Halpern was done, Helms said nothing. Nothing at all. Not, "I see," or "So that's it," or "No surprise about that." Halpern expected some sort of comment, but Helms proved again that he was a very taciturn man, not easy to read. Helms listened to the description of the CIA's biggest covert failure in ten years, a classic Cold War spoiling operation gone wrong, and then he just nodded his head.

Chapter 6

It was apparent in the fall of 1958 that Frank Wisner's tenure as DDP was over, and it was widely believed his successor would be Richard Helms. If Helms's reputation was that of a secret intelligence man, first and last, putting him on the periphery of Dulles's activist CIA, nevertheless his experience in the Directorate of Plans was unequaled, the covert operators had been dealt a jolting blow by their failure in Indonesia, and Helms had a strong coterie of supporters. This was not accidental. When Helms found someone he liked and trusted, he held on to him. In June 1954, Thomas Karamessines, an OSS and OSO veteran who had been chief of station in Greece, returned to the DDP after a year at the National War College. Helms asked what he'd like to do next. Karamessines said well, he'd spent eight or nine years in clandestine work, he thought maybe he'd like a tour of duty with the analysts and estimators. "Goddamnit," Helms said, "you guys go off to these schools and come back with a roaring case of globalitis. We need you here." And there he stayed, one of the men who thought Helms ought to be DDP.[1]

Helms himself, no less ambitious than any other man within striking distance of a top job, certainly wanted the position, thought he was well qualified for it, and discounted a remark by Frank Wisner which made the rounds at the time. Wisner, who had depended heavily on Helms's organizational talent, reportedly praised Helms as an excellent deputy, a first-rate number two man, but unsuited for the top job. But the man who would decide was Allen Dulles, and in Dulles's mind Helms had an unlikely rival, a man with less than five years' experience in the Agency, with no experience whatever in the field or in traditional spy running, but a formidable rival all the same. That was Richard Bissell, a tall, imaginative, appealing fellow—his friends often speak of him as "Dickie," whereas Helms is always prosaic "Dick"—whose air of distraction did not disguise his talents. It might be said of Bissell that he was what used to be called in the eighteenth century "a man of parts."

Richard Bissell had an extraordinary mind. Like many other high officials of the early CIA he was a perfect representative of his class—a graduate of Groton in 1928 and Yale in 1932—but it was not so much his easy demeanor, instinctive courtesy, and wide social acquaintance, but his mind which marked him for advancement in government circles. Bissell was an economist, a patrician easy with democracy, and a man as fascinated by the great world as a boy taking apart a pocket watch, and it is here that one finds the first hint of his peculiar mind.

It will not do to say simply that he was intelligent. The qualities which distinguished him were lucidity, a capacious memory, a tinkerer's love of system, and a confidence, unsettling in its coolness, that the only relevant question to be asked of a system was whether it worked. As a boy, it is said, Bissell was fascinated with trains and there was hardly a railroad line in America so obscure he could not chart its route, or tell you its exact hours of arrival and departure. He had a vast appetite for detail oddly at variance with later claims of an "appalling" memory, and once he set himself to understand how something worked, he made it his own. His genuine ability was characteristically displayed in 1964, two years after Bissell had left the CIA in public disgrace, when he was called in by the CIA and the National Security Agency to help solve a particularly knotty problem.

An important part of the NSA's huge operation was the breaking of Soviet codes, but even with the aid of its literally acres of computers this was something both difficult and expensive to do. The office for National Intelligence Programs Evaluation (NIPE), set up by John McCone in 1963, was not sure the effort was worth the money. The NSA had long been logging all Soviet message traffic at great cost in the hope a breakthrough might allow them to read back-traffic (and arguing that traffic analysis made the effort useful for the meantime), but NIPE claimed that even if the codes could be broken the intelligence take wouldn't be worth the cost. Eugene Fubini, an Assistant Secretary of Defense with the Pentagon's department of research and engineering, said that indeed it was worth the money. After the usual long, dogged, and fruitless bureaucratic wrangling, Fubini and NIPE agreed to bring in Bissell, by then head of the Institute for Defense Analysis, to settle the argument. The idea was to pick a particular Soviet code, figure out what it would cost to break it, and then ask the CIA's analysts if the result would justify the expense. The NSA was skeptical of any outsider's ability to master the arcana of code breaking, but Bissell went to work and produced an answer within a month. Later a top cryptanalyst told a NIPE official that watching Bissell work had been breathtaking; he'd met only one other man in his life with an equal capacity to absorb strange data. It was almost as if Bissell emptied his mind to make room for the new information.[2]

Problems intrigued Bissell, and Allen Dulles often gave him hard ones. His first assignment, before he joined the Agency in January 1954, had been to study ways the CIA might engage in serious troublemaking in Soviet territory, especially in the occupied countries of Eastern Europe. Bissell concluded the CIA's efforts could never amount to much more than pin-pricks, and that even those were offset by potential flareback. Later, he made a minor study of the Directorate for Intelligence, then played an anomalous but important role in the coup which overthrew Arbenz in Guatemala, a spectacular success in operational terms, and if it exacted a price in Latin American hostility, well, that was a problem for the policy-makers. But Bissell's major success, the one which confirmed his reputation in Allen Dulles's eyes, was his development of the high-altitude U-2 photo-reconnaissance plane beginning in December 1954.

From its birth in 1947 the CIA's principal target had been the Soviet Union, and while it managed to collect a great deal of disparate material on the Soviet order of battle (with the important help, especially in Eastern Europe, of Reinhard Gehlen's organization in Germany, and of the British SIS), the so-called denied areas of the Soviet bloc were barely penetrated. Traditional spies did what they could, but by all reports it wasn't much. The security services of the East were simply too pervasive and efficient.

In 1954 a presidential committee headed by James Killian, then presi-dent of MIT and chairman of the Army's Scientific Advisory Panel, ad-dressed the general question of how to deal with a surprise attack on the United States. A subcommittee on intelligence headed by Edwin H. Land of Polaroid recommended development of a high-altitude reconnaissance plane of a sort already under study by the Air Force. In November 1954, Eisen-hower approved the proposal, and the following day Allen Dulles asked Bissell to take over the CIA's part in the project. At a meeting in the office of Trevor Gardner, head of research and development for the Air Force, the CIA's part became the whole, largely because the project's success de-pended on secrecy, and because Bissell volunteered to pay for it—at least $22 million, according to Air Force estimates—from Allen Dulles's reserve fund. Before the meeting ended, Bissell called Kelly Johnson, the president of Lockheed, which had already submitted designs for a prototype, and told him the project had a go-ahead. Johnson began clearing out a hangar in Burbank, California, the next day.

A lot of CIA people distrusted Richard Bissell, thinking—especially in the light of what happened later—that his extraordinary mind was fatally flawed, that his confident enthusiasm for ambitious projects crossed the threshold of recklessness. But no one denies the magnitude of his achieve-ment in developing the U-2, a plane which many Air Force experts thought would never meet its performance requirements, would take six years to develop, and would go far beyond its budget.[3] Bissell ran the project as in effect a kind of covert operation, creating what he called a "private duchy" of eight to ten people in the Directorate for Support so exclusively under his personal control that not even Allen Dulles was allowed to read its cable traffic.

The Development Project Staff, as it came to be called, was formally inaugurated on December 1, 1954, and early the following spring Bissell and his deputy, Herbert Miller, flew out to Burbank. In a small plane with Kelly Johnson they inspected three dry salt lake pans in Nevada. When they had picked one for a training site Bissell persuaded Eisenhower to annex it to the federal atomic testing grounds so that the U-2 project might come under the Atomic Energy Commission's security umbrella. The first U-2 flew on August 6, 1955. In October six officers of the Strategic Air Command (SAC) were trained to fly the plane, and in November they, in turn, began to train civilian pilots.

At the same time Bissell fought a running jurisdictional battle with General Curtis LeMay, the commander of Strategic Air Command, who wanted to run the U-2 program himself. LeMay was a tough and thoroughly bellicose man (what was the point of swatting flies? he once asked during the early stages of American involvement in Vietnam; why not go after the manure pile—China?), but he lost the struggle. Allen Dulles and General Nathan Twining, the Air Force chief of staff, signed an agreement giving control of the U-2 program to the CIA and restricting SAC to a support role. By May of 1956 the first U-2 air wing—four planes, six civilian pilots under contract to the CIA, another two hundred support personnel—was in Turkey and ready to fly. In June, Dulles, Bissell, and Miller went to Eisenhower for permission to overfly the Soviet Union from Turkey to Norway. The following day Eisenhower's chief military aide, Colonel (later General) Andrew Goodpaster, called Bissell with Eisenhower's approval for ten days of flights.

"You mean ten *flying* days," said Bissell.

Goodpaster said absolutely not, ten days period, and it starts from now.

On the first available flying day Bissell went to see Dulles, arriving shortly before the Director's regular morning staff meeting was scheduled to begin. Dulles asked what route the first U-2 would follow. Bissell said it would pass over Moscow and Leningrad.

Dulles turned pale. Moscow! Leningrad! "Do you really think that was wise?" Dulles asked.

But the flight was a complete success. The Russians immediately picked up the U-2 by radar—Bissell had hoped the U-2 might even be too high for radar, but that hope was vain—but they were unable to do anything about it. At 80,000 feet, its cameras photographing a swathe on the ground 120 miles wide, the U-2 sailed soundlessly across the Soviet Union far beyond the range of Russian antiaircraft missiles, and it continued to fly at irregular intervals for nearly four years, until the Russians finally managed to bring one down in May 1960, on the eve of a summit conference between Eisenhower and Khrushchev.[4]

The U-2 never again flew over the Soviet Union, but by that time

Bissell's Development Project Staff in the DDS was already far along in its work on a satellite reconnaissance system, which, like the U-2, was a program picked up in its early stages from the Air Force. The original satellite project was publicly canceled, then secretly resumed in the spring of 1957 by CIA. Bissell modified the Air Force plan in two important ways. First, he switched the satellite from one in which the camera was fixed while the satellite spun, to one in which the satellite was stabilized and the camera scanned. Second, he abandoned the Air Force plan for televising the satellite's photographs and developed in its place a more complex system whereby the actual film would be jettisoned from the satellite and recovered in mid-air. With continuing refinement of the photographic equipment this eventually allowed the satellite's photographs from heights of 80 miles or more to equal U-2 photographs in fineness of resolution. Within a year after the downing of a U-2 by the Soviets the satellites had taken their place.

It would be hard to exaggerate the importance of Bissell's achievement in developing both the U-2 and the satellite reconnaissance systems. Together they completely revolutionized the business of intelligence collection, increasing American knowledge of Soviet military capacity and economic life by a quantum jump. Every square inch of Soviet territory was opened to American eyes. In the short term the Soviets might move a division, open an airfield, start building a submarine pen, or redeploy an air wing without American knowledge until the next overflight, but in the long term every aspect of Soviet military and economic activity was revealed in exquisite detail. Among other results, this allowed genuine disarmament negotiations for the first time, since it was possible for both sides (the Soviets having developed similar reconnaissance systems) to verify whether or not the other side was abiding by its agreements. Before the U-2, the principal obstacle to disarmament was verification; since its first flight, the obstacles have been mainly political.

Bissell's program brought in more hard intelligence than all previous sources put together. Arthur Lundahl's National Photo Interpretation Center (NPIC), beginning as a group of twenty interpreters in the Deputy Directorate for Intelligence in 1953, eventually expanded to include 1,200 employees and a vast computerized filing system which made it impossible for the Soviets to lay a sewer pipe in Siberia without CIA learning about it.[5] Allen Dulles was as impressed as he was delighted. Bissell had other virtues —a wide social acquaintance, a reputation for his work on the Marshall Plan, enviable connections in the State Department and on the Hill—but it was principally the U-2, and its suggestion of further breakthroughs in technical intelligence collection, which led Dulles in the fall of 1958 to ask Richard Bissell if he would be interested in Frank Wisner's job as DDP. Bissell thought it over for ten days, not sure he wanted to seal his career so permanently (as he thought) in secrecy, then told Dulles he would take the job.

From the beginning, Bissell and Helms did not get along. For one thing, of course, Helms was bitterly disappointed at missing the appointment himself. Bissell, through Dulles, asked Helms to stay on as the DDP's chief of operations, but it was a humiliating offer under the circumstances and for a while, according to one DDP officer of the time, Helms considered requesting a post overseas. But in the end, largely because he was by temperament and choice an intelligence executive, accustomed to the corridors of power, Helms agreed to stay on. However, starting off badly for obvious and natural reasons, relations between the two men deteriorated steadily. It was not so much pique of the sort expressed by Helms's secretary, Elizabeth Dunlevy, when she said, "Of course we all know Dick should have been DDP," as it was a collision of experience and of temperament.

To begin with, Richard Bissell is in certain ways an insensitive man. This is not to say that he is contentious or discourteous—far from it—but that he tends to look at the world in a mechanical way, fascinated by the way it runs, and pretty much oblivious to other things. He could be brusque enough, and it was small consolation to those he wounded that the last thing he'd intended was pain. Remembering his relationship to Helms now, he has a vaguely puzzled air, as if their cool hostility escaped him. This is no doubt partly the inevitable attempt to minimize the petty animus of bureaucratic politics, but Bissell's memory now, and his conduct then, both suggest that he either failed to notice or simply dismissed Helms's disappointment. If he had asked Helms to stay on personally, or had insisted on a long talk at the beginning of his appointment, or had recognized Helms's special expertise and requested his help, things might have worked out differently; but he did none of those things. He simply moved into Wisner's office and job, asked several young aides to assume responsibility for the overnight cable traffic (something Helms had done for Wisner), and was content to limit his contact with Helms to the Director's meetings they attended together, the regular weekly meetings with DDP division chiefs, and the occasional talk —no more than two or three a week, ten or fifteen minutes each—on practical organizational matters which amounted to housekeeping. In effect, Bissell let Helms fill in behind him, depending on him as a man might depend on a good secretary. He relied on Helms for advice on personnel appointments (and not always then, to his later sorrow), and he kept the major DDP projects and programs—the two or three things a month that were "kind of hot"—for himself.

During 1959, for example, the CIA's chief of station in Bangkok, Robert Jantzen (whom Desmond FitzGerald ten years later called "the greatest single asset the United States has in Southeast Asia"),[6] reported that the

Thai premier, Field Marshal Sarit Thanarat, wanted to invade Cambodia. Jantzen and Sarit were on such close terms they might almost have been called drinking buddies. They often talked late into the night while Jantzen, carrying a secret tape recorder because of his poor memory, was passively taking it all down. For a day or two after Sarit's threat of war, cable traffic between Bangkok and Washington was heavy, and Bissell was frequently in conference with Allen Dulles until Jantzen finally managed to talk Sarit out of his plan. Thus Bissell concentrated on the sort of problems which are described as being on the front burner—Patrice Lumumba in the Congo, a defector's report that the KGB had an agent within the DDP, a struggle in which CIA played a central role over whom the United States should support in Laos. One of Bissell's early trips abroad took him to Laos to deal with this problem, but it continued as a running battle for three years between early 1958 and 1961. At one point the chief of station in Vientiane, Henry Heckscher, ended a long and angry exchange of cables (referred to in CIA parlance as a "pissing contest") with a message to Washington in which he asked, "Is headquarters still in friendly hands?"[7]

Bissell rarely asked Helms's opinion, much less his advice, in any of these matters. A naturally loquacious man who liked to discuss the business at hand in a general, reflective way, Bissell does not remember ever having had such a conversation with Helms, and Helms apparently made no attempt to insist on being heard. As a result, Helms found himself cut off from the DDP's central preoccupations, isolated in the department he had helped to create, and undervalued to a demeaning degree. One day in 1959, not long after Bissell took over the DDP, a CIA officer in counterintelligence went to see Helms and Helms asked, in more than a purely conversational way, "What's new?" This amused the counterintelligence man: Helms was chief of ops in the DDP; who was he kidding? "You mean *you* don't know?" Helms raised up both hands, baring his teeth as he did when exasperated or striving to make a point, and said in German: "Aber keiner sagt mir 'was!"— No one tells me anything!

Worse was being forced to sit back and watch as Bissell mucked things up. Like a lot of other early CIA officials—Dulles and Wisner were not the only ones—Bissell was an anarchic administrator. He could theorize about administration for hours, eloquent on the nature of hierarchy and the way authority diffuses down through an organization. He liked to preserve time for what he called "capital formation"—improving the organization. When "Beedle" Smith had married the old OSO and OPC he had integrated both groups from top to bottom, which left each division with its own Covert Action (CA) and Secret Intelligence (SI) staffs. These were large and unwieldy, interfering, wasteful, and duplicative. Bissell wanted to cut them in half, beef up the divisions, reorganize the monitoring of cable traffic.

Or budgeting. A better planning and programming system was needed. You had hundreds and hundreds of projects, but grouping them by type was arbitrary and shallow—covert propaganda ops, covert support for left-wing political ops, etc., etc. What did *that* tell you? These didn't present an administrator with allocation decisions; they were yes-no, are they a good idea? decisions. And a system which worked for the DDP would be completely inappropriate for Angleton's counterintelligence unit. There it wasn't the project, it was the case, and each case was a person. Quite different. Bissell could speak very persuasively on these matters, said one man who often heard him do so, and then an hour later he'd go out and break *every one* of his own rules.

Helms actually knew something about handling these problems in an orderly way, but Bissell never asked his advice. Cut off as he was, he did what he could. Once, when Helms had to be out of town in 1960, he told an aide to brief Bissell on a conflict between the DDP and the DDI, giving the aide explicit instructions what to say. He knew exactly how he wanted this problem handled. But while Helms was away, the situation altered and the aide told Bissell something quite different. When Helms returned he was furious. He called the aide in. "Why didn't you say what I told you to?" The aide explained how things had changed. Helms hesitated; the anger drained out of him, and he answered in almost a musing way, "I think I can stand still for that." But it was a symptom of his impotence during Bissell's tenure as DDP. Occasionally he would discover a major operation in casual conversation. In one instance the DDP's planning officer, John Bross, dropped by to see Helms before leaving the country and found that Helms didn't know anything about it. "Thanks for telling me," he said. "I should have known about it from the first." Not usually abrasive, he grew short-tempered under Bissell. When someone came to him with a proposal of the sort he knew Bissell would want to handle himself, he sometimes said, "Why don't you take it up with Wonder Boy next door?"

The only field of substance in which Helms was given a generally free hand was in the running of agents—an undertaking requiring great tact and judgment, and one that was, as a rule, followed in minute detail from Washington. You did not simply tell an officer in the Rome station, for example, to find an agent inside the Russian Embassy and leave it at that. You wanted to know whom the CIA officer had in mind, and everything that could be discovered about him, and when the initial contact would be made, what sort of cover was being used, the exact nature of the pitch, and so on. Agent-running and counterintelligence experts in Washington were involved at every step along the way. The risk of compromise was great, and if the chances of success were generally slim, especially where the Russians were concerned, the potential rewards were of a sort unobtainable by any other means. Recruiting and running agents were the heart of traditional intelligence collection, and Helms had a reputation for being good at it. But Bissell was not complimenting Helms by leaving this intricate work to him. Instead, Bissell felt it simply wasn't worth the bother.

CIA officers who knew both men say that nothing about Bissell galled Helms more than Bissell's low opinion of the value of agents. He felt the effort involved too much spinning of wheels, too much time, organizational effort, and money for a problematic return. Say an agent in the Russian Embassy was in fact recruited, and the counterintelligence people were satisfied his cooperation was genuine; and say further that the agent was transferred to the Russian Mission to the United Nations in New York, and was privy to Moscow cable traffic, and was therefore in a position to reveal Russian thinking on something like international economic affairs to his case officer in twice-a-week meetings. What then? Even if he spilled his guts, in Bissell's view, he didn't have much to spill. Okay, Bissell might say, you get tidbits, even good tidbits, but the cost effectiveness is rather low.

Bissell had a low opinion of agent-running, and it was no secret in the DDP that Helms and other OSO veterans had an equally low opinion of Bissell's operational expertise. Bronson Tweedy, for example, one of the few OSO veterans to get an important assignment (chief of station in Vienna) in 1952 when the OSO and OPC had been merged into the DDP,[8] was the African Division chief when Bissell took over, and he frequently criticized Bissell's "ineptness" where secret intelligence operations were concerned. Even after the CIA, in collaboration with the British SIS, acquired Colonel Oleg Penkovskiy as an agent in the Kremlin in 1960, Bissell was skeptical. "How do we know this guy is on the level?" he asked Jack Maury, the Soviet Division chief who personally ran the Penkovskiy case from Washington.

Maury found this skepticism simply incredible. Penkovskiy had delivered over 10,000 pages of Soviet military documents—personal histories of leading Soviet generals, high-level training manuals, even specifications of the latest Soviet missiles. No intelligence agency in its right mind would hand over material of that quality to prove the *bona fides* of a penetration. If Bissell had known a single thing about agent-running, if it had been in his blood as it was in Helms's, he would have known immediately that the CIA had an agent here of inestimable value. But it wasn't until the Cuban missile crisis, when the take from Penkovskiy allowed the CIA to follow the progress of Soviet missile emplacement *by the hour*, and to state with bald confidence what the missiles threatened—every major city in the continental United States except Seattle—that Bissell fully realized what Penkovskiy had given him.[9] By that time, Bissell himself was gone.

But it was not solely Bissell's inexperience and indifference where agents were concerned that made the old secret intelligence operatives from OSO distrust him. Their differences had a philosophical aspect as well. Bissell liked to do things. Faced with a political problem, Bissell, with Dulles's support, looked for a clandestine solution. Like Desmond Fitz-Gerald, who frequently argued that secret information was useless as long as it remained locked in a safe, Bissell was an activist. This does not mean that he shared the attitude of certain veteran OSS paramilitary enthusiasts, who believed that the shortest distance between two points was violence. Bissell was not backward where violence was involved: he made a good-faith effort to kill the leaders of at least three countries, and sent armed men—in the case of Cuba an outright army—into two of them. But poisoned handkerchiefs and pens, sheep-dipped fighter pilots, and soldiers of fortune with sterile arms were only the most notorious tools in an inventive armory which included economic pressures, financial support, aid and training programs, propaganda, and plain persuasion. The United States was in an interventionist mood after the Second World War, and no intelligence officer, Helms included, could have lasted long or risen high with a reputation for obstruction. The Kennedys wanted Castro out of there, and when the time came Helms tried just as hard to give them what they wanted as Bissell had before him.

But Helms and Bissell differed very greatly on how to go about it. To begin with, they had differing standards of secrecy. When Helms said secret he meant *secret*—in the words of Lyman Kirkpatrick, secret from inception to eternity. Bissell meant secret from the *New York Times*, at least until the operation was successfully completed. Secrecy in intelligence collection is treated with almost religious respect. Ideally, an agent will never know the true identity of his case officer, the route of the funds which pay him, the motive behind the questions he's asked, perhaps not even the country he's working for. It's helpful if the agent believes in the cause he imagines he serves, but a wise case officer, it is said, will attempt a tighter grip than that. Ideally the agent will be dependent on his case officer in every way, for empathy in the first instance, for his very life in the last, while the case officer remains insulated from compromise. It doesn't always work out that way, but that is at least the theory.

In covert action operations it's quite the other way around. There the case officer is not so much trying to hide his agent as to help him accomplish political ends he is already pursuing on his own. The agent is more likely to know the identity of his contact, and to be in a position to embarrass him. Most important, the agent's goal is political power and influence. Far from hiding, he is trying to become visible, to make an impact, in effect to draw attention to himself. Such operations are inherently unstable, if only because the purposes of the agent and his case officer never entirely coincide. In Helms's view the CIA's role in such covert operations tends to leak out, and the larger the operation the quicker it leaks, endangering not only the security of CIA operational assets—funding arrangements, the location of safehouses, proprietary companies, techniques of cover, and so on—but something much more important: that public invisibility without which an intelligence agency cannot inspire confidence in those who trust it with their lives, their fortunes, and their sacred honor; and without which it cannot conduct the sort of operations no nation can undertake openly.

Richard Helms seems to have understood this process of exposure bet-

ter than many other high CIA officials. He disliked big paramilitary operations like the Bay of Pigs invasion and the CIA's support of the Meo army
under General Vang Pao because they were hard to keep secret, and because their exposure tended to dump in the Agency's lap the American
public's instinctive dislike of the anarchic reality of international relations,
in which power is often rawly exercised. In a word, they made the CIA
notorious, crippling its ability to do those things which can be done only in
secret. If American policymakers thought Castro was a sufficient threat to
justify invasion, fine, let the military do it. But don't risk the Agency's ability
to collect intelligence and conduct the quieter forms of coercion appropriate
to an intelligence service by asking it to do an army's job. That only forces it
upon the public's eye, inviting scrutiny, which is the one thing intelligence
services cannot survive. By assigning the CIA huge projects which the American government dared not undertake openly, the President—and the
Agency officials who tried to deliver what he asked—threatened the CIA's
ability to do anything at all.

Helms had his supporters on this point, but Bissell did not find them
congenial, and when he turned his attention to the problem of Castro in the
spring of 1960, he proceeded just as he had with the U-2: entirely on his
own. For one thing, Bissell was in a hurry. After Castro won his revolution
in January 1959, with the tacit support of an American government unhappy with Fulgencio Batista, he lost no time in alienating the U.S.
government, in a broad public way by the wholesale execution of political
enemies, more narrowly by threatening the nationalization of American
businesses and inviting Russian aid to take its place. There has been much
scholarly argument as to whether the United States forced Castro into the
arms of Russia, or merely recoiled when it discovered him heading in that
direction on his own, but there is no question that the U.S. government was
quickly disenchanted.

At a meeting of the National Security Council on March 17, 1960,
Eisenhower approved a modest CIA plan to begin training twenty-five
Cuban exiles, who might in turn train other exiles for an attempt to over-
throw Castro. The following week a meeting was held in Allen Dulles's
office, where Bissell for the first time sketched in the plan he had devised for
Castro's removal. Among the listeners were, in addition to Dulles, the
Deputy Director for Central Intelligence, General Charles P. Cabell; Tracy
Barnes, who was to be Bissell's principal deputy; David Phillips, who was to
orchestrate propaganda support for the operation; several operational officers; and Richard Helms, who said nothing, but only, in Phillips's words,
"listened carefully, often inspecting his carefully manicured fingernails. . . ."[10]

Eisenhower had approved a twenty-five-man training program, but Bissell's plan was already far more ambitious. Eventually it would include a 50-
kilowatt radio station on Swan Island, a government in exile, a rebel air
force with a base in Nicaragua, a rebel army to be trained in Guatemala,

and a full-scale amphibious landing of rebel forces in Cuba. Phillips wondered briefly why the chief of the DDP's Western Hemisphere Division, J. C. King, had not been invited. The answer, as Helms already knew and the rest quickly discovered, was that Bissell, once again, intended to run this operation as his own private duchy.

Chapter 7

It was probably inevitable that no man would leave the CIA with more personal enemies than Lyman Kirkpatrick. It was not so much Kirkpatrick's transparent ambition—he was hardly unique in that—as the nine years he spent as the CIA's Inspector General. Allen Dulles gave him the job in 1953 after he returned to the CIA in a wheelchair, crippled by polio, but at first it was not much of a job. Kirkpatrick's predecessor under "Beedle" Smith had been Stuart Hedden, who had exactly one assistant and was denied access to the Directorate for Plans, the one division which, for obvious reasons, most needed objective oversight. By the time he retired in 1965, Kirkpatrick had concluded that covert operations were as dangerous in their way as nuclear weapons. A handful of men with a bright idea could do more damage than an army, and the DDP was nothing if not filled with men with bright ideas.

After his appointment as IG, Kirkpatrick immediately asked Dulles for an extension of his writ, but until 1956 Frank Wisner successfully resisted him, arguing that the DDP's own review staff was doing very nicely and bringing in the IG would threaten security: the all-purpose argument. Kirkpatrick finally won his point after Eisenhower established the President's Board of Consultants on Foreign Intelligence Activities (PBCFIA). At one of Dulles's first meetings with the Board he was bluntly asked, "Does the Inspector General have authority over the entire Agency?" Instinct told Dulles to say yes, and from that moment Kirkpatrick did.

He began with a study of the DDP's Eastern European Division and gradually, over the years, worked his way entirely around the Agency at least twice, analyzing policy and performance and appending a list of recommendations to each study. Some of his recommendations were adopted, some not; all ruffled the feathers of DDP division and branch chiefs who resented second-guessing. Men like James Critchfield, the Near East Division chief for ten years beginning in 1961, and J. C. King, the Western Hemisphere Division chief, were sometimes called "the Barons" for their feudal prerogatives and independence, and they did not welcome Kirkpatrick's intrusion.[1]

But all this might have been dismissed as the routine abrasions of bureaucracy. The one report for which Kirkpatrick was never forgiven was his study of the Bay of Pigs. The odor of disaster was already pungent by late February of 1961, when Kirkpatrick asked Dulles in writing for permission to assign two IG inspectors to Richard Bissell's operation. He had heard enough in the halls and during his periodic working lunches with Helms to know that Bissell was thinking along the lines of D-Day, and that a lot of DDP people didn't think the plan was going to work. Kirkpatrick's request was returned almost immediately with a laconic note: "No. AWD."

After the invasion's failure in April, however, Kirkpatrick could not be denied, and with Dulles's reluctant permission he assigned his deputy and two other inspectors to work full-time on the study. In November 1961, Kirkpatrick submitted the completed report, a couple of hundred pages in length, directly to John McCone, Dulles's successor, who was already moving into the CIA's new headquarters in Langley even before the office Dulles had designed for himself had received its first coat of paint.

The reaction throughout the DDP was anger—first of all, because Kirkpatrick had not even shown Dulles, Bissell, or Tracy Barnes the courtesy of letting them see the report before it went to McCone. This was interpreted as a particularly naked and egregious attempt to ingratiate himself with the new Director. "Kirkpatrick let his ambition get the better of him on that one," said a retired CIA officer who had been no friend of Bissell. But what angered Bissell's friends even more was the report itself. They damned it as contentious, ungenerous, intemperate, and even cruel— "an outrageous performance," one of them told me years later. The DDP quickly put together a reclama[2] even longer than the original report, conceding the validity of certain criticisms—personnel had been weak in spots, security had not been as airtight as it might have been—but pointing out that the operation had not been Bissell's alone, there was blame to go around, and some of it ought properly to lodge in the White House. This point was muted in the reclama, but it certainly represented the DDP's feelings then, and they have not been moderated since.

The plan for Castro's overthrow, which Bissell outlined in Dulles's office in late March 1960 and carried out over the following year, was principally the work of a Marine colonel named Jack Hawkins, loaned to the CIA at Dulles's request by the commandant of the Marine Corps, General David Shoup, and of a DDP official named Jacob Esterline.[3] It depended heavily on exile efforts outside of Cuba (anti-Castro networks inside Cuba having proved a will-o'-the-wisp) and on a military landing which grew in scale from a paramilitary, over-the-beach operation into a conventional amphibious invasion with a fleet, an air force, and 1,400 men. If Helms had been skeptical about the original plan, he was horrified as it blossomed boldly into a major military undertaking which was clandestine in name only. He made no attempt to intervene directly—Bissell acknowledged that he "would not have welcomed" Helms's participation—but it was no secret in the DDP that Helms was getting out of the way of this one,[4] and his instincts were widely shared. At one point a group of officials at the branch chief and staff level[5] drew up a quasi-formal protest against Bissell and Barnes, with special emphasis on the latter, who had a decidedly mixed reputation within the DDP.

Tracy Barnes was an exemplar of the OSS tradition of World War II derring-do. A graduate of Groton, Yale College, and Harvard Law School, a handsome man and natural athlete, Barnes got a commission in the Air Force early in the war, then switched to the OSS, for which he parachuted into France with a paramilitary Jedburgh team. Later he was assigned to the OSS mission in Berne under Allen Dulles, who was impressed by his abilities, liked him as a friend, and once called him the bravest man he had ever known. But Barnes was also highly impetuous—when, for example, Dulles appointed him chief of station in London in 1957, he simply walked away from his cluttered desk in Germany and flew straight to England. A lot of DDP people, generally the OSO veterans, either disliked Barnes or distrusted his judgment and ability, and regarded his succession of top-level jobs as due to Dulles's weakness for an old friend and dashing figure. When the Bay of Pigs operation got under way in 1960, Barnes was chief of the DDP's psychological and paramilitary staff, and Bissell's chosen deputy for Castro's overthrow.

The criticism of Barnes was heartfelt enough, but was really only an indirect way of expressing doubts about the entire Cuban enterprise. The sticking point in the skeptics' minds—and this went for Helms too, although he was certainly not involved in the criticism of Bissell and Barnes[6]—was the blatant scale of the invasion being planned, the impossibility of hiding its sponsorship indefinitely, and the potential effect on the CIA of its failure, which looked only too likely. Well before the end of 1960, the operation was an open secret in Miami's exile community, had already been denounced by Castro, and was beginning to surface in the press of both Latin America and the United States. In January 1961, *Time* magazine even referred to a CIA political action officer in Miami, Frank Bender (the *nom de guerre* of a DDP officer named Droller), as "Mr. B." If *Time* knew that sort of detail, it was obvious that the Cuban Direccíon Generale de Inteligencia (DGI) knew a great deal more.

But if reservations about an invasion of Cuba were strong within the CIA, they did not often breach its walls. Robert McNamara, the Secretary of Defense, was completely unaware of the CIA skeptics, and Dean Rusk at the State Department, concerned about the international consequences of an intervention so blatant, did not at first realize he had potential allies within the Agency. Roger Hilsman, at that time Director of the State Department's Bureau of Intelligence and Research, says he began to worry about the operation after a conversation with Helms in which Helms gave him the impression of a headlong runaway project. Hilsman gathered that the Directorate of Intelligence, headed by Robert Amory, and the Board of National Estimates, headed by Sherman Kent, had both been completely cut out of Cuban invasion planning and that the scale of the operation was ballooning out of control. That, at any rate, was the gist of Hilsman's report to Rusk, who absorbed it in phlegmatic silence as he did so much else. In retrospect, Hilsman thought Helms was explicitly trying to warn him, even to enlist his aid.[7]

There is no evidence that Helms overtly protested Bissell's plans for the invasion of Cuba in any other forum—which makes all the more puzzling the fact that Bissell sufficiently resented his role to ask Dulles not once but twice for Helms's removal. The episode is veiled in mist, in a manner typical of bureaucratic run-ins. As described in detail by Tracy Barnes to a friend, what happened was this: Bissell went to Dulles early in 1961 and protested Helms's foot-dragging and noncooperation: they couldn't work together; Helms had to leave; perhaps a transfer to London as chief of station would ease the situation. Frank Wisner was too ill to remain in that post (he was shortly to retire), and Dulles might thereby solve two problems at once. Dulles then raised the matter with Helms, who said the tension between himself and Bissell was as much of a mystery to him as it was to Dulles. He had tried to get along with Bissell, was sure they could settle their differences, and proposed an attempt to patch things up before disrupting the DDP in the middle of a major operation. The gist of Helms's argument, as described later by Barnes, was a plea for a second chance. Dulles, who had no appetite for what amounted to firing an old friend and colleague, said okay, and persuaded Bissell to give it a try.

But it didn't work. Bissell felt the situation could not go on, and he returned to Dulles a second time to insist that Helms had to go. Dulles continued to hesitate. He astonished Lyman Kirkpatrick one day by asking what he thought of transferring Helms to London. Kirkpatrick says he was "appalled," and that he told Dulles it was unthinkable: he must not do it. The DDP needed Helms right where he was; someone had to run it and— this by implication—Bissell wasn't the man. But despite the unexpected vigor of Kirkpatrick's protest, Dulles reluctantly acquiesced to Bissell's demand. He went to Helms and gave him what amounted to a stark choice: London or out.

Helms says flatly that neither Dulles nor Bissell ever discussed with him the proposed move to London.[8] Bissell says he doesn't remember any such episode either and thinks it is probably "apocryphal," although he concedes he "would not have welcomed" Helms's advice on the Bay of Pigs and he "guesses" he knew Helms was against it—in fact, he's pretty sure Helms was "finally horrified by the scale of it, the risk of it. . . . Even Frank Wisner would have been rather horrified by it"—and he "probably resented it at the time." Bissell had taken hold of this operation himself; he and Helms were far from being in the habit of talking things over; he depended on Helms to run the spies and recommend personnel appointments. As for the transfer to London, the last thing Bissell wanted was to have "Dick's disapproval, such as it was, surfaced and clearly stated." Bissell has "absolutely no recollection" of discussing with Dulles the matter of transferring Helms. *But . . .* he *does* think that perhaps Tracy Barnes went to Dulles about this time with a proposal for Helms's transfer, and Dulles was certainly aware in any event that Bissell and Helms were not "ideal complements."

At that moment, certainly, Helms was the outsider. Dulles and Barnes had been intimate friends since working together in Berne during the war. Barnes was Bissell's trusted deputy. Bissell had been Dulles's choice for DDP, and was the morning-line favorite to replace Dulles as Director of Central Intelligence, if gout or the weight of years should ever persuade Dulles to step aside. All three men were committed to Castro's overthrow, thought they knew how to do it, and had gone too far to be touched by the unwelcome reservations of Richard Helms or other CIA officials. Helms's disenchantment was well known, but what he actually did to prompt the anger of Bissell or Barnes, or Dulles's reluctant agreement to send him to London, is harder to establish.

Helms's style was cool by choice and temperament; his instinct was to soften differences, to find a middle ground, to tone down operations that were getting out of hand, to give faltering projects one more chance rather than shut them down altogether, to settle for compromise in the interests of bureaucratic peace. He is described by friends as "a good soldier," by which they mean he might protest a policy while it was still under discussion, but once a decision had been made he would support it loyally. In the case of the Bay of Pigs, he had been deliberately excluded; it was not his job to point out flaws in a plan to which he was not even privy; and his reservations about covert action operations were presumably well known anyway.

But at the same time he could not stand entirely aside. One report says that Helms insisted on giving James Angleton's roughly one-hundred-man counterintelligence staff a role in the operation. According to one source, a single counterintelligence expert had been assigned to the Bay of Pigs project in September 1960, and the job was simply beyond him. Bissell and Barnes were not exactly indifferent to the importance of security, but the operation was moving at such a pace that its penetration by spies for Castro presented a distinct danger. Indeed, Castro's public remarks made it clear that he was already aware of at least the broad outlines of the invasion plan, and he may have known a great deal more than that. Helms was apparently prompted by two security lapses of the most egregious variety. In Mexico, where Howard Hunt was the CIA's liaison officer with the Frente Revolucionario Democratico (FRD), established by the exiles under CIA direction, a courier recruited by Hunt somehow lost a briefcase filled with incriminating documents, including a list of CIA agents and contacts inside Cuba.[9] Later, in Miami, Frank Bender committed a blunder of equal magnitude when a meeting with a Cuban politician in a motel room was overheard by a secretary next door who happened to have a brother with the FBI. She took notes and passed them on to her brother, whence they eventually got back to the CIA, much to Bender's chagrin and Hunt's delight. But it was the possibility of outright penetration that most bothered Helms and Angleton, who both remembered the early CIA disasters with WIN, NTS, and Ukrainian and Albanian émigré organizations. CIA had been badly burned at that time, but Bissell had not joined the Agency until later, had little operational experience, and did not quite appreciate what a hostile intelligence service could do to a porous operation.

The doubts of Helms and Angleton were well founded. In the days immediately preceding the invasion, Castro's police rounded up suspects throughout Cuba, perhaps as many as 100,000 altogether, who were crowded into makeshift camps. According to several sources, virtually every CIA asset on the island was caught up in the general sweep. But there was other evidence as well that Castro had learned a great deal more about CIA operations than ought to have been possible in a well-run project.

On Friday, April 21, 1961, for example, two days after the surrender of the exile invasion force, two men in workclothes—they might have been taken for window washers, say, if not for their neat Ivy League haircuts— approached a teller in the DuPont Circle branch of the Riggs National Bank in Washington with an unusual request. They asked the teller for six to eight bank checks totaling well over $100,000 to be made out in the name of Arthur Avignon. The teller was not as surprised as he might have been. Men from the CIA often arrived quietly to inspect the financial records of certain local embassies, and the teller was also familiar with several oddly active accounts in the name of groups like the National Association of Loggers, the Dry Cleaners' Association, and so on. When he had asked about these strange accounts after first going to work at the branch he had been told frankly, "Oh, those are dummy accounts."

So the teller made out the checks as requested, but was surprised, a week later, to read an Associated Press dispatch from Havana in the Washington *Evening Star* reporting a public statement by Castro in which he denounced continued CIA plotting against Cuba and specifically cited funds provided by one Arthur Avignon. The teller wondered how Castro had learned so quickly of the transaction, and of Avignon's identity.

It was to prevent just such compromises that Helms, several months earlier, had insisted that the DDP's counterintelligence staff have a role in the Bay of Pigs planning. On top of the dangers inherent in any secret operation was the additional problem of the Cubans themselves. CIA officers who worked with them say flatly that Cubans simply cannot operate in secret. But Bissell and Barnes, willing to concede the importance of security precautions in a theoretical way, were impatient with the deliberate caution of counterintelligence officers. They were trying to mount an invasion. They needed men to serve as soldiers, as well as the broad political support of the Cuban exile community, and they needed both quickly. From intelligence reports they knew that Castro was already receiving arms from the Soviet bloc, and that Cuban pilots were being trained in Czechoslovakia to fly MiG aircraft. Once Castro had a modern air force, the possibility of an exile invasion would be ended once and for all. So Bissell and Barnes resented the delays imposed by Angleton's investigators, and they blamed Helms for the fact that they had to put up with them.

In other ways, too, Helms's presence was an irritant to the Bay of Pigs planners. They felt he was protecting his own assets, advising certain favored officers not to get involved in the operation down the hall, was not moving with sufficient dispatch in providing technical support for the operation. But even more important was Helms's instinctive caution, which contrasted so sharply with the impetuosity of Tracy Barnes. The success of the Bissell-Hawkins-Esterline plan depended heavily on the exile air force, which eventually included sixteen World War II vintage B-26 bombers. Without the bombers the exiles would be unable to destroy Castro's small force of jet trainers, primitive planes compared to the MiGs he had been promised by Moscow, but lethal enough to destroy an invasion force which did not control the air.

Bissell and Barnes wanted those B-26s, and they wanted them right away. Helms, Lawrence Houston, and the DDP's support staff preferred to proceed cautiously with acquisition of the planes. Eisenhower and later Kennedy insisted that the invasion was to appear to the world as an entirely Cuban operation. This meant that the B-26s must not be traceable to the United States. But Barnes plunged into the matter in his usual headlong way, calling up friends in the air industry, giving short shrift to the problem of hiding the purchase. Words were exchanged on this matter, just as they were later concerning acquisition of the invasion fleet. Bissell and Barnes, who had originally planned to launch their invasion before Eisenhower left office, were angered and frustrated by every delay. Since Helms was not on the team, they decided to get rid of him entirely, and they finally won Dulles's consent. But events intervened, and it was Bissell, not Helms, whose career at the CIA came to an abrupt halt.

When Lyman Kirkpatrick's inspectors went to work shortly after the surrender of the invasion force on Wednesday afternoon, April 19, the CIA was in a state of demoralized disarray. It was not simply that President Kennedy was furious, the press aghast, the public stirred and confused, Congress hungry for scapegoats, the Soviet bloc triumphant. The true source of CIA despair was the magnitude of the failure itself, which was total and unmitigated. The Indonesian fiasco was an opéra bouffe next to the tragic scale of the Cuban disaster. The battle had been so unequal, the operation had gone so unequivocally wrong, that it was hard to credit the men who planned it with simple reason.

Robert Kennedy, the President's brother, arrived at the CIA within a day or two of the surrender to find out what had gone wrong, and later the President appointed him, along with Allen Dulles and Admiral Arleigh Burke, to a special commission of inquiry headed by General Maxwell Taylor. But that group was motivated less by curiosity than by renewed determination; its purpose was to find a means for Castro's removal, not to explain the failure of the initial attempt. The only serious official investigation of the Bay of Pigs itself was Lyman Kirkpatrick's.

The explanation given in the IG report which Kirkpatrick submitted to McCone in November 1961 was disarmingly simple, but to grasp a sense of its impact it is necessary to understand what the Bay of Pigs planners themselves thought went wrong. Their view, even now, is surprisingly narrow and particular. "This war *might* have been lost on the ground," Bissell said. "It *was* lost in the air."

The original plan had been for an operation truly clandestine. The first twenty-five exiles would be trained by the CIA at the U.S. Army Jungle Warfare School in the Panama Canal Zone. They in turn would train another seventy-five exiles, and all of them would be quietly infiltrated into Cuba to build a resistance with the help of dissident networks already there. But almost as soon as the initial twenty-five went to Panama in September 1960,[10] it became clear that the resistance within Cuba had been much exaggerated, and the efficiency of the Cuban security forces underestimated. Infiltrated agents were often picked up within a day or two. Communications were so bad that air-dropped supplies frequently arrived too early or late or were intercepted outright by Castro's forces. There were resistance groups in the Escambray mountains, but Castro, who had learned from his own success and Batista's mistakes, made no effort to send his troops in after them. Instead, he simply sealed off the resistance zone and proceeded to starve out the rebels. A number of Cuban exile leaders, in particular Manuel Ray (who went over the CIA's head directly to members of the Kennedy administration after January 1961), claimed the support of large networks which the CIA discovered to be inflated, unreliable, and sometimes downright imaginary. By the end of November 1960, the idea of a traditional guerrilla campaign had been abandoned for the simple reason that the exiles were too divided and disorganized, conditions in Cuba too inhospitable, and the Americans too impatient. The alternative chosen by Bissell was an invasion.

As drawn up by Jacob Esterline and Colonel Hawkins, a veteran of guerrilla warfare on Mindanao in World War II, the new plan called for a combined military and psychological effort. The invasion force—projected at three hundred in November, but it grew steadily—was to secure a beachhead while the exiles' B-26s, in control of the air following the destruction of Castro's jet trainers, were to destroy Cuba's communication and transportation network. This would have been more feasible than it might sound at first, because Cuba's telephone system was dependent on microwave relay stations highly vulnerable to air attack, as were railroad connections and broadcast facilities. The idea, drawing much of its inspiration from the successful Guatemalan operation which had literally panicked Arbenz into surrender, was to present Castro with a military threat of unknown proportions, overwhelm him with rumor and wild reports of multiple landings, encourage dissident Cubans to take up arms throughout the island, frighten Castro's borderline supporters into quiescence, and thereby generate a political crisis within Castro's government which he would not be able to contain. In effect, a real invasion was intended to defeat him psychologically by arousing fears of a far greater assault, the sort the United States could mount if it elected to do so. The problem with the plan was that its emphasis shifted from the psychological to the military as it became apparent that CIA had very few assets inside Cuba, and that Castro's government was more resolute than Arbenz's. The plan's first requirement was a successful landing, a "lodgment" on Cuban soil, and that, in Bissell's view then and now, depended on control of the air.

At this point the Kennedy administration intervened. Dulles and Bissell first briefed Kennedy on the operation in Palm Beach on November 17, 1960, and the President-elect, persuaded as much perhaps by the operation's momentum as by Bissell's considerable eloquence,[11] said he would go along with it. Dulles and Bissell told the rest of the operation officers they had a "qualified go-ahead"[12] and recruiting, suspended by Eisenhower, shortly resumed.

During the following months Kennedy repeatedly expressed reservations about the undertaking, asking the Joint Chiefs of Staff to study the feasibility of the invasion plan,[13] requesting the CIA to broaden the exile group nominally responsible for the invasion to include left-of-center leaders,[14] and insisting that the invasion site be switched from Trinidad, which was heavily populated, to the Bay of Pigs, which was not. That last change was almost enough to break the camel's back; Hawkins and Esterline both threatened to resign in protest, but were persuaded to stay.

Kennedy was principally concerned with the political consequences of the invasion: reluctant to abandon it entirely, and thus invite Republican charges he was soft on Communism, Kennedy hoped to scale down the invasion sufficiently that it might pass relatively unnoticed. He was more alarmed, in short, by the possibility of noisy success than he was by the prospect of a quiet failure, failing to see that failure itself is the noisiest thing of all.[15] But the invasion continued to balloon anyway. Bissell kept telling Colonel Hawkins that the landing force was far too small, it needed to be expanded, and as late as February 1961, another four hundred men were recruited and sent to Guatemala for training. At all but the last moment, more alarmed than ever, Kennedy told Dulles and Bissell he would approve only two air strikes, not three, and that only eight planes were to be used in each strike, not fifteen.

But even then the CIA hoped the invasion might be a success. The first strike, on Saturday, April 15, 1961, destroyed at least half of Castro's air force on the ground, a mixed bag of B-26s, Sea Furies, and T-33 jet trainers. After the strike, incredibly, Castro gathered his remaining planes, including four surviving jet trainers, on an airfield near Havana where they were lined up in a neat row, sitting ducks for a B-26's straight-line bombing pattern. At noon on Sunday, despite an uproar of protest in the United Nations over the first strike, Kennedy gave his final approval for the operation. The invasion fleet could proceed to the Bay of Pigs landing site.

A minor mystery surrounds what happened next. Some accounts say that Adlai Stevenson at the UN, angry as it dawned on him that his denials of U.S. complicity in the first air raid were in fact completely false, persuaded Rusk to urge Kennedy to cancel the second strike. A second version says that the initiative was Rusk's. Howard Hunt tells a third story.[16] On Sunday, April 16, General Cabell, the acting DCI in Dulles's absence on a speaking engagement in Puerto Rico,[17] stopped off at the CIA on his way home from a morning's golf at the Chevy Chase Club. There he found the invasion's operational planners busy with preparations for the second air strike to be conducted the following morning, April 17, as the Cuban exiles were landing at the Bay of Pigs. According to Hunt, Cabell asked who had approved the second strike, rejected the answer that Kennedy had authorized it earlier, and called Rusk to see if the President really wanted another strike following the clamor aroused by the first.

But whatever the exact origin of Kennedy's decision to cancel the second air strike, there is no dispute that he did so, that Bissell and Cabell went to protest its cancellation to Rusk at the State Department on Sunday night, that Kennedy repeated his decision on the phone with Rusk while Bissell and Cabell were sitting in the same office, that neither man chose to argue personally with the President when Rusk offered them the chance to do so, and that the CIA elected to go ahead with the landing all the same even though the operation's planners unanimously felt its success depended on unequivocal control of the air.

On Monday morning, as the landing was under way, one of Castro's jet trainers sank two ships in the invasion fleet, including the one carrying the exiles' entire reserve supply of ammunition. Later that day, realizing the magnitude of his earlier refusal, Kennedy authorized a second strike on Tuesday morning to relieve the beleaguered exiles on the beach, but the gesture was classically too little and too late. Castro's jet trainers, armed with 20-mm. cannon of which the CIA had not known, shot down three of the exiles' B-26s. That night Bissell personally urged Kennedy to authorize air cover for the exiles from a U.S. carrier off the coast of Cuba, but the most Kennedy would concede was one hour of air cover by U.S. planes over the beach. An error of timing brought the Navy's planes an hour early. When the exiles' B-26s arrived they were defenseless against the jet trainers, and two more were shot down, sealing the fate of the invasion. That afternoon the exiles on the beach, hard-pressed by Castro's air force and army, finally surrendered.

In the days immediately following the surrender, Kennedy accepted responsibility for the invasion and its failure, warned members of his administration not to start shifting the blame, of which he said there was plenty to go around, and appointed a commission to study what had happened. But at the same time he was furious with the CIA, threatening to break it into a million pieces, and as early as Tuesday, April 18, he told both Arthur Schlesinger and James Reston at a private lunch that the Agency was in for some changes. "Dulles is a legendary figure and it's hard to operate with legendary figures," he said. "We will have to do something. . . . I must have someone there with whom I can be in complete and intimate contact—someone from whom I know I will be getting the exact pitch. I made a mistake in putting Bobby in the Justice Department. He is wasted there. Byron White could do that job perfectly well. Bobby should be in CIA. . . . It is a hell of a way to learn things but I have learned one thing from this business—that is, that we will have to deal with CIA. McNamara has dealt with defense. Rusk has done a lot with State; but no one has dealt with CIA."[18]

Publicly Kennedy was taking the rap, but privately he blamed CIA for the disaster. The first casualty, logically enough, was Allen Dulles. According to many accounts, Kennedy told Dulles, "Under a parliamentary system of government it is I who would be leaving office. But under our system it is you who must go."[19]

Dulles was resigned to going, but not to taking the blame. That summer, as the rest of the CIA gradually moved into its new headquarters in Langley, Virginia, Dulles remained in his old office, so low in spirits he appeared almost physically diminished. A frequent visitor was Charles Murphy, a reporter for *Fortune* magazine, who published an article on the Bay of Pigs in the September 1961 issue, "Cuba: The Record Set Straight," which revealed in detail for the first time the Kennedy administration's fatal hesitations the previous spring. The single greatest cause of failure, Murphy said, was Kennedy's cancellation of the second air strike.[20]

Dulles's version of the Bay of Pigs has tended to stick. Even in the memoirs of Kennedy aides like Theodore Sorensen and Arthur Schlesinger, Jr., the question of the canceled air strikes is treated with the sort of pugnacious and obsessive attention reserved for vulnerable points. In almost every account of the Bay of Pigs, in fact, the air strikes loom large, with one exception: the Inspector General's report submitted to John McCone by Lyman Kirkpatrick in November 1961. Kirkpatrick does not fail to mention the role played by Castro's air force, nor the problems of security, press leaks, political infighting among the exiles, and State Department hand-wringing about the "noisiness" of an operation which by its very nature could hardly be kept quiet; and he was especially critical of Richard Bissell's refusal to ask CIA analysts what they thought of the plan.

A great deal has been made of the alleged CIA hopes for a popular uprising, as if a major cause of the failure had been an optimistic misreading of Castro's popularity. In *The Craft of Intelligence* Dulles says, "I know of no estimate that a spontaneous uprising of the unarmed population of Cuba would be touched off by the landing."[21] There could hardly have been such an estimate without a formal request of the estimators, and no such request was ever made, with one exception. That occurred shortly before the landing, when Tracy Barnes met with a number of the Bureau of National Estimate's staff members who knew about Cuba. Without mentioning the projected landing, Barnes asked the BNE people whether the Cuban armed forces were loyal to Castro. The answer which emerged in an informal discussion that lasted about an hour was that the Cuban army probably was loyal to Castro; or at any rate that the BNE had no evidence that it was disloyal.[22] What Barnes thought of this opinion is not known; what he did with it was nothing. Kirkpatrick thought the failure to ask the estimators to play a role was a mistake, and the estimators certainly concur, but he also argued that this and other obvious failings—the absence of air cover, the porous security, and so on—all paled beside the central weakness of a murkily conceived plan.

How, exactly, was the invasion supposed to "work"? Long before the invasion took place, it was clear the CIA had no assets of importance inside Cuba, that Castro was no panicky pushover like Arbenz, and that the landing force of 1,400 men was no match for the 200,000 men in Castro's regular army and militia. Until the last, Hawkins hoped that once the exiles had secured the beachhead, and Castro had been stewing in the juices of rumor, fear, and impotence for a few days, it would become possible for the exiles to break out and march on Havana. Bissell says he never shared this hope. The very isolation of the landing site, connected to the mainland through a swamp by only three causeways, would serve as equally to keep the exiles in as it would to keep Castro out.

Bissell's plan was more tentative and problematic. He hoped that the exile government could be flown to a secure beachhead, that the United States would recognize the rebels, and that "international diplomatic intervention" might provide for a cease-fire to be followed by free elections. Why Castro would accept such a proposal, from which he would have nothing to gain, it is hard to say.

There is something missing from Bissell's plan. It seems to have been his feeling—and perhaps even the heart of his plan—that the operation's momentum would force Kennedy to abandon his official neutrality and to intervene with U.S. forces, despite the fact Kennedy had sworn he would not. The pressures in such a situation would certainly have been very great. It is possible that Bissell and Dulles figured Kennedy's hand would be forced by the transparency of U.S. involvement, and the difficulty of abandoning the exiles once they had secured what the CIA always referred to as a "lodgment." Bissell says that he and Dulles had no such plan, but it is hard to see what else could have altered the balance so heavily weighted against the trapped and isolated exiles. Even with complete control of the air the exiles' B-26s could not have conquered the island alone, and the exiles were too few. The best a lodgment might have offered the Cuban people was civil war, a bitter gift.

The truth of the matter seems to be that the landing had been reduced to a desperate gamble by the time it took place. The exiles would secure their lodgment, fly in their government, raise their flag, and then wait for the world to salute. Bissell and Dulles might talk of the canceled air strikes until the cows came home, but the failure which emerged with cool logic in Kirkpatrick's report was the CIA's own. The plan was either dishonest and cynical, depending on forcing Kennedy's hand, or plain dumb. Even Dulles and Bissell seemed to know this before the landing took place. At the end, their principal argument with Kennedy for going ahead was the so-called disposal problem. If the invasion were called off, they said, what was to be done with the exile army? They were 1,400 in number, after all, had already put down an army rebellion in Guatemala with the back of their hand, and might refuse to disarm. What then? At the very least, they would trumpet the Americans' perfidy far and wide. They *wanted* to go. Bissell and Dulles led both Kennedy and the exiles down the garden path because, once they had begun, they didn't know what else to do.

Dulles deeply resented Kirkpatrick's report. The reason he gave to friends, and which has been repeated by CIA people since, was Kirkpatrick's ungenerous delivery of the report directly to McCone, but the real reason was the harshness of the report itself.[23] It no longer had the power to harm Dulles—he was already out—but it gave Bissell the final shove.

Of course, Bissell had been expecting this for some time. A month or two after the invasion Bissell urged David Phillips to turn down a job offer and join the CIA office in Mexico City instead. "Don't go to New York," he said. "Some of us will have to leave. The others must stay."[24] But as late as November 1961, Bissell's position was still unclear. McGeorge Bundy told him Kennedy wanted his resignation, and in mid-December McCone told him the same thing. But then McCone's wife died, and he was so shaken for a time that he was not sure if he could stay on with CIA at all. He asked Bissell to remain as DDP for the time being and later, after the turn of the year, McCone asked him if he'd like to stay on permanently as the first

Deputy Director for Science and Technology. McCone said he had asked the President about this, and Kennedy had said okay. Bissell says he thought it over for a few days but decided it wasn't a good idea, and resigned. The man McCone picked to replace him—the all-but-unanimous choice of everyone he asked for advice—was Richard Helms.

Shortly before Bissell formally left the CIA in February 1962, McCone held a farewell dinner for him at the Alibi Club in Washington. There were perhaps a dozen people present, including Sherman Kent, John Bross, Robert Amory, "Red" White, and Helms. There were toasts after the meal, the sort of thing usual on such occasions, expressions of friendship and regard, but all the same Bissell was at first surprised and then touched—even moved would not be too strong a word—at the grace and warmth of Dick Helms's short speech. It was as if the tension between them had never been.

Chapter 8

During the summer and fall of 1975, Richard Helms was often impatient with the staff and members of the Senate Select Committee to Study Government Operations with Respect to Intelligence Activities. When they kept coming back to the question of who authorized the CIA's unsuccessful attempts to arrange the assassination of Fidel Castro, Helms's normally cool demeanor was often frayed to the snapping point. He suspected the Committee, and its chairman Senator Frank Church in particular, of naked hypocrisy. They understood these things, he felt; they knew why the written record was so thin; they understood that the CIA did not really give a damn who ran Cuba or Indonesia or the Congo. Perhaps there was an occasional problem with CIA officers in the field in this regard; they would get involved in the local situation and forget whom they were working for. But in Washington the upper-level CIA officials worked for the President alone, they never forgot it, and one could infer pretty accurately what the President wanted by paying attention to what the CIA did.

Helms felt that the Senators on Church's committee were pretending for purely political reasons not to know this. Their questions seemed to him aimed purely at the public record. The Committee members kept asking how the CIA could undertake such monstrous acts without explicit authority. Where are the orders? they wanted to know. Where is the piece of paper which says, Do it? More than once Helms found himself with an almost irresistible urge to fire back: Senator, how can you be so goddamned dumb? You don't put an order like that in *writing*.

The Church Committee's investigation of the CIA in 1975 was an ordeal for Helms and other CIA officers. A similar committee in the House headed by Representative Otis Pike was too divided to be effective, but the Church Committee was well organized, abundantly funded, and relentless, and its appetite for CIA records violated the Agency's deepest instincts. The first principle of a secret intelligence service is secrecy. It was bad enough this ancient history was being raked up at all, but to have it raked up in public, with all the attendant hypocrisy of a political investigation conducted by political men. . . . This, truly, in Richard Helms's view, threatened to destroy the Agency he and a lot of men had spent their lives trying to build. More than Watergate, more even than a two-year cat-and-mouse game with the Justice Department over his possible prosecution for perjury, the Church Committee's investigation of CIA assassination plots left Helms with an enduring bitterness. He was convinced that all the Senators on their moral high horses understood these things. They knew who gave the orders. How could they not know, when Bissell and Helms told them in unmistakable terms—not explicitly perhaps, but unmistakably? And yet Frank Church affected not to know, and mused aloud in public that the CIA might have been off on its own like an elephant on the rampage, and only later—much later—absolved the Agency in what amounted to the merest whisper.

But that was not the first time Helms had been asked about assassinations. He'd been asked by John McCone in the summer of 1963, when Helms told him more than McCone wanted to admit later on. He'd been asked by Dean Rusk in 1966, but Rusk, despite the fact he was Secretary of State, had no right to a candid answer, in Helms's view, and Helms did not give him one. And he'd been asked by Lyndon Johnson in March 1967. Not asked idly or in passing—Dick, what about these rumors of the CIA going after Castro with the Mafia; is there anything in this? But asked directly, formally, and explicitly, in a tone and manner which did not admit of evasion, and by the one man with a right to an honest answer.[1]

The genesis of Johnson's request was typically circuitous. In January 1967, Drew Pearson, the Washington columnist, met with Earl Warren, the Chief Justice of the U.S. Supreme Court, and told him he had evidence that Castro had planned to murder John F. Kennedy. Pearson's informant was a Washington lawyer named Edmund Morgan, who had been told of the alleged plot by one of his clients, a middle-level Mafia figure named John Rosselli.[2]

A few days later Warren called the head of the Secret Service, James J. Rowley, and asked him to look into the matter. When Morgan declined to meet with Rowley—he wanted to see Warren personally—Rowley informed the FBI on February 13. Two days later the head of the FBI, J. Edgar Hoover, blandly told Rowley the FBI would be willing to accept any information the lawyer cared to volunteer. Hoover, for reasons which are unclear, apparently preferred to let the matter drop, but events prevented him from doing so. On March 3, 1967, Drew Pearson published a column which began, "President Johnson is sitting on a political H-bomb—an unconfirmed report that Sen. Robert Kennedy may have approved an assassination plot which then possibly backfired against his late brother."

Kennedy and Johnson both took an interest in this report willy-nilly, and on March 20 two FBI agents from the Washington field office interviewed Morgan at the President's request. Morgan refused to identify Rosselli as the source of the story, but told the FBI agents there were really two halves to his client's account: Castro's alleged involvement in Kennedy's murder, and his client's admitted involvement in a CIA plot to murder Castro. A summary of the agents' report was sent to President Johnson on March 22 and attached to it were three additional paragraphs outlining what the FBI already knew of CIA-Mafia attempts to arrange Castro's murder—which was plenty.

An enormous quantity of paper passes before a President's eyes every day, but this particular document arrested Johnson's attention. It is impossible to determine the exact nature of his interest now—plain curiosity, or a question picking at his mind with more particular point—but it is known that Johnson never quite accepted the conclusion of the Warren Commission that Lee Harvey Oswald killed Kennedy entirely on his own. Not long after Johnson became President, Richard Helms was one of a small group that heard him claim that Kennedy's murder was an act of retribution—not by Castro, however, a suspicion Johnson was to express later, but by unnamed persons seeking vengeance for the murder on November 1, 1963, of the President of South Vietnam, Ngo Dinh Diem.

Kennedy bore a heavy moral responsibility for Diem's death, since the generals' coup which deposed him probably never would have occurred without American encouragement and assurances. Johnson, after a trip to Vietnam in 1961, had called Diem "the Churchill of Asia," a typical exercise of Johnsonian hyperbole with a solidly practical assumption at its core that if Diem was hardly Churchill's equal in ability, he was nevertheless equally indispensable. Johnson had told Kennedy in 1961, and whenever he was given half a chance later, that Diem was all we had out there, a sentiment shared by John McCone after he took over the CIA. But Kennedy had been convinced by a small group in the State Department that Diem had to go. When Kennedy was murdered only three weeks after Diem, Johnson was convinced the two assassinations were related—"they" got Kennedy in retribution for Diem.[3]

On March 22, 1967, the day Johnson received the FBI document outlining the CIA-Mafia plots to kill Castro, the President was scheduled to meet with Richard Helms and Nicholas DeB. Katzenbach to discuss a report on the CIA's funding of the National Student Association and other private, quasi-private, and front groups.[4] Helms and Katzenbach arrived at the White House in the early evening, and at some point during their meeting, Johnson asked Helms for a detailed report about the CIA's attempts to kill Castro. But he didn't stop there; he also wanted to know the details of CIA's involvement, if any, in the murders of Diem and Trujillo. This was not a vague is-there-anything-in-this? sort of question. Johnson already knew from the FBI's report that there was plenty in it where Castro was concerned, and at the very least he suspected the CIA may have had a role in Diem's death as well.

When Helms left the White House that night, he carried a charge with him which could not be evaded. The following day he called the CIA's Inspector General, Jack Earman, into his office, and told him to make an investigation. This cannot have been a pleasant moment for Helms. He often said he only worked for one President at a time, but now he had been asked by one President to undertake what amounted to an investigation of his predecessor. Helms knew what an IG report looked like—dry, crisp, and relentlessly detailed—and of course he knew his own name would be in the report, by no means the smallest of the details, since Helms, too, had done his bit to kill Castro.

Richard Helms's lack of enthusiasm for covert operations might be dismissed as self-protective coloring, the last cynical refuge of the clandestine operator, but there is no evidence for thinking so, and a good deal to the contrary. Helms's characteristic attitude toward covert operations can be found in an incident which took place in the fall of 1964, when the CIA discovered to its alarm that four intelligence officers were prisoners of bush rebels in the Congo.

In August 1964 the Simba rebel army—if army is the right word for what amounted to a disorganized mob armed with a mixed bag of weapons —captured the river town of Stanleyville, a thousand miles from the coast and readily accessible only by air. When a mercenary army under Major Mike ("Mad Mike") Hoare, along with a group of CIA Cubans, began to advance on rebel territory in early autumn the Simbas panicked, rounded up all the whites in the territory under their control, and imprisoned them in Stanleyville—perhaps a thousand people in all, including Belgian nuns, missionaries, Western businessmen and diplomatic officials, and five Americans. One was the U.S. consul in Stanleyville, a Foreign Service officer named Michael Hoyt; the other four were a CIA team.

Their danger was extreme. The titular leader of the Simbas, Pierre Mulele, was a quasi-Catholic who baptized his followers in his own urine to make them immune to enemy bullets. Their battle cry was "Mai Mulele"— the Water of Mulele. The name they chose for themselves—Simba, meaning "lion" in Swahili—was apt; their ferocity was notorious. A group of young Simba auxiliaries called the Jeunesse, many of them only twelve or thirteen years old, were particularly infamous for their tortures. As Major Hoare's column slowly advanced along jungle roads, a Simba leader in Stanleyville announced, "We will make our fetishes out of the hearts of Belgians and Americans and clothe ourselves in the skins of Belgians and Americans."[5] Since the Simbas were already reported to have butchered some Italian prisoners and sold them for meat in the Stanleyville markets, the threat was taken seriously. The CIA was alarmed for its men, and in late October or early November 1964, John McCone called a meeting in his office in Langley to consider ways of rescuing the American prisoners in Stanleyville.

In addition to McCone, those at the meeting were Helms, the DDP; Ray Cline, the Deputy Director for Intelligence; a young DDI analyst on the Congo named Sam Adams, and a DDP officer from the African Division. Adams was to have his troubles with Helms later, at one point making a determined effort to get him fired,[6] but at that meeting he was struck by the coolness of Helms's judgment. Ray Cline knew something about the Simbas and the precariousness of the imprisoned Americans; he wanted the CIA to go in after them like gangbusters, if that's what it would take, and at first McCone was inclined to agree with him. The CIA had plenty of assets in the Congo—DDP officers, Cuban pilots, various contract mercenaries and agents left over from the Congo crisis of 1961—and Cline thought something ought to be done. In succession he suggested sending in a team through the jungle, bombing the city, a helicopter raid, a parachute drop.

Helms was against anything of the sort. He listened for a long time, then ticked off the arguments against a rescue attempt. The CIA could mount an operation all right, but then what? The Americans were in Stanleyville, but where? As soon as CIA people started to shoot the place up, the Simbas might kill the Americans. Even if a raid were successful, what about the rest of the thousand prisoners held by the Simbas? All hell might break loose. How would the rest of the world react to a narrow, high-risk operation for the exclusive benefit of five Americans? The United States had no right to risk the lives of so many others just to get its own back.

"What are the chances of success?" McCone asked.

"No better than fifty-fifty," said Helms, "because we don't really know where the prisoners are."

Then McCone asked, "What should we do?"

"Wait," said Helms.

In the end, McCone was argued around to Helms's point of view. On November 24, 1964, the prisoners were rescued in a combined operation by Belgian paratroopers and Hoare's mercenaries.

But Helms was a realist too. The business of secret intelligence had its ugly side, and for some men that was its principal attraction. Helms was not one of them, but he accepted it. Back around 1955, Allen Dulles had begun receiving reports of brutal treatment during interrogations of suspect defectors in Munich: the application of turpentine to a man's testicles, or sealing someone in a room and playing Indonesian music at deafening levels until he cracked—that sort of thing. Dulles asked Helms to investigate the situation and to write a regulation prohibiting torture.

The rule which eventually emerged was explicit: "You may not use electrical, chemical, or physical duress." (Psychological duress was okay.) What else could it say? No man with a bureaucrat's respect for the longevity of paper would write a rule saying you *can* use such means. But rules are one thing, reality another. Before concluding his investigation, Helms called a meeting of the DDP's division chiefs to ask if they had any objection to the rule. They did; they thought it ought to be left up to the judgment of the division chiefs and their chiefs of station. One of those at the meeting asked Helms: "Just what are the prerogatives of a chief of station?"

Helms's answer was a model of ambiguity: "To do the best job he can unless and until recalled for cause."

Helms's attitude toward political violence was one of lucid caution. He did not so much argue that violence was wrong—he was, after all, something in the nature of a soldier—as that it was often crude, disruptive, and ineffective. His arguments against assassination were of the same sort, and throughout his career he had plenty of chances to express them. In an early instance in the late 1940s, when Helms was in charge of FDM, the Eastern European Division of the CIA's Office of Special Operations, an agent in Europe went sour and it was suggested that the best way to handle the messy problem he posed was to kill him. The Assistant Director of Special Operations at the time, Colonel Donald Galloway,[7] argued the matter with Helms.

Helms, according to his own account, was opposed. He did not protest that killing the agent would be wrong, getting into what he has sometimes described as "the soggy mass of morality," but rather that murder will out. Somebody would have to do it, and no one could predict with confidence how that somebody would feel about it later. He might go crazy, he might go through a conversion and succumb to feelings of guilt, he might begin to blubber in his cups or send a letter to a Congressman or brood over fancied ill treatment and decide to blackmail the Agency. Things happen to people. What then? You could give some fellow a sterile gun and send him out to pull the trigger, but the Agency would have to live with the danger of exposure for the rest of time, and it wasn't worth it. Hitler, okay. But this was an agent, an irritant at worst; *it didn't make sense.*

An argument based on morality might have had Galloway looking at the ceiling and drumming his fingers on the desk, wondering, What have we got here? An argument based on caution was something else; Regular Army colonels do not rise without developing a sense of caution, and Galloway decided against killing the agent.

The CIA is not an intelligence service notorious for its quickness on the trigger. Some others are, and inevitably the word gets around. The Israelis, for example, who have responded to Palestinian terrorism by going after the people they held responsible,[8] or the Russian KGB, which murdered a number of Ukrainian and White Russian émigrés in Germany during the 1950s,[9] and a host of lesser agencies at various times, in various places, for various reasons. If the CIA had been indiscriminate in its use of murder we would know about it. Even the unsuccessful plots against Castro, involving members of the notoriously tight-lipped Mafia, were reported at least twice in the press (August 1963; March 1967) long before the Church Committee's investigation. The public record links the CIA to the specific murder of only a single man, a South Vietnamese named Thai Khac Chuyen, thought to be a double agent working for the North Vietnamese. But even in that case the CIA's role was both tangential and unproved.[10]

The literature of spies is filled with deliberate killing, and the American public probably believes that the CIA has done its share, but there is very little evidence to support such a view, and Agency people, almost without exception, flatly deny it. One of the exceptions, a CIA officer who joined the Agency in the mid-1950s, said an instructor at the CIA's training center at Camp Peary, Virginia, told one of his classes, "On occasion it's been necessary to physically eliminate someone who was a threat to the Agency." This particular officer said he took the instructor at his word then, and still believes him now, but concedes he never heard of such a killing during years of service in Hong Kong and Southeast Asia.

Lyman Kirkpatrick says he never learned of a single instance of Agency murder in his ten years as Inspector General, and claims that if he had, "I would have made a great deal of noise about it." He was referring to murder of any sort, at any level. CIA officers and contract agents carried guns in warlike situations, and used them—in Laos, say, or the Congo, or Cuba. But there were no officially authorized murders of the classic type, with silenced pistols in hotel rooms, no bombs wired up to cars, no poisoned cocktails. In the mid-1950s Kirkpatrick insisted that the Agency fire a CIA officer who had tortured suspect defectors in Munich in the mid-1950s and that the Attorney General investigate the apparent murder of an American pilot working for the CIA in Thailand in the early 1950s.[11] The Agency was cleared in that instance, and Kirkpatrick says he never even heard of another case remotely like it. Other CIA officers from every level of the Agency agree.

The Agency had its share of problems over the years: people who turned out to be working for the other side, or took off on their own, or tried to blackmail their case officers, or suffered an attack of conscience and decided to go public. But the CIA's solution to such problems, according to Kirkpatrick and other Agency people, was rarely anything worse than "termination" or "burning." Both terms have a sinister tone, but "termination" simply means dismissal, and "burning" means putting out the word to all American and perhaps allied services that X is suspect and not to be trusted. At one point in the 1950s there was talk of establishing a kind of CIA holding area—one proposal suggested an island in the Caribbean—to deal with "disposal" problems, but officials decided that the last thing the Agency wanted was a lot of angry former agents swapping stories, and nothing came of the idea. In some instances, according to CIA people, problem agents were betrayed to hostile intelligence services, or turned over to local police. Their fate could be pretty bleak, but it was not quite the same thing as murder. Other intelligence services may kill agents gone sour, or murder troublesome opponents in the field, but Agency people insist the CIA has not. They are adamant on this point.

They are speaking, of course, about murder as a deliberate act of policy, with approval sought and granted right up the chain of command from the field to the DDP, and perhaps even to the Director of Central Intelligence himself. They are not quite so positive about what goes on, in the words of one former official, "out in the boondocks." There, according to one retired officer with long experience in the Far East and in operations against Cuba in the early 1960s, a kind of unwritten rule went into effect whenever a CIA man was murdered. "One of your people gets killed in a back alley somewhere," he said. "If you know who did it you go after them, you don't ask, you're just going. Nobody back in Washington would ever have to know. . . . You know something about the Agency. Nothing would ever get into the files."

The business of intelligence, as much a part of modern nation states as a telephone system or internal revenue service, has its ugly side. The immaculate documents which go to the National Security Council do not come only from satellites and a close reading of Russian technical journals. Presidents have ways of getting their message across which go beyond State Department white papers and speeches in the U.N. Secret agents must not only be recruited but controlled. When they go sour they may be betrayed to their enemies. Clients are sometimes led out onto limbs and abandoned there. Allies of convenience are sometimes addicted to nail pliers and electric needles. Friendly intelligence services trained by the CIA in computerized file-keeping sometimes use those computers to pull the names of people they intend to kill. Helms spent thirty years in this business and accepted it. "We're not in the Boy Scouts," he often said. "If we'd wanted to be in the Boy Scouts we'd have *joined* the Boy Scouts." But the evidence, fragmentary as it is, suggests that the CIA draws the line at what is commonly meant by the word "murder."[12] Thus it was all the more surprising when, in the late 1950s, the CIA began to get orders to kill people.

Of course, talk about killing was commonplace. In 1952 a West German general had lunch in Washington with Dulles, Helms, and other CIA officials, and suggested that a way be found to assassinate the East German leader, Walter Ulbricht. The proposal was rejected.[13] As early as 1957 some American government officials were talking about "getting rid of" Ngo Dinh Diem in South Vietnam. His abuse of human rights was putting the United States in an awkward situation, just as his suppression of political opponents of every stripe was undermining his own government, but he had settled in so deeply that some of the Americans talking about getting rid of him had decided the only way was to *get rid of him*. Eventually these discussions involved the CIA; Vietnam analysts were asked to suggest a possible replacement. In late 1958, not long before he left the Agency for good, Frank Wisner discussed the "Diem problem" with another DDP official, who says neither of them was exactly keen on the idea. Diem, with all his faults, was an American ally and client. "Is it really our job to do that?" the DDP official asked Wisner.

The answer turned out to be no—for the time being, at least—because the only man with a right to issue such an order never gave it. But there was plenty of tough talk, all the same. At a State Department meeting to discuss U.S. troubles with Gamal Abdul Nasser of Egypt in late 1956 or early 1957, Allen Dulles, suddenly growing angry with a briefer's attempt to explain the situation from Nasser's point of view, turned to him and said, "If that colonel of yours pushes us too far we will break him in half!"[14]

Later, in the 1960s, a member of the President's Foreign Intelligence Advisory Board, Robert Murphy, asked why the CIA didn't kill Ho Chi Minh, since he was giving us so much trouble. Murphy asked loudly, positively, and repeatedly: Ho is the problem, isn't he? Can't you fellows do something to get rid of him? You're supposed to be able to handle things; handle him![15] Murphy was an important public official, and the DDP, Thomas Karamessines, had a tough time with his repeated demands. A CIA officer who often accompanied him said he'd heard such tough talk before and that he and other CIA officers responded with "a regular spiel you'd give these people": what good would it do? Ho's successor might be even worse. How were you going to kill Ho Chi Minh secretly? You might be able to fool the *New York Times*, Robert Murphy was told, but how were you going to deceive the Vietnamese? They'd know what happened, they'd know who did it, and they'd probably be in a position and mood to retaliate. There is a tacit truce between nations on such matters: once you start killing them, they start killing you. The CIA simply does not have the assets to kill secretly a well-guarded figure like Ho Chi Minh in a security-conscious state like North Vietnam.

Another government figure who got the regular spiel was Livingston Merchant, the Undersecretary of State for Political Affairs at the end of Eisenhower's administration. Because of his job, Merchant was a regular member of the Special Group to oversee covert operations and on November 3, 1960, when planning for the Bay of Pigs was well under way, Merchant attended a Special Group meeting where he asked "whether any real planning had been done for taking direct positive action against Fidel, Raul and Che Guevara." In the sudden absence of all three, Merchant suggested, the Cuban government would be "leaderless and probably brainless."

On this occasion the regular spiel came from General Cabell, the Deputy Director for Central Intelligence, who "pointed out that action of this kind is uncertain of results and highly dangerous in conception and execution, because the instruments must be Cubans. He [Cabell] felt that, particularly because of the necessity of simultaneous action, it would have to be concluded that Mr. Merchant's suggestion is beyond our capabilities."[16] Even through the opacity of official minutes the pattern is apparent: a hard-headed, straightforward question—what about it? if we're trying to get rid of these guys, why don't we *get rid of these guys?*—is met with a wall of spongy demurrer: it's too tough, won't work, can't predict the consequences, might blow up in our faces, etc. etc.

It is astonishing how many tough-minded men in American government have been convinced by the regular spiel that the CIA has a deep-rooted antipathy to proposals for political murder. A witness to still another episode of the sort was Armin Meyer, a career diplomat with a long history in the Near East going back to the Office of War Information, a kind of offshoot of the OSS, during World War II. In July 1958, when the government of Iraq was overthrown in a coup notable for its violence, Meyer was deputy director of the State Department's Office of Near Eastern Affairs. The following year he was promoted to director and as such was called in whenever the CIA contemplated covert operations in Iraq. The new ruler of the country was an army general named Abdul Karim Kassem, who had murdered his predecessors as well as a number of foreigners who happened to be in Baghdad at the time of his coup. On top of that, he immediately restored diplomatic relations with the Soviet Union, later lifted a ban on the Iraqi Communist party while suppressing pro-Western parties, and in many other ways invited the hostility of Eisenhower and John Foster Dulles.[17] On one occasion during Armin Meyer's tenure as director of the Office of Near Eastern Affairs, he attended a meeting in Allen Dulles's office at the CIA to discuss how the United States might remove Kassem. Meyer had attended many such meetings; they were a routine of government; but this one stuck in his mind.

During the meeting one of those present suggested that Kassem was the problem, and maybe the best way to get rid of him was to *get rid of him.* Wait a minute, Dulles said. An awful silence followed. Dulles was a man of great personal authority, and his words on this occasion had a cold and deliberate emphasis which Meyer never forgot. Dulles wanted one thing to be understood: it is not in the American character to assassinate opponents; murder was not to be discussed in his office, now or ever again; he did not ever want to hear another such suggestion by a servant of the United States government; that is not the way Americans do things.

Dulles was so clear on this point, and spoke with such evident passion and conviction, that Meyer simply could not understand how Dulles ever could have been party to an assassination plot no matter who gave the orders. Meyer knew what was in the Church Committee's reports, but he simply did not believe it, there must be some error, it was beyond Meyer's capacity to conceive that he could have been mistaken on this point, Dulles had left no room for doubt: *he would not be a party to assassination.*

The regular spiel.

The more you examine the subject, the clearer the pattern becomes. One more example ought to make it unmistakable. On August 10, 1962, during the earliest stages of what would shortly become the Cuban missile crisis, the Special Group Augmented held a meeting in the office of Secretary of State Dean Rusk to discuss Operation Mongoose, the Kennedy administration's post–Bay of Pigs plan to get rid of Castro, and Secretary of Defense Robert McNamara, a man convinced there is a rational solution to every problem, was probably astonished at the instantaneous reaction to his entirely hypothetical suggestion that perhaps the SGA ought to consider solving the Castro problem by killing him.

Edward R. Murrow, the director of the United States Information Agency, protested that this was entirely out of order. John McCone immediately backed him up. The secretary at the meeting, Thomas Parrott, did not so much as include the matter in the minutes.[18] To seal the point, McCone personally phoned McNamara later in the day and again protested that talk of assassination was completely inappropriate in such a meeting, and that he didn't want to hear any more of it.

The following day William Harvey, head of Task Force W, the CIA's end of Operation Mongoose, told McCone much the same thing: talk of murder was "inappropriate" in such a "form" and at such a "forum." McCone agreed, and described his phone call to McNamara. Thus Harvey was doubly astonished two days later, on August 13, when he got an official memo from Edward G. Lansdale, the Kennedy brothers' personal choice to run Mongoose, which explicitly requested Harvey to prepare papers on various anti-Castro programs "including liquidation of leaders." Harvey, a tough-talking former FBI agent with a gravelly voice, told Lansdale in plain terms what he thought of the "stupidity of putting this type of comment in writing in such a document." He repeated his objections to McCone the same day, and on August 14, 1962, fully briefed Helms on both the McNamara proposal and Lansdale memo and on his response. He went so far as to delete the phrase "including liquidation of leaders" from a copy of Lansdale's memo which he was passing on to Helms.[19]

The message to McNamara, and to us, ought to be loud and clear: assassination was too sensitive a matter to be discussed in official meetings or to be recorded in official memos and minutes. What those high officials who received the regular spiel failed to comprehend was the degree of secrecy which surrounded any matter as explosive as assassination. Armin Meyer, for example, was convinced by Dulles's version of the regular spiel that he would never be a party to assassination. He knew what was in the Church Committee's *Assassination Report*—roughly knew, that is; he had not actually read it—but he couldn't square what he'd heard with what he thought he knew. If he had read the report, the whole report, and most particularly the long footnote on page 181, he would have known that

Dulles's solemn disapproval was in truth nothing more than the regular spiel.

In February 1960, while the government was trying to decide what to do about General Kassem, the chief of the DDP's Near East Division [20] proposed that Kassem be "incapacitated" with a poisoned hand-kerchief prepared by the DDP's Technical Services Division. In April the proposal was supported by the DDP's Chief of Operations, Richard Helms, [21] who endorsed Kassem's incapacitation as "highly desirable." Meyer would further have known that Bissell did not act in such matters without Dulles's approval, and that Bissell was convinced—he could hardly have made this point any clearer to the Church Committee—that Dulles would not have proceeded without an order from the only man with the authority to okay an attempt on a foreign leader's life. In this instance the handkerchief was duly dispatched to Kassem, but whether or not it ever reached him, it certainly did not kill him. His own countrymen did that on February 8, 1963, by executing him before a firing squad on live television in Baghdad.

What Livingston Merchant, Armin Meyer, Robert McNamara, and others failed to understand was that official meetings in the office of the Director of the CIA, or of the Secretary of State, or of the Special Group, were hardly the place to discuss something that was really secret. From the CIA's point of view the Secretary of State's office was about as secure as the floor of Congress with a full press gallery. If you were going to plan an assassination in the Secretary of State's office, or record the discussion in the minutes, you might as well send a press release to the *New York Times*. Eisenhower and Kennedy went after two enemies in particular in the years between 1959 and 1963—Lumumba in the Congo and Castro in Cuba—but when they gave the job to the CIA they expected secrecy, and that is what they got.

Chapter 9

On April 24, 1967, the Inspector General of the CIA, Jack Earman, submitted the first section of his report on CIA involvement in assassination plots to Richard Helms, whose reaction can only have been one of queasy horror. Not only at its thoroughness and detail,[1] nor at its chilling lack of extenuating circumstance, but at the very fact it was now all down in writing. The first rule in keeping secrets is nothing on paper: paper can be lost or stolen or simply inherited by the wrong people; if you really want to keep something secret, don't write it down. The IG's report violated that rule with a vengeance. Every trace of the assassination plots scattered throughout CIA files, and all that the various CIA officials involved had been willing to say, was down in print with names—including that of Richard Helms—and dates in a document with a potential to do incalculable damage to the reputation of the CIA, two Presidents, and the United States itself. It was a classic example of the sort of paper which government officials call "sensitive," and which journalists call "explosive," and Helms did not intend that anyone other than its author and he, himself, should ever read it.

But if much was there in the IG's report, much was missing too. Helms may have consoled himself that at least the deepest secret of all—who gave the orders? and when?—had eluded the IG. And that wasn't the only point on which the IG had been compelled to confess ignorance. No secrets were ever more closely guarded than those involving the attempts of the CIA to kill a handful of foreign leaders;[2] existing accounts of what happened are oddly fragmented and suggestive, even after long official investigation. But the report which Helms began to receive in sections from the Inspector General in April 1967, expanded upon by the Church Committee eight years later, and supplemented by the recollections of CIA officers involved together indicate pretty clearly what was done, and for whom.

When Richard Bissell was forced to leave the CIA early in 1962[3] and Helms was named his heir, he discovered at the reading of the will that his inheritance was a very extensive one indeed, not simply the sum total of the DDP on paper but, more important, the fruit of those quiet conversations between two or three men[4]—Bill, would you mind waiting a bit? I've got something I'd like to discuss with you—where the plots thicken.

As Bissell's chief of operations Helms may have complained that no one ever told him anything, but in truth there cannot have been much which slipped entirely by him. The difference in 1962 was that now all the private arrangements and quiet programs—the secrets in short—were his. A secret operation, once under way, is not turned off as easily as a desk lamp. Somebody else may be reading by that light and inquire what do you think you're doing. So Helms received the secrets as he did the routine, without protest or abrupt action, in the manner of a practical and open man who only wants to get on with the job he's hired out to do, and who is apparently insensible to the possibility that what is being talked about here—the Rosselli pipe into Cuba, say; or Bill Harvey's Executive Action program—might strike the editors of the Washington *Post* as a conspiracy to commit murder. Richard Bissell must have found that passing on a secret to Dick Helms was like dropping a stone into a well.

The heart of Helms's inheritance—entrusted to him personally by John McCone at least two months before Bissell actually left the Agency—was Cuba. It was generally assumed at the time that Bissell was fired for his role in the fiasco of the Bay of Pigs, but this was only part of the explanation, the public part in fact, while the private part had to do with Bissell's continued failure to make progress in getting rid of Castro. In the fall of 1961, most particularly at a meeting in the White House, the Kennedys made it clear to Bissell they wanted Castro out of there. Then they made it clear to McCone, who had concluded early on that Robert Kennedy was the key to the administration. The President had assigned his brother the job of "dealing with the CIA." Robert Kennedy did not hang back. McCone cultivated the connection as the next best thing to intimacy with the President himself, and in the two years they worked together McCone and the Attorney General became close in the manner of men in power.

In December 1961, McCone took Cuba from Bissell and gave it to Helms, an act which reflected the Kennedys' impatience with Bissell's lack of progress. A CIA officer present at that meeting said Helms's first step was to pick up the phone and call J. C. King, chief of the Western Hemisphere Division. In late 1961 Cuba was only a desk in the Division's Caribbean Branch. Helms said, "J.C., as of here and now, Cuba is a separate branch." The Caribbean Branch chief and the Deputy Branch chief were to run the new Cuba Branch. J. C. King asked whom he was to assign to run the rest of the Caribbean. "I don't know," Helms said. "That's up to you—pick anyone you like."

From that moment on, the CIA began a determined effort to overthrow Castro under the close supervision of the White House. But this time the operation was run as a genuine clandestine operation, cautiously, secretly, and, from the point of view of all but Cuba herself, quietly. Castro was not overthrown, but neither was Kennedy embarrassed by the attempt or its failure; security was so tight that the operation, called Mongoose,[5] was not even known to exist for more than ten years. In the long run, Helms may not have done any better than Bissell before him, but he kept it out of the papers.

It is an odd fact that this should have been possible. Kennedy himself had revealed his intentions clearly enough to anyone who cared to pay attention as early as April 20, 1961, in a speech to the American Society of Newspaper Editors in which he charged that the Soviet Union viewed military power "as the shield behind which subversion, infiltration, and a host of other tactics steadily advance, picking off vulnerable areas one by one. . . . Too long have we fixed our eyes on traditional military needs. . . . Now it should be clear that this is no longer enough. . . ."[6] Eighteen months later, following the Cuban missile crisis and the ransom of the Bay of Pigs prisoners in December 1962, Kennedy all but announced what he was up to in a speech in Miami, where Brigade 2506 gave him the battle flag which had flown on the beach during the invasion. "I can assure you," Kennedy said, "that this flag will be returned to this brigade in a free Havana."[7] It ought to have been apparent that Kennedy was determined to fight fire with fire, subversion with subversion, infiltration with infiltration. But even though the Cubans understood perfectly well what was happening, and even though Miami was electric with exile activity, Operation Mongoose was run with such a professional regard for secrecy that Kennedy's assurance was dismissed as rhetoric until the truth of what he had been up to began to emerge more than a decade later.

The Bay of Pigs marked the beginning of Kennedy's determination to get rid of Castro, the moment when Fidel Castro ceased to be an enemy inherited from Eisenhower, and became his own. Kennedy's mandate to General Maxwell Taylor in April 1961 was not to fix the blame for the failure of the invasion, but to find out why it hadn't worked, so the next plan would. Taylor quickly concluded that a major reason for the failure had been Kennedy's scuttling of the Operations Coordinating Board (OCB), in February 1961. The OCB, Eisenhower's instrument for overseeing foreign operations, had a reputation as something of a paper mill, turning out reams of reports and studies which only gummed up the execution of foreign policy. In addition, Allen Dulles never entirely trusted the OCB members to keep the secrets. One Army officer in particular was distrusted by Dulles as an outright security risk.[8] But by the end of Eisenhower's second term the OCB was working smoothly, and a study committee named after its chairman, Mansfield Sprague, strongly recommended its continuation.

Kennedy, however, disdainful of the orderly, low-key, thorough staffing of foreign policy by his predecessor, did not want to hear about the Sprague report and how well things were running. He insisted his administration could do better by assigning programs to his bright young men on an ad hoc basis. So he got rid of the OCB, as well as the President's Board of Consultants on Foreign Intelligence Activities (PBCFIA). Kennedy considered them useless impediments, bureaucratic obstructions to a vigorous, activist foreign policy.

Taylor disagreed. He felt the Bay of Pigs plan had gone forward at least in part because Kennedy had destroyed the only institutional decision-making bodies—the OCB and the PBCFIA—which might have had the weight to contradict a President. When Kennedy formally asked his advisers for their personal opinions they tended to freeze, and join what they took to be the consensus.[9] Taylor's problem was to reintroduce the OCB under another name. His strategy was simple. Knowing of Kennedy's growing obsession with unconventional warfare, Taylor proposed a broad, government-wide effort to combat insurgencies from Vietnam to Latin America. The result, after Taylor joined the White House full-time as the military representative of the President on July 4, 1961, was establishment of the Counter-Insurgency Group (CI Group) which began to meet on a regular basis with Taylor as chairman early that fall.[10] The CI Group took an aggressive stance from the beginning. Chester Bowles, the Undersecretary of State for Political Affairs, would ordinarily have been a member of the group, but he was replaced by his deputy, U. Alexis Johnson, because of Bowles's known dislike of clandestine intervention in any form. Desmond FitzGerald had once said of him that giving Bowles authority over covert operations was like entrusting a ship to a captain who hated the sea.

Despite Robert Kennedy's membership in the CI Group, Taylor was in undisputed charge. Kennedy was the group's goad, not its director. During early organizational meetings Kennedy urged Taylor to include the Secretary of Labor, Arthur Goldberg, but Taylor resisted the suggestion. The group was already too large and unwieldy, he said; the Secretary of Labor's role was too peripheral. He did not say, but felt, that Goldberg was too long-winded. Kennedy's proposal was allowed to float for a matter of weeks before Taylor came to a decision at a meeting in the early fall of 1961. Taylor polled everyone present for his views on Goldberg's inclusion. One by one the CI Group members sided with Taylor: Goldberg would be out of place. The vote was overwhelming: No.

But then Kennedy reopened the argument, putting his weight into it: the President is watching what we do here, this is important, labor is part of the total approach, *I want Arthur Goldberg in this group.* And one by one those who had just voted against Goldberg reversed themselves: Well, yes, Bobby, you've brought up a good point there, maybe we'd better reconsider. When Kennedy got to General Cabell, who was sitting in while Dulles was out of the country, Cabell looked about uncomfortably and said, "Well, this is my first meeting, and I don't really know . . ."

It seemed as though Kennedy would carry the issue, but Taylor would not budge. "No," he said, "labor's role is small, the committee is too big now. I'm just not going to accept Goldberg."

Robert Kennedy was a man of considerable personal force. As the Attorney General and the President's trusted brother, he had recently been described in *Time* magazine as the second most important man in the world. When Taylor overruled him he got up slowly, slapped his papers together, headed for the door, then paused. "Well, *shit*," he said, "the second most important man in the world just lost another one." He slammed the door behind him. The windows rattled. There was a moment of silence, and then Taylor calmly resumed the meeting.

But Robert Kennedy was not easily thwarted. When the direct route was blocked, he found a way around. He grew close to McCone, and did not hesitate to call up CIA officers directly involved in the Cuban operation when he thought the committees were not working quickly enough. He often telephoned Helms to raise the temperature a bit, and sometimes even called CIA people further down the line, including William Harvey and Desmond FitzGerald, and on occasion he went so far beyond the usual channels as to call the CIA people who worked for *them*.

The first order of business for the CI Group was Cuba. The CIA was heavily involved in both Laos and Vietnam at the same time, but the covert operations launched against North Vietnam beginning in the fall of 1961 under the Saigon station chief, William Colby, were on the back burner. Cuba was where the Kennedys wanted immediate results. A second committee, the Special Group Augmented (SGA), was established to oversee Operation Mongoose, run by General Edward G. Lansdale, a counter-insurgency specialist with experience in both the Philippines and Vietnam, where he had helped Ngo Dinh Diem to consolidate his control over the country. No Kennedy program received less publicity than Mongoose, or more personal attention from the Kennedys, and in particular from Robert. The Kennedys wanted Castro out of there, and the CI Group's weekly meetings hardly had time for anything else. The fifteen members would gather at 10:00 p.m. in a conference room next door to Taylor's office. After an hour or two, half the members would leave and the remainder would convene a meeting of the Special Group Augmented. When that ended, the three members of the Special Group for overseeing covert operations would hold its meeting, with the result that John McCone, beginning in November 1961, and the other Special Group members would sometimes spend six or seven hours at a stretch in three successive meetings dominated by one priority: getting rid of Castro.

Operation Mongoose quickly became the single largest clandestine program within the CIA, but it was hardly unprecedented. In fact, it was entirely characteristic of the CIA response to the passing enthusiasms of postwar American Presidents, whose administrations tended to focus on one crisis at a time. In the late 1940s and early 1950s the CIA cranked up a huge operation against the Soviet bloc in Europe; at one time General Lucian K. Truscott II, the CIA's first station chief in Germany, had 1,200 men under him. Later, similar efforts were directed against Iran, Guatemala, Indonesia, and Cuba before the Bay of Pigs invasion failed. When Cuba slipped from Lyndon Johnson's mind the CIA switched its focus to Vietnam, and later still—for a briefer period, but with the same intensity—to Chile. In every instance the Washington bureaucracy would become obsessed with the crisis at hand, committees would proliferate, meetings would spawn meetings, paper would be cranked out by the cartload, reputations would be made or destroyed overnight, and the CIA, under the pressure of presidential demand, would search for the lever which might turn things around. Sometimes, as with Guatemala, they would find it;[11] and sometimes not. Operation Mongoose followed the pattern with eerie exactitude. For nearly eighteen months, beginning in November 1961, the Kennedy administration demanded action on Cuba. The CI Group established the Special Group Augmented, which approved Mongoose and entrusted it to Lansdale, who drew up an elaborate scenario with a precise timetable calling for a march on Havana and the overthrow of Castro in October 1962. It was all worked out on paper. The final stage of Mongoose was right there in Lansdale's charts, and it was up to the CIA under McCone and Helms to see that the plan worked.

The importance of the undertaking did not take long to establish. In the early stages of Mongoose, a CIA officer working on the operation, Sam Halpern, asked Lawrence Houston if the operation was even legal. He pointed out that the Bay of Pigs landing had been organized outside the United States at least partly in order to avoid violating the Neutrality Acts, which prohibited the launching of attacks on foreign targets from American soil. Now Mongoose was being geared up in Miami; wasn't this against the law? Houston said the answer was no: if the President says it's okay, and if the Attorney General says it's okay, then it's okay.

The CIA officers in charge of the Cuban Branch set up by Helms were appalled by the magnitude of the task. "With what?" they asked. "We haven't got any assets. We don't even know what's going on in Cuba." One of Halpern's first suggestions, submitted repeatedly to Helms's chief executive officer, Gordon Mason, was to put a major CIA officer in charge of the Cuban program to give the effort clout within the Agency. But most of the names on Halpern's list were tied up elsewhere: Desmond FitzGerald was running the Far East Division and was supposed to fight the war in Vietnam, gearing up at the same time; his predecessor Al Ulmer was in Paris and couldn't be spared, so it was decided to give the job to William Harvey, a veteran of operations in Europe including the Berlin Tunnel.[12]

Only a handful of CIA people captured the imagination of their colleagues and became legends within the Agency. Harvey was one such, a

man everyone knew but not everyone liked, a rough-voiced, imposing figure, and so fat he had the Agency's permission on medical grounds to travel
first class whenever he flew, because he could not settle his bulk comfortably
into the narrow tourist-class seats. In 1947, already a heavy drinker, he had
moved from the FBI to the CIA. He described himself (accurately) as a
three-martini man at lunch—two doubles and a single. Afterward, he sometimes fell asleep at his desk, more than once while a visitor waited patiently
for him to reawake. When he snoozed off during a meeting with McCone
the new director wanted to fire him forthwith, but was dissuaded: Harvey
was a rough diamond, perhaps, but he had his uses.

There was about him a certain single-mindedness. When he set himself
to do something he did not hold back. He once told an acquaintance that he
had been to bed with a woman every day of his life since he was twelve.
Colleagues remember him as the only CIA officer who always carried a gun.
He often left it in plain view on his desk, as if expecting to be surprised by
an assassin while at work. Sometimes he loaded the gun while he talked, or
worked the action and then let the hammer down gently, gently, but never
too gently for the visitors who watched him do it. Not just *a* gun, but a
different gun every day, from the large collection he kept in a case at home.
This habit of Harvey's has often been dismissed as an affectation or ec-
centricity, a gesture devoid of violence, but one man who knew him well in
Rome in the mid-1960s, after his failure with Mongoose, considered Harvey
a genuinely "dangerous clown." Asked why, the man said that once Harvey
expressed his position in an argument by pulling a .45-caliber automatic
from his desk drawer, pointing it between his listener's eyes at a distance of
only two or three feet, and flipping the safety.

Dulles once said of him, "That Harvey is a conspiratorial cop. The only
trouble is I can't decide if he's more conspiratorial, or more a cop." But he
was an experienced and imaginative clandestine operator, and he was a
tireless project director as long as he was given a free rein. Harvey's first job
as the head of CIA's Task Force W was to restore the agent networks in
Cuba which had been rolled up by Castro just before the Bay of Pigs
invasion. The island was penetrable to a degree because Castro's Russian
security advisers had recommended he consolidate his control of the cities
first, and leave the countryside until later. But despite the hectic pace with
which agents were sent into Cuba and recruited inside—not only exiles from
Miami sent in over the beach, but foreign businessmen and diplomats—the
Kennedy brothers were in a hurry to move yet faster. Lansdale's plan called
for a popular uprising; Harvey was trying to build an underground network
for political organizing, and to put enough agents in place to let CIA know
what was going on. But the Kennedys, like all other Presidents and high
officials dealing with the CIA, did not really understand the operational side
of clandestine activity, or the importance of time in establishing solid covert
organizations in a world all too untidy and unstable.

The Kennedys' dissatisfaction with the pace of Mongoose went to the CI Group, which passed it on to the SGA, which pressed Lansdale, who pushed Helms, who demanded results from Harvey and Task Force W. Reports and memos sent back up the line were frequently kicked back by Helms, who complained that they were not sufficiently positive in tone, not sufficiently "forward-leaning" (a Lansdale cant word). "There's a lot of ways you can write the English language to make it sound like we're moving ahead," Helms told the Cuban operators.

The sense of urgency emanating from the White House was intense. More than once Helms told Larry Houston, "My God, these Kennedys keep the pressure on about Castro." At a meeting in Bobby Kennedy's office on January 19, 1962, nearly a month before Helms officially took over as DDP, the Attorney General said that "no time, money, effort or manpower is to be spared," and that the President had told him the day before "the final chapter had not been written—it's got to be done and will be done."[13] According to the Church Committee's Assassination Report, Helms attended at least seven of the forty Operation Mongoose meetings, and he himself testified that he frequently spoke with Robert Kennedy by phone and from time to time met with him privately. Accustomed to leaving his office with a clean desk between six and six-thirty every day, Helms, after the onset of Mongoose, regularly worked late into the evening.

But despite the White House pressure the SGA and Mongoose proceeded sluggishly, not from bureaucratic indifference, but because Cuba was a hard nut to crack. Lansdale's original plan had called for an escalating effort to create an opposition to Castro inside Cuba, followed by insurgency and a general uprising. When Lansdale spoke of a march on Havana in October 1962, he meant *march*—a triumphal entry like Castro's own just three years earlier. But Lansdale's plan was a fantasy. The officers on Task Force W knew what they had begun with—something so close to nothing only a philosopher might establish the difference. Castro's effective opposition was very close to being a class without members. A number of Kennedy administration officials accused the CIA of ignoring dissident Cubans with support inside the country in favor of more pliable men the Agency could control. The CIA insisted it was only working with what it had, and that a lot of the administration's favorite Cubans could not deliver; their support networks were illusory. Harvey managed to get agents onto the island, and to recruit others in rural areas,[14] but what they told him was bleak: there would be no general uprising.

After the first few months of covert operations, Mongoose gradually shifted its emphasis from resistance-building toward sabotage, paramilitary raids, efforts to disrupt the Cuban economy by contaminating sugar exports, circulating counterfeit money and ration books, and the like. "We want boom-and-bang on the island," Lansdale said.[15] Robert Kennedy took a particular interest in efforts to sabotage the Matahambre copper mines in western Cuba, on one occasion even calling repeatedly to learn if the agents had left yet: Had they landed? Had they reached the mines? Had they destroyed them successfully? Kennedy, like Lansdale, wanted boom-and-bang, and a number of CIA officers on the operational level grew to know his voice as he called to find out how they were coming along, and to press them forward. On occasion, even his secretary called in his behalf. The Matahambre copper mines were never destroyed, despite the launching of three separate full-scale raids, but other attacks on sugar refineries, oil storage facilities, and similar targets were more successful. Still, they fell far short of wrecking the Cuban economy, even in its weakened state following the dislocations of revolution, and the paramilitary program held out little promise of Castro's overthrow.

There were three reasons for the failure. First was the inherent difficulty of the undertaking. The CIA station in Miami quickly expanded into the world's largest—six hundred case officers and as many as three thousand contract agents.[16] But Cuba is 90 miles from Key West, and a good deal farther from the Florida coast around Miami, from which most of the assaults were launched. Despite extraordinary cooperation from the Coast Guard, the Navy, and the Dade County police, these raids were hard to arrange secretly, required huge logistical backup, and were easily interrupted by weather, the phases of the moon, communications failures with agents on the island, Castro's security forces, and even the sheer cussedness of the boats themselves. "Between helicopters and boats," Desmond Fitz-Gerald once said of two of the world's most temperamental machines, "I'd rather walk."

The second reason for Mongoose's failure was that Lansdale was after boom-and-bang, while his real expertise lay in political operations of the sort he had conducted in the Philippines and Vietnam, where he had been working with the legal governments. According to several men who worked with him on Cuba, he simply did not know very much about over-the-beach operations. On top of that, he was uneven in judgment. Nutty ideas sometimes seemed to strike him as imaginative and plausible. In an early meeting with CIA people in Task Force W, he pointed to the Isle of Pines off the coast of Cuba and said, "That's what we'll do. We'll capture that island and we'll use it as our base of operations." "But Ed," said one of those present, "that's where Modello prison is. That's where Castro keeps all of his prisoners. How are you going to do that?"

Another Lansdale inspiration was to convince Cuba's Roman Catholic population that Castro had lost God's confidence. Perhaps Lansdale was thinking of the Vietnamese belief that no man can lead without "the mandate of heaven"; perhaps he was remembering the success of the "eye of God" technique he had employed in the Philippines, where helicopters had been used to broadcast messages to quasi-primitive guerrillas. Whatever its source, his plan was bold: Cuba was to be flooded with rumors that the

Second Coming was imminent, that Christ had picked Cuba for His arrival, and that He wanted the Cubans to get rid of Castro first. Then, on the night foretold, a U.S. submarine would surface off the coast of Cuba and litter the sky with star shells, which would convince the Cubans that The Hour was at hand. Walt Elder, McCone's executive assistant, named this gambit "elimination by illumination."[17] It was not pursued.

A third reason for the failure of Mongoose was William Harvey's inability to get along with Taylor and Lansdale, and later the Kennedys themselves. Having spent a lifetime in the military, General Taylor expected meticulous staffing of an operation before it was approved. Harvey, a seasoned clandestine operator, was accustomed to a freer style, taking his opportunities as he found them. Time and again he proposed an operation to the Special Group Augmented, won a kind of general okay, and concluded he was at liberty to proceed. He was wrong. Taylor expected a thick sheaf of substantiating paper before anything actually happened. A kind of three-way tug-of-war developed, with the Kennedys demanding action, Harvey pressing ahead, and the Special Group Augmented dragging along behind.

At one point during his year on Task Force W, Harvey was put on the carpet by McCone and criticized for moving too slowly. Harvey said it wasn't his fault; the SGA wanted every operation supported on paper in relentless detail, and then, as like as not, refused their approval pending an additional report or more study or a review by some third party. The SGA's deliberate rumination and chin-stroking was beginning to strike Harvey as willful and frivolous. They talked about getting rid of Castro in one year; well, how about it? In a memo to McCone, Harvey expanded in the manner to which the SGA hoped he would become accustomed: "To permit requisite flexibility and professionalism for a maximum operational effort against Cuba, the tight controls exercised by the Special Group and the present time-consuming coordination and briefing procedures should, if at all possible, be made less restrictive and stultifying."[18]

Harvey made a similar protest to Helms, who sought the help of Tom Parrott, a CIA officer on loan to the Special Group as secretary. "Harvey complains that Taylor never approves anything," Helms said. "He goes in week after week and they're all turned down. Can't you do something about this?"

Parrott could not. The various committees involved—the CI Group, SGA, and the Special Group—had all been streamlined for maximum effect. Taylor insisted that every meeting be attended by the principals involved, not by stand-in subordinates, so that decisions might be reached and acted upon immediately. But the system was not working. The officials involved had too much else on their minds, expressed their caution in demands for paperwork, and in the end shrank from the sort of all-out attack on Cuba which the Kennedys wanted. Perhaps they doubted that paramilitary raids would ever work, and were reluctant to approve actions with a maximum potential for embarrassing the United States, but a minimum chance of actually getting rid of Castro.

Whatever their reasons for proceeding slowly, the result was a logjam between the Kennedys, who continued to press for action, and the CIA, which peppered the SGA with proposals but couldn't get them approved. Robert Kennedy did his best to bridge the gap with constant telephone calls and memos. On October 4, 1962, with the onset of what would shortly become the Cuban missile crisis, Kennedy told the SGA that henceforth he would chair its meetings, and on October 16 he told Helms in a personal meeting in the Attorney General's office that the President was dissatisfied with Mongoose's progress, nothing was happening, raids on the Mata-hambre copper mines had failed, this wasn't good enough. Helms told the Church Committee years later that they were pretty direct with each other, they "used to deal in facts,"[19] and Kennedy made himself perfectly clear: he wanted to get rid of Castro, he thought the job was being botched by the Special Group and the CIA alike, and *he wasn't happy*.

But nothing worked. Taylor and the CI Group could come up with no plan for Castro's overthrow which would not require overt American intervention for the final blow. This Kennedy would not approve. The SGA, likewise, was unwilling to surrender operational control of Mongoose to Lansdale and the CIA, and for all the meetings, studies, proposals, and memoranda cranked out, in the end not much happened. Agents were infiltrated, raids took place, bombs went off, Cuban exiles were killed or captured, but Mongoose never seriously threatened Castro. It did not even come close.

Then, during the missile crisis, Harvey ran afoul of the Kennedys. The problem seems to have been one first of character and temperament. Harvey was intelligent and able, in his way, but rough, direct, and a bit of a gumshoe; it was hard to imagine him dealing with four-star generals, cabinet secretaries, or the President. He had no instinct for how such things were done. He resented, for example, Bobby Kennedy's direct dealings with Cuban exiles he'd met on his own, and felt the Attorney General's constant intervention was only mucking things up.

On one occasion, early in 1962, Harvey and Kennedy had a direct collision during a tour of the CIA's station in Miami.[20] Kennedy noticed something on the teletype which connected the station to CIA headquarters in Langley. He tore off a long strip to read, then headed for the door with the strip in his hand. Harvey had recently returned from lunch, where he drank neither more nor less than usual. Sometimes martinis made him sleepy, sometimes pugnacious. On this occasion it was the latter. He saw Kennedy heading for the door with a strip of Agency message paper in his hand and called out, Hey! Where are you going with that? Kennedy did not welcome the question or its tone. But Harvey was not about to let anyone walk off with an internal CIA document salted with message indicators and operational codes; he walked over to Kennedy and physically grabbed the strip of paper from the Attorney General's hand.

Later, at a meeting during the missile crisis when both Kennedys were present, according to a number of sources, Harvey had the temerity and professional ill-judgment to say clearly, in the midst of witnesses who were genuinely horrified at the idea of saying anything so baldly critical to a President, that the crisis was their own fault: if they'd never made an official distinction between defensive and offensive weapons, telling the Cubans and Russians alike that the United States would tolerate defensive weapons —which of course the Russians claimed the missiles to be—then none of this would have happened. That finished Harvey as far as the Kennedys were concerned. He was *out*.

But the reason given for his dismissal from Mongoose was somewhat different. At the height of the missile crisis Robert Kennedy told McCone that he wanted an immediate halt to all operations against Cuba, and Mc-Cone passed on the order to Harvey. But Harvey, making a distinction between operations and agents, and thinking that the U.S. might find itself in a shooting war and in need of all the intelligence it could get, decided on one last attempt to send some agents in. On October 21, the day before President Kennedy announced a blockade of Cuba in a television speech, a CIA team headed by Eugenio Martinez[21] landed two agents on the northern coast of Cuba. At least one other team made a similar landing the same night. Later, at a meeting of the NSC executive committee held in the Joint Chiefs of Staff war room, Harvey was asked if all operations had been halted. "Well," he said, "all but one." He told them several agents had already landed, there was no way to communicate with them, and thus no way to recall them.[22]

This confession elicited pure fury, and Harvey was yanked off Task Force W as a direct consequence. McCone wanted to fire him altogether, but Helms talked him out of it, and the following year had Harvey assigned as chief of station in Rome.[23]

In the early stages of the missile crisis the Kennedys wanted a sharp acceleration of covert raids on Cuba, but then they reversed themselves and ordered a complete halt. Within the following few months the Special Group Augmented was disbanded and replaced by the Cuban Coordinating Committee, General Lansdale quietly disappeared from the Cuban effort, Task Force W was replaced by a new CIA group called the Special Affairs Staff, and Desmond FitzGerald left the DDP's Far East Division[24] and took over the new Cuban campaign which began to gear up early in 1963. But this time FitzGerald's timetable was more flexible than Harvey's under Lansdale. In the course of 1963, with the operation going "full blast," according to several sources, the CIA carried out at least six major operations against Cuba, along with a host of lesser ones.

FitzGerald was apparently convinced that he could bring down Castro by picking away at him with these raids. He argued at length, and sometimes angrily, with subordinates who protested that the CIA's paramilitary operations were "only pinpricks." The CIA could keep up the "pressure" all right, they said, but how was the occasional destruction of a sugar refinery supposed to topple Castro? This skepticism was strongest where closest to the actual operations themselves, and the "forward-leaning" memos were all written further up the line.

There is a certain opaque quality to all of the CIA's plans to eliminate Castro. The invasion force which landed at the Bay of Pigs was too big to hide, and too small to defeat Castro's huge army and militia. Mongoose in 1962 never got much beyond an intelligence-gathering effort, and while it succeeded in raising the level of "boom and bang on the island" in 1963, noise was hardly enough to do the job. Lansdale's scenario for a triumphal march into Havana was illusory, but a lot of people who worked for Fitz-Gerald never quite grasped how his plans were supposed to work, either. FitzGerald was adamant. "You don't know what you're talking about," he told one of them. *They were going to get Castro.*

But Lee Harvey Oswald got Kennedy first. After the President's murder in Dallas on November 22, 1963,[25] the Cuban operation began to wither away. The last exile groups, boats, and maintenance facilities in Florida were not abandoned until 1965, but Lyndon Johnson never gave his full attention to the Cuban "problem." For some reason Castro did not much matter to him; he lacked all that personal fire and even vindictiveness which animated the Kennedy brothers until the last. Only two days before his murder, John F. Kennedy had been briefed by two CIA officers on the discovery of a cache of Cuban arms along the coast of Venezuela. According to one of the officers who briefed him, the President was delighted by the news, sure this was just what they needed to trigger anti-Castro action by the Organization of American States. Eventually the discovery was used to do just that, but Kennedy was gone by that time and Johnson didn't care. On April 7, 1964, he ordered a halt to all sabotage operations.

But the handwriting was on the wall earlier, in March 1964, when Desmond FitzGerald, by then the new Western Hemisphere Division Chief, visited the CIA station in Buenos Aires. There he told some of his officers, "If Jack Kennedy had lived I can assure you we would have gotten rid of Castro by last Christmas. Unfortunately, the new President isn't as gung-ho on fighting Castro as Kennedy was."[26]

Christmas, 1963. What could have "gotten rid of Castro" by Christmas of 1963?

There was a lot of talk about language at the meetings of the Church Committee. CIA officers testified that phrases like "getting rid of Castro" were only figures of speech; they merely wanted him out of the way, not dead and buried. It was a kind of shorthand, reflecting the determined spirit of the time. Perhaps they talked about "eliminating" Castro, or even "knocking him off," but they intended only to replace or remove him, not literally get rid of him. A handful of former CIA officials—notably Richard Bissell, Bill Harvey, Justin O'Donnell,[27] Richard Helms—admitted that talk of getting rid of Castro or Lumumba meant just that in one or two instances, but when they really meant "get rid of" they sometimes used a circumlocution or euphemism instead. In particular, they testified, conversations with high government officials, and especially any which might have occurred with the very highest government official, were deliberately opaque, allusive, and indirect, using "rather general terms,"[28] in Bissell's phrase.

Bissell emphasized that Dulles would have done his level best to insulate Eisenhower or Kennedy from explicit or detailed knowledge of assassination attempts. Partly, that was Dulles's job. But in a case where administrations changed in midstream, he would have been doubly cautious, and triply allusive, in order to test the water before plunging in. It would not do to tell Kennedy the CIA was trying to poison Castro before being assured that the new President would not blanch and phone the police. Bissell insists he does not *know* whether Dulles briefed Kennedy about the plots against Castro, but assumes he did. Bissell's emphasis on circumlocutions may only be intended to protect the memory of two men he admired—Dulles and Kennedy—while still making it clear the CIA was not indulging a private grudge of its own. But it is also possible that Dulles was just as indirect as Bissell suggests, so indirect that Kennedy did not quite hear what he was being told. The history of this episode is cloudier than usual. None of those involved in the plots against Castro testified to one whit more than the documentary evidence forced them to admit. In the general mist, then, it is at least possible that Kennedy was told without being told.

In his testimony Helms took Bissell's line. "I think any of us would have found it very difficult to discuss assassinations with a President of the U.S.," Helms told the Church Committee. "I just think we all had the feeling that we're hired out to keep these things out of the Oval Office."[29] He made this point repeatedly—"nobody wants to embarrass a President of the United States by discussing the assassination of foreign leaders in his presence";[30] "I don't see how one would have expected that a thing like killing or murdering or assassinating would become a part of a large group of people sitting around a table in the United States government";[31] "I don't know whether it was in training, experience, tradition or exactly what one points to, but I think to go up to a Cabinet officer and say, am I right in assuming that you want me to assassinate Castro . . . is a question it wouldn't have occurred to me to ask."[32] Bissell and Helms both insisted they had never discussed the assassination plots with either the President or the Attorney General, but at the same time they were certain they had all the authority they needed, and were in fact trying to do what the Kennedys in particular wanted done. Helms insisted Robert Kennedy "would not have been unhappy if he [Castro] had disappeared off the scene by whatever means"[33] and "I was just doing my best to do what I thought I was supposed to do."[34]

The murkiness of the record raised a certain problem for the Committee. Either the CIA had undertaken Castro's murder on its own and was indeed, in Church's words, "a rogue elephant rampaging out of control,"[35] or Eisenhower and Kennedy had ordered the CIA to attempt the assassination of foreign leaders, which the associates of both Presidents swore they had never done, and would never do. Robert McNamara said he couldn't help the Committee on this crucial point. He testified he didn't remember suggesting Castro's assassination at an SGA meeting on August 10, 1962, although he did remember McCone's phone call to protest, and he would have to take the Committee's word for it that the CIA did, in fact, try to kill Castro. He didn't know about it.

But McNamara was at the same time meticulous in emphasizing that "the CIA was a highly disciplined organization, fully under the control of senior officials of the government. . . . I know of no major action taken by CIA during the time I was in the government that was not properly authorized. . . . I just can't understand how it could have happened. . . ."[36] The dilemma was gingerly circled again and again. Kennedy administration officials had nothing but praise for the CIA's discipline; they certainly did not want to blame the CIA for this, they did not even want to blame it on a misunderstanding; and yet they *knew* the Kennedys would never have countenanced any such thing.

The CIA officials involved did not contradict them exactly, but insisted they had the authority, and yet were vague when they tried to explain where the authority came from. More extraordinary still was the restrained way in which the high officials of the CIA and of the Eisenhower and Kennedy administrations treated one another. There was no acrimonious exchange of accusation of the sort one might have expected. McNamara, typically, did not want to blame the Agency, and Helms, typically, testified he didn't want "to take refuge in saying that I was instructed to specifically murder Castro. . . ."[37] The claims of both sides were in soft opposition, and the Committee was forced to confess softly in the end that while it had no evidence the CIA had been a rogue elephant rampaging out of control, it also had no evidence that Eisenhower or Kennedy or anyone speaking in their names had ordered the CIA to kill Castro. The only indisputable fact was that the CIA did, in fact, try to do so.

. . .

The plan to kill Castro had its genesis at a strange moment in American history, one in which the top officials of the U.S. government appear in retrospect to have been in the grip of what can only be called a murderous mood. Castro was the target of the most serious and sustained attempt, but he was not alone. In 1960, when Richard Bissell asked his science adviser, Sidney Gottlieb,[38] to undertake research on assassination techniques, and when he first discussed the possibility of killing Castro with the head of the DDP's Western Hemisphere Division, J. C. King, the CIA was also trying to assassinate Patrice Lumumba in the Congo, was at the very least considering the assassination of General Kassem of Iraq, and was deeply involved with a small group of dissidents in the Dominican Republic who were planning to kill Trujillo. In September 1960, Gottlieb prepared a kind of assassination kit which included a lethal biological agent,[39] hypodermic needles, rubber gloves, and gauze masks, and then personally delivered it to the CIA station in Leopoldville, where the local station chief, Lawrence Devlin,[40] had been ordered to kill Lumumba, then in the protective custody of the United Nations.

Not long after, Bissell asked Justin O'Donnell to take over the assassination plot in the Congo, but O'Donnell, a Catholic, refused to do so on religious grounds. When Bissell pressed him anyway, he went to Richard Helms on October 31, 1960, and protested. According to O'Donnell, Helms said he was "absolutely right"[41] to refuse, but left it at that. Helms made no attempt to protest to Bissell or Dulles or anyone else, and when O'Donnell later went to the Congo on another assignment, Helms made no attempt to discover if O'Donnell had changed his mind or if the assassination plot was still under way. This was Bissell's project, and Helms did not intend to interfere.

Later, O'Donnell also protested the assignment to the Inspector General, Lyman Kirkpatrick, who not only supported his refusal but himself went to Dulles to protest. Dulles, who of course knew about the plot and had indeed authorized it, simply listened to Kirkpatrick's protest and thanked him for his views. Despite O'Donnell's refusal—Bissell apparently hoped to talk him around—the attempt continued until events overtook the CIA and Lumumba, probably on January 19, 1961,[42] was murdered by his Congolese enemies.

The CIA's involvement in the attempt to murder Trujillo was less direct, but no less deliberate. The dissidents who first made contact with U.S. Ambassador Joseph Farland during the spring of 1960 openly admitted that they intended to kill Trujillo; that was, in fact, the whole of their plan, and they asked the United States for the weapons they needed. A request for sniper rifles made to Farland at a cocktail party in Ciudad Trujillo was passed on by him directly to the CIA in May 1960, after he had returned to the United States, and was approved by both the State Department and officers at the CIA, including Helms, although the rifles were never actually sent. After Farland's recall the dissidents continued to press his replacement, U.S. Consul Henry Dearborn,[43] for help, specifically asking at various times for two hundred rifles, hand grenades, machine guns, poisons, explosives, and antitank rockets. The only weapons actually delivered, however, were three .38-caliber pistols in March 1961 and three .30-caliber M-1 carbines in April. But after the failure of the Bay of Pigs invasion the Kennedy administration changed its mind, attempted to back off from its support of the dissidents, and refused to pass on some requested machine guns which were already in the CIA station in Ciudad Trujillo. The dissidents elected to go ahead, however, and on May 30, 1961, they ambushed Trujillo's car and killed him, possibly with the pistols provided by the CIA.

But it was the attempt to kill Castro which brought the coldest, most sustained CIA efforts to engineer an assassination. The Church Committee reported that it had discovered at least eight separate plots against Castro of varying seriousness, ranging from an attempt to give him a poisoned wet suit for scuba diving to a more determined effort, through agents recruited by the Mafia, to poison his food. Some of these plots never survived the first serious discussion, but others were pushed forward over a period of years, and although none of them came close to success, it was not for want of trying.

According to Bissell, the first discussion of killing Castro occurred in the summer of 1960, when planning for the invasion of Cuba had already been under way for at least five months. Bissell recalls a vague discussion with J. C. King; they weren't planning a murder, exactly, just walking around the idea. At about that time Howard Hunt, assigned to the Bay of Pigs operation as a political action officer, made a clandestine trip to Havana for a look around and returned with a list of four recommendations. First on the list was Castro's murder. As the operation progressed, Hunt repeatedly asked Tracy Barnes about his proposal for the assassination of Castro. Barnes told him it had been put into "the hands of a special group."[44] On July 21, 1960, Barnes cabled the Havana station to ask if a newly recruited Cuban agent could handle the "possible removal top three leaders"—Castro, his brother Raul, and Che Guevara. The new agent's case officer "swallowed hard" when he read the cable, but the following day Barnes reversed himself and told the station to forget his question.

The "special group" referred to by Barnes was probably one organized by William Harvey, but that organization, never much more than a capability on paper, was not in charge of the early attempts on Castro's life. These had been assigned to the Director of Security, Colonel Sheffield Edwards, in August 1960, following Bissell's discussion with J. C. King. Edwards and another CIA officer[45] approached Robert Maheu, a former FBI agent who had frequently worked for the CIA in the past,[46] and told him the CIA would be willing to pay $150,000 for Castro's assassination. Maheu recommended a Mafia figure named John Rosselli, who agreed to go ahead with the plan, using other Mafia contacts whose gambling interests in Cuba had been confiscated by Castro in 1959. By October, Rosselli had recruited Sam Giancana and Santos Trafficante, who in turn began to recruit Cubans who might do the job.[47]

The Technical Services Division, meanwhile, was working on poisons which might be used for the murder, after Giancana had protested that a gangland-style killing would never work. In a separate but related effort in August 1960, the CIA's Office of Medical Services was given a box of Castro's favorite cigars and told to treat them with a lethal poison. They were ready in October, and delivered to someone in the Agency—it is not known to whom—the following February. The cigars may have been intended for Castro during his trip to the United Nations in September 1960. According to David Wise and Thomas B. Ross,[48] a CIA officer told Michael J. Murphy of the New York Police Department that the Agency planned to assassinate Castro with a box of exploding cigars, but then had changed its mind. Perhaps the box of cigars referred to by Murphy was the same one the Office of Medical Services had treated with botulinum toxin by October 7. Perhaps not. In any event, the Technical Services Division prepared botulinum toxin pills in February 1961, tested them successfully on monkeys, and delivered them to Colonel Edwards, who passed them on to Rosselli in Miami. Late that month or early in March, Rosselli told the CIA the pills had been given to a man in Castro's entourage, but that he had returned them after he lost his job, and with it his access to Castro. A second attempt in April failed when the agent got "cold feet"[49] and after the collapse of the Bay of Pigs invasion the Maheu-Rosselli operation went into a dormant phase.

Early that fall, however, the Mafia plot to kill Castro was reactivated after Bissell, in a meeting with both Kennedy brothers held in the Cabinet Room, was "chewed out" for "sitting on his ass and not doing anything about getting rid of Castro and the Castro regime."[50] This time Bissell bypassed Colonel Edwards and gave the job to William Harvey. Earlier in 1961 Bissell had asked Harvey to organize a unit within the DDP which might recruit agents to carry out assassinations on call—described with the euphemism "executive action," the very phrase, interestingly, which Allen Dulles later used in his memoirs to describe the " 'Murder Inc.' branch of the KGB."[51] Harvey organized the group, and on November 16, 1961, he and Bissell discussed the possibility that ZR/RIFLE, the "executive action" group, might be used for killing Castro. Bissell also told Harvey about the Mafia plot, and later Harvey briefed Helms.

In early April 1962, acting on Helms's explicit orders, Harvey asked Colonel Edwards to put him into contact with John Rosselli, and a few days later the two men were introduced in Miami by the man Edwards had assigned as Rosselli's case officer, James O'Connell. Harvey got off on the wrong foot with Rosselli by telling him to break contact on the Castro operation with Robert Maheu and Sam Giancana. Harvey had apparently decided the two men were superfluous and untrustworthy as the result of an episode eighteen months earlier, in October 1960, when the CIA-Mafia plot was first getting under way. At that time, Maheu, as a favor to Giancana, had hired a private detective to tap the Las Vegas phone of one of Giancana's girlfriends in order to discover if she was being unfaithful to him. The tap was discovered by a maid, the detective was arrested by local police, and Maheu was told to square it or else.

Later, in April 1961, with the permission of Colonel Edwards, Maheu told the FBI that the tap was connected to an operation he had undertaken for the CIA, and Edwards confirmed his story. The problem refused to go away, however, and the following year the Las Vegas wiretap episode helped the FBI to learn the rough outlines of the plot to kill Castro.[52] This all struck Harvey as a perfect example of an operation going out of control, and he decided the first step was to get rid of the clowns, Maheu and Giancana. Rosselli did as Harvey asked, and the two men met again, in New York on April 8, 1962. Before the end of the month Harvey delivered four poison pills to Rosselli in Miami. In May, Rosselli reported that the pills were inside Cuba, and later, in June, that a three-man team had been sent in to kill Castro.

But that was as far as things went. By September 1962, when Rosselli told Harvey another three-man team was to be sent to Cuba, Harvey had concluded the operation was going nowhere. He had run the operation with extreme security; none of the men who even worked for him on Task Force W knew what he was up to, or where he was going when he disappeared for a few days every month or two. Bissell had given him the Rosselli operation, Helms told him to give it a shot, Harvey decided on his own it was a will-o'-the-wisp. In February 1963, already replaced by Desmond FitzGerald as the head of the renamed Special Affairs Staff, Harvey told Rosselli the operation was over. In June the two men had a farewell dinner in Miami, which was "observed" by the FBI. The Bureau's liaison officer with the CIA, Sam Papich, told Harvey that J. Edgar Hoover would naturally be informed. Considering the nature of Harvey's business with Rosselli, this presented something of a problem. Harvey went to Helms, who agreed the best thing was to proceed one step at a time, and not to offer explanations until explanations were necessary. They decided not to inform McCone about the dinner unless Papich told Harvey that Hoover intended to tell McCone about it on his own.[53]

The reason for their coyness with McCone is unclear. According to the written record, Harvey frequently discussed the Rosselli plot with Helms during the eleven months—April 1962 to February 1963—while Harvey was running it, but both men agreed not to tell McCone what they were up to. McCone later claimed that he had known nothing about the assassination plots, and CIA documents on this episode, at least, would seem to bear him out. But a number of CIA people in a position to know, and not only those directly involved, have said in unmistakable terms they found McCone's amnesia hard to credit. He was in a position to know what was going on, and the fact no assassination memos signed by McCone could be found was better evidence of his caution than of his ignorance. Helms in particular, once the investigations began, was to be trapped between McCone's forgetfulness and Harvey's total recall, putting Helms squarely atop the traceable chain of command. So far as the record shows, during the second phase of the Rosselli plot Helms was the man in charge.

Harvey's replacement by Desmond FitzGerald in early 1963, and the scuttling of the Rosselli operation, did not end but only redirected the CIA's attempts to kill Castro. One of FitzGerald's early inspirations was fanciful and impractical, appealing to his temperamental love of the clever and the ingenious. It called for the Technical Services Division to rig an exploding seashell which would be placed on the sea floor in an area where Castro liked to go skin diving.[54] Like many CIA people, in love with the subtle and the artful, FitzGerald was fascinated by gadgets, and resented skeptics who dourly suggested they would cost too much, or would fail to work, or weren't even needed at all. At times he became downright petulant. When Sam Halpern once protested that a fancy new communications device just wasn't going to work, FitzGerald said, "If you don't like it you don't have to come to meetings anymore."

Halpern protested the seashell plan as inherently impossible to control: how could you be sure that Castro would be the one to find it? Besides, the best assassinations do not appear to be assassinations at all, while Castro blowing up on the ocean floor would point a finger directly at the United States. Similar protests had been made about the plan to give Castro a box of poisoned cigars: he might hand them all out to a delegation of visiting schoolteachers. If the idea was to kill Castro, you had to find something which would get him, and no one else.

FitzGerald's ideas weren't turning out any better than such earlier ones as the proposal to provide Castro with a poisoned wet suit to be delivered by James B. Donovan, an American lawyer negotiating the release of the Bay of Pigs prisoners. The Technical Services Division had duly purchased a suit, contaminated the breathing apparatus with tuberculosis bacilli and the suit itself with fungus spores that would cause a chronic skin disease called madura foot. Critics of this plan argued that its authors had neglected the most elementary considerations—for example, the fact that it was in effect a gift from the United States, while the idea was to *keep it secret;* or, then again, Donovan's feelings about being the gift-giver in this plot. If he wasn't let in on the plot, after all, he might try on the suit himself. In the event, Donovan gave Castro a wet suit entirely on his own, and the CIA's wet suit was destroyed.

But FitzGerald did not abandon the problem. Eventually he came up with a serious effort to use a major in the Cuban army, in contact with the

CIA since 1961, named Rolando Cubela.[55] Cubela was on intimate terms with Castro, and often saw and talked to him in his office or at official functions. He and some of his friends bitterly resented the Russian presence in Cuba and felt Castro had betrayed the revolution. From the CIA's point of view he was an ideal conspirator, a man with a public reputation as a leader in the fight against Batista, close to Castro, spokesman for a circle of dissidents, and ambitious. On top of that, Cubela had already proved himself as an assassin. In October 1956 he shot and killed the chief of Batista's military intelligence, Blanco Rico, a deed which haunted him thereafter and even resulted in a nervous breakdown. Rico had been picked as a target not because he was ruthless or cruel, but because he was a fair, temperate man; he reflected credit on Batista as a leader. Cubela was convinced that Rico knew why he was being killed, and believed that Rico had smiled at him at the very moment he pulled the trigger.

The CIA was well aware of Cubela's political and mental history, but decided to use him anyway, since he was ideally situated to engineer the one thing which might actually get rid of Castro—a palace coup. From the beginning, Cubela insisted that a coup had to include Castro's "execution." The word "assassination" disturbed him; he preferred to say he would "eliminate" Castro.[56] At various times he asked the CIA to provide him with exotic assassination devices and more mundane sniper rifles, and the CIA undertook to give him what he wanted. With Helms's approval, FitzGerald met personally with Cubela in Paris on October 29, 1963, despite protests from subordinates who argued that no high CIA official should expose himself in such a manner. Cubela had requested a meeting with Robert Kennedy, but FitzGerald satisfied him with the claim that he was Kennedy's personal representative.[57] Not quite a month later, on November 22, 1963, Cubela's case officer gave him a specially prepared "pen" which might indetectibly inject a deadly poison into Castro; the CIA recommended Blackleaf 40, a widely available toxin which Cubela was to procure on his own.[58] The assassination report says that Cubela dismissed the poison pen as a toy and insisted the CIA could surely come up with something "more sophisticated."[59]

At the end of the meeting the CIA case officer learned that Kennedy had just been shot in Dallas. During the ensuing tension and uncertainty the Cubela plot was allowed to lapse for a matter of months. Christmas 1963 came and went; nothing happened. But early in 1964 the plotting was revived, and two caches of arms—one in March, the second in June—were landed in Cuba for Cubela's use. That fall Cubela requested a sniper rifle, and the CIA told him the United States no longer wanted to have any role in the "first part"[60] of his plan—that is, in Castro's assassination. Why did the CIA change its mind at this late date? The record provides no persuasive reason, but it may have been because Lyndon Johnson was quietly sounded out—so quietly he may not have known what he was being asked—and it became evident that he wanted no part of assassination. It is certain that Johnson had not known about the earlier Mafia plots, and that Helms did not tell him about the CIA's relationship with Cubela during Johnson's own tenure as President. The important point here is that the CIA's direct involvement in Cubela's assassination plans came to an end at a time when it was probably clear they did not have the President's sanction.

But the CIA did not give up on Cubela altogether. Secretly the Agency put him into contact with Manuel Artime, the Bay of Pigs commander who had been ransomed late in 1962 and who was continuing to mount operations against Cuba with the CIA's aid. Artime provided Cubela with the requested rifle, but a plan to use it in the early spring of 1965 came to nothing. That June the CIA learned (from listening devices, among other sources) that Cubela had been talking freely about his plans to kill Castro during his frequent trips to Europe. So freely, in fact, that one CIA officer in Rome, who had maintained several contacts with Cubans on his own, also picked up word of Cubela's boasting. The warnings of the counterintelligence people were finally heeded. The CIA broke off all contact with Cubela and warned Artime that he was not to be trusted. With that, the CIA's attempts to murder Castro came to an end.

The subject of assassinations is a painful one for CIA people. On no other subject do they fight so hard to keep the secrets, and in particular the secret of presidential authority. On this point the testimony of high-level CIA officials before the Church Committee was elusive in the extreme. Helms in particular remembered next to nothing, and dismissed the rest. He never believed the Mafia plot was going anywhere. He let Harvey proceed to see if Rosselli really had assets in Cuba. The idea he might kill Castro was secondary, an afterthought. Cubela's plan to "eliminate" Castro was indulged to see if he and his associates could really put anything together in the nature of an honest plot. The Committee had obtained the Inspector General's report of 1967, but the memories of those involved halted pretty much where the documents came to an end. The Church Committee's report was detailed and lawyerly, proceeding point by point in a logical and yet a confusing manner; discussions of closely related events are sometimes scores of pages apart.

But even when one has reassembled the story in its proper order, as it happened,[61] the picture one gets is fragmentary, occasionally vivid and complete on minor points, more often bald and out of focus. The primary reason for this was the tendency of CIA officials to suffer memory lapses on all those points, which were very numerous, that had not survived in the files. In addition, of course, Eisenhower, both Kennedys, both Dulleses, General Cabell, and other high officials had died. Livingston Merchant and Admiral Arleigh Burke were too ill to testify. J. C. King and Sheffield Edwards both died during the investigation before they could testify fully. Some of the lower-level officials—William Harvey, Justin O'Donnell, Sidney Gottlieb, and others—testified at length but did not really know who gave the orders or when, and would not have presumed to ask.

Harvey, for example, said he did not mention the Rosselli plot at a meeting of the Special Group Augmented on May 3, 1962,[62] because "if" this was a White House operation, then "it was up to the White House to brief the Special Group and not up to me to brief them, and I would have considered that I would have been very far out of line and would have been subject to severe censure."[63] Harvey also said he remembered Bissell telling him that the Executive Action project had been urged on him by the White House, but that it would have been "improper" of Harvey to ask who, specifically, did the urging, and "grossly improper" of Bissell to have told him if he had asked.[64]

Even outside the confines of official hearing rooms, CIA people are uneasy with the subject of presidential authority for the assassination plots. Sometimes more than uneasy. The idea of killing a foreign leader did not seem to bother them in itself. People get killed in war; why should Castro's life count for more than anyone else's? Wouldn't the world have been a better place if Hitler had been killed in 1933? Lumumba was an unpredictable charismatic; you couldn't deal with him, and the Congo wouldn't have settled down as long as he was around. Trujillo was a bloodthirsty tyrant. What about all those people Castro put against the wall? Did they count for less than Castro himself?

CIA officials do not insist that it was an American duty to eliminate these men, but the idea of assassination itself does not much trouble them.[65] The wisdom of the undertaking was something else again. It was stupid, foolish, ridiculous, unworkable; worse than a crime, a blunder—the regular spiel. Everyone had his own adjective, none of them flattering. The best they could muster by way of justification was "the climate of the time," the Kennedys' hysteria on the subject of Castro, the eager willingness of the Cubans who were recruited seriatim to do the job. But all the same, they shook their heads in dismay.[66] More than anything else it seemed to be the sheer difficulty of assassination—that is, of a genuinely secret assassination—which left them wondering.

But on the question of presidential authority there is no such equanimity. An exception said that no one in CIA doubted for a minute that Eisenhower and Kennedy "jolly well knew," but others, more closely involved, did more than simply squirm in their chairs. Several different men, in fact, showed dramatic signs of psychological stress in discussing this point.[67] It is inconceivable that Richard Helms would ever betray himself in so unmistakable a manner. But in his testimony before the Church Committee, Helms more than once revealed an uncharacteristic degree of irritation with the Committee's insistent return to the question of authority. He was being as clear as he could: the Kennedys wanted Castro out of there, the CIA did not go off on its own in these matters, the Agency was only trying to do its job. What more could he say: Senator, how can you be so goddamned dumb? *This isn't the kind of thing you put in writing.*

And despite the Church Committee's diligent search, they never did find anything in writing. The Committee did learn, however, of three separate occasions when one or both Kennedys discussed the assassination of Castro in a manner indicating it lay heavily on their minds. The first time occurred in March or early April of 1961, just before the Bay of Pigs invasion, at the height of the first Rosselli effort to poison Castro, when President Kennedy asked his friend Senator George Smathers what he thought the Latin American reaction would be to the assassination of Fidel Castro. Smathers said he told Kennedy the murder would be blamed on the United States and on Kennedy, personally, and that he, Smathers, was therefore against it. According to Smathers, Kennedy immediately responded that he was against it, too.[68] But in mid-March 1961, before their conversation, the CIA had already given botulinum toxin pills to Rosselli in Miami, and a second batch was to be handed over on April 21.

The elimination of Castro was raised again by the Kennedys—in more ambiguous terms this time—during a meeting with Bissell in September 1961. Bissell later described the meeting to his Cuban desk officer in mid-October. He said he had been called to the White House and "raked stem to stern" by both Kennedys in the Cabinet Room, and by Robert Kennedy in particular. McGeorge Bundy, who told the Church Committee that ordering an assassination would have been "contrary to everything I know about their character," also said that when there "was something that they really wanted done, they did not leave people in doubt."[69] Larry Houston, who had briefed Robert Kennedy about the early, pre–Bay of Pigs Mafia plot, on May 7, 1962, made the same point: "If you have seen Mr. Kennedy's eyes get steely and his jaw set and his voice get low and precise, you get a definite feeling of unhappiness."[70] The Cuba desk officer got a clear impression from Bissell's description of what he'd been told by the Kennedys: they wanted the CIA to get rid of Castro, and they meant *get rid of Castro*.[71]

Castro continued to be on the Kennedys' minds that fall. On November 9, 1961, the Attorney General took Tad Szulc, then a reporter for the *New York Times*, to meet the President, who asked Szulc, "What would you think if I ordered Castro to be assassinated?" Szulc told the President it wouldn't work, and that the United States should not do such things. Kennedy said he and his brother felt the same way. In Szulc's notes of the conversation, made the same day, he wrote: "JFK said he raised question because he was under terrific pressure from advisors (think he said intelligence people, but not positive) to okay a Castro murder. Sed he was resisting pressures."[72]

Despite all the evidence gathered by the Church Committee, it never found anything like an order to kill Castro in writing, and it never found a witness who would confess explicitly that he had received such an order in person. The Committee's response to the incomplete record was to leave the question of authority hanging. Must we do the same? Lacking a smoking gun in the form of an incriminatory document or personal testimony, we can reach no firm or final conclusion, but at the same time the available evidence leans heavily toward a finding that the Kennedys did, in fact, authorize the CIA to make an attempt on Castro's life. The evidence is particularly persuasive on two points. First, President Kennedy's conversations with Senator Smathers and Tad Szulc on the subject of assassination both occurred at times when the CIA was actively trying to kill Castro with the aide of the Mafia. Second, the briefing of Robert Kennedy by Lawrence Houston and Sheffield Edwards elicited a very narrow response from Kennedy. The facts surrounding the briefing, held on May 7, 1962, are extremely complex,[73] but at its heart the episode is a simple one: a case of the dog that didn't bark. Houston told the Committee that Kennedy's anger was directed at the CIA's use of the Mafia. He made the same point even more emphatically to me. "Kennedy was mad," he said. "He was mad as hell. But what he objected to was the possibility it would impede prosecution against Giancana and Rosselli. He was not angry about the assassination plot, but about our involvement with the Mafia."[74] Perhaps Kennedy did not know the whole story,[75] Houston conceded, but he added: "All I know is that [Robert] Kennedy knew about one of them [i.e., one of the assassination plots] in very great detail."

The record is clear, then, that Kennedy was thoroughly briefed about the details of an attempt to murder Castro during his brother's presidency. The record is clear that the attempts to kill Castro continued. And the record is clear that despite his knowledge of the earlier attempt, Robert Kennedy did not protest to the CIA, to its director John McCone, to Helms, or to anyone else in the Agency for that attempt. He was mad about the use of the Mafia. Period. Would he have kept his mouth shut, and done nothing, if he had discovered that the CIA, answerable to his brother, had tried to murder a foreign leader without his brother's approval? It seems unlikely.

That was the first time the dog didn't bark. The second time occurred during the Church Committee's investigation, when Kennedy administration officials might have been expected to be publicly furious at the CIA—an executive agency, as Helms often reminded Congress when he was director—for undertaking anything so fundamental as an assassination without the President's explicit approval. Instead, they said the Kennedys they knew would never have done such a thing, and left it at that. Why were they so complaisant? Well, you can push a man keeping a secret just so far.[76]

This leads to a second question: Why did the CIA keep the secret, if we are inclined to believe there was a secret to keep? There are two probable reasons for this, and it is hard to know which deserves the greater weight. One is the tradition that secret services take the heat. The assassination report explicitly states that the Special Group Augmented was at least partially intended as a means of insulating the White House from involvement in Operation Mongoose. In addition, the concept of plausible deniability refers not only to intelligence tradecraft—that is, to the imposition of secrecy sufficient to halt even exposed operations from being traced back to the United States—but also to the insulation of the President himself, if worse should come to worst. In one of his very few public speeches Helms said, "The nation must to a degree take it on faith that we too are honorable men, devoted to her service." This statement has since been the subject of much ironic comment, and indeed any intelligence officer's claim to honor must be precisely defined to escape the charge of hypocrisy. But several people who knew Helms well said that he took his loyalty to the Presidents he had served seriously, that he felt responsible for their reputations, and that he was not about to betray their trust in him to keep the secrets.

But there is another reason CIA officials have referred only obliquely to the origin of the orders to kill Castro: they have no proof. The orders were never written down or signed. Any CIA officer who said he'd been told to kill Castro by either Kennedy or his advisers would find himself facing a great many formidable enemies indeed, without many friends to come to his aid. It would be his lonely word against that of a host of much better-known men. The CIA officials who know when the orders were given, and when, and in what words, not only don't want to betray their explicit pledge to keep quiet, they do not quite dare. They would be destroyed in the process.

The Inspector General's assassination report, ordered by Helms on March 23, 1967, and delivered to him in installments beginning on April 24, was apparently a very thorough document. It has never been published, but the Church Committee's frequent reference to it, on almost every point concerning the attempted assassination of Castro, suggests the Committee found it invaluable. The Inspector General, Jack Earman, apparently had as much trouble as the Committee when it came to the question of presidential authority, and even with regard to the roles of Allen Dulles and John McCone, but the actual plots themselves were all there, at least in outline, from the preparation of poisoned cigars in the summer of 1960, down to the final termination of all contact with Rolando Cubela five years later.

On May 10, 1967, Helms went to the White House to give Lyndon Johnson the answers to the questions he'd been asked seven weeks earlier. The only account of that meeting is Helms's own. He says he described the IG's conclusions, and that Johnson said, " 'Then you were not responsible for Trujillo?' 'No.' Correct answer. 'Diem?' 'No.' Correct answer. 'Castro, he's still alive, okay.' " At the same meeting Helms also told Johnson about the mail interception program "and some other things that were going on." Johnson's response to that was equally laconic; he just nodded and said something along the lines of, "But be careful, don't get caught."

Johnson's private response to what he'd been told must be partly inferred. A lifetime in Washington, where he'd found every story to have three or five or seven sides—anything but two—had inclined him to look for hidden explanations. He had, in fact, something of a conspiratorial turn of mind. He'd once suspected a connection between John F. Kennedy's murder and the assassination of Diem in South Vietnam. Helms started him thinking along a different track. If he was laconic in response during Helms's briefing, he was apparently putting the threes and fives together in his mind, and what he came up with was a conviction "we were running a damn Murder Incorporated in the Caribbean."[77]

Johnson had already told his aide Marvin Watson he was convinced that something more than Lee Harvey Oswald on his own was involved in the Kennedy assassination, a remark Watson passed on in a phone call to Cartha DeLoach of the FBI on April 4, 1967, whence it disappeared into the maw of J. Edgar Hoover's files. And the President made himself quite explicit to television newsman Howard K. Smith sometime before leaving the White House eighteen months after Helms's briefing. "I'll tell you something that will rock you," Johnson said, clearly thinking of what he had learned from Helms. "Kennedy was trying to get Castro, but Castro got to him first."[78]

There is no evidence that Johnson knew of the attempts on Castro's life before the spring of 1967; the very fact he asked Helms for a report indicates he did not. His remarks to others later indicate the impact of what Helms told him, and it might be wondered why he had nothing to say about the Inspector General's conclusion that the plots had lasted until the spring of 1965, well into his own presidency. But then Johnson never saw the Inspector General's report; he may not even have known it existed on paper. There was only one copy, a draft, and Helms did not bring it with him to the White House meeting on May 10. What he brought were some handwritten notes, obtained by the Church Committee, which asked Helms why the notes carried the story only up until mid-1963, about the time Harvey was having a farewell dinner with Rosselli in Miami. Hadn't Helms told Johnson about the poison pen and the guns given Rolando Cubela? "I just can't answer that, I just don't know," Helms answered. "I can't recall having done so."[79]

After his meeting with Johnson, Helms held on to the Inspector General's report for a couple of weeks, then returned it to Jack Earman with a written order. Earman was to keep the draft, but that was all he was to keep. The IG's working papers were to be destroyed. Every scrap. Every transcript of an interview, every memo, every note made by the investigators. The draft which Helms had read went into a safe, his briefing notes neatly attached to the front, and it stayed there, untouched and unread, until William Colby learned of its existence in 1973.

Chapter 10

The President is the sun in the CIA's solar system. The cabinet secretaries are usually political figures in their own right, with constituencies and interests which sometimes conflict with the President's, and the Washington bureaucracy is a great sullen rock which has seen Presidents come and go. But the Central Intelligence Agency and its director serve the President alone.

American Presidents are figures of unusual power, king and prime minister rolled into one. Their relations with men who also want to be President can be stormy, but they are figures of almost romantic appeal to the lesser men of power in Washington. They are drawn toward him; they hope to gain his confidence, to exercise the power only he can bestow, to share his hour in history. The primacy of Presidents is the great fact in the CIA's daily round. If the President does not trust or value the Agency's product, then the paper it produces ceases to have weight in government councils and it might as well unplug its copiers, because it is only talking to itself. The first duty of the DCI, then, not by statute but as a matter of practical reality, is to win the trust, the confidence, and the ear of the President. Allen Dulles had Eisenhower's but lost Kennedy's. John McCone had Kennedy's, at least in the beginning, but lost Johnson's, and Helms was close enough to the top during McCone's tenure to watch it happen.[1]

McCone had not been Kennedy's first choice. General Maxwell Taylor had been considered for a while, and after him came a New York lawyer and sometime public servant named Fowler Hamilton, but Dulles and Bissell told Kennedy they thought that choice "appalling." Roger Hilsman in the State Department had recommended Helms for the job, but Helms had no national reputation, he was not yet even DDP, and the recommendation got nowhere. Then Roswell Gilpatric in the Defense Department suggested the name of John McCone, a rich and conservative Republican who had been head of the Atomic Energy Commission and who offered Kennedy protection on his right flank. McCone was given the job.

McCone was an intelligent and decisive man by nature, with an instinctive sense for the exercise of power in Washington. His initial act was to escape a tacit trap laid (with the best intentions) by the President's Foreign Intelligence Advisory Board (PFIAB). One of Kennedy's first responses to the Bay of Pigs disaster had been to establish PFIAB, a renamed version of Eisenhower's Board of Consultants on Foreign Intelligence Activities, which Kennedy had disbanded when he took office. In July 1961, PFIAB submitted a report to Kennedy recommending a partial dismemberment of CIA and absorption of the DCI directly into the White House. While Kennedy was considering PFIAB's recommendations that fall, McCone moved into the DCI's suite in the new CIA complex in Langley, Virginia, the very day he took office to make sure he was not entrapped in the White House, which would have meant only that somebody else actually ran the CIA.

But McCone's aggressiveness, and in particular his confidence on questions of policy, strained his relations with the White House almost from the beginning. One source of that strain was Kennedy's instructions on January 16, 1962, telling him to exercise his statutory authority over the entire American intelligence community, an order which immediately threw him into conflict with the much larger military intelligence services. These had been brought under a single roof by Robert McNamara when he created the Defense Intelligence Agency (DIA) in 1961, a move much opposed by many CIA officers who felt that the military, always an adversary, would now be harder than ever to deal with. (Helms had surprised some of his fellow CIA officers—Richard Bissell in particular—by his indifference to the move.)

Early battles between the CIA and the DIA, in which McCone frequently had to call on McNamara for muscle, focused on Soviet missilery and the overall direction of overhead (by this time mostly satellite) reconnaissance programs, developed by the CIA but then turned over to the Air Force for funding and operational control. The Air Force told the CIA all it wanted from the Agency was ideas; the CIA insisted on broader authority over reconnaissance targets and the development of new gadgetry, since the instruments were designed to find what you were looking for, and the CIA and the Air Force were not always looking for the same things.[2]

According to CIA people who worked for McCone, McNamara was irritated by McCone's assumption of bureaucratic equality, and by his frequent appeals for help. He also resented McCone's tactless suggestions that McNamara (who prided himself on nothing if not management expertise) was himself guilty of administrative failures. In particular McNamara resented a McCone letter (based on studies of the DIA by the CIA's office for National Intelligence Programs Evaluation) which urged a complete reorganization of defense planning. A CIA officer who saw the letter said it was "typically McCone" in its tone: I know of your concern that the Defense Department is running a lot of useless, sloppy, irrelevant, redundant intelligence programs and I think you ought to address yourself to this problem.[3]

But the real erosion of McCone's position in the Kennedy administration grew out of his single most dramatic success. In the two weeks between July 26 and August 8, 1962, eight Soviet ships docked in Cuba, and this fact, coupled with reports of military construction and the presence of five thousand Soviet military specialists on the island, resulted in a McCone report to Kennedy that "something new and different"[4] was going on. But what? Senator Kenneth Keating had been charging publicly that the Soviet Union was planning to put nuclear missiles in Cuba. Kennedy had publicly denied it, and Roger Hilsman, in a background briefing held at the State Department on August 24, said the Russian cargoes were probably intended for "the improvement of coastal and air defenses. It may include surface-to-air missiles, which the Soviets have already supplied to Iraq and Indonesia."[5] Five days later a CIA-run U-2 flight over western Cuba photographed a construction site with two surface-to-air missiles (SAMs) already in place.

At a meeting with the President on August 22, McCone had said the Russian shipment of SAMs to Cuba might mean Keating was right. He had nothing to go on but instinct; there was as yet no hard intelligence. But what else could explain a construction site protected by SAMs? Shortly thereafter McCone remarried and left the United States for a three-week honeymoon in France. While he was gone U-2 flights continued over Cuba, but, for various reasons, there were none between September 5 and October 14 over the area of western Cuba where SAM sites had been definitely identified on August 29. Thus the Kennedy administration privately feared the worst while continuing to insist in public that it had no reason to believe missiles were being emplaced. But it didn't really know, because the CIA could find no evidence of what was, in fact, going up on those construction sites.

From France, McCone had remained in close touch with Agency headquarters. CIA agents in Cuba (the very ones sent in or recruited by William Harvey for Operation Mongoose) were reporting bits and pieces of information, but nothing decisive.[6] When facts are lacking, the best CIA can muster is an educated guess, and in mid-September McCone ordered Sherman Kent, chairman of the Board of National Estimates, to produce a Special National Intelligence Estimate on what the Soviets were doing. By this time McCone was all but certain in his mind that they had to be introducing missiles. There was simply no other way to explain the elaborate defense of the construction site in western Cuba. Sherman Kent and the BNE met on September 19, argued the matter for the better part of a day, but concluded (without dissent) that the Soviets were unlikely to have embarked on such a risky venture. Kent's arguments were basically two: the Russians had never done anything of the sort before, and the risks were too great. *It didn't make sense.*

In France, McCone was informed of the BNE's conclusion, but he refused to accept it. He was sure they were wrong. On the following day,

September 20, McCone ordered Kent to reconvene the BNE and go over the question yet again. This time the BNE had a report from a Cuban refugee who had seen what was apparently a missile tailfin assembly on a highway. (Helms had established a special group to collate reports from agents in Cuba and from refugee debriefings in Florida, which were then handed over to Ray Cline at the DDI.) A second report quoted a pilot in Castro's air force, who had said, "We will fight to the death and perhaps we can win because we have everything, including atomic weapons."[7] But even with this additional (albeit short of definitive) intelligence, Sherman Kent and the BNE reached the same conclusion: the Soviets simply would not do anything so uncharacteristic, provocative, and unrewarding.

Kent was wrong. A U-2 flight over western Cuba on October 14 brought back photos of unmistakable missiles.[8] Kent said later that not he but the Russians had been wrong: they had miscalculated a miscalculation. Even as excuses go, it was a little weak. McCone, however, had not been wrong. He had been one of the first officials in the administration to warn Kennedy what he was facing, his agency had provided the President with timely information once the missiles were identified (the CIA had actual training manuals for the operation of that particular missile, provided by Penkovskiy), and McCone had been a strong presence in the meetings of the National Security Council's Executive Committee (called Excom), which Kennedy had established to deal with the crisis.[9] McCone, in short, had every reason to feel he had enhanced his relationship with the President.

But it didn't work out that way. Once too often he remarked on his prescience about the Soviet missiles in Cuba. Of course he had been right, at a time when the CIA as a whole and Russian experts like Charles Bohlen and Llewelyn Thompson, and even the President himself, had been wrong, but he paid a price for being right. McGeorge Bundy once told a CIA official, "I'm so tired of listening to McCone say he was right I never want to hear it again." McCone's contact with the President dwindled. It was understood around town that McCone saw Kennedy once a week,[10] but this apparently ceased to be true after the missile crisis. He continued to work closely with the President's brother, but he lost his access to the President.

A further source of coolness between McCone and the administration, one which ended his tenure as DCI under Johnson, was Vietnam. On this McCone was quite outspoken. His predecessor Allen Dulles always made something of a fetish of his neutrality on policy questions. The DCI's job was to provide the facts, period. When the question of what to do about X came up at National Security Council meetings, Dulles would make quite a point of backing off. "Well, that's none of my business," he would say with a straight face. "That's the business of the Secretary of State."[11] Who was, of course, his brother. Laughter around the table.

McCone was not so coy. "Mine is not a policy job," he said, "but when asked I'll give my opinion." Give it he did, according to many accounts, strongly, confidently, and often. A CIA officer who knew McCone well said he was apt to have a martini at lunch and talk, and one of the things he talked about was policymaking in foreign affairs. In McCone's mind there ought to be a kind of troika—three equals where policy questions were concerned, a band of intimate brothers, the President *primus inter pares*, of course, closely supported by the Secretary of State and the Director of Central Intelligence. It made sense; who else had so many facts at his fingertips?

One of the issues on which McCone spoke freely was what to do about the President of Vietnam, Ngo Dinh Diem, whose autocratic style had long been an embarrassment to the U.S. government. But McCone, accompanied by Helms, had visited Diem in Vietnam in the spring of 1962, was impressed by his authority, and thought the United States should stick with him. That same year William Colby, then the Saigon chief of station, was asked to make a study of possible political alternatives to Diem. Colby, about to leave Vietnam to replace Desmond FitzGerald as chief of the DDP's Far East Division, was a friend of the Ngo brothers, and he concluded there was no one who might take their place.

Then, in mid-1963, the anti-Buddhist repressions of Diem and his brother, Ngo Dinh Nhu, brought the problem to a point of crisis. A small group in the State Department, centering principally on Averell Harriman, Roger Hilsman, and Michael Forrestal, was in favor of removing Diem from the scene. Colby's replacement as CIA's chief of station in Saigon, John Richardson, was especially close to Nhu (whose private police, the South Vietnamese Special Forces, had been organized, trained, and funded through Richardson), but the Agency was also in close contact with dissident generals through a CIA officer named Lucien Conein.[12]

Harriman, Hilsman, and Forrestal took a hard line where Diem was concerned: they wanted to support a coup which would remove him. Hilsman had fought in guerrilla campaigns in Burma during the war and thought he understood why the Vietcong were winning. His expertise did not earn him many friends; McGeorge Bundy, for example, used to call him "the confident guerrilla."[13] But with Harriman's help his arguments got a hearing in the White House, and the Counter-Insurgency Group set up by General Taylor frequently argued the wisdom of encouraging an anti-Diem coup in the spring and early summer of 1963. McCone's argument, supported by Richardson in Vietnam and Colby in the Far East Division, was that Diem was irreplaceable. Who is the alternative? McCone would ask. We've examined this question very carefully and we can't identify anybody else who could hold the country together. Diem may be a sonofabitch, but he's *our* sonofabitch. Do you know of anybody? Have you got a name? Come on now; who?

McCone particularly infuriated the State Department people with his references to "the oriental mind," something they were supposed to know all about, and they argued back that McCone was looking at the problem the wrong way round. The question wasn't who would replace Diem, but can we win with him? The answer, Hilsman and Harriman insisted, was no. These were high-level meetings, frequently including the Attorney General, Robert Kennedy, but despite all the argument the group never resolved the question. Despairing of carrying the CI Group, Hilsman and Harriman conducted an end run in August 1963. On August 21, Nhu ordered his Special Forces to attack Buddhist pagodas throughout the country, at a time when there was no American ambassador in Saigon, since Frederick E. Nolting had already left, and his replacement, Henry Cabot Lodge, had not yet arrived. The CIA reported the dissident generals' fear that they were about to become the target of assassination teams sent out by Nhu. Harriman and Hilsman immediately concluded that this time Diem had gone too far. They drafted a cable giving Lodge explicit orders to proceed with a coup, using the generals in contact with Conein, and then cleared the text by phone with President Kennedy, who was in Hyannis Port on Cape Cod. Hilsman and Harriman then "informed" other officials of the President's decision. Failing to find McCone at the CIA (and no doubt not having tried very hard), Harriman instead got hold of Richard Helms, who was at dinner with Bruce Moore, a Washington sculptor. Harriman read him the cable, and Helms responded, "It's about time we bit this bullet."[14]

When McCone and Taylor learned of the cable on Monday morning they were furious; the CI Group had never agreed to this. It was a horrible mistake. As it turned out, the generals' coup scheduled for the end of August was called off when the generals concluded that Nhu had learned their plans, but an important step had been taken all the same. McCone continued to resist plans to remove Diem, although he surrendered to Lodge's request for the recall of John Richardson as chief of station in Saigon. When one of the Vietnamese generals told Conein in early October 1963 that the generals now had three alternative plans for Diem's overthrow—of which one was assassination—McCone cabled the station[15] and explicitly ordered them to withdraw their recommendation of the plan to Lodge. At about the same time McCone met with both of the Kennedys and again urged them not to support a coup. "My precise words to the President, and I remember them very clearly, was that, 'Mr. President, if I was manager of a baseball team, I had one pitcher, I'd keep him in the box whether he was a good pitcher or not.' "[16] But Kennedy had had enough, and when the Vietnamese generals told Conein on October 28 that the moment was at hand, Kennedy allowed Lodge to assure them of American political support. The coup took place on November 1, 1963, and before it was over both Diem and his brother Nhu were murdered.

General Taylor was at the White House when news of the killings arrived. The President's advisers were all seated around the table in the

Cabinet Room, McCone among them, and they watched in silence as Kennedy received the news. In his memoirs Taylor described the President's response in a single sentence: "Kennedy leaped to his feet and rushed from the room with a look of shock and dismay on his face which I had never seen before."[17]

The following day, at McCone's regular morning meeting with the CIA's Deputy Directors and other top officials, McCone described Kennedy's reaction to the news of Diem's murder. According to Lyman Kirkpatrick, who was present at the meeting, the reaction of those in the room was not entirely sympathetic. The coup was Kennedy's idea; his administration authorized it despite repeated CIA objections. What did he expect? When a coup takes place you can't control it. Helms, too, wondered at Kennedy's dismay, and concluded later that the President had not fully understood what he had ordered. He'd okayed the August cable which first put the U.S. Embassy on the side of the dissident generals, and when a coup appeared imminent at the end of October he authorized McGeorge Bundy to tell Lodge to use his own judgment—a roundabout way of saying, It's okay with me. But Kennedy's dismay at the result convinced Helms that Kennedy had never quite hoisted this operation aboard: he'd said yes, without fully realizing what he was saying yes to.[18]

In the aftermath of Kennedy's own murder, just three weeks after Diem's, McCone was at first an almost daily visitor to the White House. But thereafter his access to President Johnson slowly tapered off. One reason was that he tried too hard; he asumed an interest in his work on Johnson's part which Johnson didn't have. The President was content with one-page summaries of foreign intelligence, and Rusk and McNamara gave him all the advice on foreign policy he wanted. McCone gradually discovered that he was not wanted as an intimate at the White House.

But Vietnam played a role here, too. Johnson inherited a large American commitment to Vietnam which was not working, and from its beginning his administration was involved in an unending attempt to decide what to do about it. Johnson tried to finesse the problem. He would take the minimum steps his advisers insisted were necessary to avoid defeat—retaliation for the Tonkin Gulf incidents in 1964, bombing of North Vietnam in February 1965; an American combat role and large numbers of additional troops that summer—but he tried to limit and disguise his steps even as he took them, as if he might slip the country invisibly into war, and save Vietnam on the sly. The result of these incremental steps was a big war in the end, just as if he had decided to go the limit in the beginning, but Johnson apparently preferred not to admit where he was heading at the various stages along the way. Naturally this involved a good deal of argument with those who preferred a clear decision, but it is hard to win an argument with a President, and McCone lost his.

McCone's position throughout this period was the one least congenial to Johnson: a strong conviction of the importance of victory, combined with deep pessimism about how we were doing, ending with a claim that only strong measures might recover the situation. Of course Walt Rostow and the Bundy brothers and a lot of other high officials contributing to the running debate in 1964 and early 1965 were leaning toward strong measures too, but McCone went further than most. In one meeting after another he insisted that if the United States was going in, it had to go in all the way. After a joint trip to South Vietnam with McNamara in March 1964, McCone told the President he thought McNamara's proposals were "too little, too late,"[19] and he continued to argue in favor of a major U.S. intervention, if there was to be intervention at all.[20]

The issue came to a head at a meeting of the National Security Council on April 1, 1965, in which Johnson approved a gradually escalating program of air strikes against North Vietnam and a shift in the mission of U.S. troops in South Vietnam to give them an active combat role. This decision marked the moment when the conflict became an American war, and Johnson stressed that he wanted no official announcement of what was in fact a turning point. McCone was at the meeting, and the following day he circulated a memo to leading government officials, arguing forcefully that the measures were again "too little, too late":

I feel that the . . . decision is correct only if our air strikes against the North are sufficiently heavy and damaging really to hurt the North Vietnamese . . . this program is not sufficiently severe. . . . With the passage of each day and each week, we can expect increasing pressure to stop the bombing. This will come from various elements of the American public, from the press, the United Nations and world opinion. Therefore time will run against us in this operation and I think the North Vietnamese are counting on this. Therefore I think what we are doing is starting on a track which involves ground force operations which, in all probability, will have limited effectiveness against guerrillas. . . . However, we can expect requirements for an ever-increasing commitment of U.S. personnel without materially improving the chances of victory. . . . In effect, we will find ourselves mired down in combat in the jungle in a military effort that we cannot win, and from which we will have extreme difficulty in extracting ourselves. Therefore, it is my judgment that if we are to change the mission of the ground forces, we must also change the ground rules of the strikes against North Vietnam. . . . If we are unwilling to make this kind of decision now, we must not take the actions concerning the mission of our ground forces for the reasons I have mentioned.[21]

This had been McCone's position for nearly a year and a half, and it was not what Johnson wanted to hear. After he left office he would quote

McCone's comments in a vindictively selective manner,[22] stressing Mc-Cone's support for really heavy bombing, and omitting every reference to its corollary—McCone's opposition to a U.S. role in the ground war, if Johnson was not prepared to go the limit.

But by that time McCone's weight within the administration had shrunk to zero. The President had pointedly dropped him from the regular Tuesday lunches, where Johnson met with his chief foreign policy advisers, a clear signal to Washington that McCone was no longer a member of the inner circle. McCone tried every way he could to win the President's ear and confidence, and for one brief moment thought he detected a new warmth when Johnson invited him to fly up to New York for Herbert Hoover's funeral on October 26, 1964. "He was as excited as a kid with a new toy," said one CIA official who worked with him. But the gesture had been hollow; Johnson apparently figured that Hoover was a conservative Republican, McCone was a conservative Republican, it was only right to invite the one to the funeral of the other. Eventually McCone realized the situation was irretrievable. "I've been trying to get Johnson to sit down and read these papers," McCone told an aide, referring to the CIA's Annual Survey of Soviet Intentions and Capabilities. "When I can't even get the President to read the summaries, it's time for me to leave."

Johnson's search for a successor to McCone was a major effort which ranged widely and lasted many months. Much of it was conducted by Clark Clifford, a Washington lawyer with almost unique access to every Democratic President since Truman, and John Macy, the head of the Civil Service Commission. Clifford and Macy thought Johnson had entrusted the job of finding McCone's replacement to them. Among the many names suggested to them was that of Richard Helms, who had the backing of a group within the CIA. Another faction supported Lyman Kirkpatrick, the Executive Director/Comptroller. McCone himself told Ray Cline, the Deputy Director for Intelligence, that he had recommended Helms, Kirkpatrick, and Cline. It's pretty clear, then, that the CIA was plumping for an intelligence professional, and preferably one who had worked his way up through the ranks. Clifford and Macy, however, were also considering outsiders like General Taylor (for the second time) and Roswell Gilpatric. But in the end Clifford and Macy were as shocked as everyone else by Johnson's abrupt announcement that the new Director of Central Intelligence would be Admiral William F. Raborn, a fellow Texan and prominent Johnson supporter during the 1964 election, who had a reputation for rapport with Congress and a hard-driving administrative style. His mastery of the PERT system—Program Evaluation and Review Technique—was credited with the success of the Polaris missile system, and Johnson apparently felt Raborn would run the CIA in the same way.

It has been a rule since the CIA's founding in 1947 that the two top jobs be divided between the military and the civilians, which meant that Raborn's Deputy Director for Central Intelligence would have to be a civilian. Johnson's choice was Helms, who thus became the first CIA officer to rise up through Agency ranks to one of the top jobs. (The significance of this fact was not lost on Lyman Kirkpatrick; he resigned, moved to Narragansett, Rhode Island, and took a teaching post at Brown University.) Raborn and Helms both flew to the LBJ ranch in Texas, where one of the dinner guests on the night of April 10 was Senator Eugene McCarthy, a sponsor of legislation to give the Senate Foreign Relations Committee a role in oversight of the CIA. McCarthy, a sometimes whimsical man, slyly asked Helms to identify the wine at dinner. Helms could not. Then McCarthy asked if Helms knew the sauce on one of the dishes, or the name of a flower in the centerpiece. Helms didn't know the answers to those questions either. McCarthy nodded in a knowing manner, and remarked that James Bond would have done better.

But Helms's mind was on other things. During that visit the President told him that if everything worked out he might expect to succeed Raborn in the fullness of time. There was no promise, but the possibility was not foreclosed. Later both Raborn and Johnson attempted to claim that Raborn had agreed to serve only one year, but the magnitude of the search makes this improbable. It is more likely that Johnson expected Raborn to be his DCI, and his swearing-in ceremony at the White House on April 28, 1965, was conducted as a major affair.

Johnson took it into his head to invite all the top officers of the CIA to the ceremony, the Deputy Directors, the head of the Board of National Estimates, a whole raft of people who had only the shadowiest existence in official Washington. One of the men in the crowd was James Angleton, who made a fetish of his anonymity. It was a source of infinite pain to Angleton when Kim Philby described him unflatteringly in a few lines in his memoirs, published a couple of years later.[23] "Oh, my God!" said Angleton as photographers trooped into the room. "Those people are going to take our picture!" He squeezed himself back into a corner, trying to hide his tall, lanky frame behind a much shorter fellow CIA officer. Then President Johnson entered the room, glanced around, and strode directly to Angleton's corner.

Angleton's is a face of exquisite refinement, finely chiseled, striking and expressive. His long mouth is so sensitive to inner mood that he can express two emotions at the same time, registering a dourness close to despair at one end, while turning up in sardonic comment at the other. But when President Johnson planted himself directly in front of Angleton, and the cameras all focused in, Angleton's face expressed nothing whatever but pure horror.

But even before his swearing-in, Raborn had been settling into his new job at the CIA, where he let everyone know he would like to be addressed as

"Admiral." Things went badly from the start. The day Johnson decided to send Marines into the Dominican Republic, Ray Cline was in the Admiral's office and heard him sign off the conversation with, "Aye, aye, Sir."[24]

Raborn's brusque military style, his complete lack of background in intelligence, and his plain ignorance about foreign affairs ("Which tribe in Liberia are the oligarchs?") all worked against him. What Johnson wanted from the CIA in Santo Domingo was up-to-the-minute information, not advice, and Raborn tried to give the President what he wanted. He overruled the objections of Helms and Desmond FitzGerald, who had replaced Helms as DDP, and ordered the placement of DDP officers directly in the centralized Operations Center, which Raborn had established along military lines to move reports from the Dominican Republic to intelligence "consumers" throughout Washington in as little as an hour. Until that time the DDI and DDP had always maintained a double-arm's-length distance from each other. That particular innovation apparently worked well, but Raborn's orders bruised professional sensibilities. Even worse, he simply did not know his way about the compartmentalized world of intelligence, and he was slow to learn. Arriving in his office one morning he flipped a switch on his interoffice communications system and got Drexel Godfrey, head of the Office of Current Intelligence.

"How are we doing down in the Dominican Republic?" Raborn asked.

Godfrey was puzzled; he hesitated.

"What's the word from all our agents?" persisted Raborn.

"Admiral, I think you've got the wrong office," said Godfrey. "This isn't Operations."

"Oh," said Raborn. "Sorry. I've got so many buttons up here I never know which one to push."

Raborn's tenure as DCI was unhappy and short. The CIA rejected him the way a human body rejects a transplant. Stories of Raborn's bumbling and incompetence began to find their way into the Washington press, evidence that the Georgetown party circuit was working overtime. A typical story from that period describes Raborn giving a talk on management technique to CIA officers in the Langley auditorium, a talk filled with characteristic Raborn humor—"I'm not one of those people who puts on his pants in the morning and thinks the whole world is dressed"—and a rambling, confused review of PERT and Polaris. It didn't make sense and it had nothing to do with intelligence. On leaving the auditorium one CIA officer turned to a friend and said, "I'm beginning to wonder if Polaris really works."

But the stories had a common theme: Raborn's dangerous combination of self-confidence—the result of years of knowing exactly where he stood in the chain of command—with the ignorance of world affairs of a man who knows only what he reads in the papers, and doesn't always read the papers. One of the Admiral's worst blunders came at a morning staff meeting where he opened the discussion with a remark that he'd just read something interesting about the Russians and the Chinese not getting along. There was dead silence around the table, according to a CIA official present at the meeting. A dozen top CIA officials stony-faced.

"No, listen, fellows, this really is really important." He turned to Ray Cline, the Deputy Director for Intelligence, and said, "I want you to do a paper on this."

Ray Cline had been studying the Sino-Soviet split ever since the Chinese had criticized the Russian response to an uprising in Poland in 1956. Perhaps no other subject had been so relentlessly analyzed, or fought over with greater heat by the estimators, in the previous ten years. They had been over this and *over* this. There was hardly a skeptic left in Washington.[25] The Sino-Soviet bloc was dead. Raborn had just announced that the world was round. Cline said politely that this matter had already been the subject of a good deal of study and there was, truly, no need of a special paper at this time.

But Raborn persisted. He wasn't sure Cline grasped the gravity of what he had discovered, and he didn't quite like Cline's independence. Cline repeated himself: the DDI had studied this subject very thoroughly. Raborn grew pugnacious. "You're not taking this seriously. I want you to send me up your papers on this. I want to see all these studies."

Cline's patience broke. "Well, what do you want me to use," he snapped, "a *wheelbarrow?*"

There were several reasons for Raborn's quick failure as DCI. One was a testy hostility on the part of the Agency itself, which jumped on every error and broadcast it throughout official Washington. CIA's pride was at stake; a lot of Agency people felt they had proved themselves during the Cuban missile crisis, they wanted an intelligence professional who might restore the reputation and élan which had existed under Dulles, the great white case officer, and they resented the imposition of someone who insisted most when he knew least. Not long after Raborn left, the wife of another naval officer, sitting next to a CIA man at dinner, asked him with real anger in her voice, "How could you have done that to poor Red Raborn?" To a degree she was right: intelligence officials had discredited Raborn in a merciless way. But the CIA had been right too: Raborn had been hopeless.

The theory behind the DCI's neutrality on questions of policy is soundly based on the observable fact that in policymaking, as in war, the first casualty is truth. When men gather to decide the fate of nations, there ought to be somebody in the room whose first loyalty is to the facts. The National Security Act of 1947 appointed the DCI to be that man. But there is a difference between neutrality[26] and ignorance, and on a question like the Dominican Republic, for example, Raborn was not simply neutral on what ought to be done; he plain didn't know.

Not long after Johnson sent in the Marines, Raborn asked Ray Cline to accompany him to a National Security Council meeting at the White House. When they arrived, they discovered that the meeting had been canceled because the President was in bed with a sore throat. "Nevertheless," Cline writes in his memoirs, "when the President learned we were there, he asked us to come over to the mansion into the bedroom, where a steamer was going and the day's newspapers were flung all over the place. The always strenuous Johnson was plainly not very ill, he was bored and he was worried about the Dominican Republic. At his request I briefed him in detail on the most recent developments. He then said, plaintively, 'How the hell can I get my troops out of this damned mess?' Admiral Raborn cheerfully observed, 'Maybe Dr. Cline has a suggestion!' "

Cline did. Not long before, Desmond FitzGerald had remarked to Cline that one man who might straighten out the mess was a former Dominican President, now in exile in New York, named Joaquin Balaguer. Cline told Johnson the troops would have to remain until a non-Communist took over. Johnson asked who that might be. Cline listed all the possibilities, dismissed them one by one for some reason or another, and concluded that Balaguer was the best man.

"That's it," said Johnson. "That's our policy. Get this guy in office down there!"[27]

It is not often we can pinpoint the moment when the light bulb goes on in the presidential mind, but before Johnson's policy was put into effect, Ray Cline was long gone from Washington, and Raborn was on his way. Cline had collided once too often with the Admiral, and in 1966 he went to Helms and asked for a station overseas. Helms, who exercised unprecedented control over the Agency during his tenure as DDCI, arranged for Cline's appointment as chief of station in Frankfurt, Germany.[28] But before he left Washington, Cline went to see Clark Clifford at the President's Foreign Intelligence Advisory Board and told him that Raborn had to go. He told McGeorge Bundy the same thing. Cline's push was only one of many; the word was out on Raborn, and early in the spring of 1966 Johnson told reporters on one of his walking press conferences about the White House grounds that Raborn was only an interim choice, the Admiral had only agreed to serve a year and now his time was up. He, Johnson, always told Raborn to bring Helms with him when he came to the White House because Helms was being groomed for the DCI's job. Maybe so, but another reason for Helms's appointment was the fact that only a year earlier Johnson had turned the country upside down looking for a Director, and the President had no appetite for going through the whole process again. In June of 1966, the first intelligence professional to work his way up through the ranks to the top, Helms was given the job.

Chapter 11

W hen Richard Helms was sworn in as Director of Central Intelligence on June 30, 1966, a lot of CIA people thought—that is, some hoped, and some feared—that the Directorate for Plans would run away with the place.[1] And indeed, according to one CIA officer, Helms as Director "ran the DDP out of his hip pocket,"[2] especially after Thomas Karamessines succeeded Desmond FitzGerald in 1967, but that was as far as it went. The DDI's fear that it would be at the beck and call of the DDP never came to pass, and while it is true that the CIA had simply grown too large to be run in such a narrow way, the real reason might be rendered down to a single word: Vietnam.

During his brief tenure Admiral Raborn had established a new position to deal with Vietnam, the Special Assistant to the Director for Vietnamese Affairs. The first man to fill the post had been Peer De Silva, a former chief of station in Saigon who had been badly injured when a terrorist's bomb had shattered the window glass in his office in the U.S. Embassy. In September 1966, Helms offered the job to a young analyst named George Carver, a short, blond-haired graduate of Yale with a gift for lucid exposition. "Carver," said one colleague, "can do more, with less evidence, than any other man I've ever known." When Helms asked Carver to succeed De Silva he said, "I can worry about Indochina or I can worry about the rest of the world. I want you to worry about Indochina."

Vietnam was Lyndon Johnson's obsession and nemesis, just as Cuba had been Kennedy's, and left-leaning "neutralists" the *bête noire* of Foster Dulles. In 1965 Johnson made two great decisions with regard to Vietnam: to initiate a campaign of bombing the North in February, and to send large numbers of American troops in July, thereby committing the United States to an American war. For the next three years his administration was under unremitting pressure from the Pentagon to extend the bombing, increase the number of troops, and (to a lesser extent) widen the war into Cambodia and Laos. Johnson gave ground on all three points, but slowly, reluctantly, even grudgingly. The war in Washington was fought with paper—CIA studies from the Office of Current Intelligence and the Board of National

Estimates, Draft Presidential Memorandums written by White House advisers, memorandums from the State Department amd the Joint Chiefs of Staff, cables from the ambassador in Saigon and the Commander of U.S. Forces in Vietnam (COMUSMACV), Defense Intelligence Agency studies, the papers of the United States Intelligence Board. The Defense Department's "History of United States Decision-Making on Vietnam," known as the Pentagon Papers,[3] four volumes and 2,800 pages in length, only lightly skimmed the surface of the ocean of paper with which official Washington waged the war. The heart of that great argument which lasted from July 1965 through March 1968—just thirty-two months—endlessly circled the two questions Johnson had opened rather than closed by his decisions in 1965: How much bombing? How many troops?

The reason for all the argument is deceptively simple: Johnson had committed the United States in effect to a military victory, but no one really knew how that was to be accomplished. The initiation of the bombing and the dispatch of troops came in response to fears of Saigon's imminent collapse in the late spring of 1965—one of the few intelligence assessments of the war on which there was genuine agreement—but there was no clear understanding of how the bombing was expected to "work," or how the troops might "win." The focus of CIA and other studies until that time had been on peripheral questions, such as the possible Soviet or Chinese response to American escalation. The bombing decision in particular had been based on nothing much better than Johnson's instinct—admittedly forged in endless official discussion—that it would demonstrate his resolve, "hurt" the enemy, somehow work. McNamara's more schematic justification was that it would bolster morale in the South and make the war more "costly" for the North, but he admitted later that neither the CIA nor the Pentagon had demonstrated in detail how the bombing would raise the "cost" to an "unacceptable level," or even if bombing could do it at all. The serious studies all came after the fact; the paper war followed the shooting war, and if Helms was to a degree distracted from the operational problems of secret intelligence collection, the subject of his special expertise and first allegiance, it was because the CIA was drawn willy-nilly into the larger paper war in Washington. Not long after Helms became DCI, McNamara got Johnson's permission to ask CIA for an ongoing study of the effectiveness of the bombing, a decision which infuriated the Pentagon and the Defense Intelligence Agency, who resented CIA's intrusion into the details of military operations. From that time forward, CIA was at the heart of the great argument.

Throughout Johnson's presidency the position of the CIA was remarkably consistent. In the first year of the big war the Agency, like the administration itself, had been vaguely hopeful. Thereafter, with few exceptions, it said—sometimes baldly, more often tentatively—that the bombing wasn't "working": it had neither broken Hanoi's resolve to press on with the war, nor severed, nor even much constricted, Hanoi's supply lines to the South. In December 1965, under pressure from the Joint Chiefs of Staff for approval of air strikes against the port of Haiphong and petroleum storage facilities, McNamara asked for a CIA study of the likely results. The answer came from Helms, the acting DCI in Raborn's absence, on December 28: "Although there presumably is a point at which one more turn of the screw would crack the enemy resistance to negotiations . . . we do not believe the bombing of the Haiphong facility is likely to have such an effect."[4] But, Helms said, it would make it harder for Hanoi to continue the war, it would increase the difficulty of moving supplies to the South, and it would reduce industrial production in the North. Wider bombing wouldn't win the war, exactly, but it would hurt.

This was a flaccid strategic notion. Von Clausewitz never argued that pain had military utility. He said the enemy's capacity for war, its armies and logistical base, was the proper target of military operations. But Johnson's ground rules in Vietnam, and especially the principle of no invasion of the North, excluded the possibility of actually destroying the enemy forces. Thus American strategy was necessarily reduced to an attempt to convince Hanoi the show wasn't worth the candle. Certainly Hanoi had shown no evidence of flexibility in this regard, but in the first year of the big war perhaps CIA, like the Pentagon, McNamara, and the President himself, felt that the awesome capacity of the Air Force to deliver bombs might turn the trick.

The following March, at the height of a renewed debate on bombing petroleum storage facilities, CIA came as close as it ever would to saying the bombing might really work. It dismissed bombing results until that time as insignificant, blaming the "highly restrictive ground rules," and more or less openly recommended mining of Haiphong and heavier bombing of the upper half of North Vietnam in a punitive campaign with "the will of the regime as a target system."[5]

In the immediate aftermath of the petroleum storage air strikes on June 29, 1966, both the CIA and the DIA were enthusiastic about the results, but by September 12 the CIA had changed its mind. The effect of the strikes had been marginal. Thereafter the CIA never again promised much result from the air war, nor, for that matter, did McNamara. CIA's position gradually jelled around a single strategic assumption: Hanoi intended to exhaust U.S. patience with the war, and no amount of bombing could do enough damage to force them to call it off.[6] Paper after paper—on proposals to hit Haiphong, or to concentrate on lines of communication (LOCs), or to restrict the bombing to the southern panhandle below the 20th parallel— ended with the CIA's belief the step would not "decrease Hanoi's determination to persist in the war."[7]

In a May 1967 study, typical of many, CIA said: "Twenty-seven months of U.S. bombing have had remarkably little effect on Hanoi's over-all strategy in prosecuting the war, on its confident view of long-term Communist prospects, and on its political tactics regarding negotiations. The growing pressure of U.S. air operations has not shaken the North Vietnamese leaders' conviction that they can withstand the bombing and outlast the U.S. and South Vietnam in a protracted war of attrition. Nor has it caused them to waver in their belief that the outcome of this test of will and endurance will be determined primarily by the course of the conflict on the ground in the South, not by the air war in the North."[8]

In another study from the same period, the CIA put its case even more strongly: "Short of a major invasion or nuclear attack, there is probably no level of air or naval actions against North Vietnam which Hanoi has determined in advance would be so intolerable that the war had to be stopped."[9]

But the CIA was not the only agency to contribute its opinion, and the running argument touched on just about every aspect of the war. Its flavor is well captured in a two-page document discovered by the Defense Department's historians in the files of John T. McNaughton, a Defense Department strategist, who listed the major points of disagreement in mid-1967 between Cyrus Vance, McNamara's deputy; General Earle Wheeler of the Joint Chiefs of Staff, the CIA, the President's National Security Advisor Walt Rostow, and the State Department's Bureau of Intelligence and Research (INR).

DISAGREEMENTS

1. Westmoreland-McNamara on whether Course A [a specific bombing program] would end the war sooner.

2. Vance-CIA on the ability of NVN to meet force increases in the South.

3. Wheeler-Vance on the military effectiveness of cutting back bombing to below the 20th parallel, and on whether it would save U.S. casualties.

4. CIA believes that the Chinese might not intervene if an invasion of NVN did not seem to threaten the Hanoi regime. Vance states an invasion would cause Chinese intervention. Vance believes that the Chinese could decide to intervene if the ports were mined; CIA does not mention this possibility.

5. CIA and the mission [i.e., the U.S. Embassy in Vietnam] disagree with Vance on whether we have achieved the cross-over point and, more broadly, on how well the "big war" is going. One CIA analysis, contradicted in a later CIA statement, expresses the view that the enemy's strategic position has improved over the past year.

6. CIA-INR on whether Hanoi seeks to wear us down (CIA) or seeks more positive victories in the South (INR).

7. INR believes the bombing has had greater effect than does CIA.

8. Vance and CIA say we have struck all worthwhile targets in NVN except the ports. Wheeler disagrees.

9. CIA cites inflationary pressures and the further pressure that would be caused by Course A. Vance says that these pressures are under control and could be handled if Course A were adopted.

10. Rostow believes that a call-up of reserves would show Hanoi that we mean business and have more troops coming—Vance believes that a reserve call-up would lead to divisive debate which would encourage Hanoi. Would not the call-up indicate that we had manpower problems?

11. Bundy-Vance disagreements on the degree to which we have contained China, whether our commitment ends if the SVNamese don't help themselves, the NLF role in political life, regroupees, and our and Hanoi's rights to lend support to friendly forces in SVN after a settlement.[10]

Throughout the paper war Helms was a bureaucratic general, chairman of the United States Intelligence Board where CIA, DIA, NSA, and the State Department's INR fought over official estimates of how we were doing in Vietnam; a regular participant in meetings of the National Security Council and of ad hoc White House groups which gathered periodically to debate the next step, whatever that might be; and after the June 1967 Arab-Israeli war, a regular participant in Johnson's Tuesday lunches. Helms, in short, was part of the inner circle, one of the dozen top officials on whom the President genuinely depended. He was not an intimate like McNamara or Rostow, perhaps, but he won the confidence and the ear of the President to a degree which had eluded John McCone, and the best single explanation for Helms's success was the CIA's handling of intelligence during the Arab-Israeli war.

At the end of May 1967, when the crisis was clearly approaching the stage of hostilities, Arthur Goldberg, the U.S. ambassador to the United Nations, vigorously protested to Johnson that intelligence estimates of Israeli strength were overly optimistic. He wanted Johnson to back off from his even-handed diplomatic efforts to force a compromise and support Israel, which was facing enemy armies on three fronts. This Johnson did not want to do. He asked the CIA for a special study of Israeli military strength. Sherman Kent and the Board of National Estimates produced one within a day, and on the evening of May 26, Helms delivered the results to Dean Rusk and Walt Rostow at the State Department. CIA said the Israelis would win a war within a week to ten days. "Do you stand by this?" Rusk asked.

Helms said he did.

"Well, to quote Fiorello La Guardia," Rusk said, "if this is a mistake, it's a beaut."

Rusk himself felt that the two sides were more evenly matched than that, and Johnson, presumably at Rusk's urging, asked Helms to go over the question yet again. The second estimate took forty-eight hours, during which the Agency won the agreement of the American military that the Israelis would indeed win within ten days. (The actual estimate was apparently a week, but the CIA's paper stretched the period a bit to be on the safe side.)[11] Based on CIA's estimates, Johnson resisted pressure for all-out public support of Israel. It was the confidence and accuracy of CIA's estimate—the Israelis won in six days—that persuaded Johnson to make Helms a regular participant at the Tuesday lunches. (But he could also be skeptical of the CIA as an institution. Going through a huge Middle East policy review not long after the war, in which CIA described "rising" Soviet influence, etc., etc., Johnson turned to an aide and wearily remarked, "Same old shit, isn't it?")[12]

The opinions Helms carried in his briefcase were never his own: he knew what his Agency knew, and thought what his Agency thought. No one hired him to figure these things out by himself, and Johnson apparently never took him aside and said, "Dick, have a drink, and tell me: How are we *really* doing out there?"

If the President had, and if Helms had answered, he might have said what he once remarked to a CIA colleague: "We just can't fight this kind of war, not against a fanatically committed bunch of guys who don't need anything except a bag of rice on their backs." He might have said that a land war in Asia was bound to be a loser, that we would have done better to fight in Vietnam as we fought in Laos, through local proxies; that the big war we had chosen to fight instead wasn't big enough, the restrictions on bombing and troop levels left us with one hand tied behind our backs—all of which Helms believed. He might have told the President what he told Tom McCoy, a CIA officer who had worked for Colby in the DDP's Far East Division before resigning to campaign for Eugene McCarthy. In June 1968, McCoy went to see Helms at the CIA to ask if the military was right about the effectiveness of the bombing.

"Sure," said Helms, "as far as it goes. Look: before the bombing they used to send three men south to get two in place. Now they have to send five. We're willing to lose planes, they're willing to pay in manpower. So it doesn't make a particle of difference. In terms of bodies, it makes a difference. There are more dead bodies. But in terms of net result, it doesn't make a damn bit of difference."

But Johnson never asked Helms for his private opinion, and Helms never volunteered it. That wasn't his job. His job was to receive questions on paper—narrow, exact questions: How many trucks does Hanoi have? How many of those trucks can we destroy with X level of air strikes? Y level? Z level?—and to respond with answers on paper. He was in charge of the men who worked out the equations in the algebra of war. It was a bloodless war of men in well-tailored suits around waxed conference tables, a briefcase full of paper propped against each chair. Helms was not a man who brought his fist down on the table and raised his voice, who pressed opponents with debaters' questions or answered criticism with sarcasm. He was the coolest of advocates, presenting his Agency's views on paper, defending them on paper, a paper general in a paper war.

The real war was in Vietnam. There the CIA fought with all the weapons developed during the activist years of the Cold War, making its first major effort not long after the French defeat at Dien Bien Phu. When the big war began in 1965, CIA stations around the world were drained of manpower to build up strength in Saigon, operating under the general cover name of the Office of Special Assistance (OSA) to the U.S. Embassy. Eventually the total exceeded a thousand, with two or three times that many contract agents, who ran a broad range of programs divided between intelligence gathering and various forms of political and covert action. One of the largest of the latter was not in Vietnam but next door in Laos, where the CIA organized an army of Meo tribesmen under General Vang Pao to resist the Pathet Lao and their North Vietnamese allies from the Meos' traditional refuge in the highlands surrounding the Plaine des Jarres.

As the war in Vietnam grew, the self-defense and intelligence-gathering activities of the Meo army grew along with it, gradually shifting toward more aggressive military actions and spoiling operations intended to harass North Vietnamese truck and foot traffic along the network of back-country trails and dirt roads known as the Ho Chi Minh Trail. From a few hundred Meos organized into small guerrilla units by half a dozen CIA officers in 1962 the Meo operation expanded to a thirty-thousand-man army with battalion-size units and operations, a fact which inevitably elicited a larger North Vietnamese effort as well. After Thailand became an important base for U.S. air strikes against North Vietnam, the Meos were given the job of defending Air Force beacons used as navigational aids on Laotian mountaintops. From a little war there grew a big war. From a limited effort to help the Meos defend themselves against the Pathet Lao, the CIA's program grew into a much larger effort to use them as an asset in the war against the North Vietnamese. The result was the destruction of the Meos as a people. Of perhaps a quarter of a million Meos in 1962, only a pitiful remnant of ten thousand escaped to Thailand in 1975.[13]

There was a moral issue involved in the CIA's Meo program, but it wasn't the one raised in the Senate Foreign Relations Committee in the early 1970s, when Stuart Symington, among others, expressed surprise, shock, and anger at their discovery of the CIA's "secret war." Symington had been thoroughly briefed as a member of the Senate Armed Services Committee as early as September 1966, when George Carver first described Vang Pao's army as part of the CIA program in Laos. Later, on a trip to Southeast Asia, Symington was the houseguest of the chief of station in

Vientiane, Ted Shackley, and he personally invited Shackley to testify before the Armed Services Committee on October 5, 1967. At the end of that briefing he specifically praised the Laotian program as a sensible way to fight a war. The CIA was spending in a year, Symington said, what the U.S. Army was spending in a day in Vietnam.

Paramilitary operations in Vietnam itself were on a somewhat smaller scale. In the early 1960s, CIA began to organize military units among the Montagnards in Vietnam's central highlands, a people traditionally held in contempt by the Vietnamese, and who were instinctively hostile to the Vietcong (and later the North Vietnamese) military units operating in their vicinity. But in the summer of 1963 the Montagnards pressed Saigon for autonomy, on the edge of full-scale military revolt (with the tacit support, it was suspected, of the Special Forces advisers whom CIA employed to run the program) and the American military assumed direct control of the operation.

The CIA was also in charge of cross-border operations to collect intelligence and harass the enemy in Cambodia and Laos, as well as more ambitious, but less effective, clandestine operations against North Vietnam itself. These latter were conducted much in the manner of earlier programs to put teams inside the Soviet bloc and mainland China. Small groups of armed men were dropped by air or sent in over the beach along the North Vietnamese coast to radio back intelligence, conduct small-scale operations which might force Hanoi to look to its own defenses, and even—a forlorn hope—encourage outright resistance to the regime. The fate of the teams which went north made the program a cynical one; not many men came back, and not much was gained. When President Johnson ordered a halt to all air operations (with the exception of reconnaissance flights and leaflet drops) over North Vietnam at the end of October 1968, resupply drops to the CIA teams were ended as well. Nine teams in place—forty-five Vietnamese—were simply abandoned. The CIA told them by radio that there were "problems with resupply," but these were being "worked out" and they should "hang in there."[14] Perhaps Johnson did not know of the men he had sent and then abandoned; CIA either failed to tell him or failed to insist that he listen. One by one the team radios fell silent. Some of the men surrendered; some were tracked down and killed; some died of starvation. The last team went off the air in 1970.

But these operations, some of them run in conjunction with the military, were only a side show to the war in the South, where the CIA's main efforts were in so-called nation-building programs—including organization of a Vietnamese Special Forces, and of two national police forces, the seventeen-thousand-man Special Branch, which operated in the cities, and the fifteen-thousand-man National Police Field Force in the countryside. Their job was pacification, a term the CIA resisted because it echoed the

French efforts of the first Indochina war, but there was something inevitable about the word and the CIA used it just as the French had, with the same results.

CIA was supposed to have special expertise in clandestine, paramilitary, and counterinsurgency warfare, and the Agency assumed the leading role in the "people's war" in the South—the attempt to fight the Vietcong on its own ground. Beginning in 1964, the CIA organized two programs to fight the war in the countryside, forty-man People's Action Teams which would work in the nation's 10,500 hamlets, and smaller Counter-Terror Teams, six to twelve men each, who would carry the war to the enemy. These penetrated deep inside Vietcong territory, occasionally making public appearances in villages which had not seen a representative from Saigon for years, but more often setting up routine ambushes or raiding suspected enemy camps. Their name quickly proved an embarrassment—counter-terror?—and they were rechristened as Provincial Reconnaissance Units.[15]

As always, from small offices big programs grow. Desmond FitzGerald, who was involved with Vietnam as chief of the DDP's Far East Division until 1963, and then as DDP between 1965 and his death in 1967, used to complain that the military did not understand Asians, or the nature of paramilitary warfare, or the utility of small programs with precise but limited aims and commensurate means. As soon as CIA got one hundred Vietnamese working effectively on some particular problem, McNamara and the military would note the first promising results, attempt to multiply the program tenfold, and end by wrecking it. Before FitzGerald died he told the Washington journalist Stewart Alsop of a meeting with McNamara in which the Secretary of Defense remarked, "You know, it's hard to make sense of this war."

"Mr. Secretary," FitzGerald said, according to Alsop's account of the conversation, "facts and figures are useful, but you can't judge a war by them. You have to have an instinct, a feel. My instinct is that we're in for a much rougher time than your facts and figures indicate."

"You really think that?"

"Yes, I do."

"But why?"

"It's just an instinct, a feeling."[16]

But McNamara was not a man who held much brief for instinct, and besides, the time for hunches was over. When Alsop published an unattributed remark by FitzGerald about McNamara's obsession with quantifying the war, McNamara immediately guessed its source and was angry. "What's FitzGerald making a crack like that for?" he asked Helms. FitzGerald remained as DDP, but he was no longer invited to brief McNamara on CIA's war, and the trend toward ever bigger programs continued.

One reason, ironically, was McNamara's resistance throughout 1967 to pressure for wider bombing. He promoted a plan for a 160-mile-long "electronic barrier" to block North Vietnamese infiltration in the area of the demilitarized zone (DMZ), separating the two Vietnams,[17] and he supported plans for a much larger and more aggressive pacification program in the South. The existing, badly coordinated programs run by the CIA and the State Department through AID were pulled together into an Office of Civilian Operations in late 1966, and then reorganized the following May under military command. Named Civilian Operations and Rural Developments Support (CORDS), the pacification effort ballooned rapidly. While General William Westmoreland was in overall charge, CORDS's first chief (known as deputy to COMUSMACV for CORDS) was Robert W. Komer, a former analyst with the CIA's Board of National Estimates, and many of its constituent programs remained under effective CIA control. One of them was the CIA-conceived and implemented Intelligence Coordination and Exploitation Program (ICEX), an effort to collect information systematically on the National Liberation Front's political apparatus throughout the South, called the "Vietcong infrastructure," or VCI, so that it might be "neutralized." Renamed Phoenix by Komer, translating from the Vietnamese words *phung hoang*, the assault on the VCI eventually became CIA's single most notorious program of the entire war.

The idea was to identify the VCI—tax collectors, supply officers, political cadre, local military officials, and the like—and then to send Provincial Reconnaissance Units (PRUs) or police teams to get the men or women singled out. This sometimes involved straightforward arrest in the cities, more often a paramilitary raid into NLF-controlled or contested hamlets in the countryside. Ideally, "neutralization" meant capture, so that each link in the chain might lead to others, but in practice death was the usual result, sometimes in the course of a firefight as a PRU team would shoot its way into an enemy camp at the first light of dawn, and sometimes through assassination pure and simple. Vietnamese veterans of the Phoenix program tell of creeping into a man's house in the night and shooting him with silenced pistols as he lay asleep in his bed.

But the system was only as good as its information, and the information was often dated, dishonest, or plain wrong. The main source was prisoners, and the CIA established a nationwide system of interrogation centers—one in each of Saigon's forty-four provinces, another in each of the country's four military regions, and three in Saigon itself. These quickly won a reputation for brutality.[18] Komer established quotas for the Phoenix units in South Vietnam's 242 districts, with the inevitable inflationary results. One was indiscriminate killing during hit-and-run raids, with every dead body arbitrarily labeled "VCI" after the fact. One CIA officer said that a good way to get an idea of what was going on was to check Phoenix program statistics for the number of Vietcong "nurses" who had been neutralized. The VC must have had more nurses than soldiers. Another method of meeting quotas was to "identify" the "VCI" killed during normal military operations; in effect, local Phoenix units simply borrowed the military's kills for its own quotas. This proved a mixed blessing, as the practice naturally inflated the number of victims which the CIA was later charged with deliberately assassinating. There have been attempts to disassociate CIA from Phoenix on the grounds that CORDS was taken over by the military in May 1967, but in fact CIA conceived and organized the program, the Regional and Provincial Officers in charge were all CIA, the interrogation centers were created and financed by CIA, and every chief of the Phoenix directorate[19] at the CORDS headquarters in Saigon was CIA, until the program was technically turned over to the South Vietnamese after the Paris peace accords in early 1973.

No man has been more closely associated with the Phoenix program, nor has defended it with greater force and conviction, than William Colby, who had been the CIA's chief of station in Saigon between 1959 and 1962.[20] His preoccupation with Vietnam continued when he succeeded Desmond FitzGerald as chief of the Far East Division in January 1963. In December 1967, Helms intended to appoint Colby the new chief of the Soviet Division, but his plans were overturned at a White House meeting with President Johnson and Robert Komer. Johnson generously offered Komer anything he wanted for the pacification program, and Komer said he wanted Bill Colby. "He can have him, can't he?" said Johnson to Helms. What could Helms say? He said yes, and in March 1968 Colby returned to Saigon as Komer's deputy at CORDS. Later that year he replaced him. "The difference between Komer and Colby," said Tom McCoy, who had been Colby's chief of political and psychological operations in the Far East Division, "was that Komer was always trying to convince you pacification was working, but Colby was trying to make it work."

Like certain French officers who had fought in Indochina and then tried to apply what they'd learned in Algeria, Colby became obsessed with the techniques of "people's war." Colby and Desmond FitzGerald were both covert political operators by temperament, but FitzGerald was an elitist, Colby a populist. One of FitzGerald's ideas in the mid-1960s was a plan to moderate Hanoi's war policy with the help of the Russians. At that time China was blocking the Russian shipments of war material to North Vietnam. FitzGerald proposed that the United States arrange an alternate route through Laos and Thailand in return for a Russian pledge to force Hanoi to back away from its policy of total victory in the South. This may sound incredible at first, but the plan was not too different from the Russian-American accommodation on Laos. Colby did not have a similar belief in high-level arrangements. He wanted to defeat the NLF on its chosen ground, among the people.

Colby's instrument was the Phoenix program. He actually wrote the Phoenix directive which Saigon's President Nguyen Van Thieu was finally pressured into adopting in July 1968, and Colby later conceded officially that Phoenix had killed—or at least recorded the deaths of—20,587 VCI.

South Vietnamese estimates, put together at a time when Saigon was trying to convince the Americans of its energy and enthusiasm, went as high as 40,000. Colby also conceded there had been "excesses"—local Vietnamese officials who used PRUs as a source of political power, units which engaged in shakedowns or released captured NLF prisoners for bribes or pursued personal vendettas under the guise of going after the enemy. But Colby never accepted the criticism of some that Phoenix failed. Quite the contrary. The North Vietnamese won the war in a conventional military campaign, Colby said after the collapse of Saigon in April 1975, because they had lost the war in the countryside. The VCI had all but disappeared; CIA won the people's war.

The CIA was everywhere in South Vietnam, a principal arm of the American government, an instrument for waging war, but it was also a political weapon. In theory the Americans were in Vietnam at the invitation of the government in Saigon, but after the removal of Diem in 1963 the government in Saigon was often a government in name only. Nguyen Khanh, who had seized power from the generals who had ousted Diem, had a slender base in the Vietnamese army but was otherwise unsupported. The air force general who replaced him, Nguyen Cao Ky, was at first not much better, and the big American war often tottered at the edge of a political vacuum. One of the CIA's jobs was to coax a genuine South Vietnamese government into being, to bring order from the political chaos, to end the factional struggles which made the Saigon governments weak and indecisive and threatened the ultimate horror: the rise to power of a neutralist faction which would strike a deal with the NLF and invite the Americans out, just as their client predecessors had invited us in. But this was no easy job. The very instability of the Saigon governments made them narrow and oppressive, little better than cliques bound by ties of family and personal loyalty who saw every broadly based popular movement, not just the NLF, as a threat to their hold on power. The effect was to promote the legitimacy of the NLF, which provided the only alternative to the military men who ruled in Saigon.

In a meeting with Colby in 1966, when Khanh's government was tottering from crisis to crisis, Desmond FitzGerald urged him to find some way to encourage a broad-based popular movement, untainted with the neutralism of the Buddhists, which might offer a legitimate democratic opposition to Khanh in the northern cities of Hue and Danang. After the meeting Colby asked Tom McCoy if he had any ideas, and McCoy said sure, he could go up to Hue and find some smart Vietnamese with ideas and a few followers. Given a little money, this fellow would hire some organizers and send them out on scooters with leaflets. Meetings would follow; support would grow; a small office would be opened. If McCoy could find a man with the capacity to draw ten people on his own, with a little help the fellow would have five hundred in three months.

And at that point the Saigon government would grow alarmed and throw the leaders of this embryonic movement into jail. There they would remain unless McCoy persuaded the chief of station in Saigon to persuade Ambassador Lodge to persuade President Johnson to persuade Dean Rusk to send a stiff note to Saigon telling Khanh to *let those guys go*.

"You know Rusk isn't going to do that," Colby said.

"And that's why I'm not going to Vietnam," answered McCoy.

The CIA involved itself in Vietnamese politics to an extraordinary degree, but it never achieved much success in the attempt to create even the semblance of healthy adversary politics, which is not something one country can easily do for another. Instead CIA's involvement turned into an intelligence-gathering operation aimed at the host government itself, as a way of keeping the Americans abreast of the chaotic and always potentially explosive political maneuvering of their clients. This was something Colby was reluctant to do, according to several accounts. James Angleton in particular had urged him to push a counterintelligence program to cut the hemorrhage of secrets to the North Vietnamese and the NLF. The first step was to penetrate the Saigon government itself, something Colby would not do. Later it emerged that the other side had as many as forty thousand agents reporting from every level of South Vietnamese society—a simply phenomenal figure; at the time of the Tet offensive in 1968 the CIA had only one high-level agent reporting on the NLF. From the point of view of pure intelligence, the other side ran circles around the CIA. Angleton blamed the failure on Colby, but did not stop there; he said the blood of American boys was on Colby's hands. But after Colby left the Far East Division, things changed and the CIA began to push a program of penetration of Saigon.

The job was an easy one. Liaison with the police, the army, and other Vietnamese governmental institutions doubled as espionage, and thereafter CIA always had far more agents inside the Saigon government than it ever had reporting on the NLF or Hanoi. CIA read North Vietnamese newspapers and captured documents and even Hanoi's radio traffic with the NLF (until they switched to a coding system called one-time pads in 1961), but it was never very successful in penetrating Hanoi or the NLF with agents. President Johnson once criticized John McCone for CIA's failure in this regard, wondering why the Agency couldn't recruit somebody like his Chinese laundryman back in Texas and send him up there. The President's Foreign Intelligence Advisory Board often raked Desmond FitzGerald and his successor as DDP, Thomas Karamessines, over the coals for the same failure.

FitzGerald told PFIAB the job was tougher than they imagined. When he'd been chief of the Far East Division he used to say that maybe the Russians were tough, but the Chinese were tougher, and the North Koreans the toughest of all; Pyongyang was just a blank on the map. After he became DDP he initiated an effort to recruit spies in the NLF, beginning in June 1966, but the difficulty soon persuaded FitzGerald to put Hanoi right up there with Pyongyang. Eventually the CIA did obtain some agents in North Vietnam,[21] but they were few and hard to run. Saigon was a piece of cake by comparison. Johnson was furious when political troubles in Saigon forced him to cancel air strikes against North Vietnam's petroleum storage facilities in March 1966, and in response CIA managed to place a tap inside the office of the President in Saigon. One CIA man believed that Johnson would not have been asked to approve such a tap. "This was not a chief of state like de Gaulle. Obviously he was a puppet, he was a client. The ambassador got the take, so he must have signed off on it. But you wouldn't have to get the clearance of the President for a tap in the office of somebody like Thieu." The transcripts of the tap were translated by the CIA in Saigon and then radioed to Langley, where a sanitized version (that is, one which disguised their origin) was prepared for the use of a small group of government officials. But two sources said that Johnson himself, a man with an insatiable appetite for information, knew of the tap, and sometimes read the actual transcripts themselves, brooding over the inconstancy of his ally.

The heart of CIA's intelligence gathering in South Vietnam, limited as the Agency was in its ability to penetrate the other side with actual agents, depended on the translation and analysis of captured documents, and on a variety of forms of technical collection. After the initiation of B-52 raids from an American air base on Guam, for example, CIA discovered that as many as 90 percent of the strikes were being compromised. Since this was an American-run operation, and Saigon was informed of the targets only at the last minute, the problem was not the notoriously porous South Vietnamese government and military. The CIA discovered that the NLF was being warned of the strikes in the following way: Russian trawlers picked up the B-52s as they approached the South Vietnamese coast (an easy process because each B-52 mission involved the transmission of as many as a thousand separate radio messages), then radioed the information to Hanoi, which in turn relayed the warning to their headquarters in Cambodia (the Central Office for South Vietnam, or COSVN in the American acronym), which passed on the word to local units. It was CIA's discovery of this procedure which helped persuade the Pentagon to shift its B-52 operations to a base in Thailand in 1966.

Richard Helms did not run the CIA's war in Vietnam. His job was to be responsible for it, just as he was responsible for everything else the CIA did around the world during his six-year tenure as Director of Central Intelligence. The war was a long way off; he had been out to see it with John McCone in the spring of 1962, and he would go again in October 1970 with George Carver, his Special Assistant for Vietnamese Affairs, but for the most part Vietnam was only a word on a great many pieces of paper which crossed his desk. Sometimes those papers were at the heart of intense controversy in Washington. One such came to his attention in the late spring of 1967. It was called 14.3.67,[22] "Capabilities of the Vietnamese Communists for Fighting in South Vietnam," and it ought to have been a routine piece of paper—*Time*-magazine-size, bound in blue with the Agency's seal on the cover, maybe thirty pages long—but the Board of National Estimates had run into a bit of a problem with a five-page section of 14.3.67 on the enemy's order of battle.

An order of battle, or OB, consists primarily of a list of the units in an army; its significance is that you can't know what's involved in fighting a particular enemy until you know how big his army is, an estimate based on intelligence gathered from agents, captured documents, and the interrogation of prisoners. In this instance it appeared that the numbers of the CIA and the Pentagon were in disagreement. Normally such disagreements would be absorbed in a footnote of dissent; 14.3.67 would say the enemy in Vietnam had x number of men in its forces, using the CIA's figure, since National Intelligence Estimates were the CIA's paper, after all; and the military would append a footnote saying they thought the proper number ought to be only $x/2$. The problem, in this case, was that the CIA's estimate was 500,000 and the military's estimate, the "official" estimate of years past, was only 270,000. There had been a similar discrepancy back in the summer of 1961 when a small group of CIA officers and Army colonels in Saigon came up with an OB for the Vietcong of 18,000. William Colby had been station chief then, and his figure was 10,000; he refused to credit the new figure or to send it on to Washington. Eventually a compromise was reached.

But a settlement of the new fight was proving more elusive: 1967 was intended to be Lyndon Johnson's year of progress in Vietnam; pressure from Walt Rostow had never been greater for "progress reports"; General Westmoreland was supposed to be winning the war. Now CIA wanted to say the enemy army, far from slipping toward the brink of defeat, was *twice as big* as we'd been figuring all along. Quite a problem. Rumors of the struggle were already beginning to circulate within official Washington, and the word from the White House was that this had to be cleared up.

So Helms convened a meeting in his office in late June 1967. Present were Sherman Kent, the chairman of the Board of National Estimates; James Graham, the CIA officer in charge of 14.3.67; and a general who represented the Pentagon. Look, said Helms, this is the most important disagreement about the war. There is a total split between the civilian and military analysts on a subject the military is supposed to know something about. We've got to come to an agreement; you fellows go back and work this out.

The problem had begun nearly a year earlier, when a young analyst in the DDI came across some documents in Vietnam which indicated the NLF was having a serious problem with desertion. The analyst was Sam Adams, a tall, solid, somewhat rumpled fellow with an air of enthusiasm, a fascination with intellectual problems, and a vast appetite for paper. One reason he loved the CIA was that it had more paper than anybody around, and Adams was never happier than when he had a stack of documents *this high* on his desk, and the answer to a problem buried somewhere within them.

Adams figured out that the NLF was losing at least 50,000 and perhaps as many as 100,000 deserters a year, a number much higher than previous estimates. If the enemy was also losing 150,000 casualties a year in military operations (a number Adams was inclined to credit, since the NLF documents he was reading tended to bear it out), and if the "official estimate" of the OB at 270,000 was correct, then clearly the NLF was on the ropes. There was no other conclusion. Adams wrote up his observations, and his superiors at the CIA were delighted. Admiral Raborn, still DCI at that time, even called Adams in for a special briefing.

But some old Vietnam hands quietly told Adams the NLF was very far from being on the ropes; recent history was littered with the reputations of men who had prematurely announced the light at the end of the tunnel. Adams began to think he'd made an error somewhere. So he decided to take another look at the OB, the softest figure in his equation, and he discovered that the "official" numbers had been floating around for years. In 1964, for example, the South Vietnamese had decided there were 103,573 guerrilla-militia in the enemy's forces, and the number went into every OB thereafter without fluctuating so much as a single digit. A 1965 CIA study in Saigon concluded there were 39,175 political cadre. A study by the Joint Chiefs of Staff—nobody could remember when it had been made, or by whom—concluded there were 18,553 service troops. The military's estimate of Communist regulars was about 110,000. None of these figures impressed Adams with their solidity. He collected another stack of documents, combed through them for months, and by December 1966 concluded that the true OB for the NLF and North Vietnamese was at least twice as big as the "official estimate"—perhaps as many as 600,000 altogether.

But much to his amazement, the Office of Current Intelligence seemed completely indifferent to his discovery. About the turn of the year 1966–1967, Adams transferred to the staff of George Carver, who sent him to Honolulu in mid-January 1967 for an order-of-battle conference which had been called by General Earle Wheeler, chairman of the Joint Chiefs of Staff, to settle the numbers once and for all. The head of Westmoreland's Order of

Battle section, Colonel Gains B. Hawkins, opened the conference by saying, "You know, there's a lot more of these little bastards out there than we thought there were." Adams figured the struggle was over; Hawkins's estimate was a total of 500,000, close to Adams's own.

The agreement did not last long. In May, when the Board of National Estimates met to write 14.3.67, the new figure of 500,000 went out the window. The DIA's representative, George Fowler, told the CIA, "Gentlemen, we cannot agree to this estimate as currently written. What we object to are the numbers. We feel we should continue with the official order of battle." That is, with the old figure of 270,000. At that point Helms convened his meeting to tell the BNE it had to reach agreement—no footnotes! —and a struggle commenced which lasted all summer. By September the military had been argued up to a new figure of 300,000, but beyond that it would not go.

In September 1967, Adams, Carver, and William Hyland (later head of intelligence at the State Department) flew to Saigon to fight over the numbers directly with the military. For three days the CIA and the military traded evidence and epithets ("Adams, you're full of shit!"), and it gradually became apparent the military simply would not agree to anything like Adams's figure. When Adams would prove one category contained more men than the military had been estimating, the military would simply reduce another category by a similar amount. In one dispute over a subcategory called the district-level service troops, a military colonel admitted he got his number by "scaling down the evidence"—arbitrarily dropping the numbers in a given unit on the grounds they represented "hangers-on" or civilians. With such techniques the military could obtain an OB just about any size it liked, and later that same day an Army officer privately told Adams what that size was. "You know, our basic problem is that we've been told to keep the numbers under 300,000."

The deadlock was finally broken on September 11, 1967, when the CIA station in Saigon received a cable for Funaro (Carver's code name) from Knight (Helms's code name) which directly ordered Carver to reach agreement. That meant accepting the military's figures. A new OB was drawn up which came to exactly 299,000, a figure established arbitrarily by dropping whole categories of enemy forces from the OB. That was bad enough, but later the military went still further, surgically removing yet another category of troops to come up with a new "official estimate" which put the OB at only 248,000—even lower than the old estimate of 270,000. Thus the Pentagon proved we were winning the war.

Back in Washington, the Board of National Estimates reconvened to write a final version of 14.3.67 and Adams told its members exactly how the new figure had been reached. Sherman Kent, chairman of the BNE, asked him, "Sam, have we gone beyond the bounds of reasonable dishonesty?"

"Sir," Adams replied, "we went beyond them last August."

But the BNE adopted 14.3.67 with the military's OB all the same, and Abbott Smith, another BNE member who was to succeed Kent as the Board's chairman, later explained to Adams that they had no choice: Helms had agreed to accept the military's figure, it was his paper ultimately, what could they do? Helms signed the estimate on November 13, 1967, and it was duly distributed to the usual offices through the executive levels of the government, one more piece of paper in the paper war.

It is worth pausing at this point to stress what happened here. The estimates of the BNE are the responsibility of the Director of Central Intelligence; they are *his* paper. If a contributor to the estimates doesn't like what's in them—in this instance, the Pentagon—then it is entitled to a footnote of dissent. The military did not convince the CIA its numbers were wrong; Carver and everyone else connected with the fight over the OB believed that Adams was right. Adams's figures, in short, were Helms's figures. They were the CIA's best estimate of the size of the army fighting the Americans in Vietnam. Nevertheless, Helms signed 14.3.67 containing the military's deflated figures, and the reason he did so is that he did not want a fight with the military, supported by Rostow at the White House. Blood between them was bad enough as it was. In the summer of 1967, CIA had provided McNamara with a huge air war study which he used during Senate hearings that August to refute military claims that the administration was keeping important targets off-limits. The bitterness of that struggle, in which Rostow sided with the military, made the OB fight look like a mild disagreement. Rostow used to write his own assessments on CIA paper before sending it on to the President—"Usual CIA bias," that sort of thing— and he insisted that estimates be rewritten, reorganized, held back. Helms signed 14.3.67 because he just did not want to fight about the OB along with everything else.

It is hard to see how else Helms's signature on 14.3.67 might be interpreted. Helms himself flatly denied he was guilty of "trimming"—agreeing to a false estimate for what amounted to political reasons—and said that after a while the argument got so complex he couldn't make heads or tails of Adams's figures. Other CIA people defended Helms, but their defense curiously tended to focus on Adams himself. In effect they charged him with making too much of a small matter; he was a nut on numbers, too insistent, a "true believer" (Carver's words), unwilling to concede that reasonable men might differ. A lot of them told Adams the same thing: in the world of intelligence (as elsewhere in government) you've got to go along to get along. But Helms's defenders made only the vaguest of claims that Adams was wrong. Perhaps the clearest expression of the CIA view came from

George Carver, who remarked that "intelligence is not written for history; it's written for an audience"—meaning that it's useless if the audience for whom it's written refuses to read it. If the White House absolutely insists on an enemy OB under 300,000, that is what it is going to get.

The battle over the OB might have disappeared into the files if the real war, in this instance, had not been following so hard on the heels of the paper war. At the end of January 1968, major units of the NLF and the North Vietnamese Army burst into Saigon and Hue and attacked just about every provincial capital and major town throughout South Vietnam, catching both the CIA and the American military almost totally by surprise. Intelligence had indicated some sort of offensive was being prepared as early as November 24, 1967, but Westmoreland thought the attack would come in I Corps along the DMZ, and no one predicted the kind of all-out offensive which took place. The CIA's daily "Situation Report" on Vietnam, called the "SitRep" and prepared by Richard Lehman in the Office of Current Intelligence, was sent to press at six o'clock on the night of January 29, 1968. In Saigon it was six in the morning of January 30; the Tet offensive had been under way for four hours. But the "SitRep" claimed that military activity had declined in the central highlands (where two premature Tet attacks had been launched the night before), and as for the rest of the country: "There is nothing of significance to report."[23]

But four hours earlier George Carver had been in his office, officially called the CIA's Related Activities Center, with Philip Habib, the State Department's Indochina desk officer, when a report from Saigon came in saying "they're attacking the Embassy." In short order Carver was on the phone with Walt Rostow, who was "quite upset" and very much wanted to know what was going on. Once Rostow got an idea he was ecstatic. He told a White House aide, Richard Moose, that the enemy had risen up, exposed his infrastructure, and was in the process of being destroyed. Moose was stunned; he thought Rostow had taken leave of his senses. But Rostow was euphoric, and wrote a draft statement for the President's signature which was confident, even heady in tone: last gasp of the enemy, desperate gamble, suicide mission, reeling under the full weight of American firepower for the first time in the war. The reports Carver was reading made him more circumspect; like Rostow's aides, Carver urged him to tone down his confidence. Maybe he was right up to a point, Carver decided later: the NLF was leading with its chin, and didn't have the horses to follow through. But at the time Westmoreland was scrambling to put out fires all over the country. Was that the moment to say the NLF was collapsing? In his mind's eye Carver saw the headlines: "48 CITIES UNDER ATTACK: U.S. CLAIMS GREAT VICTORY."

Johnson's first public response to the Tet offensive was cautious and subdued. The United States was in no danger of catastrophic military defeat; Tet was not Dien Bien Phu. But the offensive cut the ground from beneath American military strategy and contradicted the hopeful claims of the preceding months. It was obvious the bombing had neither persuaded the enemy to give up nor choked his supply lines, its two major justifications. The secrecy and coordination of the attacks demonstrated a robust military capability. It was clearly a bigger war than the American government had been estimating.

On February 4, 1968, Carver attended a meeting with McNamara, who had been going over detailed military reports that identified enemy units in action all over the country, many of them the very units which the military had scaled down or excised from the enemy OB altogether. What about this? McNamara asked Carver; "half" of these units are not even in the OB. Carver raised the OB question with Helms and later told Adams that Helms was "waffling"—he was ready to reopen the OB. On February 13, Carver cabled the CIA station in Saigon to say that the OB was going to be reopened. The "official" estimate was no longer official; they were going to refight the war of the numbers.

At the end of February, pressed by the military for approval of an additional 206,000 U.S. troops for Vietnam, Johnson asked the new Secretary of Defense, Clark Clifford, to convene a special study group to consider how to meet the troop request. That afternoon, February 28, Helms met with the Clifford group, and during the following three days he delivered three CIA studies[24] which stated that the war was far from over, and certainly not won. The papers were realistically gloomy, but they made no mention of the numbers. Clifford's conclusion from what he heard between February 28 and March 4, when he reported to the President, was that the other side could match any U.S. escalation, that no one could predict a favorable outcome from a bigger war, and that Westmoreland should not be given his 206,000 troops. In the past, as a friend and private adviser, Clifford had strongly supported Johnson's determination to fight and win the war. His reversal now shook the President's confidence, but the turning point itself—the moment when Johnson decided he had gone far enough, and would go no further—came later in March when he asked for the opinion of his Senior Informal Advisory Group, sometimes called "the Wise Old Men."[25]

At lunch on March 26, 1968, Johnson met with the Wise Old Men for the first time since the previous November and was startled when Mc-George Bundy, acting as the group's rapporteur in describing their discussion of the evening before, said that they had turned against the war and now favored a policy of disengagement. Previously, the only dove in the group had been George Ball; now their collective opinion had reversed itself. "Who poisoned the well?" Johnson wanted to know. It couldn't have been the top officials, including Richard Helms, who had met with the Wise

Old Men for dinner the night before. Johnson knew what Helms, Wheeler, Rostow, and Bill Bundy had been saying, and it wasn't anything like what the Wise Old Men were saying now. Whom else had they talked to? Well, after the senior officials departed at the conclusion of dinner on the night of March 25, the Wise Old Men had been further briefed in detail by three men: Philip Habib of the State Department, Major General William E. Dupuy of the Joint Chiefs of Staff, and George Carver of the CIA. Johnson wanted to know what those three fellows had been saying.

Two days later Helms phoned Carver from the White House and told him the President wanted to hear what Carver had told the Wise Old Men. When? Carver asked. Now, Helms said; did Carver still have his notes? He did, and he left immediately for the White House, where he was taken directly to the Cabinet Room. General Dupuy was already there, finishing up his version of what he'd told the Wise Old Men. When he was done, Carver was invited to take the chair occupied by the Secretary of Defense during cabinet meetings. He laid out his sheets of yellow legal paper, covered with notes. Helms was there, of course, as well as Vice-President Hubert Humphrey, General Creighton Abrams (who was about to succeed General Westmoreland in Vietnam), General Wheeler from the JCS, and one young man in Army fatigues whom Carver had never seen before. He hesitated a moment; he was about to give out some highly classified information; who was this fellow? Then he figured: Well, if the President wants to declassify this stuff here and now, that's up to him—and he went ahead. Later he learned the fellow in fatigues was Johnson's son-in-law, Patrick Nugent.

Carver's briefing lasted an hour and fifteen minutes, just about as long as he'd talked to the Wise Old Men. Johnson frequently interrupted him, squirmed in his chair, talked on the phone two or three times while Carver went on with his briefing, interrupted to ask another question or two, then asked, "Are you finished?" Not quite, said Carver, and proceeded. Again: "Are you finished yet?" No. Helms sat quietly throughout; Carver noticed a little smile playing across Helms's face; Johnson's restless irritation was amusing him. Finally Carver concluded and Johnson immediately jumped up and stalked from the room without a single word. But then, a moment later, he came back and pumped Carver's hand, before stalking out again, still without a word.

What did Carver tell the Wise Old Men, and repeat for the President? Carver says both briefings were identical. One point, he says, was: "You can't tell the people in Keokuk, Iowa, you want to get out and tell the North Vietnamese you're going to stick it out for two decades and make them believe you." But the heart of his briefing, according to other sources, concerned two additional points. The first was that the pacification program was a shambles.

Toward the end of each month CIA officers working for CORDS in the forty-four provinces of South Vietnam sent in reports on the progress of pacification in their area. At the end of February 1968, the reports came in routinely, were routinely processed, and were written up in a document called the amalgam, or "Monthly Pacification Report," which was routinely started on its way to the usual two or three hundred consumers. But then William Colby, about to leave Washington for Saigon to join CORDS, took a look at the report, and it was very far from routine; it said that in forty of the forty-four provinces the pacification program was going to hell. Colby immediately sent a cable to the CIA's representative at the headquarters of the Commander in Chief in the Pacific (CINCPAC) in Hawaii, an early recipient of the amalgam, telling the CIA man to destroy the document forthwith. A new amalgam was written and reproduced in only six copies. Helms convened the Board of National Estimates in mid-March, and a Special National Intelligence Estimate was produced concluding that pacification was a shambles. Half of Carver's Wise Old Men briefing was based on that SNIE. Since the CIA believed the war would be won or lost in the South, that was gloomy news indeed.

The other half of Carver's briefing concerned a familiar subject: numbers. Carver told the Wise Old Men we had underestimated the enemy by half; there were 600,000 of them. Only two or three days after listening so impatiently to Carver's briefing, Johnson went on national television to announce a bombing halt over North Vietnam, and to reveal he would not be a candidate for reelection.

Sam Adams's numbers had finally become the official estimate, but he was furious all the same. He felt that Helms was chicken, that he had caved in under pressure, that he had betrayed the CIA and his own office, and that he was in a measure responsible for the thousands of American deaths during the Tet offensive. Adams thought Helms's right to his job was forfeit, and he embarked on his most quixotic effort of all: an attempt to get Richard Helms fired.

The day after Johnson's abdication speech Adams went to the Inspector General's office and told them he wanted to file formal charges against Helms. At the end of May he delivered his indictment and asked the IG to make an investigation, determined that the new President, whoever he might be, should know what was going on at CIA. Helms told the IG to go ahead, and over the next two months IG inspectors reconstructed what had happened during the battle over the OB. On August 1, 1968, the IG completed its report.

At that point Helms took the unusual step of appointing a special board to review the IG's report; its three members—Lawrence Houston, the CIA's general counsel; John Bross; and Admiral Rufus Taylor, DDCI and chairman of the review committee—were all friends of Helms, and they quickly showed they intended to make their review careful and meticulous. Strictly by the book, as Adams himself was doing. An OCI analyst, Paul Walsh, was furious at Adams. Walsh went down to Houston's office almost daily during the review and asked Houston, "Can't we fire the sonofabitch?" Houston said no, not as long as Adams remained in channels. But the review board was in no hurry; it was hard to say when they'd be done, perhaps not even until after the election was over.

Adams grew impatient, and in mid-September he went to Houston's office and asked one of the men there if he'd be breaking any laws by personally delivering to the White House the OB memo he'd given the IG months before. Word of Adams's question quickly reached Helms on the seventh floor; he asked a top CIA official to speak to Adams. The official did, telling Adams that delivery of the memo would be "at your own peril" and that "your usefulness to the Agency will thereafter be nil." Adams said he thought he'd do it anyway, and he wrote the official a memorandum quoting his threats—he'd taken notes during the meeting. The official quickly responded that he'd been misunderstood, and besides, Adams would not have to deliver his memo himself; Helms had decided the IG report could go forward after all.

Adams waited until the election was over and the next day asked if it was now okay to send on his memo. While he was waiting for a response he brooded over Helms's delaying tactics, which had already bottled up his protest for seven months. In a chance meeting with a CIA official, Tom Parrott, a friend of Adams's father, Adams said he was tired of these endless delays. "Mr. Parrott, I think I'm going to waltz right up to the Hotel Pierre and drop this on Nixon's desk." Parrott urged him to hold back. "Don't you think this is a bit headstrong?" he asked. "Aren't you going out of channels, taking too much on yourself?" Adams took this as the advice of a friend, and decided to wait.

On November 8, 1968, Helms agreed to see Adams to discuss his protest. Adams has described their conversation:

The first thing he said to me was, "Don't take notes." To the best of my recollection, the conversation then proceeded along the following lines. He asked what was bothering me; did I think my superiors were treating me unfairly, or ·weren't they promoting me fast enough? No, I said. My problem was that he caved in on the numbers right before Tet. I enlarged on the theme for about ten minutes. He listened without expression, and when I was done he asked what I would have him do— take on the whole military? I said, that under the circumstances, that was the only thing he could have done; the military's numbers were faked. He then told me that I didn't know what things were like, that we could have told the White House that there were a million more Vietcong out there, and it wouldn't have made the slightest bit of difference in our policy. I said that we weren't the ones to decide about policy; all we should do was to send up the right numbers and let them worry. He asked me who I wanted to see, and I said that I had requested appropriate members of the White House staff and the President's Foreign Intelligence Advisory Board in my memo, but, frankly, I didn't know who the appropriate members were. He asked whether Gen. Maxwell Taylor and Walt Rostow would be all right. I told him that was not only acceptable, it was generous, and he said he would arrange the appointments for me.[26]

Helms maintained his good humor throughout Adams's effort to get him fired. At the end of their interview on November 8, Adams paused on his way out of the door, remembering that his wife had said Helms recently met her uncle down in Chapman, Alabama, and said, "Oh, by the way, Mr. Helms, how's Uncle Earl?"

"Uncle Earl? You mean Earl Magowan?" And he broke into a peal of delighted laughter at the incongruous note on which their meeting ended.

But at the same time Helms simply ran bureaucratic circles around Adams until his protest faded off into nothing. If Adams had actually gone up to the Hotel Pierre in New York, it is at least conceivable that things might have turned out differently. Nixon was uncertain whom he wanted as his Director of Central Intelligence. But Adams waited; he proceeded through channels, and it was Helms who went to New York to meet President-elect Nixon a few days after his conversation with Adams.

Helms had first met the President-elect officially at the White House on Monday, November 11, 1968, when Nixon paid a courtesy call on Johnson and received routine briefings from top administration officials. Most of them knew they would be leaving the government, of course, but Helms was in a somewhat different position as DCI, and he hoped for reappointment. The Nixons and the Johnsons had a long lunch in the White House that day and the conversation ranged widely. At one point, while the women made small talk or listened to the men politely, Nixon asked Johnson what he thought of Helms and J. Edgar Hoover.

Sometime that week Helms was invited to come to the Hotel Pierre, the transition headquarters in New York, where he was shown into Nixon's suite for a private conversation. Helms was surprised to see John Mitchell, Nixon's former law partner and campaign manager (soon to be appointed Attorney General). Nixon introduced the two men and told Helms, "Anything you can tell me, you can tell John Mitchell."

They sat down and talked for a while and Nixon told Helms he would be reappointed as DCI, and of course Helms thanked him, but!—Nixon made quite a point of this—*Helms was not to tell anyone.* This was to remain secret until Nixon chose to make a public announcement. Helms agreed, and after he returned to Washington he told only a few old friends of his tentative reappointment, stressing the need for silence.

Of course Nixon was odd, but Helms and his closest friends still could not understand his insistence on absolute silence; what did he have in mind? There was no problem with Adams's protest; that was well bottled up, and besides, if Adams had known anything about this town he'd have known a President-elect doesn't let a junior analyst in the CIA tell him whom to appoint as DCI. But rumors began to spread in intelligence circles as time went by without an appointment. Nixon had been clear enough with Helms, however; he was going to be reappointed. Surely there was no problem, unless . . . well, there was one thing, one possible problem known to Helms and very few others, and John Ehrlichman said later that if Nixon had known about it, that would have been the end of Helms.

Chapter 12

The relationship between Nixon and Helms began on the same note of Byzantine secrecy and divided loyalty with which it ended almost exactly four years later. In theory the CIA is above partisan politics, but life has a way of muddying such distinctions, and in the fall of 1968 Helms and the Agency found themselves in the middle of an intrigue which threatened to cost Nixon the election at the last moment. The details of the Anna Chennault affair have never been fully established, but even in outline the episode offers a classic example of the way in which politics and intelligence sometimes collide. While it lasted, Helms walked a fine line between the interests of the man who was President, and the man who would be.

Anna Chennault, a leader in Washington's Republican circles, was the Chinese-born widow of General Claire Chennault, who had commanded the Flying Tigers during World War II. In 1968 Madame Chennault was active in Nixon's campaign, but her real interest at the time was Vietnam, where her many friends were alarmed that the United States would grow weary of the war and abandon them to Hanoi. A particular friend of Madame Chennault was Bui Diem, who was both ambassador to the United States and Saigon's observer at the peace talks in Paris, which at that time included only North Vietnam and the United States. On June 24, 1968, Madame Chennault wrote Nixon to urge a meeting with Bui Diem. Her suggestion was turned down, but throughout the summer and fall she continued to send Nixon notes which began "Dear Dick,"[1] and met frequently with both Bui Diem and Senator John Tower, chairman of the Republicans' Key Issues Committee.

On October 11 President Johnson's negotiators in Paris told the White House that the North Vietnamese seemed to be offering a firm deal in return for a bombing halt. Johnson immediately cabled the offer's terms to General Creighton W. Abrams and Ambassador Ellsworth Bunker in Saigon for their comments. Bunker naturally asked President Thieu for his reaction, and word of the agreement's general outlines almost immediately reached Madame Chennault, probably through Bui Diem. On October 15 she wrote

Nixon, then campaigning in Kansas City, to protest the arrangement of a last-minute bombing halt.

It is not clear when President Johnson first learned of Madame Chennault's contacts with the Nixon campaign, but it may have been as early as midsummer 1968, when the CIA conducted an investigation of Richard Allen, a Nixon foreign policy adviser who had warned against a meeting with Bui Diem on the grounds of political danger. The extent of the CIA's investigation has never been determined, and its purposes never adequately explained. Allen was convinced that his phone was tapped that summer as well, but this was never confirmed. Eventually, in any case, the CIA told Johnson of Madame Chennault's efforts to establish a line of communication between the Nixon campaign and Saigon, and more particularly of her attempt to negotiate a deal in which Nixon would offer Saigon guarantees in return for Saigon's obstruction of a last-minute bombing halt which might otherwise help elect the Democratic candidate, Hubert Humphrey.

Here it is necessary to backtrack a bit. Johnson's concern with political developments in Saigon and the CIA's efforts to give him the information he wanted have already been noted. After peace talks began in Paris in April 1968, CIA agents reported regularly on the activities of the South Vietnamese observer, Bui Diem. The Agency also attempted to install listening devices in Bui Diem's office and living quarters, but a source in the DDP says the effort failed. The Agency was simultaneously keeping track of the Saigon government through its bug in President Thieu's office, and in Washington the NSA monitored radio transmissions from the South Vietnamese Embassy. Sometime that fall CIA surveillance began to pick up references to Madame Chennault's activities. Because she was a U.S. citizen, these reports were handled according to a special procedure and were not widely distributed. Several sources say the reports were written up in the office of the DDP, Thomas Karamessines, and then forwarded to Richard Helms. Helms passed them on to Walt Rostow, the President's National Security Adviser, who in turn sent them to Johnson, who liked to know what was going on.

Then, during the week which ended Sunday, October 27, the National Security Agency intercepted a radio message from the South Vietnamese Embassy to Saigon explicitly urging Thieu to stand fast against an agreement until after the election. As soon as Johnson learned of the cable he ordered the FBI to place Madame Chennault under surveillance and to install a phone tap on the South Vietnamese Embassy, which was done on Tuesday, October 29. Meanwhile, Walt Rostow pressed the CIA for what it knew about Madame Chennault's initiatives. Helms's Special Assistant for Vietnamese Affairs, George Carver, argued that Saigon did not need a deal with Nixon in order to resist the agreement Johnson was pushing. Thieu thought he was being sold down the river, and if Carver had been in Thieu's position he'd have felt the same way. But Rostow, reflecting Johnson's anger, wasn't having any; he wanted the CIA to move on this, and the CIA did so.

On Thursday, October 31, just five days before the election, Johnson thought he had an agreement nailed down in Paris, and at 6:00 p.m., shortly before his announcement of the bombing halt in return for expanded peace talks, the President called the three candidates simultaneously and told them what he was about to announce. But with Humphrey and George Wallace listening in, the President also explicitly warned Nixon he was aware of what Madame Chennault was up to, saying he didn't want any more hints to Saigon of a better deal with a new President by "some of our folks, including some of the old China lobbyists."[2]

Thieu, however, continued to balk. On Friday, November 1, he announced in Saigon that he would not send a delegation to Paris for the first session of the expanded talks, and the following day the FBI's tap on the South Vietnamese Embassy picked up a phone call from Madame Chennault. Again she urged Saigon to hold firm: they'd get a better deal with Nixon. The South Vietnamese official she talked to asked if Nixon knew about her phone call. "No, but our friend in New Mexico does," she answered.[3] On that day Nixon's vice-presidential candidate, Spiro Agnew, was campaigning in Albuquerque, New Mexico.

This time Johnson was truly angry. Late on the day after the election, Wednesday, November 6, Johnson demanded that the FBI check phone records in Albuquerque that very night to see if Agnew had called Madame Chennault. One week later, on November 13, the FBI reported that none of the five long-distance calls made by Agnew's staff that day had been to Madame Chennault. During that same period, according to several sources, Rostow continued to press the CIA for reports on Saigon's foot-dragging, but gradually Johnson cooled and the FBI and CIA efforts were allowed to lapse, although the South Vietnamese Embassy tap was not discontinued until January 6, 1969. Johnson was never sympathetic to George Carver's argument that Thieu's resistance was comprehensible, given his circumstances, but a CIA source suggests that another consideration carried greater weight in Johnson's mind. Nixon had won the election. What was Johnson to do if he discovered Nixon *had* tried to sabotage the peace talks? It was better not to know, Johnson concluded, than to know and then face the awful decision of what to do about it.

In the end Johnson simply dropped the matter. Nixon did not, and one can gauge his concern by the unseemly urgency with which Hoover attempted to escape blame for the episode. The day Nixon reappointed him at the Hotel Pierre, Hoover told the President-elect about the FBI's role in the Chennault affair, but Nixon carried away a garbled version. For several years he thought the FBI had been tapping *him*. Early in 1973 a former director of Domestic Intelligence for the FBI, William Sullivan, explained that it hadn't quite happened that way.[4] One of Nixon's first acts as President was to order H. R. Haldeman to track down the details of Johnson's last-minute peace agreement before the election. Clearly, Nixon was looking for a defense against any possible charge from Johnson that he had tried to sabotage the agreement through Madame Chennault.[5] But Nixon did not learn of the CIA's role in first directing Lyndon Johnson's attention toward Madame Chennault, nor of the CIA efforts to find out what was going on which paralleled the FBI's investigation, and his long, unexplained delay in announcing Helms's reappointment was apparently only another of the man's private eccentricities. During the investigation of the Chennault episode Helms had done his part, according to Carver, for the reason he so often cited when the interests of one President clashed with another's: he worked for only one President at a time.

On December 18, 1968, Nixon finally announced the reappointment of J. Edgar Hoover as Director of the FBI and of Richard Helms as Director of Central Intelligence. The staff in Helms's office was delighted, and they gave him a quiet champagne party to celebrate, but the four years which followed were not often happy ones, and Nixon gave his DCI ample reason to wish he had departed before the deluge.

Nixon entered the White House on January 20, 1969, in the mood of a general occupying an enemy town, bringing with him a visceral dislike and suspicion of the federal bureaucracy—partly as a Republican who had campaigned against its size for years, partly because he suspected the bureaucrats' loyalty as holdovers from the Kennedy and Johnson years, but mostly because it was in his character to see himself always as surrounded by enemies, obstructionists, and saboteurs. At National Security Council meetings Helms often heard Nixon damn "the cookie-pushers in the State Department" or bitterly accuse the Pentagon and other departments of refusing to carrying out his explicit instructions. On occasion Helms was himself the target of caustic but vague charges that the CIA had failed to accomplish some perfectly simple task. All Presidents seem to have a capacity for selective anger; Johnson was famous for his ability to tongue-lash a subordinate without mercy, and then to pick up the phone for a conversation with someone else as if nothing had happened. But Nixon's anger went deeper, and lingered; suspicion and hostility lay near the roots of his character. In his mind his enemies were legion, not only among the press, the old-money patrician establishment of the Republican party, and the government elite who had been trading top-level jobs in Washington for a generation, but closer at hand, in his own government, right down the hall.

It was Nixon's government now, but he despaired of making it his own, and more than one high official was struck by the President's willingness to demean the very men he had chosen to carry out his policies. It made him a hard man to work for. Helms and another CIA official were once trapped in Washington traffic after a meeting and got to talking about the assignment they'd just been given. Helms's companion said he didn't understand it. "There's something I've had to learn to understand," said Helms. "I've had to learn to understand Presidents."[6] What he had learned to understand was that the power of an American President is extraordinary, that the President can delegate his authority or withdraw it, as he pleases; and that no official can entirely enter a President's world. They did things for their own reasons. If you wanted to survive, you learned to understand that you did what you were told when you *didn't* understand.

So far Helms got with Nixon, and no further. The new President was an odd duck, competent in some ways, a cripple in others. Helms had first met him in the late fall of 1956, when, as acting DDP in the absence of Frank Wisner, he had briefed the then Vice-President before Nixon made a trip to Vienna, to report on the flood of Hungarian refugees crossing the border into Austria following Soviet suppression of the revolution in November. The only impressions Helms carried away from his briefing were that the Vice-President did his homework, and there wasn't much charm to the man. Time had not softened him. And yet, in Helms's view, however flawed Nixon may have been, he was President; the office justified if it did not redeem the man.

No government institution elicited Nixon's sullen suspicion more than the CIA. One of his first visits to a federal agency was to the CIA in March 1969, but it was a grudging concession. He often complained about CIA failures to warn him of something in advance, saying the Agency couldn't even keep up with the wire services. He once said to John Ehrlichman, "What use are they? They've got forty thousand people over there reading newspapers." He bitched (Ehrlichman's word) that the intelligence community was overstaffed, undersupervised, and too expensive. But the real source of Nixon's dislike was personal: he blamed the CIA for his defeat by John F. Kennedy in 1960. During the late 1950s the Pentagon had argued that Russia would soon overtake the United States in bomber and missile production, but the CIA, relying on photo reconnaissance by the U-2, proved to Eisenhower's satisfaction, at any rate, that the Pentagon was wrong. Then during the 1960 campaign Kennedy raised the issue of a "missile gap," arguing the Pentagon's position. Nixon felt he had lost the election on that issue alone, and he blamed the CIA—which Eisenhower had instructed to brief Kennedy—for failing to swing Kennedy around with its evidence. He didn't simply blame them; he suspected the CIA of deliberately withholding its U-2 data from Kennedy precisely because the issue would help defeat Nixon. This was apparently not a vaguely entertained suspicion, but a firm conviction, and as President, Nixon kept the CIA at arm's length, just as he did all the other Nixon-hating, cookie-pushing bureaucrats of Washington.

Some time before the first meeting of Nixon's National Security Council, held the day after the inauguration, January 21, 1969, Henry Kissinger informed Helms that some things would be done differently in the new administration. The Director of Central Intelligence traditionally opened NSC meetings with an intelligence briefing on the subject at hand—SALT was on the agenda the first day—and then remained for the duration of the meeting to answer any questions that might come up. Kissinger told Helms that from now on he was to leave after his briefing, instead of remaining for the debate which followed. The new arrangement was the result of a reorganization of the NSC drafted by Morton Halperin, a young defense intellectual who was already under suspicion by J. Edgar Hoover for his role in helping to turn Clark Clifford against the war the year before, and who was destined to become one of the targets of seventeen secret FBI wiretaps on government officials and newsman. Halperin's plan, designed to place the President (and Kissinger) in full control of national security decisionmaking,[7] was put into effect in its entirety, with one exception: Helms and the CIA were restored to their old role.

Helms had already picked up rumors of the plan, and was unhappy with it. The NSC was a policymaking body, and the CIA was not technically part of the policymaking apparatus; it was supposed only to submit the facts, and let others decide. Helms, never a man to insist or even raise his voice in the councils of government, was content with his role, unlike Dulles and McCone, but he didn't welcome his demotion to the rank of delivery boy in Halperin's plan. In December 1968 he protested what he took to be the new plan to Melvin Laird, the Secretary-designate of Defense, who had already approved it. Laird reflected for several days and then flew to Boston to argue with Kissinger against the CIA's exclusion. Sensing a threat to the plan as a whole if debate became general, Kissinger said okay. In this sole particular, Halperin's bureaucratic revolution would be stayed. Kissinger apparently intended to revert to the old system gradually, over a month or two, but as it turned out, Helms remained for the entire NSC meeting that first day, and then accompanied the others to lunch in the White House.

But if Helms had successfully defended his Agency's role within the NSC, he never managed to win the confidence of Nixon himself. At times Nixon's treatment of him in meetings seemed harsh to the point of cruelty. He frequently interrupted Helms with a comment or correction, sometimes in a tone which witnesses could only describe as spiteful or snide. On one occasion he corrected Helms's pronunciation of Malagasy. On another he stopped Helms in midsentence to say he'd balled up his description of who was backing whom in a local insurgency. CIA was proposing a covert intervention on one side and couldn't even get the teams straight. It wasn't the substance of the criticism which witnesses remembered; Helms certainly had a professional obligation to understand these matters aright. It was the tone of condescension.

Another source of criticism by Nixon and Kissinger was the CIA's heavy reliance on liaison with local intelligence agencies, a practice which produced a wealth of detailed information but which also tended to skew the CIA's attitudes along the lines of local obsessions. The Israeli intelligence service, for example, was well informed about Arab countries, but it naturally emphasized Arab war-mindedness, irredentism, and openness to Soviet influence, just as the South Africans looked for, and found, an infectious strain of Communist infiltration in every black nationalist organization. The result was a CIA view of the world which sometimes appeared to have been taken over entirely from third parties. It is an odd fact that the CIA was often more obsessed with evidence of Communist intrigue than Nixon himself. The President made no secret of his feelings, and one man who had attended NSC meetings on arms control since the Eisenhower administration said he often found himself acutely embarrassed by Nixon's treatment of Helms. There were no overt signs of discomfiture on Helms's part, he said, but "any criticism by your President in front of your contemporaries is a hard fall."

Part of the problem was Helms's chosen style. He liked to read his papers, thinking the written word was subtler and more exact than a spoken précis, and he prided himself on succinctness and exactitude. He heavily edited the paper which passed through his hands, and no one ever wrote for him without quickly discovering that in Helms's view, sentences do *not* begin with "However." But Johnson's appetite for foreign intelligence was quite different from Nixon's, and Morton Halperin, an NSC staff member until April 1970, said Helms took longer than he should have to sense Nixon's impatience with his broad formulations. He remembered in particular a Helms briefing on China, delivered at a meeting held at Nixon's residence at San Clemente in August 1969. Helms gave the background—*all* the background, including China's population and area in square miles. Nixon squirmed in his seat, tapping his fingers insistently on the table. He knew all that; he wanted a briefing on Chinese politics and relations with the Soviet Union, and here was the Director of Central Intelligence giving him a third-grade talk about the big country across the broad, blue Pacific.

Allen Dulles had spoken from notes at such meetings, in the manner of a man who had personally absorbed his subject, and after the formal meeting was over, he often went back to the Oval Office with the President to continue the discussion privately. He had been part of Eisenhower's political family, a genuine intimate and confidant. No relationship of that sort ever developed between Helms and Nixon. After a while Helms even found it difficult to get through to the President on the phone. Haldeman had put up a wall around the man, and Helms found himself on the outside like almost everyone else in the administration. Finally he was reduced to leaving notes for the President before his chair at NSC meetings, and even then Nixon did not always respond.

Kissinger, too, was a hard taskmaster. His demands were numerous, especially during the first months of Nixon's administration when just about every aspect of foreign policy was reopened, beginning with Vietnam. National Security Study Memorandum No. 1 was actually delivered to the CIA on Nixon's first day in office, asking a long series of questions about the war. Partly intended to prove that no policy was sacred, and partly to keep the intelligence and foreign policy communities busy while Kissinger consolidated his bureaucratic revolution, the early NSSMs ranged the world from Israel, China, and South Africa to Latin America and the Soviet Union. In response, the NSC was deluged with a flood of paper, and Kissinger was frequently critical of what he got. People who worked for Kissinger on the NSC say he was not merely disappointed with the intelligence he was getting; he was surprised at his own disappointment. He had anticipated something better. One NSC staff member remembers Kissinger with a National Intelligence Estimate from the CIA in his hand and literally screaming, "This isn't what I want!" He didn't like the analytic caution of CIA paper; he didn't like its literary style; he didn't like the burial of opposing views in one- or two-sentence footnotes of dissent, and as often as not he didn't like the conclusions. Kissinger was confident in his own abilities, and he demanded paper crisper in style backed up by appendices filled with raw data. He'd make up his own mind.

In one sense it might be argued that Helms was out of his depth in the NSC. He knew all there was to know about operating a secret intelligence agency, but he was bored by arguments over precedence in the Central Committee of the Chinese Communist party, or the exact characteristics of some new Soviet missile. Participants in meetings of the United States Intelligence Board (USIB) would sometimes notice Helms, USIB's chairman, staring dreamily off into space while the experts argued the details. Helms trusted his people on questions of that sort, but his relative lack of interest made him vulnerable at the National Security Council. Some Assistant Secretary of Defense would say: Well, what happens if you take the telemetry off missile X; will it go another 900 miles? Helms wouldn't know what the man was talking about. So he'd take the question back to the CIA for an answer, and the leader of the working group studying missile X would say, Oh, Christ, we've spent eighteen hours talking about *exactly* that.

Kissinger was especially critical of the CIA's "Annual Survey of Soviet Intentions and Capabilities," arguably the single most important piece of paper produced by the CIA. He wanted more and he wanted it better. Helms took the word back, and a major effort was made to design a new survey which would satisfy the audience of one. Helms asked for suggestions from the NSC, the State Department, and the Pentagon, and the following year the "Annual Survey" was completely reworked. In the early 1950s the "Annual Survey" had been a single, slim volume. After its latest revision it was three volumes and hundreds of pages long, with voluminous appendices, charts, and graphs. If Kissinger wanted more, Helms would give it to him.

But despite Helms's efforts to give Kissinger what he wanted, Kissinger was unhappy. To some degree his "unhappiness" was an instrument of control; his criticisms were preemptive, putting the intelligence community on the defensive. If he criticized them first, their objections would lack bite, being vulnerable to a charge of sour grapes: well, no *wonder* . . . And of course Kissinger *was* criticized, mainly for his secrecy. John Foster Dulles had always been frank with the CIA about what he was up to. When he held a meeting with a foreign official, the minutes of their conversation were given to the CIA. Kissinger kept not only his actions but his intentions secret, with the result that the NSC and the CIA were sometimes like ships passing in the night, Kissinger up to one thing while the CIA remained fuzzily uncertain of what it ought to be giving him. The failure was not one of hostility and suspicion, but an almost mechanical breakdown akin to a slipping clutch; the gears simply failed to mesh.

Kissinger's unhappiness was not all show, however. He really didn't like what he was getting. In September 1969, his chief aide, General Alexander Haig, telephoned a professional defense analyst and longtime CIA consultant at the Rand Institute in California, Andrew Marshall, to say that the President and Kissinger were not happy with intelligence. Would Marshall come to Washington as an NSC adviser for three or four months to study the problem? Marshall did, and between December 1969 and April 1970, he wrote two papers for Kissinger on reorganizing the day-to-day flow of intelligence paper reaching the White House, and on assessing its quality. Routing the paper, Marshall found, proved easier than judging what it was worth. CIA people he talked to defended themselves in the usual ways: (A) Look at this terrific stuff. (B) You don't understand how hard it is to do this sort of thing. And (C) You people are unreasonable, everybody else liked our stuff. But Marshall found that everybody else didn't like their stuff. NSC staffers from the Kennedy and Johnson administrations had been just as unhappy about roughly the same things, and government files were filled with special studies of intelligence going back to the late 1940s, all dealing with the same problems.

These were principally two. First, CIA intelligence paper tended to be pulpy with adverbs and the conditional tense. The bedrock of CIA metaphysics was not "either/or" but "maybe/if," and it drove decisionmakers from Truman to Nixon half-crazy.[8] The second problem was an infuriating coyness about the source of judgments. An estimate that the Indians were expected to behave thus-and-so would leave the policymakers wondering just how solidly this judgment could be backed up. Was it based on positive information—a report from an agent inside the Indian cabinet, say? Or was it a reasonable inference based on diverse bits of information? Or was it simply a guess founded on nothing more than some analyst's notion of the way nation-states behave? There was no way to tell from the paper itself. The style was firmly *ex cathedra*.

This problem had deep roots. The CIA was fiercely protective of its sources and methods. It certainly wasn't about to tell every junior desk officer in the government that it had an agent inside Indira Gandhi's government. The DDP didn't even want to tell the analysts that sort of thing. When a piece of information could not be divorced from its source—when the fact itself revealed where it came from—the DDP simply sat on it. If the CIA's estimators were forced to write in twilight, the policymakers naturally read their paper in deepest night.

This caution was not entirely misconceived. American governments are notoriously porous at the top. SALT negotiator Gerard Smith once called Helms to say that a story in the morning paper hadn't come from him. Helms told him not to worry. "I always call the White House first," he said, meaning that's where most of the leaks came from, and he never began a hunt for the culprit until he was sure it wasn't some high official. As a result, the CIA had learned to be cautious with details. A typical example of the danger occurred when the CIA made a reference to an agent in the Indian cabinet in a report to Nixon in August 1971, explaining that the Soviet Union had signed a friendship treaty with India in order to forestall Indian recognition of Bangladesh, then rebelling against the rule of West Pakistan. The substance of the report quickly leaked to Tad Szulc of the *New York Times*, who published the story on August 13. That same day Helms called either Egil Krogh or his assistant David Young at the White House to protest the leak, saying it put their agent's life in danger. Krogh recommended to John Ehrlichman that the CIA mount an investigation of Szulc in order to pinpoint the leak. But despite Szulc's story, the CIA's agent continued to report from inside the Indian cabinet, apparently unaware that he might have been compromised.

Then, later that year, another leak occurred which, from Helms's viewpoint, was even more egregious. With war raging in Bangladesh between Indian and Pakistani forces in December 1971, evidence began to mount that India was planning an attack on West Pakistan as well. On December 7, Kissinger asked the CIA for an estimate of the probability of such an attack. The CIA said it didn't know. But within twenty-four hours it had positive information: the CIA case officer handling the Indian politician in Gandhi's cabinet in New Delhi was told that a decision had just been reached to attack in the West. A report was immediately cabled back to Langley and forwarded directly to the White House in its raw form. Nixon was later to cite this cable as one of the few really timely pieces of intelligence the CIA had ever given him, but the Agency paid a price. The report was widely read in the White House, and its text, along with many other documents, was quickly leaked to Jack Anderson, who published them in his column in mid-December. That was the end of the agent. According to the DDP at the time, Thomas Karamessines, "he told us to go to hell."[9]

Two weeks later, in January 1972, the CIA's Office of Security began an investigation of Anderson which lasted until April and sometimes involved as many as sixteen men following the movements of the columnist and his staff. On March 17, 1972, for example, CIA officers closely observed a luncheon meeting between Helms and Anderson in Washington's Madison Hotel in an attempt to discover if Anderson was secretly taping his conversation with Helms. But even after the investigation was halted for fear Anderson would discover it, Helms continued to report to Kissinger on the problem presented by Anderson's sources. In a memo to Kissinger on October 4, 1972, Helms cited seventy-three Anderson columns based on secret intelligence documents, forty from the CIA on subjects ranging from the health of Lon Nol of Cambodia to the CIA's relationship with the Bureau of Narcotics and Dangerous Drugs, and thirty-three from the Washington Special Action Group (WSAG), a subcommittee of the National Security Council.

Thus Helms felt the CIA had reason aplenty to disguise its sources in estimates routinely circulated throughout Washington. Raw intelligence might make interesting reading at the White House, but the price was too high, leaks were too frequent, and agents too hard to recruit to be compromised in so cavalier a fashion.

Kissinger and his staff did not see things in the same light, however, and at the turn of the year 1970–1971 James Schlesinger, then the Assistant Director of the Office of Management and Budget (OMB), was asked to study the organization of the intelligence community from top to bottom. There are serious studies and there are unserious studies, said one man who worked with Schlesinger, and this one was very far from being a routine paper exercise. The President wanted results.

By March 1971, the Schlesinger group had completed a paper, blandly entitled *A Review of the Intelligence Community*, which concluded among other things that the Director of Central Intelligence's theoretical control of the community was an impolite fiction; that the total cost of intelligence, obscured by various techniques of financial sleight of hand, was at least twice the figure formally submitted to Congress; that intelligence estimates too often hid differing judgments in bland compromise; that the CIA's policy of no lateral entry of personnel had rendered the Agency almost claustrophobically insular, and that technical intelligence far surpassed political intelligence in quality.

Correcting these ills was something else again. The various agencies of the intelligence community are notoriously jealous of their independence.[10] Nixon and Kissinger pondered their reforms for some time before distributing the Schlesinger report to Helms and other Agency chiefs in August 1971, and then brooded again before announcing a reorganization of the intelligence community on November 5, 1971. As far as Helms was concerned,

Nixon took with one hand and gave with the other. A new National Intelligence Committee under the NSC was established with Kissinger as chairman, thus extending Kissinger's control of the CIA, but at the same time Helms's role as DCI was strengthened as well. Henceforth he was to *run* the whole intelligence community. Nixon personally told him, "If you have any trouble doing this, you let me know." With Nixon's intervention the plan might have worked; the National Security Agency and the Defense Intelligence Agency would only glower at a DCI, whereas they might listen to a President. But Nixon did not keep his promise. He withdrew into his White House cocoon, and Helms, anticipating failure, never seriously attempted to run the community. The new Intelligence Resources Advisory Committee, which Helms chaired, settled for simply collecting the budget requests of the various agencies nominally under Helms's control, and then forwarded them to the White House. It was the old story with a new title.

Watergate sliced open the Nixon administration like an archaeologist's trench, revealing the inner workings of government—the rivalries, intrigues, and clashes of personality—in unprecedented detail. But Watergate's awful fascination and lingering mysteries have obscured the larger preoccupation of American political leaders since the Second World War. This has centered on a rivalry with the Soviet Union which is one of history's great international contests, and whose outcome can still not be foreseen. It is hard to imagine a reconciliation, terrifying to consider a war to the finish, all but impossible to believe that it will persist without resolution forever. In its dark early years it seemed like the rivalry of Rome and Carthage, the first act of Armageddon. More recently it has seemed possible to at least hope for some sort of enduring understanding. But even if this rivalry is sometimes forgotten by the American people, whose only role is to pay for its conduct as long as it lasts, and its price if the peacemakers should fail, it has never surrendered its prominence in the mind of official Washington. The contest with Russia is what Presidents and their advisers have been thinking about for thirty years. It has been close to the heart of every international initiative from the Marshall Plan to the attempted ouster of Salvador Allende; it is why the United States has $100-billion military budgets. The quotidian details of the life of Richard Helms, whose personal history is indistinguishable from the history of the CIA, all found their source in the American rivalry with Russia. The Agency he worked for, and eventually ran, was an instrument of struggle, a tool of war in a war which preferred to be called by another name.

This ought to be an obvious point, but it has been often forgotten. The internecine conflicts among the White House, Congress, the Pentagon, the State Department, and the intelligence community, and among the ambitious men who fought for precedence within and among these separate institutions, have been so intense, and exposed of late in such detail, that it is not always noticed that the rivals of Washington are all on the same side where Russia is concerned. If Richard Helms was mired in the intrigue of Washington, spending as much time protecting his flanks from "friends" at home as he did thinking about enemies abroad, what he did was to serve the President in that larger struggle, a kind of general in a kind of war. Norman Mailer once wrote a long article about the CIA,[11] suggesting among other improbable things that the Agency might be secretly controlled by a cabal of Mormon Danites, without once mentioning Soviet missilery, oil in the Middle East, the Communist parties of Europe, Vietnam, and Chile, or Russian intentions and capabilities. This sort of blinkered vision leaves CIA people puzzled and wondering. Yes, they were in cahoots with the Mafia at one point, Howard Hunt did go to work for the White House, Howard Hughes was working for the CIA and giving Nixon money at the same time, but all that was only a kind of sideshow, the inevitable elbowing in a crowded political scene. "What does everybody think we've really been doing all these years?" one CIA man asked. "*Fighting the Cold War!*" Mailer and other cartographers of conspiracy, in the view of CIA people, are trying to unravel a quarrel between costume designers backstage at the opera, while *Götterdämmerung* is on the stage.

Of course participants in the larger struggle had begun to use it for narrower ends. War corrupts, and secret war corrupts secretly. It has not always been easy to tell where the struggle against Communism ends and the defense of American business begins. The effort to keep secrets from enemies abroad offers a tempting rationale for keeping them from political opponents at home. The keeper of the secrets acquires a certain leverage and independence; J. Edgar Hoover did not run the FBI for fifty years because he was so good at his job, but because Presidents did not dare to fire him. Johnson and Nixon both turned to the CIA, in varying degree, as an alternative to the FBI, and if Watergate had not exposed the process it is likely that somewhere down the road Directors of Central Intelligence would have begun to rival Directors of the FBI as barons of domestic power. Norman Mailer was not describing things as they were so much as things as they might become. CIA people naturally dismiss this sort of thing as a canard, but history is filled with examples of secret intelligence services which have ceased to serve and aspired to rule. The Romans repeatedly destroyed and rebuilt theirs, and the Russians in this century, after their own fashion, have done the same. At least three chiefs of the Russian intelligence services got what they gave—a bullet in the back of the head. But the fact remains that the CIA's emergence as a domestic power was very much in its embryonic stages when Watergate came along, trailing clouds of investigators, and that what Helms did until his last day in office was to serve as the President's instrument in international struggle.

It would take a separate book to describe every crisis in which the CIA played a part during the Nixon administration, but even a partial list serves to give the flavor of Helms's preoccupations. In 1969, for example, the CIA began to collect evidence that the Soviet Union was considering some sort of preemptive military attack upon China. Military skirmishing with the Chinese along the Ussuri River in March 1969 resulted in a Russian build-up along the frontier which included tactical nuclear weapons. In July, Kissinger asked for a full-scale study of the Sino-Soviet split, and during meetings of the Board of National Estimates that summer and fall two CIA analysts and General Daniel O. Graham, later head of the Defense Intelligence Agency, argued that Russia was preparing for a nuclear strike on Chinese nuclear development centers. That fall Helms told reporters in a background briefing of evidence that this was a real possibility, and some sources suggest Helms's remarks were the administration's chosen reply to quiet Soviet inquiries about the American response to such a preemptive attack.[12] But for some reason the possibility of outright war was skirted in the CIA estimate forwarded to Kissinger in November 1969, and early the following year he asked Helms for a study of that point alone.

During the same year the CIA began to collect intelligence that the Russians were building a major base for submarine tenders at Cienfuegos in Cuba, and for a while it looked as if a replay of the Cuban missile crisis was in the offing. Ehrlichman remembers an intelligence briefing held for congressional leaders on the subject in the Roosevelt Room of the White House. Charts had been prepared with the latest intelligence, but when Kissinger unveiled one which tracked Soviet ships with little dotted lines, he was startled, and a bit embarrassed, to see that the CIA's little dotted lines showed the ships were on their way home again.

In 1970 the CIA played a tangential role in planning for a military raid on Son Tay, site of a North Vietnamese prison for captured American pilots.[13] One CIA analyst who worked on the project was Anthony Riccio, a young academic who had grown restless after two or three years of being asked questions for which there were no honest answers. During the summer of 1970 he was asked what sort of arms had been provided the North Vietnamese militia in Son Tay. Riccio did not know about the planned rescue attempt but diligently searched the files for an answer all the same. There was nothing. He told his boss they'd have to confess they didn't know, and his boss, irritated, sat down right there and wrote the answer: The North Vietnamese militia in Son Tay is probably (the all-purpose word) armed with old Japanese and French rifles, pitchforks, and machetes.

When Riccio read about the Son Tay raid a few months later, he suddenly realized why he'd been asked that question. Not long after, he decided to resign from the CIA, but before leaving he requested a meeting with Helms to explain why. Helms asked what the problem was. Riccio described his frustration with orders to put together what amounted to an imaginary price index for North Vietnamese agricultural production and similar futile exercises. When he was done, Helms calmly asked if any of that really mattered.

Riccio said no, but added, his voice rising, that there was something which did matter. He described the phony estimate of Son Tay militia armament, said the militia turned out in the event to have been armed with submachine guns, and then, pointing his finger directly at Helms, said, "People's lives were at stake!" Helms sat poker-faced throughout, and when Riccio was done began talking about the generation gap.

Some of Helms's preoccupations were ephemeral, crises of the moment. But some involved enduring controversy, such as a battle (principally between the CIA and the Pentagon) over econometric estimates of Soviet military spending which began in the fall of 1971 and lasted for five years, or a long struggle in 1969 and 1970 over the characteristics of a new Soviet missile called the SS-9. That battle nearly cost Helms his job.

Kissinger and Secretary of Defense Melvin Laird both favored construction of a U.S. antiballistic missile (ABM) system, although for somewhat different reasons. But Congress was in a rebellious mood, unconvinced the ABM was really necessary. The Nixon administration launched a campaign to turn Congress around with an argument that the Soviets were building toward a first-strike capability—a force sufficient to so cripple American retaliatory response after a surprise attack that the Russians might be able to risk the consequences.[14] The argument, as sometimes happens in major disputes, narrowly focused on a specific characteristic of the SS-9: was it a MIRV (that is, a multiple independently targetable reentry vehicle—in effect, many missiles in one), or was it a MRV (pronounced *marv*, for multiple reentry vehicle, or one missile with several warheads)? Laird took the view that it didn't matter; he didn't want the Congress to lose itself in a debate on this point. "I don't distinguish between MIRV and MRV," he told Gerard Smith, the arms control expert. But there was a difference; it was hard to justify estimates of a Soviet first-strike capability unless they had MIRVs. Without them, they simply didn't have enough missiles to destroy the American Minuteman missiles which were targeted on them. Kissinger took a subtler position. He argued that the SS-9's "footprint"—that is, the landing pattern of the SS-9's several warheads—was perfectly designed to match the characteristic placement of Minutemen in threes. The controversy was not an idle or a narrow one. Kissinger needed a credible threat—Russian MIRVs, in fact or in effect—in order to get an ABM system, so as to have a bargaining chip for the SALT talks with the Soviets.[15]

The controversy centered on the CIA's insistence that the SS-9 was a MRV, and that its footprint simply did not give it the accuracy or effect of a MIRV. No first strike, and no credible threat. One National Security Council staff member said that the CIA's point of view was "highly inconvenient" to Kissinger. In late May 1969, Helms and Carl Duckett, the CIA's Deputy Director for Science and Technology, testified before the Senate Foreign

Relations Committee in a closed hearing on the SS-9. At the end of the session Fulbright observed that "It sure didn't sound like what the Secretary of Defense has been saying." Kissinger was furious. NSC staffers wondered whether Helms could survive as DCI, and one of them said that if it were not for Helms's reputation for integrity on the Hill, Kissinger would have insisted that Nixon fire him.

At that point Helms was about as far out on a limb as a DCI can get. Fulbright and other supporters in Congress even felt they had to intervene directly with Nixon and Kissinger in Helms's behalf. In the end, Kissinger settled for calling Helms into his office, where he demanded that the Board of National Estimates revise its paper on the SS-9 to include more evidence supporting CIA's view that the missile was not a MIRV. A few days later the BNE came back with a new, fatter draft which reached the same conclusions.

The CIA was right about the SS-9—Russia did not begin to MIRV its missiles until several years later—but Kissinger and Laird didn't much care who was right; they wanted a credible Soviet threat, and they did not abandon the effort to get one. Later that fall, when the CIA argued that the Soviets would not try for a first-strike capability, Eugene Fubini, a member of the Defense Intelligence Agency's scientific advisory commission, personally went to see a friend and colleague of Helms to argue that he should delete the offending paragraph. It directly contradicted Laird's public statements, it was not a matter of fact but conjecture, and Helms should not set himself at loggerheads with the Secretary of Defense. An assistant of Laird's, William Baroody, made the same point to Helms personally, and this time Helms decided to surrender the point: he deleted the paragraph from the final text of NIE 11.8.69,[16] not because he had changed his mind —his mind had never been made up one way or the other; it was the analysts who worked for him who resented surrender of the point—but because it didn't matter to him, and it did matter to Laird.

A willingness to compromise was both Helms's strength and his weakness. Some men in government—Kissinger is a good example—can so dominate debate that they force compromise on others, and rarely have to submit themselves. Kissinger's success is explained partly by the extraordinary authority delegated to him by Nixon, partly by his personal strength of character. Helms certainly did not enjoy Nixon's trust to an equal degree, and his character had been tempered by the reality of intelligence in Washington. He once told a colleague that the DCI had 100 percent of the responsibility for intelligence on paper, but spent only 15 percent of the money. To get along, he often had to go along.

One source of continuing friction was the fact that the CIA was not the only spy-runner in Washington. During the mid-1960s, the U.S. ambassador to Thailand, Graham Martin, went to a CIA official to complain of military spies running around in his backyard, causing him endless diplomatic trou-

ble at no profit. This was an old problem. A decade or so earlier, Dulles's
aide General Lucian K. Truscott II had spent years trying to persuade the
Army to let the CIA do the spy-running, especially in Western Europe. In
1958 Truscott finally won their agreement to a National Security Council
Intelligence Directive (NSCID, pronounced *n-skid*) giving the CIA primary responsibility for agent recruitment. But the problem persisted. After
Martin's complaint, two CIA officers attached to NIPE went to see the
number-two man at the Defense Intelligence Agency, Lieutenant General
Alvah Fitch, to suggest how the problem might be straightened out. They
laid out the problem: the Military Intelligence Group running Army spies in
Thailand was getting into the newspapers; there had been frequent com-
plaints from Thai intelligence officers; the quality of their reports was low.
The offending MI Group had once disseminated a report about the Chinese
Embassy in Mandalay—but Mandalay isn't the capital of Burma, and there
are no embassies in Mandalay. Another report had cited a 500,000-man
Chinese irregular army operating along the China-Burma border: 500,000!
This was absurd on its face. Intelligence reports are evaluated as to reliability: A-1 is impeccable, F-6 worthless. The MI Group in the Far East was an
F-6 paper mill. Fitch listened cordially to the complaint and promised to
look into it. Nothing was done. Later the CIA officers learned that Fitch,
personally, had established the MI Group in the Far East.

Then, early in 1972, in the wake of the Schlesinger-OMB intelligence
study, the CIA was instructed to rewrite the NSCIDs which regulated the
intelligence community. Thomas Karamessines, the Deputy Director for
Plans, saw this as an ideal opportunity to end military spy-running once and
for all. Intelligence had never been the way to the top in the military, and
the policy of frequent rotation meant that an officer handling intelligence
this week might have been running a supply depot last. Karamessines
wanted the spies to be run by CIA—all the spies. But Helms overruled him:
The military had a legitimate interest in certain sorts of intelligence the CIA
wasn't in a position to provide. Better let them run spies of their own rather
than initiate an all-out war which the military would never forgive if they
lost in the end.

Without such a willingness to compromise, Helms could never have
maintained the truce in the intelligence community. Forthcoming on some
issues, he was firm on others. In the late 1960s, for example, he refused to
give the CIA's imprimatur to the Pentagon's hugely expensive plan for a
manned orbiting laboratory, which the military hoped to slip into the intelligence budget. Another Pentagon plan blocked by Helms called for construction of a $500-million over-the-horizon radar center to be built in
England for the purpose of tracking Soviet aircraft over the Black Sea. In
addition to other problems, the center would use a huge percentage of the
electrical power in England, and its microwave transmissions would sterilize
everybody who got within two miles of the place.

But an instinct for compromise sometimes verges on indecisiveness, and probably the commonest criticism of Helms by CIA people concerned his occasional refusal—or inability, they weren't sure which—to make unpleasant jurisdictional decisions. One concerned a long-festering dispute between the Directorate for Intelligence and the Directorate for Plans. The DDI had a domestic operations division which interviewed foreign nationals in the United States. The DDP wanted to use it for spotting possible foreign agent recruits. The DDI balked. The issue went to Helms in 1967. He listened to both sides, promised he'd think it over, and did nothing. In 1970 the problem came up again. The two sides presented their cases. "All right, I've heard both your arguments," Helms said. "Leave it with me and I'll give you an answer within twenty-four hours." Well, that must be the longest day on record, said the man who described the dispute, because Helms hasn't decided yet.

The point here is that Helms's job was intelligence. He was an accepted member of the national security establishment, the director of an agency with fifteen thousand employees, the name at the bottom of National Intelligence Estimates, a man who lunched regularly with the sort of people— Senators, high administration officials, important journalists—without whose trust the CIA could not have done its job, and a servant of the President. Sometimes he did his job well, sometimes not. Both are equally hard for an outsider to judge: one must depend on the echo of his performance. Helms was generally regarded as an able DCI. Allen Dulles had said of him that he was useful and knew how to keep his mouth shut. High officials in the Johnson and Nixon administrations thought of him the same way: he kept things running; he was there when you needed him; he did not talk out of turn. One man who worked with Helms often—he could not say he knew him well—said that Helms was an ideal public servant; he wished the government had more like him. Helms never talked business after hours, unlike a lot of other men who might ramble on about Soviet missiles over dinner. Robert Amory, for example, DDI under Dulles, was famous for his volubility. His next-door neighbors used to say they hated to see winter come—without Amory puttering out in the yard, they never knew what was going on in the world. Helms stuck to his work. It was only later that Watergate turned things upside down, and elevated the quarrels of government to center stage, translating a job which was secret but routine into a mystery of Byzantine intrigue.

But if many of Nixon's officials thought Helms was doing a good job as DCI, Nixon himself did not. Like Schlesinger, he felt that the CIA's analysts reflected the bias of the liberal intellectual and academic community at large. But even worse, from Nixon's point of view, were CIA failures on matters of hard intelligence. Early in 1971, for example, the CIA told the White House that the North Vietnamese did not have reserves enough in Laos to put up more than light, sporadic resistance to a South Vietnamese foray across the Ho Chi Minh Trail. It turned out they had reserves aplenty, and the operation, Lam Song 719, was a disastrous failure. More than six hundred American helicopters were hit by North Vietnamese fire and a hundred were shot down outright. The South Vietnamese came back in wild disorder holding on to the helicopter skids, and a great many did not come back at all.

The following year the CIA predicted a North Vietnamese show of force, a "high point" in the fighting, probably in February when Nixon was in China, and probably in the central highlands. The Agency had evidence of a North Vietnamese military build-up just north of the DMZ which divided the two Vietnams, but the CIA did not anticipate an all-out conventional offensive: the North Vietnamese had never done anything of the sort before, and would be cautious about exposing regular units to the U.S. Air Force.[17] But the "high point" failed to arrive on schedule, and the CIA was puzzled. On March 27, 1972, Helms had lunch with C. L. Sulzberger of the *New York Times*, one of those men he saw regularly as a means of keeping CIA fences in good repair. Sulzberger wondered what had happened to the "high point." "We are absolutely positive it was intended," Helms told him. "And everything is still there, whenever they want to go. But we anticipated it and our bombing has been very intensive."[18]

Three days later, the North Vietnamese regular army came crashing through the DMZ and swept down into the northern provinces of South Vietnam, threatening at one point to take the old imperial capital of Hue. William Colby's reaction—he had returned to the CIA as Executive Director/Comptroller—was much like that of Rostow after the Tet offensive four years earlier. He said Hanoi was desperate and was exposing its army to a devastating defeat. Colby bet a friend they'd never take Danang, and he collected with pleasure when they didn't.

But all the same, Nixon felt challenged as never before. At the end of April he decided to mine Haiphong harbor—something the military had been recommending for years—and for a while it looked as if the offensive, and Nixon's reaction to it, would wreck the Moscow summit meeting scheduled for the end of May, when a major U.S.–USSR arms control agreement was to be signed. As things turned out, the summit was not canceled, but Nixon was angry about the CIA's mistake, however difficult the job of predicting such gambles by an opponent, and however honest the error.

But some of the CIA's errors were not quite so honest. It is not that they constituted outright lying or deception; rather they reflected a degree of cynical weariness, an overrefined sense of audience, a realistic caution about telling certain men things they didn't want to hear. When the President had decided to do something, like invade Cambodia, instinct and experience told Helms to back right out of the way. General Westmoreland and General Abrams had both argued for military operations to clear the North Vietnamese out of their sanctuaries in the areas of Cambodia known as the Parrot's Beak and the Fishhook, and after December 1966, when the U.S. Navy halted North Vietnamese supplies carried to the South in steel-hulled junks, the Pentagon argued that something would have to be done about the new supply route opened up through the Cambodian port of Sihanoukville.

The CIA insisted the effect of the new route was marginal. Paul Walsh, an analyst in the Office of Current Intelligence who had made his reputation with logistics studies, argued on the basis of intercepted radio traffic that the North Vietnamese supplies coming through Sihanoukville were only a dribble. His analysis was finely tuned: if you took the ships' turn-around time—that is, the number of hours spent in port—and multiplied it by their off-loading capacity of so many tons per hour, and then subtracted the known nonmilitary cargo, you came up with quite a small figure. Between December 1966 and early 1970, Walsh said, the total came to only 6,000 tons. The military challenged Walsh's figures, saying the total was more like 18,000 tons, and that something ought to be done about it.

The controversy over Sihanoukville was a classic intelligence war, and according to one CIA official it "raged all over town," from the Agency's Office of Current Intelligence right on up to the President's Foreign Intelligence Advisory Board.[19] Nixon was inclined to credit the military's analysts, suspecting that the real problem was the CIA's bias against the war itself. If Sihanoukville was an important North Vietnamese supply conduit, then maybe something ought to be done about it. Nixon was half-persuaded that the CIA was loading its case against Sihanoukville because it opposed widening the war. The dispute reached a kind of crisis early in 1970 when an unopened crate of Chinese-made AK-47 machine guns was captured in the Mekong Delta of South Vietnam. Serial numbers showed the weapons to be of recent manufacture. The military said, Aha! These things must have come in through Sihanoukville, since it takes months to ship material down the Ho Chi Minh Trail. Not necessarily, Walsh retorted; there was also an express route, and he pointed to an aerial photograph showing a road—to the military, it looked more like a cowpath—from Pleiku down toward the Delta. The guns must have come that way. The military said: Are you kidding? This isn't a truck route; there's grass growing in the middle of it, and it's *four feet tall*. How could some peasant supply courier haul a 200-pound case of machine guns all the way down from Pleiku?

But Walsh stuck to his analysis, and Helms stuck by Walsh, despite the heated arguments of the military and the suspicions of the President. What neither the President nor the military nor anyone outside of a tiny circle inside CIA knew was that there was very good evidence a lot more supplies were coming through Sihanoukville than Walsh's extrapolation would allow. The best evidence: reports from a spy who had access to the lading slips.

The spy had been recruited by the CIA station in Hong Kong in the summer of 1968, and after a short course in secret writing, he began sending biweekly reports to a letter drop in Hong Kong. The Hong Kong station worked largely with the China desk back at the DDP, but there was also a small section in the station devoted to Vietnamese affairs, and when it began sending the spy's reports back to the Cambodian desk there was an immediate response: congratulations all around. This is terrific stuff, keep it coming. The spy's reports were processed by the Cambodian desk and passed on in sanitized form to Paul Walsh. There they simply disappeared. Walsh had figured this thing out: the amount was 6,000 tons, the spy had to be mistaken, his reports were simply disregarded. There matters stood when Nixon began to think of invading Cambodia after the overthrow of Sihanouk on March 18, 1970.

Before the end of March the CIA learned that four VC/NVA divisions had moved into Cambodia from Vietnam, apparently to protect the sanctuaries where Hanoi maintained supply depots, hospitals, rest areas, and—somewhere—the Central Office for South Vietnam (COSVN, pronounced cos-vin), as Hanoi's military headquarters for South Vietnam was known. Intelligence reports also showed the establishment by Hanoi of a new unit called the 470 Transportation Group—"470" referring to April 1970[20]—proof the Vietnamese were giving high priority to their operations in Cambodia. The military wanted to go in after them, and Nixon was leaning in the same direction.

A few weeks earlier, the CIA's Office of National Estimates[21] had begun work on a major paper entitled "Stock-taking in Indochina: Longer Term Prospects." On April 7, 1970, Helms returned an early draft of the paper to Abbott Smith, chairman of the ONE, with the following note: "Okay, let's develop the paper as you suggest and do our best to coordinate it within the Agency. But in the end I want a good paper on this subject, even if I have to make the controversial judgments myself. We owe it to the policy-makers, I feel."[22]

A second draft of the paper was sent to Helms on April 13. It touched on the likely effects of an American invasion—purely hypothetically, no decision had yet been reached—and concluded there was some potential for disruption of VC/NVA efforts, but that the results would be neither crippling nor permanent.[23] Then, on April 21, Helms accompanied Kissinger to his regular morning meeting with the President, where he was told Nixon was planning some sort of invasion of Cambodia to disrupt the sanctuaries and put COSVN out of business, perhaps by South Vietnamese troops, perhaps by the Americans or the two together. But Helms was also warned to keep the plans secret; he was not even to tell the CIA's analysts. Nixon did not want this to get out—he was preparing himself in the usual manner for what he took to be a great decision, perhaps even a turning point in the war. He had already asked Ehrlichman for guidance on domestic matters he'd have to decide in the next month or so, because he didn't want to be distracted as the moment for decision approached. Thereafter it was a matter of weeks before Ehrlichman so much as said "good morning" to the President again.

Helms did as he was told. He kept the invasion plans to himself. Not even his Special Assistant for Vietnamese Affairs, George Carver, learned of it until a day or two before it was announced. Helms was a participant in many of the meetings which led up to the invasion. He did not argue against it, or urge that the job be done with vigor and persistence, if it were to be done at all. Later he felt Nixon had been guilty of a half-measure. A *Newsweek* column by Stewart Alsop, entitled "Semitough," struck Helms as getting Nixon just about right: he wanted to be tough, but he lacked the grit to carry through. If he was willing to go in, he ought to be willing to stay in until the job was done; but instead—as so often before, in Helms's view—he had been afraid of his own decision. These, however, were Helms's private feelings, and he didn't mention them in the meetings that preceded the invasion of Cambodia. He did not even show Nixon or Kissinger the Indochina paper which had been written by ONE, arguing later that they'd made up their minds, and it would have been unfair to the analysts, who had known nothing of the plan when they wrote their estimate. Instead, on the evening of April 29, Helms returned the paper to the ONE with a note saying, "Let's take a look at this on June 1st, and see if we would keep it or make certain revisions."[24]

This decision did not win Helms any friends. CIA analysts were so angry they wrote and circulated a petition protesting Helms's refusal to send the Indochina paper to the White House, an act of protest unprecedented in the Agency's history. Many younger CIA officers were discontented with their slow advancement, resenting the men of Helms's generation who had risen quickly in the CIA and then stayed put, circulating from job to job and blocking the career paths of officers who came later. But this protest had more behind it than the generation gap which Helms sometimes discussed with a young assistant, Robert Kiley. The Assistant Deputy Director for Intelligence, Edward Proctor,[25] was assigned to deal with the petition, but the best he could do was to keep the dissidents from going public. A leader of the dissidents, Thomas Reckford, resigned from the CIA in disgust to join the staff of the Senate Foreign Relations Committee.

Nixon, too, was unhappy. For one thing, he did not enjoy the discovery that COSVN was a will-o'-the-wisp. Kissinger and his staffers on the National Security Council had been accustomed to speak of COSVN in the same way they referred to MACV, the U.S. military headquarters in Vietnam near Tan Son Nhut air base, a huge complex sometimes called "Pentagon East." They had unconsciously assumed that COSVN was a thing, a place, a kind of underground headquarters, something concrete you might find and destroy. One of Kissinger's staffers, William Watt, called up a friend in CIA a few days before the invasion to ask what and where

COSVN was. "We don't have a triangulation," his friend said over the phone. Watt was puzzled. His friend explained that there was no fixed complex, no set of buildings with offices, files, phones; COSVN was a military unit, a group of men who moved about on trucks. Watt was stunned. The United States was about to invade a nonbelligerent country in order to destroy COSVN and no one even knew where it was. He told Kissinger what he'd learned, and Kissinger was visibly startled.[26] The very day Nixon went on the air to announce the invasion, Kissinger tried to talk him out of any reference to COSVN, but Nixon liked his speech the way it was. When the military told him later they had captured a lot of supplies, and destroyed a lot more, but never got their hands on COSVN, Nixon was not amused. He took this as one more example of CIA incompetence. The CIA tried to recover and went to work on a serious formal study of COSVN—its first—in July 1970.

But that wasn't all Nixon was irritated about. The military had also captured a cache of enemy documents, lading slips and the like, which proved in detail that the enemy had been using Sihanoukville all along. The true figure for military supply imports wasn't the 6,000 tons Paul Walsh had deduced; it wasn't even the 18,000 tons the military had estimated; it was 23,000 tons, and Nixon wanted an explanation. So did the President's Foreign Intelligence Advisory Board. Helms appointed a committee to make a postmortem on the Sihanoukville matter, and put it under the chairmanship of Walsh, who had made the original miscalculation and then stuck to it in the face of evidence from a spy and other sources to the contrary. Eventually Walsh and the DDI, R. Jack Smith, went to PFIAB to explain what had gone wrong. Smith said it wasn't such a big mistake really; all those military supplies could have been loaded aboard a single Great Lakes freighter.

But it was a pretty lame excuse, and Helms slipped one more notch in Nixon's estimation. Helms might argue that nobody could be right all the time (which is true), and that Nixon was in no mood for an Indochina stocktaking when he'd steeled himself with the movie *Patton* for a bold stroke in Cambodia (also true), and that the failure of two aspirin in the Parrot's Beak certainly wasn't *his* doing (true again), but none of that made any difference. When the President wanted something it was the DCI's job to deliver. And later that year Nixon gave Helms his toughest and least congenial assignment to date: to stop Salvador Allende from taking over Chile.

Chapter 13

There are many levels to the story of the CIA's involvement in the Chilean election of 1970, and they emerged slowly, over a period of years. One of the few men who knew the whole story was Richard Helms, and he resisted its exposure at every step of the way. Nothing that happened during his tenure as DCI was to cause him more trouble, initially with the President he served, then with the Congress which had once trusted him implicitly, and finally with the Department of Justice and the public at large. The CIA's intervention in Chile was a political spoiling operation of the purest sort. It would be a mistake to credit the CIA with too much responsibility for the wrecking of Chilean democracy; the Chileans themselves were bitterly divided over the constitutional revolution proposed by Salvador Allende. But the CIA's role was pervasive, it violated the spirit of the American political tradition, and it was undertaken at Nixon's explicit order, for reasons which seem shallow, cursory, and offhand at best. The story grew uglier as its several levels emerged, and it is not hard to see why Helms took such risks to keep it secret, beginning with his testimony at a Senate Foreign Relations confirmation hearing after Nixon had appointed him ambassador to Iran.

There was no mistaking the friendly feeling and respect felt by the committee members who talked and joked with Helms for an hour and 45 minutes on the morning of February 5, 1973. To say that they questioned him would be to misrepresent their soft inquiries. Senator J. William Fulbright, the committee's chairman, made it clear he trusted Helms as a man and had confidence in his abilities as DCI. Back in the fall of 1970, for example, Fulbright had been given a sheaf of documents suggesting there had been an alliance of convenience between the CIA and International Telephone and Telegraph (ITT) during the Chilean presidential election. Fulbright called Helms and asked what all this amounted to. Helms told him there had been no major effort down there; if the CIA had really gotten involved, things might have turned out differently. What Helms told him was true—as far as it went. It was good enough for Fulbright. He dropped the matter.

The trust Helms won from Fulbright and other congressional leaders was a considerable achievement. Helms served the President, not the Congress, and he often found himself squarely in the middle of their battles. Presidents depended on the CIA to do things which individual Senators might not like, and of which, consequently, Presidents did not want them to know. The Senate was no longer as quiescent as it had been during the "emergency" of the early Cold War. Helms frequently told the members of congressional oversight committees,[1] "We are part of the executive branch," but at the same time he managed to retain their trust with a settled policy of consistent but narrow and selective honesty. One man who often accompanied Helms to congressional briefings said he "always told the truth and nothing but the truth. But he did not always tell the whole truth."

During the days of bitterest controversy over Vietnam under Johnson and Nixon, Helms made a point of telling Congressmen the facts as the CIA saw them. He did not hesitate to send George Carver to the Hill to testify, but before Carver went the first time, Helms gave him some rigid ground rules: "Don't waffle, don't ramble, and don't guess. When you're getting into an area you feel you can't discuss, you tell them. But you also tell them as succinctly as possible the answer to the question they asked. Not the question they should have asked."

But there was a soft point in Helms's policy. Faced with an awkward question, Helms had only to fall back on his prior loyalty to the President— "Sir, I'm not at liberty to discuss that"—a ready enough escape hatch in theory, but denied in fact. Presidents did not want these battles joined. Johnson and Nixon depended on Helms—as any President depended on any DCI—to somehow avoid or get around the awkward questions. Nixon did not want a fight with Congress about what he was doing in Chile, and it was therefore Helms's delicate job both to tell the truth and to avoid giving the game away. As a result, Helms's truth was sometimes narrow and selective indeed, and in the service of Presidents he marched out onto many a limb.

On February 5, 1973, no longer director, but still a servant of Nixon as ambassador-designate to Iran, Helms marched out onto another. At that time the role of ITT in the 1970 Chilean election was being investigated by a subcommittee on multinational U.S. companies of the Senate Foreign Relations Committee. The investigation, under the chairmanship of Senator Frank Church, had been prompted by Jack Anderson's publication the previous March of ITT documents[2] indicating that the corporation had collaborated with the CIA in seeking to prevent a victory by Salvador Allende at the head of a leftist coalition. At Helms's confirmation hearing this sensitive matter was gently raised.

SENATOR (CHARLES) PERCY: Mr. Helms, this committee has established a subcommittee to study and conduct hearings into the role of multinational corporations in the conduct of American foreign policy. Would it be helpful to these hearings to meet with you before you leave? Your advice and counsel in this area would be extremely valuable to the committee. What would you suggest?

MR. HELMS: I do not think I have anything to contribute, Senator Percy, that could not very easily be acquired from any of my associates, my former associates. I am no longer Director, as you know. I ceased to be on Friday [February 2], so I am actually a free man at the moment. But I think that I would have nothing to contribute that would be of particular significance to the committee.

SENATOR PERCY: So, if we have questions, it would be best to go directly to the new director.

MR. HELMS: I think so, sir, yes. They have the records.

SENATOR PERCY: Fine.

A soft answer to a soft inquiry.

But a few minutes later Fulbright returned to the question of Chile, explicitly mentioning the alleged CIA-ITT collaboration. "Would you care to clarify that question?"

MR. HELMS: Well, sir, the Agency has connections with all kinds of companies and corporations in the United States. . . .

Fulbright said he would have hoped the CIA-ITT relationship was unique. In that case, Helms said, he wasn't quite sure what the question was.

THE CHAIRMAN: I am talking about the reports . . . that there was a very close relationship between ITT and the CIA [true; a dangerous question] or to put it another way, the CIA was using ITT for purposes of espionage, collecting data.

Wrong question. Helms was off the hook. The CIA was not using ITT for espionage. Helms explicitly denied it. Fulbright did not know how to pursue his line of inquiry. The matter lapsed. Helms had neither told a lie nor given the game away. The limb held, but this time it would not hold forever. The first level of the Chilean story was beginning to emerge.

Edward M. Korry, the U.S. ambassador to Chile from October 1967 until Nixon replaced him in October 1971, knew a great deal about the relationship of the CIA and ITT in Chile. One of the first things he did after his arrival in Santiago was to go through the files of his predecessor, Ralph

Dungan, where he found copious evidence of a huge American program, begun by President Kennedy, to make Chile a Latin American showcase for democracy that would stand in contrast to Castro's Cuba. Over the years Chile had received more American aid per capita than just about any other country in the world—Vietnam excepted—and the CIA had provided half the money spent in the 1964 election won by the Christian Democratic party candidate, Eduardo Frei.

Frei was the beneficiary not only of CIA funds given directly to his party (something he did not know), but of a CIA propaganda program intended to scare the living daylights out of Chileans at the prospect of a victory by Allende, whose Socialist Workers party was depicted as nakedly Stalinist. Posters of Russian tanks in the streets of Budapest and of Cubans in front of Castro's firing squads proliferated on Chilean walls in 1964. CIA assets in the Chilean press hammered on the same theme, while CIA election experts coached Christian Democratic party workers in American media and get-out-the-vote techniques. A quieter but equally effective CIA disinformation effort helped divide the left and keep Allende defending himself against charges which were false or half-true or even all-true—such as foreign funding of his party—but which were equally true of his principal opponent, Frei. In the end Frei's victory in 1964 was probably his own, but not its margin; the credit for that must go to the air of crisis which polarized the Chilean electorate, and which had been largely the CIA's doing.

Thus Korry inherited both an American commitment to Frei, and his program of liberal social reform, and a local CIA station well prepared for intervention in a Chilean election. But Korry also inherited the weak link in Kennedy's program for Chile—a heavy involvement by U.S. business. Back in 1963 Kennedy had persuaded David Rockefeller, chairman of the Chase Manhattan Bank, to organize a Business Group for Latin America (later renamed the Council of the Americas) which would support U.S. nation-building programs with business investments. In return, Kennedy created a public institution to ensure American firms against expropriation of their foreign holdings. The weakness of the business link lay in the fact that its heart was not with Frei's program of social reform—income redistribution, more and better schools, a fairer system of tax collection, and above all the breakup of huge landholdings for the benefit of landless peasants.

In 1964 the Business Group for Latin America, along with Chilean allies like the publisher of *El Mercurio*, Agustín Edwards, was persuaded to back Frei by a Kennedy administration official, but it went against their grain. When Nixon came to office they pressured him to drop Frei (a "Kennedy" man) and the Christian Democrats (too "leftist") in favor of a candidate of the right. As the 1970 election approached, Korry was horrified to discover that Nixon was leaning toward support of Jorge Alessandri, in Korry's view a candidate of the rich pure and simple, who proposed nothing less than the dismantling of Frei's reforms. Korry saw this as a disaster for both Chile and the United States.

There is no stranger figure in the Chilean story than Edward Korry, an intelligent and earnest but somewhat prickly man. His position is hard to unravel, not because it is contradictory in itself, but because he found himself at odds with all the other parties—those who were against the U.S. campaign to block Allende as well as those who were for it, those who investigated that effort as well as those who fought to keep it concealed. The principal American actors—Helms, Nixon, Kissinger, Senator Church, Harold Geneen of ITT, John McCone—all had their partisans; only Korry stood alone, his views too uncompromisingly his own to make him a convenient ally for any of the others.

As a journalist, Korry had covered the takeover of democratic regimes in Eastern Europe by the Russians in the late 1940s and early 1950s, an experience which left him with a lifelong distrust and dislike of totalitarian Marxist-Leninist parties. He thought Allende intended to destroy democracy in Chile, albeit through democratic means, and he wanted to stop him. But as a self-described social democrat, a believer in free elections and the natural appeal of liberal centrist parties like Frei's Christian Democrats, Korry felt that Allende's defeat was properly the work of Chileans who had voted for the center before, and, left to their own devices, would do so again. Thus Korry found himself opposed simultaneously to Allende's election and to American support for the right as an alternative. Korry was convinced that Chile would never vote for the right, and that Nixon's policy would work toward an Allende victory.

Korry's attitude toward the CIA was equally divided, or pragmatic. In Paris in the 1950s he had cooperated with the CIA when a KGB agent had tried to recruit him as a spy, stringing the agent along at some personal risk—not to life and limb, but such operations can backfire messily where reputations are concerned[3]—so that the CIA might identify the Russian's interests, learn his procedures of recruitment, and perhaps pick up a clue or two about his other assets.

But that was a glancing contact. Korry's first intimate knowledge of the CIA came during his tenure as Kennedy's ambassador to Ethiopia, where he tried to fire the local chief of station in Addis Ababa on grounds of drunkenness, incompetence, and dishonesty. Korry had already fired an Army colonel attached to the Army Security Agency for disobeying orders to remain aloof from the guerrilla war between the Ethiopians and the Eritrean Liberation Front. The colonel, a much-decorated war hero, was not only yanked out of Ethiopia, but transferred to Alaska and placed in command of a detachment of twelve men. But when Korry tried to oust the station chief in Addis Ababa, he found it tougher going—*much* tougher. He was forced to return to Washington for a full-scale hearing at the State Department, where he found himself in the position of defendant rather than plaintiff. The CIA was represented by Lloyd George, a former chief of the Far East Division in the DDP, who conducted himself like a prosecuting attorney. The State Department maintained an impeccable neutrality, and after the station chief was slapped on the wrist—tour in Ethiopia shortened by one year, then promotion, in effect, to a major post overseas—Korry realized the CIA could protect its own, and was not to be trifled with.

In Chile, Korry found himself occasionally at loggerheads with his CIA chief of station, Henry Heckscher, who was in his last post before retirement. Identified in the Church Committee hearings only as "Felix," Heckscher had worked for the CIA since its creation in 1947. In June of 1953, Heckscher had been chief of base in Berlin, where he asked CIA headquarters in Washington for permission to arm the rioters in the Eastern Zone. A year later he took David Phillips into Guatemala before the coup against Arbenz. Phillips describes him sitting on a hotel bed, calmly snipping the labels out of his clothing, the very image of a veteran clandestine operator. In the late 1950s Heckscher had been station chief in Vientiane, in the thick of a CIA–State Department struggle over the Laotian government. Heckscher, then, was a strong-minded independent, but he was a professional too, and while he questioned orders, he also followed them.

In 1961 Kennedy had explicitly placed local CIA stations under the authority of the U.S. ambassador, and Heckscher, for the most part, was content to work for Korry, but he was instinctively a man of the right, sympathetic to Alessandri and the National party, and thus skeptical of Korry's support for Frei and the center. Of the twelve CIA officers in the Santiago station, ten were devoted primarily to Soviet bloc affairs,[4] but even so, the CIA's involvement in Chilean political affairs and local propaganda programs was very extensive. Korry began to cut them back, and at the same time reduced military aid programs, halted U.S. funding of Chilean Jesuit groups, and argued that ITT and Anaconda ought to prepare for the inevitable nationalization of the copper industry, part of the program of both Allende and Frei. Korry thought the scale of U.S. involvement in Chile was distorting its political system; but he was not hostile to the CIA as such, and one of his early acts as ambassador was to perform what amounted to a personal favor for the Agency.

Not long before Korry arrived in October 1967, a Bolivian ranger unit (trained by the United States in Panama, and supported by American Special Forces troops)[5] hunted down, captured, and then murdered Che Guevara. One immediate result was a quasi-defection by Bolivian Minister of the Interior Antonio Arguedas, an agent for the CIA who fled to Chile and threatened to expose CIA operations. When the CIA learned that the chief of the Cuban intelligence agency, a red-bearded man called Bar-

barossa, was flying to Chile, it feared the worst. Helms personally asked Korry to see what he could do to isolate Arguedas, and Korry persuaded the Chilean authorities to turn Arguedas over to the local CIA station, ostensibly for an attempt to talk him into keeping his mouth shut, but more realistically as a play for time while the CIA hurriedly terminated or disguised operations in Bolivia which Arguedas was in a position to compromise. This was of course highly irregular on the part of the Chilean authorities, and it took a bit of doing; the CIA sent Korry a warm cable of thanks for his help, and later, in 1969 when Korry was briefly back in Washington, Helms invited him out to the CIA for lunch. Nothing of substance was discussed at the lunch, also attended by Cord Meyer; the occasion was purely a friendly thank-you.

As the 1970 election approached, however, Korry found himself in conflict with the CIA. As early as April 15, 1969, Helms had warned Kissinger in a meeting of the 303 Committee[6] that an early start was necessary if the CIA was to repeat its successful role in the 1964 election. Kissinger decided to let the matter ride for the moment. In Santiago, Henry Heckscher wanted to support Alessandri directly. Korry balked at that, but Heckscher persuaded him that his hands-off policy was suggesting American indifference to the cause of democracy, and was in effect helping Allende, who was receiving Russian funds. Korry and Heckscher then drafted a joint plan for a general anti-Allende campaign which would continue to bar direct support for any single candidate. Recalled to Washington for a discussion of the joint proposal at a meeting of the 303 Committee in December 1969, Korry argued that U. Alexis Johnson of the State Department was "colossally wrong" in backing a policy of remaining aloof, that an Allende victory would be a Communist victory in thin disguise, and even that an Allende government would be worse than the Castro regime, because more rigidly Marxist-Leninist. Despite Johnson's reservations about "too much" interference, the Korry-Heckscher proposal for anti-Allende "spoiling operations" was finally approved by the renamed 40 Committee on March 25, 1970.

At this point the multinational companies intervened. They did not want a general anti-Allende, scare-the-people campaign, but a more aggressive program of positive financial and technical support for Alessandri, the only candidate in the election who opposed expropriation. On April 10 a group from the Business Council on Latin America met with the Assistant Secretary of State for Latin America, Charles Meyer, to urge a major pro-Alessandri effort. Meyer, a former Sears Roebuck executive in Latin America who had been given his State Department job through the influence of David Rockefeller, was only vaguely noncommittal when the Chairman of the Board of Anaconda, C. Jay Parkinson, said his and other interested American companies were willing to put up $500,000 to block Allende. Another State Department officer present at the meeting, William Stedman, sent Korry a memorandum describing Parkinson's offer and Korry responded on April 28 with a stinging cable[7] arguing against any such involvement by U.S. business, claiming that Alessandri was a candidate of the rich who could well afford to pay for their own champion's campaign, and repeating again that U.S. support for a rightist was going to backfire against the United States.

Deflected for the moment by Korry's opposition, the multinationals changed their strategy. Instead of proceeding through the State Department, they decided to enlist the aid and expertise of the CIA. In May, John McCone, who had appointed Helms DDP back in 1962 and was now a member of the board of directors of ITT, approached Helms privately to discuss a CIA-ITT program to support Alessandri. As Director back in 1964, McCone had refused an ITT offer of funds for the Chilean election, but now he was ready to propose what amounted to the same thing. In July 1970, following a meeting of Harold Hendrix[8] with a CIA officer in Santiago, McCone again contacted Helms, who in turn arranged a Washington meeting between William Broe, chief of the Western Hemisphere Division in the DDP, and Harold Geneen, the head of ITT. Geneen offered Broe and the CIA $1 million in ITT funds for a pro-Alessandri campaign.

The various congressional committees which investigated the Chilean episode cited the ITT offer but never fully explained what it was for. Giving the CIA money, after all, is bringing coals to Newcastle. Why was the offer made? Korry and the State Department both opposed a pro-Alessandri campaign, and Kissinger duly limited the U.S. effort to an anti-Allende campaign until after the election was already over. Rejecting State Department reservations at a 40 Committee meeting on June 27, 1970—"I don't see why we have to let a country go Marxist just because its people are irresponsible"[9]—Kissinger nevertheless restricted the U.S. effort to spoiling operations and a $500,000 contingency fund, proposed by Korry ten days earlier, to "influence" the final vote of the Chilean Congress, should Allende win the election on September 4.[10] The weakness of Kissinger's strategy, as Helms suggested without emphasis at several meetings on Chile, was the weakness of any political campaign which proposed to beat somebody with nobody. It is hard not to conclude, then, that ITT's million-dollar offer, made indirectly through McCone, was actually an attempt to reach a working agreement with the CIA for a pro-Alessandri campaign which was to remain secret from Korry and the State Department, and perhaps—but this is less likely—even from the White House itself. Did McCone, a former CIA director, have reason to believe the CIA would lend itself to any such freelancing scheme? In the event, the CIA cooperated in a modified version of such a scheme, providing ITT with the names of Chileans through whom the corporation could support Alessandri on its own. According to several sources the CIA went further, and provided ITT with local introductions as well. Thus the CIA was in effect operationally supporting a policy that had

been specifically rejected, so far as the record shows, by the U.S. government. The bald facts of this arrangement were cited by the Church Committee but then more or less ignored, an omission which was to infuriate
Korry later.[11]

In the early summer of 1970 the CIA, over Korry's protest, managed to
persuade the State Department to support a preelection poll in Chile. The
result was a CIA prediction that Alessandri would win with 42 percent of
the vote. Korry took issue with this finding and reviewed the poll with the
help of embassy officers. They cabled the State Department, criticizing the
CIA for basing its poll on the 1960 Chilean census and concluding that
Alessandri would win 40 percent of the vote at best, and likely a good deal
less. The CIA then reviewed the review and stuck to its original figures:
Alessandri would win with 42 percent.

But Alessandri did not win on September 4, despite a CIA propaganda
effort which was a replay of the 1964 scare campaign. The results were:
Allende 36.3 percent, Alessandri 34.9, and the Christian Democratic candidate, Radomiro Tomic, 27.8. The reaction on the right in Chile, among the
multinationals, and in the White House was all but identical: alarm verging
on panic. Nixon and Kissinger, perhaps lulled by the CIA's poll into a
relatively low-key intervention,[12] now felt betrayed and desperate: something had to be done to stop Allende. This sentiment was fully shared by the
multinationals. Chilean publisher Agustín Edwards, a longtime ally of the
CIA, asked Henry Heckscher to arrange a meeting with Korry at the embassy. There Edwards bluntly asked, "Will the U.S. do anything militarily—
directly or indirectly?"[13] Korry was as unhappy about Allende's victory as
Edwards was, but he was dead set against anything in the nature of a coup
to keep Allende out of office. He told Edwards that the U.S. intended to
abide by the election results. Edwards, however, had other avenues to the
U.S. government, and he immediately used them. As the owner of a local
Pepsi-Cola bottling plant he knew Pepsico's chief, Donald Kendall, an old
ally and friend of Nixon. Edwards fled Chile, met with Kendall in the
United States, and prophesied general disaster if Allende were allowed to
take office. Kendall was impressed and arranged for Henry Kissinger and
John Mitchell to meet Edwards at a private breakfast on the morning of
September 15, 1970. A week earlier, Harold Geneen of ITT, also alarmed,
had asked McCone to get in touch with Helms again, but this time Helms
delayed his response, waiting to see what the White House wanted to do.

Korry, meanwhile, had picked up wind of a possible military coup as a
means of preventing Allende's confirmation by the Chilean Congress in its
vote scheduled for October 24. The commander of the Chilean armed
forces, General René Schneider, was known to be firmly opposed to any
unconstitutional attempt to block Allende's confirmation. Since the birth of
Chilean independence in 1818, democracy had been interrupted on only
three brief occasions, the last in 1932, a remarkable history in Latin America

and one which Schneider wanted to maintain. Other military officers, however, were not so punctilious. For nearly eight years the CIA had been
painting a leftist victory in the darkest possible light, and elements of the
Chilean military, like Chilean businessmen hurriedly exporting their capital
abroad, were afraid that Stalinism was around the corner.[14] One of the
early military conspirators was Brigadier General Roberto Viaux, who left
the army after an abortive coup called the "Tacnazo" in 1969, and who was
an erratic, politically irresponsible man with a beautiful, ambitious wife.
Korry had ordered the CIA to refrain from all contact with Viaux and other
military conspirators, and he later barred two local ITT men from the
embassy, Hal Hendrix and Robert Berrellez, because of their plotting with
the Chilean right. On September 12, responding to a 40 Committee request
for a "cold-blooded assessment" of the situation, Korry cabled that "our own
military people [are] unanimous in rejecting possibility of meaningful military intervention. . . . What we are saying in this 'cold-blooded assessment'
is that opportunities for further significant USG action with the Chilean
military are non-existent."[15]

Two days later, on September 14, the 40 Committee decided to gamble
on what the CIA referred to as "the Rube Goldberg gambit,"[16] an unwieldy
scheme to (A) persuade Frei to resign, (B) have his vice-president succeed
to the presidency, and then (C) "influence"—with a $250,000 CIA contin-
gency fund—the Chilean Congress to vote for Frei, who was otherwise
constitutionally ineligible to succeed himself. Korry went along with this
improbable scheme on the grounds that it depended on Frei, and thus
offered a "Chilean solution." But Heckscher had already warned Korry that
nothing of the sort could work, since CIA agents had learned that Tomic
and Allende had reached a secret deal to back the leader if either of the two
candidates should place first or second in the election. In effect, they were
collaborating to beat the right. Such a deal could hardly have been achieved
without Frei's support as leader of the Christian Democrats, but Korry
refused to believe the CIA was right in its report of the deal, and when he
learned later that the Agency *had* been right, he felt something of a fool for
ever having approached Frei with the Rube Goldberg gambit.

But in any event the gambit went nowhere, and while Korry continued
to urge Frei to think of something, at the same time he peppered Washington with warnings that only Frei and a "Chilean solution" had any chance at
all, and that a military coup by the likes of Viaux would be the height of
folly. But coup rumors continued to circulate, and Korry's suspicions were
aroused. One day Heckscher—"this normally courteous man," in Korry's
words[17]—suddenly blew up in anger at Korry's low-key intervention with
Frei, an explosion the more remarkable because the two men were not
alone, but accompanied by Korry's deputy chief of mission, Harry Shlaudeman. "Why the hell don't you twist Frei's arm?" Heckscher shouted. "You're
telling Washington you're doing it and you're not!" Korry warned Heckscher

that he'd be out in twenty-four hours if he did not calm down, and then lectured him that it was up to Frei and the Chileans to block Allende. If they couldn't find a way, the U.S. couldn't do it for them.

Heckscher later apologized, but Korry began to wonder if the CIA was up to something behind his back. He asked Shlaudeman to look into it, and Shlaudeman reported he could find no evidence that the CIA was plotting with the military on its own. He told Korry he was being paranoid.

All the same, Korry decided to fly to Washington to make his case in person. Shortly before leaving he warned Frei that a series of bombings in Santiago were the work of a right-wing group headed by General Arturo Marshall,[18] an old associate of Viaux. When Korry had asked Heckscher who was behind the bombings Heckscher told him, also mentioning the possibility Marshall might try to assassinate Allende.[19]

Back in Washington on October 13, Korry met with Kissinger and argued strongly that U.S. support for a military coup in Chile might backfire as embarrassingly as the Bay of Pigs. Viaux was simply not the sort of man to whom the United States ought to lend its support. Kissinger listened and then asked Korry if he'd like to talk to the President. Korry said he would, and the two men proceeded to the Oval Office, where Nixon met them at the door and startled Korry, as the door closed behind them, by pounding his fist into the palm of his hand and saying, "That sonofabitch, that sonofabitch!" The expression on Korry's face halted Nixon in mid-expletive. "Not you, Mr. Ambassador," he said, "you always tell it like it is. It's that bastard Allende."[20]

Nixon then commenced a monologue on how he was going to smash Allende, but afterward Korry repeated the warnings he had given to Kissinger, and despite Nixon's determination to block Allende, he appeared somewhat taken aback. He asked Korry if he'd like to attend a meeting of the 40 Committee the following day, and Korry agreed to do so. At the meeting on October 14, Korry for the third time listed his reasons for opposing any contact with Viaux or other Chilean military conspirators. Afterward, he felt the consensus of the group—Kissinger, Karamessines,[21] and John Mitchell were there, as well as the usual State Department and JCS representatives—was on his side: there was not much the United States could do to block Allende at this late hour. The assets were lacking for a direct intervention, and the Chilean allies of the United States seemed too irresolute to move on their own. Korry flew back to Chile thinking he had helped the U.S. to make the best of a bad job, and that it could now deal with Allende on a cool but correct basis, free of the consequences of a botched coup.

Korry was so convinced, in fact, that even after a group of Chilean military plotters fatally wounded General Schneider in a bungled kidnapping attempt on October 22, it never occurred to Korry that the United States might have been involved. He was satisfied that his opposition to any harebrained scheme of the sort had carried the day. His certainty was not even shaken the following March by an enigmatic encounter with C. L. Sulzberger of the *New York Times*. Korry and Sulzberger had been good friends since they had been journalists together in Europe at the end of the war, and there was nothing odd in the fact Sulzberger would stop in for an evening at Korry's official residence in Santiago. But there was something decidedly odd about Sulzberger's behavior after dinner when he quietly told Korry there was something he wanted to discuss with him. Korry said sure, what is it, Cy? Sulzberger, still in a quiet voice, said this was private, was there somewhere they might speak alone?

Now Korry was more than puzzled. Only their wives were present; what could be so secret they had to leave the room? But Korry said all right, and led Sulzberger into the library. Sulzberger closed the door, took Korry by the arm and brought him to the exact center of the room, then leaned forward and, whispering directly into Korry's ear, said he understood that Korry, personally, had killed Nixon's attempt to stage an anti-Allende coup the previous fall.

Korry was astonished. He knew Sulzberger had recently been staying with Averell Harriman in Washington, and that Harriman had been lobbying for the hardest possible line against Allende. Korry also knew that Sulzberger was, in addition, a close acquaintance of both Kissinger and Helms, but these impressive connections only made Sulzberger's question all the more puzzling. Korry told him he was dead wrong, there had been no U.S. coup plotting, nor even serious talk of a coup. Sulzberger thought Korry was being cagey; Come on, Ed, he said in effect, level with me. But Korry insisted: he didn't know where Sulzberger had picked this up, but the story was just plain wrong.

Korry was amused by Sulzberger's melodramatic air, and later he mentioned the incident to Shlaudeman, who had called him paranoid for suspecting a CIA coup gambit behind his back. See? said Korry, I'm not the only one; these nutty ideas get around. The episode struck Korry as a good example of everything that was wrong about Washington: the secrecy, suspicion, rumors of intrigue given credence by otherwise reasonable men. Korry was still convinced his views had prevailed: there had been no U.S. attempt to mount a coup.

On Wednesday, February 7, 1973, Richard Helms met again with the Senate Foreign Relations Committee in an executive session, just two days after his first, public meeting with the Committee. The Senators had a few additional questions aroused by news stories suggesting the CIA had been improperly training local American police departments, and that it had been somehow involved in Watergate.

THE CHAIRMAN: I think, Mr. Helms, in view of the nature of these questions, it would be appropriate that you be sworn as a witness, which is
customary where we have investigative questions. Would you raise your
hand and swear. Do you solemnly swear to tell the truth, the whole
truth, and nothing but the truth, so help you God?
MR. HELMS: I do, sir.

Several of the questions asked Helms that day were to cause him trouble later,[22] but none more than three totally unexpected queries from Senator Stuart Symington. Helms considered Symington a friend, with good
reason, but on this occasion Symington's sudden curiosity, on a subject
which custom reserved for the CIA oversight committee, resulted in more
trouble than Helms had ever known before. It has been suggested that
Helms and Symington had arranged their exchange in advance, so that
Helms might put an official denial of meddling in Chile on the record in a
friendly forum. This was untrue.[23] Symington asked his questions out of the
blue.

SENATOR SYMINGTON: Would you let me ask a question in context?
SENATOR PERCY: I would be happy to.
SENATOR SYMINGTON: Did you try in the Central Intelligence Agency to
overthrow the government of Chile?
MR. HELMS: No, sir.
SENATOR SYMINGTON: Did you have money passed to the opponents of
Allende?
MR. HELMS: No, sir.
SENATOR SYMINGTON: So the stories you were involved in that war are
wrong?
MR. HELMS: Yes, sir. I said to Senator Fulbright many months ago that
if the Agency had really gotten in behind the other candidates and spent
a lot of money and so forth the election might have come out differently.

Afterward Helms asked the CIA's general counsel, Lawrence Houston,
to review his testimony—a standard practice. Houston warned Helms that
his remarks on Chile might be "a problem," but Helms decided to let them
stand. "Well, please don't be so didactic next time," said Houston, meaning:
Don't be so categorical, don't slam the door, leave yourself some room to
squirm. Helms wasn't worrying about the next time. He knew that if he
changed his testimony he would only be drawing attention to the CIA's
campaign to prevent Allende's election. An even deeper secret was the
CIA's unsuccessful effort to mount a military coup in Chile to prevent
Allende from taking office after he won a plurality in the election. That was
something which Edward Korry, for one, knew nothing about. In early 1973
Korry was still on the government's side; he refused to tell the Church

Committee on multinationals anything about the CIA Chilean operation because Allende was still in office and Korry did not want to compromise the Chileans who had worked in good faith with the CIA. Helms elected to take his chances; he left his testimony alone.

But this limb was not stout enough to bear a grown man's weight indefinitely. It was already badly creaking when Ed Korry, now retired, went to see William Colby at the CIA in June 1975. A few weeks earlier, Korry had been asked for an interview by Gregory Treverton, a staff member on the recently created Senate Select Committee on Intelligence, headed by Frank Church. Korry had been expecting a call and agreed. Then he began telephoning former government colleagues—his deputy, Harry Shlaudeman; his defense attaché in Chile, Colonel Paul Wimert; Kissinger's chief expert on Latin America, Viron P. Vaky; his successor as ambassador, Nathaniel Davis, and others—in order to pin down what had really happened before talking to Treverton or appearing publicly before the Church Committee. One of the last officials on Korry's list was Colby, a man he had never met. Korry wanted to ask Colby for permission to read his testimony before the House Armed Services Committee in April 1974, when Colby allegedly had outlined CIA efforts to "destabilize" Allende's regime.[24]

At the CIA that day in June 1975, Ray Warren, who had replaced Heckscher as station chief in November 1970, introduced Korry for the first time to David Phillips, who had been chief of the DDP's Chile Task Force in September and October 1970. None of the three men—Warren, Phillips, or Colby—told Korry anything of substance about efforts to block Allende, and Colby even remarked, "If only we'd put more money into Alessandri, Allende wouldn't have been elected." Korry repeated all his old arguments against U.S. funding for a candidate of the rich, but without eliciting much response from Colby, an extraordinarily poker-faced man. He was not even able to persuade Colby to let him have a look at the April 1974 testimony, despite the fact the Church committee had it and would presumably ask Korry about it when he appeared to testify. On top of that, when Korry described his understanding of what had happened—namely, no "destabilization," no coup—Colby said nothing to disabuse him. He simply listened, and his face registered nothing whatever. Korry, to his sorrow, mistakenly concluded that Colby's expressionless gaze was intended as a kind of discreet assent, and that Korry had got his facts right. After all, Colby knew Korry was scheduled to debate the *New York Times* reporter Seymour Hersh; why would Colby let a former U.S. ambassador publicly compromise himself by denying destabilization, if he might warn him off with nothing more than a wink?

But Korry had figured wrong. The wooden face was something of a

Colby specialty, and those blank eyes behind Colby's glinting glasses expressed only one message: an absolute refusal of all comment. On July 19, 1975, when Gregory Treverton and a State Department official (and former CIA officer) named J. J. Hitchcock arrived at Korry's house in Briarcliff Manor, New York, Korry still did not know anything more about the Chilean episode than he had known five years earlier. In fact, he did not even suspect there was anything more to know.

But after Korry told Treverton that the United States had nothing to do with the military plotting which led to General Schneider's murder, or with ITT maneuvers to block Allende, Treverton asked Hitchcock, "Don't you think we can tell him?" Korry was sworn to secrecy, and then informed that in fact there had been an American attempt to foment a Chilean coup, that Korry's long-abandoned suspicions of a CIA plot behind his back had been right on the button, and that he, Korry, had been deliberately excluded from any knowledge of the attempted coup by President Nixon himself.[25] That was the first time Korry learned of Track II.

The plot had begun with a meeting in the Oval Office of the President, Kissinger, John Mitchell, and Helms on September 15, 1970, just one day after Korry had been ordered to pursue the Rube Goldberg gambit with Frei in Santiago. Helms testified later that he thought Nixon's determination to act was the doing of Donald Kendall and Agustín Edwards, who had met Kissinger for breakfast that morning. Helms knew Kendall fairly well, having seen him at Washington meetings perhaps four or five times a year,[26] and he knew that Kendall and Nixon were close, Kendall having given Nixon his first big corporate account after Nixon began practicing law in New York. But more immediately, Helms had been asked by Nixon or Kissinger—he can no longer remember which it was—to meet with Kendall and Edwards at a Washington hotel. Before the meeting, Helms called Broe to ask for somebody familiar with Chilean operations, and Broe sent a CIA officer named Ken Millian, who accompanied Helms to the meeting with Kendall and Edwards. The two men made quite an impassioned appeal for CIA help in blocking Allende, and Helms concluded that they must have made the same appeal to Nixon, with some success.

Nixon himself cited a different source for his concern about Allende. In one of his television interviews with David Frost in 1977, he told Frost that it began with a conversation with an Italian businessman, who warned him, "If Allende should win the election in Chile, and then you have Castro in Cuba, what you will in effect have in Latin America is a red sandwich, and eventually it will all be red."[27] But whatever the exact source of Nixon's fears, he made no secret of his determination to stop Allende at that meeting in the Oval Office on September 15, 1970. He outlined the dangers as he saw them, swore his administration would not "cave in at the edges,"[28] and told Helms to leave no stone unturned in the attempt to block Allende's confirmation by any means necessary. "If I ever carried a marshal's baton in my knapsack out of the Oval Office," Helms told the Church Committee, "it was that day."[29] He also carried a single page of handwritten notes which capture the tone of his instructions:

> One in 10 chance perhaps, but save Chile!
> worth spending
> not concerned risks involved
> no involvement of embassy
> $10,000,000 available, more if necessary
> full-time job—best men we have
> game plan
> make the economy scream
> 48 hours for plan of action[30]

At that point Helms thought a one-in-ten chance for success was optimistic, and nothing happened later to improve the odds. Thomas Karamessines, the DDP, felt the same way, and so did David Phillips, brought back from Brazil to head a special Chile Task Force for the duration of the operation. Henry Heckscher, the station chief in Santiago, was even more pessimistic, and he peppered Langley with his doubts[31] to such a degree that on October 7 he was ordered to stop protesting and limit his cables to what he *did*. When Heckscher continued to balk, Karamessines ordered his return to Washington. "Well," Heckscher told a friend at Langley, "I guess I've lost my job." In the event, he was not fired, but he was most unmistakably "read the riot act," according to several sources. This was something the CIA had been told to do, Langley was committed to giving it a try, and Heckscher was expected to bite the bullet and go along. When Heckscher got back to Santiago he made it clear to his deputy chief of station, Dino Pionzio, that they had no choice. The special Chile Task Force in Langley had been serious from the beginning. Helms had passed on his orders to Karamessines and Broe, and Karamessines's first instinct had been to establish the Task Force in his own suite of offices. An aide argued that this would be a dead giveaway that something major was afoot, so the mailroom registry which channeled cable traffic was moved to a conference room, and the Task Force was given space in the registry. The operation went forward, then, despite the unanimous pessimism of those most closely involved, because Helms had his marching orders from Nixon and Kissinger. "Nobody," said Karamessines, "was going to go into the Oval Office, bang his fist on the table, and say we *won't* do it." The only limits Helms imposed on the operation were those demanded by security: he was willing enough to try and fail, not at all ready for the failure to become public. Despite Korry's fear that an attempted coup might become another Bay of Pigs, not a word surfaced for nearly five years, and the operation emerged then only because another branch of the government discovered an outline of the facts and insisted on publishing them.

But secret or not, failure is failure, and Heckscher had no enthusiasm for a project with so little chance of success. The trouble, in his view, was that the CIA had nothing to work with. The local station was heavily dependent on the Embassy's defense attaché, Colonel Paul Wimert, for its contacts with Generals Roberto Viaux and Camilo Valenzuela and their coconspirators, largely because Korry had forbidden the CIA to keep in touch with dissident military officers. Colonel Wimert's contacts with the Chilean military were excellent. Wimert was a lover of horses and maintained a stable of thoroughbreds on his ranch outside Santiago where Chilean military men often came to spend the weekend. Plotting coups is not normally the work of military attachés, but Wimert was happy to oblige, demanding only one concession from Heckscher: if things went wrong, and something happened to Wimert, the CIA must promise to get his beloved horses back to the United States.

Not only was the CIA forced to deal indirectly with the conspirators, at least in the beginning, but as assets they weren't exactly formidable. Viaux in particular was an unreliable ally. Heckscher knew, and reported, that Viaux's circle had been infiltrated by the Chilean MIR, an organization of the extreme left, and as time went by, it grew increasingly apparent that neither Viaux nor Valenzuela had a plausible plan for taking power. The best they could come up with was a succession of jerry-built schemes to kidnap General Schneider in the hope that Frei, or the rest of the Chilean military establishment, might decide to act in the ensuing crisis. But even that scheme percolated erratically, despite a CIA offer to pay up to $50,000 for Schneider's successful abduction.

Helms and Karamessines informed Kissinger and his aide, Alexander Haig, of the bleak picture on a regular basis. At the end of September, Helms sent William Broe to ask Edward Gerrity of ITT for help in making the Chilean economy scream, but now ITT had cold feet and refused. Not long after, Viaux had to be dissuaded from a premature coup attempt which might wreck everything. Kissinger later told the Church Committee that a gloomy Karamessines report on October 15 led him to cancel the whole operation. Karamessines did not remember it quite the same way. The Viaux approach was abandoned, he said, but at the same time Kissinger ordered the CIA to keep the pressure on "every Allende weak spot in sight—now . . . and into the future until such time as new marching orders are given."[32] Two days later, according to one source, Karamessines was called in by Nixon and told to find a military alternative to the hopeless Viaux.[33]

On the same day in Santiago, October 17, a CIA officer told Viaux not to push too fast,[34] while Colonel Wimert met with another group of Chilean military conspirators who asked him for eight to ten tear gas grenades, three .45-caliber submachine guns, and 500 rounds of ammunition, claiming they were needed for self-protection. Wimert obtained the grenades from the CIA and delivered them to an associate of Valenzuela, who, later the same day, told Wimert that coup plans were now ready and would begin the next night with the kidnapping of Schneider following a military dinner. The plan came to nothing when Schneider left the dinner in a private car, well guarded by police. Wimert was told another attempt would be made the following night, on October 20, but that too failed, and Heckscher concluded that time had run out.

Nevertheless, Wimert delivered the promised machine guns[35] to Valenzuela's associate at a 2:00 a.m. meeting on October 22. Five hours later a group of military conspirators met for final planning of a last attempt to abduct Schneider, and at 8:00 a.m. they halted the general's car. Schneider attempted to resist, drew his revolver, and was shot and fatally wounded by his would-be abductors. He died three days later, one day after Allende's confirmation.

The Church Committee's description of Schneider's murder was punctiliously factual. Because Schneider was killed with handguns, and because the military officers to whom Colonel Wimert gave the machine guns[36] were not present at the 7:00 a.m. meeting before the botched kidnapping attempt, and because it was General Viaux who was held principally responsible for the fatal attempt by the Chilean courts later, the Committee concluded that the CIA was not implicated directly in Schneider's death. The trouble with this highly legalistic arrangement of the facts is that it obscures three points: (1) there was no clear line of division between the Viaux and the Valenzuela circles, and the Chilean courts also held the latter responsible, though to a lesser degree;[37] (2) the failed attempts of October 19 and October 20 had been carried out by the same group which fatally wounded Schneider on October 22, although Wimert's discussion of those attempts had been with Valenzuela, a fact which suggests the two generals were acting in close concert; (3) both Viaux and Valenzuela were in regular contact with the CIA, were actively encouraged to proceed with their plan for kidnapping Schneider, were promised a substantial sum of money if successful,[38] and very likely would have done nothing at all without American encouragement to move. If the CIA did not actually shoot General Schneider, it is probably fair to say that he would not have been shot without the CIA.

The day before the Chilean Congress was to vote to confirm the next President, Helms, back from a trip to Vietnam, met with the Chilean Task Force in Langley, headed by David Phillips, for a discussion which was mildly hopeful the plan might still work. "It was agreed," a CIA memorandum of the meeting said, "that a maximum effort has been achieved, and that now only the Chileans themselves can manage a successful coup. The

Chileans have been guided to a point where a military solution is at least open to them."[39]

But it didn't work out that way, just as Heckscher had predicted in a cable to Langley as early as October 9. The Chilean military rallied behind General Carlos Prats, Schneider's successor, and despite General Valenzuela's appointment as commander of Santiago province, there was no coup. Allende was confirmed on October 24.

Nixon and Kissinger were not happy with the events of September and October 1970. Far from being grateful to Helms for having made such a determined effort without so much as a word leaking to the press, they blamed him for Allende's victory. Kissinger personally asked the President's Foreign Intelligence Advisory Board to make a special investigation of the Chilean episode, and at the same time word began to spread around town that the administration was unhappy with the Agency. In December 1970, John McCone paid one of his regular visits to Langley and dropped in to see John Bross, who had handled CIA's explanations to PFIAB. McCone said he'd been to see Kissinger. "Everybody's very down on Helms for failing to take drastic action to stop Allende," McCone said.

Bross asked Helms about this, and Helms confirmed that the administration was indeed unhappy, thinking he'd failed to warn them in time of the likelihood of an Allende victory, and then had failed again to block his confirmation after the election. But in Helms's view the failure belonged at least equally to the administration, for paying no attention when he warned the 40 Committee at least a year ahead of the election that now was the time for the CIA to get involved, and to Ed Korry, for resisting a pro-Alessandri campaign down to the bitter end.

"I never got up and pounded the table and said you've got to take drastic action," Helms conceded to Bross. "I don't think that was my role. That's what we're always being criticized for—intervening in policy."

Helms thought it unfair that he should be singled out for blame in the Chilean fiasco, but at the same time he considered the matter as akin to an argument in the family, and whenever it threatened to go outside of the family he did what he could to keep the whole episode secret. He had thrown Fulbright off the scent back in September 1970, when he evaded Fulbright's question about CIA involvement with Chile and simply remarked that if the CIA had really put its weight into the election, things might have turned out differently—which was very likely true, but not, as the lawyers say, responsive. He had sidestepped an invitation to testify from Senator Charles Percy on February 5, 1973. He completely misled Senator Symington two days later. When he was called back from Iran to testify yet again on May 21, 1973, he narrowly escaped a list of 100 questions prepared by the Foreign Relations Committee staff when the hearing was held in public, a maneuver which guaranteed that the Senators—not the well-prepared staff who had been studying the Chilean episode—would be asking the questions.

It was not until January 1975 that Helms was finally cornered and forced to explain his earlier evasions. Helms explained that the CIA hadn't given money directly to Allende's opponents, that the CIA didn't try to fix the vote in the Chilean Congress because investigation had shown it couldn't be arranged, that the CIA didn't try to overthrow the Chilean government because the Agency failed to find anyone who could really do it. If there are explanations which can be called lame, these are cripples. Helms had given Symington the same "explanations" the night before his testimony back in May 1973, and Symington, a friend, had been content with them. But others preferred to describe Helms's testimony by a balder term: lies. Enough people subscribed to this definition to move the whole question to the Justice Department, but the real heart of Helms's explanation was more to the point.

AMBASSADOR HELMS: I realize, sir . . . that my answer [to a question about the attempt to bribe the Chilean Congress] was narrow, but I would like to say something here. I didn't come into the Multinational Committee [headed by Frank Church, where Helms testified on Chile on March 6, 1973, a few days before leaving for Iran] hearing to mislead you, but I have had as Director . . . a lot of problems, and one of the principal problems was who in the Congress [I] was really to divulge all of the details of covert operations to, and I must say this has given me a great deal of difficulty over the years. . . . If I was less than forthcoming it wasn't because I was being bloody-minded, it was simply because I was trying to stay within what I thought was the congressional guidelines.[40]

That was as close as Helms ever came to saying that his interrogators had no right to honest answers, because they had no right to ask the questions they had. But by this time it was not primarily the Senators whom Helms had to satisfy. The nature of his testimony—narrow in the line of duty? so evasive as to pass into the realm of lies?—was no longer academic. The matter had been referred to the Department of Justice, and the man who had hand-delivered the documents in the case was someone Helms had helped to rise in the Agency, someone who might have been considered to a degree in Helms's personal debt for his position as Director of Central Intelligence, William Colby. Helms's fight was not really with the Senators by this time—with the possible exception of Church, they had little appetite for Helms's blood—but with Colby's policy of letting out the "bad secrets." The very first of the "bad secrets"—others, of course, were coming—was a charge of perjury leveled against Richard Helms.

Chapter 14

In retrospect Watergate seems to have had the momentum of a river. The burglary of June 1972 and the investigation which followed it cut an ever-widening channel through the Nixon administration. The flood might be deflected, rerouted, or even dammed momentarily, but eventually it resumed its downward course. In trying to halt the investigation in the summer and fall of 1972, Nixon, fearful of its impact on the election in November, only succeeded in building a record of obstruction of justice which would bring him to the verge of impeachment two years later. The problem from the beginning was the burglary team itself, seven men whose patience and loyalty gradually eroded as they felt the judicial machinery closing in around them. Not two weeks after the break-in, John Dean told the Deputy Director of Central Intelligence, General Vernon Walters, that the burglars were already "wobbling," and they were never restrained for long by Nixon's parsimonious bribes and vague secondhand promises of clemency.

But for a moment in mid-September 1972, Nixon thought he had won. On September 15 the grand jury finally indicted the seven men, ignoring the officials of the Committee for the Reelection of the President (CREEP) who had paid them and given them their orders. It looked as if the case might be disposed of as the "bizarre affair" of no consequence described by the White House from the beginning. On the day of the indictments Nixon congratulated John Dean for plugging all the leaks in the White House levees. After discussing ways of keeping further investigations "buttoned up," Nixon, in a confident mood, began to talk about getting even. This was a familiar subject for H. R. Haldeman, who was also present. "I want the most comprehensive notes on all those who tried to do us in," Nixon said. "They didn't have to do it . . . they were doing this quite deliberately and they are asking for it and they are going to get it. . . ."[1] But the difficulty, as both Dean and Haldeman pointed out, was a recalcitrant bureaucracy, most of it Democratic, and just about all of it beyond the President's reach.

Well, that was all going to change, Nixon said. The Justice Department, the Internal Revenue Service, and all the rest of the departments were going to start toeing the line. When the election was over there was going to be a thorough housecleaning, a clean sweep. This was not a new notion in Nixon's mind; he was a brooding man, and the idea of seizing government by the throat had been fermenting in him for a long time. Back in 1968, at lunch with Johnson in the White House after winning the election, Nixon had asked Johnson why he'd kept on all those Kennedy people. The time to clean house had been right after Johnson's big victory of 1964. Nixon remembered the numbers precisely. Now he was about to win by an even bigger margin—every state but one—and he intended to *clean house*.[2] George Shultz, the Secretary of the Treasury, was going to get his orders; the IRS was going to get on the team or else. "The point is, I want there to be no holdovers left," Nixon said. "The whole goddamn bunch is to go out. And if he doesn't do it, he's out as Secretary of Treasury. And that's the way it's going to be played. Now that's the point. See."[3]

Nixon knew exactly what he wanted, a reorganized government which would be truly run by the White House for the first time. "I have an uneasy feeling there's no real plan developed yet. I talked to Ehrlichman about it, but he's so busy with other things. The whole plan has got to be a concerted plan to find out not only who the President appoints, but who every goddamned cabinet officer appoints, and every damned agency head appoints up and down the line."

The trouble was that the cabinet secretaries were captives of their underlings, who really ran the government. Maybe Melvin Laird appointed a few of his own people at the top of the Defense Department. "But the people who ran the Pentagon before are still running the goddamn Pentagon. . . . And this is the problem. The difficulty is you've got to do it fast because . . . after the first of the year it's too late. You've got to do it right after the election. You've got one week, and that's the time to get all those resignations in and say, 'Look, you're out, you're out, you're finished, you're done, done, finished.' Knock them the hell out of there."[4]

As always when it came to threats, Nixon was as good as his word. On November 5, 1972, the senior White House staff was called into the Roosevelt Room for what they doubtless expected to be something in the nature of a victory celebration. They were in error. Nixon came in and made a short, abrupt announcement: he wanted them all to resign. They were thunderstruck. Nixon left and Haldeman spelled it out. Things were going to change. Some would stay and some would go. They'd find out who later. For the present he wanted the resignation of every man and woman in the room on his desk before night fell. Later that day the same message was relayed to the Cabinet Room, and during the following days the word went out to the rest of the government: every presidential appointee was expected to submit his resignation. In the past, such resignations at a change of administration had been *pro forma*; this time Nixon intended that they should be genuine.

At the CIA, General Walters informed Helms he planned to submit his resignation, as ordered. But Helms told him not to do it. Only political appointments were properly covered by the President's order, Helms felt, and he did not consider running the CIA to be a political job. He did not intend to submit his own resignation, and he did not want Walters to submit his, either. Walters acquiesced.

There was probably an element of calculation in Helms's decision, a hope that Nixon would not insist if Helms made no offer to go, but he also had reason to feel he was on firm ground. The day of the election Helms had phoned Kissinger's chief assistant, Alexander Haig, to invite him to lunch. He knew Haig wasn't busy that day, and here was a chance for Helms to repay lunches with Haig at the White House. Haig came. During the lunch in Helms's office Haig asked him about his plans. Helms, dealing with the question as if it were entirely casual, said he thought perhaps his time was drawing to a close, he'd been DCI for more than six years (longer than anyone else except Allen Dulles); he'd like to stay on at least another year but then perhaps he'd be ready to leave. Haig said that sounded reasonable, another year or two, after which Helms could probably pick his own successor. Helms was not announcing a plan to leave, exactly; just discussing his job, and Haig's reaction convinced him his position was secure. It was probably with this conversation in mind that Helms decided not to submit his resignation.

But Nixon had other plans, and he had not been discussing them with Haig. Immediately after the election Nixon retreated to Camp David with Haldeman and a small staff and began the process of cleaning out the government. The firings lasted for weeks, and the sheer number of them turned the process into something as abrupt as execution. Haldeman would meet the victim of the moment, tell him his time was up, and then take him in to see the President for a final conversation. Helms's turn came on November 20.

After Helms's summons arrived he called Kissinger to ask what this was all about. Kissinger said he didn't know. Helms wondered if perhaps it didn't concern a CIA dispute with the White House Office of Management and Budget about his new system for putting together the intelligence community budget. He suggested as much to William Colby, and Colby arranged for a briefing on the dispute with OMB before Helms left for Camp David. The effort was wasted. The budget was not discussed.

Haldeman met Helms on his arrival but apparently did not tell him what Nixon had in mind, contrary to Haldeman's custom of the preceding weeks with other victims. Instead he showed Helms into a living room in the Aspen Cottage where he was directed to a seat at the end of a flowered sofa. Nixon was sitting to his left in an easy chair. Haldeman was in an identical chair at the far end of the sofa, a briefing book in his lap. Nixon's photographer came in for a routine photo of the three men, then departed.

The conversation which followed lasted perhaps 30 minutes. Haldeman said nothing, just sat and listened. Nixon wasted no time in getting to the point. He said he planned to make some changes among the top officers of his administration; people get tired, find themselves trapped in old positions, falter, give in. He wanted to bring in new blood. He planned to appoint a new Director of Central Intelligence. It was pretty abrupt and businesslike. Helms was of course surprised; he'd expected nothing of the sort. But he said all right, perhaps a good time for a changeover would be the following March, since Helms was turning sixty and that was the Agency's mandatory retirement age. Nixon hadn't known about the retirement age. They chatted a few moments more. Helms said he'd been in the OSS during the war, had spent thirty years in the intelligence business. Nixon was surprised by that too; he hadn't known Helms had been in the government all these years.

At this point Helms felt he could almost watch Nixon's mind working. The President had been vaguely under the impression that Helms was a political appointee, a Johnson man. Now he'd learned that Helms was a career intelligence officer. On the spur of the moment he asked Helms if he'd like another job, perhaps as an ambassador.

Washington was Helms's chosen ground. Until that moment he had thought he had a job. No flicker of desire to be an ambassador had ever crossed his mind, and he wasn't sure he wanted to become one now. He told Nixon he'd like to think it over. Nixon asked him where he might like to go. Helms said he wasn't sure he wanted to go anywhere, but perhaps Iran would be a logical choice. Helms was not thinking of the CIA's past role in Iran, but of something more immediately practical. It was a major post; there was something to do there; it wasn't like the big European embassies which were all run from Washington. Nixon said that would be fine, just let him know. And that was that. Helms returned to the CIA in a state of shock. General Walters took one look at his face and knew he'd been fired.[5]

A day or two later Helms saw Kissinger at a meeting in the White House and Kissinger asked, "Incidentally, what happened up at Camp David?"

Helms paused, looking for words.

"Well, hell," Kissinger said, "if you don't want to tell me, I'll call Haldeman and ask him."

"I'm not avoiding telling you," Helms said, "I'm just trying to decide which end of this thing to approach first."

Kissinger's question settled something in Helms's mind. First Haig showed no sign of eagerness for Helms's departure when they had lunch together at the CIA on election day, November 4. Then Kissinger clearly had no idea why Nixon wanted to see him at Camp David, and a day or two later still didn't know that Helms had been fired. Kissinger and Haig were the White House people who dealt with CIA, and if *they* weren't unhappy with the way he was doing his job, then Nixon must have had some other reason for firing him. Helms was certain he knew what it was. Christ, there was Haldeman sitting right there. *It was Watergate.* Nixon and Haldeman were firing him because he'd refused to save their skins back in June when the White House had wanted the CIA to quash the Watergate investigation.

By this time Helms was mad. Old friends had never seen him in quite such a state of mind before, and it only got worse when White House aide Charles Colson began spreading rumors around town that Helms was being let go because he couldn't run the Agency, he couldn't take hold of the intelligence community and run it the way the President wanted. The poisoned-tongue operation, CIA people called it. Helms's friends knew he was angry, but very, very few of them—perhaps none—could have known that Helms had concluded he was being fired by Nixon, personally, because Helms had refused to go the extra mile and help the President on Watergate. If they had known they might have wondered why he did what he did next, which was to accept Nixon's offer, saying yes, he would like to be an ambassador, and Iran was where he'd like to go.

Richard Helms did not often have cause to seek the help of President Nixon. Usually it was quite the other way around, but in March 1972 a security problem presented itself which required the President's aid. A former Russian-language specialist, analyst, and aide in the Director's own office named Victor Marchetti had resigned in an unfriendly frame of mind and had decided to write a book about the Agency. Of course the CIA had been troubled by books before. Back in 1965 two Washington journalists, David Wise and Thomas B. Ross, had written an exposé called *The Invisible Government*, but the damage it had caused had been largely political and even psychological. It was hostile in tone, and marked a permanent shift in public attitudes toward the CIA,[6] but it did not really threaten Agency security. One reason was that a copy of the book's galleys had been obtained by John Bross before publication, allowing the Agency to check it for possible breaches of security. In the event, there were not many.[7]

But Marchetti's book was something else again. He had spent years inside the Agency and knew what he was talking about. On March 12, 1972, a CIA officer in New York obtained a copy of the outline for Marchetti's book which had been submitted by his agent to nine publishers. Langley read it with alarm: Marchetti intended to tell what he knew. The CIA's general counsel, Lawrence Houston, and his deputy John Warner were asked if there was any way the Agency might block Marchetti's plans. Warner proposed a legal strategy based on the contract Marchetti had signed when he joined the CIA, promising not to reveal anything he might learn. Houston liked the approach and Helms went along. The case would have to be argued in court by the Justice Department, but at that particular moment the Department was somewhat adrift. John Mitchell had already resigned to head the Committee for the Reelection of the President, and his successor, Richard Kleindienst, was still awaiting confirmation by the Senate.[8]

Helms decided to approach Nixon directly, to ensure that the Justice Department would take the problem seriously. The President listened to Helms's argument, promised his support, and told Helms to take up the matter with John Ehrlichman. So Helms went to see Ehrlichman and repeated his story. This was important, Helms said; Marchetti was in a position to reveal a great many secrets. Like what? Ehrlichman asked. Helms gave him an example: back in 1965 a group of mountain climbers recruited by the CIA had lugged a small nuclear generator up Nanda Devi, one of the highest peaks in the Indian Himalayas, in order to power a device which would monitor the Chinese missile program, which had to be tracked from the ground. But sometime during the following winter the generator and its U–238 fuel somehow tumbled into a deep crevice and could not be recovered. It was still there in 1972.[9] If Marchetti were allowed to publish the story it would anger the Chinese, embarrass the Indian government, and might even arouse India's Hindu majority, since the plutonium could leak out of the generator and possibly contaminate the headwaters of the Ganges, a river sacred to Hindus.[10] That was just one particular, Helms said. There would be a lot of secrets in Marchetti's book.

On that occasion Nixon and Ehrlichman went out of their way to help keep the secrets; the Justice Department pressed its suit vigorously and eventually forced Marchetti to drop 168 passages from his book. But usually the favors all ran the other way. Helms had provided Nixon with information and quiet support which trod hard on the heels of the Agency's charter. It would be difficult to say exactly when Helms's responsiveness or helpfulness carried the CIA into the field of domestic operations. The process began almost imperceptibly in the early days of the Nixon administration, with delivery to Henry Kissinger of a special CIA study on U.S. student protest movements on February 18, 1969, less than a month after Nixon took office. The paper, entitled "Restless Youth," was accompanied by a letter in which Helms said, "In an effort to round-out our discussion of this subject, we have included a section on American students. This is an area not within the charter of this Agency, so I need not emphasize how extremely sensitive this makes the paper. Should anyone learn of its existence it would prove most embarrassing for all concerned."[11]

"Restless Youth" was not a study done especially for Nixon and Kissinger but a much-revised version of one originally requested by President Johnson eighteen months earlier, in the summer of 1967. Johnson had suspected that a conspiracy of some sort might lie behind the riots in Newark and Detroit that August, and he had been convinced, as much by temperament as by J. Edgar Hoover, that protest groups opposing the war in Vietnam were doing the work of international Communism. He pressed Helms to find out who the activists were seeing on their trips abroad, and where their money was coming from.

A small group in the CIA's Office of Security was already monitoring radical organizations in the Washington, D.C., area, but in August 1967, Helms expanded on their effort with the creation of a new Special Operations Group (SOG), hidden away in the DDP's counterintelligence division;[12] SOG provided the Office of Current Intelligence with material for a study on the peace movement in the United States.

The study was completed in early November, and Helms personally delivered it to President Johnson on November 15, 1967, probably at a meeting of the cabinet. It was roughly at that time, at any rate, that Ramsey Clark remembers Helms reading a study of domestic dissidents to the cabinet, a detailed but dramaless piece of work which concluded that student activism was a worldwide trend, that the issues which fueled it in the United States were the draft and Vietnam, and that it was a home-grown phenomenon without significant foreign involvement. When Helms finished reading his report both Johnson and Secretary of State Dean Rusk vigorously disputed his findings. This simply could not be the case, Rusk said: it all sounded exactly like the 1930s to him; it was naïve to think the Communists weren't behind it somewhere; the CIA just hadn't looked hard enough. Helms attempted to defend the study, according to Clark, but then backed off under renewed protest and promised the President he'd go over it again. A reworked paper was delivered to the White House on December 22, 1967, and two weeks later it was followed by another—"Student Dissent and Its Techniques in the United States"—in what Helms described in his covering letter as "part of our continuing examination of this general matter."[13]

The CIA's domestic intelligence program, renamed Operation Chaos in July 1968, expanded steadily thereafter, pacing the antiwar movement itself. Johnson insisted on the CIA's active role for two reasons. First, he and some of his principal advisers, especially Dean Rusk and Walt Rostow, were convinced that North Vietnam, Cuba, and perhaps Russia itself were not only supporting but somehow directing the movement. The CIA conceded that radicals were indeed meeting with foreign Communist leaders,[14] but insisted it could find no evidence of external control or funding. Insofar as CIA agents were investigating the foreign connections of domestic groups, and actually conducted their operations abroad, they were within the Agency's charter. It was Johnson's second demand, for evaluation of the student and protest movements as a whole, which the Agency could not legally fulfill. Theoretically this was the province of the FBI, but Hoover had steadfastly refused to analyze the information he collected, insisting that his was solely an investigative organization. While this made a kind of sense on paper, in practice it turned the FBI into the equivalent of a rumor mill, which inundated the White House and other official groups with a mélange of "fact" and hearsay—a student meeting here, a demonstration there, a "report" of guerrilla armies organizing in the Colorado mountains, etc., etc.—which raised stark visions of insurrection and sabotage without ever passing on the credibility of the threat. Facts need a context, and Hoover, whose career had been built in equal parts on publicity and the fear of domestic subversion, simply refused to say what the rhetoric of revolution really amounted to. The CIA attempted to fill the gap at Johnson's request and continued to do so after Nixon succeeded him in January 1969. Helms was well aware that this effort violated the CIA's charter, but it was both practically difficult and impolitic to say so. Helms was a "good soldier," and he was willing to break what he probably considered the letter of the law as long as no one would ever know.

This slope proved as slippery as any other. The original requests for simple analysis gradually escalated until the summer of 1970 when Helms, along with the directors of other U.S. intelligence agencies, abruptly found themselves drawing up a plan at the President's personal request for a wholesale assault on the peace and radical movements under the direction of a young lawyer and White House aide named Tom Charles Huston. By that time the pattern of compliance was well established.[15]

Inside the Agency, Helms found himself pressed from two sides, by various proposals for more ambitious domestic intelligence gathering,[16] and by simultaneous protests that Operation Chaos and related operations were outside the Agency's charter and ought to be abandoned. Despite Helms's efforts to limit Agency opposition to Chaos—in May 1969, for example, he ordered Richard Ober, head of the SOG, not to discuss his work with James Angleton, although Angleton was nominally his boss in the counterintelligence division—the internal protests were never entirely stifled. At one point two dissidents within the Deputy Directorate for Plans protested directly to an officer on the staff of the general counsel, who passed on their objections to Larry Houston. Houston discussed the matter with Thomas Karamessines, who, as DDP, was technically responsible for both the counterintelligence division and the Special Operations Group housed within it. Later, Karamessines told Houston he had talked to the dissidents personally, and had settled their doubts. In light of the continuing opposition to Chaos within the CIA, one imagines that their doubts were "settled" by a direct order. In any event, Helms found it necessary to justify the operation to all the Deputy Directors in a memorandum on September 6, 1969, defending Chaos and requiring support for the SOG "both in exploiting existing sources and in developing new ones."[17]

The White House, of course, knew nothing of the incipient rebellion within the CIA and continued to press Helms for more reports, better analysis, and a more aggressive role in domestic intelligence. According to several sources, Nixon personally told Helms that CIA analysts were being naïve about the Communists' role in protest movements, and later on, Robert Mardian, a Justice Department official with a reputation for hard-line, right-wing views, put similar pressure on Richard Ober and the SOG.

At the same time Tom Charles Huston was beginning to conceive a still bolder scheme for domestic intelligence operations. In this he was strongly influenced by his conversations with William Sullivan, the FBI's director of domestic intelligence, who was later to be summarily ousted by Hoover after Sullivan protested Hoover's caution in operations focused on the New Left. In 1970 Sullivan told Huston that Hoover, fearful of exposure and embarrassment, had halted FBI intelligence-gathering burglaries, called "black bag jobs" (a decision vigorously protested by the National Security Agency, which had depended on FBI burglars for code-books from Washington embassies); that wiretapping and bugging were being used too sparingly; and that the FBI ought to approve the recruitment of student informers who were under twenty-one, a practice banned by Hoover. Even worse, Sullivan said, was Hoover's arbitrary break with the CIA in a fit of pique over the Agency's handling of an episode in Denver, Colorado, in the spring of 1969. A professor at the University of Colorado, Thomas Riha, had disappeared in March. The local FBI office knew where he had gone, and an agent told the local CIA officer. Hoover was angry and wanted to know who the agent was. Helms refused to give him the name. Hoover's anger escalated to fury. On February 26, 1970, Helms wrote Hoover a placating letter. Hoover scribbled across the bottom: "This is not satisfactory. I want our Denver office to have absolutely no contacts with CIA. I want direct liaison here with CIA to be terminated and any contact with CIA in future to be by letter only."[18] Sullivan told Tom Charles Huston the consequences for counterintelligence in the U.S. could be nothing short of catastrophic.

Over a period of months, then, Sullivan gradually convinced Huston that Hoover had grown old and cautious, and that a vigorous new domestic intelligence program was urgently needed to check the New Left. Huston, in turn, convinced Haldeman, and through him the President, that the best solution to the problem would be to threaten Hoover's hegemony in the domestic field with an interagency effort. The result was a meeting on June 5, 1970, in the Oval Office, where Nixon himself gave instructions to the major intelligence bureaucrats—Hoover, Lieutenant General Donald V. Bennett of the Defense Intelligence Agency, Admiral Noel Guylor of the National Security Agency, and Richard Helms. Nixon made it clear he wanted a major effort against domestic dissidents, and the first meeting of the Interagency Committee on Intelligence (ICI), with Hoover as chairman, was held a few days later.

At that meeting Huston emphasized that the ICI was not to be backward in its recommendations: "Everything is valid," he said, "everything is possible."[19] Helms appointed Angleton to represent the CIA at ICI working meetings, with Richard Ober as an observer. In retrospect the deliberations of the ICI seem to have been something of a boondoggle, whatever Huston and Sullivan, the FBI's representative, may have hoped from them. The other members were simply going through the motions. Before one early meeting Huston took Helms aside and, referring to the Riha case, urged Helms to apologize to Hoover and patch things up. "We're getting along all right," Helms coolly replied.[20] Helms's refusal to welcome Huston into the real world of intelligence in Washington was typical of the ICI's efforts as a whole. But "work" proceeded quickly, all the same. The ICI's report of June 25, recommending a mail-opening program,[21] resumption of "black bag jobs," and more aggressive wiretapping, was approved by Nixon in mid-July 1970. On July 23, Huston formally told Helms and the other intelligence chiefs that their report had been accepted.

At that point Hoover proved he was a formidable opponent when it came to bureaucratic infighting. He went to Mitchell and torpedoed the bolder provisions of the Huston plan with characteristic finesse: he said he did not approve but would be glad to do his part, as long as he received explicit written authorization from the President. Mitchell realized Nixon could not put his name to any such order and called Helms on July 27, telling him to hold everything. The following day Mitchell persuaded Nixon to back off, and Helms was asked to return his copy of the July 23 memorandum authorizing the new program. The reversal, however, was more apparent than real: John Dean replaced Huston as the White House aide in charge of domestic intelligence, and an Intelligence Evaluation Committee (IEC) was established within the Justice Department to make the formal studies of domestic protest groups which Hoover had refused to do. Far from being brought around by Huston's initiative, Hoover continued to go his own way. Even before Nixon's approval of the Huston plan was rescinded, Hoover calmly halted direct liaison with the rest of the intelligence community as well (apparently so he could not be accused of singling out the CIA), and the following year he literally locked Sullivan out of his office at the FBI.[22]

The CIA's role in Nixon's domestic intelligence programs hovered on the outer edge of the Agency's charter, and occasionally crossed over. Helms tried to limit the CIA to intelligence-gathering abroad, and to describe it as a "foreign" operation even when it was domestic in fact, but the distinction was always a legalistic one. Nixon's purpose was clear: he wanted to know what his domestic opponents were up to so that he might anticipate, harass, frustrate, and discredit them. The CIA's own analysts had concluded repeatedly that antiwar activists and other domestic protesters were free of foreign control. The Agency might argue it was merely investigating possible intelligence threats by foreign powers working through domestic groups, but in fact it was contributing to an extralegal, and at times downright illegal, program to break an opposition which Nixon found politically inconvenient. The effort was only marginally successful; the American radical movement collapsed on its own in the early 1970s as a result of internal stresses, confusion of aims, and the gradual withdrawal of U.S. troops from Vietnam. The point here is that Nixon's campaign against the radicals was conducted in extreme secrecy because it fundamentally violated the tenets of American democracy, even where it was not in the strict sense illegal; that the President put his personal authority behind the program; and that Helms tried, within the limits of secrecy, to do his part. In a general way, perhaps, the Agency is supposed to protect the national security, but that is only a muffled way of saying that it is the President's most accessible arm in the conduct of foreign policy—in Helms's phrase, part of "the President's bag of tools."[23] He can use it as a navigational aid, or a Saturday night special, as he will, and a Director of Central Intelligence who tried to argue with or restrain him could not long remain in the job. Helms accepted the rules of the game right up until June 1972.

Sometime during the evening of Saturday, June 17, 1972—probably between nine and ten o'clock—Helms received a call at home from Howard Osborn, the CIA's chief of security. During Helms's tenure as DCI it was standing policy for him to be informed whenever someone connected to the Agency ran afoul of the law, and this call has been described by Helms and Osborn as strictly routine. But the implications of Osborn's message were hardly routine: a former high-level security officer of the CIA, James Mc-Cord, had been arrested at two o'clock that morning with four other men while installing wiretaps in phones at the headquarters of the Democratic National Committee in the Watergate Hotel. On top of that, Osborn told Helms, another former CIA officer named E. Howard Hunt was involved in the burglary.[24]

The CIA had been in flaps before; none could have announced itself more clearly to anyone with ears to hear. Bad enough to begin with, everything Helms learned in the following two days made it immeasurably worse. If the Watergate break-in was not the only thing discussed at the Director's regular morning meeting on Monday, June 19, it was certainly the first— "Topic A," in Larry Houston's bland phrase. "Hunt!" said Helms during the discussion. "Hell, Osborn tells me that Hunt was involved. How can that be? I haven't seen Hunt's name in the papers." But Hunt's name had turned up in the pocket notebooks of two of the Watergate burglars,[25] and he had been a suspect since Saturday night. This complicated matters considerably because Hunt, Helms knew, had been working for the White House. One subject raised at the Monday morning meeting, in fact, was the stenographic record of General Robert Cushman's conversation with John Ehrlichman a year earlier, when Ehrlichman had called the then Deputy Director of Central Intelligence to ask the CIA to help Hunt.

That brought the number of CIA people involved in the burglary to three—McCord, Hunt, and a Cuban exile named Eugenio Martinez. A veteran of Operation Mongoose, Martinez was actually still employed by the Agency at the time of the break-in, receiving a retainer of $100 a month for reporting on the Cuban exile community in Miami. After his arrest inside the Watergate, Martinez was immediately dropped from the payroll, and the following day, on Tuesday, June 20, Helms took the first public step in his campaign to put a moat between the CIA and Watergate. At an executive session of the Senate Foreign Relations Committee where Helms testified on SALT, Senator Percy asked, just before Helms ended his testimony, "Do you want to volunteer any information on Mr. Jim McCord?"

"Yes, I'll volunteer anything you would like," said Helms. "I just want to distance myself from my alumnus." A bit later he added, "I don't have—I can't conceive of what that caper was all about, I really can't conceive it."[26]

This was probably true as far as it went: what the "caper was all about" is still a subject of debate.[27] But Helms was already in a position to conceive quite clearly who the burglary team had been working for, and thus to sense the dimensions of what had happened. In particular, Helms knew a good deal about the relationship of Howard Hunt and the White House, and what he knew explains what he did.

Helms first met Hunt in 1956, when Hunt was passing through Washington on his way to a new post as chief of station in Uruguay. During the following fourteen years the two men saw each other infrequently, but Hunt conceived of Helms as a friend, admired him openly, and more than once called on him for help. In his memoirs of the Bay of Pigs operation Hunt gave Helms's code name inside the CIA—"Knight"—to David Phillips. When Phillips wrote his memoirs he conceded that he was the man Hunt called Knight, and commented, "Bestowing the name of Knight was the ultimate accolade—people who have worked in CIA will recall that pseudonym belonged to one of the Agency's most senior officers, a man Howard idolized."[28] Why Hunt idolized Helms is not so easy to explain. Helms and Hunt came from quite different traditions inside CIA, just as they differed in politics. Hunt was an activist and right-winger, while Helms was a bureaucrat, a foreign intelligence man, and a political moderate. His attitude of suspicion toward the Soviet Union, a sort of given inside the CIA, might strike outsiders as hard-line, but Helms was no ideologue. His approach to political problems was entirely pragmatic. But Helms defended Hunt on several occasions, and Hunt's gratitude was enduring.

In Uruguay in 1960, for example, Hunt had broken every rule in the book when he bypassed his immediate boss, the U.S. ambassador, Robert Woodward, and tried to extend his tour as chief of station in Montevideo by appealing directly to the President of Uruguay. Hunt's career in the CIA ought to have ended then and there, but all that happened was that he was pulled back to Washington in time to spend a few acrimonious months as political action officer on the Bay of Pigs project until Bissell fired him for refusing to take orders. He finished out the project with a low-level job working on propaganda. After the invasion collapsed, Hunt was a fifth wheel looking for a job. Helms offered him to Allen Dulles as a ghostwriter on Dulles's planned memoirs. When that fell through, Helms next proposed that Hunt serve a tour as the deputy chief of station in Madrid. Hunt accepted reluctantly; it struck him as a demotion. But even that was denied him. Fate sent Woodward as ambassador to Madrid before him, and Woodward flatly refused to have Hunt inside the Embassy. He went even further, insisting that an order be placed in Hunt's file barring him from ever again holding a job with State Department cover. Helms was irritated by Woodward's attitude and refused to be balked; he gave Hunt an "outside" job in Madrid.[29]

Before his tour in Spain ended, however, Hunt requested a transfer back to Washington because his son needed medical treatment which was unavailable in Madrid. Helms approved the transfer and assigned Hunt a new job as chief of the covert-action staff in the DDP's Western European Division. There he was not a success. "Can you imagine a right-winger like Hunt trying to deal with the Social Democrats in Germany?" asked a CIA officer, who thought one of Helms's principal administrative failings was his willingness to go on giving high-level jobs to incompetents for no better reason than a desire to avoid hurting their feelings. Later, Hunt was shifted to the Domestic Operations Division. In April 1970, apparently realizing that his career was permanently blocked in CIA, Hunt asked Helms for early retirement. Helms said okay and wrote a letter of recommendation which Hunt used to obtain a job with a Washington public relations firm, Robert R. Mullen and Company.[30] So far as is known, that was the last Helms heard of Hunt until July 1971.

During that fifteen-month period, however, Hunt was busy. Bored with his routine job in public relations, and disappointed when the firm was sold to someone invited in from the outside, he renewed a casual friendship with Chuck Colson, a fellow graduate of Brown University whose White House connections impressed Hunt. Colson, in turn, was impressed by Hunt's "leading role" in the Bay of Pigs. Lunching together often, they found themselves politically congenial and imagined that their shared taste for intrigue might make them good partners. All they needed was a project, and Daniel Ellsberg gave them one.

After the *New York Times* began to publish the Defense Department study of decisionmaking in Vietnam, known as the Pentagon Papers, in June 1971, Colson suggested that Hunt join the White House as a "consultant" in order to mount an operation which would discredit Ellsberg, and thus turn the episode into a public-relations triumph for Nixon. After all, this was exactly the sort of thing Hunt had excelled at abroad. Years before, Paul Linebarger, an expert in psychological warfare, had praised Hunt as having one of the two great "black minds" in CIA. John Ehrlichman approved Colson's plan after a meeting with Hunt on July 7, 1971, and the same afternoon he telephoned the Deputy Director of Central Intelligence, General Robert E. Cushman, to ask the CIA's help. Hunt, he said, "may be contacting you sometime in the future for some assistance. I wanted you to know that he was in fact doing some things for the President. He is a longtime acquaintance with the people here. You should consider he has pretty much carte blanche. . . ."[31]

When Hunt first went to work for the White House in July 1971, he seems to have undertaken three separate projects at once: an attempt to discredit Senator Edward F. Kennedy with new information about the Chappaquiddick scandal, a plan to discredit the Kennedys more generally by "proving" a direct and deliberate U.S. role in the murder of Diem, and an effort to embarrass Daniel Ellsberg. In all three, pursued simultaneously throughout the summer and fall of 1971, Hunt depended heavily on aid provided by the CIA. On July 22, two weeks after Ehrlichman's phone call, Hunt visited General Cushman in his seventh-floor office at the CIA and requested some special equipment for a "sensitive" interview—"a one-time op—in and out."[32]

"I don't see why we can't," Cushman said, and the following day an officer from the CIA's Technical Services Division (TSD) delivered a wig, a speech-altering device, and a miscellany of identification to Hunt at a safehouse in Washington. On July 28 Hunt suggested to Colson that the CIA be asked to prepare a psychological profile of Ellsberg, who was described by Washington rumor as being erratic and unstable. Colson passed on the idea to David R. Young, a White House aide working with the leak-plugging specialists known as the plumbers. Young, in turn, called Howard Osborn at the CIA with the request. Osborn asked Helms if they should comply, and Helms, initially reluctant, finally said, "All right, let's go ahead and try it."[33]

If Helms was wary of directly involving the CIA in White House efforts to plug security leaks, he was nevertheless glad somebody was concerning himself with the problem. When the first attempt at an Ellsberg profile proved too vague to satisfy Ehrlichman and the plumbers, Helms agreed to try again, and the following day, on August 13, 1971, he called either Egil Krogh or David Young with his own request for a leak hunt, after a *New York Times* story on India by Tad Szulc pointed a finger at a CIA agent reporting on the government in New Delhi. A couple of weeks earlier the Agency had agreed to lend the plumbers a CIA polygraph expert for the questioning of a State Department officer suspected of having leaked information which had appeared in a news story on the SALT negotiations.

But Hunt was a different matter. His requests for CIA help, beginning on July 22, suddenly escalated the following month: on August 18 he asked the CIA to lend him his old Agency secretary, at that time working in Paris.

On the twentieth, he requested a tape recorder and some alias business cards, and at about the same time—the date is not certain—he also asked for a "backstopped"[34] telephone number in New York with matching driver's license and credit cards. On the twenty-fifth, Hunt picked up the business cards and tape recorder and requested a concealed camera as well as disguise materials and identification for Gordon Liddy, who had accompanied him to the meeting. On the following day, August 26, Hunt called his contact in the Technical Services Division and asked him to pick up some exposed film at Dulles Airport the next morning, which the CIA man did.

At this point low-level officers in the CIA began to wonder, and to ask their superiors, just what Hunt was up to. The TSD had told Hunt to return the materials provided for the "one-time op," but Hunt held on to them. A protest was lodged with Cushman's executive assistant, Karl Wagner, who told TSD to refuse any further Hunt requests, and then sent Cushman a memo protesting the involvement of the unknown Liddy and Hunt's frequent demands for help, and raising the "question of [the material's] use in domestic clandestine activity."[35] Cushman called Ehrlichman, who agreed to "call a halt to this."[36] Hunt's developed film was delivered to him as promised (although the CIA retained Xerox copies in a special file marked "Mr. Edward"—Hunt's alias in dealing with the TSD), but on August 31, when Hunt called once again about the backstopped telephone number, he was told that no more help would be provided. The period during which the CIA most actively helped Hunt, then, lasted only ten days, August 18 to 27, but Hunt's other projects continued to involve the CIA indirectly.

In July, Hunt had begun a search for State Department documents which might implicate President Kennedy in Diem's murder, and at the same time he arranged to interview General Paul D. Harkins, the U.S. military commander at the time of Diem's death in November 1963, and Lucien Conein, the CIA officer who had been in contact with the Vietnamese generals behind the coup. None of these efforts turned up what Hunt was looking for, so he suggested to Colson that the CIA's Diem file be obtained by the White House. Hunt was apparently hoping that the CIA file would contain the sort of damaging cables missing from the State Department files, or that they might help him in an alternative scheme to fabricate the documents he needed. According to John Ehrlichman, Hunt gave Colson a list of about fifteen separate CIA files which might contain material embarrassing to the Kennedys. Colson passed the list on to Nixon, who gave it to Ehrlichman and told him to get the documents from Helms.

On the morning of September 22, 1971, Ehrlichman had breakfast with Helms at CIA headquarters and asked for Agency files on the Diem coup, the assassination of Trujillo, the Bay of Pigs, and the landing of U.S. Marines in Lebanon in 1958.[37] Helms was polite but evasive, telling Ehrlichman he would look into it.

This was not the first time Helms had been asked for CIA files. According to Haldeman,[38] Nixon made a request for the Bay of Pigs "file" shortly after he took office in 1969, but Helms somehow dissuaded him in mid-year. Of course there is no such thing as a single, coherent Bay of Pigs "file." Instead, there are hundreds of separate files having to do with the Bay of Pigs. At one point, while Nixon was still pressing for *the* file, the CIA told him that it did not have a copy of the Taylor Report of 1961, possibly in the hope the President would then shift his attention to the National Security Council's files. Helms says he does not remember Nixon's earlier request, but Lawrence Houston recalled it vaguely, saying there was some worried discussion of a Nixon plan to make the file "public." No one at the CIA seemed to know quite what he had in mind. The new request in September 1971, much broader in scope, was naturally more alarming, but Helms apparently hoped it would die just as the first had. This time, however, the President was insistent. On October 1, Ehrlichman again went to see Helms to ask for the files. Helms, worried that ordinary White House staffers would read the files and leak the contents, told Ehrlichman he wanted to see Nixon personally before handing them over. Ehrlichman said, "All right, but I speak for the President." Helms said he understood that, but insisted he wanted to see Nixon personally.[39]

A week later, on October 8, 1971, Helms met in the Oval Office with Nixon and Ehrlichman. After a brief discussion of Helms's relations with J. Edgar Hoover, Nixon explained why he wanted the files. An election year was rolling around and he "must be fully advised in order to know what to duck" when questions came up concerning Diem or the Bay of Pigs. Nixon assured Helms he would not "hurt the agency nor attack [his] predecessors." Helms responded that there is "only one President at a time" and "I only work for you." With that he handed Nixon an envelope containing three documents: a Bay of Pigs report by Colonel Jack Hawkins, a John McCone report on the murder of Diem, and a third file on Trujillo.[40] Nixon slipped the envelope into his desk drawer and then told Helms that in future he was to deal with Ehrlichman "as you would me."

"I'll be making requests for additional material," Ehrlichman added.

"Okay," Helms said, "anything."

Later, still worried about who would be reading the files, Helms asked Ehrlichman if they were going to be returned. When they were not, Helms asked an assistant, Kenneth Greer, to be responsible for getting the files back, but Greer failed.[41]

There is no evidence that Hunt ever saw the files surrendered by Helms, or that Helms knew anything of Hunt's attempt to discredit the Kennedys at the time, but the Agency continued to pick up intermittent echoes of Hunt's activities. In mid-October 1971, Thomas Karamessines had lunch with Hunt in Washington to discuss cover arrangements with Mullen & Company. When Karamessines had first learned of the CIA's aid to Hunt in August he had asked, "Who ordered this?" The answer—General Cushman—did not altogether satisfy him, and he insisted on being fully briefed. Not long before the lunch Karamessines had seen the photographs developed for Hunt by the Technical Services Division, pictures which one CIA officer said looked like "casing photographs" to him. Whether Karamessines shared his suspicion is not known, but he was certainly curious about the nature of Hunt's new job, and Hunt's air of elaborate mystery during their lunch together struck him as odd and troubling. "What do you do down there, Howard?" Karamessines asked. Hunt was vague in reply. "Well, you know, political work," he said, adding that he worked with Chuck Colson.

Another echo of Hunt's new job was picked up in Miami, where the CIA still maintained a major station and an elaborate network of informers among the Cuban exile community. In April 1971, Hunt had reestablished an acquaintance with Bernard Barker, a real estate salesman who had worked for Hunt in 1960 and 1961 on the Bay of Pigs operation. That August, Hunt returned to Miami to ask Barker to join him in a secret operation which turned out to be the burglary of the Los Angeles office of Daniel Ellsberg's psychiatrist.[42] One of the Cubans recruited to help in the plan was Eugenio Martinez, a veteran of hundreds of clandestine boat trips to Cuba during the Bay of Pigs operation, and, later, in connection with sabotage and agent-dropping activities during Operation Mongoose. Martinez was the only one of the Cubans recruited for the burglary of Ellsberg's psychiatrist, or the later Watergate break-in, who was still working on retainer for the CIA. Martinez was an experienced clandestine operator who understood that operations were often secret even within the CIA, and there is no evidence that he ever told his case officer about the break-in at the Los Angeles office of Dr. Lewis J. Fielding, Ellsberg's psychiatrist. Nevertheless, in November 1971, Martinez did mention that Hunt had been down in Miami recruiting people, and the following March he mentioned Hunt again, telling the Miami chief of station, Jacob Esterline, that Hunt was apparently working for the White House. Esterline was sufficiently worried to ask his superiors in Langley what was going on. On March 27, 1972, Karamessines's assistant, Cord Meyer, confirmed Martinez's report, said Hunt was on some sort of domestic assignment, and told Esterline to leave him alone—to "cool it."[43] The day after Martinez's arrest inside the Watergate, Esterline cabled a full report to Langley on Martinez.

When Helms's regular morning meeting ended on Monday, June 19, 1972, then, he knew plenty about what was going on. So far as is known, Watergate itself—that is, the actual break-in of the Democratic National Committee headquarters—was still a mystery in Helms's mind. He did not know what the burglars were after, who was paying them, or precisely who was issuing their orders. But he did not really need to know: the facts that Hunt was working for the White House, that Ehrlichman had intervened on his behalf, that his work involved the paraphernalia of classic clandestine operations, that McCord was the chief of security for CREEP, told Helms who stood to suffer from the burglars' blundering. If Helms had known less he might have made an effort to learn more. A call to McCord or Hunt, with even the barest hint of help, would have brought the whole story tumbling out. Both men were desperate. But Helms issued orders against any contact of any kind with either man, for fear the CIA would be dragged into the heart of the case. Helms preferred to remain on the shadowed periphery, and his response to the discussion of Monday, June 19, was narrow and cautious: he appointed William Colby, the CIA's Executive Director/ Comptroller, to handle the Agency's end of the investigation which was bound to follow, and he adopted a policy of withdrawal.

Colby later described Helms's guidelines as, "Stay cool, volunteer nothing, because it will only be used to involve us. Just stay away from the whole damn thing."[44] This policy was affirmed in practice almost immediately when General Cushman's executive assistant, Karl Wagner, quietly told Colby about Hunt's visit to the general the previous summer, something of which Colby had not known. Colby took Wagner to see Helms (who, of course, knew of Hunt's original requests for help, and of the call to Ehrlichman which ended the CIA's cooperation) and was told that this had nothing to do with "Watergate"—that is, with the break-in—and to keep it to himself. The CIA had no legal or moral obligation, in Helms's view, to press all sorts of "peripheral information" (Colby's phrase) on the FBI. Later, when Howard Osborn was preparing a memo which Colby was to pass on to the FBI, Helms called him and said, "About Karl Wagner, you forget about that. I will handle that. You take care of the rest of it."[45] In other words, he was hiding the fact that the CIA had been helping Hunt on orders from the White House.

It has been suggested (by Chuck Colson and H. R. Haldeman, among others) that the CIA was really "behind" the Watergate break-in, and that the Agency followed a policy of passive resistance during the investigation because it wanted to hide its guiding role. In particular, the proposition has been advanced that the CIA knew about the actual burglary before it took place. Helms himself concedes that "the Agency is large; it's impossible for me to say that nobody in the Agency, but nobody, knew anything about it." But he insists he didn't know about it, that nobody in the Agency has ever come forward to confess prior knowledge, that Hunt was not being "run" by the Agency, and that CIA was completely free of responsibility for the Watergate break-in. The evidence tends to support his claims. Hunt's work for the White House has been too densely detailed to admit doubt he was genuinely in their employ, just as CREEP's responsibility for the intelligence-gathering program which led to the break-in is too clear, deliberate, and certain to admit of a hidden hand. Watergate elicited plenty of lying, but the lion's share of it was committed by the White House. The break-in and the cover-up were the doing of Nixon and the men who worked for him, and they would hardly have tried so hard to hide their responsibility if they had ever seriously conceived that the blame might plausibly be shifted elsewhere.

The only real questions concerning the CIA's role in Watergate are how far it acquiesced in the early stages of the cover-up and, later, whether or not it pointed reporters—especially Carl Bernstein and Bob Woodward of the Washington *Post*—toward CREEP and the White House. Some Watergate historians suggest that Robert Bennett, who purchased Mullen and Company after Hunt went to work for the firm, was actually the secret informer Bernstein and Woodward called "Deep Throat." Bennett has admitted telling his case officer what he knew about Watergate on July 10, and that he talked to Woodward, but he denies he was "Deep Throat," just as Helms denies he ever authorized Bennett (or anyone else) to speak to reporters, or told him (or anyone else) what to say. Other writers have proposed James Angleton, the CIA's chief of counterintelligence, as a possible "Deep Throat," citing his reputation for extreme intrigue and expertise in manipulation, and the clandestine procedure used by "Deep Throat." This has been denied too. In the absence of evidence, the charge is only conjecture, and it ignores internal evidence in Bernstein and Woodward's reporting, and in their book *All the President's Men*, that "Deep Throat" was best informed about events in the White House and in CREEP. In addition, Bernstein and Woodward themselves would probably have exposed a CIA "Deep Throat" by now as a result of suspicion that they were being manipulated by the Agency, something they would not have been happy to learn.

This point deserves emphasis because Watergate, far from being a triumph of CIA political engineering, marks a violent break in Agency history, the first step in a process of exposure which has pretty much destroyed the unwritten charter established by Allen Dulles. Watergate was the foot in the door. The CIA had been in unwelcome spotlights before, but Watergate did what the Bay of Pigs had not: it undermined the consensus of trust in Washington which was a truer source of the Agency's strength than its legal charter, and it gave outsiders their first good look at CIA files and tables of organization. In addition, Watergate ended the long congressional acquiescence to the special intimacy between the CIA and the President, an intimacy which allowed Presidents to use CIA as they might, beholden to no one so long as congressional oversight remained a kind of charade. Watergate, in short, made the CIA fair game.

Helms seemed to have feared this from the beginning. He treated Watergate as he would the cholera, isolating the Agency from those who had been infected[46] in the hope, vain as it turned out, the disease might sweep on by. Helms's strategy worked well enough in the beginning. No CIA people were destroyed by Watergate, with the possible exception of Helms himself, other than those former agents and officers directly involved in the break-in. But the effect of Watergate was profound all the same: once congressional investigators, and the reporters in their wake, got inside the Agency's door they grew curious, restless with the narrow answers to their questions, and hungry to learn where all the personal histories led. No one learned any secrets from Helms, or from the men who worked for him as long as he was still around, but when he left he might have said, and probably felt: Après moi, le deluge.

But Helms had another reason, as well, for trying to abstract the CIA from the Watergate mess: the White House was in charge of the cover-up, and was keeping a close watch on who was telling what to whom. If Helms had been quick to forward every suspicion or tangential piece of evidence to the FBI or the federal prosecutors, the President would have known about it in short order, with predictable results. If there had ever been any doubt in Helms's mind about White House involvement in the affair, it was abruptly dispelled on Friday, June 23, not quite a week after the break-in, when he and his Deputy Director, General Vernon Walters, were summoned to the office of John Ehrlichman without explanation. Helms and Walters met for lunch together in downtown Washington, where they concluded the subject of the meeting could only be Watergate.

Walters, an amiable man whose huge fund of amusing stories disguised a shrewd mind, had built a military career on a facility for languages and discretion in the service of high officials. He had served as Nixon's translator on two crucial occasions in 1959 and 1960: during an interview with Fidel Castro in April 1959[47] and in Venezuela when the Vice-President was attacked by a mob. Nixon had appointed Walters to his post as DDCI only six weeks earlier, and Helms treated him as Presidents traditionally treat their Vice-Presidents—politely enough, while ensuring they have nothing of importance to do. At that luncheon on June 23, Walters knew only what Helms had said during the Monday meeting, that he didn't know what this caper was all about. Helms, in short, did not entirely trust Walters. Before Walters succeeded Cushman as DDCI, for example, Helms quietly arranged for the removal of the taping system which Cushman had used to record a conversation with Hunt the previous summer. The summons to Ehrlichman's office had specifically included Walters, and Helms was not sure why.

Late the previous afternoon L. Patrick Gray, acting director of the FBI, had called Helms to say that some of his men, trying to find a motive for the break-in, were wondering if it may have been a CIA operation of some kind. Helms insisted it was not, and (in Gray's words) that he had "been meeting on this every day with his men, that they knew the people, that they could not figure it out, but that there was no CIA involvement."[48] Less than an hour after the phone call, Gray mentioned the CIA theory to Dean, and he, in turn, later that same night, passed it on during a meeting with John Mitchell in the latter's office. Mention of the CIA turned on a light in

Mitchell's mind; he suggested that Dean explore the possibility of shutting off the FBI's investigation with the aid of the CIA. Either John Ehrlichman or Bob Haldeman could probably handle this, Mitchell said.

Dean thought this a good idea, since the FBI had already traced money found on the burglars to a Mexican bank and to a Republican contributor named Kenneth Dahlberg. If the FBI investigation were not halted it would quickly discover that the checks in question, totaling $114,000, had not been given directly to the burglars, but to the Committee for the Reelection of the President.[49] At eight fifteen Friday morning, June 23, 1972, Dean called Haldeman and said the FBI was closing in quickly on the CREEP connection but there might be a way out.

"The FBI is convinced it's the CIA," Dean said, according to Haldeman. "McCord and the Cubans are all ex-CIA people. Practically everyone who went in there was connected to the Agency. And now the FBI finds a Mexican bank involved which also sounds like CIA. . . . Gray has been looking for a way out of this mess. I spoke to Mitchell, and he and I agree the thing to do is for you to tell Walters that we don't know where that Mexican investigation is going to lead. Have him talk to Gray—and maybe the CIA can turn off the FBI down there in Mexico."[50]

The reference to Cubans and the CIA puzzled Haldeman and piqued his curiosity. Three days earlier, on the night of Tuesday, June 20, Nixon had called Haldeman, as he often did when he wanted to think out loud, and said the "Cuban angle" might save them yet. "Those people who got caught are going to need money," Nixon said. "I've been thinking about how to do it." He suggested "an anti-Castro fund" to be organized by his friend Bebe Rebozo; "publicize the hell out of the Cuban angle. That way we kill two birds with one stone." But then Nixon gave Haldeman an enigmatic order: "Tell Ehrlichman this whole group of Cubans is tied to the Bay of Pigs."

"The Bay of Pigs?" said Haldeman. "What does that have to do with this?"

"Ehrlichman will know what I mean," said Nixon.[51]

But if Ehrlichman did, Haldeman certainly didn't. When Dean proposed another "Cuban angle," Haldeman decided to ask about it. At five minutes after ten that Friday morning, June 23, he told Nixon where the FBI investigation was—one step away from CREEP, and closing fast—and related Dean's proposal for bringing in the CIA. Nixon mused over the idea, briefly wondering what reason to give for calling Helms in, then deciding no reason was really necessary. "Well, we protected Helms from one hell of a lot of things," Nixon said.[52] The problem, Haldeman explained a bit elliptically, was that no one quite dared to tell Gray to just stop the investigation. He needed a reason, and CIA concern for national security was just the thing.

The more Nixon ruminated on this plan, the better he liked it. "When you get in [unintelligible] people, say, 'Look, the problem is that this will open the whole, the whole Bay of Pigs thing, and the President just feels that ah, without going into the details—don't lie to them to the extent to say no involvement, but just say this is a comedy of errors, without getting into it, the President believes that it is going to open the whole Bay of Pigs thing up again. And ah, because these people are plugging for [unintelligible] and that they should call the FBI in and for the good of the country don't go any further into this case period!' "[53]

After the discussion ended at about 11:40 a.m., Haldeman went off to arrange the meeting with Helms and General Walters for that afternoon, while Nixon continued to brood over the Watergate problem. He hoped the connection between CREEP and the burglars might still be disguised, and seems to have convinced himself that the CIA could turn off the FBI investigation and end the problem once and for all. When Haldeman popped in at 1:00 p.m., on another matter, shortly before his meeting with Helms, Nixon went over the gambit one more time. "Tell them that if it gets out, it's going to make the CIA look bad, it's going to make Hunt look bad, and it's likely to blow the whole Bay of Pigs which we think would be very unfortunate for the CIA."[54]

At 1:30 p.m. Helms and Walters arrived at Ehrlichman's White House office and chatted with him for a few minutes until Haldeman arrived. The latter went right to the point: the break-in was making a lot of noise and the Democrats were trying to exploit it. The FBI investigation "was leading to a lot of important people and this could get worse";[55] was there any CIA connection with the break-in? Helms said there was not. Haldeman then said "it was the President's wish that Walters call on Acting FBI Director Patrick Gray and suggest to him that since the five suspects had been arrested that this should be sufficient and that it was not advantageous to have the enquiry pushed, especially in Mexico, etc."[56] Helms said he had already discussed the investigation with Gray the day before, and had assured him the CIA was not involved and that none of the suspects was working for the Agency.

At this point Haldeman ventured the gambit suggested by Mitchell and Dean, and honed down by Nixon. "The President asked me to tell you this entire affair may be connected to the Bay of Pigs, and if it opens up, the Bay of Pigs may be blown. . . ."

Helms's reaction was immediate. He gripped the arms of his chair, leaned forward, and shouted: "The Bay of Pigs had nothing to do with this! I have no concern about the Bay of Pigs!"

Haldeman was taken aback by the vehemence of Helms's reaction. "I'm just following my instructions, Dick," he said. "This is what the President told me to relay to you."

"All right," said Helms, calming down.[57] But inside he cannot have been calm in the least; he had just been put on notice that the President might try to pin Watergate on the CIA. If the Agency was to take the fall, then so must Helms, since he ran it. This was a threat well designed to make a man alert, and it worked. Helms, after all, had been told by Nixon that Ehrlichman spoke in his name. Now Ehrlichman and Haldeman were telling Helms to intervene with the FBI. Before the meeting ended Helms repeated that the CIA had nothing to do with the break-in—something Haldeman knew perfectly well on his own—but Helms did not object when Walters agreed to see Gray, to say that he had talked to "the White House," and to request that the FBI halt its inquiries in Mexico.

Helms and Walters left the White House together and then spoke briefly by the car waiting for them outside. There Helms put a slightly different interpretation on what Walters was to tell Gray. "You must remind Mr. Gray of the agreement between the FBI and the CIA," Helms said, according to Walters, "that if they run into or appear to expose one another's assets they will notify one another."[58]

Helms then returned to the CIA while Walters went to see Gray at FBI headquarters, where, by Walters's own account,[59] he not only reminded Gray of the delimitation agreement, as directed by Helms, but also told Gray that pursuit of the FBI's investigation in Mexico might expose CIA assets. The effect was precisely as predicted and desired: Gray told his agents not to question either Manuel Ogario or Kenneth Dahlberg, who had written the checks which were the source of the funds discovered on the burglars. The FBI's investigation, for the moment, came to an effective halt, one step short of establishing a crucial link between the burglars and CREEP.[60]

Later that afternoon Haldeman reported on the meeting to Nixon, said he had raised the Bay of Pigs as instructed, and concluded, "So at that point Helms kind of got the picture. He said, 'We'll be very happy to be helpful, and we'll handle anything you want.' "[61]

Apparently delighted with their success in enlisting the CIA, Haldeman, Ehrlichman, and John Dean decided to press their advantage. Helms had given them an inch, and they needed a mile. On Monday, June 26, Dean called Walters at Ehrlichman's request and asked the general to meet him at the White House. After checking with Ehrlichman to make sure Dean was really authorized to discuss the Watergate matter, Walters went to see him then and on the two succeeding days. By this time Walters had learned from Colby that the CIA had no connection with the Mexican lawyer, Manuel Ogario, that the Agency was not involved in the break-in, and that there was no secret message traffic coming from Mexico on CIA channels which the Agency was not reading. The latter fact convinced Walters there were no secret White House negotiations—between Nixon and Castro, say—which an investigation might compromise. In short, by Monday, Walters knew there was no good reason for the CIA to block the FBI's investigation, something he had not known at the meeting in Ehrlichman's office the previous Friday. This knowledge put Walters in a position of relative strength when he met Dean—no CIA involvement, period. In addition, Walters didn't much like Dean, he resented being summoned across town by a kid half his age, and he was appalled by Dean's naked requests that the CIA pay the burglars' bail and arrange to pay their salaries if they should be sentenced to jail. Walters did not refuse outright, but said nothing of the sort could be done without Nixon's personal order, insisted he would resign if pressed, and predicted general disaster if this sort of thing went on.

At times an almost pleading note entered Dean's voice; he was obviously in a corner and desperately looking for a way out. The meeting on Monday was followed by others on June 27 and June 28. In one of these conversations Dean attempted a new threat, saying that one of the Watergate burglars, Bernard Barker, had apparently been involved in a break-in at the Chilean Embassy in Washington.[62] Walters said he knew nothing about that. In effect, with Dean's new requests for bail money and other aid, the White House was asking the CIA to accept responsibility for the entire cover-up. This Helms and Walters would not do. They discussed Dean's requests at length after each meeting and apparently agreed to stick to the original request to the FBI, already made, but go no further. On June 28, Helms phoned Gray at the FBI and asked him not to interview Karl Wagner, the CIA officer who had pushed for the Agency's break with Hunt the previous summer. Helms had already told Howard Osborn to "forget about" Wagner, he would handle it. Clearly, Helms did not want the CIA's aid to Hunt in August 1971 to become entangled with the Watergate break-in. Two earlier CIA reports to the FBI's office in Alexandria, Virginia, about the CIA's relationship with Martinez and Mullen and Company, had promptly leaked to the papers. Helms did not want the CIA's aid to Hunt to become public by the same route. He informed Gray that Hunt had been working for Ehrlichman, and suggested Gray take it from there. After the conversation Helms told Walters in a memo that "we still adhere to the request that they [the FBI] confine themselves to the personalities already arrested or directly under suspicion and that they desist from expanding this investigation into other areas which may well, eventually, run afoul of our operations."[63]

That same day, June 28, Helms left Washington for a three-week trip to Australia and New Zealand,[64] and it is hard to read his memo to Walters as anything other than a last-minute instruction to stick to the concession they had already made. But while Helms was gone even the limited CIA-FBI agreement came unstuck. On July 5, pressed by FBI agents angry over the delay in the Watergate investigation, Gray called Walters to say he could no longer hold things up without a formal request from the CIA in writing. The Agency's role, in short, would have to go on the record. The following day Walters went to see Gray in his office and said there would be no such letter. Gray was not surprised. The two men liked each other. Both were career military officers, admirers of Nixon, anxious to do well in their new jobs, resentful of "kids" like John Dean trying to muscle them around. Both also felt the President ought to fire everybody involved in Watergate and let the law take its course.

After Walters left, Gray phoned Nixon, who was in San Clemente, and warned him that things were going terribly wrong. "Mr. President," he said, "there's something I want to speak to you about. Dick Walters and I feel that people on your staff are trying to mortally wound you by using the CIA and FBI and by confusing the questions of CIA interest in, or not in, people the FBI wishes to interview."[65]

There was a slight pause, Gray remembered. It is likely he thought the President was absorbing this shocking charge, but in fact, of course, Nixon already knew all about it—he was behind it. If Nixon had chosen that moment to tell Gray that by God national security was involved, he couldn't talk about it but his men were acting on his explicit directions and he wanted that investigation *stopped*, Gray almost certainly would have said "Aye, aye, sir," and done what he could. But Nixon was too cagey, and probably too timid, to venture on such a bold course.

"Pat," he said, "you just continue to conduct your aggressive and thorough investigation."

Gray's use of Walters's name told Nixon there was nothing further to be won from the CIA. The two men didn't like what was going on and could no longer be trusted to read between the lines and do the dirty work. From that point forward, the CIA was outside the main lines of the cover-up, and Nixon turned elsewhere for the money he needed to bribe the burglars.

But throughout the rest of the year Helms continued to hide the CIA's involvement with Hunt as best he could. In effect the CIA and the White House had arranged a marriage of convenience. Nixon wanted to hide the Hunt–White House connection, because that established clearly whom Hunt was working for. Helms wanted to hide the Hunt-CIA connection because it violated the Agency's charter and threatened to entangle the Agency in Watergate. In trying to keep the CIA out of Watergate, therefore, Helms was necessarily helping Nixon to keep Hunt at arm's length from the White House. Their motives were different—Nixon was protecting himself, Helms the Agency—but the result was the same: yard-by-yard resistance to revealing what had really happened.

Helms told Lawrence Houston about the June 23 meeting with Haldeman and Ehrlichman, but Houston did not press him to inform the federal prosecutors and Helms said nothing about the White House request until the following year. On July 7, while Helms was in Australia, Colby sent the FBI a memo about the documents and "certain other operational support items" given to Hunt the previous summer after a "duly authorized extra-Agency request."[66] This was certainly an oblique way to refer to John Ehrlichman, one of Nixon's two principal aides. When Earl Silbert, the chief prosecutor, eventually obtained the Colby memo he took one look at that opaque phrase and decided he wanted to know just who had authorized the Agency to do what. He was afraid the burglars would claim they had broken into the Watergate on CIA orders. On October 24, Helms elaborated on CIA assistance to Hunt with copies of some CIA memos and other documents delivered to the Attorney General, Richard Kleindienst, but once again Helms concealed the fact it was Ehrlichman who had originally asked for them. A month later, on November 27, Colby and the CIA's deputy general counsel, John Warner, fielded Silbert's questions about the "extra-Agency request." In Colby's own words, he "danced around the room several times for ten minutes to avoid becoming specific on this"[67] until Silbert finally pinned him down and extracted Ehrlichman's name.

Dean, of course, was closely monitoring the investigation and quickly learned of Silbert's discovery, which he passed on to Ehrlichman, who summoned Helms and Colby to his office for an explanation. Ehrlichman, at that time still in a position of great power, did not want to get enmeshed in Watergate. He was emphatic on the subject. Colby had dragged him in, and Colby had better find a way to drag him right out again. Helms and Colby agreed to do what they could. The result was extraordinary pressure on General Cushman to reexamine his memory. A first attempt did not quite go far enough; a second finally included the concession Ehrlichman wanted. "I cannot recollect at this late date who placed the call," Cushman wrote on January 10, 1973, "but it was someone with whom I was acquainted, as opposed to a stranger."[68]

Slow to tell the prosecutors about the CIA's relationship with Hunt, and who had initiated it, the Agency was also sluggish to reveal two other matters: letters received from James McCord reporting pressure on the burglars to claim they were working on a CIA operation, and its possession of Xerox copies of photos Hunt had taken while planning the Fielding break-in. The pictures had been sitting in the CIA's files since August 27, 1971, and Colby referred to them—obliquely; the FBI asked no questions—in the memo prepared for Gray in which he also disguised Ehrlichman's request for aid to Hunt. But that fall Colby began to wonder what Hunt's photographs really involved, and he asked the Office of Security to look into the matter. Proceeding from internal evidence in the photographs, the investigators established that the pictures were taken in Los Angeles, and that they were taken outside the office of a psychiatrist named Lewis J. Fielding. Colby and everyone else in the CIA insists that two and two were never put together, and that they didn't learn of Hunt's burglary of Fielding's office until May 1973, after John Dean went over to the prosecution and the cover-up began to fall apart. After brooding over the Office of Security's report on the photos for a week or so, Colby packed them up and sent them to the FBI.

Dean quickly picked up this development, and passed the word on to Ehrlichman, who was alarmed. The Fielding break-in, after all, had been approved by *him*. He asked Dean to check with Henry Petersen at the Justice Department to see if the photos could not somehow be returned to the CIA. Petersen said sure, as long as a card was placed in the files to indicate where they might be found. Dean waited until February 9, a week after James Schlesinger took over as the CIA's new Director, and then called him to suggest that the CIA ought to request the return of the photos. Schlesinger asked General Walters what he ought to do. Walters said it didn't sound like a good idea to him; an arrow would be left in the Justice Department files pointing directly at CIA. So Dean was told no once again, and the photos waited in the Justice Department's files until Dean spilled the beans. In this instance the CIA's heavy-footedness in passing on the photos was fully matched by the Justice Department's offhanded neglect in finding out what they meant. Neither agency really wanted to know.

The pattern with McCord's letters was much the same. The first—an unsigned note addressed to Helms, attached to a copy of a full letter to McCord's lawyer—arrived at the CIA on July 30, 1972, not long after Helms returned from his trip to Australia. Helms called in Lawrence Houston and Howard Osborn to ask how the Agency ought to handle the letter. The last thing he wanted to do was to give it to the federal prosecutors. Houston assured him he didn't have to; they weren't even certain that McCord had written the letter. Osborn disagreed. "It sounds like McCord and I think it is McCord," he said. He argued it was clearly relevant, and ought to go to the Justice Department. But Houston persisted. He said the letter was anonymous, they didn't know who had written it, an unsigned note was not evidence, they didn't have to turn it over.

Other letters followed, including one of December 29 in which McCord said, "I have evidence of the involvement of Mitchell and others, sufficient to convince a jury, the Congress, and the Press."[69] Taken together, McCord's letters made unmistakable what ought to have been obvious enough anyway: the burglars' silence was the result from pressure on high; they had not been working on their own; Hunt and Liddy were only middlemen in the operation as a whole, and lower-middle at that. But Helms simply instructed Osborn to hold on to the letters, and tell no one about them. It was not until May 1973, following Schlesinger's order for a IG investigation of everything doubtful in the Agency's past, that Osborn told someone else he had the letters, and they finally made their way to the prosecutors. Helms claimed then and later that he was only standing on Houston's legal opinion, these letters weren't "evidence," and in retrospect he can see he might have made a mistake. But what else could he say?

Helms has been much criticized for his role in the Watergate investigation, on the grounds that he could have done more to move it forward, and he could have done it sooner. But the whole argument is a bit surrealistic. The truth, which Helms was hardly in a position to admit then or later, seems to be that he knew perfectly well who was organizing the cover-up and why, but wanted to leave the contest to the White House and whoever chose to take it on—Congress, press, Justice Department, so long as it wasn't the CIA. Conversations with CIA people about Helms's attitude tend toward the elliptical. No CIA people involved in Watergate recanted in the fashion of John Dean, Jeb Magruder, Chuck Colson, and a host of others, with the result that accounts of Helms's strategy for dealing with Watergate all come from witnesses who are basically on his side. Their first line of defense is narrow legality: we kept to the letter of the law. The second line of defense is somewhat broader: we were trying to do the best we could in a difficult situation. The final line of defense is plain realism: here was a real good chance for Helms to lose his job and put the CIA on the President's enemies list forever, and Helms did his best to prevent both.

The facts pretty much speak for themselves. Helms hoped to keep the CIA out of this, not just out of the break-in, but out of the line of fire. One word to Nixon that Helms was whispering secrets to the Justice Department would have put the Agency and the President on a collision course. Helms did not want Nixon to think of him as an enemy. As a result he interpreted Watergate as narrowly as the mind of man could conceive, and never surrendered a dangerous piece of evidence without a fight. Besides, whom was he to tell?—Richard Kleindienst, a committed Nixon partisan and friend of John Mitchell? Earl Silbert, who was to tell the judge in the break-in trial that as best he could discover, Hunt and Liddy and the five burglars were off on their own? Pat Gray, who had invited John Dean to sit in on FBI interviews, and gave him raw FBI reports, so he might keep one jump ahead of the prosecutors?

At that point in time, as it later became the custom to say, the cover-up was pretty nearly complete, and a word to almost any of the prosecutors was only a phone call away from Nixon himself. Helms, like almost everybody else in Washington, thought Nixon had this thing wired. He was going to get away with it. And when he did, he would begin to look about him with narrow eyes for the disloyal men who had not gone along.

When Helms told Nixon that he would like to be an ambassador, and that Iran was where he'd like to go, the President granted him the job. A cable was sent to the man serving in the post, Joseph Farland, telling him his time was up. The ax was more than a bit abrupt. Farland, a Republican party stalwart who had also been ambassador to Panama and the Dominican Republic, felt harshly used. His were not the only comments. Helms's sudden departure from the CIA naturally raised questions, and these, just as inevitably, centered on Watergate. The truth—that Nixon was behind the cover-up, and that Helms's refusal to provide the White House with a way out explained why Nixon got rid of him—was still well hidden. Suspicions at the time ran in a different direction; the CIA's connections to the Watergate burglars suggested to some observers that the Agency had been behind the break-in. One reason Helms had decided to accept the post in Iran, in fact, was to avoid any implication he was leaving the government under a cloud. It was only much later, in the spring of 1976, that an altogether different explanation was proposed—slyly, in the guise of fiction—for the job Nixon gave Helms. That was the doing of John Ehrlichman, who turned to the typewriter while appealing a sentence of jail, and it is likely that nothing in Helms's long career ever angered him more.

Ehrlichman and Helms never got on well. They had the same protocol rank, which meant they often sat with each other's wives at state dinners, but Ehrlichman's manner in carrying out Nixon's orders was arrogant in the extreme. He had tried to muscle Helms into surrendering CIA files to him personally, and then got the President to back him up in the nakedest sort of bureaucratic duel. Helms's daughter-in-law, Bonnie Bottger Helms, once asked him at dinner what he thought of Ehrlichman. "I don't want to talk about Ehrlichman," Helms said, "now or ever." She froze, and never mentioned the man's name again in Helms's presence.

Part of Helms's intense dislike of Ehrlichman had to do with the latter's manner: no one could raise his chin toward the ceiling with disdain as cold, or dismiss someone with as cutting a word, as John Ehrlichman. But that is by no means the major reason for Helms's feelings. The real explanation has to do with a little joke of Ehrlichman's, a ribbing little jest for old times' sake, contained in his political thriller and *roman à clef* called *The Company.*[70]

Ehrlichman makes an improbable novelist, but he has certain talents. One is an ear for characteristic utterance: nothing captures the peculiar cadence of Richard Nixon's petty, vindictive, self-pitying soliloquies better than the passages Ehrlichman gives the President in *The Company*. Nixon's White House tapes are flattering by comparison. Another knack Ehrlichman possesses is for the suggestive marriage of the true with the merely possible in a manner that invites belief. In short, he wields a dangerous pen, and in *The Company* he describes, with considerable narrative skill, a meeting at Camp David in which a figure very like Richard Helms blackmails a President very like Richard Nixon into granting him an ambassadorial post, lest he expose the seamy details of a scandal very like Watergate. When *The Company* was published, one of its first reviewers, Lawrence Stern in the Washington *Post*, suggested that perhaps Ehrlichman was trying to tell us something.

Helms is not by nature a vehement man, but on this subject he is vehement: "I don't know what he was trying to tell us, but whatever he was trying to tell us was not true. I have not read *The Company*, but I know what the plot is and I never blackmailed Nixon in any form, manner or kind. And I'd like that to be very clear. And nobody can prove anything to the contrary because nothing to the contrary ever happened. I work for the

President of the United States. I would have been disloyal, treasonable or anything you want to call it, if I'd tried any such trick and I certainly did not. . . . I'm being a little bit positive in raising my voice . . . because I want to convey to you the fact that I mean it."

Nevertheless, Helms was for a long time reticent about his conversation with Nixon at Camp David, and about the exact chronology of his appointment to Iran. Does that mean he is lying, and that Ehrlichman was right when he implied a motive of blackmail in Helms's request for the post in Iran? Probably not, but it isn't an easy matter to settle. For one thing, whom are we to ask? The three men who presumably know are all interested parties, to say the least, and history has arranged for the impeachment of their word. Haldeman is a self-confessed perjuror and a convicted felon. Helms accepted a fine and suspended prison sentence rather than defend himself in court against charges that he had lied to the Senate. And Nixon's testimony on Watergate is so deeply mendacious as to cast a shadow of doubt over every detail of his memoirs.

All the same, there are good reasons to believe Helms on this point. First, he says it wasn't blackmail, and nobody who might know has been willing to charge openly that it was. Second, why would he blackmail Nixon for a post in Iran, in which he had no real interest, when he might have insisted on keeping his own job, in which he had a great deal? Third, what did he have to blackmail Nixon with, which would not do as much damage to himself? He wanted to keep the CIA's relationship to Hunt secret, not reveal it to the world. Was he going to expose Haldeman's appeal for CIA help in quashing the investigation, when the record showed he had gone along, at least until July 6? Fourth, to whom might Helms deliver his secrets? The prosecutors appeared to be in Nixon's pocket in November 1972. The grand jury had already been dissolved, and the Senate Watergate Committee had not yet been established. Was Helms to convene a press conference? Fifth, Helms could have picked no better way to destroy the CIA. If word had leaked out that a Director of Central Intelligence had blackmailed a President, no President ever would have trusted the CIA again. Closely read, the record reveals only a superficial opportunity for blackmail, and Helms's personal history reveals no appetite for it.

But then what is to be made of Ehrlichman's story? Was he only being malicious? Helms certainly thinks so, but there is another interpretation which might explain things better. By the time Nixon fired Helms, the President had already been blackmailed for five months straight by Hunt and the other Watergate burglars, and he still wasn't out of the woods. Early the next year, Dean would bring him the biggest demand yet—for $1 million—and Nixon wouldn't bat an eye. "We could get that. . . . And you could get it in cash. I know where it could be gotten." Nixon was accustomed to the scent of blackmail. He felt himself surrounded by enemies. He thought nothing was beyond them. He was in the habit of expressing his fears and anxieties to Haldeman and Ehrlichman, almost his only confidants.

Helms was fired at Camp David, where there was no taping system, and where Nixon spent several weeks following the election in November 1972. Whatever he told Haldeman or Ehrlichman at the time is presumably lost. But it is certain that the question of Helms's appointment was discussed. About a week after Helms had been fired he received a call from Haldeman, who said the President had been thinking things over. "He feels more positively about it and he really wants you to go," Haldeman said. When Ehrlichman sat down to write his book he may have remembered some such remark by Nixon as this: *Christ, Helms was never on our side. But we'd better take care of him, right? We can't let him get off the reservation. If Iran's what he wants we'd better give it to him. At least it'll keep him out of Washington.* In short, Ehrlichman only embellished on the fears of Nixon, who felt so threatened by what Helms knew that he assumed a threat where no threat had been made.

Chapter 15

James Schlesinger, the man Nixon appointed to replace Richard Helms, had a professorial look about him—thick white hair and craggy good looks, tweed jackets, a comfortable pipe—but he was far from being professorial in manner or temperament, and his career at the CIA was stormy and short. To begin with, Schlesinger was a confident outsider, a man with only an academic knowledge of the business of intelligence, he was replacing a respected professional, and he came with a mandate from Nixon to turn the place upside down. He showed up at Langley almost as soon as his appointment was announced, took over the Director's suite, and immediately made plans to knock down a wall and enlarge his personal office.[1] Helms moved down the hall to a small office where he and his secretary, Elizabeth Dunlevy—"I won't be needing her," said Schlesinger—began to go through Helms's files. Then in the middle of January Helms was abruptly informed that he would not be leaving on February 14, as originally planned, but nearly two weeks earlier, on February 2.

An innocent explanation was offered for the sudden change in plans: a White House swearing-in ceremony had already been scheduled for some other appointments on February 2 and the President, it was said, simply wanted to get them all out of the way on the same day. Helms was unpersuaded; he thought he was being hustled out. Larry Houston and Jack Maury,[2] a longtime CIA official who was the CIA's legislative counsel in early 1973, spoke to Schlesinger and discovered that he was equally annoyed by the accelerated changeover. They tried to persuade Helms this wasn't Schlesinger's doing, but failed.

At about the same time, on January 17, Helms received a personal letter from Senator Mike Mansfield, informing him that the Senate planned an investigation of "campaign activities"—that is, of Watergate—and asking him to preserve whatever relevant documents the CIA might possess. From Helms's point of view there were now two direct threats to the secrets: one from a Senate committee in the full glare of national publicity, which could be counted on to take the widest possible view of its mandate; and another from Nixon's man Schlesinger. Helms, of course, was already painfully aware that Nixon had a taste for rummaging about in the CIA's past, that Nixon had a history of hostility toward the Agency, and that Nixon hoped the Watergate break-in might somehow be shifted from the White House to the CIA.[3] In addition, Helms was convinced that Nixon had fired him for one reason only—because he had refused wholeheartedly to join the Watergate cover-up—and he was certainly suspicious, perhaps even convinced, that Schlesinger had been hand-picked to do what Helms would not. During his final ten days in office Helms took two last steps to protect the secrets: he ordered Sidney Gottlieb to destroy records of the CIA's drug-testing programs in the 1950s and early 1960s, and he destroyed his own files.

Throughout Helms's tenure there had been a recording system in his office which allowed him to tape discussions or telephone conversations at will. The tapes were periodically transcribed and then erased, apparently by the simple expedient of reusing them. The transcripts of these conversations, along with some other personal files, had been kept in a safe in his own office. In all, they filled the equivalent of about two file drawers, say at least 40 inches of standard 8½-by-11 sheets of typing paper, totaling perhaps four to five thousand pages. Helms told Larry Houston that he had asked Elizabeth Dunlevy to go through these documents, that he was aware of Senator Mansfield's request for the preservation of anything touching on Watergate, and that he intended to adhere to the request. He did not ask Houston if this was an adequate procedure; he simply informed him it was what he was going to do. According to Helms's testimony later, his secretary checked that entire mass of paper—all his personal records from six and a half years as Director of Central Intelligence—and found nothing related to the break-in. Nothing at all. Not one page was preserved for the Senate Select Committee. The job was finished by January 24, 1973. Every last page was destroyed.

At ten o'clock on the morning of Monday, February 5, 1973, Senator J. William Fulbright of Arkansas called the Senate Foreign Relations Committee to order in Room 4221 of the Dirksen Senate Office Building for the purpose of considering the nomination of Richard Helms to be ambassador to Iran.

THE CHAIRMAN: Mr. Helms, we are very pleased to have you this morning. Would you for the record just state what you have been doing the last ten or fifteen years?

MR. HELMS: I was working for the Central Intelligence Agency, Mr. Chairman.

THE CHAIRMAN: I am glad for it to come out at last. This has all been classified. I think this is the first time you have ever appeared before this committee in open session, isn't it?

MR. HELMS: That is correct, sir.

THE CHAIRMAN: In all these years.

MR. HELMS: All these years.

THE CHAIRMAN: Are you sure we were wise in having them in executive session?

MR. HELMS: Yes, sir. . . .

THE CHAIRMAN: Are you under the same oath that all CIA men are under that when you leave the Agency you cannot talk about your experiences there?

MR. HELMS: Yes, sir, I feel bound by that.

THE CHAIRMAN: You feel bound by that, too?

MR. HELMS: I think it would be a very bad example for the Director to be an exception.[4]

As so often before, Richard Helms was telling the truth. There can have been few senior government officials who more completely won the trust of Congressmen. His policy had been to tell the truth, not all the truth—in some instances not even most of the truth—but only the truth; and over time the legislators grew to depend on the accuracy of what he told them.

Helms's reputation for integrity extended to the Washington press corps as well. He lunched frequently with reporters like the Alsop brothers, James Reston and C. L. Sulzberger of the *New York Times*, Hugh Sidey of *Time*, the columnist Joe Kraft, Chalmers Roberts of the Washington *Post*. When Roberts retired in 1970, his successor, Murray Marder, moved quickly to establish a relationship with Helms, a man clearly well wired in the Washington establishment and one who could be trusted not to mislead. Reporters did not expect him to answer every question, only to speak what he took to be true if he elected to speak at all. In a speech (described earlier) before the American Society of Newspaper Editors in April 1971, one of the very few he delivered in public during his tenure as DCI, Helms said, "The nation must to a degree take it on faith that we too are honorable men, devoted to her service."[5] The Senators, senior government officials, and established reporters who knew Helms did not smile at this statement; they accepted him as just such an honorable man.

His reputation in the CIA, when he left in 1973, was pretty much the same. There were plenty of Agency officials who thought he was too cautious by half, too deeply committed to the arcana of intelligence procedure, too trusting of James Angleton, too quick to defer to the proprietary claims of other intelligence organizations, too slow to resolve jurisdictional disputes within the Agency itself, too ready to give second-raters like Howard Hunt a second, a third, a fourth chance.

Stories abound among old Agency people of Dulles's administrative ineptitude, Raborn's ignorance, Robert Amory's chattiness, Angleton's paranoia, Bill Harvey's pugnacity, Kirkpatrick's ambition, Bissell's erratic brilliance, Desmond FitzGerald's gadgetomania. The Agency's secrets are not so easy to plumb, but the characters of the men who ran it are accessible. If Helms had had enemies, they would be speaking up. But he seems to have passed through in the mask of a civil servant, able, devoted to his job, discreet, a bit cool and aloof. Everyone knew him; no one knew him well. One of the few genuine anecdotes about Helms comes from a man who did not like him, and he had to think a long time before he could come up with it.

Before the Director's daily meeting, the man said, Helms would read an intelligence brief describing what had come in overnight. The names of all agents, intelligence officers, operations, and the like were replaced by code words, but for the Director's convenience there were little tags attached to the edge of the page providing the true identities. One day there was an item from the chief of station in Frankfurt and the tag beside the COS's code name said "Ray Kline."

Helms allowed himself to smile broadly at this, according to the man who related the story, because the officer in charge of the brief had misspelled the name of a man who had once been something of a Helms rival until he ran afoul of a former DDI, Admiral Raborn; the name was actually "Cline," with a C. Helms paused and said, "Poor Ray. How soon they forget, how soon they forget."

A man has been stepping very lightly indeed, who has left no tracks deeper than that. Helms had his critics inside the CIA, but he was trusted. He was not loved, but he was respected. Whatever his hesitations, he was taken to be an honest man. In 1960 Helms asked one of his officers to write the speech he had agreed to deliver before a group of retired military officers on the subject of Communist espionage and subversion. The officer wrote the speech; its tone was calm: Don't be alarmed by Soviet intriguing, be patient, totalitarian systems are inherently weak, democracy will prevail in the end because it speaks to something abiding in the nature of man. Helms read the speech, then looked quizzically at the man who had written it and asked, "Do you really believe that?"

"Yes," the officer said.

Helms hesitated, thinking, then said, "Well, I *guess* I do."

Richard Helms is an elusive man. He is not quick to reveal what he thinks about things. If you were to fault him for the Agency's choice of allies and enemies during the last thirty years, he would answer that it was not the Agency's job to make policy. If you don't like what it did, talk to the men who issued the orders. Helms's view of the world was informed, but narrow and severely concrete. A lifetime of intimacy with the ways of Great Powers when they want to have their way in the world had given him something of a mechanic's attitude toward international relations, and he did not lie awake at night wondering if the CIA had a moral right to do as it did. Helms's loyalties were simple and unclouded: he was on our side. He believed in the necessity and the utility of the Central Intelligence Agency. He defended the Agency against its rivals in the intelligence community. He tried to do his job well. He left with his pension rights, his reputation, and a conviction he had no more to answer for than any other man of his generation in Washington. What happened to Helms afterward was not Helms's doing. It was life, politics, and history which were complicated, not Helms.

The web of complications was beginning to draw tight when Helms testified before the Senate Foreign Relations Committee on February 5, 1973, and again in executive session two days later. In a sense, Helms had been cut adrift. He was still working for Nixon, but he no longer quite trusted the man. His loyalties were shrinking: it was not so much the President he sought to defend as the CIA and its record. For the first time in his life, on February 7, Helms was the subject of something very like a cross-examination. He had been sworn, something which had rarely happened before. The Senators had a great many questions in mind, some of them easy to handle, like CIA training of local police departments, and some of them not so easy. Fulbright, for example, asked when E. Howard Hunt left the CIA.

"About two, two-and-a-half years ago," Helms said.

"He had no relationship to the CIA since then?"

"No, sir," said Helms. Fulbright was accustomed to greater candor than that. It is true, so far as we know, that Hunt had not been employed by the CIA since April 1970, but *no* relationship?

"What is G. Gordon Liddy's relationship with the Agency?"

"None," said Helms.

"Never?" asked Fulbright.

"Never under any circumstances."

"He never has been. I see," said Fulbright.

"Never," repeated Helms.[6]

No relationship? One of the reasons cited by Karl Wagner for urging a break with Hunt in August 1971 was the fact that Hunt brought Liddy to a meeting with a CIA officer in order to provide him with alias identification.

Senator Clifford Case had picked up vague rumors of a White House intelligence program targeted on the antiwar movement in "1969 or 1970"—Case wasn't quite sure which. He had not yet heard of the Tom Charles Huston plan by name or in detail. "Do you know anything about any activity on the part of the CIA in that connection? Was it asked to be involved?"

"I don't recall whether we were asked, but we were not involved because it seemed to me that was a clear violation of what our charter was."

"What do you do in a case like that?" Case wanted to know.

"I would simply go to explain to the President this didn't seem to me to be advisable."

"That would end it?"

"Well, I would think so," Helms said, "normally."

"Okay," said Case.[7]

Didn't recall? When a man under oath says he doesn't recall something it's a pretty safe bet either conscience or prudence is blocking him from a definite yes or no. Helms explained nearly two years later that he thought Case was talking about an *Army* domestic intelligence program. Case's acceptance of this explanation is a sign of either extreme good nature or a fundamental regard for Helms as a man.

But the rules were shifting. All the old arrangements were coming apart. Helms was not on familiar ground, and he had begun to break his own rules to defend himself and the CIA. No one told him to do this; it was instinct alone which prompted him. In the past Senator Richard Russell had exercised tight and meticulous control over the CIA's relationship with the Senate. Russell had been chairman of the Senate Armed Services Committee, one of the two Senate committees which had oversight authority for the CIA. The other was the Senate Appropriations Committee headed by Carl Hayden. Russell reached an agreement with Hayden for the two committees to exercise their function jointly, an arrangement which gave Russell great power, and which he exercised to preserve the security and the autonomy of the CIA. He trusted the CIA not to do anything he wouldn't do, and didn't pay attention to the details. Houston remembers Russell turning to an aide once during a briefing, and asking, "What does the NSA do?" He saw his role in narrow terms, not to oversee the Agency but to protect it. On one occasion during Helms's tenure Senator William Proxmire wanted him to testify before his Joint Economic Committee on a subject Helms preferred to avoid. He went to Russell for help. Russell told Helms to tell Proxmire that he, Russell, didn't think this was a good idea. Helms did so, and that was the end of it. Proxmire backed off. Russell had power, and he made it felt.

He made it felt, for example, in late 1963, after President Johnson directed John McCone to hold a press conference to publicize certain CIA findings about Soviet economic troubles. McCone gave the job to Ray Cline, the DDI, and Cline conducted the press conference as ordered. The reporters were suspicious of the whole enterprise and the coverage was uniformly critical.[8] Russell called McCone down and said he didn't think this was a good idea; if McCone persisted then Russell was going to withdraw his support from the CIA. A word was sufficient. There were no more CIA press conferences until William Colby took over the Agency in 1973.[9]

As long as Russell was alive, Helms knew exactly who had the right to ask him questions and what sort he was obliged to answer, and no other

Senator dared to challenge Russell's authority. Russell himself chose to trust Helms, and apparently never tested him with a really hard question; indeed, he once told Helms there were certain CIA operations he'd rather not even know about. Such an approach, of course, was oversight in name only, and one, furthermore, which positively invited the CIA not to be squeamish, but it was an arrangement which worked. Congress was satisfied things were under control, and the CIA thought it knew the rules. In 1966 Senator Eugene McCarthy, who later became a close friend of Helms, introduced a resolution to establish a new Senate Committee on Intelligence Operations. Mike Mansfield had tried the same thing back in 1955, but after Allen Dulles and Eisenhower hung up their phones the resolution was dead. McCarthy's resolution met a similar fate. Russell let it be known he was against it, and it was defeated in July 1966 by a vote of 61 to 28. The sense of the Senate was that it preferred not to know. As a gesture to the vanquished, Russell invited Senators Fulbright, Mansfield, and Bourke Hickenlooper to sit in on CIA briefings of Russell's joint oversight committee, but he made it clear this concession did not give them the right to take what they had learned back to the Foreign Relations Committee, and Russell had the power to make his restrictions stick. Fulbright went a time or two, but then gave it up. "There's no point in it," he told Carl Marcy, chief of the Foreign Relations Committee's staff; "they never tell you anything down there."

But all this had changed by early 1973. Russell was dead, and the new chairmen of the Armed Services and Appropriations Committees, John Stennis and Allen Ellender, inherited Russell's authority without all of his power. Stennis was if anything even friendlier and more trusting than Russell where the CIA was concerned. In late 1971, when the Agency was criticized for running a "secret war" in Laos, Stennis praised it fulsomely: "This Agency is conducted in a splendid way. . . . You have to make up your mind that you are going to have an intelligence agency and protect it as such, and shut your eyes some and take what is coming."[10]

But Stennis was also lax about holding CIA oversight hearings, and Symington, a member of the Armed Services as well as the Foreign Relations Committee, simply seized the occasion on February 7, 1973, to ask Helms a few questions which had been fermenting in the back of his mind about Chile. Helms might have said frankly, Look, Senator, this is something I'd rather not get into; or he might have waffled, but either would have let the cat out of the bag, which he did not want to do. The other Senators were as curious as Symington; it was the closest thing to a free-for-all Helms had ever encountered in the Senate, and he withdrew behind a wall of the narrowly, technically true. He didn't want to open these matters up; he wanted to shut them down, to surrender as little as possible, and to get out of the room.

At the end of the Helms confirmation hearing Fulbright said, "I think it is very healthy that you get something definitely on the record particularly in view of your leaving. I think I have covered it. You remember that famous instance in which we didn't ask Sullivan about Laos and when we asked why he didn't tell us, he said we didn't ask him about it. Is there something that I should have asked you about that I didn't to which you ought to reply?"

> MR. HELMS: Sir, let me in an effort to sort of close this, about this, Watergate business, you have asked all the relevant questions. I have no more information to convey and I know nothing about it. Honestly, I do not.
> THE CHAIRMAN: And your people other than that one man who was a consultant—
> MR. HELMS: We had nothing to do with it, honestly we didn't.

But it was too late. Helms was no longer in control of the secrets by that time, and the men who followed him did not share his regard for their inviolability. The combination of Watergate and James Schlesinger would crack open the Agency's secret history, and William Colby would finish the job. Schlesinger arrived with ideas and a mixture of suspicion and contempt for the "gentlemen's club" which had wielded and bequeathed power in the CIA since the 1940s. Schlesinger had derived a great many ideas from his study of the intelligence community two years earlier, but at their heart was a plan to gut the clandestine services. "That DDP, that's Helms's Praetorian Guard," Schlesinger told the London chief of station, Rolfe Kingsley, during a trip to England. "I'm going to bust it up."

One of Schlesinger's first acts as Director was to hold a meeting of DDP people in the Agency's main auditorium, where Helms had given a farewell speech in December. Helms had told his audience the Agency had nothing to do with Watergate, but if they had, they'd have done it a hell of a lot better. It was not praise which was on Schlesinger's mind in early February 1973, but burial. At his order the auditorium's 500 seats had been given to the DDP's younger men, an ominous sign of what Schlesinger had in mind for the older officers.

Much of Schlesinger's talk was confusing. He kept referring to the directorate of *operations*, for example. What was that? The CIA had no directorate of operations. Schlesinger said there was going to be a new emphasis on technical collection (Bissell's idea), we're going to stress analysis (Ray Cline had often proposed that very thing), of course there's a continuing need for human resources (Helms's position). What was that supposed to mean? Schlesinger was going to use bugs, newspapers, and spies; what else was there? It appeared for a moment that Schlesinger was just another outsider trying to prove he knew the jargon. But eventually Schlesinger made his way to the heart of his talk that morning, and it became brutally clear what he intended. From now on, he said, intelligence is going to be a twenty-year career. It's time to give way to young blood. Schlesinger was going to clear the place out.

The process was brutal, but many CIA people concede that it was long overdue. For a while there was talk among the old guard of putting up a fight, perhaps of bringing a class-action suit to halt mass firings. The CIA's retirement law severely limited the number of men who could take early retirement each year. If Schlesinger went over that number, the excess would be out in the cold with neither pensions nor prospects. In the corridors they were saying that by God he couldn't do it. But he could. Schlesinger called Nixon from his office while several CIA officers stood there listening. He explained over the phone there might be a fight, publicity, court cases, leaks in the papers. He asked Nixon, "How far can I go?" Nixon said he would back him all the way: clean the place out. When Schlesinger hung up the phone, it was clear to the men in the room that there would be no staying the massacre.

Like Helms, Schlesinger held a regular morning meeting with his Deputy Directors in his office, and every morning he wanted to see numbers. He didn't want excuses; he wanted the names of the people who were going. Ed Proctor, the Deputy Director for Intelligence, was frequently criticized for moving too slowly. Carl Duckett, the Deputy Director for Science and Technology, did better; he came in with a list of names every day, and the men under him began openly calling him a heartless sonofabitch. William Colby, who replaced Thomas Karamessines as head of the renamed Deputy Directorate of Operations,[11] came back to his office regularly with an echo of Schlesinger's complaint: "We aren't getting any numbers." He gave the job to Gordon Mason, chief of the DDO's Career Management Group, apparently hoping to insulate himself from the harsh decisions Schlesinger demanded. But Mason refused to let Colby off the hook. He picked his candidates for the ax carefully, but once he had put together a pile of personnel jackets he brought them to Colby and said, "Here they are, you make the decisions."

Schlesinger did not remain long at the CIA; on May 9, 1973, Nixon appointed him to succeed Elliot Richardson at the Department of Defense, who was replacing Richard Kleindienst at the Department of Justice, who was resigning because his old friend John Mitchell was finally facing indictment for his role in the Watergate scandal. But during Schlesinger's brief tenure as DCI, the shortest in the Agency's history, he fired more than a thousand CIA officers throughout the Agency, more than a hundred of them old soldiers in the DDP/DDO.

The firings came in waves. If the pace wasn't brisk enough he would do the job himself, going down a list of officers and saying, "He's been here twenty years, that's long enough, out." It was a crude method, and it got rid of some able officers along with the deadwood, but Schlesinger could not be argued with. Once a goal was met, a new one was established. At one point the CIA's director of personnel, Harry Fisher, said, "Can't we show some compassion this time?"

"Don't talk to me about compassion," said Schlesinger. "The only compassion I've got is for the American taxpayer."

Resentment of Schlesinger within the Agency reached such a degree that the Office of Security was asked to provide him with additional bodyguards. Thereafter the Director was accompanied to and from work, and a boydguard always sat in his outer office. When Schlesinger's official portrait was hung along with the others in the CIA's main corridor on the ground floor, a special closed-circuit television camera was secretly trained on the portrait and monitored from a nearby guard's office for fear some disgruntled employee would deface the painting. On one occasion the guard, watching his screen, noticed a woman stop in front of the portrait and then make a sudden movement. The guard rushed out to protect the painting and found the woman with thumb to nose, fingers waggling, giving Schlesinger a Bronx cheer.

But if Schlesinger was resented as an outsider, William Colby came to be disliked by many—not all—CIA people as something even worse, a kind of traitor who betrayed the trust Helms had shown in him, and who severely damaged the Agency during the two and a half years he ran it. Helms had given Colby just about every important job he'd held. He had recommended him as Nick Natsios's replacement as station chief in Saigon back in 1959. He appointed him chief of the Far East Division in 1963, and planned to make him chief of the Soviet Russia Division before Robert Komer borrowed him, with Lyndon Johnson's blessing, for the Phoenix program in 1968. When Colby returned from Vietnam in the summer of 1971, Helms made him the Executive Director/Comptroller, the CIA's third most important job, on paper at any rate. Colby's was a surprising rise, from one point of view. He was an OSS veteran and had joined the CIA in the early 1950s as an officer in the OPC, but he was known as a protégé of William Donovan at a time when Donovan was dismissed with condescension by Allen Dulles. Colby was a Princeton man, but he was without the social connections and gregarious charm of the other patrician Ivy Leaguers who ran the CIA in the early years. On top of that, Colby was Helms's opposite in his approach to intelligence, by temperament and choice a covert political operator, impatient with the caution and painstaking procedure of traditional intelligence collection.[12] He thought agent-recruiting, with its emphasis on the slow accumulation of operational intelligence—that is, huge biographical files on potential recruits—a laborious, wasteful, inefficient way of doing business. In particular, Colby chafed under the restraints of counterintelligence, and resented the skepticism of Angleton and his men whenever a Russian agent was recruited by luck and hard work. But Helms had promoted Colby all the same, partly for his intelligence and ability, but mostly, one suspects, for the one quality they shared in common: the belief that the CIA serves Presidents, and the willing energy Colby devoted to doing—or trying to do—whatever it was that a President wanted done.

Colby, however, was fundamentally out of sympathy with the sort of intelligence service Helms believed in, a fact which began to emerge as soon as Helms announced his departure. During the following six weeks Colby established himself as Schlesinger's chief guide and confidant within the CIA. He frequently briefed Schlesinger in his office at the Atomic Energy Commission, convinced him to drop the position of Executive Director/Comptroller, and won the appointment as Karamessines's successor. "Look," Colby told Schlesinger, according to his own memoirs, "where you are going to have your biggest trouble is with the clandestine crowd downstairs. I'm one of them. I grew up with them. Let me go down there and take care of that for you."[13]

Colby's enemies, who were both numerous and vociferous during his last three years with the CIA, would later describe his cultivation of Schlesinger as sycophancy pure and simple, the behavior of an ambitious but cynical man out for himself. This does not do justice to Colby's seriousness: Colby wanted a DDO which was leaner, more dependent on technical intelligence collection, and freer of what he took to be the melodramatics of espionage. He was, in fact, a good deal like Richard Bissell, not in personality but in practice. The old conflict between secret intelligence and political action returned with all its old force, and a new bitterness.

The mutual dislike between Colby and James Angleton was no secret in the CIA. Angleton had criticized Colby's support for the Christian Democratic party's "opening to the left" in Italy in the late 1950s. Angleton had worked in Italy for the OSS during the war, his father lived there, and he knew something about the country. Let in the Socialists, he argued, and the Communists won't be far behind. He darkly suspected that the Socialists and the Communists might have reached a secret agreement, and thought Colby's trust of the Socialists naïve. When Colby moved on to Saigon, Angleton continued to criticize him, once accusing him of failing to report a meeting with a Frenchman suspected of being an agent for the Russians. More pointedly, he blamed Colby then and later for the loss of American lives in Vietnam because Colby had neglected the importance of counter-intelligence. When it turned out later that the National Liberation Front and Hanoi had as many as forty thousand agents—a simply phenomenal figure—in place throughout the South Vietnamese military and government, from postmasters and corporals in the quartermaster corps on up, Angleton squarely placed the blame on Colby's refusal to take counterintelligence seriously back in the early 1960s. How many American soldiers had died because the other side was warned of impending operations by spies in Saigon? Angleton said there was blood on Colby's hands.

It should come as no surprise that one of Colby's first recommendations to Schlesinger was that he fire Angleton. It is nearly impossible for an outsider to decide what part of the Colby-Angleton feud was based on personal dislike, and what part on substantive disagreement. Neither man will discuss their differences candidly, for obvious reasons, and the details of charge and countercharge are impossible to pin down. But it is clear that the differences were bitter indeed. Colby thought Angleton's suspicions were close to paranoia. Friends of Angleton (and even some who were not his friends) would eventually tell reporters that Colby's more "destructive" acts as Director of Central Intelligence were entirely consistent with those of a man who was a Russian agent. This claim, backed up with supporting facts one, two, and three, is a sign of the lengths to which bitterness had gone. To an outsider, the charge against Colby seems utterly preposterous, convincing evidence, if more were needed, of the appalling deterioration of American intelligence since it began to try to explain itself in public.

Nevertheless, there is no disputing Angleton's intelligence, experience, or great knowledge about Communist intelligence services, nor his care in running operations and checking the *bona fides* of defectors.[14] But over the years Angleton had begun to see a fearful symmetry in Soviet operations around the world, the outline of a meticulous plan to insert agents in various intelligence services one by one, and then to use those established to pass on the *bona fides* of new agents. A full-scale scandal concerning penetration of French intelligence services in the early 1960s[15] convinced Angleton that the KGB's plan was extremely broad, involving the penetration of governments as well as intelligence services, so that an elaborate network of mutually supporting agents might gradually extend its control over entire governments and countries. There is no question that Russian intelligence agencies have been extremely efficient at their work. The chiefs of counter-intelligence in both Britain and Germany were working for the KGB at various times, and every major intelligence service—possibly including our own—has been penetrated by them. But Angleton's respect for Russian stratagem went far beyond the usual concession of their expertise. He thought the hoary "worldwide Communist conspiracy" was really a worldwide Communist conspiracy, and there is no way for an outsider to prove he is not right, partly because there is no easy way for an outsider to determine exactly what it is that Angleton suspects. The details were hard to come by even within the CIA. David Phillips describes a quiet Angleton overture shortly after Phillips had been named chief of the Western Hemisphere Division. Angleton took him aside and said they must set aside several hours for The Briefing. The Briefing? Exactly; Angleton would fill him in later. But somehow they never found the time, and Phillips never learned exactly what Angleton intended to include in The Briefing.

Inside the Agency, Angleton was best known for the extreme skepticism which he brought to his work. When a colleague once argued that another friendly service should be trusted with a particular piece of information,

Angleton replied, "There are no friendly services." His suspicion seemed boundless. He had been responsible for turning down an overture by the Russian spy Oleg Penkovskiy in August 1960, and later, after Penkovskiy was recruited by the British and then jointly run by the British and Americans, Angleton continued to argue that he was a provocateur. It is hard to convey just how perverse this seemed to the Soviet Russia Division under Jack Maury. Penkovskiy is credited as the single most important spy ever recruited by the Americans against the Russians. CIA people who saw the 5,000 frames of microfilmed documents provided by Penkovskiy, two pages to the frame, were dazzled by the quality of his information. The rule of thumb is that a provocateur must provide 95 percent true information if he is to be trusted and believed. The idea that Penkovskiy was a plant, and that the Russians deliberately surrendered so much true information, strikes CIA officers as insane. One man in the DDP, arguing the point with Angleton, was finally fobbed off with an appeal to secret knowledge. "You aren't cleared for certain sources," Angleton said enigmatically, and would add not another word.

This suspiciousness was characteristic, as was his tenacity once he had taken a position. He thought the conflict between Stalin and Tito was an elaborate charade to lull the West, and he is said still to believe that the Sino-Soviet split is equally a sham. Because of Angleton's brilliance, and his mastery of supporting detail in an argument, Directors of the CIA have held back from reaching the obvious conclusion: the man is unreliable. And yet, and yet . . . maybe he's right, they thought.

To argue the facts with a man convinced he has uncovered a conspiracy is to invite madness and despair;[16] and yet to ignore the facts is willful, feckless, and irresponsible, since the answer matters, and the man *could be right*. Angleton was precisely this sort of man; he was convinced the Russians exercised hidden power, and he had a genius for argument which forced his opponents to attempt to prove a negative. If a lot of CIA people simply threw up their hands, called Angleton a nut, and left it at that, a lot did not. One of his beliefs, for example, was that the KGB was in complete and utter control of the Palestine Liberation Organization. Angleton did not mean that the PLO was "influenced" by the KGB, or simply "penetrated" by the KGB; he meant that it was a KGB creature pure and simple, and his arguments were sufficiently strong to win substantial acceptance inside the CIA.

Angleton won the support of DCIs from Dulles to Helms because no one quite dared to challenge his expertise, because they were temperamentally inclined to share Angleton's extreme suspicion of the Soviets, if not his estimate of their capacity for devilish stratagem; and because they thought he just might be right. Even Schlesinger was won over by Angleton. Colby thinks the deciding factor was a shared anti-Communism, but a more likely cause was Angleton's ability to overwhelm with arcana, to plunge a new listener into the cold bath of espionage with such abruptness it took his breath away, left him disoriented, persuaded him that anyone who could survive in this frozen waste had better be trusted—better yet, left alone—to get on with the job. Colby was the first DCI who really knew something about the business of intelligence, and yet still considered Angleton's view of a noose of KGB agents slowly being tightened about the throat of the Free World as the conclusion of a man who has lost his powers of judgment.

Counterintelligence is to intelligence as epistemology is to philosophy. Both go back to the fundamental question of how we know things, both challenge what we are inclined to take most for granted, and both offer heavy advantage in debate to those who are skeptical of appearances. Angleton might be called the Bishop Berkeley of intelligence for his insistence that we cannot trust our senses, and that things are not necessarily as they appear. His method was that of the textual scholar: collation. It was his conviction that when all the facts are known, only those which are consistent are true. If a Russian defector insisted that the lighthouse visible from his schoolroom window as a boy was off to the left, when it was really off to the right, then there was something wrong with the man. Angleton's procedure was to take *everything* that a man said and match it phrase by phrase with *everything* that was known, and when he found a discrepancy, which was very often, he began to look for a motive, and he looked until he found one. Very often the motive was deception.

The three-year interrogation of the Russian defector Yuri Nosenko, who fled in late 1963 and claimed he knew Oswald was not working for the KGB, was only the most extreme of many examples. Nosenko's story was so filled with lacunae that Helms privately told Chief Justice Earl Warren in 1964 that the CIA simply could not vouch for his *bona fides*. Until 1967 Nosenko was kept under round-the-clock guard in a padded basement cell while CIA interrogators tried to decide if he could be trusted. In the end, the argument was settled by administrative fiat on the grounds that Nosenko could not be extralegally jailed forever. In this instance, Angleton apparently held the middle ground—he wasn't sure one way or the other— but the investigation was characteristic of his approach. CIA people who worked at the defector reception center in Frankfurt, Germany, describe other instances in which the stream of questions from Angleton in Washington was so meticulous, tireless, and endless they were driven half-crazy. Angleton's was a method in keeping with the man. He raised orchids, a pastime in which years may be spent in bringing a single new variation to flower. He was a patient fly fisherman, and tied his own flies, meticulous work done with fine tweezers. He polished his own gemstones and made jewelry. He became a leatherworker during a year he spent in a sanitorium with tuberculosis. He ate heavily but never seemed to gain weight, smoked heavily, stayed up late into the night.[17] At Yale in the 1930s his passion had been poetry, and he brought a certain spiritual intensity to his work in counterintelligence. He was not indifferent in the manner of a fruit sorter, tossing out the bruised apples. He felt himself to be engaged in a war between the darkness and the light. His job was to separate truth from deception, and the central enigma of James Angleton is the mystery of what it was he truly saw, when he beheld at last the fearful symmetry.

Colby had no patience for this sort of thing. Temperament did not incline him to argue with Angleton. He simply made up his mind there was no profit in this, and chucked it impatiently aside in the spirit of Samuel Johnson, who kicked a stone and said, "Thus I refute Berkeley!" In short, William Colby junked counterintelligence.[18]

But he began slowly. One of Colby's first acts as Deputy Director of Operations was to form a special study committee for reorganization of the DDO under the chairmanship of Cord Meyer, Colby's deputy, a man with something of a public reputation but never considered an operational professional within the CIA. As head of the International Organizations Division, for example, Meyer had established a web of funding groups so intimately interconnected that a single compromise—the discovery of CIA funding of the National Student Association in 1967—exposed the whole network within a period of days. The identities of scores of dummy foundations, and the groups subsidized by them, were revealed in the press. This is not exactly covering your tracks. Later Meyer had been chief of station in London, a job which demanded administrative talent and social expertise, depending as it did so heavily on liaison with British intelligence, but not much by way of secret activity. A second member of Meyer's committee, Charles Whitehurst, protested that Colby's reorganization of the DDO was "a Frankenstein monster," but Colby put it into effect anyway, doing away with the old staffs attached to each division and reducing the customary role of counterintelligence to a whisper. Schlesinger would not let him fire Angleton, but Colby took away his control over liaison with the FBI, moved the remnant of Operation Chaos before killing it entirely, cut Angleton's staff, and hoped he would get the point and retire.

Within a matter of months following Helms's departure from the CIA, the Agency's clandestine services, which he had done so much to build, had been transformed, and the bulk of his old friends and colleagues were either gone or on their way out. But it took a break in the Watergate case to really crack open the secrets of the past. On April 15, 1973, John Dean told the federal prosecutors about the burglary of Dr. Lewis Fielding's office in Los Angeles engineered by Hunt, and the following day Hunt confirmed the story when he testified before the grand jury. Nevertheless, the story was contained for nearly two weeks. On April 18, Nixon told Henry Petersen, the chief federal prosecutor, that he was not to pursue Hunt's story of the Fielding break-in. That was "national security." Petersen agreed, but a few days later he began to wonder if the Justice Department did not have an obligation to reveal the break-in to the judge in Daniel Ellsberg's trial, then being held in Los Angeles. On April 25, Petersen went to Kleindienst, the Attorney General, to argue that knowledge of the break-in constituted potentially exculpatory material which ought to be turned over to the judge. Kleindienst agreed and told the President, who was "very provoked . . . very upset about it."[19] But Nixon was in a corner; he did not dare to overrule his Attorney General, and on April 26 Judge Matthew Byrne was informed *in camera* of the break-in.

It was apparently at that time that Petersen called Larry Houston at the CIA to tell him he'd better get down to the Justice Department. "All hell's going to break loose," he said. Houston told Schlesinger where he was going and why, and Schlesinger said, "What about the psychological profile, ask about that." That was the first Houston had heard of the two psychological profiles prepared by the CIA on Daniel Ellsberg. At the Justice Department a highly agitated Henry Petersen described the break-in and its purpose: Hunt had been after raw material for the CIA's second attempt to analyze Ellsberg's motives in releasing the Pentagon Papers. Houston remembers Petersen slamming his fist into the wall and saying, "I can't believe it, how could they do this to us?" When Houston got back to the CIA he reported to Schlesinger and Colby, and Colby said, "At least now we know what Hunt was up to."[20]

Schlesinger's reaction was one of pure fury. Colby and Vernon Walters had both assured him he knew everything there was to know about the CIA's involvement in Watergate, which by this time could no longer be considered as meaning the original break-in alone, but everything which Hunt and his colleagues had done for the President. Now Schlesinger discovered that Hunt had committed a burglary with material aid from the CIA. He told Colby he was going to turn the CIA upside down and "fire everyone if necessary,"[21] but he intended to learn everything the Agency had done which might blindside him in the future. No more surprises!

Colby had a plan ready to deal with this problem. He suggested that Schlesinger issue a directive to every CIA employee instructing him to come forward with *anything* the CIA might have done which exceeded the limits of the Agency's charter. Schlesinger thought this a good idea. Colby wrote the order, Schlesinger signed it, and copies were distributed within the CIA on May 9[22]—the same day on which Nixon moved Schlesinger to the Department of Defense and appointed Colby as the new Director of Central Intelligence. The following day Schlesinger ordered Vernon Walters to prepare a complete affidavit describing his meetings with Haldeman, Ehrlichman, and Dean in June 1973, and a day or two after that Schlesinger learned of McCord's letters forwarded to the CIA the previous year. That was the last of the CIA's contacts with Watergate figures to emerge after they had been suppressed by Helms as irrelevant. But it was sufficient to put urgency behind Schlesinger's order of May 9, and reports began to pour in. Technically, the reports were directed to the Inspector General, William

Broe, who signed the final report, but in fact they proceeded first to Colby's desk.

By May 21 a 26-page preliminary summary of the reports had been prepared by Broe, who forwarded it to Colby under the title "Potential Flap Activities." And so they were. The full report, completed later, came to 693 pages in all, and it quickly acquired the *nom de scandale* of "the Family Jewels." It included just about every serious charge brought against the CIA: Operation Chaos was there, along with a sketchy account of CIA drug-testing programs (the details having disappeared when Helms ordered the files destroyed before he left the CIA), the Agency's role in the Tom Charles Huston domestic intelligence plan, training programs for local police departments, a program to recruit counterintelligence agents for the Bureau of Narcotics and Dangerous Drugs, the mail interception program, the bugging of American journalists thought to have informants within the CIA, a burglary in Fairfax, Virginia, contacts with the Watergate burglary team. Most dangerous of all was a special annex summarizing the Inspector General's Report of 1967 on the CIA's involvement in assassination plots against Trujillo, Diem, and Castro.[23]

Until that moment Colby had never heard of the IG Report, although he had been vaguely aware that assassination was something of a soft point in the CIA's past, a subject which would not bear scrutiny. In the fall of 1971 Colby had read a story in the Sunday newspaper supplement *Parade* claiming that CIA was the "only" American agency "authorized" to commit assassinations.[24] That June, Colby had been vigorously cross-examined by the Senate Foreign Relations Committee about the Phoenix program, and he had denied charges he had been running a kind of central assassination bureau in Vietnam. So Colby decided to write a letter of denial to *Parade*, lest silence be construed as confirmation. But before doing so, he quietly asked a few questions and discovered he could not fairly issue the flat, blanket denial he had planned: the CIA, he was told, had indeed been "involved" in assassination planning in Africa and the Caribbean. Precisely how involved, Colby did not learn, nor did he make an effort to find out. He contented himself with a letter of mild protest to *Parade*, and then drafted an explicit order banning assassinations which Helms signed and distributed to the Deputy Directors on March 6, 1972.[25]

Colby's response to his discovery of solid evidence of assassination plotting in the Family Jewels indicates he was of two minds. First, he volunteered what he knew to the chairmen of the four House and Senate committees with oversight authority for the CIA in June 1973, but at the same time he argued the "excesses" had all been prohibited, and the past ought to be let lie. Three of the four were willing to forget the matter, but the last, Representative Lucien Nedzi, chairman of the House Appropriations Committee, insisted on reading the entire report, all 693 pages of it. Colby only just managed to convince Nedzi the CIA would never do this sort of thing again, its house was clean, the Agency would be wrecked in the Watergate climate of 1973 if the entire contents of the Family Jewels were to be released. After a lot of argument, Nedzi reluctantly went along.

But by this time a kind of momentum had built up, and the inertia of exposure could not be restrained. The public revelation of the CIA's peripheral involvement in Watergate, suppressed by Helms for nearly a year, suggested there was more to come. Watergate itself had undermined the authority of the government, and the very fact of Schlesinger's May 9 directive had abrogated the discipline of secrecy within the CIA. It was a season for truth. Besides, once secrets are gathered together they reach a kind of critical mass and will out. When Helms had been DCI he did not merely keep the secrets; he made sure they were never gathered in one place. Colby's notion that the CIA might be cleansed by a process of quiet intramural confession brought all the secrets together in the 693 pages of the Family Jewels. Although Colby was later to be widely blamed in the intelligence community for having released the secrets deliberately, he did not precisely do this. He tried to clean house quietly and dispose of the detritus in secret, thus allowing the CIA to consume its own smoke as it had always done in the past. The weak point in the process was the number of people let in on the secrets, not just those in the offices of the Director and the Inspector General who actually took charge of the paper, but the four chairmen of the House and Senate committees briefed by Colby. Even more important were the CIA officers who had stepped sufficiently outside the hermetic mental world of the Agency to report what they took to be illegal acts. One imagines that for many of those officers their abuse reports were not the last but the first steps in rebellion, and that having reported a wrong, they began to wonder if anything would be done about it. At any rate, the very existence of the Family Jewels dispersed the secrets widely, with the inevitable result.

The CIA's role in Watergate had pointed a lot of reporters in the Agency's direction. Sometime during the year and a half between May 1973 and December 1974 Seymour Hersh of the *New York Times* got wind of the outline—but not the name—of Operation Chaos. On December 20, 1974, he went to see William Colby, who told him Chaos was not really illegal, it was targeted on the foreign connections of American dissidents, it had been fully authorized by the President, and besides, the whole program had been terminated. In short, Colby confirmed everything Hersh had discovered.

But according to several sources, Colby did not stop there. The CIA had been guilty of illegal operations, Colby confessed. For example the interception of first-class mail in New York City over a twenty-year period, a program—now terminated, like the others—which had been run by counterintelligence. Not long before his interview with Colby, Hersh had first heard the name of James Angleton from a former Colby aide, Tom McCoy.

McCoy told Hersh something about Angleton's reputation for intrigue and paranoia inside the CIA, and added that he'd told Colby back in May 1973, at the time of his appointment, the first thing he ought to do was fire Angleton. This Colby had declined to do, partly to reassure the Agency he wasn't going to continue the purge begun by Schlesinger, and partly from a healthy bureaucratic respect for what Angleton might do in response. As he suggests in his memoirs, Colby was extremely wary of Angleton.

Relations between the two men deteriorated in the following eighteen months. Colby did not like the way Angleton handled liaison with the Israelis (and indeed, where suspicion of Arab motives was concerned, Angleton made Golda Meir seem trusting). In addition Colby did not like the atmosphere of suspicion inside counterintelligence, a suspicion so extreme, Colby discovered, that Angleton had actually informed the chief of the Belgian intelligence service that the CIA's chief of station in Brussels was a Russian agent, a claim for which there was no hard—or even good—evidence. Finally, on December 17, 1974, Colby called in Angleton and told him he was to be relieved of his responsibilities for both liaison with Israel and counterintelligence, but that he might stay on as a consultant. Colby clearly hoped Angleton would take the hint and leave, but instead Angleton protested vigorously, and he was far from being a man without bureaucratic resources. So Colby took a practical step in his interview with Hersh and mentioned the mail-intercept program which Angleton had defended over the years, ascribing it to counterintelligence. Hersh put two and two together and ascribed it to Angleton. When Hersh's story was followed by Angleton's retirement before the end of the year, it was generally assumed by the press that Angleton had been responsible for Operation Chaos and was being fired in response. Eventually this misapprehension was corrected, but in the interim Angleton reached a somber conclusion: Colby had deliberately orchestrated matters in order to force Angleton out under circumstances which would prevent him from fighting back. In any event, the result was the same. Angleton left, and one of his final official acts in the CIA was a characteristically gloomy review of Communist intelligence operations, which he invariably referred to as "the threat."[26]

Two days after Hersh's interview with Colby, the *Times* published Hersh's findings under a three-column headline on the front page. With that, the slow leak of CIA secrets became a flood. The White House expected Colby to issue a flat denial, which of course he could not do. Colby had never informed the White House of the Family Jewels, something he later described as simple oversight, but CIA people say that in fact Colby kept the report to himself because he didn't want to arm Nixon with a lot of secrets in mid-1973. The result was that when Hersh's story appeared on December 22, 1974, President Ford did not know how much truth it contained, if any. The same day Colby called Ford, who was vacationing in Vail, Colorado, and told him that Hersh had distorted the record, that the "excesses" of the CIA had all ended in 1973 (following Helms's departure), and that he would provide a detailed response to the *Times* story in writing. When it was finished two days later in the form of a six-page letter, with nine annexes totaling another 58 pages, Colby took it to the White House for Kissinger to read. He also brought the Family Jewels with him that Tuesday evening, and the Secretary of State flipped quickly through its 693 pages of misdeeds until he came to the subject of assassinations. There he slowed down and read carefully. "Well, Bill," he said, according to Colby, "when Hersh's story first came out I thought you should have flatly denied it as totally wrong, but now I see why you couldn't."[27]

Kissinger took Colby's report, but not the complete Family Jewels, to Vail and briefed Ford. By that time Colby had concluded it would be better to confess everything at once (except the assassination plotting), and he had written his letter to the President with its 58 pages of annexes as a document which might be released directly to the press. Colby felt the CIA's misdeeds belonged in a category of "bad secrets" which would haunt the Agency until they were revealed for the relatively paltry wrongs he conceived them to be. Letting out the "bad secrets," he felt, would protect the "good secrets"—the names of agents, means of collection, and so on. Ford and Kissinger emphatically did not agree. Back in Washington on January 3, 1975, Ford summoned Colby to the White House for a complete briefing.

Ford was not an innocent, but he was genuinely shocked by the assassination plotting described by Colby, and it proved to be a secret too large for him. He had decided to form a commission headed by Vice-President Nelson Rockefeller to report on the allegations in Hersh's story, but the men he appointed to it were all of the sort who could be depended on for discretion. Ford and Kissinger wanted to quiet the uproar, get the lid back down, and leave the rest of the secrets in the Family Jewels. But Ford himself, brooding over what Colby had told him, was to be responsible for exposing the biggest secret of all.

On January 16, 1975, the President held a luncheon in the White House for the publisher of the *New York Times*, Arthur Ochs Sulzberger, and some of his top editors, including the managing editor, A. M. Rosenthal. At the end of an hour or so of general discussion Rosenthal asked Ford how he expected the Rockefeller Commission to win public trust when its membership was so heavily weighted by conservative figures with a history of hardline political beliefs and sympathy for the military. Ford explained with unusual candor that the Commission's mandate was strictly limited to CIA activities within the United States and he didn't want anybody on it who might stray off the reservation and begin rummaging about in the recesses of CIA history. If they did they might stumble onto things which would blacken the name of the United States and of every President since Truman.

"Like what?" asked Rosenthal.

"Like assassinations!" Ford shot back. And then it sank in on him what he had said, and to whom he had said it. "That's off the record!" he quickly added.[28]

CIA people still find Ford's blunder hard to credit. Some of them darkly suspect his indiscretion was in fact deliberate, and that he wanted the assassination story to get out for reasons of his own. What these might be is hard to fathom: the Republican Eisenhower was if anything even more intimately involved in the story than the Democrat Kennedy. But how else is one to explain the fact that a President told the CIA's darkest secret to a *newspaper?*

The *Times* searched its conscience and decided it was morally bound to sit on the story, but it did not sit very heavily; word of what had happened was not long in slipping loose, and in early February, CBS television news correspondent Daniel Schorr learned of the exchange. He was initially misled, however, by the Rockefeller Commission's study of domestic activities of the CIA; he thought the assassinations worrying Ford had been committed in the United States. Three weeks of quiet investigation turned up nothing, and he was about to abandon the story when a routine request for an interview with Colby, initiated sometime earlier, produced an appointment for February 27.

At the end of a general discussion of the CIA's involvement in Watergate, familiar ground for both men, Schorr casually mentioned he'd learned Ford was worried about CIA involvement in assassinations. Colby fell silent. He could not understand why Ford had raised the subject, and was not sure how far the President had gone.

"Has the CIA ever killed anybody in this country?" Schorr asked.

"Not in this country," said Colby, with neither inflexion nor expression. It was an unwisely narrow answer.

"Not in this country!" exclaimed Schorr.[29]

At that point Colby shut up; he would say only that assassination had been formally prohibited in 1973. Why didn't Colby simply say the CIA hadn't killed anybody? Colby's critics in the CIA suspect he wasn't really trying to kill the story, but to get it out. A more likely answer is that Colby wouldn't say what he didn't know to be true. After all, Trujillo and Lumumba had both been assassinated, and in early 1975 Colby was probably unsure of the CIA's exact role in their deaths.

From Colby's limited remarks Schorr concluded that the "assassinations" worrying Ford had actually taken place, but abroad, not at home. At first, Schorr was unsure what to do with the story because he did not know who had been assassinated, but then it occurred to him that Ford's concern was in itself a story, and the following day, February 28, 1975, Schorr went on the CBS *Evening News* at seven o'clock to break the biggest CIA story of all:

"President Ford has reportedly warned associates that if current investigations go too far they could uncover several assassinations of foreign officials in which the CIA was involved. . . . "

In Teheran, Helms was furious. It seemed to him that the Agency to which he had devoted his life was falling apart, and that the men who ought to have been its protectors were backing timidly out of the way, saving themselves from the general wreck. President Ford, Helms felt, had not only a constitutional but a moral obligation to shield the CIA, an executive agency, from outside invasion. But Ford was nowhere to be seen; he had turned the Agency over to the Rockefeller Commission and had washed his hands of the whole business. Helms was angry at Colby too. The assassination story was the final straw. One of Helms's regular correspondents was James Angleton, who often sent him news clippings or tapes of broadcasts so he might follow what was going on. Helms knew the circumstances of Angleton's departure and considered it completely unjust. He knew about the Family Jewels, believed it to have been Colby's doing, and considered it the worst sort of mistake, inviting CIA officers down the line to blow the whistle on their superiors. How could an intelligence service operate in such an atmosphere? Colby had not only collected the secrets in one place—a fundamental error! nothing on paper!—but he had passed on charges against Helms personally to the Justice Department without consulting anyone else in the government. In Helms's opinion Colby was damaging the CIA by turning it against itself and opening it to outsiders. The Family Jewels led directly to Hersh's story about the CIA's domestic intelligence program. Hersh's story led directly to the Rockefeller Commission and the just-formed Senate Select Committee to be headed by Frank Church, and before their investigations had even fairly begun, the biggest secret of all— the plotting of assassinations—was already out in the open. And finally, Helms was angry at Daniel Schorr. Back in January, when Helms had returned to testify at the opening session of the Rockefeller Commission, Schorr had waited outside his door all one morning with a camera crew. Helms thought that a cheap trick. Now he was being called back to Washington yet again, in April 1975, to testify before the Rockefeller Commission on the subject of assassinations, about which Helms knew so much but would say so little, and Daniel Schorr was the man who brought him.

By this time Helms had developed a technique for dealing with the jet lag which followed the ordeal of a seventeen or eighteen-hour flight from Iran to Washington. He changed planes in London but did not halt to rest; it seemed to work better if he pushed straight through. When he arrived in Washington in mid-afternoon he would go to the friend's house where he was staying, have dinner a bit earlier than usual, then go to bed at eight or nine o'clock and stay there until the next morning. Helms's body, still on Teheran time, would not let him sleep straight through, but he had learned to wait it out. He did not turn on the light, made no attempt to read, did not get up and pace around in the dark. He simply lay there in bed, the house and city quiet around him, and rested, and thought.

After just such a flight Helms appeared before the Rockefeller Commission staff on April 26, 1975. The next day he testified again, and the day after that, April 28, he appeared before the full Commission, which questioned him for four hours in the office of the Vice-President. When Helms emerged at last he found Daniel Schorr waiting outside with three or four other reporters. Schorr stepped forward, held out his hand, and said, "Welcome back." At that, something in Helms broke.

If there is one trait which may be said to characterize Richard Helms it is control. He does not reveal himself. He contained himself when Allen Dulles gave the job he wanted to Richard Bissell, swallowed his disappointment, stayed on in the number-two position when he had hoped to be number one. He was not a man to raise his voice or bring his fist down on the table. He was cool and exact when he reprimanded a subordinate. The words stung, said a man who knew what it was like, but it seemed entirely impersonal. "It was like a voice talking to another voice." When Sam Adams, in the fall of 1967, told Helms he was going to move heaven and earth to get Helms fired—an astonishing thing for a low-level analyst to tell the Director of Central Intelligence—Helms's only response was amused acceptance, and the meeting actually ended in laughter at a shared joke.

Both Lyman Kirkpatrick and Thomas Karamessines—the one a disappointed rival, the other a loyal, frankly admiring subordinate—used almost identical words in describing Helms's instinctive restraint. He was not a man to protest with heat, they said. "You're not going to find out if Helms ever did that," said Kirkpatrick, "unless he tells you himself, because it's not the kind of thing he'd do in front of people." Karamessines made the same point in a discussion about Chile. "If Helms ever protested to a President he did it very privately, and let me tell you, there'd be no third party to know about it." It might almost be said that Helms managed his own emotional life as he had the CIA, and kept everything within.

But on April 28, 1975, the anger broke out, and it erupted not in private, but directly outside the Vice-President's office, with three or four other reporters listening. Helms could hardly have arranged a more public explosion if it had been on television.

"You sonofabitch!" he shouted at Daniel Schorr, his face suffused with livid anger. "You killer! You cocksucker! 'Killer Schorr'—that's what they ought to call you."

Schorr was stunned. Helms strode on towards the pressroom, continuing to shout at Schorr, who followed behind. When Helms got before the cameras he cooled slightly. "I must say, Mr. Schorr, I didn't like what you had to say on some of your broadcasts on this subject. And I don't think it was fair, and I don't think it was right. As far as I know, the CIA was never responsible for assassinating any foreign leader."

Another reporter asked, "Were there discussions about possible as-sassinations?"

"I don't know whether I stopped beating my wife," Helms shot back, "or when you stopped beating your wife—talk about discussion in govern-ment, there are always discussions about practically everything under the sun."

"Of assassinations?"

"Of everything under the sun."

"But you never answered my question," the reporter protested.

"Well, I'm not trying to answer your question," said Helms, and he terminated the press conference by marching from the room.

Schorr pursued Helms down the corridor, and explained that it was not he but President Ford who had publicly raised the question of assassina-tions. At that point in his account of the exchange Schorr says that Helms cooled and apologized. Helms denies it, still angry. He did not apologize, he never apologized! He thought Schorr's was a stinking broadcast, maligning the names and reputations of CIA people who had never committed any assassinations. Helms still thinks it was a stinking broadcast, wrong and un-fair. Maybe gentlemen apologize, but Helms felt he had nothing to apol-ogize for. He did not apologize.

Helms was right, as far as we know. The CIA has never killed a foreign leader entirely on its own, with its own agents, using its own weapons, for its own purposes. After the Church Committee issued its assassination re-port on November 20, 1975, Daniel Schorr went on the air and conceded as much. "It turned out as Helms said, that no foreign leader was directly killed by the CIA. But it wasn't for want of trying."[30]

Chapter 16

In the four years Richard Helms was ambassador to Iran he made sixteen round-trips to Washington. During thirteen of them he testified
before various official bodies of investigation, beginning with the Senate
Watergate Committee, and ending with the Senate's intelligence committee.
In all he testified on something over thirty separate occasions, for a total of a
hundred hours or more. His interrogators had access to an astonishing range
of Agency files. The CIA was, in fact, subjected to the sort of scrutiny
usually reserved for the intelligence agencies of nations conquered in war.
At times Helms seemed to be the particular target of the Church Committee, which found his name on paper involving just about every CIA project
in which the Committee took an interest. When a subject in an early CIA
drug-testing program committed suicide in New York, Helms was at the
heart of the official decision to hide what had happened.[1] When it was
decided to examine mail to and from the Soviet Union, Helms went with
Allen Dulles to see the Postmaster General and clear the way. Helms knew
about the plot to kill Lumumba and said nothing, and he was officially responsible for a later attempt to kill Castro with the aid of the Mafia.[2] When
Johnson and Nixon insisted the CIA do its part to investigate the antiwar
movement, Helms went along, despite repeated internal protests that the
program was outside the Agency's charter. Helms made a good-faith effort
to block Allende from the Chilean presidency, despite his own conviction it
couldn't be done, and he accommodated the White House when it wanted
material aid for Howard Hunt. It is likely that no name shows up more frequently in the Church Committee's reports than that of Richard Helms.

But despite the long interrogation of Helms, none of the investigators
ever learned a secret from him. Although much of his testimony is still
unpublished, the frequent excerpts make him sound at times like an amnesia
victim. When investigators nailed him with a piece of paper, he answered
as he could. All the rest he had forgotten. It is said men begin life with a
tabula rasa; Helms ended it that way. On occasion this made his interrogators, staff counsel and Senators alike, short of temper. But in an odd, narrow
way, they grew to trust him. F. A. O. Schwarz, Jr., the Committee's chief

counsel, said he never knew quite where he was when he had done questioning Helms, but learned to respect him all the same.

A lot of witnesses before the Church Committee lied or feigned forgetfulness; some attempted deliberately to deceive. Almost all hewed closely to the documentary record. Colby appointed a group of CIA officers under Seymour Bolton to handle all requests for files from the Church Committee; one of these officers was Walt Elder, McCone's executive assistant when McCone had been DCI. According to several sources, including one on the Church Committee's staff, Elder told McCone which documents had been given to the Committee and what they contained, thus allowing McCone to prepare his testimony within the limits of what the Committee could prove. It was McCone's foreknowledge of the fragmentary record, according to a number of sources in both the Committee and the CIA, which allowed him to deny any awareness of the plots to kill Castro during his tenure as DCI. But Elder's attempts to protect his old boss, the sources say, went still further. He told the Committee that he had informed Helms of McCone's opposition to assassination in the summer of 1962, after Robert McNamara had proposed Castro's elimination at a meeting of the Special Group Augmented. Helms testified that he did not recall the conversation described by Elder, and added, "Let me say that in not recalling this conversation I very seriously doubt that it ever took place."[3] From these characteristic evasions, lapses of memory, hints, and suggestions the Committee and its staff concluded that the men they questioned, including Helms, knew more than they would say. Then why did many of them grow to trust Helms? For the simple reason that he never tried to convince them they knew all there was to know, when they did not.

Helms did not challenge the men who tried to extract the past from him; he never told them he felt bound by an oath of secrecy, that he would not volunteer the secrets to them or anyone else. Schwarz and the other questioners certainly did not concede Helms's right to keep silent. There was no legal case whatever on Helms's side. But after a while they understood Helms's attitude: he believed in what he had done, would attempt to explain what the investigators had already learned on their own, but would not invite anyone to share the secrets which remained.

Why did Helms keep the secrets? There seem to be three reasons. The first, clearly, is that he was at the heart of a lot of them. Talk of prosecution was in the air during the Church Committee's investigation. Helms was asked about his role in murder plots, burglaries, wiretaps, secret medical experiments, and other allegedly illegal acts. In keeping quiet, Helms was protecting himself.

The second reason is that exposure of the secrets threatened to wreck the complacent trust in the Agency's honor and good sense without which it could have no freedom of action. The CIA had been the beneficiary of a consensus of support in the United States as long as it was generally believed that the Agency took orders from the President, that he was satisfied with the way it conducted its business, and that we weren't like them. The public, in short, was content with a child's history of the world. Once it got a good look at what the Agency did, and discovered we were very much like them, the consensus collapsed. Helms thought the CIA was a necessary thing, but he did not believe the public would ever be sophisticated enough to agree if it really understood what the CIA did.

In Helms's view, the Church Committee's investigation did not open the door to reform, but to hypocrisy. He considered the Committee's expressions of shock as posturing pure and simple; the members were not really interested in making the CIA better and more efficient. They were only engaged in a morality play, they were crippling the Agency in the process, and he would not contribute to tearing down what he had built. When Helms kept the secrets, he was protecting the Agency.

The third reason is harder to explain, and is at once utilitarian and intensely emotional. Over the last thirty years one half of the CIA only supplied answers to questions—sometimes correctly, sometimes not—but the other half did things. The things it did were far from being all on the order of bribery, extortion, blackmail, murder, and so on, but they were all of the sort which cannot work unless they are secret. The importance of operational secrets is clear: those things work best which are the least expected. A device which can read human voices from the vibration of window panes, or pick up the telephone messages of Politburo members as they drive about Moscow in chauffeured limousines, is useful as long as the other fellow doesn't know it can be done. These might be called secrets of method.

But there are secrets of another order, which we might call secrets of essence. To work, the CIA's initiatives had to be hidden so that their effect would appear genuine and spontaneous, rather than contrived. If a foreign leader is known to be on the CIA's payroll he ceases to be a leader, but is discredited as a kept man. Who would be impressed by the anti-Communism of a newspaper which could not publish without CIA funds? If it was the CIA which ousted Arbenz, then it could not have been the doing of Guatemalans. Who was most opposed to the Communists in Italy—the Italians or the CIA?

The history of the CIA is the secret history of the Cold War. CIA people are cynical in most ways, but their belief in secrets is almost metaphysical. In their bones they believe they know the answer to that ancient paradox of epistemology which asks: If a tree falls in the forest without witness, is there any sound? The CIA would say no. It would agree with historian David Hackett Fisher that history is not what happened but what the surviving evidence says happened. If you can hide the evidence and keep the secrets, then you can write the history. If no one knows we tried to kill Castro, then we didn't do it. If ITT's role in Chile is never revealed, then commercial motives had nothing to do with the Allende affair. If the CIA's role in overthrowing Mossadegh remains hidden, then the Iranians did it all by themselves. If Operation Chaos remains a secret, the CIA never joined the FBI as a threat to American liberties. If the CIA's mail-opening program is never exposed, then the mails were sacrosanct. If no one knows how many Free World leaders had to be bribed, then we were something purer than the highest bidder.

So it wasn't just himself and the CIA which Helms was protecting when he kept the secrets. It was the stability of a quarter-century of political arrangements, the notion of a Free World, a "history" of American response to "aggression," a stark contrast of American "morality" with Communist "expedience," an illusion of American rectitude unclouded by reality. The true history is not the antithesis of the child's history; it is not all crime, greed, and imperial reaching. But the true history is a long way from what we tell ourselves on the Fourth of July.

The United States, the CIA, and Helms himself all did a great many things which they have not found it pleasant to defend in public. In his heart, no doubt, Helms is convinced there is a practical explanation for every one. He would not think of himself as shoring up illusions. *If no one knows what we did*, he might have told himself, *then we aren't that sort of country, the CIA isn't that sort of secret institution, and I'm not that sort of man.*

If the history of Watergate illustrated any general principle of politics and jurisprudence it is the principle that a political indictment be narrowly framed. Thus Nixon was charged with obstruction of justice—a pettifogging choice, considering the range of his abuses of his office—and Richard Helms was charged with lying. No one seriously proposed that he be charged with conspiracy to kill Castro, or conspiracy to violate the mails, or conspiracy to commit a burglary,[4] or conspiracy to obstruct justice for having withheld evidence in the Watergate matter, or any of the other doubtful enterprises in which so many people outside the CIA were equally involved—not only those in the White House who gave or transmitted the orders, but those in Congress who actively collaborated or passively acquiesced. Crimes in the legal sense might have been extracted from the facts of such endeavors, but they would have violated the Watergate principle. As a result Helms was not charged with what he did, but more narrowly for having lied about it. The man he blamed for this final episode in his public career was William Colby.

One of the items forwarded to Colby and the Inspector General, William Broe, in May of 1973 was a claim that Helms had lied to Congress about Chile. At first Colby attempted to ignore the matter, according to his memoirs, but before long he concluded an internal investigation was necessary lest he be accused of hiding a crime. With Colby's approval, Broe appointed a three-man team to examine Helms's testimony before the Senate Foreign Relations Committee and Church's subcommittee on multinationals in light of the record. The three men concluded that the CIA had certainly been heavily involved in Chile, thus establishing a discrepancy. But when the team wrote its report it went a step further and flatly described Helms's testimony as perjury, largely at the insistence of an analyst, Tom Lawlor, borrowed from the Office of Current Intelligence for the inquiry. Again Colby tried to sit on the report, but finally decided he had to forward it to the acting Attorney General, Lawrence Silberman. Larry Houston, who was about to retire from the CIA as general counsel, and John Warner, who was about to replace him, argued that neither Lawlor nor the other two men on the team[5] were lawyers, that "perjury" was a strictly legal term, that its use implied a prima facie case unsupported by the evidence, and that the word ought to be stricken from the report before it went to the Justice Department. They were lawyers, and used lawyers' arguments, but their real motive seems to have been friendliness toward Helms, and resistance to the notion the CIA ought to peach on its own. But Lawlor dug in his heels and would not be moved. He insisted that Helms's testimony had been perjury, and that the word stand. Colby declined to overrule him, and the report went to the Justice Department as written in December 1974. There it became the focus of an extraordinary three-year investigation.

From the beginning the Attorney General was the target of argument and appeal from Helms's many friends in Washington. They urged the Justice Department to decide against prosecution of Helms on two grounds. The first was fairness. If Helms had lied (which Helms's friends did not concede), he had not done so in his own interest, and he had not done so to anyone with a traditionally recognized right to ask him about covert operations in Chile. Helms had been caught in the middle of a constitutional dispute between Congress and the White House, and it would not be fair to indict him for doing what he took to be the customary duty of a DCI.

But if that was not enough, the Justice Department was told, there was a second ground for putting the matter to rest. The full record would be exposed in court, Helms would defend himself vigorously, all the participants in the Allende affair would have to testify, and the government would lose more by way of scandal, acrimony, and exposure than it could hope to gain by convicting a perjuror.[6] As described by his friends, Helms's position at this point was that of a man wrapped in the flag, with a derringer peeping out between the folds. The Justice Department apparently found merit in these two arguments. For more than a year after Colby had surrendered the CIA's documents in the case, nothing was done. Helms's lawyer, Edward Bennett Williams, was never required to so much as phone the Department. It appeared that the charge of perjury would be allowed to lapse, along with all the other abuses reported in the 693 pages of the Family Jewels.

But eventually the Justice Department, under a new Attorney General, was prodded to open a serious investigation. In 1975, Edward Korry began to suspect the Church Committee of deliberately suppressing every aspect of the Allende affair except the involvement of Nixon, the CIA, and Korry himself. Kennedy-Johnson's massive campaign to influence the Chilean election of 1964 and the deep involvement of ITT and other multinationals were being overlooked, Korry felt, to protect the reputations of the Democratic political figures involved and to help ITT secure a U.S. government payment of $94 million in December 1974 as compensation for ITT properties seized in Chile. Korry believed the payment was fraudulent because ITT had concealed its role in attempting to block Allende from office, as well as its attempts to bribe him after he had been elected.

In March 1976, convinced the Church Committee would never provide him an opportunity to present his story adequately, Korry decided to bring a civil suit for damage to his reputation. As a first step, in order to lay the legal groundwork, he wrote Attorney General Edward Levi a letter, enclosing a long account of U.S. involvement in Chile which Levi later told him was precisely what had been needed to reopen the investigation. Korry had no desire to see Helms go to jail—he liked Helms and would have been willing to testify in his behalf as a character witness—but at the same time he wanted the whole story to emerge, including those parts which Helms had evaded in Senate testimony in 1973, as well as the background which the Senate Select Committee on Intelligence had chosen to slight (in Korry's view) in its covert action report.

Korry's letter included details concerning an ITT contribution of $350,000 to the conservative candidate in the 1970 Chilean election, Jorge Alessandri, arranged through the CIA. The Justice Department, which had allowed the case to languish after Colby's report in December 1974, was prodded by Korry's letter to reopen its investigation, and a grand jury began to hear evidence in the summer of 1976, while Helms was still ambassador to Iran. An early focus of the inquiry was Harold Hendrix, the former Miami *News* reporter who had joined ITT in 1967 and who was sometimes called "Whispering Hal" by acquaintances for the sound of his voice after a throat operation. In 1970 Hendrix had represented ITT in Chile, where he had been at the heart of ITT efforts to block Allende's election. Grand jury testimony by CIA officers, as well as cables and internal memorandums subpoenaed from the Agency, allegedly turned up evidence not only of ITT's anti-Allende campaign but of plans to hide the facts in 1972 and early 1973, after it became known that Senator Church's committee on multinationals planned hearings on the Chilean episode. Hendrix was reportedly afraid the ITT-CIA connection of 1970 would emerge during the Church

Committee's hearings, and he asked the CIA how he should handle the matter.

By the late fall of 1976 the Justice Department felt it had evidence to prove Hendrix had lied to the Church subcommittee and that his friends at the CIA had helped him to work out his story. Apparently Hendrix was impressed by the evidence too. On November 5 he pleaded guilty in federal court in Miami to a misdemeanor charge of "withholding information" from Congress and at the end of the month he was sentenced to a $100 fine and three months of probation. In return for his light sentence Hendrix became a potential government witness in any further prosecution.

At this point the grand jury shifted the focus of its investigation. More witnesses were called, including John McCone, a member of ITT's board of trustees; David Phillips, the former Western Hemisphere chief and head of the Chile task force in 1970; Thomas Karamessines, a former DDP; and Helms's personal secretary, Elizabeth Dunlevy. In Teheran, Helms submitted his resignation to President Ford in the middle of October. On the day of Jimmy Carter's election in November, Ford announced that Helms would be leaving his post the first of the year. Shortly before Carter took office on January 20, 1977, probably in the first week of the month, the Justice Department formally notified Helms that he was a target of the grand jury's inquiry, a move which guaranteed that the case would not be allowed to lapse after the change in administration.

From one point of view—that of simple truth—the case against Helms was an easy one. Helms has always claimed that his testimony on Chile in February and March 1973 was literally true, that the CIA had not given funds directly to the candidates themselves, that the Agency had not tried to overthrow the Chilean government (just prevent Allende's confirmation), and so on. But Helms's denials had an air of the *pro forma*, and he never seemed to make them with much conviction. If his testimony on these two occasions was "true," after all, then there is not much meaning left in the word "lie." The Justice Department would have found it simple to demonstrate that Helms's testimony and the facts were different, and it probably could have convinced a jury that Helms knew and remembered the true facts at the time of his allegedly false testimony. The Justice Department's doubts about the case were of a different sort; it was by no means clear that a jury would reject Helms's claim he was bound by his oath as DCI to keep the secrets, and there was some difference of opinion whether prosecution would be either fair or useful.

Carter's Attorney General, Griffin Bell, said later that the Helms case was one of the three toughest he'd encountered during his first year.[7] A number of Helms's friends argued with him that the government ought to drop the case; even if a trial ended successfully in Helms's conviction, it would be an unseemly mess of charge and countercharge. Bell was inclined to go along with that point of view. No one in Washington was really very mad at Helms. With the possible exception of Frank Church, not even the Senators to whom he had allegedly lied were clamoring for his indictment. If Bell could have done so quietly, he probably would have abandoned the case.

Three things prevented him from doing so. One was the evidence turned up by the Justice Department lawyers in charge of the investigation, George A. Carver[8] and Robert G. Andary. Carver and Andary felt a crime had been committed and that they could prove it.[9] Bell could not lightly ignore the recommendation of his own prosecutors, without inviting charges he was party to a cover-up. A second problem was President Carter's explicit campaign pledge, presumably sparked by Ford's pardon of Nixon, that there would be no dual standard of justice in his administration. A final difficulty was the position of Vice-President Walter F. Mondale, who had been a member of the Senate Select Committee which investigated the intelligence community. Mondale conceded the risks of a trial, but felt an important principle was at stake: no CIA official had a right to lie to a Senate committee for what amounted to his own sweet reasons. Abandoning Helms's prosecution, Mondale argued, would be a clear signal that the administration did not really mean what it said, when it said the time had come for things to change.

The conflict between these points of view, already joined when Carter took office, was to continue for nine months before the matter was finally settled. On July 25, 1977, the issue was argued at some length in Carter's office by Bell; the chief of the Justice Department's Criminal Division, Benjamin R. Civiletti; a Civiletti assistant named Robert Kreuch; Mondale; the President; and the President's national security adviser, Zbigniew Brzezinski. The result, approved by Carter, was a break with prosecutorial custom: Bell would approach Edward Bennett Williams and propose a deal.

Early in September, Williams and an assistant went to the Justice Department and argued at length why the case against Helms should be dropped entirely. The arguments were the familiar ones: prosecution would be neither fair nor useful. Helms and his lawyers insist no threats were made of any kind, then or thereafter, but everyone involved in the case knew that the government would inevitably face vigorous discovery proceedings. Back in January George Carver had promised that the Justice Department would meet with Williams when its investigation was complete, and on September 20, in a second meeting, the promise was kept. Carver, Civiletti, Andary, and Kreuch described in detail one count of the Justice Department's proposed eight-count indictment. At one point in his testimony before Church's subcommittee on multinationals Helms had denied CIA contact with the Chilean military in September 1970. The Justice Department lawyers outlined their evidence that Helms had lied. No one at that meeting has been willing to describe the evidence in detail, but the published record amply establishes that the CIA did plot with the Chilean military. There can be little doubt that the government had a case. More important, however, was another point: the Justice Department did not intend to back off; the problem would not go away.

At that point Williams and his assistant were invited upstairs to meet with Bell. He was in a conciliatory mood. He said the Helms case had been worrying him for months; it was one of several intractable problems without happy solution which he had inherited from his predecessors. He wanted to resolve the problem, and proposed a deal: if Helms would plead nolo contendere to two misdemeanor counts, he would promise a sentence without teeth—neither jail nor fine. Williams of course did not commit his client one way or the other, and the meeting came to an end.

That day Williams called Helms and described the case against him and the deal proposed by Bell. A few days later, Helms discussed the alternatives in detail at Williams's office. There Helms raised a point which Bell had not considered: what about his pension? Helms was afraid a nolo plea would end it. But that was not Helms's only objection. During the long investigation, dragging on over the spring and summer, he had apparently convinced himself he would win in the end, and he rebelled at a public admission of wrongdoing, however muted. He was more than half-inclined to fight it out. At about that time Helms had told one old CIA colleague his mood had changed; he was no longer afraid of a trial, he thought he could win, and he wanted to vindicate himself. Indeed, after such long uncertainty he would positively welcome a trial, and a chance to state his case.

The mood did not last. Williams did not tell Helms what to do, but he made it clear the Justice Department could not be bluffed. Bell might have little appetite for it, but he would prosecute, and a trial of the case would require a major effort over a two-year period. Helms began to reconsider. He dreaded the trauma of a trial, he felt important national secrets would be exposed, and he was already restless with his imposed isolation. He wanted to resume a normal life, to speak freely on public issues, and to start a business. In the end he abandoned his hopes for vindication and authorized Williams to negotiate a counterproposal with the Justice Department: Helms would plead, if Bell would add a stipulation that there would be no threat to his pension. On October 28, the final details of the bargain were worked out by Williams, Bell, and Civiletti.

In addition to the other stipulations Williams won another concession: the Justice Department would include a paragraph explaining Helms's position in its statement to be read in open court. Helms's part of the bargain was to plead nolo to two misdemeanor charges of violating a federal statute which made it an offense not to testify "fully and completely" before Congress. In addition, the Justice Department insisted that its statement would charge Helms with having "failed to answer those questions [put to him by Stuart Symington on February 7, 1973] fully, completely and accurately as required by law."[10] The word "accurately" was not included in the statute governing Helms's plea. Williams argued against its inclusion, but the Justice Department insisted, since the real charge against Helms was that he had lied. To describe his crime in milder terms would only invite public reaction.

With the agreement settled, as it seemed, President Carter was told of the final arrangements on October 30. Only one formality remained: the selection of a judge for the case on the next morning. A lottery system had been adopted by the Federal District Court after the retirement of John Sirica as chief judge. Sirica had irritated the other judges by assigning all the important Watergate cases to himself, and his fellows, once Sirica was gone, wanted to ensure nothing similar would happen again. The luck of the draw on Monday, October 31, turned up Judge Barrington D. Parker, and at that point the deal threatened to come apart. Parker, a man of flinty character, balked at the terms and at first refused to commit himself in advance to a sentence of neither fine nor imprisonment. In the course of the morning Civiletti had three separate meetings with Williams and Judge Parker in an attempt to salvage the deal. Williams threatened to call the whole thing off. Civiletti warned him that if he did, the government was prepared to proceed with its eight-count perjury indictment. That offered a bleak prospect. Helms and Williams decided to go ahead and trust to luck and a renewed plea for leniency by the Justice Department. The formal proceeding finally got under way at three o'clock on Monday afternoon. Carter was informed of the final arrangements while Civiletti was actually in court, and Bell said later that if the President had objected, Civiletti would have been plucked from the courtroom in mid-sentence if necessary.

Civiletti began by reading the Justice Department's statement outlining Helms's offenses and explaining why it had been willing to settle for a misdemeanor plea rather than go to the expense of a trial which "might jeopardize national secrets."

Then Helms explained himself. "I found myself in a position of conflict," he said. "I had sworn my oath to protect certain secrets. I didn't want to lie. I didn't want to mislead the Senate. I was simply trying to find my way through a very difficult situation in which I found myself." He added that he understood "there is to be no jail sentence and I will be able to continue to get my pension from the U.S. government."

"This court does not consider itself bound by that understanding," Parker said. He asked Williams to prepare a background report on Helms and later scheduled sentencing for Friday, November 4. When Helms reappeared in court that day—this time surrounded by reporters, who watched his jaw set and his hands grip a podium in anger and frustration—Parker read him a stern lecture:

> You considered yourself bound to protect the Agency whose affairs you had administered and to dishonor your solemn oath to tell the truth. . . .

If public officials embark deliberately on a course to disobey and ignore the laws of our land because of some misguided and ill-conceived notion and belief that there are earlier commitments and considerations which they must observe, the future of our country is in jeopardy.

There are those employed in the intelligence security community of this country . . . who feel that they have a license to operate freely outside the dictates of the law and otherwise to orchestrate as they see fit. Public officials at every level, whatever their position, like any other person, must respect and honor the Constitution and the laws of the United States.

Parker did not concede one iota of Helms's claim of a higher duty. "You now stand before this court in disgrace and shame," he said. And then he imposed his sentence: a $2,000 fine—the maximum—and two years in jail, to be suspended.

Outside, Williams vigorously defended Helms to the reporters and television cameras. "He was sworn not to disclose the very things that he was being requested by the Committee to disclose. Had he done so, he would have sacrificed American lives, he would have sacrificed friends of ours in Chile, and he would have violated his oath."[11] Then Williams added that Helms would "wear this conviction like a badge of honor."

A reporter asked Helms if he agreed. "I do indeed," said Helms. "I don't feel disgraced at all. I think if I had done anything else I would have been disgraced."

After talking with reporters outside the courthouse for a few moments Helms drove off to Bethesda, Maryland, where he dropped in at a luncheon of four hundred retired CIA officers at the Kenwood Country Club. There he was greeted by a standing ovation. Two wastebaskets were put up on a piano and filled with cash and personal checks donated to pay Helms's $2,000 fine. The following day, Richard Helms's picture appeared on the front pages of newspapers for what would probably be the last time. Shortly thereafter he established a one-man consulting firm called the Safeer Company—"safeer" is the Farsi word for ambassador—to help Iranians do business in the United States, and with that he resumed his old Washington life revolving around lunch and the phone.[12]

The newspaper comment which followed Helms's plea in federal court focused narrowly on the question of whether or not justice had been done. Some writers thought not, dismissed Helms's view of his "dilemma," and described the Justice Department's bargain as one more chapter in the old, old story of soft forgiveness for high officials, however clear the evidence of their crimes. Others said that Helms's $2,000 fine, two-year suspended jail sentence, and the legal equivalent of a conviction were punishment enough for having kept the secrets at an unlucky moment, when the arrangements of the past were coming undone.

The debate in the press, which lasted a week or ten days, naturally focused on Helms personally, but a larger point was visible in the background. Whether Helms had got his just deserts did not matter so much (to all but him) as whether the American intelligence community had got the point. The old freewheeling days were allegedly over. Congress would no longer turn a blind eye to what the CIA did with the people's money, in the people's name. The President might continue to give the CIA its orders, but the Senate intelligence oversight committee was to be in on the secrets.

At its core the issue involved in Helms's crime was not one of honor but of the Constitution. For nearly thirty years Congress had been content to give the President blank-check authority over the intelligence community, with the result that the CIA became the President's chief instrument for conducting what amounted to a secret foreign policy. The United States had engaged in at least two wars—in Cuba and Indochina—without any real knowledge on the part, much less the advice and consent, of the Senate. This was not the way the Constitution was supposed to work, and the argument that an international emergency (that is, the struggle against Communism) justified an ad hoc approach had worn pretty thin by the time the Senate Select Committee on Intelligence finished its work in mid-1976.

So far, the principal fruits of the Select Committee's work have been a clarification of recent history, substituting for the child's history an account with a bit of the salt of truth, and the establishment of an oversight committee with its own staff and records, something the intelligence community had resisted for years. On the surface this amounted to nothing more than a reassertion of constitutional prerogatives, a simple adjustment in the machinery of government, but there was something more behind the Senate's break with the past than a practical desire to get things running smoothly. A year spent immersed in the true history of the Cold War had left the Senate with a feeling of shame. It was not the aims, or even the failures, of American policy which generated this mood; nor was it the old charge that American foreign policy was dedicated only to making the world safe for American business (although that was certainly one of its aims, and one of its effects). It was not even the "excesses" of the CIA in its zeal to do the President's bidding which convinced the Senators to break with the past, but rather the melancholy discovery that American policy had been so often callous, reckless, and offhand. Typical was the manner in which President Nixon impulsively tried to wreck the Chilean constitution to prevent Latin America from being turned into a "red sandwich," or the manner in which Kissinger tried to foment and sustain a civil war in Angola simply to convince the Russians that the American tiger could still bite. The CIA was not responsible for the cheap and fuzzy strategic thinking behind these and similar adventures (although it certainly contributed its share of supporting paper), but it was, by statute and nature alike, a docile tool of violence which allowed American Presidents to engage in acts of gross intervention, and even of war, free of the restraints imposed by the Constitution. The exercise of American power had been so heavily insulated in secrecy—not always, but too often—that Presidents were encouraged to intervene, and to approve methods they hardly dared name to their closest friends. The CIA might protest its ultimate innocence of murder all it liked; something decidedly unpleasant still lingered about the manufacture of poison dart guns, the stockpiling of lethal toxins, medical experiments on unsuspecting victims, attempts to infect Castro and Lumumba with disease, the funding and technical guidance of police organizations which tortured and killed local opponents, the support (and then abandonment) of out-of-the-way peoples in hidden wars, and the injection of corrupting sums of money into the political systems of other nations. The CIA and its defenders might argue that they do it too, they do it first, they do it worse, but these are arguments of last resort.

No official breast-beating accompanied publication of the Senate Select Committee's multivolume report, but it was clear from the Committee's conclusions that its members, as a body, felt something had gone seriously wrong. The history revealed was not the work of anything which might plausibly be called the last, best hope of mankind. When the Senate established its intelligence oversight committee it was not simply asserting its constitutional role, but implying something more as well: American Presidents would no longer be allowed to intervene callously and recklessly around the world, with the CIA providing the secret muscle. The new attitude was expressed clearly when the oversight committee began to draft a new charter for the intelligence community: at its heart was a list of prohibitions as literal and specific as the rules tacked to the cabin wall in a Boy Scout camp.

But whether things have really changed is open to question. The habits of power are not so easily broken. The worst blunders and most egregious excesses of the past tended to occur when everyone in Washington recognized the same threat and agreed that something had to be done. The Senate's intelligence oversight committee, after a year or two of skepticism, may simply join an expanded inner circle of policymakers who determine the American role in the world, and keep the secrets of the future as their predecessors did those of the past. The Carter administration's refusal to drop the case against Richard Helms was a kind of earnest that it would proceed in a different way, but at the same time it shrank from a new revelation of secrets. This fact is hard to judge. The deciding factor may have been the question of fairness to Helms, who was far from having been the prime mover in the events he refused to reveal; or pure caution about pressing a case the government might lose in court; or a deeper solicitude about the demoralized Central Intelligence Agency. Carter would not be the first national leader to find that a secret instrument of power was essential, as soon as it was in his own hands. No one in the government, and few outside it, have suggested getting rid of the CIA entirely. President Kennedy may have talked about scattering it to the winds, but that only meant giving the job to someone else, with a new title, at the head of an organization with a different name. Intelligence services are as inevitable a part of modern states as armies, telephone and postal services, or a system for collecting taxes. Outsiders might be willing to risk life without a foreign intelligence service, as we did before the Second World War, but no one in a position to decide is going to accept any such suggestion. That question is closed.

The question which remains is what the CIA will be asked to do, in addition to collecting and protecting the facts, and the spirit in which it will be used. This is not subject to legislation, and a quick answer is unlikely. Learning the truth of how we went about these things took nearly thirty years the last time around, and it may take as long again. That belongs to the future. Helms belongs to the past.

Appendix

Directors of Central Intelligence:

Rear Adm. Sidney W. Souers
January 23, 1946–June 10, 1946

Lt. Gen. Hoyt Vandenberg
June 10, 1946–May 1, 1947

Rear Adm. Roscoe Hillenkoetter
May 1, 1947–October 7, 1950

Gen. Walter Bedell Smith
October 7, 1950–February 9, 1953

Allen Welsh Dulles
February 26, 1953–November 29, 1961

John A. McCone
November 29, 1961–April 28, 1965

Vice Adm. William F. Raborn Jr.
April 28, 1965–June 30, 1966

Richard Helms
June 30, 1966–February 2, 1973

James Schlesinger
February 2, 1973–July 2, 1973

William Colby
September 4, 1973–January 30, 1976

George Bush
January 30, 1976–March 9, 1977

Adm. Stansfield Turner
March 9, 1977–

Deputy Directors of Central Intelligence:

Kingman Douglass
March 2, 1946–July 11, 1946

Brig. Gen. Edwin K. Wright
January 20, 1947–March 9, 1949

William H. Jackson
October 7, 1950–August 3, 1951

Allen Welsh Dulles
August 23, 1951–February 26, 1953

Gen. Charles Peare Cabell
April 23, 1953–January 31, 1962

Lt. Gen. Marshall Carter
April 3, 1962–April 28, 1965

Richard Helms
April 28, 1965–June 30, 1966

Vice Adm. Rufus Taylor
October 13, 1966–January 31, 1969

Lt. Gen. Robert E. Cushman Jr.
May 7, 1969–December 31, 1971

Lt. Gen. Vernon Walters
May 2, 1972–July 7, 1976

Henry Knoche
July 7, 1976–July 31, 1977

John F. Blake
July 31, 1977–February 10, 1978

Frank C. Carlucci
February 10, 1978–

Deputy Directors for Plans
(after March 1973, Deputy Directors for Operations):

Allen Welsh Dulles
January 1951–August 1951

Col. Kilbourne Johnson
1951–1952

Frank G. Wisner
1952–1958

Richard Bissell
Fall 1958–February 1962

Richard Helms
February 1962–April 1965

Desmond FitzGerald
April 1965–July 1967

Thomas Karamessines
July 1967–February 1973

William Colby
February 1973–May 1973

William Nelson
May 1973–April 1976

William Wells
April 1976–early 1977

John McMann
1977–

Notes

Introduction

1. Referred to by CIA people as "human sources." The information they deliver is called "HUMINT"—for human intelligence. Other types of intelligence are ELINT (electronic intelligence), COMINT (communications intelligence), SIGINT (signals intelligence), and so on. HUMINT is generally the thinnest, and the hardest to come by, but it is potentially the most useful. The value of HUMINT has been a subject of continuing debate in the CIA. Helms fought for it throughout his career. Other CIA officials—Richard Bissell, Helms's predecessor as Deputy Director for Plans, or Herbert Scoville, an early Deputy Director for Science and Technology, for example—held it in low esteem as little better than gossip. HUMINT enthusiasts would concede the point, while insisting that there is gossip and there is gossip, and that a spy might someday come up with the one critical fact at a crucial moment. One thing could be taken as certain, they said: if you didn't recruit spies as a matter of course, you would never get a good one.

2. Or sometimes more than one. Nazi Germany had a number of competing intelligence services whose first interest was to steal a march on their bureaucratic rivals. In the United States the CIA is not alone, but it is preeminent. Meetings of the National Security Council traditionally begin with a CIA briefing. The military intelligence services or the State Department may protest a CIA conclusion in meetings of the United States Intelligence Board (USIB), but they face an uphill battle.

3. Examples of the power wielded by local CIA officers in the Philippines and the Dominican Republic can be found, respectively, in Joseph Burckholder Smith, *Portrait of a Cold Warrior* (Putnam, 1976) and David Atlee Phillips, *The Nightwatch* (Atheneum, 1977).

4. A classic example of an intelligence failure is described in the report of a British Parliamentary committee which concluded, in 1855, "that the sufferings of the army mainly resulted from the circumstances under which the expedition to the Crimea was undertaken and executed. The Administration which ordered that expedition had no adequate information as to the armament of the forces in the Crimea. They were not acquainted with the strength of the fortresses to be attacked nor with the resources of the country to be invaded. They hoped and expected the expedition to be immediately successful, and, as they did not foresee

the probability of a protracted struggle, they made no preparation for a winter campaign. . . ." Quoted in Asa Briggs, *Victorian People* (University of Chicago Press, 1972), p. 80.

5. The three were James Schlesinger, Sherman Kent, a former chairman of the Board of National Estimates, and Walter Pforzheimer, who is famous in intelligence circles for his collection of books and documents on the history of espionage.

6. Ten or twelve hours in all. The transcript of our interviews—his were the only ones I recorded—comes to nearly 300 pages. Helms has considered writing his own autobiography, and may still do so.

Chapter 1

1. By the Senate Select Committee on Campaign Activities (that is, Watergate), the Rockefeller Commission appointed by President Ford, and the Senate Select Committee on Government Operations with Respect to Intelligence Activities, headed by Frank Church.

2. Nixon had asked for files on the Bay of Pigs, the coup that overthrew Ngo Dinh Diem in 1963, and the murder of Trujillo in 1961. For a full description of Nixon's request, see Chapter 14.

3. Walter Pincus, "The Duping of Richard Helms," *New Republic*, Feb. 15, 1975.

4. Hearings before the Committee on Foreign Relations, United States Senate, on the *Nomination of Richard Helms to Be Ambassador to Iran and CIA International and Domestic Activities* (U.S. Government Printing Office, 1974), p. 47.

5. Unlike Helms, Colby left intelligence work for several years, went to law school, and then rejoined.

6. Church Committee's *Assassination Report* (U.S. Government Printing Office, 1975), p. 105.

Chapter 2

1. Aaron Latham, "My Interview with Hitler," *More*, Dec. 1976.

2. Gardner later became the Secretary for Health, Education, and Welfare. In 1967 President Johnson appointed him to a three-man committee to review the CIA's relationship with private schools, unions, publications, foundations, and the like.

3. See R. Harris Smith, *OSS: The Secret History of America's First Central Intelligence Agency* (University of California Press, 1972).

4. Tom Braden, "The Birth of the CIA," *American Heritage*, Feb. 1977.

5. Secretary of the Navy and later Secretary of Defense, Forrestal was an intense, humorless man with troubling eyes and a slash for a mouth; his early apprehension of Soviet aggression later developed into outright paranoia. Less than a week after his replacement as Secretary of Defense in March 1949, Forrestal broke down completely, told a friend, "They're after me," and was even reported to have run through the streets yelling, "The Russians are coming. The

Russians are coming. They're right around. I've seen Russian soldiers." (Daniel Yergin, *Shattered Peace* [Houghton Mifflin, 1977], p. 208.) In May, in the Bethesda Naval Hospital outside Washington, Forrestal tried to hang himself with his dressing gown from his hospital room window, but slipped and fell sixteen stories to his death.

6. *Ibid.*, p. 214.

7. He left on June 10, 1946, after less than six months as Director of Central Intelligence (DCI), but then returned to Washington a year later and served as the Executive Secretary of Truman's National Security Council until 1950.

8. Book IV, *Final Report* of the Church Committee (U.S. Government Printing Office, 1976), p. 14. Book IV is an institutional history of the CIA written by Anne Karalekas.

9. The word "special" is almost a synonym for "secret" in the recent history of clandestine services. For example, the Special Operations division of OSS, the CIA's Special Operations Group in Vietnam, the Special Procedures Group which intervened in the 1948 Italian election, the Special Group which oversaw CIA operations between 1955 and 1964, the Special Group Augmented responsible for Operation Mongoose, the IRS's Special Services Unit which Nixon ordered to go after domestic radicals, Nixon's Special Investigations Unit (better known as "the plumbers"), the British Special Operations Executive in World War II, "special political action," the term used by the British as a euphemism for covert operations, the New York Police Department's Bureau of Special Services a.k.a. the "red squad," etc. etc. etc. Any official body with the word "special" in its name justifies a second look.

10. Yergin, *op. cit.*, p. 255.

11. After covert operations were taken over by the CIA a debate ensued between the Agency and the military as to the correct pronunciation of "covert." Was it to be "*cu*vert" as in "cover," which was technically correct but sounded British; or "*co*vert" as in "coping"? The decision was for the latter.

12. Pound was arrested by American authorities at the end of the war and charged with making pro-Axis, anti-Semitic broadcasts in Italy. It was apparently the connection with Pound that convinced some Yale professors of the 1930s that Angleton, too, was anti-Semitic. In fact, however, he befriended the postwar Jewish underground in Italy and was in charge of the CIA's Israeli desk until his forced resignation by William Colby in December 1974. Some CIA people considered Angleton almost fanatically pro-Israel. If Angleton was at all wary about Jews, it was only in the manner of many CIA people, who suspected that Jews might feel a divided loyalty where Israel was concerned. No Jew was ever appointed Israeli desk officer in either the DDI or the DDP.

13. Ray Cline, *Secrets, Spies and Scholars* (Acropolis, 1976), p. 102.

14. The U.S. maintained a similar military aid program for Chile during the regime of Salvador Allende.

15. See Arthur Koestler, *The Age of Longing* (Macmillan, 1951), which captures the feeling of many postwar intellectuals that they were living on a precipice.

16. Kim Philby, *My Silent War* (Grove Press, 1968), p. 167.

Chapter 3

1. Both magazines put Helms on the cover, *Time* on the issue of Feb. 24, 1967; *Newsweek* on the issue of Nov. 22, 1971. Both stories were friendly in tone, but pretty lean when it came to actual facts.

2. C. L. Sulzberger, *Postscript with a Chinese Accent* (Macmillan, 1974), pp. 69–70. Helms and Sulzberger seem to have been fairly close. According to E. Howard Hunt, Sulzberger published a column in the *New York Times* on Sept. 13, 1967, entitled "Where the Spies Are," which Hunt had mostly written with information provided by Howard Osborn, Director of Security. The column, which Hunt claims was lifted almost entirely from the piece he had written at Helms's request, named a number of Soviet diplomats who doubled as spies. See *More*, Oct. 1977.

3. This is a point made by the Russian defector Alexander Orlov, *Handbook of Intelligence and Guerrilla Warfare* (The University of Michigan Press, 1972). Orlov's book is a good introduction to Russian "tradecraft," the term used to describe the methodology of spying. It is a favorite word of CIA people, for whom tradecraft offers intellectual pleasures like those of chess. See Harry Rositzke, *The CIA's Secret Operations* (Reader's Digest Press, 1977); "Christopher Felix," the pseudonym of a man who worked for the Eastern European Division of the OPC in the early 1950s, *A Short Course in the Secret War* (Dutton, 1963); J. C. Masterman, *The Double-Cross System* (Yale University Press, 1972). For unloving descriptions, read Compton Mackenzie's 1933 novel, *Water on the Brain*, and Malcolm Muggeridge's memoir, *The Infernal Grove* (William Morrow, 1974).

4. This is a harsh charge, and needs some defense. I do not mean that CIA people in the field are indifferent to the fate of the peoples whose causes they support. Very often the contrary is the case. Occasionally they must be reprimanded by headquarters. But as a rule discipline obtains. The CIA officer in the field knows that he is helping the Meos or Montagnards or whomever for reasons which seem good to Washington. He knows Washington may change its mind. He is committed in advance to obeying orders. Thus he encourages out-of-the-way peoples to undertake or persist in risky courses of action knowing that he, and his country, may pack up and pull out on a moment's notice. This is morally careless. Feeling bad about such unpleasant necessity is not redemptive.

5. Critchfield, a former Army officer, joined the CIA after the war. He remained at Pullach until 1955, when he returned to Washington and eventually took over the DDP's East European Division in late 1956. He followed that with a long stint as chief of the Near East Division which earned him a reputation as one of the CIA's "barons." Despite Critchfield's five years working with Gehlen in Germany, his command of the language was never certain. Trying to make a point, Critchfield once directly translated the English proverb "A bird in the hand is worth two in the bush." The puritanical Gehlen protested at the use of such language; in German, the word for "bird"—*Vogel*—was vulgarly used to refer to girls of the most available sort.

6. Radio Liberation's name was changed to Radio Liberty after the Hun-

garian revolution of 1956 because the CIA was widely blamed for encouraging a revolution with vague promises of support which the United States was in neither the position nor the mood to make good. Liberty was considered a less provocative goal than liberation.

7. Everyone, that is, except the CIA's analysts on the Board of National Estimates, who never estimated the probability of war, in the period immediately ahead, as more than "most unlikely." But the BNE did not challenge the widespread assumption of Russia's hostile intentions. "Well, you know," said William Wright, an early BNE member, "what this comes down to is we say there isn't going to be a war next year, but we say it in the most alarming way possible." For the military it wasn't a question of whether, but when war was coming. "My God!" said DeForrest Van Slyck, an early BNE member. "If the Russians could have heard some of those Air Force generals!" In the late 1940s Van Slyck worked on a study of the prospects for war in Western Europe, called ORE (for Office of Research and Estimates, the BNE's predecessor) 91. The military felt that the economic riches of Western Europe were an irresistible temptation. Van Slyck, after months of study, concluded Moscow wouldn't see it that way: Europe's industrial base would be destroyed by a war, resistance groups would tie down huge armies of occupation, the Russians would have nothing to gain even if they should win. According to Van Slyck, the military roundly attacked his conclusions when ORE 91 was debated by the National Intelligence Authority (predecessor of the United States Intelligence Board). "We can't accept this paper," stated General Charles Peare Cabell, then chief of Air Force intelligence and later Deputy Director for Central Intelligence, according to Van Slyck. "We'll never get any budgets through."

8. See K. V. Tauras, *Guerrilla Warfare on the Amber Coast* (Voyages Press, 1962), an account of anti-Soviet warfare in Lithuania. The book was probably published with CIA funds, but is an interesting account all the same. Other sketchy accounts of these operations can be found in Heinz Höhne and Herman Zolling, *The General Was a Spy* (Coward, McCann & Geoghegan, 1972); E. H. Cookridge, *Gehlen: Spy of the Century* (Random House, 1971); and Harry Rositzke, *The CIA's Secret Operations* (1977).

9. Burke was later president of the New York Yankees and the Madison Square Garden sports arena.

10. Smith was given a new job as Undersecretary of State for Political Affairs.

11. Rositzke, *op. cit.*, p. 37.

12. Anne Karalekas cites these figures in her history of the CIA published as Book IV of the Church Committee's *Final Report*. John Bross wonders if they are accurate. He remembers a meeting between Frank Wisner, the DDP, and Frank Lindsay, head of the East European Division, in the early 1950s, where Lindsay proposed a budget for his division alone of $80 million. "Why don't we round that out and make it $100 million," said Wisner, and they did.

13. Group's Interim Report No. 2, dated May 13, 1948, on file at the Center for National Security Studies, Washington, D.C.

14. Book IV, *Final Report* of the Church Committee (1976), p. 38.

15. The official who ran the Directorate for Plans was called the Deputy

Director for Plans, or DDP for short. But the same initials were also used for the Directorate itself. Thus DDP could refer to either the group or the man who ran it. This was also the custom with DDI (Deputy Director for Intelligence, Directorate of Intelligence), the DDS&T (Deputy Director for Science and Technology), and the DDS (Deputy Director for Support).

Chapter 4

1. One such, given to Victor Marchetti by a Helms aide, Charles Enright, was *Festival for Spies* (Signet paperback, 1966), written by Hunt under the pseudonym David St. John. The best spy novels have an existential mood—Joseph Conrad's *The Secret Agent*, or Graham Greene's "entertainments," which are as bleak as the confessions of condemned men. Helms does not seem to have liked spy stories of that sort.

2. The plot of Le Carré's classic novel, in which the hero is the last to learn what is going on, does not exaggerate the role of deception in intelligence. An example can be found in the story of Noel Field, an American fellow traveler of a variety common in the 1930s. As the representative of a Quaker organization, Field had worked with Allen Dulles in Switzerland during the war, helping to repatriate refugees, many of whom later turned up as members of the Communist parties which came to power with Russian support in Eastern Europe after the war. In 1949 Field and his wife went to Poland with the idea of settling in Eastern Europe, but he was arrested as a spy, imprisoned, and then cited in many of the Eastern European purge trials of the early 1950s as a link between those on trial and the CIA, through Dulles. For the known facts of this phantasmagoric episode, see Flora Lewis's book *The Red Pawn* (Doubleday, 1965). For a more sinister interpretation, see Stewart Steven, *Operation Splinter Factor* (Lippincott, 1974), a book whose central premise apparently came from someone in the British SIS who did not like Dulles. Steven says that Dulles deliberately encouraged Soviet suspicion of Field through a CIA agent inside the Polish secret service, Joseph Swiatlo, who later defected to the West in Berlin in December 1953. Dulles's motive, according to Steven, was to spark exactly the sort of disruptive suspicion within the East European Communist parties which in fact arose, figuring it would promote nationalist resistance to the Soviet Union. That was certainly the sort of thing Dulles was attempting at the time. Field's wide contacts with East European communists, as well as his relationship with Dulles during the war, made him a perfect tool for such a plan.

I do not know what to make of Steven's book. While Dulles certainly could have dreamed up such a plan, Stalin clearly needed no encouragement where purges were concerned, and the Soviet security services might have made cynical use of Field's unique position in exactly the way Steven says Dulles did.

The interesting thing about this puzzle is that it captures one of the enigmas of intelligence, where a single fact can make all the difference. The text of a message to Swiatlo, if it came to light, for example, could rewrite a huge chunk of postwar history. The fact Steven cannot reproduce such a text is no evidence it is not still buried in the files somewhere. The plan might have been known only to Dulles and a handful of others, who might carry the secret to the grave, as Dulles undoubtedly did so many. The world view of intelligence officers involved with secret operations is characterized by a severe particularity. An intelligence analyst might look at Steven's book and say his thesis is unlikely for the following seven plausible reasons. An operations officer would be more circumspect; even if he failed to find the incriminating evidence he would continue to wonder if it were there. This gives such men an extreme open-mindedness; for them nothing is so improbable it's impossible. James Angleton, for example, is notorious for believing that somewhere deep in the bowels of the Kremlin is the super-secret text of a Sino-Soviet plan to lull the West into a false sense of security by pretending to mutual hostility. In this instance, Angleton strikes me as making the fundamental error of thinking national governments have a capacity for extreme intrigue like that which in fact characterizes intelligence agencies. They really do work up plots of dazzling complexity. But if Angleton has gone out on a conjectural limb where the Sino-Soviet dispute is concerned, there is no question intelligence services habitually look for concealed connections and hidden identities, and that they sometimes find them.

3. Wisner's secretary, hearing him muse aloud once that he'd like a new car, quietly put his salary checks aside for a year in the 1950s, and then handed them over in a bundle and said, "Mr. Wisner, here's your new car." Wisner had never noticed their absence.

4. One exception occurred in 1965, when David Phillips returned from the Dominican Republic where a delicate aspect of his job as chief of station was to get along with the FBI. Lyndon Johnson had ordered the FBI to help with security and intelligence collection (probably in order to prove he'd left no stones unturned) and Hoover was notorious for his dislike of the CIA. By chance Phillips met Helms in the gym, where Helms liked to jog. Helms asked how he was getting on with the FBI. Phillips said fine. That was that. Phillips, *The Night Watch* (Atheneum, 1977), p. 171.

5. The CIA did not have an early retirement program to handle just such situations until a few years later, when John McCone put his weight behind an effort to get one through Congress before the end of 1964. Lyman Kirkpatrick, *The Real CIA* (Macmillan, 1968), pp. 271–272.

6. E. Howard Hunt was a notorious example. For an account of Helms's many attempts to help him, see Chapter 14.

7. While I was doing research for this book, I found that just about everyone I saw knew all about me before I arrived. On three occasions an interview was interrupted by a telephone call in which I overheard something like, "Oh, hi, yes, as a matter of fact he's here right now. . . ." Letters or phone calls preceded and followed me wherever I went, and once or twice an initial refusal of an interview was followed a week later by a change of heart. "I've been thinking it over," said William Colby in one such instance, "and I guess maybe I ought to see you after all." With astonishing regularity the name of a CIA officer would elicit an answer beginning, "As a matter of fact I saw Kim at dinner just the other night . . ." or "Colby and I talked about this at his house New Year's Eve. . . ." At other times people said, "I understand you're having lunch with Johnny tomorrow," or "How'd you get along with Frank up in Boston?" Perhaps 10 percent of this is the insularity of Washington, which is referred to exclusively as

"this town" (as in: "One of the things you have to understand about this town," etc., etc.). But 90 percent of it is the especial cohesion of CIA men—the Agency receives the sort of loyalty and concern other men reserve for their old schools or friends from childhood.

8. If the CIA was gentlemanly, it was following in the British tradition. The SIS has no legal existence; it was not created by act of Parliament, and its budget is not voted upon; it is simply there. The idea that an extralegal secret service can be consonant with civil liberties is based on its traditional control by trustworthy men—gentlemen, in short. No one ever accused the Russian secret services— czarist or Stalinist—of being gentlemanly, and the traditional American attitude was that political police are necessarily a low sort. This seems to me a sound instinct; if they're not born that way, they tend to get that way.

9. For a good description of the characteristically upper-class, Ivy League, Eastern old-money connections of the CIA, see Stewart Alsop, *The Center* (Harper & Row, 1968), chap. 8. Naturally this was often resented in the ranks below. See Thomas Bell Smith, *The Essential CIA* (1975). Smith's book, which I found at the Library of Congress, was privately printed and published, with many typographical errors and unjustified margins. This makes it a bit problematic. It's friendly to the Agency, and Smith, whose name I have found nowhere else, says he submitted his manuscript to the CIA for a security check before sending it on to his printer, who appears to have been working out of someone's basement. But the book rings true, is confirmed in many particulars by other sources, and is one of the best accounts of early operations against the Soviet Union.

Smith refers to himself bitterly as a "plebe," admits the social types at the top were mostly serious and professional, and adds: "But very few such people ever recruited some politician's mistress in a bar, or operated a whole string of touchy agents in a country where Americans stand out like a sore thumb and are somewhat less than admired. Or had a last shot of booze with a couple of rock-faced ethnic types, before they got into their black jump-suits for a flight into eternity. In fact you can pretty much depend on the 'Ivy-Leaguers' to stick close to Headquarters; it can be politically unwise for an ambitious administrator to be away from the power center for a two-year tour of duty abroad" (p. 9). Sticking close to headquarters is exactly what Helms did.

10. The money was delivered by Miles Copeland, who describes the episode in *The Game of Nations* (Simon and Schuster, 1969), pp. 175 ff. Nasser used the money to build a tall structure called the Tower of Cairo. Copeland says the Egyptians on Nasser's staff referred to it as *el wa'ef rusfel*—that is, "Roosevelt's erection," after Kermit Roosevelt of the CIA.

11. For an account of intelligence wars over Soviet missilery, Sihanoukville, the Vietcong order of battle, and some other subjects, see Chapters 11 and 12.

12. See R. Harris Smith, *OSS: The Secret History of America's First Central Intelligence Agency* (1972), *passim*.

13. Harry Rositzke, *The CIA's Secret Operations* (1977), p. 13.

14. Washington *Post*, June 26, 1977.

15. David Phillips, *The Night Watch* (1977).

16. Howard Hunt, *Give Us This Day*, p. 83.

17. See *Ramparts*, Feb. 1967, for the first report of the CIA-NSA connec-

tion, and almost daily stories in the *New York Times* and Washington *Post* during following weeks for the many other CIA-supported "private" institutions. Also Tom Braden, "I'm Glad the CIA Is Immoral," *Saturday Evening Post*, May 20, 1967.

18. Frank Snepp describes the debacle in *Decent Interval* (Random House, 1977).

19. Dean Acheson, *Present at the Creation* (Norton, 1969), p. 354.

20. C. L. Sulzberger, *A Long Row of Candles* (Macmillan, 1969), p. 347.

21. After leaving the CIA, Offie went to work for the AFL-CIO in Europe. In 1972 he was killed in an air crash at London airport.

22. "On the Beaches," *Atlantic*, Oct. 1944.

23. This may sound incredible, but stories about preposterous FBI reports of suspect activities are only too common. There is no way to exaggerate the junk they passed on in their unevaluated reports, which were not unevaluated through careless oversight but at the insistence of Hoover, who said the FBI was solely an "investigative," not an analytical, agency. An aide to Donovan during World War II told me that an academic expert on Japan was once declared suspect by the FBI solely on the grounds of a report that he had a map of Japan on his wall. So he did. It was a *National Geographic* map, and in any event he was being hired as an expert on Japan. Donovan overruled the FBI and hired the man.

In a similar episode, Thomas Emerson, a distinguished scholar of the First Amendment at the Yale Law School, was shown his unevaluated FBI file by Attorney General Francis Biddle. It contained, among other items, a report from Emerson's cleaning woman that he kept books on the Russian Revolution next to his easy chair. In that instance, too, the FBI was overruled. But FBI suspects without a friend at court are not so fortunate; it takes high-level pliers just to force the Bureau to list its charges. For a fuller account of Hoover's tendencies in this line, see Sanford J. Ungar, *FBI* (Atlantic–Little, Brown, 1975) and vol. 6 of *Hearings Before the Senate Select Committee on Intelligence Activities* (Government Printing Office, 1976). Also see Chapter 14 of the present work for a description of the so-called Tom Charles Huston domestic intelligence plan, a Nixon initiative largely intended to get around Hoover's refusal to evaluate the "raw" reports collected, by the bale, by his agents.

Hoover's reason for his intransigence ought to be transparent: it gave him great power. A diligent investigator can find out something about anyone. Hoover's refusal to pass judgment on the relevance of such reports gave him the power to do injury at will. In addition, he seems to have felt a genuine suspicion of men who kept books on the Russian Revolution beside their easy chairs, or shared a platform with Harlow Shapley.

24. Harris Smith, *op. cit.*, pp. 372–375.

25. His younger brother was McGeorge Bundy, the Special Assistant for National Security Affairs for both Kennedy and Johnson, and later president of the Ford Foundation.

26. Acheson, *op. cit.*, p. 360.

27. Beacon Press, 1958.

28. There is no way to settle the unanswered questions of such episodes, but *The Care of Devils* is well worth reading for style and mood. The flavor of Miss

Press's interrogation is a good deal like Arthur Koestler's *Darkness at Noon,* a fictional account of the interrogation of an old Communist in Moscow's Lubyanka prison during the 1930s. In both books the same sort of questions were asked by the same sort of men for the same sort of reasons. The difference was that Miss Press was not imprisoned; she went home after each day's questioning, and she was fired in the end, rather than shot through the back of the neck. In May 1966, Malcolm Muggeridge published an article about her book in *Esquire* suggesting that the CIA had something to do with the original edition's faint reception, that perhaps the CIA even bought up all the copies. Muggeridge's article prompted a new paperback edition by Bantam. That fell stillborn from the press as well.

29. For a good account of British spy-running during the war, see J. C. Masterman, *The Double-Cross System* (1972). This is an especially interesting book, lucid and detailed. Mentioned in passing is the fact that a number of captured German agents were shot. One reason is that they refused to cooperate. Fair enough. They were spies, after all, and it was wartime. But another reason is that the British feared the Germans would begin to suspect something was amiss if the law of averages broke down and none of their agents was captured and executed. So some of the agents were shot, in effect, to convince the Germans the rest were genuine. Masterman is a bit oblique on this point, but the implication is clear if you read his account attentively.

30. See Chapter 3 for a description of the Russian manipulation of WIN in Poland. For a more recent case of a Russian who defected to the United States in 1959, went to work for the Defense Intelligence Agency, and then disappeared in Vienna in December 1975, see Robert G. Kaiser's stories in the Washington *Post* on July 14, 15, and 17, 1977. The defector's Russian name was Nikolai Artamonov; his name at the DIA was Nicholas Shadrin. At the time of his defection there was some question of Artamonov-Shadrin's *bona fides,* but eventually he was cleared for secret work. Then in 1966 the FBI turned him into a double agent after he had been approached by the KGB in Washington. His disappearance occurred during one of his periodic trips to meet a Russian case officer. Artamonov-Shadrin's wife thinks he was abducted by the KGB after they discovered he was really working for the Americans although pretending to work for them. But some U.S. intelligence officials think he was *really* working for the Russians—that he had been redoubled—and was simply going home after a job well done. Following the publication of Kaiser's stories the Russian press printed a story alleging that Artamonov-Shadrin had been murdered by the CIA, presumably after they discovered he was really working for the KGB.

31. Masterman, *op. cit.,* regrets the British did not realize earlier how much the Germans were giving away by the very questions they asked of their agents.

32. Another such was Heinz Felfe, chief of counterintelligence in the German BND run by Reinhard Gehlen, discovered to be a Russian agent in 1961. See E. H. Cookridge, *Gehlen: Spy of the Century* (1971), pp. 320 ff.

33. A former counterintelligence analyst told me he once spent a *great* deal of time doing a detailed study of about twenty different double-agent operations. I asked if they were ones we had been running, or ones run against us. I might just as well have asked a theologian why there is evil in the world. "Well, how do you

know?" he said with a sad and bemused smile of infinite subtlety. "That's why we made the study."

34. I asked one CIA official if the gathering of FitzGerald's friends at his funeral had presented a security problem; he said no, the Russians knew who they all were anyway.

35. According to high authority, counterintelligence experts never refer to "triple" agents.

36. A former Israeli-desk officer in the Deputy Directorate of Intelligence mentioned in passing that Jews were always faintly suspect where the matter of Israel was concerned. This intrigued me; I asked a question or two in an attempt to pursue the subject. Immediately he drew back: why did I want to know? That was all I heard about *that*. It was second nature in him to wonder about the motive behind questions, and my answer that I simply found the subject interesting did not strike him as satisfactory. Other CIA people referred to this as well. One former member of the Board of National Estimates said of Harold Linder, a Jew who worked for the BNE in the 1950s: "He was a very brilliant guy. But we were always a little concerned about his objectivity when it came to a paper on Israel."

37. Smith was testifying in a civil trial on behalf of Senator William Benton, who was defending himself in a libel suit brought by McCarthy. Smith's remark quoted here was in answer to a question posed by McCarthy's lawyer. Harris Smith, *op. cit.*, p. 369.

38. For Philby's story, see his own account, *My Silent War*, and Patrick Seale and Maureen McConville, *Philby: The Long Road to Moscow* (Simon and Schuster, 1973).

39. Stonehill, 1975.

40. See Joseph Burckholder Smith, *Portrait of a Cold Warrior* (Putnam, 1976), pp. 11 ff.

Chapter 5

1. Kirkpatrick had recommended creation of the position in a study for John McCone in 1961, and he succeeded John Bross in the job, who had held it briefly.

2. The two directives were NSC 5412/1 in March, and NSC 5412/2 in November 1955. The 5412 Committee consisted of representatives designated by the President, the State Department, and the Defense Department. The President's representative was generally his Special Assistant for National Security Affairs, the job held successively by Gordon Gray, McGeorge Bundy, Walt Rostow, Henry Kissinger, and Zbigniew Brzezinski. The State Department's representative was usually the Undersecretary of State for Political Affairs, a job filled by General Walter Bedell Smith after Allen Dulles replaced him as DCI in January 1953, and later by Chester Bowles and U. Alexis Johnson. Because of Bowles's visceral dislike of covert operations he was for a time replaced by Johnson. The secretary of the 5412 Committee, and of its successors, was a CIA official appointed by the DCI. Thus the CIA, in effect, largely controlled the committee's agenda, kept its minutes, and wrote its directives. Decisions reached

by the Committee were all forwarded to the President for final approval, which he indicated by initialing either of the two boxes marked "approve" or "disapprove." Thus every major clandestine operation of the CIA was authorized by the President in writing, a fact left unclear by the Senate Select Committee on Intelligence Activities.

3. As masters of the arts of propaganda Linebarger especially admired General Edward G. Lansdale and E. Howard Hunt; he felt they had "black minds." There is a good description of Linebarger in Joseph B. Smith, *Portrait of a Cold Warrior* (1976), pp. 86–99 and *passim*. This is one of a half-dozen books by former CIA officers published about the turn of the year 1976–1977. They were not widely reviewed, and received at best grudging recognition, but none was dismissed more curtly or rudely than Smith's. This is odd. It was the only one of that batch of memoirs which was not vetted first by the CIA (a fact which greatly angered many CIA people I talked to; one told me he'd like to read it but he'd be damned if he'd give Smith a royalty by buying a copy) and it's filled with interesting detail. My guess is that before long it's going to be hard to find.

4. Miles Copeland, *The Game of Nations* (1969), p. 184.

5. There is an interesting dispute involved in this episode. Ray Cline says the speech was obtained at "a very handsome price," and indirectly confirms the Israeli role by citing Angleton's part in its acquisition. Angleton was the Israeli-desk officer in the DDP, an organizational oddity apparently stemming from his relationship with Jewish intelligence operatives in Italy during the 1940s, when Italy served as a major transit point for Jewish refugees being smuggled to Palestine. After the publication of Cline's memoirs, Angleton told a *New York Times* reporter on the record, unusual in itself, that the speech was not "bought." But another CIA source says it was—indirectly. The CIA agreed to provide extensive financial support for the Israeli service, which in any event was an important source of CIA information about the Middle East. See Ray Cline, *Secrets, Spies and Scholars* (1977), pp. 162 ff., and the *New York Times*, Nov. 30, 1976. An independent confirmation of the Israeli role may be found in David B. Tinin and Dag Christensen, *The Hit Team* (Little, Brown, 1976), pp. 51–52. But E. H. Cookridge says in his biography of Reinhard Gehlen that Gehlen got the speech in Yugoslavia in return for helping Tito foil Stalinist plots on his life. *Gehlen: Spy of the Century* (1971), p. 303. Several CIA people told me they "thought" they remembered that it came from the Israelis.

6. Much later—in the *Times* story cited in the preceding note—Angleton claimed the CIA had been training Eastern European émigré armies for wars of liberation, and that the speech, properly used, might have served as a trigger. Indeed, it did serve as a trigger for uprisings in Poland and Hungary, but too soon; the émigrés were not "up to snuff." Other CIA sources say there was no such "plan," that the émigré armies alluded to by Angleton were nothing more than name rosters of CIA-trained Eastern European leaders who had agreed to join resistance movements in the event of general war. "The fact of the matter," said one source, "is that he [Angleton] didn't have one goddamned thing to do with it."

7. It is also typical that Cline does not mention the compromise, thus at-

tempting to preserve the secrecy of a classic CIA effort at what is called disinformation.

8. It was published on June 4, 1956.

9. One source familiar with CIA operations in Italy says that Dulles arranged for one of the paper's many owners, Langdon Thorne, to buy the English-language Rome *Daily American* with a "loan" from funds under Dulles's personal control. I was a reporter and editor for the *Daily American* from September 1965 through June 1967, and am hard put even now to see what possible advantage the CIA—or the United States—might have gained from its nuttily right-wing editorials and scanty local coverage. Those of us who worked for it always figured the paper was something of a tax-loss hobby for rich Americans who liked Rome, as we did. What their losses amounted to I cannot say, although I do know that at one time, when the paper claimed a circulation of about 32,000, it was printing only a tenth that number. But that may exaggerate its cost, since it owned an extensive job printing plant. After passing through various hands in recent years, the *Daily American* suspended publication in August 1977. But not long thereafter it resumed publication under another owner. One CIA official told me that the CIA's subsidy—about 40 percent of its operating losses—was cut off after William Colby became DCI in 1973.

10. See the *New York Times*, December 25, 26, and 27, 1977. Three paragraphs of the story of the 26th are devoted to my father, Joshua B. Powers, who ran the United Press bureau in Buenos Aires in the 1920s. Later he founded two companies, Joshua B. Powers Inc. and Editors Press Service, which engaged in business throughout Latin America. The first sold advertising space, and the second sold American newsfeatures—Walter Lippmann, comic strips, and the like. My father had known Colonel J. C. King, then an executive of Johnson & Johnson, in Argentina in the twenties, and they remained friends after King became the DDP's Western Hemisphere Division chief in 1952. When King or some other CIA officer asked him a question, as they occasionally did, he tried to answer it. He thought, and thinks, it was the natural thing for an American to do. The *Times* says that CIA sources say that Editors Press Service was a CIA propaganda outlet in Latin America. My father denies it.

11. Support for the operation was provided by the OPC's Far East Division, run at that time by Colonel Richard Stilwell, with Desmond FitzGerald as his executive officer. FitzGerald had a reputation as an enthusiast of covert operations, but is said to have been doubtful about this one. Despite its failure the CIA mounted many others during the Korean War. One CIA officer who earned a mixed reputation during that period was Hans Tofte. His job was to mount behind-the-lines operations after the Chinese intervention in November 1950. He made an impressive film of one such operation, following a paramilitary team through training to the team's actual landing along the North Korean coast in rubber rafts. The film was widely shown in government circles, the CIA was pleased with its enthusiastic reception, and Tofte's reputation soared. Until someone in a Pentagon audience noted a slight discrepancy in the CIA's—that is, in Tofte's—claim this was all actual footage of an actual operation shot by intrepid CIA cameramen. Did the CIA send its paramilitary teams ashore, as depicted in

the film, *in broad daylight?* Embarrassment all around. Tofte confessed that this was, ah . . . simulated. Later he was involved in some sort of operational fiasco in Colombia, where the CIA sent him to train government forces in the use of helicopters for a campaign to suppress a long-raging back-country civil war (200,000 dead) called *"la violencia."* By the mid-1960s, Tofte, then working for the Domestic Operations Division under Tracy Barnes, had a mixed reputation. In July 1966 a young CIA recruit, thinking of subletting an apartment from Tofte, noticed several cartons of classified documents in a closet. He informed the Office of Security. Howard Osborn went to then-Director Richard Helms, who told Osborn to get the documents. Osborn got them. Tofte then protested that the CIA had also stolen some of his wife's jewelry. He even took the charge to court, whence it reached the newspapers. This was the sort of unruly mess referred to by the CIA as a "flap." Tofte was fired in September 1966 and was followed out of the Agency shortly thereafter by the man who had hired him against much advice to the contrary, Tracy Barnes.

12. Smith, *Portrait of a Cold Warrior*, p. 242.

13. *Ibid.*, p. 118.

14. Amory resigned shortly after McCone became DCI in 1961. The story told at the CIA is that he flipped on his "squawk box" line to McCone one day and found he'd been rewired; he got one of McCone's aides instead. He was replaced as DDI by Ray Cline.

15. They included Sidney Souers, the first DCI; General Omar Bradley, Admiral Richard Connolly, General John E. Hull, Morris Hadley, a lawyer from New York; David Bruce, former ambassador to Great Britain; William B. Francke, former Secretary of the Navy; Henry Wriston, former president of Brown University and president of the Council on Foreign Relations; Donald Russell, a member of an early commission which studied the CIA; and General James Doolittle. Book IV of the Church Committee's *Final Report* (1976), p. 62.

16. *Ibid.*

17. Smith, *Portrait of a Cold Warrior*, pp. 203–204. The arrest took place in the apartment of a CIA secretary stationed inside the Embassy, borrowed for the occasion by the two polygraph experts. To conduct such an operation in such a place breaks all the rules of security. Frank Wisner, then still the chief of station in London, sent Desmond FitzGerald a stinging cable criticizing him for the disaster.

18. Copeland, *op. cit.*, p. 202.

19. It was argued that a Soviet foothold in Guatemala would be especially dangerous because of its proximity to the Panama Canal and because it would provide a landing site for Soviet bombers. In the late 1940s and early 1950s the CIA and the military had engaged in a running intelligence battle on the question of the Soviet military threat. At that time Russia had bombers which could reach the United States, but not return. The CIA argued this did not represent much of a threat; the military countered that Russia might sacrifice her bombers on one-way suicide runs, and therefore represented a threat. An airfield in Guatemala would provide a landing site for the one-way bombers.

20. In David Phillips's account of the Guatemalan operation the Project Director is referred to as Brad. The man Phillips calls Peter was Henry Heckscher,

a former chief of base in Berlin. For other accounts of the Guatemalan operation see Ernst Halperin, "The National Liberation Movement in Latin America" (an unpublished essay for MIT's Center for International Studies, an academic group which frequently did work for the CIA); David Wise and Thomas B. Ross, *The Invisible Government* (Random House, 1964), pp. 165 ff.; and *Guatemala*, a large-format paperback volume published by the North American Congress on Latin America (NACLA) in 1974. This is an extraordinarily detailed study from a Marxist perspective. It describes Arbenz's ouster as an exercise in economic imperialism pure and simple, charting the relations of the Dulles brothers, other Eisenhower administration officials, and the Dulles law firm, Sullivan and Cromwell, with American commercial interests in Guatemala, in particular the United Fruit Company. Despite NACLA's detailed charts of influence, it is not easy to see where the suspicion of the Dulleses toward Communism ends, and outrage at the expropriation of United Fruit Company land begins. It was all but an article of faith in the 1950s that Communist parties were run by Moscow, and that a presence of Communists in a government invited its takeover. The critical point in Czechoslovakia had been 30 percent.

But perhaps the most interesting published account of the Guatemalan operation is Richard and Gladys Harkness, "The Mysterious Doings of CIA," *Saturday Evening Post*, Oct. 30, Nov. 6, and Nov. 13, 1954. The Harknesses credit the CIA with the discovery of a shipload of Czech arms, aboard the Swedish freighter *Alfhem*, which landed in Guatemala on May 15, 1954. The implication was that the United States did not decide to intervene until that moment. This was untrue; Phillips began work on the operation in March. The article was one of the first on the CIA and it reflects its era. The Harknesses stated that their assignment was "to cover the Central Intelligence Agency from every angle consistent with national security and the public interest." Much of it concerns CIA efforts to detect Communist infiltrators, and one curious passage, opaque until it has been read two or three times, is at pains to explain that it is safe for the CIA to deal with avowed Communists—that is, agents in the Soviet bloc or foreign Communist parties—because the CIA uses a "cut-out," an intelligence term for a kind of intermediary between a case officer and his agent. Taken as a whole, the articles provide a kind of primer on the Cold War.

21. Eisenhower described this scene in a speech in Washington on June 10, 1963, which he delivered to the American Booksellers Association at its annual meeting. Sharing the platform with him was Allen Dulles, whose book *The Craft of Intelligence* (Harper and Row, 1963) was also published that year. The reason for Eisenhower's appearance, and for his most unusually candid account of the Guatemalan operation, was the publication of the first volume of his memoirs.

22. Phillips describes a jubilant meeting of the principal CIA officers on the operation with Eisenhower after it was over. Phillips, *The Night Watch* (1977), pp. 49–51.

23. The coup was also very much of a mixed blessing for the Guatemalans, whose history since has been one of unrelieved violence and near-anarchy. Castillo-Armas, whose government was notable for its corruption, was assassinated in 1957, as were two Guatemalans who worked closely with Phillips on the Voice of Liberation. The United Fruit Company got its land back, but the

Guatemalans got continuing revolutionary agitation in the cities and warfare in the countryside, to which the most reactionary elements in Guatemalan society responded with wholesale assassinations. A number of Americans were kidnapped or assassinated by the revolutionaries, including Gordon Mein, the U.S. ambassador, who was shot and killed in 1968. Mein had been the State Department's Indonesian-desk officer in 1957–1958, during the ill-fated coup attempt against Sukarno. Arbenz went into permanent exile, lived for many years in Cuba, and died in Mexico in 1971. One of those who fled to the Mexican Embassy, mentioned in Betty Jane Peurifoy's poem, was Che Guevara; it took him a month to get out of the country. Phillips was in Guatemala searching through captured documents, and opened a CIA file on him. He also gathered documents tending to support charges of Communist infiltration, which, selectively edited, were submitted to various congressional committees and ended up in the Library of Congress. See Herbert S. Dinerstein, *The Making of a Missile Crisis, October 1962* (Johns Hopkins University Press, 1976), pp. 6 ff. and 274n. The CIA officers involved were all promoted a GS grade, with two exceptions. One asked for a double promotion, and got none. The other was the Project Director who made an enemy of Wisner; he stayed on with CIA, but, in the words of one official who worked on the operation, "never got as dramatic an assignment again."

24. The Harkness articles, cited above, were a result of this campaign.

25. Cornell University Press, 1952.

26. Smith, *Portrait of a Cold Warrior*, p. 221.

27. Greece was one of those important CIA assignments where reputations were won or lost. Miami and Saigon were others. Their veterans tended to outstrip their rivals in the Agency.

28. Smith, *Portrait of a Cold Warrior*, p. 205.

29. Allison gives an unusually complete account of his difficulties with the CIA in his memoirs, *Ambassador from the Prairie, or Allison Wonderland* (Houghton Mifflin, 1973), pp. 293 ff. That is, it is unusual that he mentions it at all. But his candor has its limits; he describes the U.S. policy which he unsuccessfully resisted as "mostly military and covert" (p. 336). Joseph Burckholder Smith, *Portrait of a Cold Warrior*, has a good account of the early contacts with the Sumatran rebels, and of the way CIA circulated reports of their activity as a way of building U.S. government support for using them.

30. In 1956 Tony Po helped train Khamba tribesmen from Tibet, in 1958 he went to Sumatra, in 1960 he trained Nationalist Chinese paramilitary units headed for mainland China, and later in the decade he was in the Laotian countryside, where journalists discovered that some of his Meo fighting men were keeping track of the number of Pathet Lao and North Vietnamese troops they killed by cutting off their ears. Another CIA "cowboy" of this sort was William ("Rip") Robertson, who fought for the CIA behind the lines in Korea, was with Castillo-Armas in Guatemala, and directed raids on Cuba during Operation Mongoose. See George Crile and Taylor Branch, "The Kennedy Vendetta," *Harper's*, July 1975.

31. Pope parachuted safely to the ground, was captured by the Indonesians, and spent the next four years in jail. Robert F. Kennedy finally obtained his release in July 1962.

Chapter 6

1. After Helms finally did become DDP he appointed Karamessines his chief of operations in the fall of 1962, a job he continued to hold under Desmond FitzGerald. When FitzGerald died in 1967, Helms appointed Karamessines DDP. He retired from the Agency after Schlesinger became DCI in 1973 and died in September 1977.

2. Naturally I asked what Bissell's conclusions were: had the codes been breakable? Did the analysts think the take would justify the cost? My informant said simply, "That's a tough one," and fell silent. There is a special etiquette in these matters. Asked something they don't intend to answer, some CIA officials, like William Colby, baldly say, "I'm not going to talk about that." Period. Even when expected, it's a bit jolting. More frequently a refusal is disguised as a faulty memory. For example: who was the station chief in Chile during Track II? "Gee, I can't remember. Odd. I worked with him for years. Now who was that?" etc. etc. The general rule was that CIA officials would not reveal the names of CIA programs or officers not previously mentioned in public, their sources or methods. Most of the people I talked to had an astonishing capacity for knowing what was public, and what wasn't. Since the record is staggeringly large—dozens of books, scores of official reports, hundreds of magazine articles, thousands of newspaper stories—keeping things straight could have been no easy task. But from time to time a slip would be made, and someone would mention the name of a CIA officer never revealed before. I suppose my eyebrows must have popped up, because generally after such slips my informant would visibly begin to kick himself beneath the table. No such slip was ever made with the name of an agent. Even when an agent had been identified in the press—such as Rolando Cubela, a figure in one of the principal assassination plots against Castro—many CIA people insisted on referring to him by a code name. I might call him whatever I liked, but by God they weren't going to violate the Agency's confidence by confirming his identity.

A side effect of CIA people's tendency to elaborate on the public record is the fact that one learns ever more about the disasters too big to have escaped public notice, while remaining pretty much in the dark about other things going on at the same time. Whether worse or better or just different, it's often hard to say.

3. The Air Force had agreed to a price of $22 million for nineteen planes. Other estimates went as high as $26 million. Lawrence Houston, the CIA's general counsel, negotiated a contract with Lockheed for $22 million, with the proviso that more funds would be sought if they seemed necessary halfway through the project. A sliding fee was arranged—the lower the total cost, the higher Lockheed's fee. Bissell's first step was to agree to performance rather than technical specifications, which Kelly Johnson said would be a big money saver right there. The final cost of the U-2's development was $19 million.

4. The U-2 pilot shot down on that occasion, Francis Gary Powers (no relation to the author), was eventually exchanged for a Russian spy, Colonel Rudolph Abel, in February 1962. After Powers's return, John McCone convened a three-man board headed by Judge E. Barrett Prettyman, Jr., to consider formal

charges against Powers for failing to use his plane's destruct mechanism before bailing out, and for telling the Russians more than he had to after his capture. It was suggested then and later that Powers feared the destruct mechanism would destroy not only the plane but him too, as was the case with several Nationalist Chinese pilots who flew U-2s from Taiwan over mainland China. (Powers also carried, but failed to use, a poison device hidden in a silver dollar. The active agent was a shellfish toxin which cost $3 million to develop, and which later became notorious during the Church Committee hearings. Some CIA people thought Powers broke an unwritten rule when he failed to kill himself, but in fact Powers's survival, and Eisenhower's candor in acknowledging his responsibility for the flights, did much to demystify spying and make it generally acceptable.)

Powers claimed that a near-miss by a Soviet missile destroyed his right stabilizer, putting his U-2 into an inverted spin. When the escape charge of his eject mechanism failed to work he had to remove the plane's canopy manually while plunging toward the ground. By the time he was free to jump he could no longer reach the destruct switch and simply bailed out. The NSA, arguing on the basis of Soviet communications intercepts, said it didn't happen that way at all. There was a flame-out and Powers bailed out under circumstances which would not have prevented him from destroying the plane and its telltale cameras, thus allowing the United States to persist in its cover story that the craft was simply an off-course weather observation plane. But McCone's board of inquiry sent Kelly Johnson of Lockheed to look at the wreckage of the plane in Moscow, where it had been put on display by the Russians, and Johnson concluded the plane would have behaved just as Powers claimed.

The Board, which also included an Army general and John Bross as a representative of the CIA, recommended no charges be brought. The NSA protested that its version of events had to be correct, and Bross was called in to argue the board's conclusions with McCone. Unknown to him, McCone recorded his argument, which included some unflattering remarks about the NSA, and sent the transcript to the NSA for comment, an unfortunate decision which later caused Bross a good deal of trouble with NSA in his job as the head of National Intelligence Programs Evaluation.

At one point during the argument over Powers, Prettyman asked Bross if McCone was a lawyer. Bross said no; McCone was an engineer. Prettyman said aha! he thought so, and then told McCone that the evidence brought against Powers by NSA, like similar evidence of his behavior in the Soviet Union, was at best unverifiable hearsay once removed. Prettyman would not have allowed it into his courtroom. McCone accepted that argument and Powers was exonerated. Eventually he went to work as a helicopter pilot for a television station in Los Angeles, where he was killed in a crash in August 1977.

5. See Ray Cline, *Secrets, Spies and Scholars* (1976), p. 157. Of course the sword cuts both ways. The Soviets presumably know as much about us as we do about them, just as both sides know how to elude overhead reconnaissance when it is necessary to do so. During training for the U.S. Army's raid on a North Vietnamese prison compound at Son Tay in November 1970, for example, a mockup of the prison at Eglin Air Force base in Florida was dismantled during daylight hours so it would not be picked up by a Soviet Cosmos satellite which

passed over Eglin twice every day at a height of about 70 miles. The post holes for the two-by-fours which held up the prison mockup were even covered with lids so that a telltale outline of the prison would not be visible. See Benjamin F. Schemmer, *The Raid* (Harper & Row, 1976), p. 92. (This, by the way, is a brilliantly researched book, unfairly neglected for no better reason than that military derring-do under Nixon was not a popular subject. It contains the best description I've seen of the meticulous planning, training, and imaginative use of intelligence required for a successful clandestine paramilitary operation. In the event, of course, the prisoners were long gone when the raiders arrived, but Schemmer, fighting uphill all the way, will probably convince you, as he did me, that the raid, far from being a public relations boondoggle, was an entirely reasonable and honorable attempt to rescue prisoners of war.)

6. Joseph Burckholder Smith, *Portrait of a Cold Warrior* (1976), p. 204.

7. David Phillips, *The Night Watch* (1977), p. 37.

8. John Bross, then the Eastern European Division chief, gave Tweedy the assignment over the robust protests of Tracy Barnes, who wanted the job to go to someone from the OPC.

9. Penkovskiy was arrested just before the onset of the missile crisis, and was later tried and executed. CIA training of case officers now includes a 90-minute lecture by the bilingual case officer who handled the Penkovskiy case in the field. The information Penkovskiy provided on the missiles placed in Cuba included not only their range and the steps involved in bringing them to operational readiness, but their rate of refire. This information proved especially important during NSC Executive Committee discussion of a proposal to bomb the missile sites. In the event the bombers did not take them all out the first time around, Excom wanted to know, how long would it take the Russians to ready a site for a second launch? Since each missile was potentially able to account for an American city, this was no idle question. The answer was "several" hours.

10. Phillips, *op. cit.*, p. 87.

Chapter 7

1. Desmond FitzGerald was the first DDP to attempt to break up the baronies, a campaign which did not end until the mass firings of James Schlesinger in 1973, and of Stansfield Turner in 1977.

2. "Reclama" is an archaic term of Scottish law, meaning appeal. As used within the U.S. government, it refers to any written comment on, appeal from, or rebuttal of an official in-house report. In effect, it's the other side of the story.

3. In David Phillips's *The Night Watch* (1977) Hawkins is referred to as "Colonel Alcott" and Jacob Esterline is called "Cliff." E. Howard Hunt, *Give Us This Day* (1973), refers to them as "Haskins" and "Jake." Hunt also calls Phillips "Knight," which was Richard Helms's code name in CIA.

4. Victor Marchetti describes a conversation with Colonel Lawrence K. ("Red") White, the CIA's Executive Director/Comptroller, in which White, absently turning his West Point ring on his finger, said, "Do you realize there isn't one piece of paper in this whole Agency about the Bay of Pigs with Helms's signature on it?" Marchetti was puzzled; "I don't understand," he said. "You

will," said White. While not literally true, White's remark was typical of some Agency officials who felt Helms was too cautious by half. In fact, of course, Bissell had excluded Helms from an active role.

5. Each area division within the DDP was further subdivided into branches. Cuba had originally been part of the Caribbean Branch of the Western Hemisphere Division, for example. In addition, each division had its own support, covert action, planning, and counterintelligence staffs.

6. One DDP official of the time said that the protest was circulated more or less openly within the upper levels of the DDP, that it naturally excited Dulles's anger, and that it was Helms's awkward task to reprimand the protestors for getting out of line. Helms says he does not recall undertaking any such chore.

7. Helms does not remember going to see Hilsman with any such intention, but may have discussed the invasion with him in a general way in the course of routine business.

8. A couple of years later, however, Helms says he was repeatedly approached in the halls by friends saying, "I hear you're going to Rome." After a while he went to McCone and said, "I hear all over the place I'm going to Rome. Is there any truth to this?" McCone said, "Rome? I never even thought of sending you to Rome. Whose idea is this?" Helms said he didn't know, and the subject was dropped. The man who in fact went to Rome at that time was William Harvey. John Bross also remembers rumors of Helms's going to Rome, but says they were circulating before the Bay of Pigs.

About the move to London, Helms says, "Maybe Bissell was sore—I don't know, I wasn't aware of it—but Dulles didn't speak to me and Bissell didn't speak to me. Now obviously I qualify everything I say, but that's the best recollection I have, and if Bissell says anything to the contrary, I'd be glad to chat with him, because I'm not mad at Bissell, and as far as I know these days Bissell isn't mad at me."

9. The CIA eventually concluded that the briefcase had been stolen from the courier's car in Mexico City by an ordinary thief, and that its contents never reached Castro. The courier was fired and Hunt was much criticized. Hunt, *op. cit.*, p. 66, and Phillips, *op. cit.*, p. 92.

10. At State Department insistence the exile training camp was later switched to Guatemala in order to disassociate the United States even further from the whole operation.

11. Arthur Schlesinger, Jr., credits Bissell with an "unsurpassed talent for lucid analysis and fluent exposition." *A Thousand Days* (Houghton Mifflin, 1965), p. 240. Bissell is indeed persuasive. Before I talked to him, the CIA's plan for the invasion of Cuba had always struck me as plain crazy. Bissell made it sound actually workable. With further mulling it now strikes me as half-crazy— but also half-sane. It *might* have worked. This possibility shifts the central question about the Bay of Pigs from a side issue—was it feasible?—to a subject which deserves more attention: was it desirable? The more I have learned about the CIA the more it has seemed to me that the CIA has often been blamed for the simple failure of operations, when the real problem was whether they should have been undertaken in the first place. Thus, I now think that the reason the CIA justifies

our attention is not that it has pursued certain goals with questionable means, but that what it does is what policy is.

12. Hunt, *op. cit.*, p. 88.

13. The Joint Chiefs of Staff sent a team to Guatemala in late February which reported that the invasion force seemed capable enough to them. Later the JCS protested that their role had been only to review the operation, not to share in responsibility for its success or failure. Admiral Rufus Taylor, who was Deputy Director for Central Intelligence for three years under Helms (1966–1969), once told John Bross the JCS felt it had been placed in a false position with regard to the Bay of Pigs. This was the CIA's, not the Pentagon's, operation. The JCS particularly resented its putative role through Colonel Hawkins; lending Hawkins to the CIA, Taylor told Bross, was like lending someone your cook for a party. If the party failed, it was hardly fair to blame the man who lent you his cook.

14. In March 1961, as the direct result of Kennedy's intervention, the FRD was replaced by a new Cuban Revolutionary Council, which included Manuel Ray for the first time. Ray had been an official in Castro's government until November 1959, and was much resented by some exiles as a leftist, an opportunist, and a doubtful convert. But Ray was well connected in the Kennedy administration, and it insisted on his inclusion to counter charges the exiles were only *Batisteros* in disguise. Hunt's resentment of the change cost him his job as political action officer for the operation. Unlike Bissell and Barnes, Hunt identified with those Cubans who were hostile to Castro's revolution because it was a *revolution*. The position of the Kennedy administration, shared by Bissell, was that Castro had betrayed the revolution by imposing a Communist dictatorship on Cuba, despite the fact much of his support while he was still in the mountains had come from traditional liberal and democratic forces. Hunt quotes Bissell as having said of anti-Castro zealots in the Eisenhower administration, "They don't know it, but we're the real revolutionaries." Hunt, *op. cit.*, p. 83.

15. Kennedy learned. Just two days before the anti-Diem coup in Saigon in 1963, he told Ambassador Henry Cabot Lodge that he would reserve the right to change his mind until the last moment. "I know from experience that failure is more destructive than an appearance of indecision." *Alleged Assassination Plots Involving Foreign Leaders* (U.S. Government Printing Office, 1975), p. 219.

16. Hunt, *op. cit.*, pp. 195 ff. For other accounts of this episode see Charles Murphy, "Cuba: The Record Set Straight," *Fortune*, September, 1961; David Wise and Thomas B. Ross, *The Invisible Government* (1964), p. 21; Lyman Kirkpatrick, *The Real CIA* (1968), pp. 184 ff.; Schlesinger, *A Thousand Days*, pp. 272 ff.; and Phillips, *The Night Watch*, p. 107. Phillips was the only writer to have read Hunt's version of what happened, but he does not mention it.

17. Dulles felt that cancellation of his long-scheduled speech might alert Castro to the imminence of the invasion, so he kept his appointment.

18. Schlesinger, *op. cit.*, p. 276.

19. Kennedy's remark is a part of CIA's oral history. At least half a dozen high officials repeated it to me more or less verbatim, but it is not entirely clear to whom Kennedy made this remark, or when he made it. Bissell said it was made to him; others said it was made to Dulles.

20. In *Give Us This Day*, p. 216, Hunt goes out of his way to deny that Dulles was Murphy's source for his well-informed article. He says he read proofs of the article given to him by Dulles in early September and then determined that Murphy's informant was actually a White House official, whom he declines to name. This is untrue; Dulles was one of Murphy's principal sources, according to a woman in CIA who helped Dulles that summer with the book he eventually published as *The Craft of Intelligence* (1963). Hunt also worked briefly on Dulles's book—he had been recommended by Helms—but the melodramatic style he had cultivated for his novels did not sit well with Dulles, and Hunt was dropped from the project. Perhaps Hunt's denial of Dulles's conversations with Murphy was only an attempt to do his old boss a final favor.

21. Dulles, *op. cit.*, p. 169.

22. These are roughly the words a former chairman of the Board of National Estimates used to describe the BNE's answer to Barnes. The cautious qualification—"we have no evidence"—is characteristic of intelligence analysis.

23. Kirkpatrick has another explanation for going directly to McCone. He says the word in the corridors of the DDP was that the report would be a whitewash. Dulles, after all, was a legendary figure, the great white case officer, the closest thing the CIA had to a father, and the Bay of Pigs operation had necessarily been as much his as Bissell's. Kirkpatrick was determined not to whitewash a CIA failure of such magnitude that it threatened to destroy the Agency itself. He did not, but he paid a price. One of McCone's first acts as DCI was to replace Kirkpatrick as IG.

One might have thought that Nixon would have asked to see the IG report on the Bay of Pigs when he sent John Ehrlichman to ask Richard Helms for a number of CIA documents in September 1971, but he did not. Apparently Nixon did not know of the report's existence. He asked only for *a* report on the Bay of Pigs. Helms gave him the report written by Colonel Hawkins, who, of course, had been a principal planner of the operation. I do not know what was in Hawkins's report, but presumably it paid more attention to the change in landing sites and the cancellation of air strikes than Kirkpatrick's study. In any event, Helms was worried who would actually read the report he gave Nixon, and he would hardly have volunteered a detailed operational study of the sort the IG normally conducted. The security risks would be too great.

24. Phillips, *op. cit.*, p. 113.

Chapter 8

1. One retired CIA officer I talked to looked genuinely shocked when I asked if Helms might have lied to Lyndon Johnson. "I can't see him deliberately lying to the President," he said. "That would be just inconceivable." The officer was not trying to protect Helms; he had known him well but did not entirely like him. But he wanted me to understand that the Director of Central Intelligence would not lie to the President; if I hadn't got that straight I would never understand what the CIA was all about.

2. It is not clear whether or not Pearson told Warren the names of the lawyer and his client. Jack Anderson, an associate of Pearson's in 1967,

published the names in his column on September 9, 1976, when he also identified another source as the CIA officer William Harvey, who had a serious drinking problem which contributed to his departure from the Agency, and which made him notoriously voluble. See also Book V of the Church Committee's *Final Report* (U.S. Government Printing Office, 1976), pp. 78 ff.

3. A former CIA officer named Charles McCarry explored this possibility in his novel *The Tears of Autumn* (Dutton, 1974). McCarry, the best of the spy novelists to come out of the CIA, has written a trilogy about a fictional CIA officer named Paul Christopher; the other two books are *The Miernik Dossier* (Saturday Review Press, 1973) and *The Secret Lovers* (Dutton, 1977). McCarry says he spent ten years with the Agency as a "singleton," an officer working outside the usual confines of a CIA station, mostly in Europe and Africa, and his novels capture a sound feel for intelligence in the field, which involves a good deal of political intrigue, but not much melodrama.

4. The NSA connection had been revealed in the March 1967 issue of *Ramparts* magazine. After the report became public on February 13, Johnson appointed Katzenbach, Helms, and John Gardner—who had once shared an OSS office in Washington with Helms during the war—to report to him on the CIA's involvement with public institutions. Katzenbach told the Church Committee that the real reason Johnson appointed the committee was to head off a broader congressional inquiry. For a list of the CIA-supported organizations see David Wise and Thomas B. Ross, *The Espionage Establishment* (Random House, 1967), p. 155n. Tom Braden, who had once been in charge of the International Organizations Division of the DDP (1951–1954), defended the secret arrangements in a *Saturday Evening Post* article, "I'm Glad the CIA Is Immoral," May 1967. The report which Johnson discussed with Helms on March 22, 1967, was officially released on March 29.

One program omitted in Helms's report to the President was MK/ULTRA, the CIA's extensive support for research into the possible clandestine uses of LSD and other mind-altering drugs. Helms had assigned the CIA's part in the study of Agency ties with public organizations to his Executive Director/Comptroller, Colonel Lawrence K. White, who handed the job down to a staff officer. According to Victor Marchetti, the staff officer was specifically told not to include any university-connected drug research programs.

The interesting thing about this episode is that it demonstrates Helms's characteristic response when asked for an official report on Subject A—in this case, CIA ties to public institutions—which would normally be expected to expose Subject B—in this case, the CIA drug programs which were largely farmed out to university researchers. Rather than raise the issue with President Johnson, Katzenbach, or John Gardner, Helms ordered the CIA's own internal report to omit all drug programs. As a further precaution, he ordered that only one copy of the CIA's internal report was to be preserved.

It is also interesting that the government tried to suppress the relevant passages in Marchetti's book, and that it did manage to exclude 16 lines in two separate passages which may have referred to drug programs. Presumably it failed to suppress the passage mentioned above—concerning Helms's order to omit all drug programs from his report—because the CIA was unwilling to tell the judge in the case why it feared publication. See Victor Marchetti and John Marks, *The CIA and the Cult of Intelligence* (Knopf, 1974), pp. 223 ff.

Was Helms lying to the President by omitting the drug programs? Not really; or not exactly. He knew the Katzenbach Committee had a solely political motive and that its charter was not to expose and end CIA arrangements, but rather to save as many as possible. In Helms's view, the President wanted the CIA to be active and aggressive, and was far from trying "to clean it up." His mandate, in short, was to preserve and protect, and one of the things he preserved and protected was MK/ULTRA.

5. Anthony Mockler, *The Mercenaries* (Macmillan, 1969), p. 176.

6. See Chapter 12.

7. Colonel Galloway had been brought into the CIA by then-DCI General Hoyt Vandenberg (1946–1947). The Assistant Director for Special Operations (ADSO) was in charge of all CIA clandestine operations until the creation of the Office of Policy Coordination in 1948.

8. See, for example, David B. Tinnin and Dag Christensen, *The Hit Team* (1976), a detailed account of an Israeli assassination program which killed twelve Black September members in revenge for the Palestinian murder of eleven Israeli Olympic athletes in Munich in 1972. The program came to an end when the Israelis mistakenly murdered an innocent man in Norway in 1973. Also, Colin Smith, *Carlos: Portrait of a Terrorist* (Holt, Rinehart & Winston, 1977), in which Smith describes the Israeli murder of a PLO official named Mahmoud Hamchari by rigging his phone with an explosive device, then triggering it with an electronic signal after he answered and identified himself.

9. See Sanche de Gramont, *The Secret War* (G. P. Putnam's Sons, 1962), pp. 359 ff.; John Barron, *KGB* (Reader's Digest Press, 1974), chap. 13; and Richard Deacon, *A History of the Russian Secret Service* (Taplinger, 1972), chaps. 23 and 25, and *passim*. Barron's book is filled with useful information, but I'm told it includes a few tall tales as well. One of them concerns a Russian attempt to poison an enemy with barium salts; apparently this never happened.

10. Chuyen was an interpreter for the 5th Special Forces Group, headquartered in Nha Trang, which sent teams across the South Vietnamese border into Cambodia on reconnaissance missions. In May 1969, a raid on a North Vietnamese camp in Cambodia turned up a photo of Chuyen talking to an NVA officer. Polygraph tests of Chuyen seemed to confirm he was a double agent, and the Special Forces, according to several of the officers later charged with Chuyen's murder, asked their CIA liaison officer in Nha Trang what they ought to do. The CIA officer, again according to the Special Forces officers, told them that killing the agent would solve the problem—"termination with extreme prejudice," in the parlance of the time. After all, the CIA officer said, the CIA's chief of station in Saigon, Ted Shackley, "had been responsible for 250 political killings in Laos and one more wouldn't make any difference." (Henry B. Rothblatt, "Why the Army Tried to Railroad the Green Berets," *True*, March 1970. Rothblatt defended the officers charged with Chuyen's murder.)

In June 1969 the Special Forces officers killed Chuyen, weighted his body with chains, and dumped him into Nha Trang Bay. In August they were formally charged with his murder by the Army. Early in September 1969, Richard Helms told a *Newsweek* reporter the CIA's version of what happened, claiming that the CIA officer in Nha Trang told the Special Forces officers to turn Chuyen over to the South Vietnamese. Not long after Helms's background briefing, Rothblatt announced in Saigon that he intended to call Helms as a witness in the case. A couple of days later the Secretary of the Army dropped all charges. Captain Robert Marasco later admitted that he had shot Chuyen. See *Newsweek*, Sept. 8, 1969; and the *New York Times*, April 4, 1971, for Marasco's confession.

A fictional account of a similar episode can be found in *Easy Victories* (Houghton Mifflin, 1974) by "James Trowbridge," a pseudonym. This is a powerful book, unfairly neglected, the best account I've seen of what is meant by the "ugly side" of intelligence.

11. Kirkpatrick heard about the murder on a trip to Bangkok in 1952, where he'd gone to settle an OSO-OPC dispute over the recruiting of a Thai government official. He had a hard time convincing Allen Dulles the Attorney General ought to be told about the case, but eventually succeeded. Although Kirkpatrick is satisfied the murder was not the CIA's doing, the guilty party was never established.

12. This conclusion was not easily reached. One has learned to be skeptical. A few years ago Agency people would have denied with equal heat any suggestion that the CIA had ever tried to kill Castro. CIA officials seem to believe that "excesses" of that sort are not "policy," occurred only in "extraordinary" circumstances, and somehow do not count. As a result I was at first inclined to accept the general wisdom that the CIA, like other intelligence services, occasionally kills people if they cause sufficient trouble, and if their murder can be carried out secretly. When I said as much in an earlier version of this manuscript CIA people reacted so vigorously I had no choice but to reconsider the whole matter. In the end I accepted their denials of low-level agent killings for two reasons. First, I was unable to discover so much as a single example of the sort of murder referred to here. It hardly seemed fair to charge the CIA with routine homicide in the total absence of evidence. Second, I began to wonder about my own point of view. Was I so hostile toward the Agency that I actually preferred to believe the worst? I certainly opposed gratuitous violence; Agency people insisted they did too. Why couldn't I accept the possibility that on this, at least, we agreed? But as I say, my conclusion was not easily reached. It would not surprise me to learn that agent murders had, in fact, taken place; nor to hear CIA officials insist they were never a matter of "policy," occurred only under "extraordinary" circumstances, and therefore didn't count.

13. The West German general was also an opponent of Reinhard Gehlen, and argued that the CIA should stop backing him. According to an official at the meeting, Helms said, "General, we're not promoting Gehlen, we're promoting a West German intelligence service. If you don't like Gehlen, get somebody else."

14. Miles Copeland, *The Game of Nations* (1969), p. 202. According to John Marks, quoting a retired CIA official, Allen Dulles asked his brother in a similar meeting in the State Department if there was anything the CIA might do about Nasser. John Foster Dulles, according to Marks, said the CIA should "eliminate that problem." In response the CIA sent three teams to Egypt for the purpose of assassinating Nasser, without effect. Again according to Marks, the

Church Committee asked the CIA if any effort to kill Nasser had ever been made, but was told: "This Agency has no records that any teams or individuals have ever been sent to Egypt for the purpose of attempting to assassinate Nasser." Washington *Post*, Feb. 12, 1976.

F. A. O. Schwarz, Jr., confirmed that the Church Committee did investigate possible CIA assassination attempts against Nasser, but could never establish definitively whether or not they had really taken place.

15. The Church Committee was also told about the PFIAB discussions concerning the possibility of assassinating Ho Chi Minh, but decided not to mention them in its final report because the CIA had never followed them up with concrete action. PFIAB is sometimes described as if it were an "oversight" group intended to keep the Agency in line. It seems to have taken a more aggressive view of its responsibilities, and constantly urged the CIA to do more, rather than less.

16. Minutes of the Special Group meeting, quoted in the Church Committee's *Alleged Assassination Plots Involving Foreign Leaders* (U.S. Government Printing Office, 1975), p. 99. General Cabell had already been briefed on plots to kill Castro at the time he delivered the regular spiel to Merchant. See Chapter 9.

17. And no doubt Allen Dulles as well, since he was loudly blamed by several Senators for failing to predict the coup. His predecessor, General Walter Bedell Smith, had been similarly blamed by Thomas Dewey during the 1948 presidential campaign for failing to predict the riot in Bogotá, Colombia, known as the "Bogotazo." One of Helms's standing instructions to his station chiefs as both DDP and DCI was to "ring the bell"—warn him of a possible coup— because so many Washington officials assumed the CIA was asleep on the job if it missed on anything so elementary (as they thought) as a coup.

18. Parrott told the Church Committee that such a suggestion was so out of line, and disposed of so quickly, that it did not merit a place in the record. This was part of the regular spiel, too.

19. This episode is described in great detail in the *Alleged Assassination Plots*, pp. 105 and 161 ff. It was also reported by George Crile and Taylor Branch in "The Kennedy Vendetta," *Harper's*, July 1975.

20. Not named in the report.

21. Not named in the report.

Chapter 9

1. It is apparent from the Church Committee's report on assassinations that the Committee depended very heavily on the IG Report of 1967. On almost every point, especially those having to do with responsibility for the plots, the Committee was unable to press on much beyond the IG's conclusions, even with the full weight of senatorial authority, the power of subpoena, and the power to cite for contempt.

2. The Church Committee's report on *Alleged Assassination Plots Involving Foreign Leaders* (1975) deals at length with the murder or attempted murder of five individuals—Patrice Lumumba, Rafael Trujillo, Fidel Castro, Ngo Dinh

Diem, and Chilean General René Schneider. The attempt on Abdul Kassem in Iraq is mentioned in passing. The Committee concluded that the CIA was not directly responsible for the death of any of the six, although it certainly tried to kill Lumumba and Castro; was involved up to its scuppers with the Dominicans who assassinated Trujillo, and may even have been the source of the murder weapon; was fully knowledgeable of plans to overthrow Diem; and conspired with Chileans who planned to kidnap Schneider and killed him when they tried.

There is scattered evidence, in addition, that the CIA was at least in contact with groups who planned to kill Sukarno and Nasser. In the early 1960s high officials of the French government anonymously charged that the CIA had been in touch, and perhaps something more than in touch, with members of the Secret Army Organization (OAS) who repeatedly tried to kill Charles de Gaulle. The charges, which the CIA denied, and which were never substantiated, were probably the result of de Gaulle's irritation over CIA contacts with the Algerian FLN, a subject of frequent diplomatic protest.

In late 1961, for example, the CIA arranged for Frantz Fanon, author of *The Wretched of the Earth* and a theoretician for the FLN, to be flown to Washington for treatment of terminal cancer. After Fanon's death on December 6, a CIA officer named Oliver Iselin accompanied Fanon's body back to Tunis, where the FLN carried it across the border into Algeria for burial. Iselin, accompanied by another CIA officer who flew to Tunis from Geneva, according to a State Department source, was present at the funeral. This sort of thing angered de Gaulle. See Peter Geismar, *Fanon* (The Dial Press, 1971), pp. 182 ff.

3. The formal date of Bissell's departure was February 19, 1962, but of course the process of transition began a good deal earlier.

4. There were plenty of women in CIA—clerks, typists, analysts, photo interpreters, even case officers—but none ever seems to have reached a level where she might play a leading role in the sort of things which excited the admiration or outrage of her countrypersons.

5. Lansdale asked a CIA officer on the Cuba desk to find him a cryptonym for the group working on Cuba in the office of the Secretary of Defense. The officer asked the crypt people for a list of unused crypts from the Far East, figuring that would help to obscure the trail. The first two letters of a cryptonym are called the digraph; these indicate geographical area. The letters MO were the old digraph for Thailand. The CIA officer picked MONGOOSE from the list of unused crypts and passed it on to Lansdale. It was never used inside CIA.

6. Arthur Schlesinger, Jr., *A Thousand Days* (1965), p. 288.

7. *Ibid.*, p. 839.

8. This may have been General Arthur Gilbert Trudeau, head of Army Intelligence (G2) in June 1954, when he infuriated Allen Dulles by personally warning German Chancellor Konrad Adenauer of possible Communist agents inside the Gehlen organization. Dulles went to Eisenhower and demanded General Trudeau's transfer; in September 1955 he got it. Later, it was discovered that Gehlen's chief of counterintelligence, Hans Felfe, was a Communist agent. See Paul W. Blackstock, *The Strategy of Subversion* (Quadrangle, 1964), p. 107.

9. Kennedy learned from his mistakes. According to his brother in *Thirteen Days* (Norton, 1969), p. 33, he deliberately excluded himself from meetings of

the National Security Council executive committee during the missile crisis precisely so his advisers would feel free to talk.

10. Its members in the beginning were McGeorge Bundy, representing the White House; Robert Kennedy as a kind of minister without portfolio; Allen Dulles and later John McCone from CIA; the Chairman of the Joint Chiefs of Staff, General Lyman Lemnitzer; the Deputy Secretary of Defense, Roswell Gilpatric; Edward R. Murrow from USIA, and the Deputy Undersecretary of State for Political Affairs, U. Alexis Johnson.

11. In all the literature on the CIA I have been able to find only one account of an occasion on which the President told the Agency, Well done! It is a very interesting account, too, and can be found in David Atlee Phillips, *The Night Watch* (1977), pp. 49 ff. The occasion was the successful coup against Arbenz in Guatemala. Eisenhower, I am told, also called in Kermit Roosevelt for special praise, after he had succeeded in overthrowing Mossadeq in Iran in 1953.

12. The Berlin Tunnel, one of the biggest CIA intelligence-gathering achievements before development of the U-2, ran under the border between the American and Soviet zones of Berlin, ending at a major telephone cable, which was tapped for about five months between late 1955 and April 22, 1956. On that date the Russians "discovered" the tunnel and exposed it to the world. According to Harry Rositzke in *The CIA's Secret Operations* (1977), the Russians learned about the tunnel in its planning stage from an agent inside the British SIS, George Blake, but decided to let the operation go forward to protect Blake. A good account of the tunnel can be found in Heinz Höhne and Herman Zolling, *The General Was a Spy* (1972), pp. 306-313.

13. *Alleged Assassination Plots Involving Foreign Leaders* (1975), p. 141. Hereafter the *Assassination Report*. According to the report "it is probable that DDP Helms was also present" at the meeting (p. 141n.).

14. The first agent sighting of a Russian missile in Cuba, in September 1962, came from an agent recruited by one of Harvey's teams.

15. In a study of terrorism in 1977 the CIA defined international terrorism as "single actions carried out by individuals or groups controlled by a sovereign state," a pretty good description of Operation Mongoose. Times change. See the *New York Times*, Nov. 13, 1977.

16. This was the figure given by the former Deputy Director for Intelligence, Ray Cline, in "The CIA's Secret Army," *CBS Reports*, June 10, 1977. Other estimates have put the figure somewhat lower.

17. *Assassination Report*, p. 142n. Elder is not identified in the report. Ideas of this sort—pranks really—were apparently second nature to Lansdale. In 1954, shortly after the Geneva Convention which ended the first Indochina war, a Lansdale team in Hanoi secretly put sugar in the gas tanks of North Vietnamese buses. But despite all the evidence to the contrary, Lansdale was a serious man and his work in the Philippines was a model of political action.

18. Memo from Harvey to McCone, dated April 10, 1962. *Assassination Report*, p. 145.

19. *Ibid.*, p. 150.

20. Kennedy's appointment books show he spent three weekends in Palm Beach in early 1962: January 25-28, March 15-18, and April 27-28. The run-

in with Harvey probably occurred on one of these weekends. See Arthur Schlesinger, Jr., *Robert Kennedy and His Times* (Houghton Mifflin, 1978), p. 544n.

21. Martinez, a veteran of hundreds of operations against Cuba, was later arrested inside the Watergate Hotel and office complex, after being recruited for "an intelligence operation" by another CIA-Cuba veteran, E. Howard Hunt.

22. When President Kennedy was told a U-2 had wandered into Soviet air space during a later stage of the missile crisis (October 27, 1962), he said, "There is always some so-and-so who doesn't get the word." Schlesinger, *A Thousand Days*, p. 827. Harvey didn't get the word either.

23. Harvey's already serious drinking problem escalated in Rome. He spent a lot of time on sentimental weekend visits to Germany, where he'd served in his salad days. He took a dislike to one of his officers in Rome and made his life miserable there. The officer once told him, "If you don't get off the liquor you'll kill yourself." Harvey responded, "I'll live to piss on your grave, and that's what I'll do." Harvey had the officer sent home in a degree of disgrace, but one of the officer's friends in Rome gave him a personal letter to give to Helms, explaining things. When Helms read the letter he was reportedly furious and said, "If I had Harvey right now I'd ram his head right through the wall." Harvey was recalled and given a final job making a study of audio security for CIA stations, and then retired on medical grounds. When he left Rome, the station gave him a farewell party at the Hotel Flora. At the end of it Harvey walked over to the U.S. Embassy on the Via Veneto and urinated against the wall of the building. After his retirement he moved to Indianapolis, lived long enough to testify in considerable detail to the Church Committee, and then died in the spring of 1976. Harvey provides a good example of the sort of damage a long career in intelligence can do to a man's life. This is, in fact, a principal theme in the novels of John le Carré, and is one of the reasons Helms never liked Le Carré's books.

24. He was replaced by William Colby.

25. On the morning of November 22, 1963, John McCone and Lyman Kirkpatrick testified before the President's Foreign Intelligence Advisory Board. McCone was scheduled to leave Washington that afternoon for a trip to the West Coast, and he asked Kirkpatrick to round up some of the other high Agency officials for lunch before McCone left. In addition to McCone and Kirkpatrick, Helms, Sherman Kent, and several others were present in the French room—a kind of private dining room then adjoining the Director's office—when McCone's assistant, Walter Elder, came in with a flimsy in his hand saying, "The President's been shot." McCone gave the inevitable order that he was to be kept informed and then left CIA headquarters for Robert Kennedy's home nearby.

26. Joseph Burckholder Smith, *Portrait of a Cold Warrior* (1976), p. 384.

27. In the *Assassination Report*, O'Donnell is given a pseudonym—Michael Mulroney.

28. *Ibid.*, pp. 118, 121.

29. *Ibid.*, p. 149.

30. *Ibid.*, p. 150.

31. *Ibid.*, p. 151.

32. *Ibid.*, p. 152.

33. *Ibid.*, p. 151.

34. *Ibid.*, p. 152.

35. *Ibid.*, p. 158.

36. *Ibid.*

37. *Ibid.*, p. 150.

38. Later Gottlieb was promoted to chief of the DDP's Technical Services Division. At the time of the struggle over creation of the Deputy Directorate for Science and Technology a tug of war developed over the Technical Services Division (TSD). The new DDS&T insisted the TSD ought to be under its aegis; the DDP insisted the TSD should stay right where it was, close to the men who would use its gadgets. I suspect that one reason Helms and others fought to hold on to the TSD was knowledge of what was in its files—clues to a whole host of ugly operations, actual and only contemplated. To deliver the TSD with its files intact to the DDS&T would have violated a basic tenet of secrecy. DDS&T didn't need to know about this sort of thing.

39. The biological agent is not identified in the *Assassination Report*, but Gottlieb testified that he had picked it out at Fort Detrick, Maryland, from an Army Chemical Corps list of materials which would cause tularemia (rabbit fever), brucellosis (undulant fever), tuberculosis, anthrax, smallpox, and Venezuelan equine encephalitis (sleeping sickness). See the *Assassination Report*, p. 21.

40. Identified as Victor Hedgman in the *Assassination Report*.

41. *Ibid.*, p. 39.

42. This was the conclusion of a United Nations investigation. Charges of CIA involvement in Lumumba's death arose almost immediately. In 1968, when Andrew Cordier became acting president of Columbia University, the Students for a Democratic Society put together a protest campaign which accused him of helping the CIA to murder Lumumba when he had been a U.N. official in the Congo. In his book about the CIA, John Stockwell, chief of the CIA's Angolan task force in 1975, tells several anecdotes which make it clear he's not entirely convinced of the CIA's innocence in Lumumba's murder. For example, one CIA officer—unidentified—told him about an escapade in Lubumbashi, driving about with Lumumba's body in the trunk of his car, trying to decide what to do with it. Stockwell says he suspects Larry Devlin of knowing more about Lumumba's assassination than was reflected in CIA documents, or than he admitted in his testimony. See John Stockwell, *In Search of Enemies* (Norton, 1978), *passim*.

43. Dearborn supported the dissidents' plans in a letter of extraordinary candor on October 27, 1960: "One further point which I should probably not even make. From a purely practical standpoint, it will be best for us, for the OAS, and for the Dominican Republic if the Dominicans put an end to Trujillo before he leaves this island. If he has his millions and is a free agent, he will devote his life from exile to preventing stable government in the D.R., to overturning democratic governments and establishing dictatorships in the Caribbean, and to assassinating his enemies. If I were a Dominican, which thank heaven I am not, I would favor destroying Trujillo as being the first necessary step in the salvation of my country and I would regard this, in fact, as my Christian duty. If you recall Dracula, you will remember it was necessary to drive a stake through his heart to prevent a continuation of his crimes. I believe sudden death would be more humane than the solution of the Nuncio who once told me he thought he should

pray that Trujillo would have a long and lingering illness." *Assassination Report*, p. 195. The State Department was alarmed by Dearborn's letter; in future, they asked him, please forward such remarks through the CIA. His regular diplomatic cables were being distributed to at least nineteen different offices. Dearborn, incidentally, was almost certainly right; Trujillo's enemies had many reasons to kill him. But that's the sort of decision every country must make for itself. The United States certainly had no such justification for killing Castro or Lumumba, who were inconveniences to us, even though they may have been guilty of crimes against their fellow countrymen. An absolute prohibition against assassination is sensible because a government cannot be relied on to make a judicious decision about such matters, especially when it believes it will never be called to account. It has been argued—generally in private—that such prohibitions are foolish because a situation may some day arise in which an assassination truly is necessary. The argument does not strike me as a sound one; if that day ever arrives, the agency asked to perform the deed can be counted on to break the rules, just as the CIA did when the rule was only implicit.

44. E. Howard Hunt, *Give Us This Day* (1973), p. 38.

45. Identified by David Wise as James O'Connell. *The American Police State* (Random House, 1976), p. 215. The *Assassination Report* identifies him only as the chief of the Operational Support Division of the CIA's Office of Security (p. 74).

46. Among other jobs for the CIA, Maheu had once produced a pornographic film using an actor who looked like Sukarno of Indonesia. The CIA knew that Sukarno had been introduced to a beautiful blonde on a trip to Moscow, presumably by the KGB. Later, the blonde showed up in Djakarta. The idea behind the film was to offer "proof" to the Indonesians that Sukarno was in bed with the Russians. Since they could not obtain genuine proof, they decided to create it. The film itself was never intended to be shown; "We had no assets for doing something like that," a CIA man told me. But it was thought that stills taken from the film would have a convincing graininess. See the *Assassination Report*, p. 74n., and Joseph Burckholder Smith, *op. cit.*, p. 240. Maheu had also managed to scuttle a contract obtained by Aristotle Onassis for the shipment of Saudi Arabian oil.

47. Bissell and Sheffield Edwards briefed both Allen Dulles and General Cabell on the operation in late September 1960, and Dulles *may* have briefed Eisenhower during a 10-minute private meeting of the two men on November 25. *Assassination Report*, p. 112n. It is worth noting here that while Bissell was trying to organize Castro's murder in the fall of 1960, he was also pressing Justin O'Donnell to undertake Lumumba's murder. During the same period, at a meeting of the Special Group on November 3, General Cabell, the Deputy Director of Central Intelligence, who had been briefed on the Maheu-Rosselli plot in September, nevertheless gave Livingston Merchant the "regular spiel" about why the CIA considered assassination foolish, unworkable, and unwise. See Chapter 8 for a description of the meeting. The plotting of assassinations was closely held, in the CIA's term. According to the *Assassination Report*, quoting the Inspector General's Report of 1967, only thirteen people knew about the Castro plot in its early stages. That is a very small figure. In 1971 William Colby asked Howard Osborn

how many people probably knew about the surveillance ordered by Helms on Jack Anderson; the answer was fifty. Assassinations were supposed to be *secret*.

48. Writing in *The Espionage Establishment*, p. 148.

49. *Assassination Report*, p. 80.

50. *Assassination Report*, p. 141. This ought to make it clear that the Kennedys thought the CIA *could* get rid of Castro without overt U.S. intervention.

51. Allen Dulles, *The Craft of Intelligence* (1963), p. 88. One of the enduring mysteries about intelligence officials is their capacity to carry out themselves what they condemn as criminal in others. Allen Dulles once remarked, "There is something about intelligence that seems to get into the blood." Sanche de Gramont, *The Secret War* (1962), p. 132. It certainly got into his; one can watch him dusting his tracks wherever he went. In another section of *The Craft of Intelligence*, for example, he contradicts Henry Stimson, saying, "When the fate of a nation and the lives of its soldiers are at stake, gentlemen do read each other's mail—when they can get their hands on it" (p. 71). But then he adds, as if suddenly alarmed the cat is getting out of the bag, "I am, of course, not speaking here of ordinary mail. . . ." But the CIA *was* reading ordinary mail, some 200,000 letters in all, intercepted in New York. Dulles's entire book might be described as an effort to obscure the importance of political action in "intelligence"; he makes it sound as if only spies were involved, whereas the CIA was never more meddlesome than during his tenure as DCI. He was sticking to the child's history of the world.

52. Hoover's rivalry with the CIA was one of long standing, and he lost no opportunity to discredit the Agency. The *Assassination Report* is filled with needling memos from the FBI about CIA operations. On October 18, 1960, for example, not two weeks before discovery of the Las Vegas tap, Hoover sent Bissell a memo reporting that Giancana was telling friends about his involvement in a plot to kill Castro. *Assassination Report*, p. 79. This should have given Bissell pause, but he went ahead with the plan anyway, a fact which ought to be taken as tacit confirmation of the pressure Bissell felt to "get rid of Castro."

53. This is a pretty intricate understanding, and a good example of how difficult it is to keep these matters straight. Everybody was looking over everybody else's shoulder. It has been suggested that the failure of the Rosselli plot was actually deliberate, that Santos Trafficante, who ran the Cuban end of the operation through old gambling associates, was systematically reporting its details to Castro. (See George Crile, "The Mafia, the CIA, and Castro," Washington *Post*, May 16, 1976.) The web of intrigue which surrounds the American war on Castro is hard to unravel. It seems to me more likely that the Mafia was really trying to do what it had engaged with the CIA to do. Certainly the Giancana conversations overheard by the FBI in October 1960 indicated he thought he was involved in an attempt to kill Castro. The story which Rosselli told his lawyer, Edward Morgan, and which triggered the Inspector General's Report of 1967, indicates that Rosselli acted in good faith too, and there is no question the Mafia hoped to recover gambling casinos seized by Castro. But most important for our purposes here is the fact that the CIA was certainly trying to kill Castro, whatever the motives or ultimate allegiance of its chosen agents.

54. The files of the TSD were filled with compromising material of this sort. One wonders what happened to the files when the transfer of the TSD to the DDS&T actually took place after Helms left office.

55. Cubela had originally wanted to defect, but the CIA managed to persuade him to remain in Cuba as an agent in place.

56. George Crile III, "The Riddle of AM/LASH," Washington *Post*, May 2, 1976.

57. FitzGerald told the Inspector General, and Helms told the Church Committee, that Robert Kennedy had not been informed.

58. The *Assassination Report*, p. 59, says that FitzGerald was present at the November 22 meeting in Paris, but a CIA officer protested to the Committee that actually FitzGerald had been hosting a lunch for foreign intelligence officials in Washington on that date. Book V of the Church Committee's *Final Report*, published later, refers only to CIA "case officers" at the November 22 meeting with Cubela (pp. 67 ff.).

59. *Assassination Report*, p. 89. Some students of the Kennedy assassination have wondered if Cubela was acting the part of an *agent provocateur*, citing, among other things, Castro's public warning on September 7, 1963, that "United States leaders should think that if they are aiding terrorist plans to eliminate Cuban leaders, they themselves will not be safe." Crile, *op. cit.* There seems little doubt that Castro was generally aware of CIA attempts on his life. For one thing, they were an open secret in Miami's Cuban exile community, which was thoroughly penetrated by Castro's agents. One CIA officer involved in the Cubela plot also points out that Cubela did not take the poison pen device when the November 22 meeting ended; an *agent provocateur* would have, since it offered an ideal piece of evidence.

60. *Assassination Report*, p. 89.

61. Not long after I started work on this book, Sam Adams, a former CIA analyst, recommended that I compile a chronology in order to keep things straight. It took months, but the result was a fat document which eventually included thousands of entries. This helped to clarify a lot of otherwise confusing points. For example, when you put together the Kennedys' frustration with a sluggish Mongoose, the chewing-out of Richard Bissell for his failure to get rid of Castro (early fall 1961), National Security Action Memorandum 100, which discussed Castro's assassination (October 5), President Kennedy's remark to Tad Szulc that he was being pushed hard to approve Castro's assassination (November 9), the President's speech that the U.S. would never attempt assassinations (November 16), Bissell's discussion with Harvey about the Mafia plot to kill Castro (the same day), and Kennedy's approval of a stepped-up Mongoose (November 30), you begin to get the drift of what happened. A chronology is a very useful tool. James Angleton thought the Church Committee's reports were a disaster for American intelligence. Asked why, he said, "The detail given away would allow the other side to triangulate and build up a chrono that's very deep."

62. Harvey had passed botulinum toxin pills to Rosselli on April 21.

63. *Assassination Report*, p. 154n.

64. *Ibid.*, p. 184. The Church Committee learned of the Harvey-Bissell

discussion of this point from notes Harvey made at the time, and which had been quoted in the Inspector General's report of 1967. These notes were subsequently destroyed. The Committee's report does not say when, why, or by whom.

65. One exception was Thomas Karamessines, Desmond FitzGerald's successor as DDP under Helms, who said he was "pretty unhappy" about what had happened, and sounded as if he meant it. On one occasion in the late 1960s, a student in a group of college newspaper editors visiting the CIA asked him during a meeting, "Tell me, how many presidents, prime ministers, and kings have you assassinated in the last week?" Karamessines said he was furious. "I don't give a goddamn whether you believe me or not," he said, "but we've never assassinated anyone. And if we did that sort of thing, I wouldn't be working here, or sitting here." He had nothing good to say about that episode in CIA history, but then added: "It didn't happen on Helms's watch." Which, of course, it did.

66. An exception here is Richard Bissell, an uncommonly honest man, after his fashion. The Church Committee found him a tough customer, a hard man from whom to extract a concession, especially on the subject of plans to kill Lumumba, which had not been covered in the IG's report. But in his way he is forthcoming. Probably the truest picture of what happened can be elicited from his testimony by the simple expedient of deleting all the adverbs—the "possiblys" and "probablys" of which he is so fond—and then taking everything which he says "must have," "could have," or "might have" happened as established fact. Read in this way, Bissell's testimony is that Dulles got Eisenhower's okay for the first phase of the Mafia plot, that he briefed Kennedy after Kennedy became President, where he got an approval to carry on. Bissell makes no attempt to explain away what he was doing: the United States was virtually at war with Cuba, killing Castro seemed like a good idea, and that's what he tried to do. He does not appear to regret that he failed, but he does not apologize for the attempt, either.

67. Stress is not always easy to interpret, but here its source seemed to be transparent. Perhaps two examples will help make it clear. One urbane former CIA official, a model of composure and friendly interest during a four- or five-hour interview, abruptly altered when asked who it was, exactly, that told Bissell, okay, do it? He folded his arms tightly across his chest, almost as if hugging himself, drew his feet slightly up off the floor, tilted his head so far back he was facing the ceiling, shut his eyes, and said, "When they went for approval, I can't tell you." He didn't say he didn't know; he said, "I *can't* tell you." His physical posture at that moment was so odd and unexpected, so tense and desperate, I was startled into silence.

Another, similar episode took place during a conversation with a man who had spent his life in CIA, thought most of the memoirs about the Agency were self-serving rubbish, and often considered writing his own, but felt honor and old friendships prevented him from doing so. One afternoon he was talking about Bronson Tweedy, the chief of the DDP's African Division at the time of the plot to kill Lumumba. Tweedy had told both the Church Committee and old friends in CIA that until his memory had been refreshed by incriminating documents he had completely forgotten the episode. This struck me as patently incredible. The CIA man agreed. Helms, Bissell, Tweedy—"the Committee cast some pretty large asparagus at all three of them for these failures of memory," he said. "But I agree with you; it's not possible."

He had not been involved in the Lumumba episode, but he had been very much involved in one aspect of the Castro plots, and he, too, had frequently testified to astonishing lapses of memory. Naturally I asked about his own case. I hadn't been maneuvering up to it; the question simply emerged from our discussion of Tweedy. His reaction was immediate. He grew short of breath—all these years, at least one meeting a week, four or five different subjects, couldn't remember every little discussion of fifteen years before. His breath came in pants; his face went red, then pale; he began to pass his hand over his face, fretfully covering his eyes; he began to gasp. He was displaying the sort of acute distress associated with a heart attack. "Excuse me," he said abruptly. "I've got to get a glass of water." He left the room, and it was many minutes before he returned.

There are certain common elements in both these episodes. There is good reason for thinking both men knew when the orders to kill Castro were given. Both felt it unfair that the CIA had to shoulder all the blame. Both wanted me to know the CIA would never undertake anything like an assassination without a perfectly clear order. And yet both felt that honor (as well as practical apprehension of the consequences) prevented them from telling me what they knew. The result was an acute internal conflict which expressed itself—caught off guard—in dramatic symptoms of psychological stress. This isn't the kind of evidence you can take into a court of law, perhaps, but it certainly had its effect on me. It's probably worth recording here my strong feeling that two men in particular know exactly when the orders were given—Richard Helms and Richard Bissell. The others I've described almost certainly know, too, but Helms and Bissell probably received the orders personally.

68. *Assassination Report*, pp. 123–124.

69. *Ibid.*, p. 157.

70. *Ibid.*, p. 133.

71. Much later this meeting was described to Thomas Karamessines by the Cuba desk officer. Karamessines told me he thought that's when Bissell got an order to kill Castro. The Church Committee also learned of the meeting, but heard it described in somewhat less explicit terms. Bissell told the Committee he did not recall that particular meeting, but agreed that the Kennedys had in fact told him to "get off your ass about Cuba." But they did not tell him to kill Castro, he would not have tried it without "formal and explicit approval," and besides, the entire effort was not really renewed until after he had turned over the DDP to Richard Helms in February 1962. *Ibid.*, p. 141.

72. *Ibid.*, pp. 138–139. The conversations with Smathers and Szulc indicate Kennedy was certainly troubled by the matter, but if he was absolutely clear in his mind that it was wrong it does not seem likely that he would have invited the reaction of two knowledgeable but disinterested outsiders. The fact that Kennedy said he was against it, too, in both instances, should not be taken at face value. Maybe he was against it, but even if he had been for it he probably would not have tried to argue Smathers and Szulc around. When McCone cabled Saigon in October 1963 that he didn't want the U.S. to support an assassination attempt against Diem, Henry Cabot Lodge responded that he was in full agreement. *Ibid.*,

p. 221. When Justin O'Donnell protested an order to kill Lumumba to Helms, Helms responded he thought O'Donnell was "absolutely right." *Ibid.*, p. 39. There seems to be a pattern here.

73. The episode is described in three different sections of the *Assassination Report*: pp. 77–79, pp. 103–104, and pp. 125–134. Briefly, what happened was this: A man hired by Robert Maheu to wiretap a Las Vegas apartment in October 1960 was arrested by local police. Maheu told the FBI the tap was connected to a CIA operation, and Sheffield Edwards subsequently confirmed the story on May 3, 1961. Some months later, however, the FBI discovered that a girlfriend of Giancana's, Judith Exner, had been calling President Kennedy on Giancana's home phone. This was brought to the President's attention and the relationship lapsed, but it apparently helped to retrigger the FBI's interest in the wiretap case, which also involved Giancana, since the Las Vegas tap had been placed on the phone of another Giancana girlfriend, Phyllis McGuire. Hoover insisted that the CIA explain fully why it opposed prosecution. Houston and Sheffield Edwards briefed the Attorney General on the pre–Bay of Pigs plot on May 7, 1962.

74. Houston also said that Kennedy's fears were groundless because Rosselli had told Houston he wouldn't spill the beans to prevent a routine prosecution. "Hell, no, the only thing that would make me tell about the CIA plot to kill Castro would be if they try to extradite me." Which is what happened. When Rosselli told his lawyer about the plot in 1967 he was facing deportation charges, and the charges were still pending at the time of Rosselli's murder.

75. Kennedy was not told that a second phase of the plot was under way—a new batch of pills had been given to Rosselli in April. Houston says that the head of Staff D in the DDP told Edwards that the plot was over, and that Edwards told him the same thing. That, he says, was why a memo sent to the Attorney General on May 14, 1962, made no mention of the ongoing effort. But the memo had been read by both Harvey and Helms, who were in charge of the second phase of the poison-pill plot. Why they sent a deliberately inaccurate memo to the Attorney General is a mystery. The Church Committee pointed out in its report (p. 131) that Kennedy's appointments calendar for May 7 (the day of the Houston-Edwards briefing at 4:00 p.m.) stated "1:00—Richard Helms." The Committee asked Helms if he had met secretly with Kennedy that day to give him the full story before Houston and Edwards arrived with their "official" but incomplete version. Helms said he had not, and if he had he would have remembered it because "I would have been conniving or colluding, and I have no recollection of ever having done anything like that."

76. It ought to be added here that on October 29, 1962, Hoover sent the Attorney General a memorandum about an underworld informant of the FBI who had stated confidently that he could arrange Castro's assassination. Hoover and Kennedy had frequently discussed the CIA's plot at the time of the Houston-Edwards briefing, had agreed that use of the Mafia for such an undertaking was foolish to say the least, but had never condemned assassination as such. Knowing Kennedy's feelings on the subject, Hoover did not hesitate to offer the FBI's good offices where the CIA's had failed. Hoover's memo to Kennedy concluded: "The informant was told that his offer is outside our jurisdiction, which he acknowl-

edged. No commitments were made to him. At this time, we do not plan to further pursue the matter. Our relationship with him has been most carefully guarded and we would feel obligated to handle any recontact of him concerning this matter if such is desired." *Final Report*, Book V, p. 10n.

77. Leo Janis, "The Last Days of the President," *Atlantic*, July 1973. Johnson made the remark to Janis in an interview in 1971.

78. *New York Times*, June 25, 1976.

79. *Assassination Report*, p. 179.

Chapter 10

1. The single greatest fear associated with the CIA, among government officials as well as the public, is that the Agency will slip its moorings and go off on its own. This has never happened in an important way. Even in the case of Laos between 1957 and 1961, sometimes cited as an example of CIA independence, it appears that CIA support for a rightist government in conflict with the State Department's backing for a neutralist regime in fact represented, first, a dispute between Washington and the field, and, second, an instance, one of many, in which the President elected to use the CIA without fully informing the State Department what he was up to. See David Wise and Thomas B. Ross, *The Invisible Government* (1964), chap. 9, and Arthur Schlesinger Jr., *A Thousand Days* (1965), pp. 325 ff. It is important to remember that no Director of Central Intelligence has ever approached the independence of J. Edgar Hoover. Almost all of the DCIs, in fact, lost the confidence of their Presidents and were fired or replaced: Hillenkoetter by Truman, Walter Bedell Smith by Eisenhower, Dulles by Kennedy, McCone and Raborn by Johnson, Helms by Nixon, Colby by Ford, and George Bush by Carter. Presidents have a lot more influence on what the CIA does and says than the other way around.

2. A good account of this struggle, sanitized of the sometimes bruising human conflict involved, can be found in Book IV of the Church Committee's *Final Report* (1976), pp. 74 ff. Not mentioned, for example, is the fact that Herbert Scoville resigned as the CIA's Deputy Director for Science and Technology, having lost a battle in the course of the war, which did not end until 1965.

3. Great bureaucratic battles can sometimes turn on small episodes. One such was the McCone-McNamara battle over the rank of a military representative to the National Intelligence Programs Evaluation (NIPE). McCone wanted a three-star general, who would come with a flag for his office and military aides, and would thus carry a bit of weight. McNamara said the job could be handled by a two-star general. Finally a compromise was reached: McCone would get only a two-star general, but he could have his pick.

4. Schlesinger, *A Thousand Days*, p. 798.

5. Elie Abel, *The Missile Crisis* (Lippincott, 1966), p. 17.

6. An intelligence postmortem showed that of 200 reports of possible missile sightings by agents, only six were in fact reliable; the rest were of SAMs and other military hardware. Herbert Scoville of the DDS&T argued from this fact that the

utility of agents was much overrated, and that scientific intelligence collection methods—in this instance, the U-2—worked best.

7. Abel, *op. cit.*, p. 24.

8. Kennedy sent various CIA officials with copies of the U-2 photos to allied countries so they might see for themselves the threat was a serious one. Sherman Kent accompanied Dean Acheson to visit de Gaulle, for example. R. Jack Smith, later a Deputy Director for Intelligence, went to see Konrad Adenauer in Bonn. At the meeting Adenauer was introduced to "Mr. Smith." The chancellor sighed, shook his head at the ways of intelligence agencies the world over, and said, "Immer Schmidt"—"Always Smith."

9. During Excom meetings McCone was particularly impressed with the ability of Theodore Sorensen; when Sorensen was nominated by Carter to head the CIA, McCone was one of the few old CIA people to support him for the job.

10. McCone's weekly meetings are described—incorrectly—as fact by Anne Karalekas, the author of the Church Committee's institutional history of the CIA. *Final Report*, Book IV, p. 73.

11. R. Harris Smith, *OSS* (1972), pp. 375–376.

12. Much later, one of the generals who had been active in the coup opened a restaurant in Washington. In the spring of 1978 a friend took me to the restaurant and introduced me to General Tran Van Don. We chatted for a few moments. Then my friend happened to mention Lucien Conein's name, and the general pointed to a candle-lit table at the rear of the restaurant. There Conein sat over his dinner, a heavy man with almost platinum-white hair, staring dreamily off into space.

13. The dislike of Hilsman seems to have been general, but his memoir of the Kennedy years, *To Move a Nation* (Doubleday, 1967), makes painful reading alongside the blind, arrogant optimism of many of the official studies included in the Pentagon Papers. Hilsman knew what he was talking about. My own guess is that Hilsman's approach probably wouldn't have worked either, but he seems to have been unusually free of that fascination with American muscle which led Dean Rusk, Robert McNamara, and the U.S. military down the garden path. Rusk once said that when a Great Power like the United States decides to *push*, the other side will damn well *budge*. Helms has said, "After all, strength in this world isn't what it actually is; it's what your enemy thinks it is." Maybe that's the case where missiles are concerned, but in Vietnam Hanoi's strength was what it was, and they were stronger in the ways that counted than we were.

14. Accounts of the coup can be found in John Mecklin, *Mission in Torment* (Doubleday, 1965); Hilsman, *op. cit.*; the *Gravel Edition of the Pentagon Papers* (Beacon Press, 1971); and the Church Committee's *Assassination Report*, pp. 217–223.

15. William Colby actually drafted the cable sent in McCone's name.

16. *Assassination Report*, p. 221.

17. General Maxwell Taylor, *Swords and Plowshares* (Norton, 1972), p. 301.

18. It is impossible to know the true nature of Kennedy's reaction to Diem's murder; the evidence is too fragmentary. But the subject bears some thinking. At

first glance, one might question Kennedy's sincerity. He almost certainly approved an attempt on the life of Castro (just as Eisenhower probably had before him); why react so strongly when the same thing happened to Diem? The answer seems to be that Diem's status as an American ally and client made all the difference. It is one thing to kill an enemy, quite another to kill an inconvenient friend. If the idea behind standing fast in Vietnam was that it would reassure American allies around the world, killing Diem hardly contributed to the cause.

It seems to me that Helms was right; Kennedy didn't understand what he was doing. In the first place, he seemed overconfident as to the ease with which Diem's ouster might be engineered, giving insufficient thought to the inherent violence of any coup. But that was a relatively narrow failure of understanding; much broader was his failure to sense the emotional consequences of the murder of a national leader. The CIA was equally blind, and the officers involved still do not seem to have grasped what makes assassination wrong. The rest of us are in a much better position to weigh this matter as a result of Kennedy's own murder. The shock to the entire country has been incalculable. Even now, more than fifteen years later, the assassination is an open wound. A national leader is not just another man or woman, an individual like any other. To some degree he embodies his whole country, and his murder necessarily inflicts the deepest and most general psychic injury. This is why assassination has a special name, and why it is wrong. The evidence strongly suggests that Kennedy, in his ignorance, tried to do to Cuba what his own murder did to us, and I can't help thinking there was a kind of rough justice in the event. This is a harsh thing to say, but I think Kennedy himself might have agreed. To say that a man who lives by the sword shall die by it does not mean simply that he runs the danger of meeting a more adroit swordsman. It means that he has chosen the world of violence, and has no right to protest when violence chooses him.

19. Lyndon Johnson, *The Vantage Point* (Holt, Rinehart & Winston, 1971), p. 119.

20. This seems to have been the principal official conclusion from the American mistakes in Vietnam, a fact which is bound to cause us trouble in the future. McNamara's strategy of "graduated response" is not likely to be tried again. Next time, watch out.

21. *Gravel Edition of the Pentagon Papers*, Vol. III, pp. 352–353.

22. Johnson, *op. cit.*, p. 140, quoting apparently from a personal memo from McCone on April 28, 1965, the day McCone left office.

23. "We formed the habit of lunching once a week at Harvey's where he demonstrated regularly that overwork was not his only vice. He was one of the thinnest men I have ever met, and one of the biggest eaters. Lucky Jim! . . . Our close association was, I am sure, inspired by genuine friendliness on both sides. But we both had ulterior motives. . . . Who gained most from this complex game I cannot say. But I had one big advantage. I knew what he was doing for CIA and he knew what I was doing for SIS. But the real nature of my interest was something he did not know." Kim Philby, *My Silent War* (1967), pp. 164–165. Philby's brief descriptions of Frank Wisner, William Harvey (whom he calls William J. Howard, and describes falling asleep from too much drink after din-

ner), and other CIA officials are dipped in acid. The portraits are vivid, but Philby's history is unreliable. He suggests at one point, for example, that the CIA might have been responsible for the murder of Stepan Bandura, the Ukrainian leader, even though he must have known that a Russian defector named Bogdan Stashinski had confessed to Bandura's murder in 1961. Perhaps he cannot discredit Stashinski altogether, but even a soupçon of doubt. . . . The world of intelligence is hermetic. Hostile services are constantly sending each other little messages which are extremely difficult for an outsider to read. For example, someone told William R. Corson that Israeli intelligence had detected the activities of Burgess, Maclean, and Philby, and that the CIA and SIS were thus in a position to play them back to the KGB—that is, to use them as conduits for false information. The best one can say for this is that it is not impossible. Maclean was stationed for a time in Cairo, where the Israelis were active and might have uncovered his true allegiance. But it is much more likely that Corson was simply used to send Philby the CIA's equivalent of a valentine. (See Corson, *The Armies of Ignorance* [The Dial Press, 1977], p. 328.) Another such message was sent by Miles Copeland, who remarked that Philby could return home if he liked, a suggestion hardly likely to make life easier for him in Russia. *Without Cloak or Dagger* (Simon & Schuster, 1974), p. 183.

24. Ray Cline, *Secrets, Spies and Scholars* (1976), p. 212.

25. James Angleton was the last hold-out, but as late as 1967 the chief of the Soviet Division in the DDP asked a young case officer how he could be so *sure* the Sino-Soviet enmity was real.

26. This neutrality is a slippery thing. All the DCIs have stuck to it, up to a point, if only because Presidents and their Secretaries of State and Defense are jealous of their role as advocates and arbiters. But on the very broadest issues of national policy—anti-Communism, for example—all have been equally warm. The DCI is on board with the others, and his neutrality is limited to ways and means. The great postwar disasters of American foreign policy, especially those of Cuba and Vietnam, were not the result of mechanical failures—too much of this, not enough of that—but of consensus at the top on a wrong policy. For this reason most of the recent reforms of the intelligence community amount to little more than tinkering. Executive orders against assassination and the subversion of democratically elected governments are a step in the right direction, but the best they can achieve is a limit on egregious excess the next time the policymakers, with the DCI in close harmony, all agree on a mistake.

27. Cline, *op. cit.*, p. 213.

28. Cline's official cover in the post was Special Adviser to the American Embassy. As chief of station in Taipei he had been director of the U.S. Naval Auxiliary Communications Center. These facts come from *Who's Who in America*, 39th Edition, 1976–1977. A fair number of CIA people are listed in *Who's Who*. For example, William Colby, Drexel Godfrey, David Phillips, John Maury, Robert W. Komer, Al Ulmer, Nick Natsios, General Richard G. Stilwell, Russell Jack Smith, John Bross, and Lewis Lapham. I can't quite figure why some are, and some aren't. Chiefs of station usually have foreign service cover, but they aren't all listed.

Chapter 11

1. The Directorate for Intelligence is said to have been especially apprehensive on this point, fearing it would be asked to back up DDP operations with special studies and the like.

2. Book IV, *Final Report* of the Church Committee (1976), p. 66.

3. *Gravel Edition of the Pentagon Papers* (1971).

4. *Pentagon Papers*, vol. 4, p. 65.

5. *Ibid.*, p. 71.

6. As early as 1960 and 1961 North Vietnamese officials were asking foreign visitors how many years of war the Americans wanted. Ten? Twenty? They could have all they liked. See Bernard B. Fall, *The Two Vietnams*, 2d rev. ed. (Praeger, 1967), and Jean Lacouture, *Between Two Truces* (Random House, 1966). The proper time to have gauged North Vietnamese determination was before the bombing began.

7. Helms to McNamara, June 1, 1967, *Pentagon Papers*, vol. 4, p. 12.

8. *Ibid.*, p. 168.

9. *Ibid.*, p. 180.

10. *Ibid.*, p. 188.

11. ". . . the advice of an Intelligence officer will almost always tend to err on the side of prudence." Sir Kenneth Strong, *Men of Intelligence* (Cassell-Giniger, 1970), p. 22.

12. Roger Morris, *Uncertain Greatness* (Harper & Row, 1977), p. 12.

13. A CIA officer who worked with the Meos between 1962 and 1966 told me he developed a deep liking and respect for Vang Pao, and often warned him that he should assume the Americans were going home in three years. But the war simply overwhelmed Vang Pao. The CIA officer, a young Princeton graduate who left the Agency after his years in Laos, said he'd often thought about the fate of the people he'd tried to help. "What has happened to an honorable and likable people . . . ," he said, and hesitated. "It's pretty grim." When he returned from Laos in February 1966, William Colby told him that four years of jumping out of planes was enough: he ought to quit. That convinced him. Then he had a one-hour meeting with Helms, who was interested to hear his impressions of what was going on out there. "What if Vang Pao dies? That sort of thing." Vang Pao left Southeast Asia before the general collapse of April 1975, and as of the spring of 1978 was living in Missoula, Montana.

14. Ben Schemmer, *The Raid* (1976), p. 40.

15. Terror is not supposed to be an American way of war. It was certainly a Vietcong way. If there is a moral question involved here—and there is—it does not so much concern the question of fighting fire with fire as it does the morality of adding American fire to a Vietnamese conflagration. These were American programs, conceived, organized, financed, and run by Americans. The Vietnamese had to be pushed every step of the way, a paradigm of the war as a whole. Without the Americans there would have been no division of the country in 1954, no American client in Saigon, no Tonkin Gulf incidents, no Vietnamese army, no

Counter-Terror Teams, no Phoenix program, no bombing, and no war. CIA was hardly responsible for this long horror; the Agency was only one more doctor on a medical team thinking up heroic measures to preserve life in the moribund.

16. Stewart Alsop, *The Center* (1968), p. 145.

17. For a detailed description of the barrier, see Paul Dickson, *The Electronic Battlefield* (Indiana University Press, 1976), chap. 2; and the *Pentagon Papers*, vol. 4, pp. 112 ff.

18. Frank Snepp describes the long interrogation of a North Vietnamese secret operative captured in Saigon in December 1970, Nguyen Van Thai. Bit by bit, using extreme psychological pressure, the CIA and South Vietnamese slowly extracted from him who he was. Shortly before the collapse of Saigon, in April 1975, Thai, at the suggestion of "a senior CIA official," was flown out over the South China Sea and jettisoned at 10,000 feet. *Decent Interval*, pp. 31 ff.

19. Evan J. Parker, Jr., 1967–1969; John H. Mason, 1969–1970; John S. Tilton, 1971–1972.

20. His predecessor was Nicholas Natsios, chief of station in Saigon from 1956 until Colby's arrival. Natsios, a veteran of CIA operations in Greece (1948–1956), also served as chief of station in Korea (1962–1965), Argentina (1965–1969), the Netherlands (1969–1972), and in Iran under Helms.

21. See Schemmer, *op. cit.*, and Snepp, *op. cit., passim*.

22. 14.3 was the code number for the CIA's annual estimate on Vietnam; 67 referred to the year in which it was issued.

23. A week earlier, on January 23, Helms had delivered his annual briefing to the Senate Foreign Relations Committee, a kind of world roundup. When Carl Marcy of the Committee's staff, one of only two staff members allowed to attend CIA briefings, read about the Tet offensive in the morning's papers he remembered Helms's briefing a week earlier and thought to himself, "Well, goddamn, we didn't hear one thing about that." After the CIA failed to predict the Tet offensive, a postmortem was performed to pinpoint what went wrong; Helms gave the job to the man who had announced there was "nothing of significance to report" four hours after the offensive began—Richard Lehman.

24. "The Outlook in Vietnam," dated February 26, 1968, which predicted heavy losses on both sides without any major change in the overall military situation; "Communist Alternatives in Vietnam," dated February 29, which predicted either steady pressure or a major effort; and a series of responses to questions Clifford had asked, dated March 1, which concluded that "our best estimate is that . . . the overall situation ten months hence will be no better than a standoff." See *Pentagon Papers*, vol. 4, pp. 550 ff. One of Helms's documents cited "a recent high-level defector" as saying that Moscow would not reduce its aid to Hanoi, and that it would fight for access to Haiphong. Helms said the report "conflicts sharply with the present judgment of the intelligence community and is undergoing extremely close scrutiny." But Llewellyn Thompson, the U.S. ambassador to Russia, was reporting the same thing. *Ibid.*, p. 242.

25. The Wise Old Men were Dean Acheson, George Ball, General Omar Bradley, McGeorge Bundy, Arthur Dean, Douglas Dillon, Henry Cabot Lodge, Robert Murphy, General Matthew Ridgway, General Maxwell Taylor, and Cyrus Vance.

26. Sam Adams, "Vietnam Cover-up: Playing War with Numbers," *Harper's*, May 1975. Adams is currently writing a book about his years with the CIA which promises to be the best book ever written about the process of intelligence. It is extraordinarily detailed; but Adams has agreed to submit it to the CIA for clearance on security grounds, and there is some question in my mind if the book will fully survive the process. This account of his war with the numbers is based on his *Harper's* article and my interviews with Adams and a number of other CIA officials.

Chapter 12

1. The fullest account of the Chennault affair is to be found in William Safire, *Before the Fall* (Doubleday, 1975), pp. 88 ff. Safire quotes several memos and letters indicating that Nixon understood what Madame Chennault was up to, but he concludes that there is no evidence Nixon actually attempted to sabotage the Paris agreement.

2. George Christian, *The President Steps Down* (Macmillan, 1970), p. 104.

3. *New York Times*, June 27, 1973.

4. Nixon was hoping to use the charge as a Watergate defense, arguing that other administrations had engaged in political taps too. See J. Anthony Lukas, *Nightmare: The Underside of the Nixon Years* (Viking, 1976), pp. 383 ff.

5. Haldeman got nowhere. Some of the critical papers, he says, had been carted off by Leslie Gelb when he moved from the Defense Department to the Brookings Institution.

6. David Atlee Phillips, *The Night Watch* (1977), p. 223.

7. The heart of the plan was to give Nixon (and Kissinger) authority over the drafting process of papers even before they reached the NSC, the idea being that NSC control over what went into the papers it received would offer control over what came out. Halperin's reorganization is described in Roger Morris, *Uncertain Greatness* (1977), pp. 78 ff.

8. The best-kept secret of intelligence is that more often than not they simply don't know. Sometimes the failure is a mechanical one, as it was in the case of Czechoslovakia, already mentioned, when the CIA simply "lost" certain units of the Russian army in Poland for two weeks during the late summer of 1968. After those units invaded Czechoslovakia the CIA was much embarrassed. In October 1968 the President's Foreign Intelligence Advisory Board called in Helms for an explanation. He told PFIAB that he was not "happy with those two weeks," but that the CIA would have done better "if West Germany had been the target rather than Czechoslovakia." (*Report of the House Select Committee on Intelligence*, published in the *Village Voice*, Feb. 16, 1976, p. 77.) But more often the failure has to do with the inherent difficulty of deciding what someone is going to do, when he may not know himself until the last minute, and when you have no spy in a position to tell you. The principal work of analysts, in fact, is to infer what intelligence agencies don't know.

9. The CIA eventually concluded that Anderson's source was Navy Yeoman Charles E. Radford, who was also passing NSC documents to the Joint Chiefs of

Staff. The episode was exhaustively investigated by the Senate Armed Services Committee. See *Transmittal of Documents from the National Security Council to the Chairman of the Joint Chiefs of Staff*, Parts 1, 2, and 3 (U.S. Government Printing Office, 1974).

10. "It is difficult, if not impossible, for anyone who has not been directly involved with the hidden conflict between rival intelligence bureaucracies to believe how bitter this conflict is, and the extreme forms it may take. . . . In Ankara, Turkey, during World War II, rivalry between two competing Nazi covert intelligence organizations was so bitter that each was turning in or denouncing to the Turkish police the agents of the other. . . . Although the example cited above may appear extreme to the uninitiated, those with experience in this area will recognize it as typical. Anyone who believes that the rivalry between civilian and military intelligence agencies is any less intense today than it was between, say, comparable bureaucracies under the Nazi regime is either remarkably naive or has led a very sheltered bureaucratic life." Paul W. Blackstock, *The Strategy of Subversion*, pp. 106–107. This is the best general discussion I have found of covert political intervention—frank, practical, and unsanctimonious.

11. *New York*, August 16, 1976.

12. Helms says he received no instructions to that effect; the subject simply came up in conversation. In his memoirs Haldeman says that the Russians not only planned to strike China but asked the United States to support the plan. Despite his confusion of certain details—for instance, thinking aerial photos of a tactical rocket called the "Scaleboard" showed stockpiles of nuclear bombs—I suspect that Haldeman was right. See H. R. Haldeman, *The Ends of Power* (Times Books, 1978), pp. 89 ff. The suggestion of a Russian approach to the United States can also be found in John Barron, *KGB* (1974), p. 3.

13. After the raid it was charged that the intelligence failure to spot the removal of the prisoners had been CIA's fault. Helms protested to Fulbright that this wasn't true, the operation had been under military control from start to finish (which was true), and Fulbright defended the Agency against the charges. But at times the CIA was coy with the military about their own agents and operations in the area. An excellent account of the raid can be found in Ben Schemmer, *The Raid* (1976).

14. The balance of terror rests on what Robert McNamara called mutual assured destruction, referred to by an eerily appropriate acronym as MAD. The idea is that all-out spasm war is extremely unlikely so long as both sides know they will be destroyed in the process. Hence peace depends on precariousness, and anything which tends to protect one side—ABM systems, for example—makes war more likely.

15. This whole subject is interesting and complicated. A good account of the first stage of the talks, with passing references to the SS-9 controversy, can be found in John Newhouse, *Cold Dawn: The Story of SALT* (Holt, Rinehart & Winston, 1973).

16. "We believe that the Soviets recognize the enormous difficulties of any attempt to achieve strategic superiority of such order as to significantly alter the strategic balance. Consequently, we consider it highly unlikely that they will attempt within the period of this estimate to achieve a first-strike capability, i.e., a

capability to launch a surprise attack against the U.S. with assurance that the USSR would not itself receive damage it would regard as unacceptable. For one thing, the Soviets would almost certainly conclude that the cost of such an undertaking along with all their other military commitments would be prohibitive. More important, they almost certainly would consider it impossible to develop and deploy the combination of offensive and defensive forces necessary to counter successfully the various elements of U.S. strategic attack forces. Finally, even if such a project were economically and technically feasible the Soviets almost certainly would calculate that the U.S. would detect and match or overmatch their efforts." *Foreign and Military Intelligence*, Book I of the Church Committee's *Final Report* (1976), p. 78. The paragraph was tacked back onto the estimate as a footnote by the State Department's representative at a meeting of the United States Intelligence Board. When Helms testified before the Church Committee on this episode he dismissed the controversy as a tempest in a teapot, said he had been willing to leave the question of motives up to Laird on this point, and added that in any event USIB paper was the DCI's paper, he signed it, and he could strike something out if he thought it a good idea at the time. One man who knew Helms well said this sort of thing should occasion no surprise; no man could rise high in a bureaucratic job without knowing when it was time to compromise his views; this, clearly, was one of those times. Helms stood fast on the characteristics of the SS-9, but gave in on the inherently pulpier question of what the Soviets were up to, which was what Kissinger and Laird were really interested in all along. As things turned out, Kissinger got his ABM—by one vote in the Senate—and as a direct result won a SALT agreement on limiting ABMs. It's a complicated world.

17. The CIA's failure to predict Hanoi's offensive was not an isolated error. Perhaps the most interesting thing I discovered about the Agency, in fact, is the probability that it would fail to predict even a major attack upon the United States if some other country should ever decide to launch one. This is a notable weakness in an intelligence organization which was founded largely in response to the American failure to foresee the Japanese attack on Pearl Harbor, and not, as is sometimes suggested, in order to mobilize for the Cold War. We shall assume, for the sake of argument, that Russia has decided, in a time of crisis, that this is the moment we've all been dreading: they're going to attack. I take it as a given that the CIA would have no spy in a position to tell us positively and definitively that the decision had been reached. Not even Oleg Penkovskiy, the best agent the CIA ever recruited inside Russia, was in a position to inform us that Khrushchev had decided to put missiles into Cuba in the summer and early fall of 1962. The same goes for listening devices and code-breaking capabilities. CIA people may smile mysteriously when asked about assets inside the Kremlin, but mystery is their stock in trade. The truth is the CIA does not have any assets which would give explicit warning of a Russian decision to attack the United States.

The question, therefore, would be handed over to the analysts, whose job is to figure things out in the absence of positive knowledge. The analysts have two principal tests for judging a hypothesis about what someone is going to do: Is there a precedent? And does it make sense? These are entirely reasonable questions. Faced with the problem of what someone is going to do, it is natural to ask if Possibility A—in this case, a nuclear assault on the United States—is the sort of thing he has done in the past, just as it is natural to ask if he might reasonably expect to gain anything from it. In our case the answer to both questions must be no. The Russians have certainly never launched a nuclear attack on the United States, or even seemed close to the verge of doing so, and indeed have been characteristically wary of war in the past. Would it be reasonable for them to do so? Of course not. They would be all but obliterated in response. What could they possibly gain commensurate with what they would lose? It's out of the question. Hence the analysts would predict no attack.

This is not an idle observation. There is plenty of evidence to back it up. Over the years the analysts have proved themselves good at divining the truth in situations where nations act in an accustomed manner for reasonable ends. But on at least four separate occasions the CIA has failed to anticipate military offensives precisely because they were unprecedented and didn't make sense: before the Cuban missile crisis in 1962 (when Sherman Kent and the BNE twice predicted that no offensive missiles would be placed in Cuba because Khrushchev had never done anything so provocative before, and stood to gain nothing commensurate with the risk); before the Tet offensive in 1968 (during a period of such relative quiet the CIA didn't even know the question ought to be asked); before the North Vietnamese invasion of South Vietnam in March 1972; and before the Arab-Israeli war of October 1973 (when the analysts argued explicitly that the Arabs had never attacked in such a manner before, and that it didn't make sense because they couldn't hope to win). The pattern is the same in all four cases: no spy, no precedent, no reasonable hope of gain—and the wrong answer. It is hard to escape the conclusion that if surprise offers an advantage in nuclear war, it's there for the taking.

18. C. L. Sulzberger, *Diary with a Chinese Postscript* (1974), pp. 69–70.

19. The fight over Sihanoukville provides a good example of the gap between the worlds of the insiders and the outsiders. At one time the intelligence community was all but obsessed with the Sihanoukville question, but there was hardly a peep about the controversy in the press.

20. One of the CIA's first positive indications that Hanoi intended to wage a war in the South was discovery that it had established the 559 Transportation Group—May 1959—to reactivate the Ho Chi Minh Trail. CIA people found it hard to take seriously the public debate over whether the war was a local insurgency in the South because it knew Hanoi was actively engaged in the war, just as we were.

21. The Office of National Estimates was the support staff of the Board of National Estimates, until William Colby abolished both and established a new system of National Intelligence Officers responsible for estimates about the world's various regions.

22. *Foreign and Military Intelligence*, p. 80. The language is interesting. Helms was telling Smith to attempt to get the various analytical components of the CIA to agree on the paper's conclusions, but not to water it down just for the sake of agreement, as often happened in the estimating process. In short, keep the maybe–could be–would be's to a minimum.

23. This was the CIA's estimate of almost every American initiative throughout the war: everything works, but nothing works enough.

24. *Foreign and Military Intelligence*, p. 80. June 1, 1970, was the date by which Nixon later publicly promised to withdraw all American forces from Cambodia.

25. Proctor replaced R. Jack Smith as DDI, and was later appointed chief of station in London.

26. William Watt was one of a number of National Security Council staff members who resigned in protest of the invasion of Cambodia. When he called up high government officials he'd worked with to say goodbye he found it hard to get past their secretaries, until he came to Helms, who invited him to lunch. Watt considered this a characteristic sign of graciousness on Helms's part. It is easy to collect stories of this sort about Helms; people did not often know him well, but they liked him.

Chapter 13

1. There were four of these, one each on the House and Senate Armed Services and Appropriations Committees. None met regularly, kept its own records, had its own staff, or carried out its role either aggressively or skeptically. All seem to have conceived of their job as protecting and defending the Agency. They often explicitly declined to be informed of "sensitive" operations or projects, and DCIs from Dulles forward tended to entertain them with "dog and pony shows"—briefings heavy on spookish gadgetry, huge blow-ups of Russian missiles stamped "TOP SECRET," spy stories, and the like. The serious contacts between the CIA and the Congress tended to be with individual members, and their relationship was one less of oversight than of quiet cooperation.

2. These documents had a strange history. They were first delivered to Fulbright on the Senate Foreign Relations Committee on September 24, 1970, by Warren Unna, a Washington journalist. Fulbright called Helms to ask what was going on, but otherwise did nothing. The same batch of documents was also given to *Time* magazine, which likewise ignored them, and to the columnist Charles Bartlett, who mined them for an attack on Allende. Helms thinks it was the same batch of documents which provided Church's subcommittee on multinationals with all of its ammunition at the hearing where Helms testified on March 6, 1973. See Washington *Post*, Nov. 13, 1977; and Victor Marchetti and John Marks, *The CIA and the Cult of Intelligence*, pp. 330–331.

3. One reporter who cooperated with the CIA and lived to regret it was Sam Jaffe, an ABC television correspondent. When his connection to the CIA became public he was more or less blacklisted by network television. See Robert Friedman, "The Reporter Who Came In from the Cold," *More*, March 1977.

4. This is apparently characteristic of CIA operations abroad, partly because Russian Embassy staffs offer the richest recruiting ground for agents, mostly because it is the Soviet-American struggle for power which dominates U.S. policy and the preoccupations of the CIA. During the Church Committee hearings Senator Philip Hart asked David Phillips, a former chief of the DDP's Western

Hemisphere Division, "Are we picking on the small countries?" Phillips answered, "Senator, it has been my experience that throughout this time there is one country that's not a small country, and that most of the covert action, direct or indirect, even though it's done in a third country, is proposed and approved and executed within the framework of our conflict with the Soviet Union." (Vol. 7 of the Church Committee hearings, *Covert Action*, p. 90.) When the CIA was criticized for failing to predict the Libyan coup of 1967, some Agency people blamed James Angleton because the local CIA officers in Tripoli were all out chasing Russians on counterintelligence missions.

5. One of whom was later involved in the Green Beret murder case in Vietnam. See Chapter 8, note 10. The CIA's file on Guevara, started by David Phillips in Guatemala after the ouster of Arbenz in 1954, had grown fat by 1967, but most of the recent additions were rumor and surmise. After Guevara disappeared from Cuba in the spring of 1965, one school of thought held that he had been murdered by Castro. Rumors of his presence in the Congo were not confirmed until after he was gone, and he was said to have appeared in an astonishing range of places around the world, including New York City. When Thomas Karamessines delivered a report in the late spring of 1967 that Guevara was in Bolivia, Helms was openly skeptical. "Oh, really? How many times does this make?" But later that summer Guevara's presence was confirmed through captured documents and other means, and a Cuban communications specialist working for the CIA, Julio Gabriel Garcia, was with the Bolivian group which captured and killed him. The CIA presence was reported at the time, and it was assumed that Guevara's death was the Agency's doing. Every source agrees, however, that Garcia, the CIA station chief in La Paz, and Langley all argued against his execution. In the end the Bolivian President, René Barrientos, decided that Guevara dead would be less trouble than Guevara alive and the inevitable object of a worldwide clemency campaign. Garcia sent the CIA a long, admiring account of Guevara's last hours. For a summary, see Marchetti and Marks, *op. cit.*, pp. 138 ff.

6. Previously called the Special Committee, its name was changed after publication of the Wise-Ross book *The Invisible Government* in 1965, and then changed again in February 1970 to the 40 Committee. Despite its frequent name changes the group has always had substantially the same membership and method of operation.

7. Korry's cables were characteristically long, definite in tone, and energetic in language. At the CIA they were referred to as "Korrygrams." One man who read a lot of them said they "always began with a bang, and never ended with a whimper."

8. Hendrix, a former Miami reporter who won a Pulitzer Prize in 1963 for his account of the Cuban missile crisis, reported to have been heavily based on information provided by the CIA (as is my own book), was a "public relations" employee of ITT. Far from being a routine writer of press releases, however, Hendrix was something in the way of being a secret operative for the company.

9. Roger Morris, *Uncertain Greatness* (1977), p. 241. In Kissinger's view the Chileans were "irresponsible" because the center and right declined to submerge their differences in a joint campaign for one candidate to oppose Allende.

This, of course, was to put the American view of things ahead of the Chileans'. As Korry never tired of saying, 60 percent of the Chilean electorate—that is, the combined supporters of Allende and Radomiro Tomic, the Christian Democratic candidate—opposed the right. To expect a Tomic-Alessandri alliance was to misread Chile, which was why Korry was willing to oppose Allende, but against support for Alessandri. Kissinger's remark was deleted from Victor Marchetti and John Marks's heavily censored account of the Chilean episode in *The CIA and the Cult of Intelligence*, pp. 38 ff., in addition to 70 other lines in 10 separate passages. These cut the heart from the story eventually revealed in part by the Church Committee two years later.

10. If any of the candidates were to win an absolute majority that would be that, but under the Chilean constitution the Congress had the right to choose between the two top vote winners in the event no one won a clear majority. By custom, however, the Congress in the past had always voted to confirm the candidate who came in first.

11. It is, of course, entirely possible that Helms informed Kisssinger of what the CIA was doing and that Kissinger approved it as a way of getting around State Department objections without a lot of argument. But since Kissinger and McCone were both angry at Helms later for botching the anti-Allende campaign, it is hard to know either what happened or for whom, exactly, Helms was working. Given the enigma of Nixon, it is possible that even Helms did not know. In this episode, as in so many others, just about everybody wanted *something* done, but wanted somebody else to do it.

12. Helms insisted later he had warned them in plenty of time to gear up for a major effort, a claim supported by the record. But he has also implied that he warned Nixon and Kissinger that Allende was going to win. It is my distinct impression that CIA was complacent on this point, convinced by its poll that Alessandri was going to win.

13. Edward Korry, "The Sell-Out of Chile and the American Taxpayer," *Penthouse*, March 1978.

14. Korry thought there was a pretty good chance of this. The heart of his objection to the Church Committee's investigation was that it presented a selective, partisan, anti-Nixon "morality fable in which American officials were all Nazi-like bully boys cuffing around decent Social Democrats." (*Covert Action*, p. 33.) The CIA's estimators for the most part took a calm view of Allende's regime—far calmer than the one pictured in the Agency's propaganda—while Kissinger insisted, in a background briefing on September 16, 1970, that Allende portended the death of Chilean democracy. Chilean views were mixed. Ultraleftists, whose provocative programs kept Allende in a state of near-constant political crisis, thought he was too timid. So did Castro, who urged Allende to seal his revolution in blood. The Christian Democrats were worried, but expected to win the next election. The right was convinced the end was at hand. In a situation where local opinion was so divided, it seems presumptuous of the United States to have decided what was really going on. In any event, the regime which ousted Allende did all that had been feared of him, and more.

15. *Assassination Report*, p. 230.

16. *Ibid*. Was it Helms who named the Rube Goldberg gambit? It is a tiny

irony that Helms attended an honorary dinner for the eighty-seven-year-old cartoonist following the opening of a show of his work at Washington's Museum of History and Technology on November 24, 1970, just one month after Allende's confirmation.

17. It was not Korry who told me Heckscher's name. That he declined to do, saying he didn't think it fair. I eventually figured it out through a chain of inference too long to go into here, but when I finally got the answer during an interview with a CIA officer I instinctively burst out, "Then it was Henry Heckscher!" This embarrassed the man I was talking to, and made him worry that now Heckscher was going to blame *him*. Finding out details of this sort can be an extraordinarily tedious process.

18. The CIA, without Korry's knowledge, had contacted General Marshall in the last week of September, but concluded he was one of those men with glittering eyes who are too unstable—because too passionately committed—to serve as allies. When Heckscher told Korry who was behind the bombings in Santiago he failed to mention the Agency's contacts with the man. Korry then passed the information on to the Frei government, without telling Heckscher. Thus Marshall's contact with the CIA in late September 1970 led directly to his arrest on October 17, 1970. Betrayal, in one form or another, is at the very heart of the world of intelligence.

19. Not the first mention of such a possibility. Korry says that a West European ambassador to Chile had asked him directly if the CIA could arrange for Allende's assassination. The Church Committee investigated various assassination attempts made on Allende without finding any U.S. involvement. Thomas Karamessines, in the thick of coup plotting in Washington, said that at no time did Kissinger or Nixon ever so much as mention such a possibility.

20. Washington *Post*, January 10, 1977.

21. Helms was off on a trip to Vietnam, Thailand, Laos, and Japan with George Carver. He was out of the country from October 7 until October 21.

22. Especially one by Senator Clifford Case, who had learned of the so-called Huston plan—Case did not know it by that name—and who asked Helms if the CIA had played a role. Helms set something of a record for narrowness of answer with a response which certainly sounded like "no." Later, he explained that his "no" was simply intended to deny any CIA involvement in domestic spying by the *Army*. The question can be found on p. 43 of the Senate's confirmation hearings, and Helms's later "clarification" at a hearing on January 22, 1975, *CIA Foreign and Domestic Activities* (U.S. Government Printing Office, 1975), p. 18.

23. Helms was still trying to keep the cork in, but his effort did not work for long. Church's subcommittee on multinationals was about to reveal something of the first level of the CIA's Chilean operation in 1970, the CIA's support for an anti-Allende spoiling operation. After the story emerged, Helms was called back to Washington by the Foreign Relations Committee to explain his earlier denials. One of the first things he did after his arrival was to see Symington on Sunday, May 20, 1973, so he might explain his precise meaning three months earlier, when he had answered Symington with a flat no, instead of yes, but.

Helms was scheduled to testify before the Foreign Relations Committee the following day. Symington wasn't angry with him and suggested that Helms request the hearing to be held in public rather than in executive session, so that Helms could in effect speak for himself rather than depend on the Senators' version of his remarks afterward. Helms was reluctant to risk this; once Senators got into a hearing they could ask anything they had a sweet mind to. So Symington proposed they visit the home of Senator Henry Jackson, one of Symington's colleagues on the CIA oversight committee, and ask his advice. Jackson agreed with Symington: better to hold the session in public and face the Senators' wandering inquiries than to answer to Foreign Relations Committee staff members, who might have done their homework. Helms finally said okay, and then called Fulbright to request the change. Afterward Symington left for an engagement and Helms stayed on for dinner at the Jacksons'.

Three years later, while Jackson was running for President in 1976, the story of their meeting leaked in a way that made it appear Jackson, Symington, and Helms had been working out the details of Helms's testimony. Jackson did not appreciate the implication or the publicity. He called Helms and asked what the hell was going on. Helms said the story certainly didn't come from him. (Reasonable enough: by that time Helms was facing a serious threat of criminal prosecution for his answers to Symington's three questions.) "Oh," said Jackson, "it's Stuart, I guess." Helms and Symington both deny any attempt to orchestrate Helms's testimony on Chile on February 7, 1973; Helms had asked for the meeting on Sunday, May 20, 1973, precisely in order to apologize for having "misled" Symington.

Some of Helms's friends later claimed there had been an element of collusion between the two men, trying to help Helms out of his legal difficulties by suggesting he couldn't have "lied" to Symington, because Symington knew the truth. It was also said that Kissinger had explicitly instructed Helms in what to say. These helpful comments were made while the Justice Department was still considering perjury charges against Helms, and were transparently intended to alarm the Justice Department about the messy consequences of an indictment, an effect they doubtless had. I think the truth was simpler: Helms did not need permission or prodding to give the answers so many others would call lies. Evading such questions was part of his job.

24. Colby's testimony had been read by another member of Congress, Representative Michael Harrington, a critic of the CIA, who exercised a neglected right of Congressmen to read the testimony before any committee. Helms had avoided just such problems by asking the official stenographer to stop recording his remarks when he described secret operations. Colby had neglected this precaution. Before Harrington was given Colby's transcript, however, he had to sign a secrecy waiver. Later, he wrote a letter describing Colby's testimony to the chairman of the House Foreign Affairs Committee, Representative Thomas Morgan, whence it was promptly leaked to Seymour Hersh of the *New York Times*, which published an outline of the testimony on September 8, 1974. Colby denied then and later that he had used the term "destabilization," claiming that the CIA's efforts were intended only to sustain the anti-Allende forces until the 1976 election. See David Atlee Phillips, *The Night Watch* (1977), pp. 252 ff.

25. One reason for his exclusion had been the CIA's frank claim that Korry

could never be talked into going along, to which Nixon's response had been okay, don't tell him. This was unusual, but not unprecedented. CIA operations had also been kept secret from ambassadors in Burma in 1952 (under Truman), and in Indonesia in 1958 (under Eisenhower).

26. Kendall was a member of the Business Council—not to be confused with the Business Council on Latin America—which had been created by Averell Harriman and which met with Washington officials, including Helms, at regular intervals throughout the year.

27. *New York Times*, May 26, 1977. Pretty thin bread for a pretty thick sandwich. Nixon gave a somewhat different answer to the Senate Select Committee: "There was a great deal of concern expressed in 1964 and again in 1970 by neighboring South American countries that if Mr. Allende were elected President, Chile would quickly become a haven for Communist operatives who could infiltrate and undermine independent governments throughout South America." *New York Times*, March 12, 1976.

28. Morris, *op. cit.*, p. 242.

29. *Assassination Report*, p. 228.

30. *Covert Action*, p. 92.

31. Cable of September 23, 1970: "Bear in mind that parameter of action is exceedingly narrow and available options are quite limited and relatively simple." Cable of October 1: "Feel necessary to caution against any false optimism. It is essential that we not become victims of our own propaganda." Cable of October 7: "Urge you do not convey impression that Station has surefire method of halting, let alone triggering coup attempts." *Assassination Report*, p. 239.

32. *Ibid.*, p. 242.

33. Karamessines described this meeting to the Church Committee but said he could not remember exactly when it had taken place—only that it was sometime between October 10 and October 22, when Helms was out of Washington. It has been suggested that the Nixon-Kissinger claim they called a halt on October 15 was simply an attempt to escape responsibility for the murder of Schneider on October 22, but there is evidence to support them: (1) Korry saw Nixon on October 13, and the 40 Committee on October 14; (2) Nixon ordered Karamessines to drop Viaux on October 15; (3) C. L. Sulzberger was told that Korry had personally quashed a projected coup in Chile. What Nixon and Kissinger may have failed to realize was the fact it is easier to get the CIA moving than to halt it. A kind of local inertia gets under way, and things grind steadily forward after the policymakers have shifted their attention elsewhere.

34. The officer was one of four sent to Chile early in October under the guise of "third-country nationals"—in other words, as something other than Chileans or Americans. They were intended to beef up the local station, to take over contact with Viaux from Colonel Wimert, and to further ensure secrecy of the whole operation by the fact they were "clean"—that is, unknown to local security officials and other interested parties. The local CIA officers were by this time "dirty"—well known for what they were.

35. These had been sent to the Santiago station via diplomatic pouch on October 19.

36. After the shooting of Schneider, the machine guns were returned to the CIA, which "deep-sixed" them.

37. Valenzuela was sentenced to three years of exile in June 1972. Viaux was sentenced to twenty years in prison and five years of exile.

38. Viaux was promised $20,000 and $250,000 in life insurance; Valenzuela was promised $50,000.

39. *Assassination Report*, p. 246.

40. *CIA Foreign and Domestic Activities*, p. 13.

Chapter 14

1. *The White House Transcripts* (Viking, 1974), p. 63.

2. "Yes, you won by—what was it, 61, 62 percent?—the biggest majority anyone ever won by. That would have been the time for you to clean house." Lady Bird Johnson, *A White House Diary* (1970), p. 734.

3. H. R. Haldeman, *The Ends of Power* (1978), pp. 171 ff. Haldeman quotes from transcripts which were not made public by Nixon.

4. *Ibid.*

5. The details of Helms's firing by Nixon and his appointment as ambassador to Iran were not easy to establish. Helms has consistently refused to discuss it at length on the grounds that it was a privileged conversation with the President. The following typical exchange on the subject took place at a hearing of the Senate Foreign Relations Committee on May 21, 1973, after Helms had been recalled from Iran:

SENATOR PERCY: Do you have anything you would like to say with respect to your own belief as to why you suddenly left the CIA after many years of distinguished service? Was there a request by you to take an ambassadorial post or did you have a desire to leave the Agency?

MR. HELMS: I do not know how I can answer that question without repeating the entire conversation that the President and I had.

SENATOR PERCY: I think that should be a privileged conversation. (*Nomination of Richard Helms to Be Ambassador to Iran and CIA International and Domestic Activities* [1974], p. 74.)

In an interview with David Frost on May 22, 1978, Helms added that at the Camp David meeting Nixon offered him a job as ambassador somewhere, and that he—Helms—suggested Iran, but said he wanted to think it over. I also discussed the subject with Helms at some length, and with several of his friends. Neither Haldeman nor Nixon mentions it in his memoirs. Colby told me that no one at the CIA knew why Helms had been summoned to Camp David, unless it was to discuss the budget. In his memoirs, General Vernon Walters describes the look on Helms's face after he returned. *Silent Missions* (1978), p. 604.

6. Perhaps the last friendly book by an outsider was Sanche de Gramont's *The Secret War* (1962), which emphasized the "threat"—that is, the actions of hostile intelligence services in the Soviet bloc. Since then Americans have been more preoccupied with what we're doing to them than with what they're doing to us.

7. Within the Agency the Wise-Ross book was ridiculed by Sherman Kent in a review published in a house magazine called *Studies in Intelligence*. Who is in this so-called invisible government? he asked. Not Fu Manchu or Professor Moriarty, it turns out, but the Undersecretary of State for Political Affairs, the Deputy Secretary of Defense, the Deputy Director of Central Intelligence, the President's Adviser on National Security Affairs. These, of course, were the members of the Special Group. But the Agency took the book seriously, and managed to persuade *Time*'s bureau chief in Washington to abandon plans for a cover story on it.

8. This would normally have been a routine matter, but Kleindienst was the target of questions about presidential pressure to drop an antitrust case against ITT.

9. And is still there now.

10. A good account of this adventure, based on interviews with the climbers, can be found in Howard Kohn's article, "The Nanda Devi Caper," *Outside*, May 1978.

11. *Report of the Rockefeller Commission*, p. 134.

12. Colby thinks Helms deliberately placed it there for reasons of internal secrecy. The group in the Office of Security was disbanded in late 1968 after the Washington metropolitan police created their own internal security division, but the Special Operations Group (SOG) grew steadily, eventually including a staff of 52 who opened subject files on 7,200 individual Americans and 6,000 political organizations. In all, more than 300,000 names of people and groups found their way into the 13,000 subject files. In October 1969, SOG began to recruit agents for operations abroad; in the course of training three of them also reported on New Left and black militant groups in the United States. The operation was finally closed down in March 1974, under William Colby. See the *Report of the Rockefeller Commission, passim*, and J. Anthony Lukas, *Nightmare: The Underside of the Nixon Years*, pp. 38–40. The Special Operations Group was run by Richard Ober, the CIA officer Helms had assigned to handle the Agency's inhouse investigation at the time of the National Student Association flap in February 1967. That was the base of his expertise in domestic radical movements.

13. *Report of the Rockefeller Commission*, p. 133.

14. Representatives of Students for a Democratic Society (SDS), for example, traveled to Hanoi in 1965, met with North Vietnamese officials in Bratislava, Czechoslovakia, in the summer of 1968, and met with Cuban and North Vietnamese officials in Havana in the summer of 1970. In the mind of a man like Hoover, this would establish a sinister pattern. The SDS's explanation was not sinister but simple: Of course we go to see the North Vietnamese; we're on their side.

15. Huston, an admirer of Thomas Jefferson and Alexander Hamilton, justified his domestic intelligence program as a prudent attempt to head off a much more severe reaction later on. He was handling domestic intelligence matters for the White House as early as June 1969, when he requested and obtained yet another CIA study of dissidents, this one entitled "Foreign Communist Support to Revolutionary Protest Movements in the United States." Like its predecessors, the study concluded that there wasn't any.

16. These proposals came initially from the Office of Security, which drew up a plan called "Project 1" for penetrating domestic groups. It was rejected by Helms in March 1968 and replaced by "Project 2" for the domestic training of agents who would then be used abroad.

17. *Report of the Rockefeller Commission*, p. 136. But the doubts persisted. In 1970 the Management Advisory Group, made up of fourteen mid-level CIA officers, criticized Chaos and was reassured by Helms it had been properly authorized. Another memorandum defending the program was distributed by Helms on December 5, 1972, two weeks after Nixon had fired him, in response to a critical revew of Chaos by William Colby, then the Agency's Executive Director/Comptroller.

18. David Wise, *The American Police State* (1976), p. 265. Wise gives a good account of what is known about the Riha affair on pp. 258–273.

19. *Report of the Rockefeller Commission*, p. 123.

20. Wise, *op. cit.*, p. 271.

21. The CIA had been checking, and later opening, mail between Russia and the United States since 1952. In 1958 the FBI discovered the program when it approached the Post Office with a proposal for a mail-opening program of its own; thereafter it shared the CIA's take. There is no evidence that Presidents Truman, Eisenhower, or Kennedy were ever informed of the mail openings, although Dulles and Helms briefed two Postmasters General, in 1954 and in 1961. Helms says that he also personally informed President Johnson of the program on May 10, 1967, when he reported on the CIA Inspector General's investigation of CIA assassination plots. According to Helms, Johnson warned him not to get caught. They didn't, until William Colby revealed the program to Seymour Hersh of the *New York Times* in December 1974, allegedly as a means of engineering Angleton's retirement. Nixon apparently did not know about the mail-opening program at the time of Huston's report. If Nixon had asked about it, Helms presumably would have told him, but he was not about to confide the secrets to a low-level White House staffer like Tom Charles Huston. Later, in June 1971, Helms discussed the program with Attorney General John Mitchell. There is a lesson for Presidents in this: if they want to know what their intelligence agencies are up to, they had better send a known confidant of recognized power, or better yet, go themselves.

Less than two weeks after Helms's departure from the CIA in February 1973, the mail-opening program was halted by the new Director, James Schlesinger, against the protests of Angleton but presumably with the support of William Colby, who was shortly to replace Karamessines as Deputy Director for Operations—the DDP having been renamed as one of Schlesinger's first acts as DCI. See the *Report of the Rockefeller Commission*, pp. 101–115, and Edward Jay Epstein, *Legend: the Secret World of Lee Harvey Oswald* (Reader's Digest Press–McGraw Hill, 1978), p. 272. Epstein's book, incidentally, is the best description in print of counterintelligence operations by the CIA.

22. The IEC staff met on 117 separate occasions between January 29, 1971, and May 4, 1973. The group was formally disbanded in July 1973 by Assistant Attorney General Henry Petersen. See the *Report of the Rockefeller Commission*, pp. 116–129. On November 9, 1977, Sullivan was killed in a hunting accident

near his home in Sugar Hill, New Hampshire. It has been suggested there was more to Sullivan's death than met the eye. An excellent report by Jeff Goldberg and Harvey Yazijian, "The Death of 'Crazy Billy" Sullivan," *New Times*, July 24, 1978, establishes pretty clearly—to me, at any rate—that Sullivan's death was entirely accidental.

23. Helms interview with David Frost on May 22, 1978, p. 112 of the complete transcript.

24. Question has been raised about Helms's account of when he first learned of the Watergate break-in. A freelance writer named Andrew St. George, a man with at least some connection to intelligence circles, claimed that Helms was informed by a CIA "watch officer," not Howard Osborn, and that the conversation had gone like this:

HELMS: Ah, well. They finally did it.

WATCH OFFICER: It's a pity about McCord and some of those guys.

HELMS: Well, yes. A pity about the President, too, you know. They really blew it. The sad thing is, we all think, that's the end of it, and it may be just the beginning of something worse. If the White House tries to ring me through central, don't switch it out here, just tell them you reported McCord's arrest already and I was *very* surprised. (Lukas, *op. cit.*, p. 285.)

This strikes me as being utterly unlikely. The first rule of intelligence security is compartmentalization: the greater the secret, the fewer in the know. The last person to be in the know would be a routine watch officer, and yet St. George suggests Helms would casually discuss a secret of this magnitude with such a figure. In addition, the tone is all wrong. The watch officer was reporting the bungling of an operation in which the CIA's involvement was transparent. The roles of McCord, Martinez, and Hunt in the Watergate break-in have caused the CIA generally, and Helms personally, endless trouble. Helms seems to have anticipated exactly such trouble from the very beginning. This was a disaster of the first magnitude, but St. George makes Helms sound as if he thought it a matter of no consequence. Finally, the White House did not call Helms about the break-in until Friday, June 23, 1972, six days after the arrests, and the reason it called him then has been established in abundant detail.

A second account of when Helms first learned about the Watergate break-in was provided by Carl Rowan in a newspaper column published in the Washington *Star-News*, May 11, 1973. Rowan said he had met Helms and his wife Cynthia at a movie screening a couple of days after the break-in, that they discussed the case in a casual way, and that Helms said, "Cynthia and I had been up late and had just fallen asleep when they telephoned me to tell me that these fellows had been arrested in the Watergate." Rowan took this to mean that Helms had been up late on Friday night, June 16, and that he was called in the wee hours of Saturday, June 17—that is, within an hour or two of the arrests. This would suggest the CIA learned of the arrests from some other source than the FBI or the Washington police. Hunt, of course, was on the loose after the arrests that Saturday morning, and *could* have called someone in the CIA. Helms was frequently questioned on this point during the Watergate investigations; he and Howard Osborn, the man who phoned him, both testified repeatedly that the call was made at about nine thirty or ten o'clock in the evening, on Saturday, June 17, about eighteen hours after the arrests. Neither Hunt nor anyone in the CIA has ever testified to anything else, so the matter must rest there.

25. Hunt's name was also found on a personal check for $6.36 made out to the Rockville, Maryland, Country Club, which he inadvertently left behind the night of the break-in.

26. Percy read these remarks into the record at Helms's public testimony before the Senate Foreign Relations Committee on May 21, 1973. Since the CIA by custom retains the transcripts of all congressional briefings, Percy must have asked the Agency for the June 20, 1972, transcript to see what it was Helms had said.

27. Specifically, what were the burglars after? Almost every observer finds it hard to grasp their motive in tapping Larry O'Brien's phone at the DNC, an office he rarely used. Some writers have suggested the tappers wanted to learn what O'Brien knew about Nixon's relationship to Howard Hughes, and in particular if he had known about the $100,000 which Hughes had contributed to Nixon through Bebe Rebozo, who held the money in his own safe deposit box. Haldeman suggests that Nixon asked Colson to find out, and that Colson, in turn, gave the job to Hunt and Liddy. Colson denies it. The Hughes theory merely wraps a mystery inside an enigma, further complicating the puzzle. There is no question the break-in grew out of plans for a Republican intelligence-gathering effort, and that it was unhappiness with the results of an earlier tap which led to the June 17 attempt. The target makes sense if you assume Hunt and Liddy thought the DNC was where the secrets were, or at least enough secrets to satisfy John Mitchell.

28. David Atlee Phillips, *The Night Watch* (1977), p. 88n.

29. CIA stations have two sorts of American personnel, those with "inside" jobs who are formally attached to the Embassy under State Department cover, and who deal more or less openly with the local intelligence services; and those with "outside" jobs under commercial or other civilian cover, who have no overt connection to the U.S. government and may or may not be known to the local intelligence service. The outside officers remain nominally under the authority of the local ambassador, but are once removed.

30. Mullen at one point claimed that Helms and the CIA had put pressure on him to hire Hunt; later he reversed himself and said nothing of the sort had happened. No evidence has turned up to indicate Mullen's initial claim was correct. Mullen & Company had a tangential role with the CIA through provision of cover for agents working abroad, principally in Scandinavia. Hunt's covert security clearance was maintained after he left the Agency so that he might handle cover arrangements in Mullen's absence, something he seems to have undertaken on only two occasions. Helms says he did not know Mullen personally, and that he did not even know Mullen & Company was being used for cover until some time after the break-in, when publicity surrounding Hunt's connection with the firm brought an end to the relationship. See *Report of the Rockefeller Commission*, pp. 173 ff.

31. Lukas, *op. cit.*, p. 109. Ehrlichman's remarks were transcribed by Cushman's secretary, listening in on a "dead key." The offices of Helms and Cushman were both fitted with taping systems which could be turned on by either man whenever he wanted to record a general conversation in his office or a

discussion over the phone. Since February 1971, the President's office and phone were also connected to recording systems, but in Nixon's case the systems were automatic and recorded everything. A tape transcript of Cushman's conversation with Hunt on July 22, 1971, was destroyed in January 1973, at a time when Helms did not consider it to have anything to do with "Watergate"—that is, with the break-in per se. A copy of the transcript was later discovered, however. So far as I know, none of Nixon's recorded conversations from the preburglary period has been made public, with the exception of fragments from a meeting between Helms and Nixon in October 1971, to be discussed below. When these are eventually released they will presumably establish just how closely Nixon followed the work of his "plumbers," and whether or not he knew of their switch to intelligence gathering for CREEP after the beginning of 1972. Whatever may have been on tapes made in Helms's office is, for the most part, lost forever.

32. Lukas, *op. cit.*, p. 110.

33. *Ibid.*, p. 124.

34. "Backstopping" identification means arranging for its verification if someone should check it out.

35. *Report of the Rockefeller Commission*, p. 180.

36. *Ibid.*

37. Why the Lebanon file was included is not known, since the landing occurred before Kennedy took office. It may have been on the list simply to disguise the anti-Kennedy thrust of the request as a whole. Ehrlichman says he browsed through all the files but found the one on Lebanon the most fascinating for the extreme care Eisenhower had taken with "downfield blocking"—clearing things in advance with Britain and France. He discussed the landings with Nixon, who fell into a reminiscent mood, describing the National Security Council meetings on the episode at length. The other files did not seem to stick in Ehrlichman's mind with the same vividness. Helms does not remember any Lebanese file.

38. Haldeman, *op. cit.*, pp. 25–26.

39. *Report of the Rockefeller Commission* (pp. 190 ff.) says the White House called in Helms, but both Helms and Ehrlichman agree that it was Helms who insisted on the meeting. The *Report* also says that Helms gave some of the files to Ehrlichman on October 1, refusing to hand over only the Diem file. Helms says he held on to all the files until his meeting with Nixon. Ehrlichman does not remember whether Helms surrendered any of the files on October 1 or not. Helms told the Rockefeller Commission that there must be a tape of his meeting with Nixon on October 8, since it had apparently been quoted by Walter Pincus in a *New Republic* article, "The Duping of Richard Helms," published in the issue of February 15, 1975. For obvious reasons, however, the Commission—which had been appointed by Nixon's successor, Gerald Ford—elected to ignore the tape and to depend instead on a CIA memorandum of the meeting written by Helms. The Commission criticized Helms for surrendering the files, and recommended that future DCIs be figures from outside the government who would have sufficient authority to resist such requests. Helms condemns this conclusion as thoroughly unfair, asking how any DCI could properly refuse a President access to files which were, in fact, his.

40. Nixon did not request either the IG report on the Bay of Pigs written by

Lyman Kirkpatrick or the 1967 IG report on assassinations. Helms says Nixon did not know of the existence of either document.

41. The three documents, as well as the one on Lebanon which Ehrlichman remembered so clearly, are presumably still somewhere among Nixon's impounded papers.

42. This was part of Hunt's effort to discredit Ellsberg. After the CIA's first psychological profile of Ellsberg seemed too thin for Hunt's purposes, he suggested that the FBI or the Secret Service steal the files which Ellsberg's psychiatrist, Dr. Lewis J. Fielding, had refused to surrender voluntarily to the FBI. Liddy told Hunt that was out of the question; Hoover had banned black bag jobs back in 1966. So Hunt proposed that he recruit some old CIA contract officers in Miami, and do the job himself. Egil Krogh drew up a plan, Ehrlichman approved it, and on September 3, 1971, Hunt, Gordon Liddy, and three Cubans burglarized Fielding's office, apparently without finding what they were looking for.

43. Wise, *op cit.*, p. 236.

44. William Colby, *Honorable Men*, p. 321.

45. Wise, *op. cit.*, p. 249.

46. One possible exception to this policy occurred on Monday, June 19, 1972, the same day Helms and his principal deputies and aides met to discuss Watergate for the first time. On that day a CIA contract officer named Lee R. Pennington, Jr., who worked for Howard Osborn on a $250-a-month retainer, went to McCord's house and helped McCord's wife to burn McCord's files. According to Pennington, he then called Osborn to report what he had done, but the CIA and Pennington both insisted later that he had been acting on his own; McCord was a friend and Pennington was only trying to help. Whether this is true I do not know. There is no question, however, that the CIA attempted to hide its connection to Pennington. When the FBI asked Osborn for a report on "Pennington" in August 1972, the Bureau was given a description of one *Cecil* Pennington. The Agency's relationship to the correct Pennington did not become known until January 1974, when an officer working for the CIA's Inspector General went through the files of the Office of Security. Osborn wanted to lift Pennington's file before the IG could get to it, but two men working for Osborn insisted it be left where it was. See Wise, *op. cit.*, pp. 255–256. This is the only known post-break-in contact between the CIA and any of the Watergate burglary team, and the evidence is sufficient only to establish it as a contact once removed. But even if Osborn, or both Osborn and Helms, authorized the episode, it does not really alter our view of what happened thereafter. Helms, and the Agency at his direction, were trying to get out of the way.

47. After the interview Nixon said the U.S. could not tolerate Castro's regime. For some reason General Walters does not mention this interview in his memoirs, *Silent Missions*.

48. Lukas, *op. cit.*, p. 312.

49. This, of course, would have been a disaster. It was tough enough trying to convince the public that five men inside the Democratic National Committee headquarters, including the chief of security for CREEP, in fact had nothing to do with CREEP. Once the burglars' money was traced to CREEP, the Committee would have to insist on something more incredible still—that CREEP had given

$100,000 or more to the burglars without knowing what the money was for. One amazing aspect of the whole episode is that CREEP's hollow denials stood up for as long as they did. John Dean thoroughly deserved the congratulations which Nixon gave him in September 1972, when it became clear there would be only seven defendants—the five burglars, plus Hunt and Liddy.

50. Haldeman, *op. cit.*, p. 31.

51. *Ibid.*, pp. 24–25. At that early date Nixon could have learned of the Bay of Pigs "connection"—Howard Hunt—from only one source: Chuck Colson, who had recruited Hunt for the "plumbers."

52. The transcript of the June 23, 1972, conversation was finally released on August 5, 1974, just four days before Nixon resigned. Nixon later claimed (in March 1976) that he had been thinking of the legal support the administration had provided for the CIA in its effort to block publication of the Marchetti book. Helms says he does not know what the President had in mind; the only favor he could remember was a Nixon offer to let him use Camp David one weekend, an offer Helms declined.

53. Lukas, *op. cit.*, pp. 313–314. The phrase "for the good of the country" comes from Haldeman's version of Nixon's remark (*op. cit.*, p. 33).

54. *Ibid.*

55. Walters described the meeting at some length in a memo for his files written on June 28, 1972, following three successive meetings with John Dean on June 26, 27, and 28. By that time it was abundantly clear this episode was a potential minefield. Helms himself preserved no memo of the conversation. Haldeman's version of the meeting can be found in *The Ends of Power*, pp. 37–38. See also Lukas, *op. cit.*, p. 314.

56. Walters's memo, quoted in Lukas, *ibid.*, p. 314.

57. Haldeman, *op. cit.*, p. 38. Helms told David Frost he didn't shout. Helms's voice does not often run away with him, but it happens occasionally, and I think this must have been one of those times. Walters's memo makes no mention of Haldeman's remark about the Bay of Pigs, but Helms described it during an appearance before the Senate Foreign Relations Committee on May 21, 1973. "Mr. Haldeman made some incoherent remark about the investigation running into the Bay of Pigs and I said I was not concerned about the Bay of Pigs, that was years before, and I had no interest or concern about it any further." (*Nomination of Richard Helms . . .* , p. 85.) By Haldeman's own account, he did not understand Nixon's reference to the Bay of Pigs at the time, and still does not understand it now. In his memoirs he speculates that "Nixon might have been reminding Helms" of the CIA's attempts on Castro's life, which the CIA had never reported to the Warren Commission, and which "may" have triggered a successful Castro attempt to kill Kennedy. "It's possible," Haldeman says, that Nixon knew of the CIA plots from William Sullivan of the FBI (*op. cit.*, pp. 39–40). That strikes me as pretty heavy use of the conditional tense. It's apparent that Nixon was aware of Hunt's role in the Bay of Pigs, something he presumably learned from Chuck Colson, but there is no evidence Nixon knew about the assassination plots, and Hunt's book about the Bay of Pigs, *Give Us This Day*, indicates he did not know about them either. Helms told me specifically that Nixon did not know of the 1967 IG investigation of the plots. I think it more

likely that "the whole Bay of Pigs thing" was intended as a crude threat by Nixon which worked initially but backfired in the long run.

58. Lukas, *op. cit.*, pp. 314–315. In his testimony on May 21, 1973, Helms recalled his words slightly differently: "I told him that I thought that he should limit his remarks to Director Gray to saying if any investigations in Mexico run into CIA operations that in keeping with the delimitation agreement between the CIA and the FBI that he simply notify us that this had occurred." (*Nomination of Richard Helms . . .*, p. 85.) Nixon wanted Walters to tell Gray to halt the investigation, which Walters agreed to do, and in fact did do. Helms wanted him to see Gray as directed, but to stop short of asking specifically for a halt in the investigation. In this way the CIA might follow the President's orders without assuming responsibility for a halt in the investigation. Helms, clearly, was walking a fine line. He understood perfectly well why Nixon wanted the investigation halted, not in detail, perhaps, but in general. His main concern was not whether Nixon would be successful or not, but to ensure that the CIA did not have to do the dirty work.

59. Walters, *op. cit.*, p. 589.

60. Haldeman's guess that Gray was looking for a way to be "helpful" seems to have been right. Manuel Ogario was a Mexican, but how could an interview of Kenneth Dahlberg have compromised the CIA? Dahlberg was a Midwestern businessman, but Gray halted his interview anyway. In for a penny, in for a pound.

61. Leon Jaworski, *The Right and the Power* (Reader's Digest Press, 1976), p. 258.

62. This charge has never been satisfactorily cleared up.

63. Lukas, *op. cit.*, p. 317. The protective coloring of this memo is transparent. Helms was not going out on a limb to say the FBI's investigation *would* intrude onto CIA territory, only that it *might*.

64. Helms says the trip had been long scheduled and was entirely routine; no DCI had ever been to that part of the world before.

65. There was no phone-taping system at San Clemente, so this call was not recorded. Gray reconstructed it from memory. Lukas, *op. cit.*, p. 318.

66. Wise, *op. cit.*, p. 249.

67. *Ibid.*, p. 250.

68. *Ibid.*, p. 251. Colby had known it was Ehrlichman who called because a transcript of Cushman's recorded conversation with Hunt said so. Cushman finally admitted it in public on May 11, 1973, saying he had recently discovered the minutes of a meeting with Helms in which he had reported the call. On February 4, 1974, Karl Wagner said he had discovered the actual notes made of the conversation, as recorded by Cushman's secretary. But of course they all knew from the beginning it was Ehrlichman who made the call asking the CIA to help Hunt. Keeping Ehrlichman's name out of it was an attempt to accommodate the White House, and to continue to hide the CIA's aid for Hunt on matters which were "sensitive"—that is, potentially explosive—but unrelated to the Watergate break-in itself.

69. Wise, *op. cit.*, p. 255, and Lukas, *op. cit.*, p. 361. McCord was sending the letters to an old friend in the Office of Security, Paul F. Gaynor.

70. Simon & Schuster, 1976.

Chapter 15

1. Schlesinger annexed a private conference room, known as the French Room, which had separated the DCI's office from the DDCI's.

2. Maury had been chief of the Soviet Division in the early 1960s before moving to Athens as chief of station, where he remained until after the colonels' coup in April 1967. An excellent account of his tenure in Greece, and of the CIA in that country generally, can be found in Lawrence Stern, *The Wrong Horse* (Times Books, 1977).

3. Nixon's men, Haldeman, Ehrlichman, and Dean, had tried to involve the CIA in the cover-up in the two weeks immediately following the break-in, with a limited success. The copies of McCord's letters being forwarded to the CIA indicated the attempt was continuing. The CIA's role in Watergate is going to be a subject of debate for the rest of time, at least partly because Nixon and other White House figures continue to suggest that Watergate was somehow the CIA's doing. When Haldeman's memoirs were published early in 1978, Nixon's former aide Herb Klein called Helms to say he was planning to review the book for his old newspaper, the San Diego *Union*, and to ask Helms if there was any truth in Haldeman's broad hints of a CIA role in the burglary. Helms, of course, said there was not, and Klein said he had not taken the charge seriously anyway. He had been in the White House for several months after the break-in, and he did not remember Haldeman, Ehrlichman, or Colson ever suggesting a CIA connection at the time. That was evidently a later invention. It seems to me that there are three reasons to discount the charges: (1) The claims are entirely consistent with Nixon's effort in June 1972 somehow to involve the CIA in the cover-up. At that time the White House wanted practical help in turning off the FBI and in raising money for the burglars. The attempt now is more ambitious, to blame the break-in directly on the CIA. (2) The evidence for CIA responsibility is entirely circumstantial and thin. The most that could plausibly be squeezed out of it is that the CIA knew more about Hunt's activities than it has let on. But there is quite a jump from knowing about Hunt's activities to directing them. (3) The evidence for White House and CREEP responsibility for the break-in is detailed and well established. Many of those involved have confessed to their role, and Nixon's part in the cover-up is thoroughly recorded on the White House tapes. The emphasis on finding a "smoking gun" during the preimpeachment inquiry is an indication of how solid the evidence had to be before the House of Representatives would act, not of its ambiguity. The fullest accounts of the CIA's role in Watergate are to be found in J. Anthony Lukas, *Nightmare: The Underside of the Nixon Years* (1976), *passim*, and David Wise, *The American Police State* (1976), chap. 7. Both writers speculate that the CIA may have known more than it has confessed, always a pretty safe guess where the CIA is concerned, but with all the diligence in the world, they have failed to establish anything more than a tangential CIA role, and an attempt to hide the CIA's help for Hunt. Watergate was Nixon's doing.

4. *Nomination of Richard Helms to Be Ambassador to Iran and CIA International and Domestic Activities* (1974), pp. 1–2.

5. During that same speech, delivered on April 14, Helms said, "And may I

emphasize at this point that the Statute [that is, the National Security Act of 1947] specifically forbids the CIA to have any police, subpoena or law-enforcement powers, or any domestic security functions. . . . We do not have any such powers and functions; we have never sought any; we do not exercise any. In short, we do not target on American citizens." The text of Helms's speech, entitled "Global Intelligence," can be found in *Vital Speeches*, May 15, 1971.

6. *Nomination of Richard Helms . . .* , p. 26.

7. *Ibid.*, p. 43.

8. Ray Cline describes the press conference, but not Russell's objections, in *Secrets, Spies and Scholars* (1976), pp. 204 ff.

9. Colby held a similar press conference, the same thing happened, and he abandoned the practice as well.

10. Victor Marchetti and John Marks, *The CIA and the Cult of Intelligence* (1974), pp. 328–329.

11. Karamessines had announced his resignation on the same day Helms announced his, December 22, 1972. Karamessines left on March 1, 1973, a few days after the DDP was officially renamed the DDO, with the result that he was both the last DDP and the first DDO. He died in retirement in 1978.

12. The devotion to secrecy in these procedures can be carried to great lengths. One example: the recruiting of Russian spies is obviously given a high priority by the CIA, and operations are closely monitored from Langley. After the pitch is finally made, the result is cabled to Langley. The answer is almost always the same: We failed. Later, another cable is dispatched by secret channels describing in detail what really happened. Colby is said to have considered this sort of precaution excessive and unnecessary.

13. William Colby, *Honorable Men* (1978), p. 332.

14. Counterintelligence is wearing work, demanding a prodigious memory, patience, great psychological sensitivity, and the capacity to live with uncertainty forever. The best account of a counterintelligence case is to be found in Edward Jay Epstein's book about Lee Harvey Oswald, *Legend* (1978). Epstein clearly was fascinated by the CIA's difficulties in deciding whether or not Yuri Nosenko was a genuine defector. Epstein comes down on the side of skepticism, perhaps because his informants all seem to have been partisans of Angleton, as well as suspicious of Nosenko, and of the men who finally accepted Nosenko as a genuine defector. But the argument is clearly stated, and the inherent difficulty of assessment convincingly evoked. A fictional portrait of Angleton can be found in Aaron Latham's novel *Orchids for Mother* (Little, Brown, 1977). Best is the description of Angleton's methods of interrogation.

15. Leon Uris described this episode in fictional terms in his novel *Topaz*. A factually vague but interesting account can also be found in P. L. Thyraud de Vosjoli, *Lamia* (Little, Brown, 1970). De Vosjoli was the French SEDECE's liaison in Washington for several years in the early 1960s, and he is credited by some CIA people with having provided first-rate intelligence on Cuba at the time of the missile crisis. Others dispute the claim. He does not mention Angleton's name, but the two men are said to have been close.

16. Samuel Johnson once insisted to Boswell of the ease in taking a skeptic's position. "If a man were now to deny that there is salt upon the table, you could

not reduce him to an absurdity. I deny that Canada is taken, and I can support my assertion with pretty good arguments. The French are a much more numerous people than we; and it is not likely that they would allow us to take it. — 'But the Ministry tell us so.' — True. But the Ministry have put us to an enormous expense, and it is their interest to persuade us that we have got something for our money. — 'But we are told so by thousands of men who were at the taking of it.' — Ay, but these men have still more interest in deceiving us. They don't want you should think they have gone a fool's errand; and they don't want you should think the French have beat them, but that they have beat the French. Now suppose you should go over and see if it is so, that would only satisfy yourself; for when you come home, we will not believe you. We will say you have been bribed. — Yet, for all these plausible objections, we believe that Canada is really ours. Such is the weight of common testimony." *Boswell's London Journal* (McGraw-Hill, 1950), pp. 301–302.

17. I once called Angleton for an interview shortly before noon on a spring day and was told by one of his children that he was still asleep, because he had been up all night making jewelry.

18. Henry Knoche, the DDCI after both Angleton and Colby were gone and the Agency was being run by Stansfield Turner, told old friends bleakly, "We have no counterintelligence now." For a lot of CIA people this made about as much sense as walking barefoot through a snake farm.

19. Lukas, *op. cit.*, p. 449.

20. There is a chronological discrepancy here which I cannot explain. In his memoirs Colby claims he first learned of the break-in from a newspaper account he read while in Bangkok in early May 1973 (*op. cit.*, p. 337). Vernon Walters was also on a trip to the Far East at that time; he says he was ordered back to the CIA by a cable from Schlesinger which arrived in Taipei on May 8 or 9 (*Silent Missions*, [1978], p. 605). Helms says he first learned of it from a story in the *International Herald Tribune*, which he read on a trip to Shiraz, Iran, on May 13, 1973 (*Nomination of Richard Helms . . .* , p. 64). The Fielding break-in was revealed in open court by Judge Byrne on April 27, 1973. Houston seems to think Colby first learned of the break-in the day Houston talked to Henry Petersen.

21. Colby, *op. cit.*, p. 338.

22. In his memoirs Colby says this was Schlesinger's idea, and in one sense, of course, it was; without his signature it could not exist. But I was pretty clearly told by two men working closely with Colby at the time that it was his idea, that the order was written by him, and that he insisted on personally handling the results. It would be a minor point, if Colby's responsibility for the May 9 directive were not taken by many old CIA people as one of the two major counts in the general indictment charging him with wrecking the Agency. Colby later argued that it was not the "bad secrets" themselves that were wrecking the Agency, but their piecemeal revelation, and the suspicions they fed of yet more horrors to come. By the time of the Church Committee investigation in 1975, Colby said, things had gone too far to be righted by a whitewash.

23. The attempt to kill Lumumba had not been investigated by the CIA in 1967, apparently because Johnson had not thought to include his name when he asked for a report from Helms. Where Castro, Diem, and Trujillo were concerned

the Church Committee had a relatively easy time of it, once F. A. O. Schwarz, Jr., realized that Colby was referring to a CIA study of some sort and demanded a copy of it. Lumumba was more difficult; according to Church Committee staff members, every document required painful extraction.

24. Colby, *op. cit.*, p. 311.

25. "It has recently again been alleged in the press that CIA engages in assassination. As you are well aware, this is not the case, and Agency policy has long been clear on this issue. To underline it, however, I direct that no such activity or operation be undertaken, assisted or suggested by any of our personnel. . . ." *Assassination Report*, p. 282. Colby issued a similar order under his own name on August 29, 1973.

26. David Atlee Phillips describes the scene in his memoirs, *The Night Watch* (1977), pp. 264–266. One of Angleton's objections to the *Report of the Rockefeller Commission* was that it had reduced a long "threat assessment" to a single paragraph.

27. Colby, *op. cit.*, pp. 394–395.

28. Daniel Schorr, *Clearing the Air* (Houghton Mifflin, 1977), pp. 143–144.

29. *Ibid.*, p. 144. Colby also describes the encounter, more briefly, in *op. cit.*, pp. 409–410.

30. Schorr, *op. cit.*, p. 160. Schorr's account of his encounter with Helms is described on pp. 147–148.

Chapter 16

1. No one in the CIA seems to have considered any other response. Larry Houston describes writing the most blistering memo of his career after he learned what had happened, but once that was out of the way he secretly arranged for a pension to be paid to the widow of the man who killed himself, Dr. Frank Olson. Houston's job was often that of clearing up the debris of CIA disasters. When some CIA contract pilots were killed at the Bay of Pigs he handled that too, and was pleasantly surprised when the secrecy of his arrangements proved durable. His job was not to keep the CIA out of trouble, but to get it out of trouble after it had got into it. When Houston asked Angleton why he had never been consulted about the mail-opening program, Angleton told him, "We only went to you when we had a problem, and we didn't have a problem."

2. That is, Helms authorized men working for him to attempt it, and no one has been able to establish that anyone above Helms ever told him to proceed. John McCone, the Director at the time, professes he knew nothing about it, and Helms did not contradict him, just as he made no claim that either of the Kennedys told him to do it either.

3. *Assassination Report* (1975), p. 106n.

4. On February 19, 1971, the CIA, with the aid of local police who served as lookouts, broke into a photographic studio in Fairfax, Virginia, in order to check on a CIA employee suspected of stealing documents.

5. One was Scott Breckinridge, the deputy Inspector General; I have not been able to learn the name of the third man.

6. When I first began to work on this book (before the charges against

Helms had been resolved), a number of his friends told me that his testimony had been cleared by the White House, and that Nixon, Kissinger, former officials of the CIA, and several Senators would be implicated in a more general conspiracy to keep these matters secret before the courts were finished with the case. Helms told me (after the charges had been settled) that this wasn't true, and that he had not asked anyone to tell me or anyone else anything different. In his Senate testimony he had been trying to tell the literal truth without giving the game away, but he had not rehearsed his testimony with the White House, ITT officials, John McCone, or anyone else, and he did not threaten "to bring down Kissinger," as had been charged. He said he did not know why I had been told the opposite, unless it was from the desire of friends to help out by suggesting he was only a good soldier carrying out orders. Helms said he was the one charged with keeping the secrets, and he did not need to ask anyone how he ought to testify. I'm not quite sure how to resolve this contradiction, if indeed there is a contradiction. I was told that Nixon, Kissinger, and a few others had better *watch out* if Helms were indicted. I was told that Williams made it clear to the Justice Department the defense would be vigorously conducted, if it came to that. Helms said he did not threaten to bring anyone down. Perhaps there is no contradiction, and Helms did not have to threaten a mess, because there already was a mess.

7. The other two were potential cases against FBI agents for illegal wiretaps and burglaries, and the investigation of South Korean influence-buying in Washington.

8. No relation to the CIA official of the same name.

9. The crime was perjury. It was suggested in a number of news stories during this period (by Joe Trento in the Wilmington, Delaware, *Sunday News Journal* of December 19, 1976, and by Seymour Hersh in the *New York Times* of December 23, 1976) that the Justice Department was also gathering evidence to support a charge of conspiracy to commit perjury. What that evidence might have been has never been revealed. Helms says he does not know anything about it, and that he was never threatened with indictment for conspiracy as well as perjury.

10. The statement also charged Helms with failing to answer questions before the Church subcommittee on multinationals on March 6, 1973, "fully and completely"—dropping the word "accurately." In that instance, evidently, the Justice Department did not think it had quite such a good case.

11. This is pure hyperbole, with no basis in fact. Helms himself never made any such claim, although he did say he was reluctant to reveal the CIA operations against Allende while Allende was still in power. Williams was apparently just carried away by the moment. Helms, of course, might easily have avoided lying to the Senate without threatening anybody's life. It was not lives Helms was protecting, but the secret of American intervention in Chile.

12. Within a year, however, Helms's business was to be reduced to a trickle by the Iranian revolution, which caught him completely by surprise.

Bibliography

The literature on spies is enormous, and much of it is of uncertain reliability. The books listed here by no means exhaust the subject, but they include all the recent memoirs of former CIA officers, as well as other accounts I found especially useful.

Elie Abel, *The Missile Crisis* (Lippincott, 1966).

Dean Acheson, *Present at the Creation* (Norton, 1969).

Philip Agee, *Inside the Company: CIA Diary* (Stonehill, 1975).

John M. Allison, *Ambassador from the Prairie* (Houghton Mifflin, 1973).

Stewart Alsop, *The Center* (Harper & Row, 1968).

John Barron, *KGB* (Reader's Digest Press, 1974).

Louise Bernikow, *Abel* (Trident Press, 1970).

Paul W. Blackstock, *The Strategy of Subversion* (Quadrangle, 1964).

Douglas Blaufarb, *The Counter-Insurgency Era* (Free Press, 1977).

Ben C. Bradlee, *Conversations with Kennedy* (Norton, 1975).

Clyde W. Burleson, *The Jennifer Project* (Prentice-Hall, 1977).

George Christian, *The President Steps Down* (Macmillan, 1970).

Ray Cline, *Secrets, Spies and Scholars* (Acropolis, 1976).

William Colby, *Honorable Men* (Simon & Schuster, 1978).

E. H. Cookridge, *Gehlen: Spy of the Century* (Random House, 1971).

Miles Copeland, *The Game of Nations* (Simon & Schuster, 1969).

————, *Without Cloak or Dagger* (Simon & Schuster, 1974).

William R. Corson, *The Armies of Ignorance* (Dial, 1977).

Richard Deacon, *A History of the Russian Secret Service* (Taplinger, 1972).

Sanche de Gramont, *The Secret War* (Putnam's, 1962).

Peer de Silva, *Sub Rosa: The CIA and the Uses of Intelligence* (Times Books, 1978).

Paul Dickson, *The Electronic Battlefield* (Indiana University Press, 1976).

Herbert S. Dinnerstein, *The Making of a Missile Crisis* (Johns Hopkins University Press, 1976).

Allen Welsh Dulles, *The Craft of Intelligence* (Harper and Row, 1963).

Francis Dvornik, *Origins of Intelligence Services* (Rutgers University Press, 1974).

Edward Jay Epstein, *Legend: The Secret World of Lee Harvey Oswald* (Reader's Digest Press, 1978).

Rowland Evans and Robert Novak, *Nixon in the White House* (Random House, 1971).

"Christopher Felix," *A Short Course in the Secret War* (Dutton, 1963).

Thomas M. Franck and Edward Weisband, eds., *Secrecy and Foreign Policy* (Oxford, 1974).

Peter Geismar, *Fanon* (Dial, 1971).

Gravel Edition of the Pentagon Papers (Beacon Press, 1971).

H. R. Haldeman, *The Ends of Power* (Times Books, 1978).

Roger Hilsman, *To Move a Nation* (Doubleday, 1967).

Heinz Höhne and Hermann Zolling, *The General Was a Spy* (Coward, McCann & Geoghegan, 1972).

E. Howard Hunt, *Give Us This Day* (Arlington House, 1973).
————, *Undercover* (Berkley-Putnam's, 1974).

Leon Jaworski, *The Right and the Power* (Reader's Digest Press, 1977).

Haynes Johnson, *The Bay of Pigs* (Norton, 1962).

Lady Bird Johnson, *A White House Diary* (Holt, Rinehart & Winston, 1970).

Lyndon Baines Johnson, *The Vantage Point* (Holt, Rinehart & Winston, 1971).

Bernard Kalb and Marvin Kalb, *Kissinger* (Little, Brown, 1974).

Robert F. Kennedy, *Thirteen Days* (Norton, 1969).

Lyman B. Kirkpatrick, Jr., *The Real CIA* (Macmillan, 1968).

Maj. Gen. Edward G. Lansdale, *In the Midst of Wars* (Harper and Row, 1972).

Flora Lewis, *The Red Pawn* (Doubleday, 1965).

J. Anthony Lukas, *Nightmare: The Underside of the Nixon Years* (Viking, 1976).

Victor Marchetti and John D. Marks, *The CIA and the Cult of Intelligence* (Alfred A. Knopf, 1974).

J. C. Masterman, *The Double Cross System* (Yale University Press, 1972).

Patrick J. McGarvey, *CIA: The Myth and the Madness* (Dutton, 1972).

John Mecklin, *Mission in Torment* (Doubleday, 1965).

Anthony Mockler, *The Mercenaries* (Macmillan, 1969).

Roger Morris, *Uncertain Greatness* (Harper and Row, 1977).

Robert Moss, *Chile's Marxist Experiment* (David and Charles, 1973).

John Newhouse, *Cold Dawn: The Story of SALT* (Holt, Rinehart & Winston, 1973).

North American Congress on Latin America, *Guatemala* (1974).

Bruce Page, David Leitch, and Philip Knightly, *The Philby Conspiracy* (Doubleday, 1968).

Kim Philby, *My Silent War* (Grove Press, 1968).

David Atlee Phillips, *The Night Watch* (Atheneum, 1976).

Sylvia Press, *The Care of Devils* (Beacon Press, 1958).

L. Fletcher Prouty, *The Secret Team* (Prentice-Hall, 1973).

Harry Howe Ransom, *The Intelligence Establishment* (Harvard University Press, 1970).

Harry Rositzke, *The CIA's Secret Operations* (Reader's Digest Press, 1977).

Ben Schemmer, *The Raid* (Harper and Row, 1976).

Arthur Schlesinger, Jr., *Robert Kennedy and His Times* (Houghton Mifflin, 1978).
————, *A Thousand Days* (Houghton Mifflin, 1965).

Daniel Schorr, *Clearing the Air* (Houghton Mifflin, 1977).

Peter Dale Scott, Paul L. Hoch, and Russell Stetler, eds., *The Assassinations* (Vintage, 1976).

Patrick Seale and Maureen McConville, *Philby: The Long Road to Moscow* (Simon & Schuster, 1973).

Senate Foreign Relations Committee, *Hearing on CIA Foreign and Domestic Activities* (U.S. Government Printing Office, 1975).
————, *Hearing on the Nomination of Richard Helms as Ambassador to Iran* (U.S. Government Printing Office, 1974).

Senate Select Committee on Government Operations with Respect to Intelligence Activities, *Alleged Assassination Plots Involving Foreign Leaders* (U.S. Government Printing Office, 1975).
————, *Covert Action Report* (U.S. Government Printing Office, 1975).
————, *Hearings* and *Final Report* (U.S. Government Printing Office, 1976).

Colin Smith, *Carlos: Portrait of a Terrorist* (Holt, Rinehart & Winston, 1977).

Harris Smith, *OSS* (University of California Press, 1972).

Joseph Burckholder Smith, *Portrait of a Cold Warrior* (Putnam's, 1976).

Thomas Bell Smith, *The Essential CIA* (privately printed, 1975).

Frank Snepp, *Decent Interval* (Random House, 1977).

Lawrence Stern, *The Wrong Horse* (Times Books, 1977).

Stewart Steven, *Operation Splinter Factor* (Lippincott, 1974).

John Stockwell, *In Search of Enemies* (Norton, 1978).

Maj. Gen. Sir Kenneth Strong, *Men of Intelligence* (Cassell, 1970).

K. V. Tauras, *Guerrilla Warfare on the Amber Coast* (Voyages Press, 1962).

Maxwell Taylor, *Swords and Plowshares* (Norton, 1972).

P. L. Thyraud de Vosjoli, *Lamia* (Little, Brown, 1970).

David B. Tinnin and Dag Christensen, *The Hit Team* (Little, Brown, 1976).

Transmittal of Documents from the National Security Council to the Chairman of the Joint Chiefs of Staff, Parts 1, 2, and 3 (U.S. Government Printing Office, 1974).

Vernon Walters, *Silent Missions* (Doubleday, 1978).

David Wise, *The American Police State* (Random House, 1976).

————, *The Politics of Lying* (Random House, 1973).

———— and Thomas B. Ross, *The Espionage Establishment* (Random House, 1967).

————, *The Invisible Government* (Random House, 1964).

The White House Transcripts (Viking, 1974).

Daniel Yergin, *Shattered Peace* (Houghton Mifflin, 1977).

Index

A NOTE ABOUT THE AUTHOR

Thomas Powers was on the staff of United Press International when he won a Pulitzer Prize in 1971 for his reporting on the case of the young Weatherman terrorist Diana Oughton. This work was the basis for his first book, *Diana: The Making of a Terrorist;* his second book, *The War at Home,* was published in 1973. Powers lives in New York City with his wife and three daughters.

A NOTE ON THE TYPE

The text of this book was set in Caledonia, a Linotype face designed by
W. A. Dwiggins. It belongs to the family of printing types called
"modern faces" by printers—a term used to mark the change in style
of type letters that occurred about 1800. Caledonia borders on the
general design of Scotch Modern, but is more freely drawn than
that letter.

Composed by Maryland Linotype, Baltimore, Maryland.
Printed and bound by The Haddon Craftsmen,
Scranton, Pennsylvania.

Typography and binding design by Virginia Tan